The Dred Scott Case

THE DRED SCOTT CASE

Its Significance
in American Law and Politics

DON E. FEHRENBACHER

New York
Oxford University Press
1978

Copyright © 1978 by Oxford University Press, Inc.
Second printing, 1979

Library of Congress Cataloging in Publication Data

Fehrenbacher, Don Edward, 1920–
    The Dred Scott case.

    Includes index.
    1. Slavery in the United States—Law.   2. Scott,
Dred.   3. Slavery in the United States—Legal status of
slaves in free states.   4. United States—History—
1849–1877.   I. Title.
KF4545.S5F43   346'.73'013   78-4665
ISBN 0-19-502403-6

Printed in the United States of America

For Virginia with love

Preface

Dred Scott v. Sandford, which Abraham Lincoln called "an astonisher in legal history," remains to this day the most famous of all American judicial decisions. Nearly all of the significant commentaries on the text of the decision were written soon after it appeared in print. One man who undertook such a critique was Daniel D. Barnard, a New York lawyer and old-line Whig who had served in Congress and as minister to Prussia. In the spring of 1858, Barnard confided to a friend that he had encountered difficulty in setting bounds to his project. "My first idea," he said, "was to comprise all I wished to say in a moderate pamphlet. . . . But my study of the case, and my investigations, have caused the subject to grow in my hands to such an extent that I do not see very well how I can thus limit myself." Instead of a pamphlet, he concluded, it would be necessary to write a book of some two or three hundred pages. This more ambitious undertaking never reached completion, however, perhaps because it continued to grow in his hands.

My own experience in writing about the Dred Scott decision has been somewhat similar to Barnard's. That is, I began work with an article in mind, decided to turn it into a very short book, signed a contract with Oxford University Press for a book of moderate length, and eventually submitted a manuscript three times as long as the one contracted for. Over the years—too many years—the book grew and changed in my hands, becoming something considerably more than a history of the Dred Scott case, though something considerably less than a comprehensive history of the sectional conflict over slavery. Unlike Barnard, I seem to have brought my enterprise to a conclusion and can now take up the pleasant task of acknowledging the help given me along the way.

Charles A. Lofgren lent a hand in the beginning with some preliminary bibliographical work. My colleague Carl N. Degler has from time to time suggested sources of information, and the treatment of early American slavery in the first chapter has benefited from his criticism. I have depended heavily at times on the work of Walter Ehrlich, a leading *Dred Scott* authority who will soon publish his own book about the case and who generously made available to me his file of newspaper comments on the decision. At Stanford, in addition to financial assistance from the Institute of American History, I have received much help from members of the office staff of the Department of History and from the staffs of Green Library and the Law School Library. As either a visitor or a correspondent, I am indebted to staff members at a good many other institutions, including the Library of Congress, the National Archives, the Library of the United States Supreme Court, the Missouri Historical Society, the Maryland Historical Society, the Ohio State Library, the Historical Society of Pennsylvania, the University of North Carolina Library, and the University of Virginia Library.

I am grateful also to the editorial staff of Oxford University Press for all the hard work associated with publication, and especially to Sheldon Meyer for his encouragement, advice, and patience. Fortunately, the Press secured the services of Robert W. Johannsen and William M. Wiecek as outside readers, and the book is much improved as a result of their valuable criticisms and suggestions. Carol Clifford served expertly as research assistant, checking the accuracy of quotations and citations. My wife, Virginia Fehrenbacher, has shared the work of checking accuracy, has carried the heaviest burden of proofreading, and has contributed in many other ways to the enterprise of authorship.

About six of the twenty-three chapters were written during a sabbatical year, 1975–76, when I held a National Endowment for the Humanities Fellowship. Chapter 22 incorporates part of my article, "Roger B. Taney and the Sectional Crisis," *Journal of Southern History*, XLIII (November 1977), 555–66, copyright 1977 by the Southern Historical Association. I am grateful to the managing editor, S. W. Higginbotham, for permission to reprint this material.

A hallowed but perhaps excessively altruistic tradition requires that my sincere thanks to persons and institutions named above must be accompanied by a statement absolving them of responsibility for whatever errors of fact and judgment, of commission and omission, may blemish the pages that follow. As it happens, error has been a conspicuous feature of the *Dred Scott* story from the beginning. The name of the defendant was misspelled in the title and throughout the official report of the case. An "Agreed Statement of Facts," upon which counsel based their arguments, contained a number of inaccuracies. Mistakes are common in most historical writing on the subject. For example, in an influential article published many years ago by the distinguished constitutional scholar Edward S. Corwin, there are four factual errors in one paragraph summarizing the background of the case; and a similar summary in a recently published book on the American judicial system contains five such errors. I have no sense of being immune from this plague of inaccuracy that seems to afflict students of the Dred Scott decision. My best hope is that I may have corrected some tiresome old errors and made some interesting new ones.

Stanford
May 15, 1978   Don E. Fehrenbacher

Contents

PART THREE   CONSEQUENCES AND ECHOES

The Dred Scott Case

Introduction

O n Friday morning, March 6, 1857—a crisp, clear day for residents of Washington, D.C.—public attention centered on a dusky, ground-level courtroom deep within the Capitol. The Senate chamber directly above was quiet; Congress had adjourned on March 3. The inauguration ceremonies of March 4 were over, and James Buchanan had begun settling into his role as the fifteenth President. Now it was the judiciary's turn to be heard, as though the three branches of government were passing in review before the American people. Ordinarily, the Supreme Court carried on its business before a small audience and with only perfunctory notice from the press, but today the journalists were out in force and the courtroom was packed with spectators. A murmur of expectancy ran through the crowd and greeted the nine black-robed jurists as they filed into view at eleven o'clock, led by the aged Chief Justice. Acrimonious debate in the recent Congress had once again failed to settle the paramount constitutional and political issue of the decade. The Court, however, was ready to terminate the long struggle over slavery in the territories and, incidentally, decide the fate of a man named Dred Scott.

Neither of the two litigants was present in the courtroom. Scott remained at home in St. Louis, still a hired-out slave eleven years after he had taken the first legal step in his long battle for freedom.

1

As for his alleged owner, John F. A. Sanford languished in an insane asylum and within two months would be dead. But then, both men had been dwarfed by the implications of their case and were now mere pawns in a much larger contest.

Roger B. Taney, who in eleven days would be eighty years old, began reading from a manuscript held in tremulous hands. For more than two hours the audience strained to hear his steadily weakening voice as he delivered the opinion of the Court in *Dred Scott v. Sandford.* * Other opinions followed from some of the concurring justices and from the two dissenters. When they were finished at the end of the next day, only one thing was absolutely clear. Nine distinguished white men, by a vote of 7 to 2, had decided in the court of last resort that an insignificant, elderly black man and his family were still slaves and not free citizens, as they claimed.

What else had been decided was fiercely debated then and ever afterward. Critics argued that on some points Taney did not speak for a majority of the justices. Yet none of his eight colleagues directly challenged Taney's explicit assertion that his was the official opinion of the Court, and in popular usage on all sides the "Dred Scott decision" came to mean the opinion read by the Chief Justice. Critics also insisted that Taney's most important pronouncement was extrajudicial, but only the Court itself, in later decisions, could legally settle such a question by accepting or rejecting the pronouncement as established precedent. Rightly or not, permanently or not, the Supreme Court had written two new and provocative rules into the fundamental law of the nation: first, that no Negro could be a United States citizen or even a state citizen "within the meaning of the Constitution"; and second, that Congress had no power to exclude slavery from the federal territories, and that accordingly the Missouri Compromise, together with all other legislation embodying such exclusion, was unconstitutional.

Public reaction was prompt and often intense, as countless lawyers, politicians, editors, and preachers reached for their pens or cleared their throats for oratory. The outpouring of comment gath-

* The defendant's name, John F. A. Sanford, was misspelled in the official Supreme Court report.

ered into three major streams of opinion. Most conspicuous by far was the roar of anger and defiance from antislavery voices throughout the North, well illustrated in the notorious remark of the New York *Tribune* conceding the decision "just so much moral weight as . . . the judgment of a majority of those congregated in any Washington bar-room."[1] From southerners, in contrast, came expressions of satisfaction and renewed sectional confidence at this overdue vindication of their constitutional rights. Meanwhile, northern Democrats and certain other conservatives were confining themselves, for the most part, to exclamations of relief at the settlement of a dangerous issue and pious lectures on the duty of every citizen to accept the wise judgment of the Court.

In the years immediately following, the response to the decision proved to be much more important than its direct legal effect. As law, the decision legitimized and encouraged an expansion of slavery that never took place; it denied freedom to a slave who was then quickly manumitted. But as a public event, the decision aggravated an already bitter sectional conflict and to some degree determined the shape of the final crisis.

There is irony here, of course, if one views the Court's action as an effort at judicial statesmanship, intended to bring peace but instead pushing the nation closer to civil war. In this light, the Court majority appears incredibly unrealistic—indeed, so foolish as to pour oil rather than water on a fire. Yet Taney's opinion, carefully read, proves to be a work of unmitigated partisanship, polemical in spirit though judicial in its language, and more like an ultimatum than a formula for sectional accommodation. Peace on Taney's terms resembled the peace implicit in a demand for unconditional surrender. As one scholar has written, "The Dred Scott decision was nothing less than a summons to the Republicans to disband."[2]

Thus perceived, the decision falls logically into place as one unusually bold venture in a desperate struggle for power, rather than being an evenhanded effort to resolve that struggle. And under close study it proves to be no less meaningful as a historical consequence than as a historical cause.

There are sharply defined historical events through which, like the neck of an hourglass, great causal forces appear to flow, emerging converted into significant consequences. Strictly speaking, this is illusion, and the translation is essentially a verbal one; for "cause" and "consequence" are subjective categories that serve to simplify and make intelligible the highly complex relationships among objective historical phenomena. Yet all explanation, being in some degree selective and synthetic, is to some degree a distortion of reality. The hourglass construct at least incorporates the flow of time and is chronologically sound. Like biography, moreover, the history of a single event provides a firm and convenient vantage point from which to observe the sweep of historical forces. The principal fallacy to be avoided is a tendency to view one's subject as the matrix of forces when it is usually instead a mere channel of their passage.

The Dred Scott decision, for example, was the Supreme Court's first invalidation of a major federal law. It is therefore a landmark in the history of judicial review. But the power to declare an act of Congress unconstitutional had frequently been asserted or implied in earlier decisions, and the existence of such power was widely assumed by the American people. That the power would have been exercised eventually, if not in 1857, seems about as certain as that someone else would have discovered America if Columbus had failed to do so. Thus the Dred Scott decision should probably be regarded as a prominent point of reference, but not as a major turning point, in the development of judicial review. And yet, since it was in 1857 that the Supreme Court first took this important step, it was in 1857 that Americans for the first time had to consider the operational scope and meaning of judicial review in national politics. What was the effect of such a decision beyond the specific judgment rendered? To what extent, for instance, would it inhibit the subsequent deliberations of Congress, and what recourse was left for the bitter critics of the decision? The heated argument of these constitutional questions had unmistakable political consequences.

The answer of Republicans like Abraham Lincoln was that a decision so defective in its logic, so contrary to precedent, and so repugnant to a large part of the population did not immediately become binding on the other branches of the government or upon the American people as settled law of the land. Republicans, for their part, would not defy the decision but instead work to have it reversed. This reversal obviously could be accomplished only by changing the personnel of the Supreme Court, which in turn depended upon control of the presidency. Thus the South's judicial victory was to be challenged at the polls, and southerners had another strong reason to fear a Republican in the White House. That is one plainly observable link between the Dred Scott decision and the secession crisis of 1860–61.

There were other links, of course, such as the divisive influence of the decision within the Democratic party and its reinforcement of northern fear of an "aggressive slave power." No doubt the Dred Scott decision is of historical significance primarily because of its place in the configuration of forces and events that produced the Civil War. But the decision also has revelatory value in the study of other forces at work and other historical problems. For instance, unlike Taney's pronouncements on slavery, which defended a minority section with partisan fervor, the racial theory underlying his opinion was majoritarian. For proof of the Negro's degraded status, he relied heavily upon examples taken from the free states. Without the northern record of increasing discrimination he would have found it much more difficult to exclude Negroes from citizenship. Thus, although the principal conclusions of Taney's opinion were soon wiped away by the Civil War and subsequent constitutional amendments, the spirit of the opinion survived for a century in the racial sequel to emancipation.

Furthermore, although the Dred Scott decision was essentially a vain effort to turn back the clock of civilization and permanently legitimate a "relic of barbarism," in at least one respect it had a distinctly modern ring. American courts in the late twentieth century are no longer mere constitutional censors of public policies fashioned by other hands. They have also become initiators of social change. Government by judiciary is now, in a sense, democracy's non-democratic alternative to representative government when the latter bogs down in failure or inaction.[3] The Dred Scott decision nevertheless remains the most striking instance of the Supreme Court's attempting to play the role of *deus ex machina* in a setting of national crisis. The deci-

sion, in fact, provided an early indication of the vast judicial power
that could be generated if political issues were converted by definition into constitutional questions.

Much of the American past clung to the Dred Scott case, and
some of the American future was embodied in it. But this had not
always been true. For most of its eleven-year history, Scott's legal
struggle for freedom aroused scarcely any public interest as it proceeded by an anomalous route from a Missouri trial court to the
Supreme Court of the United States. In the beginning, it posed a
fairly simple legal problem for which precedent seemed to provide a
ready-made solution. At each stage of litigation, however, new and
bigger issues were injected into the case. Thus it grew steadily more
complex and in the end became critically important to the entire nation.

The confusion still surrounding the case reflects the confusion
with which it was handled by the Court, and both are attributable in
part to its legal complexity but in larger measure to the enormous
range of its scrutiny and implication. In his opinion, Taney issued
pronouncements on the relationship between the Constitution and
the Articles of Confederation, on the limits of congressional power, on
the geographic extent of the Bill of Rights, on constitutional authority
for territorial expansion, on the rights of private property, on comity
between states, and on the nature of the Federal Union. He defined
the power of naturalization, the legal status of Indian tribes, and the
criteria for citizenship, state and federal. He introduced a new meaning of "due process" into federal law and virtually rewrote the privileges-and-immunities clause of the Constitution. These, moreover,
were merely connotative aspects of the opinion.

The three *principal* subjects with which Taney dealt at length
were: (1) the Negro race generally and free Negroes in particular; (2)
the institution of slavery; and (3) the territorial system. Of these, the
first is not mentioned at all in the Constitution; the second is referred
to in three separate passages, but never by name; and the third is
treated in one brief and ambiguous clause. The textual basis for constitutional interpretation was therefore meager. In each instance,
moreover, there was a peculiar hybridism that fostered confusion.

The so-called free Negro, though not a slave, was excluded from many of the privileges and opportunities associated with American freedom. Slaves were in some respects persons and in other respects property. And territories were likewise something betwixt and between, being neither colonies nor self-governing states but rather a distinctive American combination of the two.

Altogether, the Dred Scott case was legally complex and invited a judicial investigation of remarkable scope into matters of perplexing ambiguity for which the constitutional guidelines were often vague and discrepant. The Court, as a consequence, had much freedom of choice and found it easy to treat broad political and historical questions as though they were legal issues susceptible of judicial settlement. Indeed, citation of legal rules and precedents was only a secondary bulwark of Taney's opinion, which depended primarily upon the interpretation of American history that he proposed to write into constitutional law.

Such an event cannot be examined in any narrow context without the risk of considerable misunderstanding. For it is integrally part of a complex pattern of thoughts and actions extending far backward and well forward in time from the year 1857. Studied in breadth and depth, the Dred Scott decision becomes a point of illumination, casting light upon more than a century of American history.

I

OUT OF THE PAST

Race, Slavery, and the
Origins of the Republic

The first African Negroes in the British North American colonies were brought ashore at Jamestown from a Dutch ship in 1619. The irony in the date has often been pointed out. During that same year, Virginians organized the first representative assembly on the continent, and thus, in a sense, slavery and self-government arrived simultaneously. But the agency of Dutch mariners in this initial transaction likewise has symbolic meaning, for it illustrates the international origins of the slave system in the United States.

During the next few decades, additional Negroes in relatively small numbers were brought to Virginia and introduced into the other English colonies. Their status at the time is far from clear, but it was apparently not uniform. Some were held in bondage only for a period of years and then received their freedom, much in the manner of white apprentices and indentured servants. To be sure, perpetual and hereditary servitude became the rule soon enough, and by the 1660s it was being formalized in colonial laws. Yet the inadequacy and inconsistency of records for the earliest years have left room for the argument that the first Negroes in British America were essentially servants rather than slaves and that institutionalized slavery was a somewhat later development. Associated with this historical problem is a chicken-or-egg controversy over the relationship between slavery and race prejudice.

According to Gunnar Myrdal, for example, Negroes in British North America were first treated as indentured servants and then, beginning in the middle of the seventeenth century, "were pushed down into chattel slavery while the white servants were allowed to work off their bond." Furthermore, this momentous change was justified for a time in cultural terms and on biblical authority—that is, "the Negro was a heathen and a barbarian, an outcast among the peoples of the earth, a descendant of Noah's son Ham, cursed by God himself and doomed to be a servant forever on account of an ancient sin." Not until later did the defense of slavery become also "biological in character."[1] In short, first came the Negro, then the institution of slavery, and finally racism of the kind that asserts the genetic inferiority of the Negro.

It does indeed appear that a fully articulated theory of biological (and therefore permanent) black inferiority did not emerge until the second quarter of the nineteenth century. The theory, it also appears, developed in close association with the southern defense of slavery as a "positive good" and in response to the intensified abolitionist crusade personified by William Lloyd Garrison.[2]

Thus racism in its ultimate, intellectualized form became a conspicuous part of the rationale for slavery only after nearly two centuries of slavery's existence as an institution, and slavery itself had been institutionalized and legalized only after several decades of the Negro's presence in the English colonies. This double time-lag might seem to indicate a slow evolution of race prejudice as a concomitant, or perhaps even as an outgrowth, of the slave system. Yet enslavement, whenever it began, was imposed selectively on a racial basis. Would the Negro alone have been "pushed down into chattel slavery" without the pressure of strong preconceptions and elemental feelings amounting to rudiments of the full-blown racial doctrine perfected in the nineteenth century? Slavery and race prejudice were no doubt perpetuated and mutually strengthened by the continuing resonance between them, but, for the origins of each, one must look past the formalities of enacted law and elaborated theory into the dimmer realm of private, seldom-expressed attitudes, random thoughts, and unrationalized behavior.

In one respect, at least, Negro servitude and white servitude in colonial America were radically different from the start. That is, all Negroes arrived as captives, having been hunted down on their native soil and shipped in chains across the ocean to be "tamed" like wild creatures for their regimen of forced labor. Of course, much white servitude was also involuntary, but as punishment for crime or sometimes as the result of kidnapping carried on outside the law. Only in the case of Africans was captivity the normal and universal prelude to servitude. Purchasers of Negroes during the early colonial years were merely new receivers in a traffic that already had a long history. Their willingness to buy indicates that they had been conditioned to accept the fundamental assumption of the slave trade: that Africans, by their nature, were fair game for capture and uniquely fitted for servitude.

To be sure, colonial servitude, white and black, took root in response to the practical need for cheap, controllable labor, especially on southern plantations. Yet the economic explanation of slavery, which becomes increasingly valid with the growth of the institution, does not fully account for its origins. For one thing, there is the question of why slavery at an early date penetrated New England, where no strong need for it existed.[3] And even in the southern colonies, slavery acquired firm legal status well before Negroes replaced white servants as the principal labor force. In other words, the installation of slavery appears to have preceded the rise of a pressing economic need for it. The institution was not born of necessity but was instead a mere convenience at the time of its introduction into the English mainland colonies.

The low profile of African slavery during the early decades of English settlement is not surprising in view of the small numbers involved. By 1649, for example, there were still only three hundred Negroes in Virginia. Here is one obvious reason why the establishment of uniform legal rules for slavery did not begin until 1660. Before that time, the institution was simply not significant enough to warrant such attention. Furthermore, since no ready-made English

law of slavery existed, it is scarcely surprising that the status of the
first Negroes should have been vague and varied or that a period of
adaptation should have preceded the legal incorporation of this alien
institution.[4]

Neither is it surprising that biological theory should have been
much less prominent in the early justification of slavery than reference to scriptural authority and emphasis on the contrast between
Christian civilization and heathen savagery. Seventeenth-century
men were not yet equipped to distinguish systematically between nature and nurture. They commonly blurred the difference by using
words such as "instinctive" and "natural" to describe what was cul-
turally ingrained, while for a long time there was some doubt that
even skin color was a hereditary characteristic. Moreover, the Bible
itself stood as a barrier to any notion that Negroes were a separate
and lower order of creation; for in Adam and Eve, God had fashioned
the ancestors of all mankind. Yet, at the level of feeling below rational
discourse, the first generation of colonial Americans did harbor the
rudiments of just such a notion. This is plain enough in their actions,
if not in their words. Evidence of a repugnance for racial mixture appears early in colonial records, and the first laws forbidding miscegenation were passed at about the same time as the first laws forma-
lizing slavery.[5] In addition, the swiftness with which Negro servitude
was made not only lifelong but *hereditary* indicates deep-rooted assumptions essentially biological in character.

What seems remarkable about the origins of American slavery is
the speed with which the institution took shape and received legal
sanction, considering the relatively small number of Negroes involved
and the lack of precedents in English law. One major influence after
1640 was the example set in the British West Indies, where the commitment to African slavery proceeded even more rapidly than on the
mainland.[6] But in both instances the speed of institutionalization is
incomprehensible except as a reflection of established racial attitudes
that were part of the colonials' European heritage. More than a century of observing Spanish and Portuguese practices had conditioned
Englishmen to accept African slavery as a normal accessory of colonial
empire.

Whichever took root first in European thought, the association of Africans with slavery and the assumption of black inferiority had become firmly set and intertwined with each other before the first Negroes were landed in Virginia. So it was in the beginning and so it remained on the eve of the Civil War. One of the truly striking aspects of Roger B. Taney's opinion in the Dred Scott case was his inability to dissociate free Negroes from slavery. His discussion of their legal status invariably slipped over into a consideration of their racial ties with slavery. Manumission did not alter the fact that they were members of a race regarded as "beings of an inferior order" who might "justly and lawfully be reduced to slavery."[7]

By the eve of the American Revolution, slavery was not only legally established in all thirteen colonies but so firmly implanted in the southern colonies that Negroes constituted about 40 per cent of their population. The theoretical foundations and essential nature of the institution were much the same from Maine to Georgia. Yet the daily life of a New England house servant bore little resemblance to the life of a field hand on a South Carolina rice plantation. There were significant variations even in the legal structure of the institution from colony to colony, and slavery in practice took many forms, reflecting many varieties of social context and individual personality.

In all the colonies, African slavery was lifelong and hereditary, with a child of mixed free and slave parentage assuming at birth the status of its mother.[8] At law, a slave was reduced in considerable degree from a person to a thing, having no legitimate will of its own and belonging bodily to its owner. As property, a slave could be bought and sold.[9] As animate property, he could be compelled to work, and his offspring belonged absolutely to the master. Thus a slave was in some respects like a domestic animal, being an item of wealth, virtually a beast of burden, and a creature requiring constant supervision and restraint.

No doubt the problem of restraint accounts for much of the sectional variation in the degree to which slavery suppressed individuality. Slave codes of New England and the middle colonies, for example, were generally less elaborate and severe than those with which apprehensive southerners fenced in their swelling black populations.[10] Southern slaves, unlike many of their northern counterparts could not own property, or contract legal marriages, or testify against white persons in court. These privileges would have been incompatible with the mass control necessary in the South. New England, in contrast, could indulge its Puritan conscience and treat its few thousand slaves more leniently without jeopardizing white security.[11]

Yet even in the South, classification of the slave as property could go only so far before it was overtaken by the ineluctable fact of his humanity. Both conscience and interest dictated that in certain respects he must be treated as a person. In perhaps the most obvious instance, criminal law held the slave fully responsible and punishable for his own misdeeds, like any free man. Furthermore, the principal moral justification for slavery—that it lifted savages up toward civilization and heathen up to Christianity—certainly contemplated slaves as men, and men, indeed, with immortal souls. Plainly, in law as well as in life, a slave was both person and property. This dualism often proved embarrassing for slaveholders and confusing for lawmakers, but southerners learned that it could also sometimes be advantageous.

II

Introduction of the peculiar institution into the thirteen colonies had been essentially undeliberate and uncontroversial. There were objections now and then, but until the latter part of the eighteenth century, "slavery remained a largely unexamined fact of life."[12] By the 1760s, however, new currents of liberal thought from the European enlightenment, which contributed so much to the ideology of the American Revolution, were also encouraging uneasy reflection on the rationale of slavery. And then the rhetoric of the colonial struggle with England brought out in strong relief the ugly paradox of freedom and servitude in America.

It was not merely the difficulty of assimilating slavery to the natural rights philosophy and the rising humanitarian spirit of the age. What nagged at the consciences of some Americans was the way in which the language of colonial resistance to England could be read as an indictment of slaveholding. In fact, the metaphor of the colonial argument was often drawn from the realities of the slave system. Thus, in 1774, Samuel Adams rejected "servile compliance" with the Boston Port Act; a mass meeting in Farmington, Connecticut, declared, "We scorn the chains of slavery"; and George Washington accused the British of "endeavouring by every piece of art and despotism to fix the shackles of slavery upon us."[13] The alleged victims of British oppression had victims of their own and used them for analogy. Was there not, then, a foul hypocrisy at the heart of the Revolutionary movement? "Blush ye pretended votaries for freedom! ye trifling patriots!" exclaimed one antislavery writer, "for while you are fasting, praying, nonimporting, nonexporting, remonstrating, resolving, and pleading for a restoration of your charter rights, you at the same time are continuing this lawless, cruel, inhuman, and abominable practice of enslaving your fellow men."[14]

If words are read for their plainest meaning, slavery was incompatible with the fundamental assumption of the Declaration of Independence—that all men are created equal and endowed by their creator with the inalienable rights of life, liberty, and the pursuit of happiness. Yet, although the Revolution triumphed, slavery survived and entered the nineteenth century with renewed vitality. Among various explanations of this apparent contradiction, two were rehearsed on the prairies of Illinois in 1858. Abraham Lincoln maintained that the Declaration meant literally what it said, but as an ideal to be striven for, rather than as an actual condition. Thus the document, while it did not signal the end of slavery, nevertheless pointed imperatively toward eventual abolition of the institution. Stephen A. Douglas replied that the Declaration had nothing whatever to do with Negroes. The assertion that all men are created equal referred exclusively to white men of European birth and descent. Thus there *was* no contradiction between the Declaration and African slavery.[15] Douglas, in his interpretation, was merely repeating what Chief Justice Taney had recently said in the Dred Scott decision.

Actually, neither side in the argument could offer evidence sufficient to carry conviction. Lincoln and Douglas were both mistaken in assuming that there was anything so simple and so explicit as a

Revolutionary consensus on the subject of the Negro's place in the order of the universe. White Americans of the eighteenth century were simply not in the habit of thinking much about the Negro at all, except as the raw material of slavery. In addition, a generation busy with revolution, war, and nation-building could spare little sustained attention to a problem of marginal relevance and no practical urgency. The meager evidence available suggests that a systematic poll in 1776 would have produced considerable disagreement on the question of whether black men were included in the philosophy of the Declaration.[16]

In the circumstances, then, the antislavery tendencies of the Revolutionary decades were not inconsiderable and amounted to a new departure. State after state took steps to end the African slave trade, though effective enforcement proved to be another matter. Abolition of slavery itself was achieved in New England and Pennsylvania, and it seemed only a matter of time in New York and New Jersey. Further south, the revulsion against slavery was in large measure confined to expressions of hope for eventual abolition. But Virginia in 1782 gave strong encouragement to private manumissions by removing earlier restrictions upon them, and both Maryland and Delaware subsequently followed her example. During the war, slaves numbering several thousand were enlisted in military service, with freedom as their ultimate reward. By the 1790s, abolition societies had appeared in every state from Virginia northward, with prominent men like Benjamin Franklin, John Jay, and Alexander Hamilton in leading roles. And the climax came in 1787 when slavery was prohibited in the Northwest Territory with scarcely a dissenting vote.[17]

It is true that the antislavery manifestations of the Revolutionary era were to some degree reflections of interest as well as conscience, and a moral force that proves inadequate is in any case often suspect.[18] One can see in this early movement against slavery, despite all its achievements, the general contours of a revolution which failed—failed, however, not because its supporters lacked *sincerity* but rather because they lacked the *intensity* of conviction that inspires concentrated effort and carries revolutions through to success. The great men of the time gave the movement their sympathy and some promise of leadership but always had other more pressing claims on their attention. Also, they were inhibited by their desire for continental unity, by a tender concern for the rights of private property, and, in the South, by racial fears that made universal emancipation difficult to visualize. In the end, there was a strong disposition to settle for moral gesture and a reliance on the "benevolence of history."[19]

What this incomplete revolution did produce, of course, was a more or less formal division of the new nation into slaveholding and nonslaveholding states—all at the very time when the foundations of a national government were being laid. The division proved to be a remarkably even one, both in number of states and in population.[20] It was also ominously geographical, reinforcing old economic differences between the North and the South. The elements of sectional conflict were thus assembled, as James Madison later pointed out more than once to members of the Constitutional Convention.

Slavery at the time of the Convention was therefore in a somewhat disorderly process of becoming strictly a sectional institution, and men's minds were likewise in a transitional, unsettled state on the subject. Only in Massachusetts and New Hampshire (for all practical purposes) had slavery disappeared. Rhode Island, Connecticut, and Pennsylvania had installed programs of gradual emancipation, but similar efforts in New York and New Jersey had thus far been unsuccessful.[21] Yet Madison counted eight of the thirteen states (including Delaware) as nonslaveholding, and there was some reason to think that gradual abolition might even cross the Mason-Dixon line into Maryland.[22] In a context of so much change and uncertainty, the men of Philadelphia were not very well prepared to make indelible decisions about slavery for themselves and their posterity.

III

Slavery had in fact been an obstacle to American union since the beginning of independence, contributing especially to the financial weakness of the Articles of Confederation. Efforts to apportion the expenses of the Confederation among the states according to their populations had foundered on the question of whether slaves should be counted in the enumeration. Instead, the Articles as finally adopted provided for apportionment according to the value of real estate—a formula that proved unworkable.[23]

At the Constitutional Convention, the first major struggle was between large and small states over the distribution of legislative power. But after the Great Compromise began to take shape, establishing proportional representation in one house while retaining state equality in the other, the old sectional dispute about counting slaves promptly resumed. The stakes had changed, however, and so both sides more or less reversed their previous arguments. When it had been a question of apportioning governmental expenses according to population, northerners had insisted that slaves be included in the enumeration; southerners had replied that slaves were property and therefore to be excluded. Yet in 1787, when apportionment of seats in the House of Representatives was the issue, southerners wanted slaves to be counted equally with free men, but northerners emphatically disagreed and in some instances even asserted that slaves must be regarded as property.[24]

Ready at hand, however, was a familiar design of compromise—the so-called federal ratio, which, although approved by Congress in 1783, had never been put to use.[25] Now brought forward in the Convention, it provoked a brief but lively debate before winning acceptance by the narrow margin of 6 states to 2, with 2 delegations divided. By the terms of this settlement, both representation and direct taxes would be apportioned among the states "according to their respective numbers," determined by adding to the total of free persons "three fifths of all other persons."[26]

The three-fifths compromise, having become, according to Rufus King, "the language of all America," went over rather smoothly in the Convention and in the state ratifying conventions that followed.[27] As the years passed, however, it looked more and more like a major victory for the South, especially when the link with direct taxes proved to be unimportant. The federal ratio consistently augmented southern representation in the House by 30 per cent or more. This enormous electoral bonus for slaveholders seemed increasingly anachronistic and unjust in an age of developing democratic tendencies. Yet, in spite of growing northern resentment, the ratio never became a critical public issue, partly because it was too securely locked into the constitutional system.[28]

The political effects of the three-fifths compromise were plain enough, but what did the compromise say or imply about the nature and status of slavery within the American constitutional system? Certainly, by its reference to "other persons," the clause gave formal recognition and perhaps a measure of legitimation to the existence of a system of bondage in the country. But did this mean that the clause recognized and legitimated the property-holding aspect of the system? Is it true that the Convention, by accepting the three-fifths rule, granted "representation to property in slaves"?[29]

The affirmative answer eventually adopted throughout the South rested on a combination of palpable fact and plausible inference. That is, the three-fifths clause, which unquestionably referred to African slavery, officially recognized the existence of the institution (fact). In doing so, moreover, the clause recognized the institution *as it existed*—in all its aspects, including that of property-holding (inference). But what this interpretation ignored was the possibility that some of the framers (and perhaps a majority of the framers some of the time) intended to give slavery only a limited kind of constitutional recognition. At one point in the Convention proceedings, for instance, James Madison, a slaveholder who had supported the three-fifths compromise and who certainly regarded slaves as property in Virginia, nevertheless declared that it would be "wrong to admit in the Constitution the idea that there could be property in men."[30]

The muddled thinking of some delegates about the meaning of the three-fifths clause is well illustrated in a statement made by Charles C. Pinckney of South Carolina during the debates on ratification:

> We were at a loss, for some time, for a rule to ascertain the proportionate wealth of the states. At last we thought that the productive labor of the inhabitants was the best rule for ascertaining their wealth. In conformity to this rule, joined to a spirit of concession, we determined that representatives should be apportioned among the several states by adding to the whole number of

free persons three fifths of the slaves. We thus obtained a representation for our property; and I confess I did not expect that we
had conceded too much to the Eastern States, when they allowed
us a representation for a species of property which they have not
among them.[31]

Here was the slaveholder's easy leap from viewing slaves as "inhabitants" to viewing them as "property." The last sentence in this passage contradicted what had gone before, being essentially propaganda
for local consumption in the struggle to win ratification. The earlier
sentences, on the other hand, constituted a fairly accurate summary
of the historical origins of the three-fifths clause.[32]

The confusion resulted not only from the association of *slavery*
with property but also from the association of *representation* with
property in eighteenth-century thought. Among Convention delegates there was widespread acceptance of the Whig principle that political representation should to some extent reflect differences in
wealth.[33] But while the principle had been applied to individuals in
the suffrage and office-holding qualifications of the various states, no
one, as Pinckney said, had found a practical way to compute the
"proportionate wealth" of the states themselves. The best alternative,
it seemed, was simply to count the producers of wealth—that is, to
use population as an index of property values in the states. "What was
done," says J. R. Pole, "was to melt property and persons into a
single concept . . . but numbers became the sole instrument of mea-
surement."[34] Thus, in the apportionment of representation and direct
taxes, slaves were not treated as property any more than free persons
were treated as property, but both were regarded in part as measures
of wealth. The three-fifths compromise did not necessarily imply that
a slave was 60 per cent human being and 40 per cent property. Instead, it incorporated a differential estimate of his wealth-producing
capacity *as a person*. It reflected a widespread belief in the relative
inefficiency of slave labor.[35] Therefore, neither in its wording nor in
its historical context does the clause lend significant support to the
property-holding aspect of slavery. Perhaps this is why it received no
mention whatever in Taney's Dred Scott opinion.*

* See below, pp. 352–53.

Slavery provoked only one other major disagreement in the Convention, and it was over the future of the African slave trade. Delegates from Georgia and the Carolinas insisted vehemently that their states must be free to permit the trade or prohibit it, as they chose. This would require a special restriction on the general powers of Congress to lay taxes and regulate foreign commerce. The issue divided the South, for Virginia's delegates, as a matter of both interest and conscience, wanted the traffic suppressed. The outcome, after extensive debate, was a compromise finally worded as follows:

> The migration or importation of such persons as any of the states now existing shall think proper to admit, shall not be prohibited by the Congress prior to the year one thousand eight hundred and eight, but a tax or duty may be imposed on such importation, not exceeding ten dollars for each person.[36]

An earlier version set the cut-off date at 1800. The eight-year extension was approved by a vote of 7 to 4, with the three New England states and Maryland joining the three southernmost states in the majority. There is little evidence to support the cynical view later adopted by Taney that the New Englanders were motivated primarily by a desire to protect the slave-traders of their own region. One of the North Carolina delegates, Richard Dobbs Spaight, later explained: "The limitation of this trade to the term of twenty years was a compromise between the Eastern States and the Southern States. South Carolina and Georgia wished to extend the term. The Eastern States insisted on the entire abolition of the trade."[37] The voting alignment, in short, did not reflect attitudes toward the slave trade as much as it did degree of willingness to compromise.[38]

In spite of its circumlocution, the purpose of the clause was obvious, and Congress at the first opportunity prohibited importation of slaves.[39] But here again, as in the case of the three-fifths compromise, one must ask what the passage indicated about the status of slavery in the American constitutional system.

By the slave-trade clause, according to Chief Justice Taney in 1857, "the right to purchase and hold this *property* is directly sanctioned and authorized for twenty years."[40] Even if this were true, there would remain the question of whether the implications of the sanction could have any legal force beyond the time limit set for the sanction itself. But the clause actually authorized nothing except a tax on the importation of persons. Otherwise, it merely stayed the hand of Congress in the latter's exercise of a power presumably granted elsewhere in the Constitution. It would have been just as accurate to say that the clause authorized the future abolition of the slave trade and thus amounted, by Taney's own logic, to a delayed repudiation of the slave system. Some delegates did in fact regard the clause as a major step toward total abolition.[41]

Whether intended or not, the vagueness of the clause lent variety to its interpretation. Thus the awkward euphemism for slaves could be read as including free immigrants also. And for the sets of dual phrasing ("migration or importation" and "tax or duty") there were several explanations: (1) They merely reflected the lawyer's habit of saying everything at least twice. (2) They were intended to include and distinguish between free immigrants and slaves. (3) They were intended to include and distinguish between entry from abroad and movement across state lines (thereby confirming the power of Congress, after 1807, to regulate or prohibit the interstate slave trade). (4) They were an acknowledgment of the slave's dual status as person and thing. (5) They were an attempt to straddle conflicting sectional views of the slave's fundamental nature.[42] Certainly the use of the word "importation" and the very idea of collecting a duty on imported slaves seemed to recognize the property-holding aspect of slavery. But it was a recognition scheduled for cancellation in twenty years. Even the authority to impose a tax or duty was symbolically ambiguous, as Congress soon discovered. Measures unsuccessfully introduced in 1789 and again in 1804–6 were defended on the antislavery grounds that taxation would constitute a public censure of the slave trade, and they were opposed on the antislavery grounds that such taxation would degrade human beings by classifying them as merchandise.[43]

Neither the three-fifths clause nor the slave-trade clause offered slavery any positive protection under the Constitution. The fugitive-slave clause, on the other hand, became the basis for the most notorious kind of federal intervention in behalf of the institution. According to a modern scholar, it gave "a nationwide sanction to the right to property in slaves." This, of course, was precisely the view that Taney would take in 1857.[44]

Yet the wording scarcely invites such an interpretation:

> No person held to service or labour in one State, under the laws thereof, escaping into another, shall, in consequence of any law or regulation therein, be discharged from such service or labour, but shall be delivered up on claim of the party to whom such service or labour may be due.[45]

Read literally, the clause seems to include apprentices and other persons bound to service for a limited period. Thus, unlike the three-fifths clause, it drew no distinction between free and non-free persons. And its terminology, unlike that of the slave-trade clause, carried no connotation of property. Not in what it said, but only in how it was universally understood, did the so-called fugitive-slave clause acknowledge the existence of slavery in America.

The clause was not a significant issue in the Convention. Introduced late in the proceedings by a South Carolina delegate, it aroused little debate and received unanimous approval. There is little evidence to support the assertion frequently made in later years that without the clause the Constitution would have failed. As originally proposed, the clause would have amended the section on interstate flight from justice by requiring "fugitive slaves and servants to be delivered up like criminals." The final version became a separate paragraph of Article Four, placed immediately following the flight-from-justice paragraph, and its phrasing reflected the influence of a similar provision recently written into the Northwest Ordinance.[46]

Placement of the fugitive-slave clause in Article Four, rather than in Article One, suggests that it was designed as a limitation on state authority and not as an extension of federal power and responsibility. That is, the purpose was to guard against personal-liberty laws, rather than to provide for a national fugitive-slave law. The very language of the clause seems plainly directed at the states, not at Congress. Nevertheless, both Congress and the Supreme Court eventually came to the opposite conclusion.[47]

IV

Of course there were other passages in the completed Constitution
that would come to bear upon the institution of slavery—including
the privileges-and-immunities clause, the territory clause, and the
provision for admission of new states. But none of these passages
were directed at slavery, and none contributed even by implication to
defining its constitutional status.[48] Furthermore, the three clauses
that did deal with slavery seemed to embody no ruling principle except compromise for the sake of union. "Intent of the framers" is in
this instance probably a fiction, not merely because some of the
framers were in sharp disagreement about the constitutional status of
slavery but because so many of them had never given the problem
systematic consideration. Even Madison, with all of his awareness,
proves to be hopelessly ambiguous on the subject.[49] Yet if the text
and historical context of the three clauses fail to reveal a clear intent,
their want of coherence does not entirely obscure a certain elemental
drift or tendency.

To begin with, the Constitution neither authorized nor specifically forbade the abolition of slavery. It dealt only with certain pe-
ripheral features of the institution. All three of the slavery clauses
treated slaves as "persons," and just one (the three-fifths clause) expressly differentiated between free and unfree persons. None used
the word "property." One (the slave-trade clause) contained language
that seemed to reflect the property-holding aspect of slavery, but
another (the fugitive-slave clause) seemed almost to repudiate ownership of men by designating a slave as a "person held to service or
labour," and an owner as "the party to whom such service or labour is
due." The temporary nature of the slave-trade clause made it a dubious sanction for perpetual slavery. In addition, the operation of the
clause was restricted to the original states, and this, together with
congressional enactment of the Northwest Ordinance, indicated a
disposition to make slavery the exception rather than the rule in an
expanding nation.

Perhaps most revealing of all was a last-minute revision of the
fugitive-slave clause. As it came from the committee of style, the

clause began: "No person legally held to service or labour in one state." The revised version read: "No person held to service or labour in one state, under the laws thereof." Because of its contextual ambiguity, the word "legally" would have permitted the inference that the Constitution explicitly affirmed the legality of slavery. The framers, in shifting to the phrase "under the laws thereof," lent strong support to those antislavery spokesmen of a later day who would insist that slavery was without national existence and strictly the creature of local law.[50]

The pattern that emerges is one of acknowledging the legitimate presence of slavery in American life while attaching a cluster of limitations to the acknowledgment. Abraham Lincoln was perhaps overreaching the evidence when he declared that the fathers of the government intended to put the institution "in the course of ultimate extinction." Yet he may have been much closer to the mark than those southerners who insisted that the right to hold slaves as property was "distinctly and expressly affirmed in the Constitution."[51]

One returns finally to the striking fact that in the three clauses dealing with slavery, the word itself was deliberately avoided. This should not be dismissed as mere fastidiousness. The law inheres most essentially in the text of the document, not in the purposes of those who wrote the document, although the purposes may be consulted to illuminate obscure meaning.[52] The sharp contrast here between text and purpose has its own significant effect, whether intended or not. It is as though the framers were half-consciously trying to frame two constitutions, one for their own time and the other for the ages, with slavery viewed bifocally—that is, plainly visible at their feet, but disappearing when they lifted their eyes.[53]

Slavery in the
American Constitutional System

From time to time at the Constitutional Convention there had been confrontations between a slavery interest and an antislavery sentiment. The interest was concentrated, persistent, practical, and testily defensive. The sentiment tended to be diffuse, sporadic, moralistic, and tentative. This distinction between interest and sentiment remains appropriate for at least the first half-century of national history. An antislavery interest of significant proportions was slow to develop, even slower than a proslavery sentiment.

Antislavery sentiment received considerable lip service even from the slavery interest in the early years of the Republic, and the first American constitutions, including those of the slaveholding states, made no direct mention of the peculiar institution.[1] Constitution-making, after all, was a noble enterprise, infused with a good deal of political philosophy and moral grandeur. Overt recognition of slavery did not fit well with solemn discussion of fundamental law, the social compact, and bills of rights. In the day-to-day operations of government, however, interest would usually have the advantage over sentiment.

American Negro slavery had originated in international custom and colonial practice, reinforced by the express or implied support of the English government. Over the years, however, the institution had acquired a legal structure consisting essentially of local common and statute law in the thirteen colonies. Slavery under the new federal Constitution of 1787 remained almost entirely the legal creature of local (state) law. In this respect it was not unlike marriage, property-holding, inheritance, and other basic social institutions, except that state authority extended beyond protection and regulation to the power of annihilation. That is, abolition of slavery by legislative action was conceivable everywhere in the United States, while abolition of marriage or private property was not. The principal reason for this significant difference may have been the fact that slavery, unlike marriage and property, had no clear-cut sanction in natural law. Indeed, a widespread belief that slavery was contrary to natural law (and thus existent solely by force of positive law) penetrated deeply even into southern thought and jurisprudence.[2]

The abolition of slavery in the North during and after the Revolution tells us a good deal about the structure of the early Republic. This "first emancipation" was a striking expression, not only of state sovereignty but also of legislative supremacy; for in most instances it was achieved by statutory means. State governors played no important part in the achievement, and state judiciaries offered no resistance of any consequence.[3]

State control of slavery was exercised as an inherent or residual power carried over from colonial times and lodged primarily in the legislature. Disillusionment with legislative dominance began to set in not long after the Revolution, however, and state constitutions were increasingly written or rewritten to instruct legislatures more precisely in their duties and to lay more definite restrictions on their power. Among the slaveholding states, this trend encouraged the injection of references to slavery into written constitutional law. Thus the constitution of Arkansas at the time of its admission to statehood in 1836 authorized the general assembly to regulate slavery in a number of ways, while at the same time declaring that it should "have no power to pass laws for the emancipation of slaves, without the consent of the owners."[4]

More important than the incorporation of some statute law into constitutional law was the process of converting much common law and custom into statute law and organizing the latter systematically into digests or codes. Codification of a sort had begun in the early colonial period, and it soon came to embrace the institution of slavery. In 1680, for example, Virginia enacted a general police law "for preventing negroes insurrections." It grew more elaborate with subsequent additions and was drawn upon to some extent by several other colonies and slaveholding states in the construction of their own slave codes. South Carolina in 1712 likewise enacted comprehensive legislation for controlling the "barbarous, wild, savage natures" of Negro slaves, using the law of Barbados as its model. A revised and enlarged version, enacted in 1740, was then taken over, with some modifications, by Georgia during the years 1755 to 1770.[5]

The general law passed by Georgia in 1770 became the basis for the slave code of the state. Accumulating legislation was summed up from time to time in penal codes and in various digests. On the eve of the Civil War, the Georgia legislature authorized preparation of a comprehensive code of state laws, "whether derived from the Common Law, the Constitutions, the Statutes of the State, the decisions of the Supreme Court, or the Statutes of England, of force in this State."[6] Prepared by a commission that included a leading national authority on slave law, Thomas R. R. Cobb, and adopted on December 19, 1860, in the midst of the secession crisis, this code may be taken as a kind of antebellum climax in the legal history of slavery.

The code was divided into four principal parts, each having important provisions related to slavery. Part One, devoted to the structure of state government, included a detailed chapter on the patrol system with which slaves were kept in bounds. Part Two, the civil code, began with a section on "different kinds of persons" that defined the character of slavery and laid down some of the basic principles governing the institution, such as the incapacity of slaves to own property and the rule that children of slaves followed the "condition of their mother." A chapter entitled "Of Master and Slave" ran to forty sections—one of which, for example, guaranteed slaves a day of rest on Sunday, while another forbade manumission except by legislative act, and still another provided for retaliation against northern states that refused to return fugitive slaves. Elsewhere in the civil code there were sections regulating the hiring of slaves and forbidding slaves to enter into contracts. Part Three, the code of legal practice, contained a chapter detailing the proceedings to be followed in suits for freedom. Part Four, the penal code, included a separate code for slaves and free Negroes. One article of this unit listed the crimes for which, when committed by blacks, capital punishment was mandatory or discretionary. For instance, conviction of raping a white woman, which meant a prison sentence of two to twenty years for a white offender, carried a mandatory death penalty for Negro offenders. Even attempted rape of a white woman by a black man could be punished with death, at the discretion of the court. On the other hand, rape of a slave or free Negro by a white man was punishable "by fine and imprisonment, at the discretion of the court." Another division of the penal code listed the "offences relative to slaves" that could be committed by any free person—such as treating a slave cruelly, selling a slave intoxicating liquor, and supplying books to a slave.[7]

The slave codes of the South varied substantially from state to state and underwent frequent legislative revision. The state laws, moreover, were supplemented by a large body of local regulations, and of course for the average slave the most important law was likely to be the set of rules laid down and enforced by the master on the plantation.

The accumulation and codification of statutory law pertaining to slavery did not, as one might expect, diminish the volume or significance of judicial lawmaking on the subject. For despite all the drafting of so-called codes, the American states (except Louisiana) remained firmly within the common-law tradition, in which judges constantly manufacture law during the process of applying existent law to individual cases.* The very increase in the body of statute law on slavery meant that there was more text for judges to interpret (statutory construction) and more likelihood of their finding conflicts between statute and constitution (judicial review). Furthermore, there were times when statute law did not cover a case, necessitating

---

* Even in Louisiana, with its civil-law tradition, the law of slavery was scarcely less influenced by judicial interpretation than in the rest of the country. See below, pp. 59–60.

a resort to other authorities, such as natural law or the common law of England.

The complexity of slavery and its numerous ambiguities, such as the dual status of the slave as person and property, produced many of those legal gray areas that encourage and often necessitate judicial lawmaking. For instance, in criminal law, the slave was regarded essentially as a person, responsible and punishable for his offenses. But did this mean that he could be tried under any part of the criminal code, or only under those parts that either pertained exclusively to slaves or expressly included them? In the absence of clear legislative determination, the question had to be dealt with judicially as it arose in specific cases, and the answers varied from court to court and state to state.[8]

The law of private rights (civil law), on the other hand, treated slaves primarily as property, and even though a slave was punishable as a person for any crime he might commit, he was not suable as a person for any injury he might do. Damages, if they were to be collected at all, had to be collected from the slaveholder. But was a master legally liable for the injurious acts of his slave, just as he might be for damage done by his livestock? Here, too, there were both affirmative and negative answers, provided in some states by statute but in others by judicial decision; and even the statutory provisions soon acquired a significant judicial gloss.[9]

Furthermore, even in civil cases where the slave's status as property was not in dispute, there could be disagreement about the class of property to which he belonged. The statute law of the subject was often highly ambiguous. In 1820, for instance, the Kentucky Court of Appeals declared: "It is true, that by the positive law of this country, slaves are declared to be real estate; but by the same law, there are to that rule so many exceptions, that they may, at least in common parlance, and by common intent, be sufficiently described as personal estate."[10] Such statutory confusion is, in its practical effects, a grant of judicial power.

In behavioral terms, the so-called law of slavery was the work, not only of those persons who drafted it but also of everyone charged with enforcing it—including sheriffs, constables, patrols, judges, jailors, masters, and overseers. But as a body of written rules, it was primarily the work of state legislatures and state appellate courts, with the latter standing first in the sheer bulk of their contribution. Jacob D. Wheeler's *A Practical Treatise on the Law of Slavery*, published in 1837, is nothing more than a compilation of selected court decisions, and Thomas R. R. Cobb's much better known book on the subject cites court cases more often than any other kind of authority. In one of the monumental achievements of American scholarship, Helen Tunnicliff Catterall abstracted most of the appellate cases concerning American slavery, and the number runs, by a conservative estimate, to more than five thousand.[11]

II

The content of this state law of slavery, which was in a small degree constitutional but for the most part of legislative and judicial origin, has been described in all of its detail and variety by numerous historians. In fact, any book on slavery is likely to have at least one chapter on the law of slavery.[12] Recently, moreover, the subject has been studied in depth by a number of legal scholars.[13] Here, it is sufficient to note certain major characteristics and tendencies discernible in a cluster of fifteen systems that were similar but by no means uniform, and stable but by no means unchanging.

General police laws and penal codes for the governance of slaves had been well developed in the Old South by the end of the colonial period and were ready for appropriation by new slaveholding states as they entered the Union, beginning with Kentucky in 1792 and Tennessee in 1796. The law of slavery as it moved westward tended to lose some of its severity—not because westerners were more tender-hearted but because the times were becoming more enlightened. Thus the slave code of Arkansas was considerably less severe than the codes of Virginia and South Carolina, which, locked in the colonial tradition, remained the harshest in the South.[14] At the same time, the severity of the codes was often mitigated by executive clemency. In Virginia, for example, it appears that a majority of death sentences for slaves were commuted to transportation.[15]

For slaves as well as free men, the cruel physical punishments of earlier times were eliminated or at least diminished in the criminal law of the nineteenth century. The list of capital offenses grew longer as a consequence, however, and the inappropriateness of imprisonment for slaves left whipping as the standard punishment for lesser offenses. The Georgia Code of 1861 specified that jailors and constables should be paid one dollar "for whipping a negro," but set the limit at thirty-nine lashes, not "inhumanly" done.[16]

Perhaps the most notable development in the slave law of the nineteenth century was the increasing procedural protection given slaves accused of capital offenses. In many southern states this came to include nominal equality with white persons in respect to the rights of trial by jury and appeal, the right to counsel, and immunity from coerced self-incrimination. The changes were wrought by legislative action and by certain enlightened appellate judges, some of whom insisted upon bringing the slave generally within the protection of the common law. Such ameliorative tendencies did not reflect any erosion of proslavery conviction in the South; for in protecting a slave's person one also protected a master's property, while at the same time offering refutation to the abolitionist indictment of slavery as totally unjust and inhumane.[17]

Slaves as the victims of physical attacks and other mistreatment by white persons were likewise better off in the nineteenth century, though here the progress seems pathetically slight by modern standards. Under colonial law, the killing of a slave in the course of chastisement or in a fit of passion was a minor offense at most and seldom punished. Even for willful, malicious homicide the prescribed penalty was ordinarily no more than a fine.[18] Beginning with a North Carolina law of 1774, all of the slaveholding states eventually imposed death as the punishment for deliberate murder of a slave. South Carolina did so at last in 1821, but the same law declared that anyone killing a slave in "sudden heat and passion" should, upon conviction, pay a fine of no more than $500 and be imprisoned for no more than six months.[19] Non-fatal abuse of slaves was occasionally punished under the common law of the general criminal code, and by the 1850s most states provided statutory protection of some kind. The Georgia Code of 1861, for instance, defined excessive whipping and various other cruelties as misdemeanors, punishable by fine or imprisonment at the discretion of the court. Furthermore, the code declared: "On second conviction, such person shall be declared incapable of holding slave property in the State."[20]

But the enforcement of these protective laws was difficult and infrequent. For one thing, no southern state permitted a slave to testify against a white person. Thus, conviction of a white offender required white testimony strong enough to convince an all-white jury, and that seldom materialized. In a study of nine southern states from 1830 to 1860, A. E. Keir Nash discovered only forty-seven appeals of white persons convicted of killing or injuring slaves—an average of about one such appeal per state every six years. The fact that thirty-four of those appeals were denied indicates, as Nash maintains, "exemplary fairness" on the part of the appellate courts; but the figures may also reflect the fact that only extremely flagrant cases of assault on slaves ever came to trial. Indeed, as Nash points out, the death or injury of a slave at the hands of someone other than his master was much more likely to result in a civil suit for property damage than in a criminal prosecution.[21]

The ultimate purpose of the slave codes was to prevent insurrections and other dangerous forms of servile resistance, such as arson and poisoning. Southern legislatures grappled continually with the problem of security, becoming especially active in the 1830s after the Nat Turner rampage and the emergence of Garrisonian abolitionism. Much of the security legislation laid restrictions on white behavior considered subversive in its influence on slaves. Laws forbade teaching slaves to read and write, trading with slaves, gambling with slaves, or supplying them with liquor, guns, or poisonous drugs. In addition, severe penalties were established for the utterance of abolitionist doctrines and the circulation of abolitionist propaganda. According to an Arkansas statute of 1850, for instance, a person could be sentenced to a year in jail just for publicly denying the right of property in slaves; and he could be imprisoned up to five years for inciting slaves to rebel or distributing literature to that end. This latter penalty was actually rather mild, however, for in some states the same offense was punishable by death.[22]

The fear of insurrection was also reflected in southern hostility to free Negroes, who were widely regarded as a subversive influence on slaves, by their example if not by any actual intent. With increasing severity, most of the slaveholding states endeavored to eliminate this dangerous social element by forbidding or discouraging manumission; by compelling manumitted slaves to leave the state; by prohibiting immigration of free blacks from other states; and by subjecting the resident free black population to additional restraints and disabilities amounting virtually to persecution.*

If this state law of slavery—constitutional, statutory, and judicial—were the whole story, then even in all its great bulk and variety it would be a relatively simple story of each state's enforcing its own law within its own jurisdiction. The complexity results in large part from the interplay, overlapping, and conflict among these and other jurisdictions. For one thing, there was the remarkable extent to which slavery, though given very limited recognition in the Constitution, became a matter of concern to the federal government in the routine conduct of its business. For another thing, there were the legal problems arising when the laws of more than one jurisdiction became applicable to a single case. "Conflict of laws," a major category of jurisprudence, embraces matters of fundamental social importance, such as the status and force within one state or nation of a contract signed, a marriage celebrated, a will made, or a court judgment rendered under the authority of a different jurisdiction. It extended most frequently to the institution of slavery in instances where it appeared that a Negro was free by the law of one state and a slave by the law of another.[23]

III

It might seem that in a nation already plainly becoming "half slave and half free" in 1789, the new federal government ought to have followed a policy of scrupulous neutrality and detachment, leaving slavery entirely to the responsibility of the slaveholding states. Technically, the Constitution would have permitted adoption of such a

*On manumission and the free black, see below, pp. 48–50.

policy, but various influences and circumstances conspired not only to involve the United States government with slavery but to make it in some degree a sponsor and protector of the institution.

The pressure of the slavery interest on the federal government was greatly enhanced, for instance, by the location of the national capital on the north bank of the Potomac River and by the predominance of southern leadership in the public affairs of the new nation. The city of Washington was from its inception a slaveholding community, and it remained so by the express volition of Congress, which in 1801 decreed that the laws of Virginia and Maryland should continue in force within the District of Columbia.[24] Thus the only sizable area of the country exclusively and permanently under United States jurisdiction acquired its own slave code, established and enforced by federal authority. One finds a federal judge in 1807 sentencing a slave convicted of robbery to be "burnt in the hand and whipped with one hundred stripes." And one finds another in 1856 instructing a jury that assault and battery on a slave is not indictable unless done in such a manner and such a place as to constitute a public nuisance.[25] The fact that many early presidents, cabinet members, and congressmen were owners of slaves likewise tended to normalize and legitimate the institution on a national basis. Some northern residents and visitors found it painful that the United States should thus present a slaveholding aspect to the nations of the world. But for others the experience of living daily in the presence of slavery may have softened the image of a system that in the District of Columbia "wore perhaps its mildest face."[26]

Federal jurisdiction over western territories also helped implicate the United States government in the maintenance and promotion of slavery. To be sure, the first Congress did re-enact the Northwest Ordinance with its famous antislavery article, and later Congresses resisted strenuous efforts to have the article suspended. But much of the proslavery pressure came from territorial officials appointed by the President, and with their encouragement both the Indiana and Illinois territories established indenture systems amounting to quasi-slavery. Congress, although it had the power to disallow such flagrant violations of the spirit of the Ordinance, did not choose to do so. Fur-

thermore, beginning in 1790, Congress gave its acquiescence to the
expansion of slavery into the southwest. There, as in the District of
Columbia, slave codes adopted under federal authority were enforced
by federally appointed officers and judges.

The conduct of foreign affairs was still another realm of responsibility that involved the federal government in the sustention of slavery. The Washington administration, for instance, had inherited from
the Confederation government the task of persuading Great Britain to
recompense slaveholders for slaves carried off by British forces at the
close of the Revolution. To demand such compensation was obviously
to affirm that slaves were property, and yet men of antislavery sentiment like John Adams, Gouverneur Morris, and John Jay allowed
themselves to be enlisted in the enterprise. Jay's Treaty of 1794 included no British concessions on the issue, however, and the omission was a major cause of the southern hostility that almost defeated
the treaty in the Senate.[27] A similar problem on a smaller scale presented itself after the War of 1812, and again the United States government pressed vigorously for the compensation of owners whose
slaves had fled to British forts and warships. This time the effort succeeded. After more than a decade of negotiations in which John
Quincy Adams played a major role, Britain gave up the struggle and
paid indemnities totaling over a million dollars.[28]

In various other ways and in numerous incidents, the problem of
fugitive and resistant slaves impinged upon American foreign relations. Thus, Adams as secretary of state lent the assistance of his office
to southerners trying to extradite fugitives from Canada. In a more violent intervention several years earlier, the Madison administration
authorized the destruction of a fort in Spanish Florida held largely by
escaped blacks who were allegedly enticing other slaves in nearby
Georgia to flee from their masters. Nearly all the occupants of the
fort, numbering some three hundred men, women, and children,
were killed or fatally wounded during the attack.[29]

Slave ships on the high seas could also spell trouble for the
United States government in its relations with foreign powers. During the 1830s, slaves from several distressed or shipwrecked coasting
vessels were rescued in British West Indian waters and promptly set

free. The Jackson and Van Buren administrations, in language that sometimes became menacing, repeatedly demanded compensation for the slave-owners. At one point the government insisted that under American law slaves were property and no different from inanimate property. The British government eventually agreed to pay the slave-owners, but only for those human cargoes liberated before abolition took effect in the British colonies.[30]

Anglo-American relations were further embittered in 1841 when slaves aboard the *Creole*, en route from Virginia to Louisiana, staged a mutiny and took the ship to Nassau in the Bahamas. This time it was Daniel Webster, secretary of state in the Tyler administration, who labored in vain to have the slaves returned to the United States. Again the British stood firm, though a claims commission many years later awarded a small indemnity to the American owners.[31]

The case of the *Amistad* was substantially different, involving a Cuban ship taken over in 1839 by mutinous slaves and eventually brought into an American port. It soon came to light that most of the slaves had been carried off from Africa in violation of treaties suppressing the international slave trade. The Spanish government nevertheless demanded return of the slaves, and the Van Buren administration tried earnestly to comply. Because of salvage claims, however, the issue went to trial in a federal district court and reached the Supreme Court in 1841, the year of the *Creole* affair. With only one justice dissenting, the Court declared the Negroes to be free men. Yet, as Carl B. Swisher says, there was an "odd sequel" to the *Amistad* story in the continued refusal of the executive branch of the federal government to accept the Court decision as final. Presidents Tyler, Polk, Pierce, and Buchanan all recommended payment of reparations, but Congress never made the appropriation. These presidential efforts to appease Spain were probably not unconnected with the chronic presidential desire for annexation of Cuba.[32]

IV

The executive branch of the federal government became involved in the *Amistad* affair because of presidential responsibility for the conduct of foreign relations; the federal judiciary became involved because of its admiralty and maritime jurisdiction as specified in the Constitution. In these ways and others (such as the jurisdiction of federal courts in suits between citizens of different states), the regular duties of office—indeed, the very structure of government—brought federal officials frequently into association with slavery. It is unlikely that a complete detachment, if attempted, could have been achieved and maintained; but at the same time it appears that from the beginning the federal government gave slavery more support than law or circumstances required.

A further case in point is the act of Congress usually referred to as the Fugitive Slave Law of 1793. The relevant clause in the Constitution, as we have seen, was rather vaguely phrased in the passive voice and located elsewhere than among the powers delegated to Congress. A person "held to service or labor" in one state and escaping into another, it said, must be "delivered up" when claimed by the party to whom the service or labor was due. That the clause necessitated or even authorized congressional implementation is open to question. Enforcement might have been left to interstate comity or to the federal judicial process.*

The first session of the first Congress apparently saw no pressing need in 1789 to include a fugitive-slave law in the great body of fundamental legislation with which it was then setting the federal government in motion. Not until four years later did the second session of the second Congress take action on the subject, and it did so more or less gratuitously.

No outbreak of fugitive activity had inspired a slaveholders' demand for legislation. The act of 1793 resulted instead from a quarrel between Pennsylvania and Virginia over criminal extradition. But since fugitives from justice and fugitives from service had been dealt with side by side in the Constitution, it seemed logical to do so again in implemental legislation. And so Congress passed "An Act respecting fugitives from justice, and persons escaping from the service of their masters."[34] The first half of the law, dealing with criminal ex-

* Daniel Webster, in his famous Seventh of March speech during the crisis of 1850, said of the fugitive-slave clause: "I have always been of the opinion that it was an injunction upon the States themselves."[33]

tradition, proved to be essentially declaratory. Whenever the governor of a state demanded the return of a fugitive from justice who had fled into another state, it was to be the "duty" of the governor of the second state to comply. The law provided no means of compelling a governor to perform his duty, and it is unlikely that any such compulsion would have been permissible under the Constitution. Interstate extradition thus remained what it had been before the act was passed—a matter of interstate comity.[35]

The second half of the law had more teeth in it and was less deferential to state sovereignty. It authorized a slave-owner or his agent to cross a state line, seize an alleged fugitive slave, take the slave before any federal judge or local magistrate, and there, upon proof of ownership, receive a certificate entitling him to return home with his captive. Financial penalties were provided for interfering in any way with the recovery of a fugitive. The act as a whole passed in the Senate without recorded opposition and in the House by the overwhelming majority of 48 to 7.[36]

And so, with scarcely a serious thought about the implications of its action, Congress voted to invade state sovereignty for the benefit of the slaveholder, issuing him a kind of vigilante's license to enforce his rights himself with a minimum of formality.* The law set aside normal legal process, such as the writ of habeas corpus and trial by jury. Its evidential requirements were loose, oral testimony being sufficient. It gave the alleged fugitive no protection against self-incrimination and no assurance that he could testify in his own behalf. It specified no time limitation; so an alleged slave could be claimed many years after his alleged escape. Furthermore, there was nothing in the text of the legislation to discourage a pursuer from taking his captive back home without bothering to obtain a certificate. The act was in fact an invitation to kidnapping, whether as a result of honest error or easily contrived fraud.

The early "personal liberty laws" enacted by many northern

---

*Perhaps based upon the common-law right of "recaption," which permitted recovery by personal effort of property wrongfully taken or of a wife, child, or servant wrongfully detained, provided that it was accomplished without breach of the public peace. The difference here, however, was that the right of recaption was made extraterritorially effective within another jurisdiction.[37]

states were in large degree anti-kidnapping laws and often so entitled. Their purpose was not to flout the federal law of 1793 but rather to strike some kind of balance between the rights of slaveholders and the rights of free Negroes threatened by that law.[38] To southerners, who were in the habit of classifying free Negroes with slaves, the priorities seemed clear enough. The right to recover fugitives, they maintained, had been given a preferential place in the Constitution and could not be impaired by any authority for any reason. As interference with recapture increased in the free states, southerners intensified their demands for more effective federal action in the slaveholder's behalf. Congress responded in 1818 with a proposal to amend the act of 1793, giving additional advantage and protection to a slaveholder in pursuit of a fugitive. Both houses passed the bill, but with differences in detail that could not be resolved, and so it never became law.[39]

Meanwhile, certain federal and state courts, in the process of enforcing the act of 1793, were turning aside challenges to its constitutionality, begging the question of its threat to the security of free Negroes, and contributing to the myth that the fugitive-slave clause had been indispensable to the success of the Constitutional Convention and the creation of the Union. In the federal circuit court for Pennsylvania, Justice Henry Baldwin declared, "The foundations of the government . . . rest on the rights of property in slaves."[40] By 1842, the "historical-necessity thesis" had become so well accepted in high judicial circles that five out of seven Supreme Court justices reiterated it in the single case of *Prigg v. Pennsylvania*. Joseph Story, for instance, said that the fugitive-slave clause unquestionably "constituted a fundamental article, without the adoption of which the Union could not have been formed."[41] Thus the clause, by reason of its supposed indispensability, was elevated into a special category as one of the "fundamental articles" of the Constitution.* State and federal judges in the North, faced with the unpopular task of enforcing the

---

*John Codman Hurd, noting that this "method of constitutional interpretation" did not receive judicial sanction in any other class of case, commented: "A court has no right to discriminate provisions of the Constitution as more or less essential to its existence, much less to distribute the powers of sovereignty according to such view."[42]

Fugitive Slave Law, often appealed to the principles of legal positivism, insisting that moral objections to slavery must not be allowed to override the majesty of the written law. Yet the tendency of many judges to treat the fugitive-slave clause as a kind of higher law *within* the Constitution was itself an expression of highly moralistic assumptions about the value of the Union.[43]

V

Among Supreme Court decisions dealing with slavery, *Prigg v. Pennsylvania* rivals *Dred Scott v. Sandford* in historical importance. It is well known that the opinion of the Court, delivered by Justice Story, released state governments from the obligation to enforce the fugitive-slave law of 1793; that the consequences of the release provoked a renewal of southern demands for stronger federal legislation; and that those demands were eventually satisfied in the Compromise of 1850. The *Prigg* decision was thus in one respect a concession to state sovereignty, with an antislavery purpose that backfired.[44] What has perhaps received too little attention, however, is the remarkable extent to which the decision, in its own substance, carried forward the involvement of the federal government in the protection of slavery.

Edward Prigg had been convicted on kidnapping charges in Pennsylvania for taking a recaptured fugitive slave back to Maryland without obtaining the required certificate. Story reversed the judgment and invalidated the Pennsylvania statute under which Prigg had been indicted, finding it in conflict with the federal law of 1793 and with the Constitution. In the course of reasoning his way to this conclusion, he laid down a number of weighty rulings:

1. *Slavery was entirely a creation of municipal (domestic) law and could claim no recognition within another jurisdiction as a matter of international right, though it might be granted some degree of recognition as a matter of international (or interstate) comity.* This part of Story's opinion won applause in certain antislavery circles; yet it had the effect of concentrating in the federal government total responsibility for enforcement of the allegedly indispensable fugitive-slave clause. Without that clause, said Story, "every non-slaveholding State

in the Union would have been at liberty to have declared free all run-
away slaves coming within its limits, and to have given them entire
immunity and protection against the claims of their masters; a course
which would have created the most bitter animosities, and engen-
dered perpetual strife between the different States."[45]

2. *The fugitive-slave clause of the Constitution, aside from any
implemental legislation, was self-executing.* That is, it gave every
slaveholder the "positive, unqualified right" to recapture a slave by
private effort anywhere in the Union, and to do so without interference from any quarter, provided that no breach of the peace were
committed. This right of self-help, said Story, was universal in the
slaveholding states, and the fugitive-slave clause made it equally effective in all the free states. The slaveholder, in short, carried the law
of his own state with him when he pursued a fugitive into a free state.
The implications of such extraterritoriality were startling, though
Story left them unexplored. His ruling had the effect, for instance, of
compelling free states to accept the slave-state principle that a Negro
or mulatto was a slave unless he could prove otherwise. One-half of
the nation must sacrifice its presumption of freedom to the other
half's presumption of slavery, and the historic English principle of *in
favorem libertatis* was reversed where fugitive slaves were concerned.[46]

3. *The fugitive-slave law of 1793 was constitutional.* Here, Story
concentrated entirely on the relatively easy task of demonstrating that
congressional power to enact such legislation could reasonably be inferred from the fugitive-slave clause. For every act of Congress, however, there are two constitutional tests. The first is whether the Constitution authorizes it; the second is whether the Constitution forbids
it. What Story coolly ignored was the argument of counsel for Pennsylvania that the law of 1793, in certain of its provisions, violated personal rights guaranteed by the privileges-and-immunities clause, by
the Fourth Amendment, and by the due-process clause of the Fifth
Amendment. In this manner, free Negroes wrongfully or dubiously
claimed as slaves were denied some of the fundamental protections of
the Constitution.

4. *The power to legislate for enforcement of the slave-holder's*

right of recovery was vested exclusively in Congress. Nothing in the nature of the *Prigg* case necessitated such a pronouncement, and nothing in the text of the fugitive-slave clause justified it. Furthermore, the principle of federal exclusiveness could obviously cut either way in the slavery controversy, depending upon how vigorously Congress exercised its exclusive power. Both sides were accordingly somewhat worried about where the doctrine might lead. Chief Justice Taney, who concurred in the decision and with much of Story's opinion, dissented at this point. State governments, he insisted, were constitutionally restrained only from legislation and other action *interfering* with a slaveholder's property rights in his slave; they had the power and even the obligation to assist in *protecting* those rights.[47] Twenty-five years later, Taney would come to a similar conclusion regarding federal power over slavery in the territories.

The element of racism in the *Prigg* decision, though fundamental, was relatively inconspicuous. It consisted in the Court's silent refusal to pay any attention to the kidnapping problem—a refusal that would have been inconceivable if the victims had been white. Similarly, the proslavery nationalist tendencies of the decision were somewhat obscured by the fact that for a time it worked the other way, as various northern legislatures enacted laws forbidding state officials to participate in the recovery of fugitive slaves.[48] Despite these antislavery consequences, the *Prigg* decision, enunciated by an avowedly antislavery New Englander, was another major indication of the extent to which the United States government had voluntarily become the guardian of slaveholding rights everywhere outside the territorial limits of slaveholding law.

The fugitive-slave clause, implemented in the law of 1793 and given added force and meaning in court decisions, came to have a significance that transcended the problem to which it was addressed. The number of slaves actually escaping over the years made little difference.[49] What mattered most to southerners was legitimation of their *right* of recovery, for it came to be an "indispensable foundation" of the proslavery argument.[50] In the long-running debate between the enemies of slavery and its defenders, neither side maintained a consistent position on the question of national power versus state sovereignty. Both shifted ground whenever it suited their intrinsic purposes to do so. For southerners especially the issue was critical and delicate. At times driven by circumstances to invoke federal protection of their slaveholding rights, they were nevertheless extremely reluctant to endorse any increase in federal authority over slavery, fearing that the power to protect could too easily be converted into the power to destroy. Even the Fugitive Slave Act of 1850, although passed in response to southern demands, made some southerners uneasy because of its expansion of federal authority.[51] Yet the federal fugitive-slave complex as a whole (that is, the clause, the legislation of Congress, and the judicial enforcement) provided the South with the basic formula for claiming federal protection of slavery while denying federal power to interfere with slavery.

Federal enforcement of the fugitive-slave clause treated slaves essentially as property and thus constituted federal acquiescence at an early date in the southern definition of slaveholding as a form of property-holding. This acquiescence, though not required by the language of the clause itself, was repeatedly confirmed in judicial decisions. For example, Story in his *Prigg* opinion referred to slaves as "this species of property."[52] The fact that slaves were regarded as property *under federal law* proved highly advantageous to the South in the constitutional debates on slavery in the territories. In addition, the federal fugitive-slave complex gave the southern law of slavery an imperial, extrajurisdictional force within the free states, thereby furnishing a precedent for similar claims to extrajurisdictional rights within the federal territories. The effect was to make slaveholding rights to some degree national in scope, overriding even the sovereignty of the states.

Yet the federal government undertook its fugitive-slave responsibilities, not by virtue of any authority delegated to Congress in Article One, Section Eight, of the Constitution but rather as the guarantor of slaveholding rights outside the jurisdiction of slaveholding law—and therefore as virtually the extrajurisdictional *agent* of the slaveholding states. In some respects, then, the federal fugitive-slave complex provided a working model of John C. Calhoun's theory of the Union as a compact among sovereign states in which the federal government, being the mere "common agent" of those states, had certain protective obligations where slavery was concerned but possessed no power to interfere with the institution anywhere.[53]

Whether so much federal intervention in behalf of slavery accorded with the letter and spirit of the Constitution was a matter of disagreement even among abolitionists, some of whom insisted that the Convention of 1787 had sold the nation's soul to the slaveholder, while others maintained that it had written essentially an antislavery document.[54] What seems worth stressing, however, is the extent to which the framers were indeterminate in their treatment of slavery, leaving Congress and the other branches of government much freedom of choice as a consequence. That federal power should have become in many ways a bulwark of slavery was a development permitted but not required by the Constitution. It reflected not only the day-to-day advantage of interest over sentiment and the predominance of southern leadership in the federal government but also the waning of the liberal idealism of the Revolution.

The Pursuit of Freedom

A side from the fugitive's hazardous road to an uncertain future, there were various legal ways for a slave to escape into freedom. The pale southern counterpart of northern emancipation in the aftermath of the Revolution was a substantial increase of individual manumissions. Indeed, it appears that during those early decades of the Republic, more slaves may have been freed in the South than in the North, where universal emancipation was under way. One piece of evidence supporting such an estimate is the fact that the free black population of the South grew at a faster rate than the free black population of the North.[1]

Manumission, being an exercise of the property-holder's inherent right to renounce ownership of his property, presumably needed no express sanction of law, but like all property rights it was subject to regulation in the public interest.[2] Even in colonial times, certain legislative restrictions had been laid on private emancipation. A Virginia law of 1691, for instance, required the owner who freed a slave to pay for his transportation out of the colony. South Carolina later enacted similar legislation but allowed it to lapse. In 1723, a more stringent Virginia law prohibited manumission entirely, except for "meritorious services" confirmed by the governor and council. Beginning the same year, North Carolina adopted a series of restrictive acts, establishing the "meritorious services" test and requiring

that freed Negroes leave the colony within six months or face re-
enslavement.[3]

Then, in 1782, with the spirit of the Revolution triumphant,
Virginia removed her principal barriers to manumission, and Delaware and Maryland followed suit a few years thereafter. North Carolina, to be sure, maintained her restrictive policy, but elsewhere in
the South of 1790 private emancipation was relatively unimpeded by
law. The main limitation was the requirement by many states of security for liberated slaves who, because of age or infirmity, were likely
to become public charges.[4] Thousands of slaves were individually
manumitted in the next two decades, and during that time the free
black population of the South grew three times as fast as the white
and slave populations.[5]

But a reaction soon set in. Free Negroes were, after all, an
anomaly in a slaveholding society. Their presence in increasing
numbers seemed likely to cause dissatisfaction in slave quarters and
perhaps inspire slave resistance. The black rebellion on the island of
Santo Domingo was a frightening spectacle for southerners in the
1790s, and its leaders were recently freed slaves. The shadow of
Santo Domingo fell across Virginia in 1800 with the discovery of
Gabriel Prosser's plot to lead a band of fellow slaves in an insurrectionary attack on Richmond. Apparently no free blacks were involved
in the conspiracy, and yet Virginians, with Santo Domingo in mind,
put free blacks at the center of their racial apprehensions. One of the
consequences was a law passed in 1806 requiring that manumitted
slaves leave the state within twelve months.[6]

Several other southern legislatures had already passed new laws
restricting manumission in one way or another, and this became the
dominant trend of the next half-century. Many states eventually followed Virginia's example in requiring the removal of liberated slaves,
and some insisted that bond be posted to guarantee such removal. A
number of states canceled the slaveholder's right to free his slaves privately by will, deed, or contract, making manumission instead a public act that could be performed only by a judge in court or by means
of special legislation. More and more states also prohibited slaves
from hiring out their own time, thereby discouraging the practice of

achieving freedom through self-purchase. Hostility to manumission grew even stronger as the sectional conflict entered its final stages in the 1850s. Louisiana and Tennessee required guarantees that freed slaves would be sent out of the United States, and by the end of the decade several states had forbidden manumission absolutely.[7]

Yet, despite all efforts at curtailment, manumissions continued. They reportedly numbered some three thousand in the year 1860, for example, and the figure was probably an underestimate.[8] This does not mean that a significant abolitionist tradition persisted in the South, for antislavery conviction seldom appeared to be the reason for manumission. Rather, freedom was often given as a reward for faithful service. Even more often, perhaps, the slaveholder was simply freeing his own children born to a slave concubine.[9] Many of the southern laws aimed at restricting manumissions were poorly enforced, and exceptions were frequently made by courts and legislatures. It has been estimated, for instance, that about one-fourth or one-third of Virginia's free black population in 1860 was living there in violation of the removal act of 1806. Furthermore, anti-manumission laws could be circumvented in a number of ways. Thus, a slaveholder might take his slaves into a free state and liberate them there. More common was the practice of simply turning a slave loose to fend for himself without the formality of manumission. Such quasi-free slaves became fairly numerous in the urban South, and by the 1850s their number in St. Louis may have included Dred Scott.[10]

II

Unintentional manumission was also possible. It could occur as a result of a slave's merely being moved from one slaveholding state to another in violation of law.[11] More significant, however, were the claims to freedom that sometimes arose when slaves were taken into states or territories where slavery was prohibited. What happened to the legal condition of a slave entering a nonslaveholding jurisdiction? And if he later returned to a slaveholding state, what counter-effect did that return have upon whatever change of condition had been wrought by his stay in the free state or territory? By the early decades of the nineteenth century, this problem of the status of slaves residing or once resident on free soil had already become one of the classic issues in the legal history of slavery.

Actually, it was not just a single issue but rather a complex cluster of issues. For one thing, it included the substantive question of which law should prevail and the jurisdictional question of who had the final word about which law should prevail. Still another question of crucial importance was whether the purpose and duration of the slave's residence on free soil made any significant difference in its effect on his status.

To the substantive question there were three basic answers, each subject to qualification:

1. *The law of slavery remained attached to a slave when he entered a free state; his status did not change.* This was admittedly the case with fugitive slaves by explicit provision of the Constitution, but how much further did the extraterritorial force of slaveholding law extend? Obviously it must at some point yield to the sovereign power of the free state; otherwise, slavery would be a national institution.

2. *The slave taken by his master into a free state became a free man and remained so permanently, wherever he might go thereafter.* This amounted to: (A) a rejection of the extraterritoriality of slavery, except in the case of fugitives, and (B) an assertion of the extraterritorial effect of emancipation. Proposition A, if not otherwise qualified, would mean that a slaveholder manumitted his slave the moment the two of them set foot on free soil. Proposition B, the principle of "once free, forever free," had strong roots in natural law and the European civil law tradition.

3. *The slave taken into a free state became free in the sense that his master lost the power to control him, but upon his returning to a slaveholding state, the status of slave reattached to him.* This amounted to minimizing or completely denying both the extraterritorial rights of slavery and the extraterritorial force of emancipation.

The jurisdictional question was essentially whether, in a suit for freedom, the forum state had an uninhibited right to apply its own law or whether it could be compelled to apply the law of another state. Such compulsion could come (as it did with respect to fugitive slaves) only from the federal government in the form of an act of Congress or a decision of the Supreme Court. Although the jurisdictional question might arise in a free state, it was more likely to become urgent in a suit for freedom brought by a slave who had been taken into a free state and then returned to a slaveholding state. The specific issue then presented was whether the emancipatory effect of the free state's law would be enforced extraterritorially by federal power, or whether the slave in returning to the slaveholding state reverted totally to its jurisdiction.

The jurisdictional principle of *reversion* was often linked with the substantive principle of *reattachment* (number 3 above). It is nevertheless important to maintain the distinction between the two. The principle of reversion could be confirmed in the end only by the United States Supreme Court, or conceivably by act of Congress, but even if it were confirmed, a slaveholding state might embrace or reject the principle of reattachment.*

As for the purpose and duration of a slaveholding intrusion into free territory, there were numerous varieties of the one and gradations of the other. The primary distinction recognized, however, was between residence temporary enough to be classified as "sojourning" and residence permanent enough to constitute "domicile." The dividing line could be difficult to draw in specific cases, but the distinction, as we shall see, provided the basis for a tacit sectional compromise of some duration.

Underlying the specific substantive question of which law should prevail was the more general problem of the legal and philosophical character of slavery. Discussion of the subject usually led beyond the American constitutional system to English common law and the law of nature. Underlying the specific jurisdictional question of who had the final word was the more general problem of interstate relationships. Discussion led by analogy to the law of nations, especially as expounded on the European continent, and to the branch of that jurisprudence known as the conflict of laws.

*Without using the terms, Taney clearly distinguished between the principle of reversion and the principle of reattachment in his Dred Scott opinion. See below, p. 386.

The problem of the extraterritorial status of slavery had arisen several times in eighteenth-century England, eventually drawing forth the famous decision of Lord Mansfield in *Somerset v. Stewart* (1772). Somerset, a slave taken from Virginia to England, ran away from his master, only to be recaptured and consigned to a ship's captain for sale in Jamaica. Brought before the court of the King's Bench by a writ of habeas corpus, Somerset was ordered released on the ground that nothing in the positive law of the realm authorized his imprisonment aboard the departing ship.[12]

That was, in strictest terms, the whole of the matter, except for a few general statements reportedly included in Mansfield's brief oral opinion. The enormous, persisting influence of the *Somerset* decision on American legal thought is in fact nothing less than astonishing when one considers its limited scope, even in England, and its limited relevance to the interstate aspects of slavery in the United States. For one thing, the primary question confronting Mansfield was whether slavery had legal status in England, given the absence of explicit statutory provisions on the subject; whereas, in the United States, that was not a matter at issue, slavery being for the most part expressly protected or prohibited by positive law. Furthermore, the decision did not outlaw slavery or free the 14,000 slaves then resident in England. It merely declared that English law provided no sanction for holding a slave against his will with the intent of sending him out of the country.[13] Quite obviously, then, it did not settle the question of whether Somerset would remain free if he returned to Virginia. In any case, the problem was not one of comity between equal sovereignties but rather one of internal imperial relations between Britain and her own slaveholding colonies.

The language attributed to the English jurist proved far more important than the decision rendered. Slavery, he allegedly declared, was such an extreme form of personal dominion and, indeed, "so odious" that it could be given legal status only by the positive law of the country in which it was used. Thus *Somerset*, in the words of William M. Wiecek, "burst the confines of Mansfield's judgment."[14] Over the next half-century there developed an extravagant tradition, nourished by some leading English jurists, that the decision had outlawed slavery in Britain, and that, accordingly, any slave brought into the country became a free man the moment he set foot on English soil.[15]

In America, *Somerset* and its legend contributed significantly to the antislavery tendencies of the Revolutionary era. It became a major weapon in the arsenal of abolitionism, lending support to the argument that slavery was contrary to natural law and without legal status beyond the boundaries of the jurisdiction establishing it by positive law.* Yet the *Somerset* doctrine, with one simple adjustment, also fitted into a formula of sectional accommodation. Southerners, for the most part, were willing to accept the doctrine in so far as it applied to slaves *domiciled* by their masters on free soil; northerners, in turn, generally agreed that it should not apply to instances of transit, sojourn, or temporary residence.

In some northern states, such as Pennsylvania and New York, sojourning rights were acknowledged and specified by statute; in others, such as Ohio and Illinois, the same effect was achieved by implicit understanding. Furthermore, northern state judiciaries offered no serious challenge to sojourning during the early decades of the Republic. It was a matter of "hospitality," said a Pennsylvania judge, pointing out that many "southern gentlemen . . . attended with their domestic slaves" were accustomed to spending the summer months at watering places in the state. And as late as 1843 the Illinois supreme court confirmed the right of transit with a slave, declaring that a denial of such comity would "tend greatly to weaken, if not to destroy the common bond of union amongst us."[17]

Southern courts, for their part, consistently ruled that a slave taken to live permanently in a free state or territory was thereby emancipated. More than that, they consistently held that such freedom vested in the former slave and could not be rendered void by his return to a slaveholding state. That is, the southern courts did not invoke the principle of reattachment and embraced instead the princi-

---

*Certain abolitionists, such as Richard Hildreth and Lysander Spooner, carried the argument further, insisting that *Somerset,* by confirming the illegality of slavery in England, likewise confirmed its illegality in the colonies, since the latter were forbidden to pass laws repugnant to the laws of England.[16]

ple of "once free, forever free." Furthermore, in several of these
decisions, the judge even echoed some of the broader philosophy of
Somerset, declaring that slavery was contrary to natural law and susceptible of establishment only by positive law—a doctrine that southern spokesmen later repudiated. What historians have too often failed
to emphasize, however, is that this pattern of southern liberalism was
developed within an explicitly restricted context. Court decisions in
favor of freedom were limited almost entirely to instances of permanent slaveholding residence on free soil in more or less flagrant defiance of state or federal law.* Very often the court expressly discriminated between sojourning and domicile, making it plain that only the
latter worked emancipation.[19]

The sectional accommodation thus incorporated two of the three
possible answers to the substantive question of which law should
prevail. In the case of sojourning, the law of slavery remained attached to a slave when he entered a free state; in the case of domicile, the law of the free state emancipated him, and irreversibly so.
Within this formula of compromise, be it noted, there was no place or
need for the third answer—the principle of reattachment.†

Eventually, however, the period of accommodation gave way to
one of "disintegration." Legal historians are substantially in agreement as to what happened. First, they say, many northern states
began to apply the *Somerset* doctrine in its more extreme version by

---

*The most notable exception was Louisiana, with its civil law tradition. There slaves
were more than once liberated after temporary residence in France, where the law of
1791 did not permit sojourning. On the other hand, in freeing a slave woman who
had been in Ohio, a Louisiana court concluded that her owner had gone to Ohio
"with the intention of residing there."[18] It should be emphasized that we are concerned here with cases of unintentional manumission by residence in a free state.
There were also numerous instances of deliberate manumission by sending slaves to
free states.

† Of course, the dividing line in this compromise was not as clearly defined as the 36°
30′ line in the Missouri Compromise. The length of residence was not in itself
conclusive, except in those states like Pennsylvania and New York that fixed statutory
time limits to sojourning. Intent as well as length of stay could be important. For instance, a slaveholder who voted in a free-state election gave clear indication of regarding himself as a permanent resident. The Missouri supreme court explored the problem in a series of cases.[20]

withdrawing the right of sojourn and transit; then, in retaliation, southern states repudiated their earlier liberalism and began "to refuse freedom to slaves who had established a free state residence and had returned to a slave state."[21] But the evidence, as we shall see, does not support the second half of this formulation. There *was* no general southern repudiation of the earlier tacit understanding. Scholars have fallen into error by failing to keep an eye on the difference between sojourning and domicile.[22]

The difference is critically important, not only in legal terms but also as a matter of chronology. The sectional accommodation had developed at a time when slavery or quasi-slavery still existed in most of the border free states such as Pennsylvania and Illinois. Sojourners then encountered little hostility or supervision. Indeed, public permissiveness and the laxity of law enforcement encouraged a certain amount of illegal slaveholding residence on free soil. Consequently, a good many cases reaching southern appellate courts during that earlier period involved slaves who had plainly been domiciled in free states or territories. In the decades after 1830, however, fewer slaveholders risked losing their slaves by holding them on free soil for extended lengths of time.* Most of the cases arising in the later antebellum period therefore involved sojourning or transit, rather than domicile. In short, what had changed by the eve of the Civil War was not so much the quality of southern justice as the nature of the demands laid upon it.

III

The northern states were the first to turn away from the tacit understanding. They began to abrogate it in the 1830s, at a time when antislavery sentiment was crystallizing into a sustained antislavery movement. By the middle of that same decade, Joseph Story had published his famous treatise on the conflict of laws, a work of synthesis rather than innovation but immensely influential nonetheless. In brief, Story rejected certain theories of extraterritoriality derived from

---

*A notable exception was Caifornia's most famous slave case, *Ex parte Archy* (1858).[23]

Roman civil law and gave emphatic utterance instead to the principle that every sovereign state had absolute control over what law should be enforced within its boundaries. Foreign law might well be received and applied, but only voluntarily as a matter of comity and not *ex proprio vigore* or by virtue of any moral compulsion. And furthermore, no nation could be expected to enforce an external law that was "incompatible with its own safety, or happiness, or conscientious regard to justice and duty."[24] The Story doctrine, as it affected interstate relations in the United States, plainly confirmed the jurisdictional supremacy of the forum state. Plainly, too, the doctrine could cut both ways in the mounting sectional struggle over slavery, but it seems first to have strengthened a northern revulsion against extending comity to slaveholders.

In 1836, the Supreme Judicial Court of Massachusetts freed a six-year-old slave girl who had been brought into the state by her mistress on a visit. Chief Justice Lemuel Shaw rejected an appeal to interstate comity put forward by the young defense counsel, Benjamin R. Curtis. Slavery, Shaw declared, was contrary to natural right and dependent upon local law for its "existence and efficacy." To extend comity in such cases would mean permitting any amount of slaveholding residence short of outright domicile, and that, being repugnant to state policy, was "inadmissible." Shaw was no abolitionist, and he carefully delimited his decision. It did not, he said, apply to fugitive slaves; nor did it apply to any slave who voluntarily returned home with his master. Shaw also withheld judgment on whether the decision covered transit and accidental intrusion. Nevertheless, sojourning had been pronounced illegal in Massachusetts.[25]

Soon other northern states took similar action. One year later, a slave held "temporarily" in Connecticut for some twenty-four months was awarded her freedom by the supreme court of the state. In the 1840s, New York and Pennsylvania repealed their laws permitting sojourners to remain for nine and six months, respectively.[26] Southerners bitterly resented these demeaning barriers being raised against slaveholding travel into the free states, and they set about defending themselves against what a Georgia judge called "the foul . . . spirit of modern fanaticism."[27]

One thing lending strength to their defense was a fairly recent English court decision that trimmed back the more extravagant ramifications of the *Somerset* tradition. The case of *The Slave Grace* (1827) involved a slave woman who had accompanied her mistress on a one-year visit to England and then returned willingly to Antigua. In the Court of Admiralty, Lord Stowell ruled that Grace, although free in England, had resumed her status as a slave once she was back in Antigua. Stowell thus rejected the idea that emancipation was irreversible, enunciating instead the principle of reattachment as a restrictive corollary to the *Somerset* doctrine.[28] But Grace's case, more clearly than Somerset's, had been one of sojourning rather than domicile.[29] That it was so regarded in the United States seems beyond question. Justice Story, in an exchange of correspondence on the subject, assured Stowell that the *Grace* decision was "impregnable" and universally approved by the American bar. In Massachusetts, he added, "the state of slavery is not recognized as legal; and yet, if a slave should come hither, and afterwards return to his own home, we should certainly think that the local law would re-attach upon him, and that his servile character would be re-integrated."[30] Given the terms of the tacit sectional accommodation then functioning, it is utterly impossible that Story could have been associating the *Grace* decision and the principle of reattachment with anything but temporary slaveholding residence in a free state.

The question, at any rate, was largely an academic one for Americans in 1827. Southerners, as we have seen, had no need for the principle of reattachment so long as northern states continued to agree that temporary residence in a free state did not change a slave's legal status. Later, when northern courts and legislatures began to outlaw sojourning, southern judges began to make use of Stowell's formulation, but only as a defense against the new northern doctrine of immediate, foot-on-the-soil-of-freedom emancipation. Scholars have persistently misread this defensive strategy as a southern counter-repudiation of the old tacit accommodation. One historian, for instance, says that "in later years Southern courts rejected *Somerset* in favor of *Grace*." What he fails to make clear is that the earlier southern courts applied the *Somerset* principle to cases of permanent slaveholding residence in free states, and the later courts applied the *Grace* principle to cases of temporary residence.[31] Another legal historian declares that the high court of Kentucky made an "abrupt reversal" in two decisions delivered within a year of each other (1848–49).[32] Investigation reveals, however, that the court, with good reason, found the first case to be one of domicile and the second case one of sojourn. In earlier and later decisions, it should be added, the Kentucky court consistently drew the same distinction in ruling for or against freedom.[33]

One Kentucky case, *Strader v. Graham*, became better known than the others because it alone among all such state court decisions was appealed to the United States Supreme Court.[34] Aside from that unique distinction, the *Strader* case conformed to the pattern already described. It involved slave musicians who had been taken temporarily into Ohio, and the Kentucky court accordingly ruled against the claim of emancipation, citing the Stowell principle of reattachment. In 1851, the United States Supreme Court dismissed the case for want of jurisdiction, but Chief Justice Taney in a dictum declared, "The condition of the negroes . . . as to freedom or slavery, after their return, depended altogether upon the laws of that state [Kentucky]."[35] Taney thus followed Story's rationale in the matter of conflict of laws.* He confirmed the jurisdictional principle of reversion, but not, except by sufferance, it should be noted, the substantive principle of reattachment.

It is true that in 1846 the Louisiana legislature passed a law declaring: "No slave shall be entitled to his or her freedom under the pretence that he or she has been, with or without the consent of his or her owner, in a country where slavery does not exist."[37] The phrasing seems comprehensive and conclusive, but Louisiana had previously been very liberal in defining the kind of foreign residence that worked emancipation, and the 1846 statute did nothing more in

---

*In an earlier case, involving a corporation engaged in interstate business, Taney had already echoed Story in declaring that the extension of comity was always a voluntary act and "inadmissible" when contrary to a nation's policy or prejudicial to its interests. He had added, also following Story, that silence usually implied the extension of comity.[36]

practice than bring the state into line with the rest of the South. This
is clear from subsequent judicial interpretations. Without exception,
the supreme court of Louisiana continued to approve claims to freedom based on extended residence in nonslaveholding states or countries.[38] When the court ruled against freedom in *Conant v. Guesnard*
(1850) and in *Liza v. Dr. Puissant et al.* (1852), it did so with regard to
slaves who had sojourned only two or three months in France. The
chief justice in the course of his *Liza* opinion reiterated the old, familiar formula. "This court," he said, "has held the status of a slave to be
changed by a residence in a country in which slavery did not exist,
when the residence, with the consent of the master, had a character
of permanency, but not that the status was affected by a transit for a
temporary purpose."[39]

Except in Missouri, as a result of the Dred Scott case, there appears to have been no decision of a southern appellate court that denied a suit for freedom in a clear-cut case of permanent residence on
free soil.* On the eve of disunion seven years later, the high court of
Mississippi angrily renounced comity with Ohio because of the latter's
"negro-mania," but it did so in a suit to recover a legacy, rather than
in a suit for freedom.[40] Southern states, to be sure, responded vehemently in other ways to the mounting antislavery offensive—for instance, by tightening laws against immigration of free Negroes and by
further abridging the wretchedly few rights and privileges of the resident free black population. But there was no sweeping repudiation by
southern judiciaries of the old tacit sectional accommodation on the
status of slavery in nonslaveholding jurisdictions.

Meanwhile, the northern assault on sojourning privileges
reached its climax in a half-forgotten New York case of the 1850s that
caused much excitement at the time. In *Lemmon v. The People*
(1860), first decided in the trial court in 1852, the state freed a

---

* See below, p. 660. Such cases, it should be emphasized, were unlikely to arise in
the later antebellum period; for few slaveholders were willing to risk losing their
property in this manner, and any Negro who did gain a claim to freedom by virtue of
longtime residence on free soil was not likely to risk it by returning to the hostile
legal environment of a slaveholding state. The exceptional cases in Missouri, though
decided in the 1850s, were based on events taking place in the 1830s.

number of slaves that were merely in transit from Virginia to Texas by coastal vessel. "It marked," says one legal scholar, "the uttermost expansion of the libertarian implications of *Somerset*."[41] To southerners it seemed that they were being treated more and more like lepers, and their resentment soon found expression in the documents of secession. The Mississippi resolutions of November 30, 1860, for example, declared that the northern states had "insulted and outraged our citizens when travelling among them for pleasure, health or business, by taking their servants and liberating the same . . . and subjecting their owners to degrading and ignominious punishment."[42]

IV

Although manumission was prohibited or severely restricted in much of the South by the late antebellum period, suits for freedom were still generally permitted and often carefully provided for by statute. The number of such suits prosecuted in trial courts is unknown, but according to one tabulation, state supreme courts heard 670 appeals during the entire slaveholding era. Decisions were rendered in 575 of these cases, with Negroes winning their suits 57 per cent of the time.[43]

Black "freedom" in a slaveholding state, however, was in many respects little more than a special category of slavery. The southern free Negro lived in a precarious world cramped between two fairly distinct boundaries—the legal line separating him from the great mass of blacks and the color line separating him from the great mass of free men. More often than not, it was the color line that determined his status and treatment in any specific circumstance.

At the end of the Revolution, free Negroes probably constituted less than 1.5 per cent of the South's total population and less than 4 per cent of its black population. By law and custom in the colonial period they had been assigned an inferior social status and deprived of many rights and privileges possessed by white persons. Yet the process of exclusion and degradation had been a haphazard one, and it varied extensively from colony to colony. For example, Virginia denied Negroes the right to vote in 1723, but Maryland did not do so during the colonial period. On the other hand, Maryland was the only colony that formally barred Negroes from militia service. Of course social pressure often served as the agency of repression when the law did not, but with the exception of prohibitions against miscegenation, there was nothing approaching uniformity in southern racial policies before the Revolution.[44] Moreover, the free Negro of colonial times, although scorned and in many ways deprived, had not yet become a serious cause for alarm and therefore enjoyed more freedom from surveillance than he did in the antebellum period.[45]

But with the free black community growing more rapidly than other elements of the population, and with southerners becoming ever more fearful of slave revolts, the racial restraints increased in number and severity. One by one, the southern states formally disfranchised the free Negro, North Carolina being, in 1835, the last state to do so. They excluded him from jury service, and in most of the South he could not testify against a white person (although a slave could testify against him). His freedom of movement came under heavy restriction as other states forbade him to immigrate and his own state required him to register, carry freedom papers, and, in the lower South especially, have a guardian appointed by law.

Increasingly, free Negroes were equated with slaves in southern law. The Georgia Code of 1861 declared: "All laws enacted in reference to slaves, and in their nature applicable to free persons of color, shall be construed to include them, unless specially excepted."[46] Among other things, this meant that free Negroes were subject to search without warrant and to trial without jury for all but capital offenses. They were denied the right of assembly and forbidden to own or carry arms. They were barred from professions and many trades by laws, high license fees, and extralegal pressures. They were excluded from schools, and it was a crime to teach a free Negro to read or write.[47]

In addition, there was always a danger of slipping back into slavery. The free Negro had to be able at all times to produce proof of his status or risk losing it, and in most southern states he could be reduced to temporary or permanent servitude for a variety of offenses, beginning with mere vagrancy. Georgia law required that tax-delinquent Negroes be hired out "from year to year," during which time their status would be the same as that of slaves. The state code also declared: "The punishment of a free person of color for immigrating into this State, in violation of its laws, shall be sale into perpetual bondage."[48]

It is true that such regulations were often ignored or evaded by Negroes and indifferently enforced by southern officials, but it is also true that the free Negro's legal disabilities were supplemented with a good deal of informal coercion and discrimination in his local community. Free Negroes were widely regarded as a subversive influence on slaves and as potential agents of abolitionism. In the upper part of the Old South there was also much apprehension about their sheer numbers and rate of increase. Nowhere, says Ira Berlin, was the fear of an eventual free black majority more intense than in Maryland, the home state of Roger B. Taney.[49]

In the North, free Negroes were often regarded collectively as a nuisance but seldom as a serious menace. Freer than their southern counterparts from linkage with slavery and from the danger of re-enslavement, they nevertheless lived marginal lives as a despised and deprived minority. Social pressure restricted them largely to menial labor. More than 90 per cent of them were disfranchised. Their children either attended segregated schools or were barred entirely from public education. Some states, such as Illinois and Indiana, forbade their entry. Some forbade them to testify in cases involving white persons. Outside of New England, the legal disabilities of the northern Negro generally became more severe as the slavery controversy became more intense. Thus, the constitution of Oregon, admitted as a free state in 1859, declared emphatically: "No free negro or mulatto not residing in this State at the time of the adoption of this Constitution shall ever come, reside, or be within this State, or hold any real estate, or make any contract, or maintain any suit therein." The fact that these northern black laws were poorly enforced took much of the sting out of them, to be sure, but the threat of enforcement hung in the air, adding to the precariousness of life for the free Negro. In one notorious instance, a Cincinnati effort to enforce the Ohio black laws requiring registration and posting of bond drove more than a thousand Negroes into flight from the city.[50]

The Constitution of the United States, though it provided some basis for the federal government's support of slavery, contained no authority for federal discrimination against the black race. Yet Congress in 1792 excluded Negroes from the militia and in 1810 denied them the right to work as mail carriers. By congressional action, free Negroes in Washington, D.C., were disfranchised, excluded from certain kinds of business activity, and made subject to many of the laws regulating slaves. From time to time, Congress also disfranchised blacks in the territories.[51] The executive branch, though it never developed a consistent and comprehensive racial policy, added discriminatory edicts of various kinds, such as those excluding Negroes from the Navy and Marine Corps in 1798 and denying them pre-emption rights on the public lands in 1856.[52]

V

With racial discrimination so pervasive in American law and society, there inevitably arose the question of whether free Negroes were citizens of the United States and of the states in which they lived. It was an issue clouded not only by the free Negro's intermediate status between slavery and freedom, and by the variations in his treatment from New England to the Deep South, but also by the vague and flexible meaning of the word "citizen" itself. Adding further to the confusion was the problem of the undefined relationship between state citizenship and national citizenship in a federal republic.

No longer "subjects" of the British crown, Americans in the Revolutionary era began to speak of themselves as "citizens" of their respective states and their new nation. The term appeared in both the Articles of Confederation and the Constitution, but it was not given authoritative and precise definition until after the Civil War.[53] In its broadest and perhaps most common usage during the early national period, "citizen" meant any domiciled inhabitant except an alien or a slave.[54] Sometimes, however, the word was used to designate only

those "active partners" in a sovereign community who possessed all
its civil and political rights and privileges, including suffrage and eligibility to hold public office.[55] This definition, strictly applied in the
early nineteenth century, would have excluded not only women,
children, and most free Negroes, but also many white male adults
who could not meet religious and property-holding qualifications for
voting. In very strictest terms, it would also have excluded naturalized citizens, who could not become president or vice president and
were barred from service in the Senate and House of Representatives
until they had been naturalized for nine and seven years, respectively.

It is easy enough to demonstrate that the stricter definition of citizenship did not universally prevail. Women, for example, although
not allowed to vote, were recognized as citizens for the purpose of
bringing suit in federal courts, and foreign-born women were capable
of becoming citizens of the United States through naturalization or
even through marriage.[56]

At times, free Negroes were likewise recognized in the language
of the law as falling within the circle of citizenship, broadly defined,
and this was especially true during the early decades of national independence. For one thing, the fourth article of the Articles of Confederation, approved by the Continental Congress in 1778, treated
the word "citizens" as interchangeable with the word "inhabitants." It
declared that the "free inhabitants" of each state should be entitled to
"all the privileges and immunities of free citizens in the several
States." A proposal from South Carolina that the word "white" be inserted in this clause was defeated by a vote of 8 states to 2.[57] Five
years later, in the abortive amendment on apportionment of taxes
that first introduced the three-fifths ratio, Congress referred to "white
and other free citizens."[58] At about the same time, the Virginia legislature repealed an earlier law limiting citizenship to white persons
and provided instead that "all free persons born within the territory of
this commonwealth" should be entitled to all the rights, privileges,
and advantages of citizenship.[59] Moving into the early nineteenth
century, one finds an act of Congress in 1803 prohibiting the importation, in violation of state law, of any Negro who was not "a native, a

citizen, or registered seaman of the United States." The same year, a resolution of the House of Representatives referred to "such American seamen, citizens of the United States, as are free persons of color."[60]

Evidence of this kind is by no means consistent, however, and it can too easily be mistaken for proof of a racial equalitarianism that did not exist. For instance, the above-mentioned refusal of the Continental Congress to inject the word "white" into the fourth article of the Articles of Confederation has been interpreted as follows: "Delegates from eight states, therefore, insisted that *their black* citizen-inhabitants be equally received as citizens throughout the Confederation."[61] But it seems clear that the 8-to-2 vote reflected no such majoritarian devotion to interracial equality. Congress, hoping to avoid the necessity of resubmitting the Articles to the states, rejected *all* proposed amendments, including one that would have *removed* the word "white" from the apportionment of militia quotas.[62]

The Revolutionary generation's disposition to view the Negro as racially inferior and unassimilable was plainly exhibited in the federal statute of 1790 that limited naturalization to "free white persons," as well as in the first stirrings of the colonization movement.[63] Yet the legal issue that would later arise to plague legislators and jurists was not what the founding fathers had thought of the free Negro as an element in the American population, but rather what status they had actually accorded him in American law. And the evidence is that by implication, sufferance, and inadvertence they often classified him as a citizen. For instance, neither the Ordinance of 1787 nor the first constitutions of Kentucky (1792) and Tennessee (1796) discriminated against Negroes in civil rights or suffrage, and citizenship could reasonably be inferred from the failure to do so.[64]

Whatever such permissiveness may have owed to the liberalizing influence of the Revolution, it primarily reflected the fact that free Negroes were at first too insignificant in number to be taken separately into account every time a constitution or statute was drafted. As we have seen, however, the rapid growth of the free black population during the post-Revolutionary period inspired the legal imposition of many new racial restraints and disabilities. This increase of racial repression in turn raised perplexing questions about the status of the free Negro and the meaning of citizenship.

In 1820, Justice Benjamin Mills, speaking for the Kentucky Court of Appeals, ruled against the validity of a statute that subjected free Negroes to summary punishment of thirty lashes for lifting a hand against a white person. Free persons of color, said Mills, were in some measure "parties to the political compact" and entitled to many—though not all—of the benefits that it provided. The law, accordingly, was contrary to the state constitution.[65] Eighteen years later, in a decision that attracted much public attention, Justice William Gaston of the North Carolina supreme court declared that free Negroes born in the state were citizens of the state. At the same time, however, he held that a racially discriminatory law passed in 1831 did not violate the North Carolina constitution.[66] In 1844, Justice Frederick Nash of the same court upheld the constitutionality of a state law forbidding free Negroes to carry guns without having obtained a license to do so. "The free people of color," he said, "cannot be considered as citizens in the largest sense of the term, or, if they are, they occupy such a position in society as justifies the legislature in adopting a course of policy in its acts peculiar to them; so that they [the acts] do not violate those great principles of justice which ought to lie at the foundation of all laws."[67]

In each of these cases the problem was one of the free Negro's rights under *state* law. Justice Mills, Gaston, and Nash were all struggling to define the Negro's intermediate position between slavery and freedom in such a way as to guarantee him certain fundamental rights without lending support to any claim of complete equality before the law. Mills and Gaston both regarded the occupants of this middle ground as state citizens of a sort. Nash was not so sure, and other jurists emphatically disagreed. Thus, in another Kentucky case, *Amy v. Smith* (with Mills dissenting), the court held that to be a citizen, one must "enjoy *all* the privileges and immunities appertaining to the state," whereas the free Negro was "almost everywhere, considered and treated as a degraded race of people."[68]

The essential question, then, was not whether the free Negro should be classified as a citizen and freed from racial disabilities but, rather, whether the free Negro, given the fact of his racial disabilities, should be classified as a lower order of citizen or simply as a non-citizen. This issue, if it had been strictly a matter of *state* law and *state* citizenship, would have amounted to little more than a dispute over terminology. But any use of the word "citizen" in connection with free Negroes provided the basis for a claim that they were protected by the first paragraph of Article Four, Section Two, of the Constitution: "The citizens of each State shall be entitled to all privileges and immunities of citizens in the several States." Plainly, recognition of the free black as a citizen within the meaning of this clause would have been incompatible with racial policies established throughout most of the country, and with southern efforts to fortify the slave system against subversion. It is therefore not surprising that most of the prominent judicial rulings *against* Negro citizenship were made in cases in which rights had been claimed under the privileges-and-immunities clause.[69]

For one thing, if the clause did in fact protect free Negroes, then state laws prohibiting or severely restricting their immigration were constitutionally indefensible. Virginia had enacted such legislation as early as 1793, and a number of other states followed her example during the first two decades of the nineteenth century.[70] But the issue did not become a cause of national discord until the final stage of the Missouri controversy in 1821.* As authorized in the famous compromise of the preceding year, a Missouri convention set about writing a state constitution and put in a clause calling for prohibition of Negro immigration. With the sectional struggle fiercely renewed as a consequence, antislavery leaders used the issue of Negro citizenship as the basis for one last effort to prevent the admission of Missouri. They failed, however, and had to settle for a meaningless compromise drafted by Henry Clay, which left unresolved the question of whether free Negroes were included in the citizenry protected by the privileges-and-immunities clause.[71] Rarely, in the decades that followed, did the subject of Negro citizenship again provoke serious debate in Congress. The South had nevertheless been made sensitive to the issue and given one more cause for alarm.

* For the earlier stages of the Missouri controversy, see below, pp. 100–113.

Late in that same year, 1821, two members of the Monroe cabinet took up the question that Congress had contrived to evade. Secretary of the Treasury William H. Crawford, a Georgian, wrote to Attorney General William Wirt, a Virginian, asking whether a free Negro could command an ocean-going vessel operating out of Norfolk, given the requirement that such commanders must be citizens of the United States. Wirt answered in the negative: "It seems very manifest," he said, "that no person is included in the description of citizen of the United States who has not the full rights of a citizen in the State of his residence." Therefore, free Negroes living in Virginia were not citizens of the United States. Thus Wirt subscribed to the principle that federal citizenship depended on state citizenship and also to the hard-line view that only persons enjoying complete civil and political equity could be regarded as state citizens. By discussing just the status of Virginia Negroes, Wirt left open the possibility that blacks in several New England states could qualify for national citizenship, but even so, his criterion excluded at least 95 per cent of the free black population of the country.[72]

About six months after Wirt presented his opinion to Crawford, the insurrectionary plot of Denmark Vesey, a former slave who had freed himself by self-purchase, was discovered and crushed in Charleston. The South Carolina legislature responded to the outcry of an angry and frightened white populace by tightening its restrictions on free Negroes. One of the new security measures required that black crew members of any ship coming into port must be arrested and held in jail until their vessel departed. This policy, eventually adopted with variations by a half dozen other southern states, affected black British sailors as well as Americans and caused friction in Anglo-American relations until the coming of the Civil War.[73]

In 1823, Justice William Johnson of the United States Supreme Court, while on circuit court duty in his home state of South Carolina, ruled that the Negro seamen act was unconstitutional. Attorney General Wirt came to the same conclusion in an official opinion written the following year. Both men, however, regarded the law as an invasion of federal authority over foreign relations and over foreign and interstate commerce. Neither gave any consideration to the rights of free Negroes under the federal Constitution.[74]

Despite these rulings and despite strong pressure from Secretary of State John Quincy Adams, South Carolina retained and enforced the Negro seamen law. The nationalism expressed by Johnson and Wirt was in any case already losing ground throughout much of the South. In 1831, Attorney General John M. Berrien, whose home state of Georgia now had a Negro seamen law of its own, presented a lengthy opinion overruling Wirt and pronouncing the South Carolina statute constitutional. In effect, Berrien held that state police powers, protected in the Tenth Amendment, took precedence over federal power to regulate commerce. He too ignored the question of the rights of free American Negroes.[75]

Soon Roger B. Taney replaced Berrien as Jackson's attorney general. Further trouble with Britain, this time over a North Carolina Negro seamen law, elicited from him an opinion of some four thousand words, to which he added a long supplement twelve days later. Taney, unlike Wirt and Berrien, took up the subject of free American Negroes and concluded that they had no rights under the Constitution at all:

> The African race in the United States even when free, are everywhere a degraded class, and exercise no political influence. The privileges they are allowed to enjoy, are accorded to them as a matter of kindness and benevolence rather than of right. They are the only class of persons who can be held as mere property, as slaves. . . . They were never regarded as a constituent portion of the sovereignty of any state. . . . They were not looked upon as citizens by the contracting parties who formed the Constitution. They were evidently not supposed to be included by the term *citizens*. And were not intended to be embraced in any of the provisions of that Constitution but those which point to them in terms not to be mistaken.[76]

Thus Taney, in 1832, formulated the same harsh racial doctrine that he would proclaim from the bench twenty-five years later. But his opinion had no influence outside the little circle of men around Jackson, because for some reason it was never published along with other opinions of the attorney general.[77]

The Berrien and Taney opinions placed the Jackson administration firmly on the side of the South in defense of the Negro seamen laws, and subsequent British protests were met with the reply that the matter was "beyond the reach of any power vested in the President." James Buchanan, as Polk's secretary of state, not only reiterated the assertion of executive impotence but also threatened abrogation of the commercial convention of 1815 unless the British ceased to make demands which, if complied with, said Buchanan, would result in a dissolution of the Union.[78]

The strongest efforts in behalf of black American sailors were made in the early 1840s. A committee of the House of Representatives, responding to a memorial from 150 citizens of Boston, condemned the Negro seamen acts on several grounds, including their incompatibility with the privileges-and-immunities clause. The argument of the majority report was conservatively designed, however, to take advantage of the loophole in Wirt's opinion. That is, the right of protection under the clause was claimed only for Negroes, such as those of Massachusetts, who were regarded as citizens in their own states. The minority report, citing *Amy v. Smith* and similar state court decisions, insisted that Negroes were nowhere citizens because nowhere did they enjoy all the rights of the white citizens. The House in effect upheld the minority by tabling the resolutions accompanying the committee report.[79] Thereupon, the state of Massachusetts undertook to institute suits at Charleston and New Orleans in order to test the constitutionality of the seamen laws. But the distinguished lawyers sent to both cities had to give up their missions under threat of mob violence. Resolutions passed by the South Carolina legislature referred to the Massachusetts agent, Samuel Hoar, as "the emissary of a foreign Government," who must be expelled because of his seditious purposes.[80]

The nature of citizenship, state and national, and whether it included free Negroes, remained unsettled issues when the Dred Scott case reached the Supreme Court a decade later. Although certain abolitionist theorists had developed a doctrine of paramount national citizenship, the general tendency was to regard state citizenship as primary, with United States citizenship deriving from it.[81] This made it reasonable to maintain that at least *some* free Negroes, being recognized as citizens in their own states, were entitled to protection under the privileges-and-immunities clause. Yet no federal court or high state court had expressly endorsed the claim, and several state courts had expressly rejected it.[82]

Southern spokesmen in responding to the claim often contended that since no Negro anywhere possessed *all* the rights and privileges of citizenship within his state, no Negro could be entitled to *all* the privileges and immunities of citizens in other states. But this line of reasoning, as we have seen, raised some difficult questions about the status of women, children, and many white adult males. It was therefore sometimes reinforced or replaced by the more general argument that Negroes, having been no part of the sovereign American people who founded the nation, were not citizens of the United States and could claim no protection under the Constitution.[83]

Meanwhile, the increasing use of the corporate form of business organization was opening up the question of whether a corporation, as an "artificial being," had the legal status of a citizen. In 1839, the Supreme Court, with Taney delivering the decision, rejected the contention of counsel that a corporation was a citizen within the meaning and protection of the privileges-and-immunities clause.[84] Five years later, however, the Court upheld a claim that corporations were citizens within the meaning of the diverse-citizenship clause of Article Three, Section Two, and thus capable of being litigants in the federal courts.[85] Taken together, these two decisions had the effect of declaring that a corporation was a citizen in one respect but not in another.

Perhaps, then, the same could be said minimally about Negro citizenship. That is, since free blacks had access to the courts in their own states, were they not citizens at least to the extent of having access, like corporations, to the federal courts under the diverse-citizenship clause? It would have been reasonable to think so. There are indications that free Negroes did sometimes appear as parties in federal suits without being challenged on racial grounds. Indeed, the leading attorney in one such case was Roger B. Taney.[86]

Yet southerners, always hostile to any influence that might weaken their system of racial control, were generally unwilling to allow any linkage between the word "Negro" and the word "citizen."

Thus, the Georgia legislature by unanimous resolution in 1842 declared that free Negroes were not citizens of the United States and that Georgia would "never recognize such citizenship."[87] Two years later, in the midst of the frenzy over Hoar's mission, the South Carolina legislature empowered the governor to use the militia, if necessary, to prevent the release by writ of habeas corpus of any person imprisoned under the Negro seamen act.[88] This meant that South Carolina was prepared to invoke military force to prevent federal judicial intervention in behalf of Negro seamen claiming the protection of the privileges-and-immunities clause. No northern state ever went that far in resisting enforcement of the fugitive-slave laws.

∽ 4 ∾

Expansion and Slavery
in Early National Politics

T he problem of territorial government and its relationship to
slavery arose in the 1780s, when the first state cessions of
western lands made it clear that the central government of
the new United States was about to take on certain attributes of an
empire. Earlier, Virginia had reasserted her vast transappalachian
claim but at the same time had felt some need to reconsider it in the
light of the movement for independence from Britain. Republican
government, according to the theory of the day, was unsuitable for
the exercise of sovereignty over such a broad domain. So Thomas Jefferson, in his several drafts of a state constitution, boldly provided for
the creation of "new colonies" which would be "free and independent" of Virginia and of "all the world." As finally adopted, the
Virginia constitution of 1776 failed to go that far, but it did acknowledge the possibility that one or more territories might be "laid off,
and Governments established Westward of the Allegheny Moun-
tains." At this early date, the status of slavery in the western wilderness was not an issue, and neither Jefferson's drafts nor the adopted
constitution said anything on the subject.[1]

In 1777, the Continental Congress approved the Articles of Confederation, but they remained unratified for more than three years
because of a controversy over western lands in which the two principal antagonists were Virginia and Maryland. Both states were acting

74

in the interest of speculative companies, and the burning issue between them was not so much who should govern those lands as who
should own them. Maryland, ostensibly speaking for the six states
that had no western claims, insisted that the transmontane region, "if
wrested from the common enemy by the blood and treasure of the
thirteen States, should be considered as a common property." Here
was the original "common-property doctrine," which John C. Calhoun and other southerners would later translate to the constitutional
defense of slavery in the territories. It referred primarily to the West
as real estate, as a great reserve of potential wealth which, in the
Maryland view, should be used for the benefit of all the states, instead of a favored few. The real bone of contention, in short, was the
substantial income expected from the sale of western lands over the
years. The *political* disposition of the West aroused little dispute.
There was not much sentiment in favor of extending the jurisdiction
of the seaboard states into the Mississippi Valley and even less in
favor of creating a system of permanent colonial dependencies. The
Maryland legislature was not only echoing Jefferson but giving expression to a general consensus when it proposed that western territory "be parcelled out by Congress into free, convenient, and independent governments." Clearly, an "independent" government
could not be the "common property" of other governments, and so,
just as clearly, the common-property doctrine was in the beginning
strictly an economic concept and not a political one.[2]

Early in 1780, with Maryland still holding firm against ratification, New York put added pressure on Virginia by offering to cede
her own extensive but dubious western claim, which was based upon
her alleged jurisdiction over the Iroquois Nation. By this time, a
number of leading Virginians were convinced that their state should
offer some kind of compromise which would protect its basic interests
and yet satisfy Maryland. The answer appeared to be cession with
certain reservations and conditions. In September 1780, Congress
approved a committee report calling for cessions from the land-claim-
ing states and at the same time urging Maryland to ratify the Articles.
A congressional resolution adopted some five weeks later plainly dealt
with and distinguished between the economic and political aspects of

the expected cessions. As real estate, the ceded lands would be "disposed of for the common benefit of the United States." As territory or dominion, they would be "settled and formed into distinct republican States, which shall become members of the Federal Union, and have the same rights of sovereignty, freedom, and independence, as the other States."[3]

On January 2, 1781, the Virginia assembly passed an act ceding all of the state's claims northwest of the Ohio River, while at the same time retaining its rights in Kentucky, both as to soil and as to jurisdiction. Two months later, Maryland's delegates in Congress signed the Articles of Confederation, and the United States of America, after five years of provisional government, were at last operating under their first federal constitution. But the Virginia cession included conditions on land disposal that proved unacceptable to the Confederation Congress. Another long delay followed. Not until March 1, 1784, did a modified offer of cession win approval in Congress by a narrow vote. With this transfer, the national domain came into existence, and a system of government, as well as a system of land disposal, became a practical necessity for the region we call the Old Northwest.[4]

The Confederation Congress had already begun to prepare for such a responsibility, and a committee headed by Jefferson was ready on March 1 with its "plan for the temporary government of the Western territory." According to this ambitious design, the entire transappalachian region between the thirty-first and forty-seventh parallels would be divided into at least fourteen states, approximately equal in size and rectangular in form. The population of each state was to be, from the beginning, almost entirely self-governing. Congress would intervene only to authorize and to facilitate the progress of a state through two preliminary stages before it finally became a full-fledged member of the Confederation, equal in every respect to the original states.[5]

To these general provisions, Jefferson added five restrictions. The first, for example, was that the new states should "for ever remain a part of the United States of America." The fifth declared, "That after the year 1800 of the Christian era, there shall be neither slavery nor involuntary servitude in any of the said states, otherwise than in punishment of crimes, whereof the party shall have been duly convicted to have been personally guilty."[6] Thus the issue of slavery in the western territories was first formally raised before the national legislature, not to be finally disposed of until seventy-eight years later.

On April 19, a North Carolina delegate moved to strike out the antislavery provision. According to the rules of the Confederation Congress, this meant that the affirmative votes of at least seven states would be required to retain the provision. A total of fourteen delegates from the seven northern states voted unanimously for retention, but New Jersey had only one man present, and so, again according to the rules, its vote did not count. Nine delegates from four southern states cast seven votes against retention and two in favor. Jefferson was outvoted in the Virginia delegation, and the two North Carolina members were divided. Consequently, the vote by states was six for and three against retention of the antislavery provision—not enough to save it. The voice of a single individual, Jefferson later wrote, "would have prevented this abominable crime from spreading itself across the country."[7] So it happened that the Ordinance of 1784, as finally enacted, contained no reference to slavery.

Before its passage, however, several delegates came to realize that the ordinance made no provision for government during the earliest phase of settlement. Accordingly, an amendment was incorporated in the final version, as follows: "That measures not inconsistent with the principles of the confederation, and necessary for the preservation of peace and good order among the settlers in any of the said new states, until they shall assume a temporary government as aforesaid, may from time to time be taken by the United States in Congress assembled."[8] This was the first modest assertion of congressional authority to govern the West directly.[9] Eventually, of course, much of the conflict over slavery would be acted out in an often abstruse and seemingly interminable debate over the extent of federal power in the territories. The next year, Rufus King of Massachusetts renewed the proposal to prohibit slavery in the West. On the question of commitment, sixteen delegates from seven northern states voted unanimously in the affirmative. The Maryland delegation was divided two to one in favor, and the other southerners were six to one against. The vote by states was eight to three for commitment. On April 6, 1785, King and the other members of the committee submitted a resolution excluding slavery from the West but at the same time providing for the recovery of fugitive slaves escaping into that region. Thus the two most abrasive issues associated with the institution of slavery—territories and fugitives—were joined together for the first time on the national scene.[10]

The King resolution never came to a vote in Congress, however, perhaps because it was already becoming apparent that the Ordinance of 1784 itself would never be put into operation. Jefferson's plan, with its simultaneous creation of so many new states in a still predominantly empty wilderness, was simply impractical for the needs of the time. But in these first efforts to prevent the expansion of slavery there are some points worth special notice. For one thing, the Jefferson-King proposal would have prohibited the institution throughout the *entire* transmontane region, including Kentucky and the unceded claims farther south. It was no doubt this comprehensiveness that provoked such a sharp sectional division on the proposal—a division more or less along the Mason-Dixon line, even though there were still slaveholding states to the north of it in the 1780s.[11] Furthermore, it was the northern delegates who maintained a perfect sectional solidarity in the voting on the question. The few doughfaces at this time were all from the South.

The impression encouraged by Jefferson that Congress in 1784 and 1785 came within a hair's breadth of excluding slavery permanently from the entire West is no doubt mistaken. The movement of slaveholders into Kentucky and Tennessee had already begun, and Congress had no effective means of enforcing a law against it. Moreover, the states south of Virginia probably could have compelled the repeal of any such prohibition simply by continuing to withhold cession of their western lands. In fact, North Carolina made an abortive offer of cession on June 2, 1784, and one of the conditions attached was that Congress should make no regulations tending to emancipate slaves in the ceded area.[12] This maneuver had obviously been provoked by Jefferson's antislavery effort in Congress a few months earlier.[13] For the Old Southwest, that effort came both too early and too late—too early with respect to land cessions, too late with respect to the westward migration of slaveholders.

After Jefferson left Congress to become the American minister at Paris, his friend James Monroe took the lead in preparing a more workable version of the Ordinance of 1784. The report of Monroe's committee on May 10, 1786, was in a sense a partial first draft of the famous Northwest Ordinance. It proposed a fairly detailed, two-stage plan of temporary government for "such districts" as should be "laid out by the United States." The plan called for much more centralized control than Jefferson had intended, and, except for the promise of eventual statehood, it closely resembled the old British colonial system. As for slavery, even though Rufus King was a member of the committee, the report said nothing on the subject.[14]

Several times during the ensuing year, the Monroe plan was debated, recommitted, and revised. Monroe himself left Congress, and Nathan Dane of Massachusetts became the most influential member of the committee. At last, on July 11, 1787, Congress received a draft that it was willing to approve. The proposed measure included a resolution repealing the Ordinance of 1784, and a recent change of title made it explicitly applicable only to "the territory of the United States North West of the river Ohio."[15] Even so, there had as yet been no renewal of the Jefferson-King effort to keep slavery out of the region. Then, at virtually the last moment before passage on July 13, Dane moved an addition to the five "articles of compact between the original States and the people and States in the said Territory." His sixth article read as follows:

> There shall be neither Slavery nor involuntary Servitude in the said territory otherwise than in the punishment of crimes, whereof the party shall have been duly convicted; provided always that any person escaping into the same, from whom labor or service is lawfully claimed in any one of the original States, such fugitive may be lawfully reclaimed and conveyed to the person claiming his or her labor or service as aforesaid.[16]

Surprisingly, this antislavery amendment won prompt approval, and the ordinance as a whole was then passed by a unanimous vote of the eight states present. Only three of those eight states were northern; only one (Massachusetts) had itself actually abolished slavery.[17] In short, the first legislation discriminating against slavery in the West was the work of a predominantly southern Congress. Yet the South had been strongly opposed to the antislavery efforts of Jefferson in 1784 and King in 1785. What, then, could have produced such a dramatic change of heart in 1787?

For one thing, of course, the fugitive slave section of the article gave the South something in return. But that was scarcely an equivalent concession and had at any rate failed to lure southern support when King first proposed it in 1785.

Another answer is that Congress, by prohibiting slavery only in the region north of the Ohio, was tacitly sanctioning expansion of the institution into the Southwest. Article Six, according to this view, may have been as much a proslavery maneuver as an antislavery triumph.[18] But the problem here is one of perspective distorted by hindsight. The decision to legislate only for the Northwest was made at a time when the text of the proposed ordinance contained no mention of slavery. It therefore carried no implication of dividing the West between slavery and freedom. The subsequent failure to exclude slavery from the Southwest was implicit, not in the Ordinance of 1787 but rather in the patterns of western settlement and the realities of political power. The Ordinance, after all, forbade slavery in every part of the West that had come under congressional jurisdiction.[19] As precedent, it pointed toward the Wilmot Proviso, not the Missouri Compromise. Besides, why should southerners have tried to protect their peculiar institution in the Southwest (where it was already secure) by the devious means of outlawing that institution in the Northwest? Why not simply prevent *any* restrictions on the expansion of slavery, as they had done in the past and were perfectly capable of continuing to do? There is no evidence that the last-minute addition of Article Six was necessary to secure passage of the Ordinance, and neither evidence nor logic supports the view that southerners unanimously accepted an explicit proscription of slavery in the Northwest to establish, unnecessarily, an unstated presumption about the rights of slaveholders in the Southwest.

Still another explanation is that the antislavery provision of the Ordinance (enacted by Congress in New York on July 13) and the three-fifths compromise of the Constitution (adopted by the Convention at Philadelphia on July 12) were the principal features of a grand "Compromise of 1787"—the one abolishing slavery forever in the Northwest, the other sanctioning slavery "more decidedly than any previous action at a national level."[20] But the evidence of such intercity cooperation is slender, and the chronology seems wrong, since Article Six was not introduced by Dane at New York until the three-fifths compromise had already been approved at Philadelphia. Besides, as we have seen, the three-fifths formula was no innovation in 1787 and had in fact been enacted by Congress four years earlier, but had never gone into effect.[21] This is not to deny that in both Congress and the Convention there was general recognition of the need for some amount of sectional adjustment. Yet, as anything more than a statement of the general climate of opinion, the "Compromise of 1787" lacks substance and is certainly not to be compared to the compromises of 1820 and 1850.

Perhaps the key to understanding southern action in 1787 is the fact that the South was not then obviously destined to be a minority section and, indeed, hoped to become the majority section. It was expected, for instance, that the Northwest would be settled largely by southerners who would remain pro-southern in their politics.[22] Furthermore, the line between slavery and freedom was not yet clearly drawn, abolition being still not begun in New York and New Jersey; and economic considerations were not always aligned to a proslavery-antislavery axis. For example, some southerners apparently favored prohibition of slavery in the Northwest to discourage competition from that region in the production of tobacco and indigo.[23] Most important of all, disagreement over slavery was less intense, as well as less intersectional, than it would later become.

The southern outlook in 1787 was therefore much different from what it would be in the 1850s. Criticism of slavery, pitched well below the Garrisonian level of fury, carried less of the menace associated with it in later years; and southerners were less worried about their political strength within the Union. In short, the morally vulnerable section had not yet become the politically vulnerable section of the Union.

Another mystery about the Ordinance is why no one at the time

challenged the power of Congress to enact it. Madison in *Federalist*
38 said that the measure was passed "without the least color of constitutional authority," a view that was subsequently echoed by Taney in
the Dred Scott decision and by numerous historians. Of course it is
by no means certain that Madison was right, for one could argue that
the authority to administer ceded western lands had become, by common consent, a part of the Articles of Confederation, and indeed a
precondition for their functioning at all. But at any rate, the most
striking thing is Madison's comment that this alleged usurpation went
unnoticed. "No blame has been whispered," he wrote, "no alarm has
been sounded." Whether legal or extralegal, the power of Congress
to take action in the matter seems to have been universally conceded.[24]

II

The Ordinance of 1787 was in some respects what Jefferson had intended, but it set up a system of colonial control far different from the
virtual self-government that he had envisaged in 1784. The first stage
of the system can only be called autocratic, and the second stage,
though it provided for a representative assembly, nevertheless included extensive checks on frontier democracy. The governor would
be appointed rather than elected, for example. The council of five
would be appointed by Congress from a list of ten nominated by the
territorial legislature. The governor had an absolute veto over legislation, as well as the power to convene, prorogue, and dissolve the assembly. According to one leading authority, the Ordinance was contrary to the liberal perspective of the time—"as undemocratic and
centralized as it was feasible to secure."[25] But whether it should be
regarded as a liberal or a conservative document, the Ordinance did
plainly amount to a strong assertion of congressional control over the
West in the matter of temporary government preceding statehood
and without any direct reference to the problem of land disposal.

In October 1787, the Confederation Congress implemented the
Ordinance by appointing the territorial officials and providing for their
salaries.[26] At Philadelphia, meanwhile, the Constitutional Convention

was giving somewhat belated attention to the problem of the West. Provision for the admission of new states had been included in the Virginia plan, with which the work of the Convention began, and also in the report of the committee of detail, submitted on August 6. But nothing was done about territorial government or western lands until James Madison on August 18 proposed a number of additions to the powers of Congress, the first two of which were:

> To dispose of the unappropriated lands of the U. States.
> To institute temporary Governments for New States arising therein.[27]

It would be difficult to believe that Madison, drafting these proposals, did not have in mind the equivalent legislation of the Confederation Congress—that is, the Land Ordinance of 1785 and the Northwest Ordinance of 1787, enacted just five weeks earlier.

Much subsequent controversy would have been avoided if Madison's phrasing had been retained, but the Convention telescoped his two propositions into one clause that proved to be ambiguous: "The Legislature shall have power to dispose of and make all needful rules and regulations respecting the territory or other property belonging to the United States." The question that later arose was whether the rule-making authority applied only to the disposal of public land or whether it included the power to establish territorial government. Everything in the record supports the latter interpretation. The Convention approved the clause on August 30 without debate and probably without dissent. There is no evidence that any delegate thought a major alteration had been made in the substance of Madison's proposals, and a decision *against* granting Congress the power to provide temporary government would surely have inspired discussion, especially in view of the recent passage of the Northwest Ordinance.[28]

The territory clause does not appear to have been a matter of controversy during the process of ratification. Madison in *Federalist* 43 referred to it as "a power of very great importance," which he associated specifically with the preceding clause providing for the admission of new states. On August 7, 1789, the first Congress under the Constitution, without any challenge to its authority, re-enacted the

Northwest Ordinance, making some necessary modifications, but including the antislavery provision.[29] Nineteen members of the Constitutional Convention were sitting in this congress, and a twentieth, George Washington, signed the law as president.[30] It seems clear enough that no one then doubted the power of Congress to govern the West and prohibit slavery there. The one thing not entirely clear was whether this power derived from the statehood clause, from the territory clause, or, as Madison apparently believed, from the two clauses combined.[31]

The head start thus apparently given to antislavery in the West was soon offset in several ways. For one thing, in spite of the plain language of the Ordinance, slaves already held within the Northwest Territory were exempted from the legislative prohibition by the executive interpretation of Governor Arthur St. Clair. This converted an abolition measure into a mere ban on further importation of slaves. Although he met opposition on the issue from at least one of the territorial judges, St. Clair's high-handed action won silent acquiescence from Congress and the President.[32] The precedent thereby established would be cited seven decades later in the struggle over the Lecompton constitution for Kansas.*

A number of reasons were adduced for this impairment of the antislavery clause of the Northwest Ordinance, including alleged previous commitments to the French population of the territory and several references in the Ordinance itself to "free inhabitants," which seemed to imply the continuing presence of an unfree class.[33] St. Clair relied primarily, however, on a natural rights argument against *ex post facto* interference with property ownership. Speaking of the Ordinance as the "constitution" of the territory, he said:

> So far as it respects the past, it can have no operation, and must be construed to intend that, from and after the publication of the said Constitution, slaves imported into that Territory should immediately become free; and by this construction no injury is done to any person, because it is a matter of public notoriety, and any person removing into that Colony and bringing with him persons

*See below, pp. 458–84.

who were slaves in another country, does it at the known risk of their claiming their freedom; whereas, on the other hand, had the Constitution the effect to liberate those persons who were slaves by the former laws, as no compensation is provided to their owners, it would be an act of the Government arbitrarily depriving a part of the people of a part of their property.[34]

Here we see one of the early steps in a process whereby the federal government recognized the property-holding aspect of slavery—a recognition permitted but certainly not compelled by the Constitution. At the same time, however, the distinction drawn by St. Clair had its antislavery side; for in denying that prospective enforcement of the antislavery provision constituted any invasion of property rights, he rejected a stock southern argument of later times—one that Taney would incorporate in his Dred Scott opinion.

St. Clair's interpretation of the Ordinance, amounting virtually to amendment, had some justificatory basis in the general American hostility to retroactive legislation, but it cleared the way for a series of more flagrant violations. In 1803, the governor and judges of Indiana Territory (comprising the whole of the Northwest except Ohio) established an indenture system that differed little from chattel slavery except for certain legal technicalities.[35] The territory soon entered its second stage, and the legislature elaborated the system to the extent of providing a rudimentary slave code.[36] In 1809, the governor and judges of the new Territory of Illinois adopted the indenture system along with the rest of the laws of Indiana.[37] These developments lent substance to the later assertion of Stephen A. Douglas that popular sovereignty, whether installed as official policy or not, was a fact of life on the American frontier.

Indiana Territory abolished indentures in 1810 (though not retroactively), but in Illinois, with its heavily southern population, the system took firmer root. The Illinois constitution of 1818, while prohibiting slavery, provided for the enforcement of all indentures previously made and authorized continuation of indenturing on a one-year basis, presumably renewable. Congress, on the eve of the great Missouri controversy, accepted this dubious compromise with servitude and admitted Illinois as a "free" state.[38] A subsequent effort to revise the constitution in favor of slavery was supported by the legislature but rejected by the voters. Vestiges of the indenture system nevertheless remained in the state for another generation, and the code of black laws accompanying it survived until the end of the Civil War.[39]

Meanwhile, Congress was also using the Northwest Ordinance as a model for territorial government in the region south of the Ohio River, but with a crucial difference. By 1789, slavery had already emplanted itself firmly in the transappalachian districts of Virginia and North Carolina that would soon become the states of Kentucky and Tennessee. Accordingly, when North Carolina ceded its western land to the federal government in December of that year, it did so on the condition that "no regulation made or to be made shall tend to emancipate slaves." Some antislavery objections were brushed aside in the House of Representatives, and Congress accepted the cession with the condition attached. Shortly thereafter, Southwest Territory was organized along the same lines as the Northwest, but with the antislavery clause deleted.[40]

In the circumstances, it would have been extremely difficult for Congress to do otherwise. There were strong reasons for avoiding delay in the completion of North Carolina's cession, and the well-established presence of slavery in Kentucky, beyond the reach of federal authority, no doubt militated against the possibility of prohibiting it farther south.[41] Kentucky, indeed, was the critical factor in a passive decision against trying to confine slavery to the original states, as Jefferson had proposed in 1784. Its westward-moving pioneers, well exemplifying Turnerian theory, were simply too far ahead of national policy-making to be overruled. When Kentucky entered the Union in 1792, slavery advanced officially to the banks of the Mississippi River.[42]

Thus, with very little controversy, the members of the first Congress voted in effect to extend the Mason and Dixon line westward along the Ohio River. Without being entirely conscious of doing so, perhaps, they officially adopted a policy of having two policies regarding slavery in the western territories. This, of course, was the formula that would be more expressly installed as national policy in the Missouri Compromise of 1820. North of the Ohio, slavery was forbidden by federal authority in a way that prefigured the Wilmot Proviso and the platform of the Republican party. South of the Ohio, Congress did *not* establish or protect slavery in federal territory. It merely refrained from prohibiting the institution or exercising any kind of authority over it. This omission had the effect of leaving decisions about slavery to the local population, although in Tennessee the results of the decision were foregone. In later years, such restraint on the part of the federal government would be called "nonintervention," and its implied corollary would be made explicit as "popular sovereignty."

As early as 1790, then, congressional action foreshadowed three of the four principal policies that were to be advocated in the late 1840s as solutions to the problem of slavery in the territories. The only policy not at least partly operative at this time was the one deriving from the theory that Congress lacked the constitutional power to exclude slavery from the territories. The very condition attached to the North Carolina land cession seems to indicate a general assumption in 1789 that what Congress had done north of the Ohio River it had the power to do south of that river, unless restrained by formal agreement.[43]

For all practical purposes, the short history of Southwest Territory came to an end with the admission of Tennessee (as another slave state) in 1796.* But at about the same time Spain relinquished its claim to the Yazoo strip, approximately a hundred miles wide and extending across what is now southern Mississippi and Alabama.† Congress in 1798 therefore proceeded to organize Mississippi Territory. Again, as in 1790, the legislation followed the form of the Northwest Ordinance, with the antislavery provision deleted. It may seem strange that after the establishment of slavery in Kentucky and Tennessee there should have been an effort to abolish the institution farther south, but the Yazoo strip was in a sense newly acquired territory, offering the opportunity for a new beginning. A motion to strike

*The narrow South Carolina cession remained as the unorganized "Territory South of Tennessee."

†By Pinckney's Treaty (Treaty of San Lorenzo), signed in 1795 and ratified in 1796, but not fully executed until 1798. The region was also claimed by Georgia until 1802.

out the deletion, offered by George Thacher of Massachusetts in the House of Representatives, set off the first recorded congressional debate of any significance on the subject of slavery in the territories.[44]

Southerners had already been antagonized early in the session by the reception of an antislavery memorial from a group of Quakers, whom Nathaniel Macon (North Carolina) and John Rutledge (South Carolina) accused of trying to foment servile insurrections.[45] Now, in response to the Thacher amendment, Rutledge asked angrily whether it was proper "on every occasion" to put southerners in an "odious light." The debate became in several respects a preview of others that would follow over the next sixty-three years. For instance, the issue cut across party lines, as Thacher, a Federalist, received his strongest support from two Republicans, one of whom was Albert Gallatin. Also, the issue tended to unite the South and divide the North. The sharpest attack on the amendment came from Harrison Gray Otis, like Thacher a Massachusetts Federalist, who declared that if it were approved, "an immediate insurrection would probably take place, and the inhabitants would . . . be massacred on the spot."[46]

Concern about the possibility of slave revolts was sharpened, of course, by the black revolution then in progress on the island of Santo Domingo. But the argument that antislavery agitation had the purpose and effect of inciting slaves to murder their masters would become a standard southern article of faith, subsisting through the years more often on apprehension and rumor than on solid fact. Other arguments in this early legislative debate also have a familiar ring. For example, two Virginians insisted that the expansion of slavery would ameliorate the condition of slaves by thinning out their numbers in areas of high concentration. Thacher maintained, on the other hand, that the nation ought to honor the principles upon which it was founded, at least when establishing "a government for a new country"—words that Abraham Lincoln would echo in his debates with Stephen A. Douglas.[47]

In two important respects, however, the argumentation of 1798 differed markedly from that of the antebellum years. First, many southerners were then still speaking of slavery as a national misfortune which, though presently ineradicable, would surely disappear in some far-off, better future. Second, Thacher's proposal to prohibit slavery in Mississippi Territory was denounced as unwise, unjust, and impracticable, but not as unconstitutional.[48] The amendment in any case had no chance of passing. When the vote was taken, only eleven of Thacher's colleagues supported him in this last effort to delimit slavery east of the Mississippi River.[49]

Georgia, meanwhile, continued to claim the Yazoo strip along with the rest of her western lands, all of which the state finally ceded in 1802. The articles of agreement and cession included an anti-antislavery provision similar to that extracted by North Carolina in 1790. Three members of Jefferson's cabinet negotiated and signed the agreement for the United States—namely, James Madison, who had said in 1787 that it would be "wrong to admit in the Constitution the idea that there could be property in men"; Albert Gallatin, previously one of the strongest antislavery spokesmen in Congress; and Levi Lincoln, onetime attorney for Quock Walker in the case that had helped bring slavery to an end in Massachusetts. There had now fully emerged the curious paradox of political liberalism linked with the defense of slavery.[50]

Acceptance of Georgia's terms of cession amounted to a final stamp of defeat on Jefferson's plan of 1784, which would have excluded slavery from the entire transappalachian region. Instead, the West, like the East, was to be partly free and partly slaveholding, with the Ohio River as the dividing line. All of this had been effectively determined before Jefferson entered the White House, and it was probably beyond his power to cancel the arrangement, even if he had wanted to.

III

In 1803, the whole question was opened up again with the purchase of Louisiana, an area more than twice as large as the transappalachian West. The long struggle over slavery in the territories now entered the second of its three major phases. Jefferson, who had once tried to confine slavery to the seaboard states, could now try, if he wished, to prevent the institution from becoming permanently established west

of the Mississippi River. He had the advantage of his presidential authority and prestige; settlement of the vast region had barely begun;
and there were no state claims to be used as leverage against a federal
antislavery policy.

Yet Jefferson in power did nothing to advance the antislavery
cause, except in the matter of terminating the African slave trade, and
he seems to have had no qualms of conscience about signing a law
that made Louisiana a slaveholding territory. Himself one of the select group of southern planters who owned more than a hundred
slaves, he had for many years been publicly silent on the question of
abolition, while continuing to express occasionally in private correspondence his heartfelt but more or less theoretical opposition to
human bondage. Indeed, the Ordinance of 1784 proved to be the last
public act of his life directed at the prohibition or circumscription of
slavery in the United States. A quarter of a century had passed since
his assertion in the Declaration of Independence that all men are
created equal, and a middle-aged Jefferson, shocked by the excesses
of the black revolution in Santo Domingo, had allowed racial preconceptions and fears to blunt his lifelong hatred of slavery as the greatest of all injustices. By the time of his inauguration, he had settled
into the not entirely uncomfortable conclusion that the enormous
problem was beyond the power of his own generation to solve and
must be left to the indefinite future—to the stream of human progress.[51]

Jefferson, moreover, had won the presidency by carrying 82 per
cent of the electoral vote of the slaveholding states and 27 per cent of
the electoral vote of the free states. He headed a political party of
predominantly southern interest, but one that needed northern allies
and thus had good reason to muffle the sectionally divisive issue of
slavery. Northern Jeffersonians such as Albert Gallatin were under
strong though usually silent pressure to restrain whatever antislavery
feelings they may have harbored.[52] They and their successors, the
northern Jacksonians, remained for the next sixty years the pivotal element in sectional politics. Painfully vulnerable to partisan and sectional cross-pressures in any controversy over slavery, they produced
two contrasting types, each critically important. One was the acquies-

cent "doughface," whose influence served, along with the three-fifths clause, to convert a southern minority into a southern political majority in all three branches of the federal government. The other type was the maverick antislavery Democrat, who would eventually contribute so much leadership to the Free Soil and Republican parties.

In the midst of the Jeffersonian silence, then, the principal antislavery voices in national politics during the first decades of the nineteenth century were certain northern Federalists—men no doubt motivated in part by moral imperatives but also fully aware that they were probing a weak spot in the armor of the enemy. The rhetorical egalitarianism of a slaveholding elite was too conspicuously anomalous to escape sarcasm and ridicule. As one Federalist versifier put it:

> These despots boast of Liberty
> Of *Freedom and Equality*,
> And yet O! *dire disgraceful* clan,
> They tread in dust their fellow man.[53]

But the Federalists, unlike the later Free Soilers and Republicans, were not a party generated and unified by an antislavery purpose, and they made no planned, collective effort to exploit the issue of the expansion of slavery. Their principal complaint was against the three-fifths clause, to which they attributed their defeat in 1800, and they expended much energy in useless denunciation of its malign influence on American politics. Furthermore, the fact that many Federalists had bitterly opposed the acquisition of Louisiana lent the semblance of obstructionism to Federalist gestures against slavery in the territories.

Previous legislation had already established the rule that slavery could go anywhere in federal territories where it was not positively forbidden by federal law. This was doubly true of Louisiana, where slavery had been legal under both French and Spanish rule, and where the inhabitants, according to the treaty of acquisition, were guaranteed "the free enjoyment of their liberty, property, and the religion which they profess." The Jefferson administration could therefore erect Louisiana as a slaveholding territory simply by passing an organic act that contained no prohibition against slavery.[54] Such a measure was introduced in December 1803 by Jefferson's trusted friend, Senator John Breckinridge of Kentucky. A Connecticut Federalist named James Hillhouse assumed the role of antislavery leader and stirred up heated debate with a series of amendments offered near the end of January.[55] The official record of roll-call votes and the informal record of discussion both reveal that senatorial perceptions of the slavery problem, regardless of party or section, were to an astonishing degree unstable, confused, and idiosyncratic.[56]

The first of the Hillhouse amendments proposed merely to forbid importation of slaves into Louisiana from places outside the United States. A similar restriction had been imposed on Mississippi Territory, and all of the southern states except South Carolina now prohibited foreign slave trade within their own borders.* The proposal accordingly won acceptance by a vote of 21 to 6, but only after extensive debate. The opposition came from two Georgians and four New Englanders. One of the latter was John Quincy Adams.

Next, Hillhouse in his maximum effort offered an amendment providing that no male slave taken into the territory after a date to be specified should be required to serve more than one year beyond his twenty-first birthday (eighteenth, in the case of females).[57] This proposal fell considerably short of enacting outright abolition.[58] For one thing, it did not touch the status of some thirty thousand slaves already living in Louisiana.[59] Nevertheless, the effect would have been to limit severely the growth of slavery west of the Mississippi. The amendment failed by a vote of 17 to 11—with northern Republicans and northern Federalists more or less evenly divided among them-

| | REPUBLICANS | | FEDERALISTS | | TOTALS | |
	YES	NO	YES	NO	YES	NO
North	6	5	3	3	9	8
South	1	8	1	1	2	9
Totals	7	13	4	4	11	17

*South Carolina too had abolished the foreign slave trade in the 1780s, only to reinstate it in 1803.

selves, while a fairly solid South provided the margin of defeat. This time, both senators from Massachusetts, Adams and Timothy Pickering, voted in the negative.

Unsubdued by the setback, Hillhouse promptly offered still another amendment to the Breckinridge bill. The first part of it, obviously aimed at the South Carolina loophole, forbade the importation into Louisiana of any slaves that had arrived in the United States after May 1, 1798. The second part was more severe, placing a restriction on the domestic slave trade as a commercial enterprise. It prohibited the introduction of slaves into Louisiana by anyone except a citizen who was their bona fide owner and was taking them there for his own use. The Senate agreed to divide the question and quickly approved the first section, 21 to 7. The second section was also approved, 18 to 11, but only after two more days of discussion. Adams on both occasions again cast negative votes.[60]

The bill as a whole passed the Senate, 20 to 5 (Adams in the negative), and the House of Representatives, 66 to 21. The House added a number of amendments, including one offered by James Sloan of New Jersey prohibiting all admission of slaves into Louisiana, "as well from the United States, as from foreign parts." This renewal, in effect, of Hillhouse's defeated second amendment won approval by the slim margin of 40 to 36. The Senate refused to concur, however, and the House seems to have receded without a struggle from its briefly held advanced position. As finally signed into law by Jefferson on March 26, 1804, the measure organized the area south of the thirty-third parallel (substantially, the later state of Louisiana) into "Orleans Territory," with officers and council all appointed by the President. The remainder of the vast region, containing only a few settlers, was designated the District of Louisiana and attached for administrative purposes to Indiana Territory. These were all temporary arrangements, however, for the final section of the act specified that it was to be in effect just one year, plus the duration of the following session of Congress.[61]

Hillhouse, though accused of merely pursuing his earlier opposition to the Louisiana treaty, seems to have been fairly straightforward and practical in his purpose. "I consider slavery as a serious evil," he declared, "and wish to check it wherever I have authority." He had the shrewdness not to harp on the moral iniquity of the institution but rather to stress the dangers of insurrection and the vulnerability of a slaveholding society in time of war.

John Quincy Adams, in view of his later record as an antislavery leader, is somewhat more difficult to fathom, but it appears that in 1804, at the age of thirty-six, he was simply not much interested in the problem of slavery. At one point in the debates, he said: "Slavery in a moral sense is an evil; but as connected with commerce it has important uses. The regulations offered to prevent slavery are insufficient, I shall therefore vote against them." Adams objected most strenuously to the administration's Louisiana legislation because it allowed the people of Louisiana no voice in their own government and proposed to tax them without their consent. His argument in some respects anticipated that of Stephen A. Douglas and other later advocates of "popular sovereignty."[62]

The senator most confused by the issue was Stephen R. Bradley, Vermont Republican. Bradley at first wanted to preserve a Jeffersonian silence while allowing slavery to extend into Louisiana. "It is a right they claim," he said, "and by the treaty we are bound to grant it to them." Furthermore, he believed that Congress should provide only a general government for the territory and "ought not to descend to particulars." As the debate progressed, however, Bradley with increasing vehemence offered antislavery reasons for his conduct. He spoke and voted against the amendment prohibiting foreign slave trade in Louisiana on the grounds that it was an "insufficient" restriction, that it acknowledged the "principle of slavery," and that it would only encourage the slave states to "send their vicious slaves" into the territory. As an avowed "enemy" of slavery, he was ready to assist the southern states in a program of abolition. "But that time," he added, "is not yet come—the public mind is not ready for it—and I think we had now better do nothing upon the subject." Four days later, however, when Hillhouse proposed his second, bolder amendment (the maximum effort), Bradley spoke and voted in its favor. Then came the third Hillhouse amendment, divided by the Senate into two sections. Bradley declared that he abhorred slavery and would "on every occasion" vote against the institution, whereupon he joined the majority in approving the first section. But the next day he announced his opposition to the second section (which provided that only bona fide owners could take slaves into Louisiana) on the grounds that it acknowledged the justice of slavery—"like a law regulating theft or any other crime." Called to account for his "extraordinary conduct" by a Virginia senator, he said, "I have not changed my sentiments. I was unwilling to have the question stirred. I was desirous of shutting my eyes against the subject—but since I am compelled to act, I will vote in favor of *liberty.*" He then reversed his announced intention and cast his vote with the majority in support of the second section. The erratic Bradley, scurrying from one position to another, could be viewed as an apt caricature of the northern Democrat (Jeffersonian and Jacksonian), pulled in one direction by party and in another by section, whenever the issue of slavery arose.[63]

The most strenuous opponent of the Hillhouse amendments was James Jackson of Georgia. He acknowledged that the country as a whole would be better off without slavery and said that he would "join to *export* all the slaves." But having them, he added, "we cannot with safety or policy free them." As for Louisiana, he argued that it could not be settled without slave labor; that the decision should be left to the people of the territory; that the treaty with France forbade the Hillhouse restrictions; and that the senators "must decide not on the morality but policy of the case."[64]

The sense of slavery as a repulsive but ineluctable fact of life hangs heavily over the debates on the Hillhouse amendments, which also reveal that in Congress antislavery was widespread as a vague sentiment but scarcely had existence as an organized movement. Twelve of the senators participating in the discussion asserted or acknowledged the immorality or undesirability of slavery, but only three of them supported the second Hillhouse amendment, and only Hillhouse himself voted for all of his amendments. There were, to be sure, seven *other* senators who voted for all of the amendments, but none of them, according to the admittedly imperfect record, gave Hillhouse any help in the debate.[65]

Several features of the struggle over the Hillhouse amendments deserve special notice. One is the frequent reference, by northerners as well as southerners, to the danger of slave insurrections and the high cost of security in a slaveholding society. Events in Santo Domingo had plainly inspired a renewal of concern about slavery on other than humanitarian grounds. Another thing worth noting is the continued absence of any challenge to the constitutional authority of Congress over the territories, although a few senators did suggest that restrictions on slaveholding would violate rights guaranteed in the treaty with France. Samuel Smith of Maryland expressed a common point of view when he said, "We have a constitutional right to prohibit slavery in that country, but I doubt as to the policy of it."[66]

But most striking of all is the failure of antislavery men in Congress to propose excluding slavery from the northern part of the Louisiana Purchase. It seems incredible that such a move would not have occurred to someone, in view of the precedent already established east of the Mississippi and the decision to divide Louisiana, attaching the huge upper part to Indiana for temporary administrative purposes. Most of the Louisiana slaves were concentrated in Orleans Territory, and prohibition of slavery north of the thirty-third parallel might well have won majority support, especially if linked with acquiescence in slavery south of that line. Perhaps the reason for the omission must be sought in the desultory, uncrystallized nature of the antislavery sentiment itself, but it also appears that the solution of the dividing line—the policy of having two policies—had not yet fully impressed itself on the American consciousness. The consequences of the omission were in any case immense; for the whole west bank of the Mississippi had been opened to slavery, and frantic efforts in 1819–20 to repair this earlier neglect proved only partly successful.

Hillhouse in effect had sought a compromise along functional rather than geographical lines, and the magnitude of his achievement ought to be recognized. Although his second amendment (the maximum effort) failed, his first and third amendments became a part of the law that Jefferson signed. Together, they prohibited not only the foreign but the domestic slave trade in a territory where the institution of slavery was already so well established that slaves constituted half the population. This was the strongest antislavery restriction imposed on any portion of the Deep South between 1733 and 1865.* In the hostile environment of Orleans Territory in 1804, however, the restriction was probably unenforceable. Certainly there is no evidence that the Jefferson administration made any serious effort to enforce it, and within a year, the barrier against the domestic slave trade was quietly removed.

So quietly, in fact, that the action largely escaped public notice at the time and scholarly attention thereafter. No mention of it appears in the everlasting diary of John Quincy Adams or in the monumental history written by his grandson Henry.[67] Since the Breckinridge law of 1804 was expressly temporary, Congress in its next session took up a bill "further providing" for the government of Orleans Territory. In three days near the end of the session, at a time when congressional interest centered on the exciting climax of the impeachment trial of Justice Samuel Chase, the measure was passed by the Senate and the House without roll-call votes and apparently without significant debate.[68] The legislation raised Orleans to the second territorial grade by authorizing a representative assembly. It also provided that the inhabitants were to enjoy all the rights guaranteed by the Northwest Ordinance and enjoyed by the people of Mississippi Territory, specifically exempting Orleans from the antislavery article of the Ordinance. Territorial officials were not slow to conclude that these clauses wiped out the Hillhouse ban on domestic slavetrading. Thus Orleans was fully assimilated to the rest of the slaveholding South.[69]

At the same time, Congress enacted legislation converting the "district" of Louisiana into a first-stage territory. Inhabitants of the west bank of the Mississippi feared an effort to limit or abolish slavery in the region, but none materialized. No senator or representative proposed that this new West be divided between slavery and freedom, as the old West had been. Neither Hillhouse nor any other northern man tried to obtain restrictions on slavery in Louisiana Territory in exchange for surrendering the antislavery restrictions previously imposed on Orleans. Instead, the Louisiana bill as presented

*The prohibition against slavery imposed in 1733 by the trustees of Georgia was gradually relaxed and finally repealed in 1747.

Orleans Territory
1804–1812

to the Senate carried the same provisions affecting slavery as those
contained in the Orleans act, including exemption from the antislavery article of the Northwest Ordinance. Then, in a somewhat
mysterious late-hour move on February 28, 1805, the Senate
amended the bill to the extent of completely altering its character.
There is no evidence of antislavery motivation at work, but the revised version omitted all reference to the Northwest Ordinance and
Mississippi Territory. It neither authorized slaveholding nor laid any
restriction upon the institution, thus leaving it, presumably, still legal
under previous French and Spanish law. This measure passed the
Senate on March 1 and the House on March 3, without a roll-call vote
in either case.[70]

    Slavery, as a consequence, quietly took deeper root in Louisiana
Territory, and by 1810 the slave population had reached 3,000.
Across the Mississippi in Illinois Territory, the southern-born governor, Ninian Edwards, expressed a desire to be transferred to Louisiana, so that he could "have the benefit" of his slaves.[71] In response
to petitions from various inhabitants of the region, a committee of the

House of Representatives on January 22, 1810, reported a bill elevating Louisiana to the second territorial level. In the manner of the Mississippi and Orleans organic acts (and of the Louisiana bill of 1805 in its original form), the measure guaranteed the people of the territory all rights specified in the Northwest Ordinance, but exempted them from the antislavery provision. If enacted, it would have constituted an explicit federal sanction of slaveholding in the entire trans-Mississippi West. Instead, the bill died in the committee of the whole, and slavery continued its sturdy growth in the territory under the blanket of silence preferred by Senator Bradley and Thomas Jefferson.[72]

In 1812, having admitted Orleans Territory as the state of Louisiana, Congress enacted legislation changing the name of Louisiana Territory to Missouri Territory and raising it to the second grade. A motion to prohibit the admission of slaves, offered in the House by Abner Lacock of Pennsylvania, was defeated emphatically. The act contained no reference to the Northwest Ordinance or its antislavery article. Four years later, amendatory legislation raised Missouri to a still higher grade by providing for popular election of the council as well as the assembly, but no effort was made either to inhibit or to sanction slavery.[73] Missouri remained slaveholding territory by virtue of congressional default.

Thus, territorial legislation for the Louisiana Purchase between 1803 and 1819, as it affected the problem of slavery, seems almost wantonly anomalous. By far the strongest efforts to inhibit slavery were made in the organization of Orleans Territory at the southern tip, where the institution was already firmly implanted; while for the remainder of the region, stretching northward to the Canadian border, only one brief and ineffectual antislavery gesture appears on the record. Moreover, all other territories of the period were expressly assimilated to the Northwest Ordinance, with the antislavery article either reaffirmed (Indiana, Michigan, and Illinois territories) or excluded (Southwest, Mississippi, and Orleans territories). But the organic acts of 1805 and 1812 for Louisiana-Missouri Territory, while using the Ordinance as a model, scrupulously omitted all reference to it. This avoided the necessity of reaffirming or excluding the antislavery article. The effect was to establish in its purest form a policy that would later be called "nonintervention."

IV

Antislavery sentiment of the kind manifested in the strong support for the Hillhouse amendments of 1804 probably became more difficult to sustain during the mounting crisis in foreign relations that culminated in war with Great Britain. Indeed, an argument apparently used against the Lacock motion in 1812 was that it tended further to divide the nation at a desperately critical time.[74] The ending of the war did not immediately inspire a surge of antislavery effort, however. As late as April 1818, a proposal to forbid slavery in all states thereafter admitted met swift defeat in the House of Representatives.[75] Yet, within ten months, antislavery elements trying to recover ground passively yielded during the preceding fifteen years had provoked the first major sectional controversy over the expansion of slavery.

Through the years historians have offered a variety of reasons for this sharp turn of events. Any satisfactory explanation of the Missouri crisis is likely to be a complex one, taking into account such factors as the state of the American party system and the social influences of evangelical Protestantism. Certainly it made a great difference to have the war ended and Europe at peace after a quarter-century of revolution and conflict. The internalization of American interest after 1815 and an accompanying renewal of national self-scrutiny drew attention once again to the great anomaly of slavery in a republic allegedly dedicated to freedom.

More specifically, northerners in considerable number seem to have awakened suddenly to the realization that the national prospect had somehow become weighted in favor of slavery. For one thing, federal prohibition of the African slave trade, from which much had been expected, was obviously having no significant effect on the viability of domestic slavery, and talk of the institution as an undesirable but impermanent necessity was becoming more and more perfunctory. But it was when he looked at a map that the man of antislavery sentiment found the most cause for alarm. Rapid expansion of the cotton kingdom had produced the new slaveholding state of Mississippi and would soon produce the new slaveholding state of Alabama.* These accessions, to be sure, would ostensibly do no more than offset the recent admissions of Indiana and Illinois, but the latter two were in fact tainted with slavery. Illinois, especially, still hung in the balance. Its high officials were proslavery men, and the chief architect of the Missouri Compromise would be one of the two slaveholding senators from this "free" state. In a sense, the beginning of the Missouri crisis was signaled in November 1818 when Representative James Tallmadge, Jr., of New York denounced the Illinois constitution as insufficiently antislavery. About one-third of the northern congressmen joined him in voting against admission.[76] And if the antislavery restriction in the Northwest Ordinance was not entirely effective, beyond the Mississippi there *were* no such restrictions. The boundaries proposed for the state of Missouri would carry slavery more than two hundred miles northward from the mouth of the Ohio River. Furthermore, American expansion had plainly not ended with the Louisiana Purchase. Florida already seemed ripe for acquisition and would surely be a slaveholding territory. Also, by a convention signed in October 1818, Britain acknowledged the right of the United States to participate in occupying the Oregon country. Did this mean that slavery would eventually be planted on the Pacific coast?

Settlement of Missouri Territory had proceeded most rapidly in the region stretching from the mouth of the Ohio River northward to the valley of the Missouri. Admission of a new state of Missouri would therefore necessitate erecting a new territory farther south in the less populated region centering on the Arkansas River. If the latter had been settled first, the slavery issue perhaps could have been resolved without great difficulty by admitting Arkansas as a slaveholding state and reorganizing the rest of Missouri as a free territory. But in the actual circumstances, where antislavery restriction was relatively easy to justify in constitutional terms, it was harder to justify in geographical

* Mississippi was admitted to statehood in 1817; Alabama was admitted in 1819, during the early stages of the Missouri controversy.

terms (the territory of Arkansas), and vice versa (the state of Missouri).

It is strange that the functional connection between Missouri and Arkansas should receive so much less attention from historians than the formal connection between Missouri and Maine.[77] The House of Representatives began consideration of the bill for the admission of Missouri on February 13, 1819. It passed the measure on February 17, having added the antislavery proviso known as the Tallmadge amendment. On that very same day, the House took up the bill for the organization of Arkansas Territory, passing it on February 20 after several antislavery amendments had failed. In the other chamber, the two bills were reported from committee on successive days, February 22 and 23. The Senate struck the antislavery clauses from the Missouri bill on February 27 and passed it on March 2, whereupon both houses refused to yield and the issue was put off to the next session. Meanwhile, on March 1, the Senate had defeated an antislavery move against the Arkansas bill and passed it into law.[78]

The two measures thus went through both houses virtually in tandem, and debate on them tended to intermingle. For example, Louis McLane of Delaware, while speaking against the antislavery amendment to the Arkansas bill, took up the question of whether Congress had the power to lay down conditions for admission to statehood—a subject relevant to Missouri but not to Arkansas.[79] On the other hand, argument in the extended struggle over Missouri would sometimes turn irrelevantly to the meaning of the territory clause.[80] The resulting confusion was never entirely dissipated. Justice John A. Campbell in his Dred Scott opinion, for instance, would devote several pages to showing that the Tallmadge amendment to the Missouri bill had been "unconstitutional and subversive," despite the fact that the amendment had never become law and bore no relation to the issues before the Court.[81]

The great constitutional question that the Supreme Court attempted to answer in the Dred Scott decision was whether Congress had the power, exercised in the Missouri Compromise, to prohibit slavery in the territories. Throughout most of the Missouri controversy of 1819–20, however, the legislation under consideration was not the Missouri Compromise but rather the Missouri statehood bill with the Tallmadge amendment attached.* The amendment proposed to place a perpetually binding condition on the admission of a new state. This issue, though sometimes bobbing to the surface in subsequent phases of the slavery controversy, would never again become the focal point of a sectional crisis.† The territorial issue did not properly arise in relation to the Missouri bill until the proposal of the 36° 30′ compromise in February 1820, though it was directly posed a year earlier in the Arkansas bill.

In previous debates on slavery in the territories, as we have seen, the constitutional power of Congress had scarcely come into question. But the Tallmadge amendment was more difficult to justify in constitutional terms because it proposed to place on one state a disability not placed on all states. And beyond the question of whether Congress had the power to *impose* such a discriminatory restriction lay the question of how the restriction could be *enforced* after Missouri became a sovereign state. The amendment thus tended to turn the Missouri struggle into a constitutional debate, and the close association between the Missouri and Arkansas bills apparently encouraged some members of Congress to consider also the constitutional aspects of the problem of slavery in the federal territories.

No doubt there were other reasons for the shift of emphasis. For example, the judicial activism of the Marshall Court reached a climax in the year 1819 with a series of decisions that provoked widespread public discussion of a constitutional nature. Most notably, *McCulloch v. Maryland,* in which John Marshall presented his classic statement of the case for broad construction of congressional power, was argued

*The Tallmadge Amendment of February 13, 1819, provided, "That the further introduction of slavery or involuntary servitude be prohibited, . . . and that all children of slaves, born within the said state, after the admission thereof into the Union, shall be free but may be held to service until the age of twenty-five years."

† According to many southerners, the same issue arose in the struggle over the admission of Kansas under the Lecompton constitution in 1857–58. However, in the case of Missouri, no one doubted that a majority of the people of the territory wanted admission as a slaveholding state. The real issue in the Lecompton controversy was whether the proposed constitution represented the will of a majority of Kansans. See below, p. 464.

at the very time that the Arkansas and Missouri bills were being considered in the Senate.* But then it was perhaps inevitable that once the Constitution had been written and generally accepted, the political theorizing of the founders' generation should give way to the narrower activity of constitutional exegesis in the age of Webster, Clay, and Calhoun. From the beginning, moreover, there had been a tendency on the part of any party or element finding itself in the minority to convert political issues into constitutional issues. The Jeffersonians had done so repeatedly in the 1790s, and New England Federalists followed their example after 1800. Southern members of the House of Representatives in 1819, after many years of suffering only occasional antislavery reproach, were shocked to find themselves suddenly in the minority on the Tallmadge amendment. Accordingly, they began to talk more than ever before about limitations on congressional authority to interfere with the expansion of slavery.

Not that debate on the Arkansas bill was cast exclusively or even primarily in constitutional terms, but it did contain rudiments of argument that would one day appear in the Dred Scott decision. That is, several southerners insisted that Congress lacked the power to prohibit slavery in the Louisiana Purchase. One or more of them anticipated Justice Catron in maintaining that such prohibition would violate the treaty with France; anticipated Justice Campbell in arguing that it would deny inhabitants the right of self-government; and anticipated Chief Justice Taney in insisting that it would constitute an illegal seizure of property.[82]

The voting on the Tallmadge amendment seemed to indicate the sudden emergence of an antislavery majority in the House of Representatives. The amendment was approved in the committee of the whole, 79 to 67, and on the floor of the House in two parts: 87 to 76 for the clause prohibiting the "further introduction" of slavery into Missouri, and 82 to 78 for the clause liberating at age twenty-five all slaves born in the state after its admission.† Yet when the House then

---

*The *McCulloch* decision was handed down March 6, 1819. In February, the Court had delivered its decisions in *Dartmouth College v. Woodward* and in *Sturges v. Crowninshield*, both also highly controversial.

†The Tallmadge amendment, it should be noted, would have left unchanged the status of some ten thousand slaves already in Missouri. It therefore confiscated no

turned promptly to the Arkansas bill, where restrictionism stood on firmer constitutional ground, the antislavery advantage melted away. It appears that the determination of some northerners may have been weakened by the fierceness of the southern response to Tallmadge's amendment. For instance, Thomas W. Cobb of Georgia threatened disunion, saying, "We have kindled a fire which . . . seas of blood can only extinguish." Edward Colston of Virginia complained about the presence of a black face in the gallery, called the whole debate improper as being on too "delicate" a subject, and suggested, in effect, that one New Hampshire congressman deserved hanging for trying to incite servile war.[83]

It was in such heated atmosphere, with the Missouri bill (including the Tallmadge amendment) having just been sent on to the Senate, that John W. Taylor of New York proposed to modify the Arkansas bill by applying virtually the same restrictions as those in the Tallmadge amendment. At this point, a few northerners changed sides and helped to defeat the proposal. The first part, which prohibited further introduction of slaves into Arkansas, failed by a single vote, 71 to 70; the second part, which liberated at the age of twenty-five all slaves born in Arkansas after its admission, was first approved, 75 to 73, but then, upon reconsideration, defeated, 89 to 87.[84]

Taylor did not give up. He tried again to prohibit the further introduction of slaves into Arkansas. And when that effort failed, 90 to 86, he offered another amendment forbidding the introduction of slavery into any part of federal territory lying north of 36° 30'.[85] Whether he realized it or not, this was an especially shrewd move; for it tied the permission of slavery in Arkansas to the prohibition of slavery in Missouri, thus strengthening the case for the Tallmadge amendment in the Senate. If he had been successful, Taylor might well be known to history as the author of the "Arkansas-Missouri Compromise." Instead, the proposal never came to a formal vote. Several congressmen favored the idea of a dividing line but wanted to draw it farther north or farther south. A Tennessean said that it was unconstitutional; a Virginian, that it should be brought forward as a separate bill; a Pennsylvanian, that he would oppose *any* concession

property and could scarcely be seriously regarded as a violation of the Louisiana treaty.

to slavery. Taylor, seeing no chance of success, withdrew his amendment, and the Arkansas organic act was passed without restriction
concerning slavery.

By failing to attach antislavery amendments to *both* measures,
the House gave up any possibility of using one as leverage to elicit
senatorial approval of the other. The Senate simply passed the Arkansas bill while refusing to accept the Missouri bill unless the Tallmadge amendment were deleted. A last-minute effort to prohibit further introduction of slaves into Arkansas was defeated, 19 to 14.
Every southern vote was negative; every northeastern vote was affirmative. Four of the six senators from the Old Northwest voted with
the South and made the difference. The House, confronted with the
Missouri bill again, refused to allow deletion of its antislavery amendment, though the vote was close, 78 to 76. On this note of sharp sectional division, Congress adjourned, and the issue went to the country.[86]

That first flurry of excitement over Arkansas and Missouri lasted
scarcely three weeks and was confined largely to the halls of Congress. In those days of slow communication it took much longer to
awaken popular interest nationwide. But by the autumn of 1819, an
antislavery crusade was taking shape in many northern states, and the
demand for exclusion of slavery from Missouri echoed in mass meetings, pamphlets, editorials, and legislative resolutions. Some Federalist leaders appear to have seized upon the issue for partisan advantage, but the movement can perhaps also be understood as a
manifestation of the patrician reformism that was becoming a hallmark
of the era.[87]

From Missouri, meanwhile, came angry protests against the efforts at restriction and the resulting delay of admission.[88] The
strength of proslavery sentiment there must have made it obvious
that no one could turn Missouri into a free state. The work of salva-
tion had begun much too late, and the best that the antislavery forces
could hope for was some kind of *quid pro quo*. Thus, soon after the
sixteenth Congress assembled in December 1819, it was the antislavery leader John W. Taylor who made another attempt to construct a compromise. Again he proposed a dividing line between

freedom and slavery—this time the Missouri River, which would have split the state of Missouri—and again he had to acknowledge failure.[89]

At this point, the incipient state of Maine entered the scene and promptly became a sectional hostage. Maine had long been a part of Massachusetts and, with the latter's consent, now applied for admission. The House passed a bill for that purpose on January 3, 1820. The Senate amended it by adding a Missouri enabling act unencumbered with restrictions on slavery. The object, plainly, was coercion of the House, and in order to make the yoking of the two measures more acceptable there, the Senate added another amendment offered by Jesse B. Thomas of Illinois. It declared slavery to be "forever prohibited" in the remainder of the Louisiana cession lying north of 36° 30'. This was in fact the same dividing line that Taylor had proposed a year earlier to compensate the South for the Tallmadge restrictions on slavery in Missouri. Now it was being offered to the North as compensation for removal of those restrictions. The House responded by twice refusing to accept the Senate's package, and as late as March 1, by a vote of 91 to 82, it passed a new Missouri bill of its own, with a slavery restriction included. Yet, the very next day, at the recommendation of a conference committee, the House retreated and approved the compromise that it had previously rejected. The critical vote, on deletion of the antislavery clause from the Missouri bill, was 90 to 87. Fourteen of the majority's votes came from northerners.[90]

This would happen again thirty years later—the House giving in to the Senate and giving up an antislavery proviso that it had repeatedly insisted on. In both cases, the extended bitterness of the controversy and the apparent threat of disunion persuaded some men to give ground. For example, Charles Kinsey of New Jersey changed over to the proslavery side near the end of the Missouri struggle, saying that a northern victory would be "an inglorious triumph, gained at the hazard of the Union."[91] But in addition, some antislavery men probably recognized that the Thomas amendment was just about the most they could realistically expect to gain, Missouri having been lost to slavery a good many years earlier.

In later years, the phrase "Missouri Compromise" was often used inaccurately to designate the Thomas amendment, which in fact had been just one-half of one side of the Compromise. Historians have perpetuated the confusion. The Kansas-Nebraska Act of 1854 is commonly spoken of as having repealed the Missouri Compromise, whereas it actually repealed only the Thomas amendment, and that only as it applied to Kansas and Nebraska. The other parts of the Missouri Compromise were unrepealable, there being no way to revoke the admission of a state. The resulting ambiguity is largely responsible for the argument over which section contributed more support to the Compromise. Thus, according to Glover Moore (1953), it was "an agreement between a small majority of Southern members of Congress and a small minority of the Northern ones." But Homer Carey Hockett (1955) insisted that "the Compromise was passed by a majority in which the Northern members outnumbered the Southerners who voted with them." Both scholars had their figures straight, but Moore was talking about the whole compromise package, consisting of the Missouri bill (without slavery restriction), the Thomas amendment, and the Maine bill; whereas Hockett was talking about the Thomas amendment alone.[92]

The Thomas amendment, a grossly uneven division of the remaining federal territory, had been presented originally by a northern antislavery leader. Northern members of Congress voted for it, 115 to 7 (Senate: 20 to 2; House: 95 to 5). As a separate measure, it would have been opposed by southerners with similar solidarity, but proslavery strategists eventually brought it forward as an offer of part of the price to be paid for the admission of Missouri as a slave state. The question of whether to make this concession divided the southern membership in Congress, a membership that had otherwise displayed a high degree of unity wherever slavery was concerned. Southerners voted for the Thomas amendment, 53 to 45 (Senate: 14 to 8; House: 39 to 37). This was, in a sense, a measure of southern willingness to compromise. The northern membership, on the other hand, voted overwhelmingly against the compromise package, 105 to 18 (Senate: 18 to 4; House: 87 to 14).[93] Thus, when northerners later talked about the "sacred Missouri Compromise," they were referring either to a three-part settlement that their section had emphatically opposed, or to the one part of the settlement that had been most emphatically a southern concession.

Neither house engaged in extensive debate on the Thomas amendment, and consequently the great constitutional issue of later years never became a matter of critical importance during the Missouri controversy. Yet, during the long and wide-ranging argument, there were numerous references to the territorial aspect of the slavery question. Early in the session, when he was renewing his effort to prohibit further introduction of slavery into the trans-Mississippi region, John W. Taylor said that he knew of no member "who doubted the Constitutional power of Congress to impose such a restriction on the Territories." Although the assertion apparently went unchallenged at the time, subsequent debate proved it to be mistaken, as a number of southerners either denied or at least questioned congressional power to forbid slavery in the territories. Among those who did so were Charles Pinckney of South Carolina, one of the framers of the Constitution, and John Tyler of Virginia, a future president.[94]

Glover Moore concluded that "almost half" of the southern membership was unwilling to acknowledge the power as a matter of principle, although "somewhat more than half would vote for it in the form of a 'hoss trade' compromise."[95] From the beginning, then, there was southern ambivalence toward this northern invention, the 36° 30' line; and however accurate or inaccurate Moore's estimate may be, it is at least clear that the debates on the Missouri Compromise brought, more or less incidentally, the first significant challenge to the constitutional power of Congress over slavery in the territories.

Not surprisingly after so much discussion of the subject, when the Missouri enabling act came to President James Monroe for his signature, that strict constructionist consulted his cabinet about the eighth section of the measure (the Thomas amendment). According to John Quincy Adams, then secretary of state, there was general agreement that Congress had the power to impose the 36° 30' restriction, though several, including John C. Calhoun, could not find explicit authority for it in the Constitution. With Adams alone dissenting, the cabinet also agreed that the phrase "forever forbidden" actually meant only for the duration of the territorial period.[96] It is astonishing that southerners should have permitted the word "forever" to be used in the Thomas amendment; for it seemed to mean literally that the antislavery restriction would carry over after each territory north of 36° 30' became a state. Southerners appeared to be surrendering here the very principle for which they were fighting so desperately in opposing antislavery restrictions on Missouri—namely, the principle of state equality. One can only conclude that Thomas, in phrasing his amendment, drew somewhat thoughtlessly on the tradition of the Northwest Ordinance.

The strongest opposition to the 36° 30' restriction came from the state of Virginia. Both Virginia senators voted against it, and, in the House of Representatives, eighteen Virginians contributed almost half of all the negative votes. They received emphatic moral support from the two greatest living Virginians. Thomas Jefferson had virtually invented the idea of prohibiting slavery in the American West, but now, thirty-six years later, he opposed the restrictive portion of the Compromise, adducing the "diffusion" argument that the expansion of slavery would ameliorate the condition of the slave. Madison wholeheartedly sided with the South in the Missouri controversy and questioned the constitutionality of the 36° 30' restriction.[97]

These attitudes can be explained in various ways—as manifesting the conservatism of the elderly, for instance; or as resulting from the strong suspicion (which Monroe shared) that the Missouri agitation was essentially a Federalist scheme to split the Republican party; or as reflecting the economic interest of Virginia, a slave-surplus state, in the continuing expansion of the peculiar institution. But in addition, the proslavery pronouncements of Jefferson and Madison signalized the depth and unity of southern commitment to slavery by 1820. The Missouri crisis had strikingly revealed just how solid the South could be on this issue. Southerners in Congress voted 83 to 1 against the first part of the Tallmadge amendment and 81 to 2 against the second part. Their voting on the proposed antislavery amendments to the Arkansas bill was about the same.[98]

Statistically emphatic, the southern response to the antislavery efforts of 1819–20 was also emotionally excessive. Jefferson's colorful phrase, "fire bell in the night," has become a cliché, endlessly quoted but seldom analyzed. It is true that for more than a decade, owing primarily to the foreign crisis and war, the slavery issue had been considerably muffled, but even so there was much precedent for raising the question of the status of slavery in new territory. After the debates accompanying the organization of Mississippi and Orleans territories, after the recent controversy over the admission of Illinois, it was scarcely accurate to compare the Missouri struggle to an alarm breaking the silence of the night. Jefferson used far stronger language, however, saying that the crisis filled him with "terror"—indeed, with worse apprehension than any he had felt "in the gloomiest moment of the revolutionary war."

> I considered it at once as the knell of the Union. . . . I regret that I am now to die in the belief, that the useless sacrifice of themselves by the generation of 1776, to acquire self-government and happiness to their country, is to be thrown away by the unwise and unworthy passions of their sons, and that my only consolation is to be, that I live not to weep over it.[99]

All of this despair was poured out in response to proposals for doing nothing more than what Jefferson himself had proposed to do in 1784. Although his rhetoric is ambiguous, he must have been referring to the antislavery movement in Congress when he also spoke of "unwise and unworthy passions" and of "treason against the hopes of the world." Yet, in the same breath, he continued to pay lip service to the ideal of universal freedom. "I can say, with conscious truth," he wrote, "that there is not a man on earth who would sacrifice more than I would to relieve us from this heavy reproach, in any *practicable* way."[100]

Most southerners in Congress likewise continued to go through the motions of deprecating slavery, but their words over the years had come to sound increasingly hollow, especially when they insisted that nothing could be done about the problem, and that it was dangerous to try or even talk about trying. Justice, said Jefferson, was in one scale and self-preservation in the other. One can detect some-

thing of the tension felt by many southerners in a passage from a
speech by Robert W. Reid of Georgia. With a perfect *volte-face* in
the middle, it begins with high-flown rhetoric and ends in passion:

> I would hail that day as the most glorious in its dawning, which
> should behold, with safety to themselves and our citizens, the
> black population of the United States placed upon the high emi-
> nence of equal rights, and clothed in the privileges and immuni-
> ties of American citizens! But this is a dream of philanthropy
> which can never be fulfilled; and whoever shall act in this country
> upon such wild theories, shall cease to be a benefactor, and be-
> come a destroyer of the human family.[101]

The Missouri crisis apparently came at a time of internal crisis for
many southerners who had begun half-consciously to readjust their
conceptions of the future of slavery in the United States. Many simply set the great day of ultimate extinction infinitely far ahead in time,
but a few took the logical step of praising as a public good what so
many were already defending as a necessity. Some were obviously in
transit, such as the future vice president Richard M. Johnson of Kentucky, who said that slavery was a "necessary evil . . . not incompatible with true religion." Various speakers insisted that slaves were
generally a happy breed; several took their listeners back to ancient
Greece and Rome in defense of slavery on historical grounds; and a
number turned to the Bible for testimony that the institution was part
of God's plan. The oratory was often florid, as in the appeal of Senator
James Barbour of Virginia for submission to the divine will: "The
same mighty power that planted the greater and the lesser luminary
in the heavens, permits on earth the bondsman and the free. To that
Providence, as men and Christians, let us bow. . . . it is a link in that
great concatenation which is permitted by omnipotent power and
goodness, and must issue in universal good." A speech by Senator
William Smith of South Carolina may have been the most emphatic
statement of the emerging southern attitude. "That gentleman," exclaimed Benjamin Ruggles of Ohio after listening to it, "justified slavery on the broadest principles, without qualification or reserve. This
was taking entirely new ground."[102]

Missouri's struggle for admission did not end with passage of the enabling act in March 1820, but the second crisis and compromise involved the status of free Negroes rather than the expansion of slavery.[103] The latter question had been settled with a formula that would presumably also be suitable for any additional territory that might be acquired. Politically and constitutionally, slavery in the territories became more or less a moot issue, and sectional hostility found other avenues of expression.

∾ 5 ∾

Expansion and Slavery
in a Continental Republic

T he Missouri crisis, it has been said, "introduced the antislavery issue into American politics."[1] But in fact, the
issue was more or less continuously present in the consciousness of American political leaders from the very beginning of
the Republic, and often enough before 1819 it had broken through
the surface of congressional business. Perhaps in part because of Jefferson's overwrought imagery, the Missouri controversy appears in
textbook history as a sudden, interruptive event, full of meaning for
the future but somewhat anomalous in the context of its own time. It
is true that the controversy does not fit easily into an "Era of Good
Feelings" or an interval of "postwar nationalism." Unlike the crisis of
1850, it did not arise inevitably from the consequences of a war
recently ended, and it had no inflamed aftermath like northern reaction to the Fugitive Slave Act, nor a spectacular sequel like the
Kansas-Nebraska controversy.

Yet the Missouri affair was actually not an isolated eruption but
instead the most prominent part of a sequential pattern. One major
reason for the intensity of the controversy was the belatedness of the
antislavery effort, impinging as it did upon the highly sensitive principles of state sovereignty and state equality. Missouri *as a territory*, it
has been shown, inspired less argument over slavery than did Mississippi Territory in 1798, Orleans Territory in 1804, or Arkansas Terri-

114

tory in 1819. Missouri *the incipient state* was belatedly controversial, and doubly so because of its geographical position as a rather northerly sectional borderland. It was, in fact, the only one of the so-called border states to have been a part of the territorial system.

The success of the Missouri Compromise resulted primarily from its having left no other such borderland anywhere on the horizon, together with the fact that neither northerners nor southerners were at this point prepared to insist, on moral or constitutional grounds, that all federal territory should be uniformly closed or uniformly open to slavery. The 36° 30′ line had little to do with the success of the Compromise, for it merely stipulated realities that everyone acknowledged. If the territorial issue did cease for a time to be provocative, it was not because of the Thomas proviso or a decline in sectional feeling about slavery but essentially because of the nature and location of the remaining federal territory.

For a third of a century after the Missouri Compromise, the western half of the Louisiana Purchase remained unsettled and unorganized, supposedly set aside permanently as Indian country. Iowa Territory, created in 1838, with slavery forbidden, was too far north to provoke southern opposition. Florida, acquired by treaty from Spain in 1821, was too far south to invite a serious antislavery effort. Arkansas Territory, bounded on three sides by slave states, had already been conceded to slavery. Yet, even in these conditions, some controversy arose. Framers of the bill for the organization of Florida Territory in 1822 copied it from the Orleans act of 1804, including the Hillhouse provision that no slaves could be taken into the territory except by bona fide owners. Southerners in the Senate managed to get this clause deleted, but only by a vote of 23 to 20.[2] Arkansas applied for admission in 1836 with a constitution prohibiting legislation "for the emancipation of slaves, without the consent of the owners." There were complaints that the clause would make slavery "perpetual" in the state, and John Quincy Adams, now a congressman from Massachusetts, offered an amendment stating that nothing in the act should be construed as congressional assent to the article on slavery and emancipation. The legal effect of this merely declaratory proviso would have been doubtful, and it failed in any case. The Arkansas admission bill passed easily by votes of 143 to 50 in the House and 31 to 6 in the Senate.[3]

With the subsidence of the territorial issue after 1820, the history of the slavery controversy tends to move away from Congress and national politics for a time, but not entirely so. There was a long running debate, for instance, on proposals for federal assistance to the African Colonization Society.[4] In 1824, the Senate, after heated argument, emasculated a convention signed with Great Britain for stricter enforcement of laws against the international slave trade.[5] The year following, Rufus King, in his last antislavery flourish, proposed to the Senate that proceeds from the sales of public lands be used to finance a program of emancipation and colonization. Senator Robert Y. Hayne of South Carolina in a vehement response denied that Congress had power to create such a fund, which would constitute a threat, he said, to the "peace and harmony of the Union."[6] In 1828, the House of Representatives spent an astonishing amount of time debating a private bill that raised some fundamental questions about the status of slavery in the United States. The measure proposed to remunerate the owner of a slave impressed into federal service during the War of 1812 and wounded as a consequence. Was this the same as having one's property damaged? No, replied a number of northerners; for under the Constitution slaves were persons, not property. This stirred the wrath of various southerners, including Edward Livingston of Louisiana, the transplanted New Yorker who would soon become Andrew Jackson's secretary of state. "Slaves not property!" he exclaimed. "What are they then? If they are not property, then they are free." The southern defense of slavery throughout the discussion was eloquent and emotional, but it retained some of the old apologetics. "Slavery, in the abstract, I condemn and abhor," said William Drayton of South Carolina. Nevertheless, "it was part of our inheritance—from which we can no more deliver ourselves, than we can from the miasma of our swamps."[7] Soon, even such theoretical concessions to the antislavery principle would go out of fashion among southern politicians.

The most important consequence of the Missouri struggle was the bitter memory of it. Slavery remained a haunting presence in national politics, unmentioned much of the time, but inspiring many apprehensive glances over the shoulder. Behind the emerging partisan alignments and behind many issues of the period were strong sectional purposes, and at the core of sectional consciousness, especially in the South, was the problem of slavery.[8] Still, if partisanship often masked sectional motives, it also discouraged sectional excess. Like its Jeffersonian predecessor, the triumphant Jacksonian coalition of 1828 was essentially a southern-based party—proslavery at heart, but quietly so in order to accommodate its robust northern wing. The opposition, developing into the Whig party with a somewhat more northerly center of gravity, found it no less expedient to repress the slavery issue in the interest of building a southern constituency. Thus the exigencies of party formation in the Jacksonian period tended to push slavery out of national politics. Yet certain external forces already at work would eventually produce a stronger counter-pressure.

The most striking development, of course, was the rise of radical abolitionism as exemplified in the person of William Lloyd Garrison and signalized by his launching of *The Liberator* in Boston on New Year's Day, 1831. Partly an outgrowth and partly a repudiation of earlier antislavery efforts, this new movement was in some respects another victory of the nineteenth century over the preceding age of neoclassic restraint and rationalism. The transformation has sometimes been described as a shift from "gradualism" to "immediatism" in the struggle against slavery, but the terms are not entirely appropriate.

Gradual emancipation was a practical, conservative process working reasonably well in New York, New Jersey, Pennsylvania, Connecticut, and Rhode Island. But the "gradualism" represented by the colonization movement and still embraced theoretically by many southern slaveholders was obviously impractical, except as a gesture, and better described as "eventualism," because it relied less on the will of men than on the benevolence of time. Meanwhile, in spite of the closure placed on importation of slaves, the slave population of the country continued to grow, not gradually but rapidly. By 1830 it had reached 2 million. Furthermore, even the workable gradualism of the Middle Atlantic States and southern New England dealt with slavery as an institution, rather than with slaves as human beings. The solution was statesmanlike in that it avoided social upheaval, and it was conservative in that the slaveholder received substantial compensation, in the form of service, before he surrendered any property. But gradual emancipation, from the slave's point of view, was cruelly unjust. It usually meant that the older generation must live on in bondage to the end of its days and that the younger generation must serve as much as twenty-eight years before becoming free. In the eyes of the new breed of abolitionist, every slave had a right to be *immediately* free.

Although immediatism seemed to imply instantaneous, universal emancipation, even Garrison acknowledged the distinction between what was called for and what might be expected. "Urge immediate abolition as earnestly as we may," he wrote, "it will, alas! be gradual abolition in the end."[9] Immediatism, with its origins in evangelical Christianity, was not so much a program of action as it was a state of urgent conviction, to which all men must be brought, concerning the evilness of slavery. Out of the passion of their own commitment, but also as a deliberate choice of strategy, the new abolitionists set forth to destroy slavery by direct, personal assault upon everyone associated with the institution and everyone acquiescing in its existence. Their inflammatory rhetorical style won some converts but made many enemies, in the North as well as the South. The effect was to intensify greatly the antagonism over slavery that had never been entirely absent from American life, to aggravate southern fear of slave revolt inspired by northern agitation, and to evoke a related phenomenon of transcendent importance that can perhaps best be labeled "southern rage."

Zealotry was nothing new among opponents of slavery, however, and although radical abolitionists grew steadily in numbers after 1830, they continued to be a very small part of the total population. It was by rising to a new level of dedication and organization that they managed to become a dynamic, disruptive element in American society. Except among the Quakers, earlier antislavery activity had often been a secondary concern of busy men of affairs and therefore not entirely free of dilettantism. The new, Garrisonian breed made the war on slavery the central factor in their lives. They thus professionalized the movement, and, in spite of their alleged anti-institutional bias, they institutionalized it. Opposition to slavery for the first time became, in its own small way, an interest as well as a sentiment, and the slaveholding interest felt the difference immediately.

Still another significant difference between the old and the new was in racial attitudes. Henry Clay, during the debate on the Arkansas territorial bill in 1819, had declared that northern antislavery men seemed to be suffering from "Negrophobia."[10] It was an interesting diagnosis, in view of the fact that later critics of slavery—Republicans as well as abolitionists—were much more likely to be charged with Negrophilia, but Clay appears to have been substantially accurate. With the uprising on Santo Domingo fresh in mind, fear of the Negro in mass numbers as a dangerous, half-sleeping giant was expressed frequently by northerners like James Hillhouse in the early congressional debates over slavery. Not surprisingly, these apprehensions were felt even more strongly by southerners, including Clay himself, who supported the African colonization movement on the grounds that the ultimate alternative would be social upheaval amidst "shocking scenes of carnage, rapine, and lawless violence."[11] The early abolitionist movement, gradualistic in outlook and heavily concentrated in the upper South, allied itself closely with the colonization program, thus offering solutions to the twin problem of Negro slavery and Negro unassimilability. The latter might be attributed to natural inferiority, or to the irreversible effects of slavery, or to ineradicable white prejudice, but it was in any case the fundamental assumption of an abolitionism that condemned slavery primarily as a threat to the security of the nation rather than because of its injustice to slaves.[12]

The new abolitionists, rejecting not only the gradualism but the racial conceptions of the colonization movement, proceeded on the assumption that slaves after emancipation would remain on American soil as full-fledged members of American society. No doubt such a purpose was much easier to adopt in Boston than in the cotton kingdom, but it was nevertheless a remarkable leap of conscience and faith—faith not only in the capacity of the black race to surmount its disadvantages but also in the capacity of the white race to outgrow its prejudices. It was an unrealistic expectation thoroughly in the spirit of romantic perfectionism, but no more unrealistic than the expectations of the colonizationists.

The racial equalitarianism openly embraced by Garrison and many other abolitionists after 1830 added a provocative new element to the slavery controversy. It intensified the fury of southern reaction and was apparently the principal stimulus to an outburst of violent anti-abolitionist activity in the North.[13] Moreover, all antislavery men, however moderate, thereafter became vulnerable to the charge of being "Negro-worshippers"—a charge that few politicians could afford to leave undenied. In the famous Illinois senatorial campaign of 1858, for instance, Stephen A. Douglas repeatedly associated Abraham Lincoln with "Negro equality," and despite Lincoln's vehement denials, it may have made the difference on election day.

II

By 1836, the new wave of abolitionism had turned Congress into a battleground over the receipt of antislavery petitions there and the postal delivery of antislavery literature in the southern states. It had also contributed heavily to turning most of the South into a closed society of closed minds where slavery was concerned. With Nat Turner's rebellion of 1831 (essentially a two-day massacre of plantation families) still a fresh memory, southerners tended to view all abolitionist propaganda as incendiary in purpose. By a combination of state laws and connivance of federal officials, they achieved substantial success in closing down mail circulation of objectionable publications.[14] The South also tightened its system of control over slaves and free Negroes. It treated peddlers and other travelers from the North with increasing suspicion and sometimes with harassment. Some states, such as Virginia, passed severe laws punishing advocacy of abolition. Vigilance committees ferreted out subversives, administering whippings and other chastisements. By 1837, there were no southern abolition societies remaining in existence, and from the South came importunate demands that northern states curb the abolitionist invective originating within their borders.[15] The defense of slavery as a positive good was replacing the old argument that it was an unfortunate but inescapable legacy. Jeffersonian ambivalence would no longer satisfy the dynamic elements of either section. If slavery was evil, then slaveholders must be evildoers—on that point the new southern militants were in agreement with the new abolitionists. They viewed all moral denunciation of slavery as impeachment of their honor, virtue, and human decency.

But it was the swelling volume of antislavery petitions and the notorious "gag rule" imposed in 1836 (formally so by the House of Representatives and informally by the Senate) that brought slavery truly to the center of congressional politics for the first time since the Missouri crisis. Thus began the eight-year struggle in which John Quincy Adams, with all the brooding passion of an Old Testament prophet, made himself the scourge of the slaveholding South—detested and feared, but at the same time grudgingly respected.[16]

The political consequences of the gag rule are well known. As a defense of slavery, it proved to be foolish strategy; for it inspired the abolitionists to more heroic efforts and brought them support from many non-abolitionists who believed that a fundamental right was in jeopardy.[17] The resulting uproar never entirely subsided during the next quarter-century; for at this point the sectional controversy over slavery became virtually continuous.

On March 15, 1836, in the midst of the first struggle over the gag rule, the Senate confirmed the nomination of Roger B. Taney as chief justice by a vote of 29 to 15. The division was largely partisan rather than sectional, with Webster, Clay, and Calhoun listed among the opponents. Later that same spring, an army medical officer in Illinois took his Negro servant with him up the Mississippi River to a new assignment in federal territory where slavery had been forbidden by the Missouri Compromise. The historical convergence of these two unrelated but nearly simultaneous events lay twenty years in the future, but to a considerable degree the forces that would bring them ultimately together were visible in the petitions controversy.

Before 1836, antislavery petitions had been handled expeditiously, usually by reference to committees which took no action on them. But the tone as well as the substance of the documents so in-furiated many southerners that they wanted to cut off all reception of them in Congress. Not even the House gag rule, requiring automatic tabling of all antislavery petitions, would satisfy men such as Calhoun, James H. Hammond, and Henry Wise; for tabling still extended a measure of recognition. The petitions had to be turned away at the threshold, Hammond argued, in order "to put a more decided seal of reprobation on them."[18] Here, in fact, was the heart of the sectional conflict, the real issue that would drive the nation to civil war—not the regulation of territories or the recovery of fugitive slaves, but, quite simply, northern denunciation of slavery and whether it could be silenced. "Abolition and the Union," said Calhoun, "cannot coexist."[19]

Southerners demanding outright rejection of all antislavery peti-tions justified such severity on the ground that no one had a right to petition Congress for legislation not within its delegated constitutional authority. The primary target of petitioners in 1836, however, was slavery in the District of Columbia, and there the Constitution em-powered Congress "to exercise exclusive legislation in all cases what-soever." These words were more emphatic and explicit than the phrasing of the territory clause. They seemed clearly to invest Congress with municipal powers in the District similar to those pos-sessed by state governments and their subsidiaries, including the power to establish or prohibit slavery. Many southerners were ac-cordingly satisfied to have interference with slavery in the District labeled merely undesirable, but others insisted vigorously that it would be unconstitutional, giving a variety of reasons. For instance, in a notable anticipation of Taney's Dred Scott opinion, Calhoun in-voked the Fifth Amendment provision against deprivation of life, lib-erty, or property without due process of law. Due process, he de-clared, meant jury trial, and "were not the slaves of this District property?"[20] In a series of resolutions introduced December 27, 1837, Calhoun also set forth his theory that the federal government was created as the "common agent" of the sovereign states with the duty of "strengthening and upholding" the domestic institutions of those states. Slavery, he declared in a speech, was actually "as much under the protection of the Constitution" in the District of Columbia and in the territories as it was "in the States themselves."[21]

In this manner Calhoun laid the basis for that convenient contradiction whereby southerners, especially in the late 1850s, were able to maintain that slavery was a local institution beyond the power of Congress to restrain in any way, and yet at the same time deserving of full protection in the territories by direct force of the Constitution itself. Thus "nonintervention" could be converted at will to mean intervention. But from the revealing debates on the right to petition for the abolition of slavery in the national capital it becomes clear that the defense of slavery by men of the Calhoun school, in spite of their frequent references to the Constitution, was essentially transconstitutional—an appeal to a southern version of higher law. For the ambiguity that impaired the force of the territory clause was entirely absent from the District clause, and yet the conclusions of the Calhoun school were the same in each instance. Slavery was untouchable and, indeed, unmentionable except in respectful, protective tones.

The Senate, accepting four of Calhoun's six resolutions, endorsed his definition of the federal government as the creature and agent of the sovereign states, but to his disappointment it took a stand against abolition in the District of Columbia on grounds other than lack of constitutional authority.[22] Calhoun, in fact, had nothing approaching united southern support for his extremist position. Many strong party men—Whigs and Democrats—together, regarded him and his followers as troublemakers, but not in the same sense as the "fanatics" and "lunatics" at the other extreme. The abolitionists, held primarily responsible for the ceaseless quarrel over slavery, were treated with less tolerance. For instance, when Joshua Giddings of Ohio in 1842 offered a series of antislavery resolutions that were no more vehement or unreasonable than those presented by Calhoun, the House of Representatives punished him with a formal vote of censure.[23]

With each new Congress after 1836, northern support for the gag rule diminished; yet it continued in effect for eight years and became more severe in 1840. For a time, the growing intensity of the slavery controversy was substantially offset by the growing tensile strength of party allegiance. No political leader was more determined to keep the

lid on the slavery issue than Martin Van Buren, elected president as
Andrew Jackson's successor in 1836, the very year in which the gag
rule was first imposed. But in that same year another outside force
began to operate in such a way as to broaden the base of the antislavery movement and intensify sectional antagonism in Congress—
namely, the renewal of American expansion, which promised eventually to reopen the question supposedly closed by the Missouri Compromise. Calhoun raised the territorial issue in his resolutions of
December 1837, and he did so because by that time petitions against
slavery in the District of Columbia were outnumbered by petitions
against the annexation of Texas.[24]

III

A dubious American claim to Texas as part of the Louisiana Purchase
had been relinquished in the Florida treaty of 1819–21. Later, there
were complaints about this "surrender," especially in the Old Southwest, and they became all the more bitter during the 1830s when the
negotiator of the treaty, John Quincy Adams, emerged as a zealous
opponent of slavery in the House of Representatives. Actually, Adams
had been very reluctant to give up Texas in 1819, and during his
presidency he tried in vain to buy the province from newly independent Mexico. Jackson made the same effort without success.[25] Meanwhile, American settlers had begun to enter Texas in the 1820s,
drawn there by generous Mexican land grants. Predominantly southerners, they took their slaves along and kept them even after Mexico
formally abolished slavery in 1829. So when Texas, after fighting and
winning a war for independence in 1836, requested annexation to the
United States, it did so as a slaveholding republic.

Long before the Texans made their application, antislavery
spokesmen in and outside of Congress had launched a fierce campaign against annexation, charging that the revolution in Texas was
part of a slaveholders' plot to enlarge the domain and power of their
peculiar institution within the United States. Adams, putting aside his
old enthusiasm for expansion, warned that seizure of Texas would
provoke foreign war and civil conflict in which the war power of

Congress could be used against slavery even within the southern states—a prophecy that eventually proved to be not far off the mark.[26] The threat to Democratic party unity in the abolitionist crusade, together with the danger of driving Mexico to a declaration of war, induced Jackson and Van Buren to deal cautiously with the Texas question. Annexation, as a consequence, was postponed for nearly a decade.

Public attention turned to other problems, notably the Panic of 1837 and an extended aftermath of economic depression, but interest in the annexation of Texas never entirely subsided, and by 1843 it had been emphatically revived. Sam Houston, who favored annexation, had returned to the presidency of Texas, and he was able to exploit a growing American concern about British designs on Texas. There was also a new enthusiasm for territorial expansion, soon to be associated with the phrase "Manifest Destiny." The overland movement of settlers to Oregon and California had begun, and the whole North American continent suddenly seemed barely large enough domain for the American eagle. No less important were the vagaries of politics. John Tyler, a pseudo-Whig who succeeded to the presidency in 1841 after the death of William Henry Harrison, broke with Henry Clay and other party leaders over the issue of re-establishing a national bank. In the hope of gaining some measure of glory for his administration and perhaps gathering a new political following, Tyler set out to acquire Texas.[27] Negotiations progressed slowly, however. Not until April 1844 did Tyler lay a treaty of annexation before the Senate, and by that time Americans were in the midst of a presidential campaign, with Texas as the central issue. Both of the expected nominees, Clay and Van Buren, promptly published letters opposing immediate annexation. Calhoun, now secretary of state, killed whatever slight hope there may have been for the treaty by defending annexation on proslavery grounds in an imprudent letter to the British minister in Washington. He thereby made it difficult for any northern senator to support the treaty, which was soundly defeated on June 8 by a vote of 35 to 16.[28]

The Texas question, like the Missouri controversy, involved the issue of the expansion of slavery but not the issue of congressional power in the territories. In some respects, it produced a mirror image of the typical dispute between the sections; for, in this case, it was the northerners who were resorting to strict construction of the Constitution and talking about disruption of the Union if annexation should be consummated. The amount of reliance on constitutional argument is a notable feature of the anti-Texas crusade. It was not enough to denounce annexation as a slaveholders' plot to extend their dark empire, or as an act of international villainy that would surely plunge the United States into war, or as an acquisition that would destroy the Union. In addition, men as dissimilar as Joshua Giddings and Daniel Webster felt it necessary to maintain that the constitutional authority to annex Texas was lacking. "I, for one," said Giddings, "deny the constitutional power of this government to amalgamate the political destinies of this people with those of Texas or any other foreign government." Webster, ordinarily an advocate of broad nationalism, took the same strict-constructionist view. He justified the acquisition of Louisiana and Florida on grounds of national necessity (thereby divorcing himself from the Federalism of his youth) and then added: "No such necessity . . . requires the annexation of Texas."[29]

The argument that national interest had occasionally required Congress to go beyond its constitutional authority was a way of escaping the force of precedent and the legal principle of estoppel. It would later be used to great advantage by southerners trying to explain away southern support of the Missouri Compromise. The disposition to convert public issues into constitutional issues was nothing new in American politics, but it became an especially prominent feature of the slavery controversy during the 1840s. For southerners, the claim to equal rights under the Constitution served to offset the vulnerability of slavery to moral reproach. Calhoun in 1850 would provide the ultimate formula: Unjust laws are unnecessary laws and, therefore, unconstitutional.[30]

Texas by 1844 had thus replaced the District of Columbia as the primary focus of the slavery controversy. More than that, the Texas question decisively altered the course of American history because of its influence on one of the most crucial of all presidential elections. Hostility to annexation probably cost Van Buren the Democratic nomination and may very well have made the difference in Clay's narrow defeat by James K. Polk. At any rate, contrary to all expectations when the year began, an enthusiastic expansionist was elected president on a platform calling for "the reoccupation of Oregon and the reannexation of Texas." Tyler, interpreting the outcome as a referendum in favor of his policy, recommended annexation of Texas by joint resolution instead of treaty. This maneuver circumvented the need for a two-thirds majority in the Senate. In spite of strong opposition from Whigs and some antislavery Democrats, the desired resolution passed both houses of Congress at the end of February 1845, just in time for Tyler to sign it triumphantly before he left office.[31]

The resolution was approved by the House, 120 to 98; by the Senate in amended form, 27 to 25; and then by the House again, 132 to 76. These figures offer a striking contrast to the virtual unanimity with which the acquisition of Florida had been approved a quarter of a century earlier. To be sure, the alignment of voting was more partisan than sectional and reflected sharp differences of opinion about expansion per se. Nevertheless, it was primarily the slavery issue that had made expansion such a controversial matter where Texas was concerned. Any careful study of the annexation movement will expose the inaccuracy of the view that it was merely a proslavery project; but this in no way changes the fact that antislavery feeling was the dynamic, dominant element in the opposition to annexation.[32]

One significant feature of the resolution, in view of the fact that it received the support of all southern Democrats voting on it in the House and Senate, was that it included a reaffirmation of the Missouri Compromise restriction. Texas claimed an enormous area, and a small part of that claim extended north of 36° 30'. The annexation measure provided that as many as four additional states might, with its consent, be formed from Texas. Any such states lying south of the Missouri Compromise line must be "admitted into the Union with or without slavery, as the people . . . may desire." Also, in any state or state formed north of the line, slavery was prohibited, but this clause amounted to little more than a gesture. Since nearly all of Texas lay south of 36° 30', the essential purpose of reaffirming the Missouri Compromise line was to make sure that any subdivision of the state

would leave slavery secure. Yet, in accomplishing their purpose,
southerners theoretically acknowledged the power of Congress to
exclude slavery, not merely from a federal territory but from a new
state entering the Union. The latter was the very power that southerners had denied so vehemently during the Missouri struggle.[33]

The two major historical consequences of the Texas question,
however, were that it brought Polk to the presidency and it brought
Mexico and the United States into conflict. Given the brute force of
American expansionism, the extravagance of Texan boundary claims,
and the imprudence of Mexican policy, the war may have been unavoidable no matter who occupied the White House. But a war
merely to hold all the land claimed by Texas would not have necessitated the conquest of California or the capture of Mexico City. Polk
may or may not have been responsible for making the war, but he
was certainly responsible for the kind of war that it turned out to be.
His prompt dispatch of General Stephen Watts Kearny to Santa Fe
and Los Angeles indicated plainly enough that a war of territorial
aggrandizement had begun.[34] And so, just eight weeks after the declaration of war, David Wilmot introduced his famous proviso.

IV

Historians have devoted much attention to the authorship of the Wilmot Proviso and the motives of its supporters. One is sometimes
given the impression that it came like a bolt from a cloudless sky,
reviving an issue that had been dead since 1820. Yet the Proviso controversy was a logical extension of the recent struggle over the annexation of Texas—an extension, however, in which party solidarity
proved less resistant to the pressures of sectional antagonism. Radical
antislavery elements within Congress and outside of it were still bitter
about Texas and determined to resist further encroachments of the
"slave power." Nothing can be more certain than that *someone* would
have raised the question of the status of slavery in any territory
wrested from Mexico by military force. The only puzzling thing about
the Proviso is that it was introduced at such an early stage in the war
by a northern Democrat who had not previously been associated with
the antislavery cause.[35]

It must be remembered, however, that most of the antislavery Whigs in Congress were opponents of southwestern expansion, resolved to resist any conquest of territory from Mexico, and the Proviso, much as they might like its antislavery character, was plainly an expansionist document, acknowledging the likelihood and propriety of such conquest. More than that, it was offered as an amendment to an appropriation of $2 million requested by Polk on August 8, 1846, for the obvious purpose of facilitating the acquisition of California and New Mexico.* As for those antislavery men who *favored* expansion (principally northern Democrats), their best strategy would seem to have been waiting until a treaty of annexation had been signed before raising the question of slavery. Furthermore, it could be argued that slavery was illegal in Mexico and would remain so in any ceded area unless Congress provided otherwise by positive enactment. From this point of view, the Proviso was unnecessary, and, indeed, it tended to yield important vantage ground; for if it failed to pass, that failure could be interpreted as a repudiation of Mexican law and an implied acquiescence in the extension of slavery.[37]

It is therefore easy enough to understand why the Proviso did not originate with one of the well-known antislavery radicals in Congress. Historians have convincingly shown, moreover, that Wilmot acted for a group of northern Democrats inspired by other motives besides their dislike of slavery. For various reasons, they shared a growing animosity toward Polk and the South. Some resented the Oregon Treaty, signed with Great Britain in June, and the President's recent veto of a rivers-and-harbors appropriation. In each of these two cases, the blow had fallen most heavily on the Northwest, and in each the heavy hand of southern influence seemed all too visible. Polk's hostility to internal improvements at federal expense reflected the strict constructionism so dear to the old South. As for Oregon, nearly half of it had been surrendered after the great expanse of Texas had

*The Wilmot Proviso read as follows: "*Provided*, That, as an express and fundamental condition to the acquisition of any territory from the Republic of Mexico by the United States, by virtue of any treaty which may be negotiated between them, and to the use by the Executive of the moneys herein appropriated, neither slavery nor involuntary servitude shall ever exist in any part of said territory, except for crime, whereof the party shall first be duly convicted."[36]

been secured for slaveholders, and now southerners expected to obtain still more slave territory from the Mexican adventure. The Proviso, in the circumstances, seemed an appropriate retaliation. But the center of disaffection was probably New York, where Van Buren Democrats like Preston King were still unhappy about the defeat of their leader in the national convention of 1844. They regarded themselves as mistreated by Polk and feared that they were losing ground to the Whigs in state politics because national party policies compelled them to carry too much proslavery weight. The Proviso, for these men, was "a defensive, not an aggressive movement," intended to restore sectional balance in a party leaning heavily southward and to "justify the Mexican War to the northern electorate."[38]

The reasons why certain northern Democrats decided to introduce the Proviso will by no means suffice, however, as an explanation of why nearly all northern votes in the House of Representatives were cast in its favor. The distinction is important and seldom made. Even anti-expansionists placed their antislavery feelings first and voted for the Proviso. Men such as John Quincy Adams who considered it unnecessary nevertheless voted for the Proviso. Northerners who had favored the Oregon compromise voted for the Proviso, and northerners who had opposed the rivers-and-harbors bill voted for the Proviso. Northern Democrats joined northern Whigs in voting for the Proviso. Whatever one may say about its "origins," the Wilmot Proviso was essentially what it appeared to be—a remarkably strong expression of antislavery sentiment and an effort to keep slavery out of any territory that might be seized from Mexico.

The introduction of the Proviso on August 8, 1846, cannot be called a "fire bell in the night." It came at the end of a decade of almost continual controversy over slavery, and it raised an issue made irrepressible by the kind of war Polk had instituted against Mexico. It did not revive the question of the extension of slavery; that had already been done in the struggle over Texas. Even the *territorial* aspect of that question had arisen two days earlier when the House of Representatives added an antislavery amendment to a bill for the organization of Oregon Territory, with all but seven southerners voting *no* or abstaining.[39] The Proviso at this stage, moreover, was a little too premature to provoke a sectional crisis. No one yet knew what territory it might apply to, and public attention was caught up in the excitement of a war just begun. But soon the need to provide government for Oregon, then the Treaty of Guadalupe Hidalgo, and finally the problem of gold-rush California would make the issue of slavery in the territories increasingly unavoidable and undeferrable.

In any case, this first skirmish over the Proviso was exceedingly brief. It came at the very end of a session of Congress that had lasted eight months. Debate in the House was limited to ten minutes per speaker and two hours altogether. At the end of the allotted time on a hot Saturday evening, members voted 83 to 64 for the Wilmot amendment and 86 to 64 for the $2 million bill to which it was attached. In neither instance was there a roll call, but on the intervening motion for engrossment of the bill, the *ayes* and *nays* were recorded. They showed southerners opposed, 67 to 2, and northerners in favor, 83 to 12, with 8 of the 12 negative northern votes cast by unyielding anti-expansionist Whigs. Thus it can be said that only 6 congressmen out of 164 really crossed sectional lines in the voting.

	N. DEM.	N. WHIG	S. DEM.	S. WHIG
Yes	52	31	0	2
No	4	8	50	17

$2 MILLION BILL WITH PROVISO ATTACHED: ENGROSSMENT

The measure did not reach the Senate until the final hour of the session on Monday, August 10. There it died at the hands of John Davis, a Massachusetts Whig, who filibustered until the hour of adjournment arrived. Apparently he did so to prevent the Senate from striking out the Proviso and returning it to the House in time for the latter to acquiesce.[40] The notion that Davis made an enormous blunder, preventing an antislavery triumph, seems utterly unfounded. The bill, as long as it included the Proviso, had little chance of passing the Senate in the few minutes available, and southerners probably would have prevented its even coming to a vote. Beyond those barriers, moreover, lay the presidential veto power. But even if the Proviso had become law in 1846, it simply would have accelerated a crisis that in fact took several years to reach its full fury.[41]

The war, rather than the Proviso, was the principal issue of the state and congressional campaigns of 1846. The Whigs made important gains, notably in New York, where their candidate for governor defeated the incumbent Silas Wright, leader of the Van Buren or "Barnburner" wing of the state's Democrats. This repulse seems to have further convinced many Barnburners that they must take a firmer antislavery stand in the future.[42] When Congress reconvened in December, however, Polk delayed renewing his request for a special appropriation, and so for a time there was no legislation to which the Proviso could conveniently be attached. Instead, the territorial issue flared up first over Oregon.

During the previous session, the Senate had failed to act on the House bill organizing Oregon Territory. In January 1847, the House took up a similar measure that again included an antislavery clause. Southerners, responding in advance to an expected renewal of the Wilmot Proviso, began openly to use Oregon as a hostage. Armistead Burt of South Carolina, following instructions from Calhoun, proposed adding the words, "inasmuch as the whole of the said territory lies north of 36° 30' north latitude," thus by implication extending the Missouri Compromise line to the Pacific. Yet, in his accompanying argument, Burt insisted that Congress had no constitutional authority to prohibit slavery anywhere. The Compromise line, though extralegal, he added, should nevertheless be accepted as a basis for sectional peace. Burt thus demonstrated the anomalous Calhoun straddle between theory and expediency that would become a familiar southern posture in the months that followed.[43]

Few northerners would vote for the Burt amendment, and it was soundly defeated, after which the Oregon bill, with its antislavery clause intact, again passed in the House and died in the Senate.[44] Thus a striking reversal is readily apparent. In 1820, the Missouri Compromise line had been a concession made to the North as part of the price for the admission of Missouri as a slave state, and nearly half of the southern representatives had bitterly opposed it. In 1846, extension of the line was demanded by southerners as the price for organization of Oregon as a free territory, and nearly all of the northern representatives opposed it. One reason for the change, of course, was that much more of the land at stake in 1846 lay south of 36° 30′ than had been the case in 1820.

Debate on the Oregon bill and the Burt amendment included some heated discussion of congressional power in the territories. Before it was over, Robert Barnwell Rhett of South Carolina, the epitome of proslavery extremism, came forward with a statement of the southern doctrine that is associated primarily with Calhoun. Only the states possessed sovereign power, he maintained. The territories did not belong to the federal government but instead were the "joint property" of the states. Congress therefore had no authority under the Constitution to exclude some states and their people from equal access to and enjoyment of the territorial property. This was the distinctively southern answer to the Wilmot Proviso, and the battle had thus been fiercely renewed even before the day that Wilmot rose to renew his historic amendment.[45]

On January 22, one week after passing the Oregon measure, the House received from committee a bill appropriating $3 million for "extraordinary expenses" that might be incurred in making peace with Mexico. Debate began in earnest on February 8. Wilmot, who had given notice of intent a week earlier, launched a new crusade for the Proviso with the first of nearly thirty speeches in which the slavery question overshadowed the substance and purpose of the bill itself.[46]

By this time, with New Mexico and California subdued and with Winfield Scott's expedition against Vera Cruz under way, the eventual acquisition of considerable Mexican territory seemed reasonably certain. Meanwhile, petitions opposing the extension of slavery were pouring in from northern citizens and from a number of northern legislatures, while the Polk administration was making every effort to bring northern Democrats into line with its policies. Southerners, fully anticipating reintroduction of the Proviso, were ready to pounce upon it. Their mood had been well expressed by Congressman Shelton F. Leake of Virginia after the defeat of the Burt amendment. The House of Representatives, he complained, had become "a magnificent abolition society." The Missouri Compromise was obviously considered "as no longer of any obligation," and, in any case, he had grown "sick and tired of compromises." The South, he warned, would never submit to the subjugation apparently planned for it.[47]

The day of decision in the House was February 15. Supporters of the Proviso, breaking through a net of parliamentary objections, presented it formally as an amendment to the $3 million bill. Two efforts to substitute extension of the Missouri Compromise line ended in failure, after which the House accepted the antislavery amendment and passed the appropriation bill by identical votes of 115 to 106. With eighteen northern Democrats joining southerners in opposition, administration pressure was obviously having some effect.[48]

The Senate, meanwhile, had been considering its own $3 million bill and continued to do so, taking no action on the House measure except to bury it in a committee.[49] But four days after the House approved the Proviso, Calhoun responded in the Senate with a set of resolutions embodying the already familiar "common-property" doctrine: Congress, as the "joint agent" of the sovereign states, had no power to prevent the citizens of any states from "emigrating with their property" (i.e., slaves) into the territories, which were the "common property" of the states. In his accompanying remarks, the South Carolinian declared that the Proviso, if enacted, would ultimately give the free states an overwhelming proponderance in the Union. Such a destruction of sectional balance, he warned, would mean "political revolution, anarchy, civil war, and widespread disaster." The South must be done with compromises and take its stand upon the solid rock of the Constitution. And if even the Constitution should fail to provide adequate protection, what then? Calhoun answered the question only obliquely, but in words more revealing than a direct threat of disunion:

> I am a planter—a cotton planter. I am a southern man and a slaveholder; a kind and a merciful one, I trust—and none the worse for being a slaveholder. I say, for one, I would rather meet

any extremity upon earth than give up one inch of our equality.
. . . What! acknowledge inferiority! The surrender of life is nothing to sinking down into acknowledged inferiority.[50]

The Calhoun resolutions were never called up for consideration,
but the Senate passed its own $3 million bill unencumbered with any
reference to slavery. The measure came before the House on March
3, the last day of the session. Administration influence now prevailed
as members voted 102 to 97 against adding the Proviso and passed
the bill without it. Thus the House gave in to the Senate on the slavery issue, just as it had done in 1820, and as it would *not* do again
until 1850. Polk had his $3 million, but the territorial problem re-
mained unsolved.[51]

V

The Wilmot Proviso transformed American politics, and, together
with the doctrine articulated by Calhoun, it constituted the "territorial shears" that would one day sever the Union.[52] At the same time,
there were influences tending to counteract the divisive and inflammatory effects of the slavery controversy. For one thing, between the
extremes represented by Wilmot and Calhoun stood many men temperamentally disposed to be peacemakers, mediating differences and
drafting programs of compromise. In addition, the party system had
its own imperatives which continued to moderate sectional passions,
as both Democratic and Whig organizations struggled to hold themselves together and retain their bi-sectional constituencies. Members
of Congress went home in March 1847 to a chorus of often furious
comment on the recent battle over the Proviso, but they went home
also to the grass-root beginnings of a presidential campaign in which
party victory seemed to depend upon finding some formula of compromise or evasion with which to bridge the sectional rift.

The Whig solution proved to be nothing more than the nomination of General Zachary Taylor—a slaveholding southerner to counterbalance the party's northward leaning, and a military hero who
presumably transcended the political conflict over slavery. The Dem-

ocrats, on the other hand, embraced two compromise formulas and for a time were divided over which one was better. Polk's secretary of state, James Buchanan, tied his presidential aspirations to advocacy of the Missouri Compromise line. But that was a somewhat threadbare solution, already rejected emphatically on several occasions by the House of Representatives. Many Democrats therefore became increasingly receptive to a solution that had the double advantage of being conveniently ambiguous and of seeming more innovative than it really was. Vice President George M. Dallas was the first candidate who proposed "leaving to the people of the territory . . . the business of settling the matter for themselves," and Senator Daniel S. Dickinson of New York introduced resolutions to the same effect when Congress met in December 1847. But it was Lewis Cass who made the doctrine of popular sovereignty peculiarly his own in a public letter dated Christmas Eve and addressed to A. O. P. Nicholson of Tennessee. The Democratic nomination of Cass in May 1848 signified an informal endorsement of the doctrine, even though it was not at this time incorporated into the party platform. With Martin Van Buren heading the ticket of the new Free Soil party, slavery for the first time in American history became the leading issue of a presidential contest. The results of the election scarcely constituted a mandate, however. The voters, by a relatively narrow margin, elected Zachary Taylor, the one candidate not committed to any of the four solutions to the territorial problem—not the Proviso, or the Calhoun doctrine, or popular sovereignty, or extension of the Missouri Compromise line. The voice of the people had been heard, but the message was Delphic.[53]

The Proviso controversy turned American history into a new channel, but the extent to which it inspired a new set of political principles about slavery has been overstated by historians and generally misunderstood. One is given the strong impression that popular sovereignty and the joint-property theory were invented at this time. Allan Nevins has insisted, for example, that Calhoun "executed an about-face" in 1846–48, having never before challenged the power of Congress over slavery in the territories. Robert R. Russel goes further to assert that "in the 1840's three virtually new views of the powers of

Congress as to slavery in territories were presented to the public"—namely, the "free-soil doctrine," the "Calhoun doctrine," and the "Cass doctrine."[54] However, the cluster of doctrines that seemed to emerge during the 1840s was actually a blending of old and new, and it is important to understand the nature of that blend.

Generally speaking, practice had preceded theory, and as a matter of practice, Congress from the beginning had had three functional choices. It could prohibit slavery in federal territory; it could establish and protect slavery; or it could refrain from laying down any rules regarding slavery. In practice, the third option meant leaving the decision to be made by the persons settling a territory. They did so, informally at first, simply by bringing or not bringing slaves with them, and then officially, through the action of their territorial government. In short, the practical effect of nonintervention by Congress was popular sovereignty in the territories; they were national and local aspects of the same policy. Along with these three functional alternatives, Congress had the further option of making different provisions for different territories. That is, it could adopt a policy of having more than one policy.

Not until 1861 did Congress seriously consider legislation establishing and protecting slavery in a federal territory. During the preceding three-quarters of a century it employed the other two alternatives in rather haphazard combination. Jefferson's Ordinance of 1784, which contemplated the exclusion of slavery from all of the transappalachian West, would later serve as a shining precedent for advocates of the Wilmot Proviso,[55] but it never went into effect. Instead, as we have seen, Congress by 1790 had settled for a policy of prohibition north of the Ohio and nonintervention to the south.* In the case of the Louisiana Purchase, however, this precedent was not at first followed. A policy of nonintervention silently prevailed throughout the whole of Louisiana until 1820.† Then antislavery sentiment forced a westward extension of the dual system, with slavery expressly forbidden north of 36° 30′ and nonintervention silently con-

* See above, pp. 86–87.

† Orleans Territory, 1804–5, is a slight exception, of course. See above, pp. 96–97.

tinued south of that line. The Missouri Compromise thus renewed
and formalized the policy of having two policies, but one of them—
nonintervention—remained largely a matter of implication. In annexing Texas twenty-five years later, Congress reaffirmed the 36° 30′ restriction and for the first time said something definite about the rights
of persons south of the line. The joint resolution provided that any additional states formed from that region were to be admitted "with or
without slavery," as the people might desire. This offered clear confirmation that popular sovereignty had always been understood to prevail in territories where slavery was not prohibited.

If such a "compromise" seems rather lopsided in favor of the
North, with slavery forbidden on one side of the line and merely permitted on the other, it was all the South wanted or needed in the
early decades of the Republic; for the westward movement during
those years was lopsided in favor of the South. The outpouring of
southern settlers nearly made slave states of Indiana and Illinois in
spite of the Northwest Ordinance. Texas was settled and independent
a year before Michigan entered the Union. Down until 1861, no free
state was ever formed out of territory in which nonintervention had
been the rule. In practical terms, nonintervention had meant popular
sovereignty, and popular sovereignty had always meant slavery.

It scarcely needs to be said that the Wilmot Proviso amounted to
moving the Missouri Compromise line southward to the southern
boundary of the United States, as ultimately defined in the Treaty of
Guadalupe Hidalgo. What seems to have escaped notice, however, is
that popular sovereignty amounted to nothing more than moving the
line northward to the Canadian boundary, thereby returning to the
very policy in force before 1820, against which so many northern
congressmen had rebelled when Missouri presented itself for admission. The fact that popular sovereignty nevertheless received its
strongest support in the free states, while many southerners continued to prefer the Compromise line at 36° 30′, gives some hint of
the practical, theoretical, and psychological complexities inhering in
the sectional controversy over slavery in the territories.

Three of the four doctrines current in the 1840s had already been
put into practice by 1790, but what little debate they aroused during

the early years was over considerations other than their constitutionality. It seems to have been generally assumed, without any need for open expression, that Congress possessed the authority to do virtually anything it wished concerning slavery in the territories. Principles were appealed to along with expedience—but not constitutional principles. The policy of prohibiting slavery inevitably received much support on moral grounds; nonintervention could be justified as a recognition of the right of local self-government; and the policy of having two policies sprang from the dictates of intersectional equity.

Congressional power over slavery in the territories first came under challenge in a significant way during the Missouri controversy. Relatively few voices were raised on the subject, since it was not the central constitutional issue of the crisis.* Nevertheless, in the remarks of men such as Charles Pinckney and John Tyler, one finds the rudiments of the subsequent "Calhoun doctrine," although Calhoun at the time endorsed the constitutionality of the Thomas amendment prohibiting slavery north of 36° 30'.[56] According to Nevins, Calhoun continued to support the Missouri Compromise for another quarter of a century, then "swung to a new position" in 1846–47. Neither the evidence nor one's sense of what is credible will permit acceptance of such an interpretation, however. The great change in Calhoun's thought and feeling about the future of the slaveholding South had taken place much earlier. His theory of the nature of the Union, conceived no later than 1828 and matured during the nullification crisis of 1832–33, was ready for use shortly thereafter when slavery once again became a burning issue in Congress. By 1837, as we have seen, he and a number of other southerners were prepared to deny federal power to prohibit slavery, not only in the territories but even in the District of Columbia. The "Calhoun doctrine" and the cluster of attitudes associated with it emerged in response to the abolitionist crusade of the 1830s, although its full articulation was not called for until the expansionism of the following decade revived the dormant territorial issue.[57]

So none of the four principal solutions to the territorial problem

* See above, pp. 102–3.

offered in 1847–48 were innovations. The Calhoun doctrine, to be sure, was much newer than the other three, and, significantly, it alone originated in constitutional theory and had never been put into practice. The other three solutions had begun as political policies, implemented with scarcely any overt attention to the constitutional implications. But by the 1840s, partly as a result of the Calhoun example, it had become the fashion and almost a necessity to justify any sectionally controversial proposal in constitutional terms. The crucial change in the slavery controversy occurring during the 1840s was therefore not the introduction of new principles or formulas, but rather the constitutionalizing of the argument. Once that process was completed, a long step would have been taken toward the Dred Scott decision.

The ultimate purpose of such argument, moreover, was not merely to claim constitutional sanction but to impose a constitutional imperative—that is, to demonstrate that only one proposed course of action was permitted by the Constitution or, better yet, that it was virtually compelled by the Constitution. According to the Calhoun doctrine, for instance, the other three options were all unconstitutional and, more than that, the Constitution *required* the federal government to protect the property (including slaves) of state citizens everywhere within its exclusive jurisdiction. The effect was to make slavery national except where interdicted by the sovereign power of a state.

On the other hand, the policy of prohibition, originating in the Northwest Ordinance, was at first adopted as a matter of legislative discretion, not of constitutional compulsion, and everyone more or less silently acknowledged the existence of such discretionary authority. What argument occurred in the early years was therefore set in the following pattern, with the words in parentheses usually understood rather than expressed:

A: Congress (has the power and) ought to prohibit slavery in the territories.

B: Congress (may have the power but) ought not to prohibit slavery in the territories.

Beginning with the Missouri controversy, however, the pattern underwent a change, as some southerners shifted the debate from political to constitutional grounds:

A: Congress has the power and ought to prohibit slavery in the territories.

B: Congress does not have such power.

The third stage was reached in the late 1840s, when the argument began to become one of competing constitutional imperatives:

A: The Constitution itself forbids the establishment of slavery in the territories.

B: The Constitution and the sovereign rights of the southern states require that slavery be protected in the territories.

The principal antislavery imperatives were proslavery arguments turned upside down. Thus, the due-process clause of the Fifth Amendment, to which southerners occasionally appealed, with emphasis on the word "property," could be invoked by northern radicals like Salmon P. Chase, with emphasis on the word "liberty." "Slavery," Chase wrote in 1844, "never has lawfully existed in any territory of the United States since the adoption of that amendment which declares that no person shall be deprived of liberty without due process of law."[58] This argument was incorporated into the platforms of the Liberty party in 1844, the Free Soil party in 1848, and the Republican party in 1856 and 1860. Also, southern insistence that the Constitution, with two very specific exceptions, delegated Congress no power to legislate concerning slavery—an argument that had proved especially serviceable during the controversy over the admission of Missouri—could be turned to northern advantage with the proposition that Congress had been delegated no authority to introduce or permit slavery where it did not previously exist. This principle was of course extremely important in relation to the Mexican Cession, where, unlike Louisiana and Florida, slavery had been abolished by the preceding regime. Like the due-process clause, the legal definition of slavery as a creature strictly of local law was a blade that cut two ways.

In the official dogma of all the antislavery parties, then, the Wilmot Proviso likewise became a constitutional imperative, with the other three territorial formulas denounced as not only politically unacceptable but legally impossible. Yet antislavery argument, because its ultimate appeal was to a still higher, moral imperative, never secmed as narrowly legalistic as the Calhoun doctrine.

Nonintervention, which in practice meant popular sovereignty, had been installed in 1790 as a proslavery policy for the Southwest. Southerners from time to time had defended it as a matter of intersectional equity and territorial self-government, but no elaborate constitutional justification seemed necessary for a policy of abstention. In the fashion of the 1840s, however, Lewis Cass did his best to infuse a measure of constitutional compulsion into the principle of nonintervention. He did so by adopting a line of argument that some southerners had taken as early as 1820, and that Roger B. Taney would follow in 1857—that is, an exceedingly narrow interpretation of the territory clause as referring only to property and not to jurisdiction. According to this theory, any general legislative power exercised by Congress in the territories derived from the clause providing for the admission of new states. Such power could not be extended beyond the "creation of proper governments for new countries," together with "the necessary provision for their eventual admission into the union, leaving, in the meantime, to the people inhabiting them, to regulate their internal concerns in their own way."[59] The Wilmot Proviso, Cass maintained, was therefore not only unwise (because of the sectional discord it caused) and unnecessary (because California and New Mexico were unsuited for slaveholding); it was also without constitutional authority.[60]

Popular sovereignty as a discretionary congressional policy had been simple enough, but as a constitutional doctrine it proved to be elusive and equivocal. For most of the next decade, Cass explained and went on explaining what he had said, or had meant to say, in the Nicholson letter. He acknowledged that he had first intended to vote for the Proviso, then had turned against it for practical reasons of state before finally becoming convinced that it was unconstitutional. He added the startling assertion that the primary influence bringing him to that conviction had been a newspaper article written by Justice John McLean.[61] That McLean, later an emphatic, even angry dissenter in the Dred Scott case, should have been the inspiration for an assault on the constitutionality of the Wilmot Proviso, is not so much a historical paradox as a striking example of the confusion that descended on the issue of slavery in the territories, once it became constitutionalized.

Cass, in fact, somewhat altered McLean's meaning to serve his own purpose. The heading given the justice's essay, as it appeared in the *National Intelligencer*, was "Has Congress Power to Institute Slavery?" He did indeed embrace the narrow interpretation of the territory clause, declaring that it referred only to land and conferred no power to legislate concerning slavery. His aim, however, was to demonstrate that slavery could not be reintroduced into territory acquired from Mexico—not, at least, until such territory achieved statehood. McLean took the radical position that slaves were recognized as property only by state law, not by the federal Constitution. Slavery was local, freedom was national, and the federal government accordingly had no power to establish slavery anywhere. The Proviso, in short, was inherent in the Constitution and thus not strictly necessary as legislation. McLean, it will be seen, had constitutionalized the principle of nonintervention and made it into an antislavery weapon. In the process, he did undercut the Proviso movement, but at the same time he lent no support to popular sovereignty.[62]

As constitutional theory, nonintervention proved difficult to defend; for in addition to certain logical shortcomings, it went against a strong grain of precedent and gave rise to conflicting corollaries. Cass, himself a territorial governor for eighteen years, ignored the virtually unlimited control that Congress had regularly exercised over the territories. Although the structure of territorial government had been substantially democratized by the 1840s, this trend was offset in organic acts and other legislation that imposed increasingly detailed congressional supervision and restraint. For instance, Congress frequently restricted or utterly forbade the incorporation of banks and the borrowing of money by territorial legislatures. In 1838, it even undertook to regulate the tolls of a canal company chartered in Wisconsin Territory. The Cass doctrine also ignored the fact that in every organic act Congress reserved the right to disallow any territorial law. By this legislative veto alone, it possessed the means to sponsor or prevent the establishment of slavery in a territory. So if Cass was right, scores of federal territorial laws having nothing to do with slavery were unconstitutional.[63]

The Cass argument was also in conflict with what appeared to be the most relevant judicial precedent. Chief Justice John Marshall, in *American Insurance Company v. Canter*, had designated the territory clause as the most likely among several possible sources of "unquestioned" congressional authority over the territories. "In legislating for them," he added, "Congress exercises the combined powers of the general and of a State government."[64] A decade later, in his *Dred Scott* dissent, Justice McLean cited the Marshall opinion with approval, having by then considerably altered his views on congressional power in the territories.[65]

In practice, nonintervention on the part of Congress had meant popular sovereignty for the territory, but this was not necessarily true of nonintervention as a constitutional principle. For if Congress merely *withheld* its authority to prohibit or establish slavery, it would imply an intention to leave the decision in the hands of the territorial population. But if Congress *lacked* such authority, how could it be exercised by a subordinate government which Congress had created? Cass, Stephen A. Douglas, and other advocates of popular sovereignty would struggle for years with this difficult question. One ingenious answer eventually fashioned by Douglas was that there were certain powers which Congress could exercise but not confer, and other powers which Congress could confer but not exercise, with the latter category including "domestic" legislation for the territories. More often, popular sovereignty was equated with the right of self-government claimed by American colonies in the eighteenth century. But this, of course, was an appeal to the principles of the Declaration of Independence, rather than to the legal authority of the Constitution, and in a sense it amounted to a "higher law" argument. Both of these formulations, it should be emphasized, were utterly out of touch with the historical realities of territorial policy.[66]

To the constitutionalized version of nonintervention (that is, the principle that Congress lacked the constitutional authority to legislate concerning slavery in the territories) popular sovereignty was therefore a possible but by no means a necessary corollary. Beginning with the same principle, as we have seen, Justice McLean reached the conclusion that the Constitution, of its own force, excluded slavery from the territories. Historically more significant, however, was John C. Calhoun's use of the principle to reach the opposite conclusion that the Constitution, of its own force, *protected* slavery in the territories. This was the South Carolinian's response to the northern argument that slavery, having been abolished by Mexico, could not be reestablished in ceded Mexican territory except by positive legislative enactment. In effect, he was asserting not only that slavery automatically followed the Constitution, but also that the Constitution automatically followed the flag—a proposition of doubtful validity that would still be in dispute a half-century later.[67]

It is a matter of some importance that the Calhoun and Cass doctrines went a certain distance together before diverging; for northern and southern Democrats could talk about "nonintervention" and have different corollaries in mind. This was the first of two ambiguities with which the party would hold itself together until shortly before the Civil War. Eventually, the party did more or less endorse the Cass corollary of popular sovereignty, whereupon that term suddenly acquired a convenient doubleness of meaning. This second ambiguity was associated with the question of *when* the people of a territory could begin to exercise their popular sovereignty. Cass and Dickinson had obviously intended that the decision concerning slavery might be made by a territorial legislature as soon as it came into existence. That was the orthodox northern version for which Stephen A. Douglas later became the pre-eminent spokesman. The southern interpretation, carefully camouflaged until the 1850s, held that the territorial decision could be made only at the time of admission to statehood. Before that time, accordingly, no authority could prohibit slavery in the territories. This version was nothing other than the Calhoun doctrine slightly reworded, and it made a mockery of the phrase "popular sovereignty."[68]

Of the four major territorial formulas under discussion in 1847–48, the one that could not be erected into a constitutional doctrine was the proposal to extend the Missouri Compromise line to the Pacific coast. That is, because of its biform nature there was no way of making such an extension constitutionally imperative; for, if the Compromise-line formula was constitutional, so too must be the two policies that it combined. Perhaps this unfashionable theoretical deficiency is one reason the idea of extending the 36° 30′ line faded away as a viable alternative in the sectional conflict.

Of course, a great deal of the debate over slavery in the territories was conducted at the level of interest and expediency, rather than at the level of constitutional theory. To many politicians favoring sectional conciliation, extension of the 36° 30′ line seemed the obvious solution at first. Douglas, a political pragmatist if there ever was one, turned to popular sovereignty only after failing in several attempts to get the Missouri Compromise solution accepted. But popular sovereignty did not in itself constitute an ultimate disposition of the problem and therefore was not truly a substantive compromise. Instead, it simply transferred the decision-making responsibility from Congress to the territorial legislatures. It dealt with a vexed issue by banishing it to the wilderness. The hard-headed expediency of the strategy was what appealed to realists like Douglas, who had little interest in the labyrinthine paths of constitutional argumentation.

Yet, constitutional questions, once raised, had a logical priority and often seemed to become psychologically compelling for men in public life. Even Douglas in the end would yield to the pressure and write a long, tedious article defending the constitutionality of popular sovereignty.[69] Furthermore, the progressive constitutionalization of the debate tended to make popular sovereignty seem absurd. For, even if the territorial inhabitants were indeed the persons best qualified to choose between slavery and antislavery as a matter of practical local considerations, they were undoubtedly among those least qualified to decide questions of high constitutional theory for the nation. The next inference was soon reached—that Congress should transfer the vexed issue not to territorial legislatures but to the federal judiciary. A constitutional imperative might or might not, at the discretion of Congress, be embodied in legislation; it could be enforced only in a court of law.

VI

When Cass, Taylor, and Van Buren were nominated for the presidency by their respective parties in May and June 1848, the Treaty of Guadalupe Hidalgo had confirmed Mexico's cession of the Southwest, and gold had been discovered in California. In Congress, the principal territorial problem continued to be Oregon, where American settlers were still living under the extralegal provisional government that they themselves had established five years earlier. Southerners persisted in the strategy of holding Oregon as a hostage until the status of slavery in the Mexican Cession had been determined. Debate accordingly ranged over the whole embittered subject of congressional power and territorial policy. It dominated the session and intruded frequently upon other legislative business. Especially in the House of Representatives, a member obtaining the floor during discussion of some appropriation bill would often seize the opportunity to speak his piece on the great issue of the day.[70]

Douglas, now chairman of the committee on territories in the Senate, as he had been in the House, introduced a new Oregon bill on January 10, 1848. One section declared that the existing laws of the provisional government (which included a ban on slavery) would remain in force until altered or repealed by the territorial legislature. The effect was to establish popular sovereignty, with every indication that it would mean the continued prohibition of slavery. This satisfied neither the vehemently antislavery senators, who wanted the prohibition made explicit in terms of the Northwest Ordinance, nor the militantly proslavery senators, who were unwilling to let Oregon become a territory without at the same time settling the issue of California and New Mexico.[71] The intensity of feeling between these two elements even before the measure came up for consideration is revealed in a notorious exchange on the Senate floor between John P. Hale of

New Hampshire and Henry S. Foote of Mississippi. Foote invited Hale to visit Mississippi, where he would soon "grace one of the tallest trees of the forest, with a rope around his neck, with the approbation of every virtuous and patriotic citizen." Foote himself would gladly "assist in the operation." Calhoun, joining in the quarrel, compared Hale to "a maniac from bedlam."[72]

On June 27, at the urging of President Polk, administration spokesmen launched another effort to link the Oregon bill with extension of the 36° 30' line. But the proposal made little headway against strong opposition from both sections and the knowledge that it had slight chance of success in the House. Calhoun delivered a speech setting forth his own brand of nonintervention as a constitutional imperative. Neither Congress nor any territorial legislature, he insisted, had any power to prohibit slavery during the territorial period. Nowhere did the federal government possess such sovereign authority— not even in the District of Columbia, where, he said, sovereignty remained with Maryland.[73]

With all progress seemingly halted, the Senate accepted a proposal from John M. Clayton of Delaware for reference of the Oregon bill to a select committee of eight. Chosen by ballot, the membership was half northern and half southern, as well as half Whig and half Democratic. It included Calhoun but not a single leading antislavery man.[74] Under Clayton's leadership, the committee labored and brought forth a substitute measure, bicephalous in nature and called a compromise, although there was much justice in the complaint of one northern senator who said, "This bill is no compromise; it is no compromise at all."[75] In dealing with Oregon, the committee simply followed the original Douglas bill, validating the provisional laws already in effect and confirming the power of the territorial legislature to amend or repeal them. The later sections of the measure established territorial organizations in New Mexico and California. There, the legislatures were *forbidden* to pass any law "respecting the prohibition or establishment of African slavery." At the same time, the Constitution was extended to the two territories and special provisions were made for review by the Supreme Court of any lawsuit testing the status of slavery in either of them. Thus, popular sovereignty was to be explicitly conferred on Oregon but explicitly denied to New Mexico and California.[76]

What the committee in a sense had tried to do was yoke together the Cass and Calhoun versions of nonintervention. The one referred to Congress only and led to popular sovereignty; the other referred both to Congress and to the territorial legislature, thereby denying popular sovereignty and relying on the direct force of the Constitution. Paradoxically, however, in order to ensure *territorial nonintervention* with slavery in New Mexico and California, the bill embodied a degree of *congressional intervention* that seemed incompatible with the Calhoun doctrine. But logical consistency was at a discount, even for Calhoun, who supported the Clayton measure in spite of having reservations concerning it. What the committee had sought and found, after giving up on the 36° 30' line, was a new formula of sectional compromise—one which, like popular sovereignty, transferred the substantive problem to other hands. In Clayton's own words, "It was thought that by this means Congress would avoid the decision of this distracting question, leaving it to be settled by the silent operation of the Constitution itself."[77]

Actually, of course, there is no such thing as a "silent operation of the Constitution," and a few days later, Clayton put the matter more precisely. "The bill," he said, "leaves the entire question which is in dispute to the Judiciary."[78] Constitutionalization of the struggle over slavery in the territories had at last been pursued to its logical conclusion, but the motives for doing so were primarily opportunistic. In their theoretical foundations there was a vast difference between leaving the question to the territorial legislature elected by the local population, and leaving it to nine judges in Washington, elected by, and responsible to, no one. Yet, as political expedients for evading a troublesome responsibility, the two formulas had much in common, and this was not the last time they would appear together in the same legislation.

But exactly *what* question did the Clayton bill leave to the judiciary? Not, as one is led to believe by most historical accounts, *not* the classic question of whether Congress had the power to prohibit slavery in the territories. That could be tested judicially only with an

act providing such prohibition.* What the Clayton bill in effect submitted to judicial disposition was the question of the status of slavery
throughout the Mexican Cession *in the absence of* congressional and
territorial legislation on the subject. The answer, presumably, would
be in terms satisfactory either to Wilmot or to Calhoun. Either Mexican antislavery law remained in effect until superseded by positive
legislation; or the Constitution, *proprio vigore*, superseded Mexican
law and carried with it the right to hold slaves in the conquered territory.

The thought of putting so much at risk in a single court action
inspired considerable apprehension. Many northerners believed that
the southern majority on the Supreme Court would surely close ranks
and hand down a proslavery decision. But there were also southerners who feared that, as a matter of law, the antislavery cause might
prove to be the stronger.[79] Some realists, moreover, challenged Clayton's sanguine prediction that "the people, being law-abiding," would
submit to the decision of the Court because it occupied "the highest
place in their confidence." Instead, said a North Carolina Democrat,
"the moral influence of the Court must be forever destroyed in one
section or other of the Union." Prophetically, a Tennessee congressman declared: "If the decision should be against the North, the North
would not abide by it. They would agitate the country a great deal
more than they do now on the subject."[80]

Consideration of the Clayton bill, it should also be noted, took
place during the heat of the presidential campaign, and there was
consequently much calculation of its potential effect on party fortunes
as well as on sectional discord. The Senate passed the measure on
July 27 by a vote of 33 to 22, with the majority overwhelmingly Democratic and southern.[81] But any senators who expected the House to
endorse their "compromise" were quickly disabused. With scant
courtesy it was laid on the table the very next day. Then the House

---

*It is conceivable, to be sure, that the Court might have invalidated the provision for-
bidding the territorial legislature to take any action, giving as its reason the lack of
congressional power over any aspect of slavery in the territories. That was scarcely
what the Clayton committee had in mind, however.

took up and passed its own Oregon bill, with the provisions of the Northwest Ordinance included.[82]

Many senators were furious at this cavalier treatment. Andrew P. Butler of South Carolina called the House bill "a masked battery, from behind which the institutions of the South were to be assailed." His advice to his own constituents, he said, "would be to go to these new Territories with arms in their hands . . . and take possession of the lands which they had helped to acquire."[83] The Senate majority, still unwilling to give in, passed the House bill only after amending it to include extension of the Missouri Compromise line. Every southerner present in the Senate voted for that amendment, which, according to prevailing southern theory, was unconstitutional.[84] But this time, unlike the case of the $3 million bill, it was the House that remained firm, promptly rejecting the 36° 30′ amendment. On August 12, the Senate receded by a vote of 29 to 25, and Polk reluctantly signed the measure, explaining at length that he did so only because all of the area concerned lay north of the compromise line. Oregon Territory had at last been organized, and with slavery prohibited there, but the festering problem of the Southwest remained unsolved.[85]

∾ 6 ∾

The Territorial Question, 1848-1854

T he presidential campaign of 1848 was in certain respects a very strange contest. It took place while Congress was engaged in a sustained and bitter struggle over the extension of slavery; yet both major parties did all they could to smother or evade the issue in their platforms and nominations. The Whig party offset its northern, antislavery leaning by nominating a southern slaveholder who took no clear public stand on the issue.[1] The Democratic party offset its southern, proslavery tendency by nominating a northerner whose pronouncement on the issue was conveniently susceptible of different interpretations in different regions.* Even the Free Soil party, while emphatically endorsing the Proviso principle, blurred its image by nominating Martin Van Buren and thus partly

---

*An effort to attach the Calhoun doctrine to the Democratic platform failed when the convention, by a vote of 216 to 36, rejected the following resolution offered by William L. Yancey of Alabama: "That the doctrine of non-interference with the rights of property of any portion of the people of this confederation, be it in the States or in the Territories, by any other than the parties interested in them, is the true republican doctrine recognized by this body." It is an indication of how much the Calhoun and Cass doctrines had in common that this anti-Cass resolution should have been mistaken by some historians as an effort to inject popular sovereignty into the platform. The speech with which Yancey introduced the resolution made it quite plain that his target was popular sovereignty.[2]

converting an antislavery crusade into a Barnburner reprisal against Cass.*

Efforts to play down the territorial question proved futile, and the campaign resolved itself into an odd combination of partisan and sectional advocacy. Each of the two major parties claimed in each section that its own candidate was the more reliably proslavery or antislavery, as the case required. Their success in this strategy of dualism was roughly equal. The Democrats carried eight northern and seven southern states; the Whigs carried seven northern and eight southern states; but Zachary Taylor received the larger number of electoral votes.† Americans for the first time had elected a president totally without political experience.

Congress assembled for its short session in December 1848 with the meaning of the recent election unclear, but knowing that control of the administration would soon pass into Whig hands and that gold had been discovered in California. Democratic leaders were therefore doubly eager to settle the territorial issue before Polk left the White House. Yet, from the opening day it was clear that the deadlock between House and Senate remained unbroken. None of the familiar formulas of compromise had any chance of success, and party leaders were driven to seek new avenues of circumvention. One possibility was simply to by-pass the entire territorial stage of the state-making process. On December 11, Stephen A. Douglas introduced a bill to organize the whole Mexican Cession as one huge state, with the provision that Congress might later create additional states out of the area lying east of the Sierra Nevada. When this inventive but unrealistic proposal got nowhere, Douglas suggested admitting only California. Then, as chairman of a select committee, he presented still a third plan creating two states, with California to be admitted immediately and New Mexico when it had sufficient population.[4] Frustrated at every turn, the Little Giant would soon find his direct-admission approach to the problem taken over by the Whigs and their new president.

*Cass's candidacy in 1844 had been instrumental in the defeat of Van Buren for the Democratic nomination.[3]

†Van Buren polled about 10 percent of the popular vote but won no electoral votes.

The House of Representatives, meanwhile, was showing its mettle by reaffirming the principle of the Wilmot Proviso, reviving the issue of slavery in the District of Columbia, and drafting a territorial bill for California with slavery prohibited by invocation of the Northwest Ordinance.[5] Passage of a resolution calling for abolition of the slave trade in the District of Columbia inspired a caucus of the more militant southerners, from which there emerged Calhoun's famous "Southern Address."[6]

An eloquent document saying nothing really new, the "Address" was essentially the rhetorical climax of a political move that failed. In it, the South Carolinian, now sixty-six years old, catalogued antislavery aggressions from the time of the Northwest Ordinance. He warned that exclusion of slavery from the territories would eventually produce a free-state majority so overwhelming as to make universal emancipation constitutionally feasible. He pictured the consequences of such a revolution in apocalyptic terms and closed with some vaguely menacing talk of southern resistance as the ultimate defense.[7] Calhoun's purpose, like that of the Free Soilers and later that of the Republicans, was to fashion a sectional party strong enough to make good its demands in national politics. In his view, the tyranny of northern majority rule could not be sufficiently curbed by appeals to minority rights under the Constitution and necessitated creation of an organized and powerful coercive minority. His famous principle of the "concurrent majority" was in essence a doctrine of political power, not of constitutional law. Many southerners distrusted Calhoun, however. He was a man still a little ahead of his time. Only 48 out of 121 southern members of Congress were willing to sign his manifesto, and only 2 of those were Whigs.[8]

In its territorial theory, the "address" adhered closely to Calhoun's doctrine of nonintervention as a constitutional imperative. "The Federal Government," he declared, "has no right to extend or restrict slavery, no more than to establish or abolish it. . . . What then we do insist on, is, not to extend slavery, but that we shall not be prohibited from immigrating with our property, into the Territories of the United States, because we are slaveholders." The distinction here was extremely subtle, and in the end it would prove impossible to maintain. If a person's right to "immigrate" with his "property" were interfered with, where would he find protection? Congress could scarcely enact protective legislation without thereby tending to "extend" or "establish" slavery. Territorial legislatures, according to the Calhoun view, had no powers greater than those of Congress in this respect. Self-protection by force of arms, as suggested by Senator Butler, was the kind of lawless solution that would prevail for a time in Kansas. The only other conceivable alternative was protection through the courts of law. Thus, by its very nature, the Calhoun doctrine generated pressure toward a judicial disposition of the territorial question. And since reference to the judiciary would itself be an intermediate and open-ended decision, rather than a conclusive one, it was regarded sympathetically by many congressional moderates who did not embrace the Calhoun doctrine. For these same reasons, however, and also because of the personnel of the Supreme Court, antislavery men, with a few exceptions, remained suspicious of proposals to "leave the question to the judiciary." In fact, they grew increasingly fearful that slavery might be slipped into the territories through some constitutional back door. The California bills introduced by Douglas, for instance, included a clause extending all applicable laws of the United States over the incipient state. This was a more or less standard provision, but some antislavery leaders now detected in it a possible basis for legalization of slavery.[9]

It is only against this background that one can understand the astonishing furor produced in both houses near the end of the session by the "Walker amendment." During consideration of a major appropriation bill, Senator Isaac P. Walker of Wisconsin offered an extraneous amendment extending the Constitution and applicable laws of the United States over the territory acquired from Mexico and authorizing the President to establish temporary means of government there. Young and inexperienced, Walker was apparently acting under southern influence.[10] At the very least, his proposal would definitely abrogate the antislavery law of Mexico in the region, and it provided a statutory basis for promotion of the Calhoun doctrine that slavery in the territories was under the protection of the Constitution.

There followed a long, confused debate in which Daniel Web-

ster, among others, argued that the Constitution was made for the
states alone and could not be extended wholesale to the territories,
while Calhoun insisted that the Constitution followed the flag. Antislavery senators opposing the Walker amendment placed themselves in a vulnerable position, for, as Calhoun gleefully pointed out
several times, such opposition seemed to acknowledge his major contention that the Constitution was a "shield to the South."

> It is an implied admission on the part of those gentlemen that, if
> the Constitution does extend to the territories, the South will be
> protected in the enjoyment of its property. . . . I hold it to be a
> most important concession. It narrows the ground of controversy
> between us.

Northerners denied that any such concession had been made, but
they were probably unwise in allowing the discussion to be shifted
from the status of slavery in the territories to the status of the Constitution in the territories. What about powers forbidden to Congress,
Calhoun asked Webster, anticipating the approach of Taney in the
Dred Scott decision. "Can you establish titles of nobility in California? If not, if all the negative provisions extend to the Territories,
why not the positive?"[11] Even the historian Hermann E. von Holst,
despite his strong anti-southern bias, concluded that Calhoun was the
winner in this debate.[12]

The South Carolinian nevertheless carried his argument almost
to the point of contradicting himself. In dealing with the Wilmot
Proviso, he had minimized the territorial power of Congress, but
now, when the antislavery spokesmen had turned strict-constructionist, he demonstrated the flexibility of the property-rights doctrine. The territories belonged to the states of the Union, he declared, "and we, as the representatives of those thirty States, have the
right to exercise all that authority and jurisdiction which ownership
carries with it."[13] Here, in this apparent inconsistency, one finds the
groundwork being laid for the ultimate southern doctrine of the
1850s—that state sovereignty made slavery a national institution, and
that the Constitution made Congress powerless to prohibit or es-

tablish slavery in the territories but fully empowered and unconditionally obligated to protect it.[14]

The Walker amendment passed the Senate by a narrow margin, and the appropriation bill to which it was attached reached the House of Representatives just two days before adjournment. From that moment until a few hours before Zachary Taylor took the presidential oath, the Capitol was a scene of turmoil, as tempers flared, insults flew, blows were exchanged, and gavels pounded away futilely in both chambers. The House predictably rejected the amendment. A conference committee failed to reach agreement. The House then voted to replace the Walker amendment with a substitute more to its own liking; but the Senate preferred instead simply to recede from the Walker amendment, and the appropriation measure was thus passed with no territorial rider attached. Meanwhile, the House had approved its own bill organizing California as a territory, with slavery forbidden, but the Senate, by a vote of 28 to 25, refused to take it up. An angry and exhausted Congress adjourned at 7:00 a.m. on March 4, leaving the embittered question to its successor.[15]

II

During the next nine months, the sectional quarrel over slavery reached the level of a national crisis. The Gold Rush made California's need for stable government more desperate every day. Trouble was also brewing over the extravagant boundary claims of Texas, which extended as far west as Santa Fe. By the end of the year, nearly every northern legislature had passed resolutions endorsing the principle of the Wilmot Proviso, and in many cases they included demands for the abolition of slavery in the District of Columbia.[16] Most inflammatory of all was the southern awakening to the fact that in Zachary Taylor the nation had elected a kind of doughface in reverse. Taylor, who came increasingly under the antislavery influence of William H. Seward, adopted as administration policy the idea of by-passing the territorial issue by admitting California and New Mexico directly to statehood. This plan had originated with Douglas, a Democrat, but it also proved attractive to certain congressional Whigs anxious to preserve sectional harmony within their party after its capture of the presidency.[17]

In April 1849, Taylor sent a Georgia congressman to California as his special agent, with instructions to encourage preparation for statehood. Californians, however, had already begun to take matters into their own hands. Neglected by Congress, they resolved to erect their own government without federal authorization. General Bennett Riley, the provisional governor, sensibly decided to direct the movement, rather than oppose it. A constitutional convention, elected at his order, met at Monterey in September and drafted a state constitution with slavery prohibited. Under the authority of this document, voters went to the polls in November and elected a governor, a state legislature, and two congressmen. The legislature, convening in December, chose John C. Frémont and William M. Gwin as the state's two senators. Thus, when the new Congress met that same month, it was confronted with a *fait accompli* on the Pacific coast.[18]

Southerners unhappy at this turn of events had already been displeased by other presidential words and actions. In August, for instance, Taylor angered proslavery expansionists when he issued a proclamation calling a halt to plans for a filibustering invasion of Cuba. Shortly thereafter, he told an audience at Chambersburg, Pennsylvania, that "the people of the North need have no apprehension of the further extension of slavery," and that the need for a Free Soil party "would soon be obviated." Such remarks could not fail to convince many people of the South that the White House, for the first time in American history, sheltered a president actively hostile to the slaveholding interest—and a renegade southerner at that.[19]

The natural results were a weakening of the Whig party in the South and a strengthening of the movement for southern unity. Early in the year, the South Carolina legislature passed a resolution inviting other slaveholding states to co-operate in resisting the Wilmot Proviso. Throughout the state, local meetings appointed "committees of vigilance and safety" whose functions bore a marked resemblance to those "committees of correspondence" that had sprung up on the eve of the Revolution. The North, Calhoun asserted, must be presented by a united South with "the alternative of dissolving the partnership or of ceasing on their part to violate our rights." The best means of offering this choice, he thought, was a southern convention, and from Mississippi in October came the ominous call for such a convention to meet in Nashville on the first Monday in June 1850.[20]

That the crisis of 1850 was truly a secession crisis can scarcely be doubted. Even after the great Compromise had been engineered, disunion efforts continued in more than one southern state. If Taylor had lived to pursue his own territorial plan with all the executive power at his command, the disaffection in the South would have been widespread and probably decisive.* Our retrospective knowledge of his unexpected death, and of how it cleared the way for compromise, makes it especially difficult for us to understand how desperate the situation seemed when the thirty-first Congress assembled on December 3, 1849.

Along with sectional antagonism, there was the added disadvantage that neither major party had full charge of the government. A Whig occupied the presidency, and the Democrats retained control of the Senate. In the House of Representatives, no party could claim a majority, and a dozen or so Free Soilers held the partisan balance of power. A bitter contest over the election of a speaker lasted nearly three weeks, and the House at times, according to its reporter, was "like a heaving billow." Then, with Democrat Howell Cobb of Georgia installed in the chair by a plurality vote, members spent another full month wrangling over rules and other officers. Twenty ballots were required to choose a new clerk, and, after fourteen roll calls failed to produce a doorkeeper, that problem was laid aside for the session. The end of January drew near before even the President's annual message could be given official attention. Meanwhile the sectional crisis deepened.[22]

With the House in such disarray, there was all the more reason for the Senate, which had always been the more compromise-minded of the two, to take the lead in formulating a plan for sectional conciliation. In addition, the senatorial membership provided an illustrious

---

*Whether it would have been better to have the showdown in 1850, rather than in 1860, is a different question. Most historians believe that the North profited from the ten-year reprieve, but Holman Hamilton has doubts about it.[21]

cast for what was to be the most famous legislative event in American history. Henry Clay had returned to join Webster and Calhoun in one last appearance of the celebrated triumvirate. Benton, Cass, and Douglas were still there, together with the legendary Sam Houston. Jefferson Davis, in some respects a younger version of Calhoun, had taken his seat in the previous Congress, while William H. Seward and Salmon P. Chase were new antislavery arrivals. Other names, lesser known but of historical significance, stand out on the roster— Lincoln's future vice president, Hannibal Hamlin, for instance; John Bell of Tennessee, presidential nominee of the Constitutional Union party in 1860; Pierre Soulé, forever associated with the Ostend Manifesto; Daniel S. Dickinson, one of the putative fathers of popular sovereignty; James M. Mason of Virginia, one of the two Confederate emissaries figuring in the Trent affair; and David Atchison of Missouri, who later played a major role in the struggle over Kansas.

The achievement of compromise in 1850 is a familiar story, complete with moments of high drama, such as Calhoun's dark valedictory, presented just twenty-seven days before his death, and Webster's seventh of March speech, which earned him the praise of men yearning to save the Union and the scorn of men who hated slavery. Clay provided the general formula of compromise in a set of resolutions introduced on January 29. He advocated admission of California with its antislavery constitution, and, as counterbalance, the organization of Utah and New Mexico Territories without restrictions on slavery. Similarly, reduction of the area of Texas would be balanced by federal assumption of the Texas debt, and prohibition of the domestic slave trade in the District of Columbia would be balanced by passage of a more effective fugitive-slave law.[23]

After many weeks of debate the resolutions were referred to a select committee headed by Clay, which reported on May 8, lumping the California, territorial, and Texas proposals together in one "omnibus bill," while dealing with the fugitive slave and slave trade problems in separate measures. The strategy of the omnibus was apparently based upon the assumption that men of both sections would feel stronger about what they favored in the bill than about what they opposed. However, as Douglas remarked, the device "united the opponents of each measure instead of securing the friends of each." [24] Accordingly, at the end of July, the omnibus was knocked to pieces on the Senate floor. An exhausted Clay went off to rest, and Douglas assumed the leadership of the compromise effort.

In several respects, the chances of success had improved. The Nashville Convention in early June proved less militant than expected, merely advocating extension of the Missouri Compromise line in preference to the Clay plan. Then the sudden death of Taylor on July 9 removed a major obstacle to compromise, and his successor, Millard Fillmore, was entirely in sympathy with Clay and Douglas. Furthermore, a surge of support for compromise throughout the country could be felt in the halls of Congress. Between July 31 and September 16, the Senate passed the compromise in six separate measures embodying the principal features of the original Clay resolutions. In no instance was the voting really close. The overall total of *yeas* was nearly double that of *nays*, with excessive abstentions on the New Mexico and fugitive-slave bills. [25]

In the House it was not so easy, of course. There, the New Mexico bill and the Texas boundary and debt bill were joined together in a "little omnibus," which became the critical test. From September 4 to September 6, the chamber was in an uproar. Northern and southern opponents of the bill tried to delay action upon it. Some of the roll-call votes were "perilously close," and on one occasion the Speaker broke a 103-103 tie. Efforts to attach the Wilmot Proviso proved fruitless, and at last the measure passed, 108 to 97. Everything that followed was anticlimax; for everyone knew that the compromise had succeeded. The House took only eleven more days to pass the other four bills admitting California, organizing Utah Territory, prohibiting the slave trade in the District of Columbia, and providing a new system for the recovery of fugitive slaves. Only the Utah vote was even reasonably close. [26]

Most historians have paid comparatively little attention to the brief role of the House in rubber-stamping the set of measures fashioned with so much drama and difficulty in the other chamber. Yet the Senate had always favored compromise, and perhaps the question most needing to be answered is why it took nearly eight months to approve substantially the same formula that Clay had presented in January. One influence, unquestionably, was the high value that the age placed on oratory, and the feeling of nearly every senator that for the sake of his standing back home, he must, at this obviously historic moment, be heard formally and at length. What needs to be explained about the House, on the other hand, is why it deserted a position previously clung to with great tenacity. Indeed, the most startling feature of the Compromise of 1850 is that the House should have twice surrendered the principle of the Proviso and, in addition, passed the inflammatory Fugitive Slave Law by a comfortable margin. It is therefore important to note that this House of Representatives, more than most, was a transient body. More than half of its members were new members, nearly half of whom would not be re-elected. Inexperienced and lacking the direction of a party majority, the House was all the more amenable to senatorial influence, and to the widespread popular desire for compromise that had been inspired by senatorial oratory.[27]

No more than one-fourth of the members of Congress can be said to have voted for the Compromise of 1850, but by joining forces with the sectional supporters of each bill, they assembled the necessary majority six times in the Senate and five times in the House—not to mention all the preliminary votes taken. Only four senators and 28 representatives voted for all the compromise measures. If one discards the Texas bill in the Senate as not relevant to the slavery controversy (defensible but arguable), one more senator is added to the list. It is not surprising to discover that of these 33 men with "perfect" scores, 26 were northern Democrats and four were southern Whigs, the two political groups that suffered most severely from the strains of sectional conflict.[28]

The criterion used here is too strict, however; for a good many true supporters of compromise failed to vote on all of the measures. Even Douglas, conveniently but innocently, according to his biographer, missed the roll call on the Fugitive Slave Act. If one defines a supporter of compromise as a member who voted for at least four of the five measures and opposed none of them, then the totals rise to 14 in the Senate and 47 in the House. Of these 61 compromisers

MEMBERS VOTING FOR ALL FIVE COMPROMISE MEASURES (Texas Bill in Senate Not Included)				
	ND	NW	SD	SW	TOTAL
Senate	2	0	1	2	5
House	24	1	1	2	28
Totals	26	1	2	4	33

MEMBERS VOTING FOR FOUR OR FIVE COMPROMISE MEASURES AND AGAINST NONE (Texas Bill in Senate Not Included)				
	ND	NW	SD	SW	TOTAL
Senate	9	0	2	3	14
House	29	6	4	8	47
Totals	38	6	6	11	61

(constituting about 21 per cent of the entire membership), 38 were northern Democrats, and eleven were southern Whigs.[29]

As the lower table indicates, just 17 of the 61 compromisers were southerners. Furthermore, 13 of those 17 came from the three border states of Delaware, Kentucky, and Missouri. Sam Houston, pursuing the same independent course that he would follow in the secession crisis a decade later, was the only one of the 61 from any of the seven states of the deep South. Virginia, North Carolina, and Tennessee supplied one apiece. Thus, only four members of Congress from the eleven states of the future Confederacy (whose total representation exceeded 90) can be classified as supporters of the Compromise. It has been well called "the Armistice of 1850."[30]

III

The antislavery strategy that failed even in the House, despite presidential support until Taylor died, had been to push through a separate bill for the admission of California. From the beginning of the session, California assumed a place similar to the one previously oc-

cupied by Oregon in the sectional conflict—that is, admittedly closed
to slaveholding, but held as a hostage to prevent further success of
the Wilmot Proviso.[31] Thus the territorial issue remained alive, for
the most part, only in regard to the predominantly arid region then
called New Mexico, but including present-day Utah and Nevada,
most of Arizona, and parts of Colorado and Wyoming. In this context,
it is not surprising to find some realists like Webster concluding that
the Proviso game had ceased to be worth the candle. The law of nature, he declared, "settles forever, with a strength beyond all terms of
human enactment, that slavery cannot exist in California or New
Mexico."[32] In California, moreover, the law had apparently already
taken effect, thereby providing positive proof of its validity. This was
a line of argument frequently used by supporters of compromise and
had, in fact, been incorporated by Clay in his set of resolutions.

Few antislavery men were fully persuaded by this theory of
climatic limitations on the expansion of slavery; for the historical
record plainly revealed that the institution had established itself in a
variety of physical settings—indeed, wherever it was not positively
forbidden by law. Some southerners likewise refused to concede that
nature had barred slaveholders from the Southwest. Jefferson Davis,
for example, insisted that Negroes were much better fitted than white
men for labor in the gold mines.[33] Nevertheless, the repeated assertion that the slavery question, as it applied to Utah and New Mexico,
was a mere abstraction may have weakened resistance to compromise
in some moderate antislavery circles. Of course, the "mere abstraction" argument presumably cut two ways and should have weakened
southern resistance also. But southerners were generally convinced
that even in a purely symbolic struggle, they had far more at stake
than their opponents. "Ask yourselves if it is right," said Albert Gallatin Brown of Mississippi, "to exasperate eight millions of people upon
an abstraction; a matter to us of substance and of life, but to you the
merest shadow of an abstraction."[34]

A thing of vital substance and yet of merest shadow may be difficult to visualize, but the dubious logic of Brown's appeal is less significant than its emotional intensity. Southerners felt hounded by the
antislavery crusade. They spoke increasingly of the "degradation"

with which they were confronted. Anger, wounded pride, and a half-suppressed panic were pushing many of them to the edge of hysteria, and the territorial issue had come to symbolize a struggle for survival. "The South," said Brown, "cannot, will not, *dare* not submit. . . . The consequences to her are terrible beyond description." What southerners wanted, fundamentally, was an end to agitation of the slavery question; what they were fighting ultimately to preserve was their self-respect.[35]

The absolute minimum was repudiation of the proscriptive principle embodied in the Wilmot Proviso. The Proviso meant disunion. Southerners had begun saying so even during the speakership contest in December, and the threat echoed and re-echoed through the many months of debate that followed. If disunion in turn meant war, then, as a Virginia congressman put it, the fighting would be "between men contending for their firesides, and the robbers who are seeking to despoil them of their rights, and degrade them before the world."[36]

Southerners, with few exceptions, maintained that the Proviso was not only unjust but unconstitutional, and that slaveholders had a legal right to take their "property" into any federal territory. Many added, however, that in the interest of peace and preservation of the Union, they were willing to settle, extra-constitutionally for extension of the Missouri Compromise line to the Pacific. But some, like Jefferson Davis, insisted that the old formula be modified to include positive protection of slavery, rather than mere nonintervention, south of the dividing line.[37]

Of course, everyone knew by now that the Missouri Compromise solution had no chance of success, and northern Democrats supporting compromise pinned their hopes instead to the concept of popular sovereignty. For Cass, as we have seen, the doctrine was a constitutional imperative; for Douglas it was a matter of discretional policy. That is, Cass believed that Congress had no power to regulate slavery in the territories, whereas Douglas believed that Congress had the power but should not use it. They agreed that the decision must be left to the territorial population, acting through its elected representatives in the territorial legislature. This Cass-Douglas version of popular sovereignty met a cool reception among southerners,

however, and some of them pronounced it "worse than the Proviso."[38]

At this point, certain curiosities and anomalies in the controversy
over the territories seem to cry out for special notice. To begin with,
the dividing-line principle, offered in 1820 to northerners as part of
the price for admission of a slaveholding state (Missouri), was now
demanded by southerners as the minimum price for admission of a
free state (California). The continuing southern preference for the 36°
30' solution can perhaps be attributed to implications of sectional
equality in the dividing-line concept. Nevertheless, the preference is
astonishing when one remembers that, in its traditional form, the 36°
30' solution combined the principle of the hated Wilmot Proviso with
the principle of nonintervention, which in practice had always meant
popular sovereignty.

On the other hand, it must be noted that northern strategy, after
preventing a compromise that would have prohibited slavery north of
36° 30', then allowed a compromise that permitted slavery as far
north as the 42nd parallel! In fact, the Oregon, California, New Mexico, and Utah Acts of 1848–50 had the practical effect of extending the
Missouri Compromise line as follows: northwest to 42°, west to the
northeastern corner of California, and south along California's eastern
boundary to the Mexican border. On one side of that line slavery was
prohibited, and on the other side it was permitted, just as in the original Missouri Compromise. By extending the line in this strange way,
rather than straight along 36° 30' to the Pacific, Congress excluded
slavery from southern California but permitted it throughout the
whole of New Mexico and Utah territories.[39]

Quite clearly, successful compromise required a non-Proviso settlement of the territorial question to balance the admission of California as a free state. Yet the anti-Proviso elements in Congress could
not agree upon an alternative. Neither the Calhoun doctrine, nor the
Missouri Compromise line, nor popular sovereignty could command
majority support. Henry Clay realized from the beginning that the
only possible solution was nonintervention, pure and simple—that is,
the organization of New Mexico and Utah territories without any
mention of slavery whatsoever. Now, nonintervention, being actually

TERRITORIES IN 1848–1850

Line Between Freedom and Nonintervention

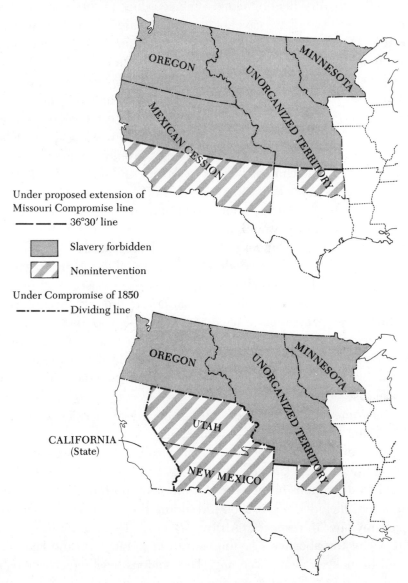

just a half-doctrine, had a splendid elusiveness about it. The meaning of the term seemed to vary, said Jefferson Davis, "as often as the light and shade of every fleeting cloud."[40] According to the southern version of nonintervention, slaveholders could enter a territory without interference throughout the territorial period; then, at the time of admission to statehood, a constitutional convention would make the choice between establishing and prohibiting slavery. To Cass and Douglas, on the other hand, nonintervention meant that the territorial legislature, as soon as it was organized, could establish or prohibit slavery. To Clay himself, nonintervention in New Mexico and Utah meant that the antislavery laws of Mexico would remain in effect, thus reinforcing the climatic barrier to slavery and making the Proviso doubly unnecessary.

Ultimately, of course, nonintervention by Congress meant that some other authority would have to intervene. That authority, in Clay's view, was the federal judiciary. Did Mexican law continue in force until explicitly superseded? Did a territorial legislature have the power to establish or prohibit slavery? Did the Constitution protect slaveholding in the territories as a matter of property right? Such questions, being essentially legal in nature, should be left to "the proper and competent tribunal—the Supreme Court of the United States." Clay's solution to the territorial problem, like that offered by Clayton two years earlier, was to convert a political issue into a constitutional case at law.[41]

But some southerners, resentful at having to sacrifice the whole of California to antislavery, were reluctant to settle for nothing better than an even start in what one of them called the "mutilated remnant" of the Mexican Cession.[42] Against Clay's wishes, the New Mexico and Utah sections of the omnibus bill, as reported from the select committee, included a provision forbidding the territorial legislatures to pass any law "in respect to African slavery." This was an idea taken right out of the abortive Clayton compromise but with the language altered to make it more sweeping. The obvious legal effect would be to outlaw the Cass-Douglas version of popular sovereignty and thus to push the slavery issue toward a judicial decision. In political terms, however, it was a provision bound to make the achievement of compromise more difficult. Even so, Jefferson Davis was still not satisfied. Though willing that the Supreme Court should have final disposition of the question,[43] he nevertheless worried about what would happen in the meantime. Slaveholders would presumably be able to settle in Utah and New Mexico without legal interference but also without receiving any protection from the territorial legislatures. This seemed likely to discourage southern migration as too risky, with the result that the entire region would eventually be turned into free states. And even if a proslavery court decision were swiftly obtained, how could it be enforced in the territories if the legislatures were unable to pass any laws for that purpose?

Davis accordingly proposed an amendment authorizing the territorial legislatures to "protect" slavery, though not to "introduce or exclude" it—the assumption being, of course, that the institution would introduce itself.[44] Although he did not succeed, a substitute offered by John M. Berrien of Georgia attracted five more votes and carried, 30 to 27. Three northerners who switched sides provided the margin of victory.[45] The Berrien substitute brought the measure even more closely in line with the Clayton compromise by replacing "in respect to African slavery" with the provision that no law should be passed "establishing or prohibiting African slavery." The obvious intention was to accomplish Davis's purpose by implication, leaving room for the territorial legislature to recognize the existence of slavery and provide for its protection. This, to Davis, was the proper meaning of "nonintervention."[46]

The voting on these two amendments constitutes a revealing measure of attitudes toward popular sovereignty among opponents of the Wilmot Proviso. Southerners rejected the principle almost unanimously; for only one senator from the slaveholding states, Thomas

	NORTH		SOUTH		TOTAL	
	YES	NO	YES	NO	YES	NO
Davis amendment	1	28	24	2	25	30
Berrien amendment	4	25	26	2	30	27

Hart Benton, voted against both amendments. At the same time, only three northern Democrats failed to oppose both amendments, and only one voted in favor both times. He, ironically, was Daniel S. Dickinson of New York, often credited as one of the authors of the doctrine of popular sovereignty.

John P. Hale, the militant Free-soiler, saw the point of the Berrien amendment immediately and tried unsuccessfully to close the proslavery loophole by adding the words "or allowing" to the phrase "establishing or prohibiting." Then Douglas moved to strike the Berrien phrase itself and thereby remove all reference to slavery, as Clay had originally planned. The motion failed, 21 to 33, with southerners in opposition, 26 to 2. One indication of the confusion prevailing is that at this point Davis and Hale found themselves allied on the negative side.[47]

Although the Berrien amendment plainly favored the Calhoun doctrine at the expense of popular sovereignty, not every southerner was as yet fully satisfied. David L. Yulee of Florida, appealing to the precedent of the Clayton compromise, offered an amendment extending the Constitution and laws of the United States over Utah and New Mexico territories. Senators must have groaned inwardly at this revival of the Walker amendment, which had inspired so much useless theorizing and sectional animosity during the final days of the previous Congress. The debate indeed recapitulated much of that earlier argument about whether the Constitution followed the flag. Some southerners insisted that the Yulee proposal was necessary; others labeled it unnecessary but harmless; still others said that it was unnecessary and dangerous. Yet all except three of them helped carry the amendment by a vote of 30 to 24.[48]

At this point, events took an interesting turn. Heretofore, southerners had been the principal advocates of turning the territorial issue over to the Supreme Court, for only in that way, presumably, could the Calhoun doctrine be established as the law of the land. But the omnibus bill, as it stood, meant that neither congressional nor territorial legislation would exclude slavery from Utah and New Mexico, leaving an antislavery court decision as the only remaining hope of Proviso forces. Consequently, Hale, the Senate's harshest critic of the

Supreme Court, offered an amendment taken directly from the Clayton compromise and designed to ensure access to the Court in all cases involving the legal status of slavery. After some technical discussion, the Senate gave its approval without serious opposition. The effect was to waive the usual minimum-property-value requirements for carrying a case to the Supreme Court, as follows:

> Except only that in all cases involving title to slaves, the said writs of error or appeals shall be allowed and decided by the said Supreme Court, without regard to the value of the matter, property, or title in controversy; and except, also, that a writ of error or appeal shall also be allowed to the Supreme Court of the United States from the decision of the said Supreme Court created by this act, or of any judge thereof, or of the district courts created by this act, or of any judge thereof, upon any writ of *habeas corpus*, involving the question of personal freedom.[49]

Next, Pierre Soulé of Louisiana proposed an amendment, the language of which he derived from the joint resolution for the annexation of Texas. In final form, it read: ". . . And, when admitted as a State, the said Territory, or any portion of the same, shall be received into the Union, with or without slavery, as their constitution may prescribe at the time of their admission." This clause, approved after extensive debate by the overwhelming vote of 38 to 12, is the one most often quoted by historians summarizing the Compromise of 1850.[50] But precisely what did it signify?

Many northern senators, including some who voted with the majority, regarded the amendment as constitutionally superfluous and politically useless—superfluous in that it affirmed a right already generally acknowledged, and useless in that it was essentially an attempt to bind the action of a future Congress. Viewing it in similar fashion as nothing more than a "promise," one twentieth-century historian has quite rightly declared that the Soulé clause "was certainly not the 'crux of the compromise.' "[51] If there was such a thing, the crux of the compromise consisted simply in admitting California as a free state and organizing the remainder of the Mexican Cession without the Wilmot Proviso.

Yet Alexander H. Stephens later called the Soulé amendment "the turning point" upon which "everything depended" in the compromise effort. The news of its adoption, he added was "well calculated to make a nation leap with joy."[52] And, indeed, one finds in the pages of debate a curious intensity of feeling about this declaratory clause. "Having been offered," said one senator, "it ought not to be rejected. Such a step . . . would be mischievous, in the extreme, in its influence upon the public mind of the South."[53] Legally nugatory though it might be, the amendment plainly carried implications of great emotional force.

Soulé himself explained that his purpose was to "feel the pulse of the Senate" on the question of whether any more slaveholding states were ever to be admitted to the Union. One of his southern colleagues added that the clause would draw "a broad line between the Abolitionists in this Chamber . . . and those who stand by the Constitution." But Soulé at one point also maintained that his amendment, like the rest of the compromise, would be a compact, "binding *in future.*" He meant binding, not in law but as a pledge of honor, with the threat of disunion serving as the sanctional force. Here, in fact, one gets a preview of sectional politics in the next decade, with southerners forever calculating the value of the Union and testing it, like ice on a river in early spring, to see how much proslavery weight it would still bear. Here, also, was a view of the compromise legislation as a set of pledges negotiated like an international treaty, the violation of which would lead to sovereign reprisals. "Whenever," said William R. King of Alabama, "there is found a majority in both Houses of Congress in favor of prohibiting the admission of a State into the Union because its people choose to have slavery . . . the days of this Republic are numbered." The key concept was that between sovereignties there must be equality. On this very same day, June 15, in the House of Representatives, Robert Toombs put the matter in flaming words that must have reminded his audience of Patrick Henry:

> I stand upon the great principle that the South has right to an equal participation in the territories of the United States. . . .

> She will divide with you if you wish it, but the right to enter all or
> divide I shall never surrender. . . . Deprive us of this right and
> appropriate this common property to yourselves, it is then your
> government, not mine. Then I am its enemy, and I will then, if I
> can, bring my children and my constituents to the altar of liberty,
> and like Hamilcar, I would swear them to eternal hostility to your
> foul domination. Give us our just rights, and we are ready, as ever
> heretofore, to stand by the Union. . . . Refuse it, and for one, I
> will strike for *Independence*.[54]

But there were other important implications in the Soulé amendment. As Roger S. Baldwin of Connecticut complained, it embodied
the southern interpretation of the territorial status of slavery in the
prescribed absence of positive legislation establishing or prohibiting
the institution. That is, the clause assumed the nullity of Mexican antislavery law and the validity of the Calhoun doctrine that slavery followed the Constitution, which in turn followed the flag. For how else
could slavery enter the territories and necessitate the eventual choice
provided for in that amendment?

Even more significant was the way in which the Soulé amendment reinforced the previously approved Berrien amendment. The
latter forbade the territorial legislatures to establish or prohibit slavery. Soulé's clause fixed the proper time for establishing or prohibiting. The two fitted together perfectly, and Henry S. Foote insisted
that together they constituted true Democratic doctrine. The Soulé
amendment, he declared, was "the precise principle of the Nicholson
letter." Lewis Cass, the author of the Nicholson letter, had emphatically stated otherwise in Foote's presence just twelve days earlier, but
he was now apparently not in his seat, and no other northern Democrat raised any objection as Foote continued:

> We have declared, in unison with that letter, in the most explicit
> terms, that it belongs exclusively to the people of the Territories
> to determine for themselves what they will do with the subject of
> slavery, *at the period of their admission into the Union*. That is the
> clearly asserted doctrine of the Democratic party of the United
> States, and was so recognized and understood, during the canvass
> of 1848, everywhere.[55]

Dickinson, the very next senator to speak, said not a word about Foote's erroneous explication of the Nicholson letter; nor did anyone else. Here, in the words spoken and left unspoken, was the cement of ambiguity and dissimulation with which the Democratic party would manage to hold itself together for another eight years—namely, two sectionally different definitions of "popular sovereignty."

Up to this point, the principal amendments to the territorial legislation, even the one offered by Hale, had strengthened the southern hand. But then, on July 30, Moses Norris of New Hampshire renewed the Douglas proposal to strike out the Berrien amendment and thus, presumably, permit the territorial legislatures to "establish or prohibit" African slavery. In the heated debate that followed, one southerner protested, significantly, that such action would be "incompatible" with the Soulé amendment. Another said that he would just as soon vote for the Wilmot Proviso as for the pending measure with the Berrien amendment removed from it. Several others argued, however, that the change would substantially improve the chances of the compromise effort as a whole. When it came to a vote the following day, the Norris motion to strike out was approved, 32 to 20. Six southern Whigs, five of whom had voted the other way on the Douglas motion two months earlier, provided much of the margin of victory.[56] It was in this form that the territorial measures were passed as separate bills, after the breakup of the omnibus. With the Berrien amendment gone, the only specific references to slavery remaining in the text were those facilitating appeals to the Supreme Court (the Hale amendment) and promising eventual admission to statehood with or without slavery (the Soulé amendment).

What, then, had been enacted in the Utah and New Mexico bills, and what was their relationship to the Compromise of 1850 as a whole? A generation ago, Robert R. Russel addressed himself to these questions in a learned, perceptive, and dogmatic article that seemed for a time to be the last word on the subject.[57] The principal conclusions of the article are as follows:

1. The legislation installed popular sovereignty in Utah and New Mexico. That is, "the territorial legislatures were given full power to legislate on slavery, subject to a possible veto by the governor or a possible disallowance by Congress."

2. "The territorial acts did not open the territories to slavery. They neither explicitly nor implicitly recognized the alleged constitutional right of slaveholders . . . to take slaves into the territories. . . . There was only a bare chance that a large enough number of Southern people friendly to slavery would migrate into the territories to get laws enacted in one or both territories legalizing slavery."

3. "Congress did not try to wash its hands of the question of slavery in the territories and leave it to the Supreme Court. . . . The appeals provisions meant only that Congress recognized that a case might be got up to test the extent of its power to legislate on the subject . . . and that Congress was willing to have its powers so tested in the courts."

4. The territorial legislation was not a concession offsetting some other part of the compromise, but rather a compromise in itself, containing "mutual concessions," and it would be "futile to attempt to say which side came off the better" in the two acts.[58]

Each of these generalizations, however, is either mistaken or in need of careful qualification. Russell speaks of "the great skill with which the slavery provisions of the territorial bills had been framed," but in fact they were written haphazardly and with confused purposes. Certainly it is erroneous to depict popular sovereignty as the studied intention of the legislation. After months of maintaining its resolve to *forbid* popular sovereignty, the Senate, at the last moment and almost capriciously, reversed itself and removed the ban. The effect was a noncommittal silence which could be regarded as permitting popular sovereignty by default, especially in view of another clause declaring that the legislative power of the territory should "extend to all rightful subjects of legislation." But southerners, who provided two-thirds of the senatorial vote for the Utah bill, were generally insistent that slavery was subject to prohibition by territorial action only at the time of admission to statehood, and they could point to the Soulé amendment as explicit confirmation. The territorial measures, in short, were open-ended—adaptable either to popular sovereignty or to the Calhoun property-rights doctrine, but legitimizing neither on an exclusive basis.[59]

Of course the territorial acts *did* open Utah and New Mexico to slavery in precisely the same way that Mississippi Territory had been opened to slavery in 1798 and Arkansas in 1819—by withholding any prohibition against it. The fact that slaveholders, as Webster and others predicted, did not take advantage of the opening is an entirely different matter. It resulted from the nature of the country, not the nature of the legislation.

Congress, while attempting to fashion an expediently vague political settlement of the territorial issue, did in fact wash its hands of the constitutional aspects of that issue. Russel's contention that in the section on judicial appeals it was merely providing for a rather remote contingency is not borne out by the debates, in which there were frequent references to a judicial disposition of the territorial problem. This was Clay's solution, certainly, and the uses made of the Clayton compromise indicate how much the judiciary figured in senatorial expectations. Even Cass, the advocate of popular sovereignty, at one point cried out, "If the South think they have rights there under the Constitution, in God's name, let the Supreme Court determine the question."[60]

For four years, the antislavery majority in the House of Representatives had refused to organize any territories without the Wilmot Proviso attached. Now that barrier had been swept away in legislation that not only rejected the Proviso but accommodated the Calhoun common-property doctrine as well as popular sovereignty. A region once closed to slavery by Mexican law was now presumably open to slavery by virtue of American law. It is therefore difficult to agree with Russel that there were "mutual concessions" here. The Utah and New Mexico laws constituted a southern victory, offsetting the admission of California. They were limited in their meaningfulness by the external factor of climate, rather than by anything in their texts. Jefferson Davis voted for the Utah bill, and so did 82 per cent of southerners in both houses; 62 per cent of the northerners voted against it.

The problem of slavery in Utah and New Mexico ceased to be significant, however, as soon as the Compromise of 1850 was passed. Slaveholders simply did not migrate to either territory. The census of 1860 reported no slaves in New Mexico and twenty-nine in Utah, together with a "free colored" population of a hundred or so in the two territories combined.[61] New Mexico nevertheless perversely became the only jurisdiction in American history to enact a slave code for a slaveless society. This action was taken in 1859 as a response to the Dred Scott decision, and it reflected the growing southern influence in New Mexico as a consequence of the territorial appointments made by Presidents Pierce and Buchanan.[62] The territorial acts of 1850 did have an important indirect effect on the sectional conflict over slavery, but it was felt in Kansas rather than in Utah or New Mexico.

IV

The Compromise of 1850 inspired sighs of relief throughout the country and was grudgingly welcomed even by many men who disliked some of its provisions. The resounding victory of Franklin Pierce in the presidential election of 1852 was in some degree a measure of popular support for the principle of "finality"—which meant that the last word had been said about slavery as a national issue.

Yet it quickly became apparent that in some northern states, militant minorities were determined to resist enforcement of the Fugitive Slave Act at every opportunity. Equally clear and ominous was the fact that in much of the South, "conditional Unionism" had more or less officially emerged as a majoritarian sentiment. Southerners, as David M. Potter has observed, rejected secession itself for the time being but embraced the principle of secessionism.[63] The so-called Georgia Platform, drafted by a state convention in December 1850, became the sectional credo of the next decade. Accepting the Compromise (without fully approving of it) as "a permanent adjustment," the platform then listed the conceivable northern aggressions, any one of which would justify southern resistance, even to the point of disrupting the Union. The principal ones were: legislation abolishing slavery in the District of Columbia, or forbidding slavery in the Territories of New Mexico and Utah, or suppressing the interstate slave trade; repeal, substantial modification, or non-enforcement of the Fugitive Slave Law; and refusal to admit a new state because of the existence of slavery therein.[64]

Stephen A. Douglas was nevertheless convinced that the settlement would endure. The proceedings of the new session of Congress were "dull & quiet," he reported with great satisfaction in January 1851. "There is very little attempt at agitation & excitement upon the vexed question of slavery. . . . Public opinion is becoming sound & enlightened upon this question and the abolitionists are already reduced to a state of despair."[65] It is also important to note that, in spite of the ambiguous phrasing of the territorial bills, Douglas firmly believed that the Compromise of 1850 had installed the principle of popular sovereignty. More than that, he persuaded himself against a good deal of evidence that he had "always advocated the right of the people in each State and Territory to decide the slavery question for themselves."[66]

Douglas still did not regard popular sovereignty as a constitutional imperative. That is, he refused to agree with Cass that Congress lacked the power to establish or prohibit slavery in the territories. He argued instead that the question "ought to be left to the decision of the people themselves," and he gave essentially three reasons for doing so. Popular sovereignty, he maintained, was the wisest public policy; it was in accord with democratic principles; and it was a recognition of the inevitable.[67] In an attack on the principle of the Wilmot Proviso, Douglas argued that it was the will of the people, rather than the Northwest Ordinance, that excluded slavery from Illinois. "A law passed by the national legislature to operate locally upon a people not represented," he declared, "will always remain practically a dead letter upon the statute book, if it be in opposition to the wishes and supposed interests of those who are to be affected by it, and at the same time charged with its execution."[68] Here was the essence of the "Freeport doctrine," which Douglas would turn to a different use eight years later in seeking to salvage popular sovereignty from the devastating effect of the Dred Scott decision.

Douglas was therefore temperamentally and ideologically ready, when pressed by circumstances, to replace the Missouri Compromise restriction with the principle of popular sovereignty. By 1854, efforts to establish a territorial government west of the Missouri River had become entangled with the controversy over proposals for building a railroad to the Pacific. A bill passed by the House of Representatives early in 1853 for the organization of Nebraska Territory contained no mention of slavery or the Missouri Compromise, but everyone assumed that the institution was still forbidden north of 36° 30'. The Senate refused to pass the measure, and southerners provided most of the opposition.[69]

With the movement of settlers across the Missouri River into what had so recently been called "permanent Indian country," there was considerable local agitation for territorial organization. According to the "railroad interpretation" of the Kansas-Nebraska Act, however, Douglas wanted such organization immediately in order to strengthen the hand of those supporting a central route for the proposed Pacific railway, and so he resolved to bring in a territorial bill more attractive to southerners in its treatment of the slavery problem.[70] The neatness of this explanation may have lent it more credibility over the years than it really deserves; for the absence of territorial organization was only a technical objection to the central route as far as the southern argument was concerned. The real objection, as Douglas and everyone else knew well, was that southerners wanted a southern route, and there is not the slightest evidence that passage of the Kansas-Nebraska Act altered that objection. Besides, the motives of Douglas alone no longer seem as significant as they once did, for some historians have come to believe that he was "not really in command of the situation."[71] A more important question is why fifty-eight northern Democrats in Congress voted to erase the 36° 30' line and admit slavery into a region where it had been forbidden for thirty-four years. Was the Pacific railroad uppermost in their minds? If so, one might expect a determined simultaneous effort to push through a railroad bill. But, as Douglas's biographer notes, when a committee reported such a measure in March 1854, "it excited little interest." In fact, ironically, the Nebraska bill pre-empted so much time and energy as to discourage consideration of railroad legislation during that year.[72] Furthermore, if the Kansas-Nebraska Act was indeed visualized as the preliminary step in the authorization of a Pacific railroad, it proved to be a great miscalculation. Seven years later, little progress had been made toward realization of the project.

As soon as one puts aside the dubious assumption that to explain the Kansas-Nebraska Act it is sufficient to explain the motives of Stephen A. Douglas, the railroad question falls into its proper perspective as one of a number of influences at work. Perhaps the most important factor of all was the very existence of the anomaly, conspicuous on any map, of a great region in the heart of the continent, possessed by the nation for a half-century but still ungoverned. In addition, there were vigorous local pressures from Missouri and Iowa for development of the Nebraska country, and increasing travel across the plains inspired demands for better protection against the Indians. The federal government, moreover, was geared for ready response to such influences. Each house of Congress had its standing committee on the territories whose most important work had always been the organization and supervision of territorial governments. And the Senate committee in particular was headed by a man dedicated to a vision of westward expansion in which railroad-building was just one of the major considerations.

But a sectional barrier had appeared, and it amounted to the Wilmot Proviso in reverse. Southerners, many of whom had declared that a policy of "no more slave states" would mean disunion, were now seemingly committed to a policy of "no more antislavery territories." They wanted erasure of the 36° 30' line, the extension of which they had so warmly advocated in 1850 as the best formula of compromise. The critical difference, of course, was that in 1850, a substantial part of the land in question had been south of the line, whereas in 1854, most of the land in question lay north of the line. However unlikely migration of slaveholders into Nebraska country may have seemed, southerners by 1854 were strongly disposed to regard any overt federal prohibition of slavery as a moral reproach of unbearable weight.

Thus, a mounting pressure for territorial organization of the Nebraska region—pressure coming from more than one source—was meeting stubborn sectional resistance. But the most important question is why both the pressure and the resistance were yielded to by the House of Representatives in a manner that would have been unthinkable a half-dozen years earlier; for the House, which had so often tried to *impose* the Wilmot Proviso everywhere in the territories, now agreed to *repeal* the equivalent of the Proviso affecting an area of several hundred thousand square miles. One quite simple explanation is that the House had ceased to be well balanced in its partisan makeup and was now overwhelmingly Democratic. The Whigs in just four years had declined from approximate parity to barely 30 per cent of the total membership, and most of the decrease had been among northern Whigs, who had always been the backbone of the antislavery element in the chamber. Also, within the dominant but faction-ridden Democratic party, the Kansas-Nebraska measure swiftly became a standard of party orthodoxy, used especially to test the loyalty of free-soil elements that had ostensibly returned to the fold, receiving lavish patronage rewards for doing so.

Most important of all, perhaps, was the high standing of the Compromise of 1850 and the Democratic commitment to it as a kind of treaty between North and South which must be observed in spirit as well as in letter. To southerners already angered by resistance to the Fugitive Slave Act, the most significant achievement of 1850 had been rejection of the Wilmot Proviso. Yet the dead hand of the past in the form of the Missouri Compromise restriction was now reaching out to impose the Proviso on newly organized territory, and that seemed utterly incompatible with the spirit of 1850.

Actually, the popularity of the Compromise resulted largely from its general pacificatory effect, not from any principles that could be inferred from its specific provisions. In short, the clearest violation of the spirit of the Compromise would be *any* action that revived the slavery controversy. Douglas seems to have been at least dimly aware of this fact at first, but in the heat of the legislative struggle he allowed it to be forgotten.

On January 4, 1854, he reported a bill for the organization of Nebraska as one big territory stretching from 36° 30′ to the Canadian boundary. The measure incorporated the slavery provisions of the Utah and New Mexico Acts while making no reference to the Missouri Compromise restriction, which was presumably still in force. The familiar Soulé clause declared that "when admitted as a state or states, the said territory . . . shall be received into the Union, with or without slavery as their constitutions may prescribe." There were the same provisions for easy access to the Supreme Court in slavery cases; and, as in the Yulee amendment of 1850, the Constitution and laws of the United States were extended over the territory. The effect at this point was curiously similar to that achieved four years earlier: Popular sovereignty was implied but not plainly established, and the status of the Missouri Compromise restriction, like the status of Mexican antislavery law in 1850, was left undefined and to be determined either by the territorial legislature or by judicial process.

In attempting pragmatically to neutralize the Missouri Compromise restriction without formally repealing it, Douglas awakened the anger of antislavery men and yet fell short of satisfying many southerners. After various negotiations and conferences in which President Pierce assumed an important role, the Illinois senator on January 23 presented a new bill establishing two territories instead of one and explicitly declaring the restriction to be "inoperative and void." It was to this measure that Salmon P. Chase and other antislavery radicals responded with the denunciatory "Appeal of the Independent Democrats," which set the tone of utmost bitterness for the long struggle that followed.[73]

One clause in the Kansas-Nebraska Act justified voiding the Missouri Compromise restriction on the grounds that it was "inconsistent with the principle of non-intervention by Congress with slavery in the territories" as embodied in the Compromise of 1850. During the legislative debate, Douglas went even further to argue that the Compromise of 1850 had legally "superseded" the Missouri Compromise in respect to slavery in the territories. The Missouri principle of having a dividing line between freedom and slavery had been defeated, he said, by northern votes, and that had created a need for a new kind of compromise based on the principle of self-government.[74]

The foundations of this argument were very weak. For one thing, it assumed a uniformity of principles in the government of territories that had never existed in American history. During the Jefferson administration, for example, slavery had been expressly forbidden in Indiana Territory, expressly unforbidden in Mississippi Territory, and totally unmentioned in the organization of Louisiana Territory.

Even more conclusive is the complete lack of evidence that any members of Congress in 1850 thought that the Utah and New Mexico Acts would have any effect on the status of slavery in Nebraska country. Instead, the Compromise of 1850 had included a reaffirmation of the Missouri Compromise restriction as it had appeared in the joint resolution for the annexation of Texas. Furthermore, efforts in 1850 to include repeal of the 36° 30′ restriction in the compromise package were ruled out of order as unrelated to the legislation under consideration.[75]

But perhaps the most fundamental weakness of the "supersession" argument is one that has gone largely unnoticed—namely, the falsity of the assumption that there was something new in the principle of nonintervention as it appeared in the territorial acts of 1850. Douglas mistakenly referred to 36° 30′ as a dividing line between freedom and slavery, but, as we have seen, the accurate terms are be-

TERRITORIES IN 1854

The Line Between Freedom and Nonintervention
After the Kansas-Nebraska Act

☐ Slavery prohibited*
▨ Nonintervention
—·—·— Dividing line

tween freedom and nonintervention.* The critical error is viewing the
Compromise of 1850 without including the Oregon bill of two years
earlier. Together, they constituted an extension of the old policy of
having two policies, instituted in 1787–90 and renewed in 1820, with
the principle of prohibition on one side of the line and the principle of
nonintervention on the other. The Compromise of 1850, it has been
said earlier, had the effect of extending the Missouri Compromise line
while moving it northward to 42° in Utah Territory. Congress in 1854
then extended the area of nonintervention northward all the way to
the Canadian boundary in Nebraska Territory, but not in Minnesota
to the east or in Oregon to the west.† The policy of having two
policies remained intact, but the dividing line between freedom and
nonintervention (once the Ohio River and 36° 30′) now varied in latitude from 42° to 49°.

The Kansas-Nebraska Act, to be sure, went beyond the Compromise of 1850 in attempting to establish popular sovereignty as a corollary to nonintervention. One clause declared that the "true intent and
meaning" of the act as a whole was "not to legislate slavery into any
Territory or State, nor to exclude it therefrom, but to leave the people thereof perfectly free to form and regulate their domestic institutions in their own way, subject only to the Constitution of the United
States." But what, precisely, did this passage mean? Did it authorize
the territorial legislatures to establish, recognize, or prohibit slavery,
as Douglas believed? It must be remembered that southerners, with
a few exceptions, were either lukewarm or hostile toward the Cass-
Douglas version of popular sovereignty, and many of them would
later find it easy enough to argue that the "people" of a territory could
take action only through a constitutional convention called to prepare
for statehood. Before that time, according to this southern version,

---

*What clouds our vision is the fact that in every instance before the Civil War, the
policy of nonintervention produced a slave state. But that was not a necessary consequence of the law itself, and we are talking about legal policy. Douglas's "supersession" argument was a legalistic one.

†Washington Territory, carved out of Oregon Territory in 1853, is a curiously indistinct case. Slavery remained excluded there, but apparently by virtue of popular sovereignty rather than by extension of the Northwest Ordinance, as in Oregon.[76]

pure nonintervention would prevail, with slaveholders free to enter the territory at will. It is highly significant that an amendment proposed by Philip Phillips of Alabama, which would have obviated much subsequent argument, was not incorporated into the bill. The amendment declared: "That the people of the Territory through their Territorial legislature may legislate upon the subject of slavery in any manner they may think proper not inconsistent with the Constitution of the United States." Here was clarity, if it had been truly desired. Instead, the more ambiguous phrasing won acceptance; for only by such evasion could the Democratic party be held together.[77]

Equivocal, then, at best, in the degree to which it established popular sovereignty, the Kansas-Nebraska Act, like the Utah and New Mexico acts which it imitated, also looked toward a judicial settlement of the slavery controversy. Addition of the totally superfluous phrase, "subject only to the Constitution," was a reminder of the fact that beyond the uncertain authority of the territorial legislature stood the certain authority of the Supreme Court. Vagueness in legislation is a kind of delegation of power, and the very vagueness of the Kansas-Nebraska Act invited, if it did not authorize, an eventual judicial disposition of a difficult issue. During the debates, there was considerable speculation about the outcome of the expected Court decision.[78] Under the Kansas-Nebraska Act, however, it would not have been possible to secure a judicial test of the power of *Congress* over slavery in the territories; for the act renounced the use of that power. Instead, it was the power of the *territorial legislature*, the principle of popular sovereignty, and perhaps the validity of the Calhoun doctrine that would have been tested in the envisioned court case. The power of Congress could be tested only where it could be challenged—that is, where it was operative.

It is doubly inaccurate to speak of the Kansas-Nebraska Act as the "repeal of the Missouri Compromise." In the first place, as we have already seen, the 36° 30′ line was not *the* Compromise and cannot even be considered *a* compromise. It was part of one side of the Compromise, being the major concession from the South to the North with which Missouri was ransomed and admitted to the Union. But in addition, the emphatic clause declaring the Missouri Compromise restriction to be "inoperative and void" formed part of a section extending the Constitution and laws of the United States *specifically* to Nebraska and Kansas. Did the clause also apply to Minnesota Territory, covered by the Missouri Compromise and organized since 1849 with slavery forbidden? Textually, one might argue either way, but certainly neither Douglas nor any other congressional leader claimed that nonintervention, by virtue of the Kansas-Nebraska Act, now prevailed at the headwaters of the Mississippi. It is therefore also of questionable accuracy to say that the Dred Scott decision of 1857 invalidated a law that had already been repealed in 1854. For the case involved Scott's residence, during the 1830s, in what later became Minnesota Territory, and there is not the slightest evidence that the Kansas-Nebraska Act had any effect on the antislavery law operative in Minnesota.[79]

The debates on the Kansas-Nebraska bill ranged over the whole of the slavery controversy—its history, moral conflict, and constitutional theory. Southerners frequently justified their support of the measure by arguing that the Missouri Compromise restriction was unconstitutional. These were in many cases the same men who, as recently as 1850, had urged extension of the 36° 30' line as the best means of resolving the sectional conflict. Yet perhaps even more anomalous was the spectacle of radical antislavery men appealing to the sanctity of the venerable Missouri Compromise, which they had consistently rejected as a basis for further conciliation.

Paradoxical, too, is the fact that, although southern pressure in Congress produced the Kansas-Nebraska bill, the South as a whole displayed little enthusiasm for it at first.[80] But the fierce antislavery attack on the measure provoked a reponse in kind, and soon another sectional crisis had developed. One can easily forget, however, that the Kansas-Nebraska bill was a partisan as well as a sectional issue, receiving the official support of a Democratic administration and the approval of a heavily Democratic Congress. Actually, 93 per cent of southern Democrats, southern Whigs, and northern Whigs voted *with* their sections, whereas 56 per cent of northern Democrats voted *against* their section and with their party.[81]

VOTING ON KANSAS-NEBRASKA BILL, TWO HOUSES
COMBINED

| | NORTH | | | SOUTH | |
	DEM.	WHIG	F.S.	DEM.	WHIG
Yes	58	0	0	70	22
No	46	52	5	3	8

The Kansas-Nebraska bill passed the Senate easily on March 3, 1854, by a vote of 37 to 14. In the House of Representatives, however, it took nearly three months for administration forces to whip enough northern Democrats into line. On May 22, the effort succeeded, 113 to 110, and Franklin Pierce signed the measure eight days later, thereby writing the label on his entire presidency. The two major consequences were a revolution in the party system and a civil war in Kansas.

Toward Judicial Resolution

T he bitter reaction against the Kansas-Nebraska Act throughout the North spelled disaster for the Democratic party in
a mid-term election year. Its huge majority in the House
of Representatives melted like snow during a sudden thaw. More
than 70 per cent of the party's free-state seats were lost. Only seven
of the forty-four northern Democrats who had voted for the bill won
re-election. Never until the days of Franklin D. Roosevelt would the
party fully recover from this defeat into which it had been led by
Stephen A. Douglas.[1]

The fate of the Whig party in the North is more difficult to
fathom, for it suffered curiously from having been on the right side of
the issue. Tainted with nativism and already in partial dissolution, it
seemed to have been given, in the Kansas-Nebraska Act, a last almost
miraculous chance to survive—not as a national party any longer but
as the antislavery party of the North. Whiggery, however, simply
could not turn the party revolution to its own advantage, and the
reason becomes clearer when one considers the blow administered in
Illinois to the political ambitions of Abraham Lincoln. The voters of
Illinois made clear their repudiation of the Kansas-Nebraska Act by
electing an "anti-Nebraska" majority to the state legislature in the autumn of 1854. In the ensuing contest for a seat in the United States
Senate, most of that majority supported Lincoln. He received forty-

five votes on the first ballot, just five short of victory. But five anti-Nebraska Democrats, unwilling to vote for a Whig, gave their support instead to Lyman Trumbull and clung to him through the subsequent ballots with rising success, until on the tenth ballot he was elected.[2] Obviously, anti-Nebraska strength could not be maximized under the Whig banner, and that fact counted heavily, though not everywhere immediately, in the reorganization of parties throughout the North.

Conversion of the spontaneous, loosely organized anti-Nebraska movement of 1854 into the new and permanent Republican party actually proceeded at different speeds in the various free states and was not entirely completed even by 1860. The virtually simultaneous national emergence of political nativism in the form of Know-Nothingism (officially, the "American party") further complicated an already confused situation and enabled the Democracy, in spite of its weakened condition, to capture the presidency one more time.

The Republican party should not be viewed simply as the Free Soil party writ large; for it became a *major* party, and that made a critical difference, not only in the sectional conflict but in the nature of the antislavery movement as well. In the South, the Georgia platform was augmented with a new justification for secession, one that proved to be more important than all of the other items on the list. The election of a Republican president, many southerners began to say in 1856, would mean dissolution of the Union.[3]

The Republican party incorporated and increased the varieties of antislavery sentiment in the United States. Perhaps the oldest variety was that associated with national pride and the traditions of the Revolution. However bitterly divided on the issue of slavery they may have been at home, Americans presented to the rest of the world the face of a slaveholding nation, and that made a mockery of their asserted belief that the United States had a special mission to lead mankind into a better, freer way of life. An Ohio congressman gave the sentiment apt expression during the struggle over the Wilmot Proviso. "It is," he said, "inconsistent with the genius of our institutions, and injurious to the character of the United States, to extend slavery."[4] Essentially an abstraction, antislavery as a form of patriotism was nevertheless widely diffused throughout the free states and can even be discerned in the radical Garrisonian slogan, "No union with slaveholders!" For most Americans, however, love of country meant a willingness to make some concessions in order to preserve the Union. Thus, in the case of men like Abraham Lincoln, patriotism had the effect of both inspiring and moderating antislavery feeling.

Opposition to slavery as an institution harmful to the nation also took the more practical form of economic argument. That "relic of barbarism," as the Republican party officially labeled it, was said to be a backward, inefficient mode of production constituting an enormous barrier to economic progress because it tied up needed capital and degraded free labor. There was probably more rhetoric than motive in the "free labor" appeals of Republican politicians, but they may have had significant effect at the polls.[5]

Of course, opposition to slavery also drew much of its energy from the conviction that the institution was morally wrong. But the mere theoretical acknowledgment of the wrong of slavery had long been a comforting, meaningless genuflection, indulged in universally and especially by many southerners, who, even in the 1850s, did not put the habit entirely aside. It was a different matter, however, when moral conviction focused on the injustice of slavery to the slave, as in the case of most abolitionists. Slave-centered antislavery, with its hunanitarian sympathy for creatures classified and treated partly as human beings and partly as livestock, was a dynamic force widespread in the North. The very intensity of abolitionist sympathy somewhat obscures the extent to which it was more mildly and sometimes even passively shared by millions of people in the free states.

But along with sympathy for the victims of injustice, there was also much hostility to slaves embedded in Republican hostility to slavery. Few Americans of the 1850s were entirely free of a physical repugnance for Negroes founded on an assumption of black inferiority in the endowments of nature and in the purposes of destiny. Antislavery racism was especially strong in the states and territories of the Northwest, where, it has been suggested, the very mobility of society made white men more apprehensive about "Negro equality."[6] The term "free soil" had, from the beginning of its usage, contained implications of "lily white," although it would be a distortion to say that this was its primary meaning. Opposition to the westward exten-

sion of slavery did include opposition to the westward migration of
the Negro as far as westerners themselves were concerned. State and
territorial laws forbidding or severely restricting black immigration
provide conclusive evidence on this point. And Republicans generally
were fond of the argument that the territories should be reserved for
the labor of free white men.[7] Nevertheless, racism as a Republican
motive has probably been exaggerated in some recent scholarship.
For one thing, there has been a tendency to generalize too readily
from the racist posture of some Republicans; and for another, it is too
often forgotten that antislavery politicians, as a matter of political survival, were usually compelled to disclaim any commitment to racial
equality. The racial preconceptions that Republicans shared with
other Americans do not, in fact, explain their opposition to slavery
but do help us to understand the limitations of that opposition.[8]

In still another way, some Republicans were antislavery without
being, in any meaningful way, pro-Negro—that is, in their anger at
southern power and its consequences in national politics. They could
see nothing but selfishness in southern opposition to internal improvements, homestead legislation, and other measures desired in
the North. They had heard too many threats of disunion and seen too
many displays of southern arrogance, reflecting the habit, it was said,
of whipping slaves into obedience. Out of the antislavery crusade
grew a stereotype of the slaveholding southerner as a man who put on
a show of chivalrous conduct, but underneath was cruel and cow-
ardly, rendered brutal by the institution that he cherished. For instance, when an Arkansas congressman assaulted Horace Greeley
near the Capitol in January 1856, the Chicago *Tribune* commented:
"He had been accustomed to lashing male, and knocking down female
slaves, in the State from whence he came. . . . Fresh from women-
whipping, those cotton lordlings import their plantation airs and manners to the federal city."[9] Four months later, when Preston Brooks of
South Carolina made his more famous attack on Charles Sumner, he
dramatically confirmed the image of the slaveholder that antislavery
newspapers had fashioned from a combination of fact and fiction. To a
considerable degree, Republican hostility to slavery was actually a
hostility to the "slave power."[10]

Of course, no individual's antislavery convictions were likely to be exclusively of the patriotic or economic or moral or humanitarian or racist or sectionalist kind. Each man acted from his own peculiar mixture of motives. And in addition to all the objective reasons for opposing slavery, there were undoubtedly subjective forces at work, such as the psychological satisfaction accruing from participation in a cause.[11] All of these influences had been present before 1854; yet the rise of the Republican party added something new and crucial.

On an earlier page it has been suggested that antislavery for a long time was primarily a sentiment, whereas proslavery from the beginning was a powerful interest. The abolitionist organizations to some degree and on a small scale constituted an antislavery interest, but not in the same sense as the Republican party after 1854. For the Republicans began immediately to capture statehouses and legislatures, not to mention making a strong run for the presidency as early as 1856. In the process, the party drew support, not only from all kinds of antislavery men, but also from many men who cared less about slavery than about winning elections and distributing patronage. Diffuse antislavery sentiment had at last been converted into a major, organized political interest, with its own self-sufficient reasons for survival and growth. Moreover, because of its utterly sectional nature, Republicanism differed from other major parties in its attitude toward agitation of the slavery question. For the Federalist, Jeffersonian, Democratic, and Whig organizations, all aspiring to be national in scope, there had always been good reason to reduce sectional tension; but Republicanism, as the very circumstances of its birth testified, had a stake in the continuance of the slavery controversy. That is one of the central facts in the history of "bleeding Kansas."

II

Before 1850, a congressional policy of nonintervention, whenever adopted, had always led to the establishment of slavery in the respective territories and states because the policy had been generally limited to regions lying aross the path of southern migration that were more or less suitable for plantation agriculture. By 1854, it could already be seen that the effect of such a policy in Utah and New Mexico would probably be different, and nobody seriously expected slavery to take root in Nebraska. Kansas, however, was plainly a borderline case, unlikely to become the goal of a large-scale and sustained migration of slaveholders, and yet almost certain to be heavily influenced for a time by the adjacent proslavery population of western Missouri.

The troubles began with the first territorial elections. There had been a widely publicized movement in the Northeast to organize "emigrant aid societies" and save Kansas from slavery. This provided the excuse for an invasion of illegal voters from Missouri, who secured the election of a proslavery legislature. At its first session in the summer of 1855, the legislature enacted a severe slave code. By then, however, a considerable number of bona fide settlers had arrived from nearby free states. The militants among them repudiated the "bogus legislature" and in the autumn organized their own rival government at Topeka. Thereafter, Kansas suffered under the rule of two governments, each in its own way illegitimate.[12]

President Pierce supported the official, proslavery government in Kansas. He denounced the Topeka government as "revolutionary" but took no decisive action to suppress it, and neither he nor the federal authorities in the territory seemed capable of ending the intermittent violence that reached its peak in May 1856 with the so-called "sack" of Lawrence and John Brown's retaliatory murders on Pottawatomie Creek. Sensationalized Kansas news filled the Republican press, to the increasing embarrassment and anger of the Democrats. With each party in effect supporting its own faction in the bedeviled territory, Kansas became a kind of violent extension of the approaching contest for the presidency.

The thirty-fourth Congress, elected in the aftermath of the struggle over the Kansas-Nebraska bill, assembled on December 3, 1855, with Kansas and presidential politics very much on its mind. A confrontation between proslavery and free-state forces in the territory, given the inflated name "Wakarusa War," was actually under way when the session began.[13] The Democratic party had lost control of the House of Representatives, which, as in 1849–50, entered upon a long, tiresome contest over the choice of a Speaker. This time the struggle lasted through two months and 133 ballots before the members, by a plurality, finally elected Nathaniel P. Banks of Massachusetts, a Know-Nothing recently turned Republican.[14] By then, the national party conventions were near at hand, and presidential campaigning had begun in earnest, with Kansas obviously destined to be the overriding issue of the canvass. Democrats had to wrestle with the embarrassing problem that two of their leading candidates, Pierce and Douglas, were intimately associated with the measure which had so recently proved disastrous in its effect on the party's fortunes throughout the free states. The debates in Congress, especially when they involved Douglas, Seward, or one of the other prominent aspirants, became, like the strife in Kansas, an aspect of the presidential campaign.

It was at this time that the case of *Dred Scott v. Sandford,* which had been on the docket for more than a year, finally came before the Supreme Court. Oral argument began on February 11, just nine days after the election of Banks as Speaker of the House had been hailed by Republicans as their first great national victory. The Court held conferences on the case intermittently during the next several months, while members of Congress were engaging in still another fierce and longlasting oratorical battle over the question of slavery in the territories. The justices, all political men to some degree, read their newspapers and in some cases, no doubt, followed the legislative debate in the *Congressional Globe.* Most of them mingled freely with political leaders in Washington and privately exchanged opinions on the issues of the day. With the territorial question now laid squarely before them, it seems likely that the members of the Court paid especially close attention to the proceedings of Congress in 1856.

The debate was launched by Franklin Pierce in his annual message to Congress of December 31, 1855. Embittered by the ruinous effect of the Kansas controversy on his administration and his personal popularity, Pierce closed the message with a harangue placing the entire blame for the sectional conflict on the critics of slavery. "While the people of the Southern States," he said, "confine their attention to their own affairs, not presuming officiously to intermeddle with the social institutions of the Northern States, too many of the inhabitants of the latter are permanently organized in associations to inflict injury on the former by wrongful acts, which would be cause of war as between foreign powers."

The President acknowledged no merit in the moral opposition to slavery, which he described as a "passionate rage of fanaticism and partisan spirit," and just one of many "wild and chimerical schemes of social change which are generated one after another in the unstable minds of visionary sophists and interested agitators." He offered his own emphatically pro-southern history of the territorial issue, during the course of which he pronounced the Missouri Compromise restriction of doubtful legality. It was, he said, "in the estimation of many thoughtful men, null from the beginning, unauthorized by the Constitution, contrary to the treaty stipulations for the cession of Louisiana, and inconsistent with the equality of these States." Pierce, who later spent some time in the company of Roger B. Taney during a summer vacation at Fauquier White Sulphur Springs, Virginia, had thus provided the Chief Justice with a presidential opinion on the central constitutional issue of the Dred Scott case.[15]

Several weeks later, Pierce sent to Congress a special message on Kansas, taking the proslavery side, denouncing the Topeka government as revolutionary, and recommending legislation that would authorize Kansas to prepare for statehood in the near future. The Senate referred the recommendation to its committee on territories, still presided over by Douglas, who responded on March 12, 1856, with a report of forty-one printed pages. This report, which Douglas himself read in its entirety to the Senate, served admirably as a campaign speech in a day when presidential candidates did not ostensibly make campaign speeches. In it, significantly, for the first time, he undertook to provide a constitutional imperative for his principle of popular sovereignty.[16]

Douglas followed the example of many southerners, and of Cass as well, in maintaining that the territory clause of the Constitution referred only to property and therefore conferred no power of government. He then separated himself from Cass by rejecting the latter's contention that congressional authority to govern the territories derived from simple necessity. Anticipating Taney's reasoning in the Dred Scott decision, he concluded instead that the authority must be implied from the expressly delegated power to admit new states. But to Douglas this meant that territories were essentially incipient states, to which the rule of state equality fully applied. The organic act for a territory, he declared, "must contain no provision or restriction which would destroy or impair the equality of the proposed State with the original States, or impose any limitation upon its sovereignty which the constitution has not placed on all the States." More specifically, the organic act "must leave the people entirely free to form and regulate their domestic institutions and internal concerns in their own way, subject only to the constitution of the United States."[17]

The latter passage was taken, of course, from the text of the Kansas-Nebraska Act, but with the notable addition of the word "must." What had been set forth in 1854 as "the true intent and meaning of this act" now became the true intent and meaning—indeed, the *command*—of the Constitution itself. In other words, Douglas now maintained that the repeal of the Missouri Compromise restriction in 1854 had been dictated by constitutional necessity, joining southerners in the conviction that Congress possessed no authority to enact such a restriction.[18] Thus, one full year before the Dred Scott decision, its most important conclusion had already been reached by Democratic leaders of both sections.[19]

That Douglas, a man for whom theory had always been secondary to practical achievement, should now find it expedient to constitutionalize the principle of popular sovereignty is a striking indication of the increasing formalism and casuistry in the public debate over slavery. "The constitution," said one editor, "threatens to be a subject of infinite sects, like the Bible."[20]

As a sect leader, Douglas was in fact proclaiming a major doctrinal revision while insisting that it had ever been so. The effect was to convert *popular sovereignty,* with its theoretical roots in the Lockean individualism of the Revolution, into *territorial sovereignty,* a constitutional theory stressing the corporate rights of an organized territory and, in effect, wiping out the distinction between territories and states. In this respect, Douglas was returning to the outlook of

Jefferson in 1784, but ignoring the history of territorial legislation over the intervening seventy years.

The quarrel that later developed between Douglas and southern Democrats over interpretation of the Dred Scott decision tends to obscure the fact that his committee report of 1856 anticipated certain important parts of Taney's opinion, including the ruling that the Missouri Compromise restriction was unconstitutional. It is important to understand, however, that by 1856, as compared with the years of the Wilmot Proviso, the question of congressional power over slavery in the territories had lost some of its relevance and emotional force. This had once been essentially a sectional issue between North and South. Few northerners in Proviso times had challenged the power of Congress to prohibit slavery in the territories, though they might question the wisdom of doing so.* Now with Douglas leading northern Democrats into the constitutional camp of the South, the question of congressional power became essentially a partisan issue between Democrats and Republicans. Yet, despite numerous oratorical and editorial exchanges on the subject, it was to some extent an academic, or at least a dormant, public issue. The Proviso principle, after all, had been rejected by Congress in 1850 and then had been rolled back from Kansas and Nebraska in 1854. Only in Minnesota and the Pacific Northwest did it still presumably apply. For southerners, accordingly, there was no urgent reason to press the issue, and for Republicans there was little use in doing so until restriction again became *politically* feasible. In short, with Congress having virtually disclaimed any *intention* of prohibiting slavery in the territories, the question of congressional *power* in the territories receded somewhat into the background of the sectional controversy.

The paramount public issue of 1856 was the turmoil in Kansas and who had caused it, involving primarily questions of fact and policy, rather than constitutional law. The only constitutional question of any urgency did not arise between Democrats and Republicans, but, instead, between the northern and southern wings of the Democratic party. First, there was a preliminary problem of statutory construc-

---

*Cass was the most prominent exception, of course.

tion—namely, whether the Kansas-Nebraska Act authorized the territorial legislatures to establish or prohibit slavery. If it did, then there followed the question of whether the territorial legislatures could constitutionally exercise such authority. For Democrats, generally anxious to maintain a semblance of party unity in an election year, this was a touchy subject which they would have preferred not to talk about. But Republicans could readily see the advantage of forcing the Democrats to confess their sectional disagreement on the issue. So the Douglas version of popular sovereignty replaced Republican Provisoism as the focus of constitutional argument.

What *was* the "true intent and meaning" of the Kansas-Nebraska Act regarding the power of the territorial legislature over slavery? The senator who pursued Douglas most relentlessly with this question was his new Illinois colleague, Lyman Trumbull, sitting in the seat that Abraham Lincoln had hoped to occupy. Douglas detested Trumbull as a renegade Democrat, and Trumbull fully returned his enmity. Douglas men in the Illinois legislature had gotten up a flimsy challenge to Trumbull's election, and not until March 5 did the Senate, by a vote of 35 to 8, declare him entitled to his seat.[21] On March 12, Douglas read his Kansas report, concluding with the announcement that he would soon bring in a bill to prepare Kansas for statehood. Two days later, Trumbull attacked the report in a speech of several hours, giving considerable attention to Douglas's constitutional argument.[22] He ridiculed the idea that the thirty-seven sections of the Kansas-Nebraska Act and all previous territorial legislation had been based entirely, as Douglas now maintained, on congressional power to admit new states. What, for example, he asked, did the definition of jurisdiction for a territorial justice of the peace have to do with admission to statehood? He also denounced the "constant attempt to make prominent the equality of the States, as if somebody doubted it, and to assimilate States to Territories." This, he said, was "only calculated to confuse the mind." Then Trumbull pointed out that the report, like the Kansas-Nebraska Act, did not say precisely *when* the people of a territory could make the decision about slavery. Had the territorial legislature been empowered to do so, or did the authority rest solely with a constitutional convention on the eve of statehood, as most southerners maintained?

Douglas reported his promised bill for Kansas statehood on March 17 and opened debate on the measure three days later in a set speech that was partly a reply to Trumbull. For two and one-half hours he held the attention of a full chamber and crowded gallery, but during that time he said nothing in response to Trumbull's question about the ambiguity of the Kansas-Nebraska Act; and, as his biographer notes, "He wisely avoided being drawn into a constitutional discussion by making no further mention of his attempt to base popular sovereignty on legal and constitutional grounds."[23]

The Douglas bill furnished the basis for senatorial debate on Kansas during the next three months. Curiously premature, the measure set forth the procedures for the admission of Kansas to statehood when its population reached 93,420, the current ratio for one seat in the House of Representatives. However, the population in 1856 probably amounted to no more than half that figure. Douglas was thus introducing an enabling act several years ahead of the time when it would be needed. The practical effect would be to continue the rule of proslavery territorial government, ignoring its questionable origins and egregious conduct. The attitude of Seward and other Republican leaders was even more unreasonable; for they demanded immediate admission of Kansas under the Topeka constitution, ignoring the lack of sufficient population as well as the illegitimate origins and partisan nature of the Topeka government.[24] Quite obviously, the Douglas bill would never get through the House, and the Seward proposal had no chance in the Senate. Yet the debate continued.

On May 2, Judah P. Benjamin of Louisiana delivered a speech, much of which was in the vein of southern extremism, with its peculiarly distorted view of American history. For instance, he said of the Missouri Compromise: "Scarcely had it been passed when it was broken by nearly every northern State." And of the territorial question: "All admit that the power to legislate for the Territories is nowhere given in express terms in the Constitution."[25] But then Benjamin took up the question that Trumbull and others had posed, and he laid out the formula for holding the Democratic party together during a presidential year. Supporters of the Kansas-Nebraska Act, he declared, were in agreement even about their one point of disagreement:

All agreed upon the right of a State to enter into this Union whenever it had sufficient population, and had formed a republican constitution, whether that constitution established or prohibited slavery. That provision was, therefore, inserted in the bill. All agreed
that it was prejudicial to the best interests of the country that the
subject of slavery should be discussed in Congress. All agreed
that, whether Congress had the power or not to exclude slavery
from the Territories, it ought not to exercise it. All agreed that, if
that power was owned by us, we ought to delegate it to the people
whose interests were to be affected by the institutions established
at home. We therefore put that into the bill.

Then came the point upon which we disagreed. Some said, as I
say, Congress has no power to exclude slavery from the common
territory; it cannot delegate it, and the people in the Territory
cannot exercise it except at the time when they form their constitution. Others said, Congress has the power; Congress can delegate it, and the people can exercise it. Still others said—my honorable friend from Michigan [Lewis Cass] said—that the power to
legislate on that subject was a power inherent in every people
with whom the doctrine of self-government was anything more
than an empty name. On this proposition we disagreed; and to
what conclusion did we come? We said, in this bill, that we transferred to the people of that Territory the entire power to control,
by their own legislation, their own domestic institutions, subject
only to the provisions of the Constitution; that we would not interfere with them; that they might do as they pleased on the subject;
that the Constitution alone should govern. And then, in order to
provide a means by which the Constitution could govern, by
which that single undecided question could be determined, we of
the South, conscious that we were right, the North asserting the
same confidence in its own doctrines, agreed that every question
touching human slavery, or human freedom, should be appealable
to the Supreme Court of the United States for its decision.[26]

Of course, no such agreement had ever been explicitly concluded. Benjamin's account was a mixture of fact and fiction—a pre-
scription for 1856, rather than an accurate historical reconstruction of
what had happened in 1854. Not surprisingly, both Douglas and Cass
promptly praised the speech, the latter calling it "magnificent and

patriotic."[27] The Benjamin formula incorporated the northern statutory construction of the Kansas-Nebraska Act, while leaving the constitutional construction to the Supreme Court. This meant that the territorial legislature did possess the power to prohibit slavery, *if that power could be constitutionally given.* The qualification, it should be noted, had always existed, whether stated or not. What the South gained was added emphasis upon it. Not all southern Democrats were willing to accept the Benjamin formula with its substantial concession to northern sentiment.[28] Nevertheless most members of the party could readily see the political advantages of adhering to the formula, and Republicans could readily see the necessity of demolishing it.

III

On May 12, the Supreme Court ordered a re-argument of the Dred Scott case, thereby postponing its decision until the next term, after the presidential election. Soon public attention was diverted by the attack of Preston Brooks on Charles Sumner and by the outbreak of violence in Kansas, including the attack on Lawrence and John Brown's retaliation at Pottawatomie Creek. These events were still fresh when the national party conventions assembled in June.

The Know-Nothings had already nominated Millard Fillmore for president in February, but the party had been split by the slavery question, and a substantial portion of its northern members would soon join the Republicans. At Cincinnati, in early June, the Democratic convention chose James Buchanan on the seventeenth ballot. This was not a victory for the South, which preferred Pierce or Douglas. The platform, on the other hand, vaguely embodied the southern interpretation of the Kansas-Nebraska Act by stressing "nonintervention" and the right of a territorial population to accept or reject slavery at the time of framing a constitution for statehood. Later events tend to cloud the fact that the Cincinnati convention produced a northern candidate on a southern platform.[29] Buchanan, however, was a political trimmer without strong antislavery conviction and would take the southern side as soon as it seemed safe to do so.[30]

Two weeks later, the Republican convention met at Philadelphia.

Still struggling for the inclusiveness of a major party, the Republicans passed over all their leaders and nominated instead a national celebrity, the explorer John C. Frémont. The only serious challenge to Frémont came from the conservative supporters of Justice John McLean, whose presidential aspirations had reportedly been one reason for the postponing of the Dred Scott decision. The Republicans, in fact, made the meaning of their party much clearer in the framing of a platform than in the selection of a presidential candidate. It declared that the Constitution (no specific clauses named) conferred upon Congress "sovereign powers over the Territories of the United States for their government," and that in the exercise of these powers it was both the right and duty of Congress "to prohibit in the Territories those twin relics of barbarism—Polygamy and Slavery." This presented the orthodox free-soil doctrine in the tradition of the Northwest Ordinance—that is, Congress possessed the power of exclusion and, as a matter of good policy, ought to exercise it. The reference to polygamy was, of course, a sly thrust at popular sovereignty and the Kansas-Nebraska Act, with its declared intention of leaving the territorial population "perfectly free to form and regulate their domestic institutions in their own way." Marriage being no less "domestic" than slavery, this seemed to be a pretty firm guarantee that Brigham Young could continue to maintain his remarkable household. Democratic embarrassment at being thus associated with Mormon polygamy would soon have its own startling consequences.[31]

But the Republicans, like Douglas, felt the constitutionalizing pressure of the times and the consequent need to convert their political policy into a constitutional imperative. They accordingly adopted also the argument of Salmon P. Chase and certain other party radicals that slavery was illegal in the federal territories by virtue of the due process clause of the Fifth Amendment. This formulation ruled out popular sovereignty and in a curious way revived the strategy of the abortive Clayton compromise, though with different constitutional presumptions. The effect was to reinforce the expectation already widespread among Democrats that the fundamental sectional differences over slavery would ultimately have to be settled in the courts. There is, moreover, some minor historical irony in the fact that the due process clause, which would soon figure prominently in Taney's Dred Scott decision, received mention only from the Republicans in the platform-writing of 1856.

On the subject of Kansas, Republican wrath overflowed. The platform listed and denounced the "atrocious outrages" allegedly committed by proslavery elements in the territory. It charged the President and his administration with "high crime against the Constitution, the Union, and humanity." And it reiterated the demand of Republican congressional leaders for immediate admission of Kansas with the Topeka constitution.

The threat of Republicanism convinced even militant southern leaders that Kansas must somehow be pacified before the presidential election in November. Robert Toombs accordingly came forward in late June with a plan that seemed fairer than anything either side had previously supported. The plan incorporated the Republican idea of admitting Kansas to statehood at an early date, without restriction as to minimum population. Under the supervision of five commissioners appointed by the President, there was to be a new census of the territory and a new registration of voters. A convention elected in November would meet in December to draft a state constitution. Admission could presumably be consummated before the adjournment of Congress in March 1857. Thus Toombs proposed to wipe the slate clean and begin anew, repudiating both the "bogus" proslavery territorial government and the "revolutionary" Topeka organization. The measure truly deserved to be called a compromise.[32]

Republicans nevertheless greeted the Toombs bill with suspicion and hostility. "Gentlemen tell us that the commissioners will be fair men," said Senator William P. Fessenden of Maine. "What authority have we for that?" Certainly, nothing in Pierce's record encouraged the belief that he would administer the law impartially, and the ultimate test of fairness would not come until after the presidential contest had been decided. Many Republicans agreed sincerely with Henry Wilson of Massachusetts when he insisted that the bill was intended to make Kansas a slaveholding state. Yet Republicans were also fully aware of the partisan advantage to be gained from a continuation of the turmoil in Kansas, and their opposition to the Toombs compromise left them vulnerable to the charge of playing politics with the lives of settlers in Kansas. "An angel from heaven," Douglas exclaimed, "could not write a bill to restore peace in Kansas that would be acceptable to the Abolition Republican party previous to the presidential election."[33] These words received loud applause from the Senate gallery, and the Democrats did have the better of the controversy, even though their legislation failed. No less politically motivated than their opponents, they had nevertheless made the right gesture. The Toombs bill seemed fair, and the opposition to it seemed unreasonable. After passing the Senate easily enough, it was turned aside contemptuously in the House, but one suspects that it won some critically important votes for Buchanan in the fall.[34]

The Republican campaign of 1856 was essentially a sequel to the anti-Nebraska crusade of 1854, with the emphasis now on the allegedly disastrous consequences of the Kansas-Nebraska Act, as administered by the Pierce administration. In addition, some Republicans continued to exploit the conspicuous ambiguities in Democratic territorial theory. Congress had scarcely reconvened after the Cincinnati convention before Trumbull resumed his pestering of Douglas on the subject. Did the territorial legislature of Kansas have the power to exclude slavery? He, Trumbull, doubted whether Douglas could be induced to answer the question. But Douglas and several other northern Democrats did respond by reciting the Benjamin formula. The Kansas legislature, they said, had been invested with all the power over domestic territorial affairs that Congress could rightfully confer. Whether that included the power to prohibit slavery was a constitutional question, which Douglas solemnly refused to answer on the ground that it belonged exclusively to the Supreme Court. Congress, he said, ought not to "coerce and dragoon that court" in the performance of its duty. He himself had too much respect for the Court to discuss judicial questions in the Senate.

As a political expedient, the argument was brilliant, but Trumbull quickly exposed its logical absurdities. "Every law which we pass," he said, "is subject to the scrutiny of the Supreme Court of the United States, whenever a case properly arises." Why, then, was it a legislative function to declare that the people of Kansas Territory were "perfectly free to form and regulate their domestic institutions in their own way," but not a legislative function to say more precisely that the territorial legislature might establish or prohibit slavery? Were not both equally subject to judicial review? Douglas, after all, had never hesitated to render judgment on other constitutional questions. For example, he had voted to extend the Fugitive Slave Law over Kansas Territory in spite of the fact that the Constitution provided no specific authorization for doing so.* "This," said Trumbull, "involved a constitutional question which my colleague had no difficulty in deciding." Moreover, the Kansas-Nebraska Act as a whole might some day come before the Supreme Court for review, and yet Douglas had offered some emphatic comments on that subject in his report read to the Senate on March 12. Did he have any qualms then about trespassing on the prerogatives of the Court?

> My colleague can spend days in arguing the power of Congress to establish a territorial government; he can study the Constitution until he derives that power from the clause authorizing the admission of new states into the Union. . . . He has no trouble in deciding that constitutional point. . . . How is it that he can give a judgment here on all these constitutional questions; but when he comes to the very one about which one opinion is proclaimed in the North, and another in the South, he says he has no opinion?[35]

Trumbull pressed the issue again during the debate on the Toombs bill in early July. He offered first one amendment and then another interpreting the Kansas-Nebraska Act as endowing the territorial legislatures with the authority to regulate slavery. But Cass, Douglas, and other northern Democrats rejected this confirmation of their own version of popular sovereignty. In each instance, they quite rightly observed, the Trumbull amendment was irrelevant to a bill that dealt with statehood rather than with territorial government.[36] Trumbull's proposal was also superfluous, they insisted, because it conferred no power not already granted in the Kansas-Nebraska Act. It "expressed the true idea," Douglas acknowledged, but unneces-

---

*The fugitive-slave clause of the Constitution refers only to slaves escaping from "one State . . . into another."

sarily and improperly, and Trumbull's sole purpose, he charged, was to provide material for Republican use on the campaign stump. The extent of territorial power over slavery was a judicial question, he reiterated. Cass and other northern Democrats echoed him—"a judicial question, a judicial question," and the phrase became a kind of political incantation for warding off the curse of Republicanism. The two versions of the Trumbull amendment were defeated, 34 to 9 and 34 to 11, with not a single Democrat voting in the affirmative.[37]

Now, the refusal of Democratic senators to yield an inch on this point is especially striking because the general party strategy was to give the Republicans no good excuse for opposing the Toombs bill. In pursuit of this policy, they made substantive concessions that seemed sufficient to insure a free-state triumph in Kansas. Why balk, then, at accepting the Trumbull amendment, which, according to Douglas himself, merely recapitulated a provision of the Kansas-Nebraska Act? The answer is that the amendment, which could have had no significant effect on the operation of the Toombs bill, was designed to break down the fragile unity of the Democratic party which the Benjamin formula symbolized.

The Congress of the early 1850s, it has been said, hoped to "rid itself of the vexing territorial issue" and therefore did everything possible "to foster a judicial resolution of the problem."[38] Indeed, according to one legal historian, the Supreme Court undertook the Dred Scott decision "only upon explicit invitation of Congress," thereby "accepting the buck which Congress and the statesmen had passed."[39] The second statement is less accurate than the first, however, and the distinction between the two, though inconspicuous, is nevertheless exceedingly important. In fact, the "judicial question" talked about so much in Congress was not the same as the question before the Supreme Court. The buck passed and the buck accepted were subtly but significantly different.

The constitutional question before the Court in the Dred Scott case was the one that divided Republicans from Democrats, especially southern Democrats—namely, whether Congress had the power to prohibit slavery in the territories. The constitutional question repeatedly thrust on the Court in 1856 by supporters of the Benjamin formula was the one that divided northern Democrats from southern Democrats—namely, whether a territorial legislature had the power to prohibit slavery. Ever since the failure of the Wilmot Proviso, the question of congressional power had been largely a theoretical issue in legislative debates; for the constitutionality of a power can be tested judicially only by exercising it, and Congress, after establishing Oregon Territory, had ceased to enact, or even consider, legislation prohibiting slavery in other territories.* The question of territorial power, on the other hand, was a troublesome and even dangerous domestic issue within the Democratic party, exploited assiduously by Republicans and therefore referred to the judiciary as a matter of Democratic strategy. But this question simply did not arise in the Dred Scott case. The gears therefore did not mesh. What Democrats were turning over to the Supreme Court was the task of defining popular sovereignty; what the members of the Court were about to pass judgment on was the constitutionality of the Wilmot Proviso.

Most southerners, to be sure, assumed that the two questions were intimately related. They insisted that if Congress lacked the power to prohibit slavery in the territories, it certainly could not delegate that power to a territorial legislature. But Cass and Douglas obviously did not accept this inference, and no northern Democrat could do so without finding himself in trouble with his constituents. In fact, neither sectional wing of the Democratic party could accept the other's definition of popular sovereignty. This meant that the Benjamin formula would work just so long as it was not carried to execution. Talk of referring the question of territorial power to the Supreme Court might promote Democratic unity for the presidential campaign, but an actual Court decision on the subject was likely to have the opposite effect and redound to the advantage of the Republicans. It would serve the same divisive purpose that Trumbull had hoped to achieve in his interrogations of Douglas.

It therefore appears that the political need for a judicial pro-

---

*Washington Territory remained free soil after its separation from Oregon Territory in 1853, but by congressional confirmation of territorial law, rather than by congressional prohibition in the tradition of the Northwest Ordinance. See pp. 639–40.

nouncement on slavery in the territories was to some extent an illusion. Kansas, the principal danger area in 1856, would be little affected by such a pronouncement, for the troubles there were not
essentially constitutional, and Kansas, in any case, had by general
consent become a statemaking problem rather than a territorial problem. Exclusion of slavery by congressional authority, prevailing only
in Minnesota and the Pacific Northwest, was not a concrete issue of
any significance in 1856, and a Court decision, one way or the other,
could scarcely have much effect upon those regions. Exclusion of slavery by territorial authority prevailed nowhere (except arguably in
Washington Territory), and any judicial ruling on the subject would
have a destructive effect on Democratic unity.

Still, the pressures for judicial intervention in the mounting sectional conflict over slavery, though somewhat illogical, were nevertheless very strong. As we have seen, the tendency to constitutionalize the territorial issue dated back many years. It was reinforced
in 1856 by the peculiar needs of the Democratic party and especially
by the strategy of unity through evasion, as embodied in the Benjamin formula, with a consequent increase in talk about "leaving it to
the Supreme Court." The Court, furthermore, was the one major
agency of government that had not yet tried its hand at resolving the
conflict. More than a few Americans apparently believed that at its
command, agitation of the slavery question would subside and the
years of crisis would come to an end. Indeed, some members of the
Court itself seem to have harbored the belief that it possessed some
such extraordinary power.

The Taney Court
and Judicial Power

Years of political pressure for a judicial settlement of the slavery controversy undoubtedly had their effect on the collective judgment of the Supreme Court in its handling of the Dred Scott case. But the boldness with which it acted also reflected public understanding of the nature of judicial power and the Court's own sense of strategic responsibility in the American constitutional system.

There is no simple historical explanation for the extraordinary power of the judiciary that eventually became a "distinguishing characteristic of the American system of government."[1] One can find its sources, for instance, in the functioning system of English law as transplanted to the colonies, in the constitutional nature of the British colonial empire as perceived by eighteenth-century Americans, in certain aspects of pre-Revolutionary argumentation over colonial rights, and in the formal structure of the federal republic created between 1776 and 1789.

The place to begin, perhaps, is with the fact that by the early seventeenth century the English judiciary, in the words of one legal historian, "had come to occupy a position of pre-eminence in the English constitution unmatched in any other European country."[2] The great common-law tradition, in which the judge was the central figure of authority, crossed the Atlantic with every shipload of English colonists, even though the body of the common law, in all its patchwork complexity and technical detail, was never more than fractionally "received" by the American commonwealths.[3] The law of the common-law tradition, which included much English local law as well as the common law itself, was essentially judge-made law, but not self-admittedly so. In theory, the judge was merely the expositor of an existing body of law consisting partly of statute but deriving largely from general custom made legitimate by its long survival. In practice, the judge relied on the memory or written record of what other judges had decided in earlier, similar cases, sometimes making reasoned adjustments to suit new circumstances. Thus the judge followed precedent but also occasionally set precedent (that is, made law) in response to the changing legal needs of a changing social order.[4]

Each judicial decision accordingly became one of the "building blocks of law."[5] But in addition to the enormous accumulation of discrete cases that could be sought out and cited as precedents for other discrete cases, the process of law-building gradually produced certain basic patterns of procedural rules and general principles that formed a significant part of the "unwritten" English constitution. These general principles of common law, often identified in eighteenth-century Anglo-American thought with the first principles of natural law and natural rights, came to be regarded (in the words of John Marshall) as a great "substratum of the laws"—that is, a foundation of justice more elemental and pervasive than any enacted law, even a constitution. In the common-law tradition, then, not only was the judicial power of central importance, but also, much of the country's fundamental law was developed by judges in the course of deciding ordinary legal disputes between private individuals.[6]

The common-law tradition did not, however, include a functioning system of judicial review. That is, neither in England nor in colonial America did courts make a practice of invalidating legislation on the ground of its repugnance to fundamental law. In England, where the concept of separation of powers was never institutionalized, judicial review would have been incompatible with the principle of parliamentary supremacy as it became established after 1688. In America, the colonials themselves had only occasional reason to want restraint placed on the power of their provincial assemblies, and imperial officials had other, more effective means of imposing or securing such restraint.* Furthermore, the emergence of judicial review during the late eighteenth and early nineteenth centuries was in some degree a response to a legislative activism seldom manifested during the colonial period. In those times of much slower social change, legislative responsibilities were primarily managerial, with little expected in the way of innovation. For example, the Massachusetts General Court in 1761, according to William E. Nelson, "passed only three acts that were arguably legislative in the sense that they changed law or made new law." Nelson adds that whenever a statute did make a significant change in substantive law, the legislature nearly always justified its action in a preamble, "demonstrating that the new statute was not really a change at all but a mere extension of . . . the law's fundamental principles."[8] In the presence of such conservatism there was not much need for judicial review.

At the same time, certain features of the British colonial system no doubt helped to prepare American ground for the introduction of judicial review. The colonial charters, for example, served as prototypes of written constitutions, conferring and limiting governmental power. The British empire, moreover, was in some respects a functioning federal system, and colonials became accustomed to having their local laws subject to disallowance by the central authority of the Privy Council. In its judicial capacity, the Privy Council also heard appeals from colonial courts and upon a number of occasions took the validity of colonial legislation under advisement. In the most notable of these cases, which has been somewhat extravagantly called "the one clear-cut precedent for the American doctrine of judicial review," the Council voided a Connecticut intestacy act on the grounds that it violated the law of England and the colony's charter as well.[9]

It was in the polemics of pre-Revolutionary resistance to British authority that Americans, invoking both natural law and the princi-

---

*Colonial courts, to be sure, did exercise some supervisory control over local officials, and a statute could often be held in line with common-law precedent by the manner in which it was judicially construed.[7]

ples of English common law, developed a coherent theory of constitutional limitations on legislative power. To be sure, much of this argument proved at first to be mere rhetoric sent into battle against Parliament. When the Revolution began, its circumstances tended generally to enhance legislative supremacy in the various colonies. Fundamental law there might be, but American legislatures of the 1770s and 1780s were much like Parliament in assuming that interpretation of the fundamental law was exclusively a legislative responsibility. It is true that Pennsylvania and New York, in their constitutions of 1776 and 1777, respectively, lodged the power of constitutional review with specially created bodies—a "council of censors" in the one instance and a "council of revision" in the other. For the most part, however, the first state constitutions, while paying some lip service to the principles of constitutionalism and separation of powers, actually reflected and reinforced the Revolutionary tendency toward legislative supremacy. Nearly all of them were drafted by provincial congresses that mixed constitution-making with ordinary legislative business. With but few exceptions, the executive authority in these constitutions was weak, and the judiciary was subject in some degree to legislative domination. This concentration of power in the legislative branch was inconsistent with the trend of American political theory, and it also proved highly unpopular in practice. The assemblies passed too many laws, and much of their handiwork seemed ill-considered and unjust. "The acts of almost every legislature," said a Maryland jurist in 1784, "have uniformly tended to disgust its citizens." Here was a threat of tyranny from an unexpected source, and James Madison led in the outcry against it. "The legislative department," he wrote in *Federalist* 48, "is everywhere extending the sphere of its activity and drawing all power into its impetuous vortex. . . . it is against the enterprising ambition of this department that the people ought to indulge all their jealousy and exhaust all their precautions."[10]

One of the earliest reactions against the drift toward legislative domination took place in Massachusetts. There, in 1778, the towns rejected a constitution drafted by the General Court. They did so partly on the ground that the fundamental charter of a commonwealth ought to be the work of a special convention, separate from the legislature and drawn directly from the people. The Massachusetts constitution of 1780 was accordingly prepared by just such a body, and America's invention of the constitutional convention thereby became virtually complete.[11]

By the middle of the 1780s, moreover, there was a growing conviction among thoughtful Americans that if their constitutions, however drafted, were to have effective force as restraints on government, they would have to make the theory of separation of powers more of a reality by strengthening the executive and judicial departments. The judiciary benefited especially from this gradual change in the climate of opinion, and judges in several states during the decade even ventured tentatively onto the ground of judicial review by holding statutes, or parts of statutes, to be unconstitutional and unenforceable.[12]

It was in this context of disillusionment with legislative supremacy and of renewed commitment to separation of powers that the men of 1787 assembled at Philadelphia to write a new federal constitution. The resulting document, emphatically declaring itself to be the "supreme law of the land," enlarged the powers of the national government and established within it a strong executive and an independent judiciary. According to the theory of separation of powers, each department should be, not only independent, but capable of protecting itself against encroachments by the other departments. This, in the view of Alexander Hamilton, was a major purpose of the presidential veto and the legislative power of impeachment.[13] The judiciary was not expressly provided with any such weapon of self-defense. But in the Constitutional Convention there appears to have been some agreement with the observation of Elbridge Gerry that the judiciary would have "a sufficient check against encroachments on their own department by their exposition of the laws, which involved a power of deciding on their constitutionality."[14]

Beyond this narrow conception of judicial review as an instrument of self-defense for the "least dangerous" branch of government, there were the more expansive views of men like Hamilton, who assumed from the beginning that the courts of justice must be the principal guardians, not only of their own independence, but also of the integrity of the Constitution—especially against legislative excesses. Judicial review so broadly defined could not have been introduced into the text of the Constitution without considerable resistance. Madison, for one, would surely have opposed it. Instead, the idea was left to be developed by inference and practice until it became, in the end, the most remarkable of all the "implied powers" of the Constitution.[15]

II

A constitution is a document in which the sovereign people both confer power on government and limit the power of government. The limitations are set to some extent by the very contours of the power conferred, but also by specified prohibitions on government, such as those included in a bill of rights. The *positive* or power-conferring clauses of a constitution are ordinarily not self-executing. They require further action, such as implemental legislation, in order to have the force of law. Federal taxes, for instance, are authorized by the United States Constitution, but they are imposed only by act of Congress. On the other hand, a *negative* or power-limiting clause, such as the one forbidding *ex post facto* laws, is usually self-executing and therefore directly enforceable in the courts.* Much depends, of course, upon whether constitutional provisions are construed broadly (loosely) or strictly. Broad construction, so often associated with "implied powers," is commonly thought of as promoting expansion of legislative authority, but this actually holds true only with respect to the positive clauses of a constitution. Upon reflection, one quickly realizes that broad construction of the negative clauses of a constitution will tend to restrict legislative authority. It would scarcely be an exaggeration to say that the enormous power exercised by the Supreme Court of the United States in the twentieth century proceeds largely from broad interpretation of certain negative provisions of the federal

---

*Edward S. Corwin speaks of the "Constitution as instrument" and the "Constitution as symbol" to draw the same distinction, but the terms "positive" and "negative" seem clearer and were good enough for John C. Calhoun.[16]

Constitution—most notably, the First and Fourteenth amendments.

All American constitutions, state and national, incorporate the principle of limited government, called "constitutionalism." In each instance they create a government, describe its working parts, and define the relationship between government and people. But the Constitution of the United States is more complex in that it also incorporates the principle of partly decentralized government, called "federalism." It defines the political relationship between the nation and the states. The contours of federalism, like those of constitutionalism, are indicated in both positive and negative clauses of the Constitution. Least ambiguous are certain powers expressly delegated to the federal government and expressly forbidden to the states, such as coinage of money. In a number of important instances, however, the framers neglected to draw the line between state and federal authority with any precision. For example, one clause empowered Congress to establish "uniform laws on the subject of bankruptcies throughout the United States." But was this power intended to be exclusive, or, in the absence of congressional action, could the states enact bankruptcy legislation of their own?[17] Many such questions arose in the early decades of the Republic, testifying to the fact that in the work of defining the federal relationship, the Constitution itself was only a beginning.

One further complication must be noted. If the principle of federalism is diagramed as a horizontal line connecting state and central governments, then the principle of constitutionalism may be represented by vertical lines connecting those governments with their respective populations. That is, the new Constitution of 1787, with its Bill of Rights, protected the American people against excesses of the *national* government; for protection against excesses of their *state* governments, the people depended primarily upon their state constitutions and accompanying state bills of rights. Yet, in the federal Constitution there were certain exceptions to this general design. Several clauses laying prohibitions upon the states (such as the one forbidding laws that would impair the "obligation of contracts") were interventional rather than distributional in purpose. These clauses did not contribute to marking off the boundary between central and local au-

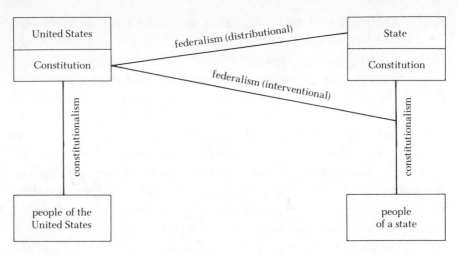

thority; instead, they *intervened* between each state government and its people, for the latter's protection. Such intervention, which applied the principle of constitutionalism in a context of federalism, was obviously an invasion of state sovereignty, viewed with apprehension by many Americans of 1787 for whom state loyalty remained the highest form of patriotism. And there one approaches the core of the federal problem that so perplexed the framers at Philadelphia. How were the various constitutional restrictions on state power to be made effective—and, indeed, how was federal law generally to be enforced—without serious impairment of state sovereignty?

The critical operational question in this respect was whether the central government should continue to function through the agency of the state governments. Experience had already shown that it could not do so effectively without some kind of coercive control. Madison and the other authors of the "Virginia plan" accordingly proposed that Congress be empowered to disallow state laws and, more than that, "to call forth the force of the Union against any member of the Union failing to fulfill its duty under the articles thereof."[18] But the Convention rejected this solution, with its unpleasant echoes of British coercive policy on the eve of the Revolution. Instead, the delegates chose to create a federal government that would have its own agencies of enforcement, thus by-passing the states and operating directly upon the people. State government and federal government would consequently function side by side, independent of one another, and each supreme within its own designated sphere of power.

Yet, even if that proved sufficient as the means of compelling individual obedience to federal law, there remained the problem of how, without direct coercion, the state governments could be held faithful to the Constitution of the United States. The solution eventually adopted by the Convention was a clause that seemed relatively innocuous and had, in fact, been brought forward by anti-nationalists, who obviously did not realize the amplitude of its potential force:

> This Constitution and the laws of the United States which shall be made in pursuance thereof; and all treaties made, or which shall be made, under the authority of the United States, shall be the supreme law of the land, and the judges in every State shall be bound thereby, anything in the constitution or laws of any State to the contrary notwithstanding.[19]

By itself, this "supremacy clause" could be read as relying upon *state judges* to uphold the federal Constitution against the legislatures of their own states, simply because they were bound by oath to do so. Elsewhere, however, the framers provided that the power of the *federal judiciary* should extend to all cases in law and equity arising under the Constitution, laws, and treaties of the United States. This seemed to mean that the Supreme Court would have authority to review state court decisions involving the federal relationship, and in the Judiciary Act of 1789, Congress expressly invested the Court with such authority.[20] As a consequence, the American judicial system assumed a pyramidal shape that was more or less inconsistent with the design of dual federalism, in which state and federal governments presumably functioned side by side, independent of one another. State legislatures were not accountable to Congress; governors were not accountable to the president, but state courts were, in certain crucial respects, accountable to the federal Supreme Court. In the structure of judicial power after 1789, the United States was as much a unitary as a federal state.

The authors of the Virginia plan also gave consideration to the problem of holding Congress within constitutional bounds and preventing its encroachment upon the other departments. They proposed that a "convenient number" of federal justices be associated with the executive in a council of revision possessing the power to veto legislative acts. Three times the Convention considered the proposal and rejected it, preferring instead to lodge the veto power exclusively with the president. One of the various reasons offered for doing so was that the judiciary ought not to have a double negative on legislation and that in the course of applying acts of Congress, it would examine their constitutionality. During the contest over ratification, this expectation was repeated by several members of the Convention, including Hamilton, Oliver Ellsworth, and James Wilson. Ellsworth, in the Connecticut ratifying convention, neatly summarized the two basic kinds of judicial review that could be inferred from the Constitution:

> If the general legislature should at any time overleap their limits, the judicial department is a constitutional check. If the United States go beyond their powers, if they make a law which the Constitution does not authorize . . . the national judges . . . will declare it to be void. On the other hand, if the states go beyond their limits, if they make a law which is a usurpation upon the general government, the law is void; and upright, independent judges will declare it to be so.[21]

So the foundation of American judicial power was well and truly laid in 1787, even though its full potential would not be realized until the middle of the twentieth century. The Constitution, to begin with, was itself *law* to be enforced. Its negative provisions in particular were enforceable directly by the courts and perhaps in no other way. The framers, whatever the mixture of their intentions in rejecting disallowance, coercion of states, and a council of revision, had left primarily to the judiciary the task of protecting the Constitution against encroachment by Congress, the president, and the state governments. They had done so more or less by default, rather than as an act of crystallized volition. In fact, judicial responsibility resulted almost automatically from their having created a *hierarchical* order of law, in which the federal Constitution was superior to federal legislation, and both took precedence over state legislation. That is, in any ordinary case at law, a court might be called upon to say whether a right claimed under a statute must give way to a right claimed under a constitution or other superior law. To accept the responsibility of making such a decision was in itself an exercise of judicial review, no matter how the court should eventually rule. The word "ordinary," moreover, needs special emphasis. Unlike the great modern expansion of presidential power, so much of which is associated with extraordinary executive action initiated in times of crisis, modern judicial power in the United States has been constructed gradually and often unobtrusively during the routine performance of regular judicial duties.

From all this it should be clear that "judicial review" is a term of complex meaning used to designate an institutional pattern of complex origin. In its most familiar usage, the phrase signifies a decision of the federal Supreme Court declaring an act of Congress to be unconstitutional and therefore void. Such "true" or "coordinate" judicial review at the national level (call it Type A-1) is addressed to the principle of constitutionalism and has its counterpart at the state level in court decisions invalidating state laws as contrary to state constitutions (Type A-2). Perhaps most important historically, however, is "federal" or "hierarchical" judicial review (Type B), addressed to the principle of federalism, in which a state law may be set aside on the ground that it violates the federal Constitution or conflicts with a federal law or a treaty. Although judicial review may be exercised by lower as well as higher courts, the final decision in a Type A-2 case will usually be made by a state supreme court, and in Type A-1 and Type B cases (which involve rights claimed under the federal Constitution), by the United States Supreme Court.

But aside from these basic categories, there are other important variations in the meaning of the term "judicial review." Debate on the intent of the framers has too often been beside the point; for it seems clear that most of them, whether approving or not, did expect the Supreme Court to exercise, in some degree, the power of reviewing federal and state legislation with an eye to its constitutionality.

The main problem associated with judicial review is not the question
of its legitimacy but rather the need to determine its scope and
force.[22]

By way of illustration, one may begin with *Hayburn's Case*
(1792), in which a number of federal judges refused to perform duties
assigned to them by act of Congress, insisting that those duties were
not judicial in nature. Here, then, was judicial review in its narrowest
sense, used as a means of self-defense, with the rights at stake being
those of the judiciary itself.[23] Next, in a hypothetical case, let us
imagine an act of Congress (or a state legislature) increasing the penalties for a certain crime and making the change retroactive. Such a
law would directly affect the administration of justice, and it would be
a clear violation of the *ex post facto* clause, one of those negative
provisions of the Constitution that are enforceable directly and perhaps solely in the courts. Thus a decision holding the law unconstitutional and void would likewise represent a relatively limited assertion
of judicial power. Finally, and in contrast, let us consider the central
issue of *McCulloch v. Maryland*, decided by the Marshall Court in
1819—namely, whether Congress had acted within its constitutional
authority in chartering the Second Bank of the United States. Here,
the judiciary was not defending itself against encroachment; the statute in question did not involve the administration of justice; there was
no indisputably clear conflict between the law and the Constitution;
and the relevant constitutional clauses were of the positive or power-
conferring kind, not requiring judicial implementation. Furthermore,
the theoretical problem at the heart of the matter—whether the
power to establish a bank could be inferred from some other, specifically delegated power by way of the necessary-and-proper clause—
was as much a political question as a legal one; and it is not clear to
this day that the answering of it belonged any more rightfully to the
Supreme Court than to Congress.

Thus the Marshall Court in its *McCulloch* decision exercised
judicial review of a much more expansive kind than that ventured in
the *Hayburn* case. And the fact that it *upheld* the constitutionality of
the bank law does not cancel the fact of review itself but instead illustrates the important point that judicial review has been a legitimating

as well as a curbing influence in American political development.[24] In other words, the full significance of judicial review cannot be calculated solely from the sum total of those court decisions invalidating legislation. And neither, it should be added, can the dimensions of judicial power be measured exclusively in terms of judicial review. In the process of statutory construction, judges shape much of the law into its final form. Without any question of constitutionality arising, a court may divert legislation far from its original intent and even render it virtually inoperative.

The frequency and scope of judicial review have depended largely upon the will of the judiciary itself—that is, upon the extent to which, through the years, it chose to embrace activism or self-restraint. But the force or effect of judicial review has always depended in addition upon how much acceptance it might win and how much resistance it might encounter within the judicial system, from other departments of government, and among the people at large.[25] Acceptance, from the beginning, implied much more than mere compliance with the judgment rendered, and it was this outward reach of judicial review that provoked strong resistance. The critical question was whether interpretation of the Constitution is pre-eminently a judicial function, in which the word of the Supreme Court is final (barring constitutional amendment) and binding on all other public officials in the country. Thus it was a question, and nothing less, of who possessed the ultimate power to determine the fundamental structure of the Republic. For, in the words of an Anglican bishop spoken seventy years before the framing of the Constitution: "Whoever hath an absolute authority to interpret written or spoken laws; it is he who is truly the lawgiver to all intents and purposes and not the person who wrote or spoke them."[26]

III

The Supreme Court, during its first decade of existence, heard no more than a handful of cases each year, and few of those were in any way historically significant. The justices worked hardest in their circuit court duties, an increasingly arduous service from which members of the Supreme Court did not escape until late in the nineteenth century. Both of the first two chief justices, John Jay and Oliver Ellsworth, went off to Europe on diplomatic missions while continuing to hold their judicial posts. Jay, during his six-year tenure, also sought the governorship of New York on two occasions and resigned from the Court when his second effort proved successful. All of this tended to bear out Hamilton's prediction that the federal judiciary would be "beyond comparison the weakest of the three departments of power," having at its disposal "neither force nor will but merely judgment." Yet Alexis de Tocqueville in the 1830s concluded that the Supreme Court was "placed higher than any other known tribunal." No nation in history, he said, had "ever constituted so great a judicial power as the Americans."[27]

What the early Court needed most of all was a clearer vision of its essential role in the constitutional system and a firmer hold on its bases of power. That proved to require the seasoning of time, as well as the genius of John Marshall. For one thing, it took time to achieve a sufficient measure of aloofness from current party politics, and the appointment of Marshall, an intense partisan, did not make the matter any easier. The problem down until 1801 was that the members of the Court were too cozily a part of the Federalist regime and too willingly agents of Federalist policy. The election of Jefferson freed the Court from a suffocating relationship with Federalism but placed it squarely in the path of Jeffersonian hostility. Judicial independence, which had been yielding to seduction, now seemed more in danger of outright destruction; for the threat of impeachment and other reprisals hung heavy in the air. Yet it was during those years of peril that Marshall, with his most famous constitutional pronouncement, laid out the classic rationale for judicial review in general and for Type A-1 judicial review in particular. His argument came down to the twofold assertion that the Constitution, being law, must be interpreted by the judiciary, and, being supreme law, must prevail over statute whenever the two were in conflict.

The bold words of *Marbury v. Madison* were strictly declaratory, however. In practical terms, the decision settled no important point of law. It was essentially a brilliant political maneuver, combining ingenuity and prudence in such a way as to rebuke the executive power while avoiding a direct confrontation with it.* To put the matter as briefly as possible, Marshall held that the Jefferson administration was in violation of law and subject to correction by court order, *but* that the Supreme Court itself could not issue a writ of mandamus as requested, even though authorized to do so by the Judiciary Act of 1789, because that authorization was an unconstitutional expansion of the Court's original jurisdiction and therefore null and void.[29] Thus *Marbury v. Madison,* while setting forth the doctrine of judicial review in comprehensive terms, was itself an exercise of the narrowest kind of judicial review (like *Hayburn's Case*) in which the judiciary interpreted that part of the Constitution applying directly to its own duties.

Furthermore, the court over which Marshall presided for another thirty-two years never again expressly invalidated even so small a part of an act of Congress, although upon occasion it did take a question of constitutionality under review.† The *Marbury* doctrine remained prominently on the record, well respected but more or less dormant. The Marshall Court, after all, was generally disposed to foster the expansion of national power, rather than to curb it. But there were additional reasons for the quiescence of Type A-1 judicial review. One of them was that early presidents used the veto power primarily as a constitutional check, thereby reducing the need for judicial review. Also, the energies of the young republic were heavily concentrated until 1815 in the area of foreign relations, where federal power was less susceptible to challenge. Even Jefferson's strict-constructionism usually stopped at the water's edge. In domestic affairs, at the same time, the federal government confined itself to a very limited range of activities, leaving most of the regulation of society to the states. Congress tended to be constitutionally conservative; only

---

*A far better target for the Court, if it had wanted to challenge Jeffersonian power, would have been the Judiciary Act of 1802, which the justices bitterly disliked because it returned them to circuit duty. Yet, in *Stuart v. Laird,* decided just six days after the *Marbury* case, the Court discreetly upheld the constitutionality of the act.[28]

†*Hodgson v. Bowerbank*, 5 Cranch 303 (1809), may by inference be classified as a case of judicial review of federal law, but the wording of the official report is obscure.

rarely did it enact laws that might be open to challenge in court. Here, as in the case of colonial assemblies, the relative lack of legislative activism reduced the pressure for judicial review.

Despite the fame of *Marbury v. Madison*, the main contributions of the Marshall Court to American constitutional development were associated, not with constitutionalism at the national level, but rather with the federal-state relationship. Most fundamental was the Court's successful exercise of its authority to review state court decisions, as provided in Section 25 of the Judiciary Act of 1789. By repeatedly upholding and enforcing that authority against vigorous state opposition (most notably in *Cohens v. Virginia*), it confirmed the principle and the pyramidal structure of judicial nationalism.[30]

Meanwhile, the Court had also been asserting its power to invalidate state legislation. In *Ware v. Hylton* (1796), even the pre-Marshall Court had struck down a Virginia statute on the ground that it violated the treaty of peace with Britain. But it was *Fletcher v. Peck* (1810) that best exemplified Type B judicial review. With Marshall as its spokesman, the Supreme Court for the first time declared a state law to be in conflict with the federal Constitution. *Fletcher v. Peck* is thus the state-level equivalent of *Marbury v. Madison*, and the contrasts between them are highly significant. *Marbury* involved the right of one man to his commission as justice of the peace, and it resulted in the invalidation of one minor section of a federal statute. *Fletcher* intervened in the notorious Yazoo land fraud case originating in the wholesale corruption of the Georgia legislature, and it accordingly affected the financial claims of a large number of people. The decision invalidated a state law rescinding the corrupt land grants in question, and it did so by expanding the contract clause of the Constitution, beyond the intent of the framers, to include public grants as well as private contracts. In short, *Marbury* was a gesture that the future would invest with much greater relevance and force; *Fletcher* was a real exercise of judicial power having immediate and extensive impact.[31]

Fletcher v. Peck proved to be a typical Marshall case; for most of the Court's other leading decisions during his tenure involved judicial review of state laws. The list includes *McCulloch v. Maryland, Dart-*

mouth College v. Woodward, Gibbons v. Ogden, Sturges v. Crown-inshield, and *Craig v. Missouri.* We are speaking here of the triumph of judicial nationalism—that is, the Court's effective assertion of the power to review decisions rendered by state courts and to review laws passed by state legislatures. While the right of review was consistently maintained, the substance of review did not always run against state authority. Sometimes the Marshall Court upheld the constitutionality of state legislation. But the general tendency of its principal state-federal decisions, as everyone knows, was to expand the range of national power while restricting the power of the states. Marshall himself was not only a judicial nationalist but also a political nationalist in the manner of Hamilton, Webster, and Clay. These two kinds of nationalism were not necessarily inseparable, however, and they have sometimes been confused in discussions of the Supreme Court. Judicial nationalism was in fact an independent force that could be brought to bear in support of particularism or sectionalism.

Among the decisions of the Marshall Court on state-federal relations, one can readily identify some that were essentially distributional and others of the interventional kind. In *Gibbons v. Ogden, Osborn v. Bank of the United States,* and most strikingly in *Brown v. Maryland,* the Court was concerned with establishing the boundary between state and federal legislative authority.[32] But in cases such as *Fletcher v. Peck, Dartmouth College v. Woodward,* and *Green v. Biddle,* no delegated powers of Congress were involved.* Instead, the Court set the Constitution itself, like a protective screen, between state legislative power and the people affected by that power. The constitutional issue in most of these interventional decisions was whether state law violated the contract clause. In its broad application of the clause for the protection of vested property rights, the Marshall Court most clearly revealed the social conservatism that reinforced and perhaps in some degree inspired its political nationalism.[34]

A high percentage of the great Marshall decisions were concen-

---

*There were a few cases that involved both distributional and interventional federalism. *Sturges v. Crowninshield,* for instance, was a contract clause case, but it also raised the question of the dividing line between federal and state authority in regard to bankruptcy legislation.[33]

trated in the period from 1819 to 1824. Those were the Court's years of maximum cohesion and power, when its nationalism briefly suited the national mood.* Soon, the political environment became more hostile, and new appointments eroded the internal unity that Marshall had so carefully nourished. The Court, during his last years as chief justice, spoke with less authority and gave ground before the dynamic forces of Jacksonianism and particularism. Most notably, it adopted a more permissive attitude toward state legislative power. Thus the transition from the Marshall Court to the Taney Court was begun before Marshall's death.[35]

But the Supreme Court, in making such adjustments and strategic withdrawals as prudence might seem to advise, did not relinquish any part of its essential right to decide constitutional issues coming before it. In fact, the prestige and power of the Court were often fortified during relatively quiet intervals when it aroused little controversy; for then the justices best fitted their Olympian public image as "keepers of the covenant, and therefore touched with its divinity."[36] The Court's bases of power were secure when Marshall died. Over the years it had made many enemies and sustained much bitter attack, but none of the various efforts to curb its authority ever came close to succeeding. In 1830, for instance, the House of Representatives considered a bill to repeal Section 25 of the Judiciary Act of 1789 and defeated it by a vote of 138 to 51.[37] And significantly, President Andrew Jackson, whose hostility to Marshall and defiance of the Court are among the authentic elements in the Jacksonian legend, gave no support to this measure or to any other aimed at weakening the institutional structure of the federal judiciary.[38]

IV

Roger B. Taney was already fifty-nine years old when sworn in as chief justice in March 1836, and because of chronic ill health it seemed unlikely that he would enjoy a long tenure. "His constitution," said a colleague in 1844, "is exceedingly feeble and broken."

*From 1812 to 1823, the Court's membership remained unchanged—the longest such period in American history.

For another twenty years close friends and casual acquaintances went on describing Taney's physical condition in such terms. President after president took office with the expectation that before the end of his term he would probably have the naming of a new chief justice.[39] Taney's ailments were real enough, but he fussed about them excessively and wore an air of persistent invalidism that grew more pronounced with advancing age. Six feet tall, flat-chested and stooped, with homely features and irregular, tobacco-stained teeth, he was an unimpressive figure until he began to speak. Then, without oratory or gesture, he held his audience by the force of his reasoning and conviction. According to a contemporary, he spoke with "so much sincerity . . . that it was next to impossible to believe he could be wrong." Taney himself had the same difficulty. A leader of the Maryland bar is said to have complained of his "infernal apostolic manner," and as chief justice there were times when he reminded men of the Pope, speaking "ex cathedra, infallibly."[40]

Taney was provincial in his outlook and experience, never having traveled very far beyond the narrow boundaries of Maryland. One of the friends of his youth was Francis Scott Key, whose sister he married in 1806, more than eight years before the writing of "The Star-Spangled Banner." Taney was a Roman Catholic who bitterly resented the nativism that came to flourish in his home state. He was also one of that curious breed, a former Federalist turned Jacksonian Democrat. From the Whig point of view, he reeked of partisanship, having served as Jackson's hatchet man in the Bank war. "The pure ermine of the Supreme Court is sullied by the appointment of that political hack, Roger B. Taney," said a New York newspaper.[41] Yet Taney on the bench quickly demonstrated judicial capacities of a high order. Eventually, it is said, even his old political adversary Henry Clay acknowledged his fitness to succeed John Marshall.[42]

Taney, like Marshall a soft-spoken man of urbane manners and simple tastes, presided gently but firmly over the Court, and his judicial opinions, written in a plain, dry style, were much praised for their lucidity and pointedness. At the same time, Taney displayed little of his predecessor's remarkable talent for achieving consensus. Marshall, after much effort, had succeeded in replacing the custom of *seriatim* opinions with a system in which he, or another justice appointed for the task, delivered the "opinion of the Court." Often it was the *only* opinion presented. Dissent sometimes occurred, but it was much less frequent than in later periods of the Court's history. The semblance of internal unity undoubtedly contributed to the growth of judicial power.* It was usually achieved by discussion, concession, and compromise, in which Marshall himself, like a good committee chairman, set an example of flexibility. The system began to disintegrate in Marshall's last years, however. Its constraint did not suit the temper of Jacksonian individualism, and Taney, a less flexible man than Marshall, probably could not have restored it even if he had been disposed to try. Multiple opinions accordingly became more and more common, especially in cases of major importance. Dissent caused little confusion, but multiple concurring opinions often made it difficult to determine what part of the designated opinion of the Court had enough support from other justices to be considered *ratio decidendi*, binding as precedent in lower courts.†

Scholarly debate about the Taney Court has often centered upon the question of how sharply it changed the course of American constitutional development from the direction set by the Marshall Court. Three decisions rendered in 1837 seemed to signal a "judicial revolution" overturning the structure of nationalism and economic conservatism that Marshall had engineered.

In *Charles River Bridge v. Warren Bridge*, with Taney himself delivering the official opinion, the Court narrowed the protection given corporate charters by the *Dartmouth College* decision. In *New York v. Miln*, the Court ruled that a New York law impinging on foreign commerce was a valid exercise of the state's "police power." And *Briscoe v. the Bank of Kentucky* upholding the issuance of state bank notes, though technically distinguishable, was in practical terms a direct reversal of *Craig v. Missouri*.[44] In each instance, the Court upheld the constitutionality of a state law, and each time it seemed to do so in contravention of one of the major Marshall decisions.[45] Jus-

---

*Jefferson thought that Marshall's "habit of caucusing opinions" had strengthened his hand and proposed that Congress require a return to the *seriatim* system.[43]

†This was a major problem in *Prigg v. Pennsylvania*, as we have seen above, p. 45.

tice Story, now a lonely dissenter, saw the old constitutional order crumbling under revolutionary assault and viewed the future of his country with deepening despair.[46]

But the fears of Story and other Whigs soon proved to have been exaggerated, and in the perspective of history the supposed "revolution of 1837," like Jefferson's "revolution of 1800," became something less definitive and more complex, in which change of considerable significance took place within an elemental flow of continuity. Furthermore, the change that did occur under Taney's leadership was only partly a doctrinal repudiation of the Marshall synthesis and partly also a judicial response to accelerating social change. One ineluctable reality of the Jacksonian era was the expansion of business enterprise; another was the rising public expectation of economic intervention and social control on the part of government, especially state government. These were by no means incompatible tendencies. The Taney Court in the *Charles River Bridge* case did not simply rule in favor of state power and against corporate rights. The decision in fact upheld the claims of one corporation against those of another, and besides, state power was far from being inherently hostile to corporate enterprise. Corporations, after all, were artificial entities created and nurtured by state law; and state economic legislation was as often promotional as it was regulatory in purpose.[47] The implicative effect of the *Charles River Bridge* decision was to allow state governments somewhat more latitude in adjusting the law to new economic realities. In certain later decisions, the Taney Court significantly improved the legal status of corporations—for example, by recognizing them as citizens to the extent of being able to bring suit in federal courts.[48]

During the Taney period, constitutional issues coming before the Supreme Court continued to be predominantly matters of state-federal relations, involving judicial review of state legislation rather than acts of Congress. In its distributional decisions (including a series of important commerce cases beginning with *New York v. Miln*), the Court steered a middle course, often upholding the state law in question but sometimes striking one down because of its intrusion on federal authority.[49] In its interventional decisions, the prime example of

Charles River Bridge should not be allowed to obscure the fact that
the Taney Court on a number of other occasions proved willing to invalidate state laws as violations of the contract clause. Nevertheless,
the general trend was toward less judicial restraint on state legislative
authority than the Marshall Court had been disposed to apply.[50]

This does not mean, to be sure, that the Taney Court was willing
to relinquish the power of review or any part of it, even though the
Jacksonian bias ran strongly against judicial supremacy. On the contrary, this is where the lines of continuity with the Marshall era
become most plainly visible—in the unflagging determination to exalt
federal judicial power and consolidate the role of the Supreme Court
as final arbiter of constitutional issues. Indeed, it may be said that in
certain decisions expanding its own jurisdiction, the Taney Court
displayed a more avid judicial imperialism than its predecessor.[51]
Whenever historians present evidence to show that Taney was something of a "nationalist," much of it turns out to be evidence of his
judicial nationalism, an outlook scarcely uncommon among Supreme
Court justices at any time.[52]

The Taney Court, then, without renouncing any of its power of
review, tended to use the power sparingly where the constitutionality
of state legislation was at stake. Here one recognizes in operation the
principle of "judicial self-restraint," which, it has been said, was
Taney's "great contribution to the law and custom of the Constitution."[53] But "judicial self-restraint" is a phrase of multiple meaning,
and in Taney's case it is associated less with a disposition to presume
constitutionality than with the doctrine of "political questions." That
doctrine, although commonly regarded as Taney's invention in *Luther
v. Borden* (1849), had been foreshadowed in a number of Marshall
and earlier Taney opinions. "The powers given to the courts of the
United States by the Constitution," said Taney in 1838, "are judicial
powers and extend to those subjects only which are judicial in their
character; and not to those which are political."[54] Accordingly, some
kinds of conflict, being essentially political in nature, were beyond
the capacity of the judiciary to resolve and must be dealt with by the
legislative branch of government. "The overriding consideration,"
says Bernard Schwartz, "was to steer clear of political involvement."

Most of the time, he tells us, Taney managed to carry the Court with him in the exercise of such prudence, but there came a day when the "rule of abnegation" gave way to stronger influences. "The *Dred Scott* case was the one occasion when Taney yielded to the temptation, always disastrous, to save the country, and put aside the judicial self-restraint which was one of his chief contributions to our constitutional law."[55]

Thus the conception of Taney as a major prophet and successful practitioner of judicial self-restraint leads easily to the view that the Dred Scott decision was an unfortunate aberration, a false step out of character and into the "political thicket." The purpose, it is often added, was above reproach; for Taney and his Court committed their "blunder in statecraft" with the high hope that it would "allay the conflict between North and South."

> He endeavored to settle by judicial decision what debate in Congress and on the hustings could not settle but only disturb. He tried to avert the revolutionary disruption of a social and economic system. He was playing for high stakes, he played his trump card to maintain the old constitutional arrangements and prevent disunion—and he failed.[56]

Presumably, then, the course of judicial wisdom would have been to treat the issue of slavery in the territories as though it were a "political question" and avoid rendering a decision on it.* This would have been somewhat like returning the ball to the server's court; for political leaders in the majority party, it will be remembered, had been busy converting the same issue into a "judicial question." But in any case, the "aberration" theory is more catchword than explanation, and it does not bear up well under the pressure of facts.

For one thing, there is little evidence that the decisions of the Taney Court were actually governed in any significant or systematic way by the principle of judicial self-restraint. As a precept formally

---

*Owing to certain technical features of the Dred Scott case, Taney and his fellow justices, if they had so wished, could have avoided the territorial issue without formally invoking the doctrine of political questions or the principle of self-restraint in any other guise.

invoked, restraint was often mere rationalization; as a pattern of judicial behavior, it was the consequence of other influences, not the prime motivational force itself. The three major decisions of 1837, all upholding the constitutionality of state laws, may be said to exemplify judicial self-restraint, but they reflected the Court's attitude toward banking, corporations, and states' rights, not a philosophy of judicial power.

The semblance of restraint also emanated in some degree from the Court's political affinity with the dominant political party. For Taney, unlike Marshall, government was more often than not in the hands of political friends. This was especially true of the national government, which the Whigs seldom controlled. And during the period of Democratic ascendancy, from 1829 to 1861, the national government continued to operate within a very narrow functional range, offering little challenge to the principle of constitutionalism. Thus the fact that the Taney Court waited twenty years before declaring an act of Congress unconstitutional must be attributed to lack of provocation rather than to judicial self-restraint. (The Chief Justice would reveal the extent to which he was, at heart, a judicial activist when control of the federal government passed into hostile Republican hands in 1861.) But if coordinate judicial review, applying the principle of constitutionalism, was unneeded at the national level, it flourished at the state level throughout the Taney period and had long since won general public acceptance.[57] And what the state courts were doing almost as a matter of routine, the Supreme Court would certainly not hesitate to do when the appropriate occasion arose.

Furthermore, when the Court invoked the doctrine of political questions or otherwise embraced the principle of self-restraint, it did not do so to avoid critical public issues or to "steer clear of political involvement." The cases, by and large, were legally peculiar rather than politically sensitive. They often seemed strange beyond all precedent, or unmanageable by judicial means, or likely to involve the Court in a demeaning confrontation.[58] *Luther v. Borden*, to be sure, was an outgrowth of an important political event, the Dorr War in Rhode Island, but the struggle had ended and lost much of its controversial edge long before the Court decided the case in 1849.

Taney's opinion, moreover, was scarcely a model of judicial self-restraint. Stating the political-question doctrine in its most memorable form, he held that the Court lacked authority to dispose of the substantive issues in the case; yet at the same time he discussed those issues in such a way as to come down emphatically on the side of the victorious anti-Dorr faction in Rhode Island.[59] *Luther v. Borden* thus illustrates the point that a judicial refusal to rule may be no less political in its purpose and impact than a vigorous exercise of jurisdiction. What the doctrine of "political questions" really signified was not that issues with strong political implications were to be evaded by treating them as non-justiciable but rather something nearer the reverse—that certain anomalous, thorny, and perhaps ultimately non-justiciable issues could be conveniently set aside by labeling them political.

A constitution is as much a political as a legal document, and every constitutional decision is therefore to some extent a political act. At the same time, members of the Taney Court were predominantly politicians, appointed for political reasons in an intensely political age, and their partisanship, though it might be muted, was never entirely smothered by the proprieties of judicial office. Justices for the most part no longer participated as openly and actively in politics as they had during the Federalist period, but the Taney Court was nevertheless decidedly a Democratic court. Of the fourteen members appointed from 1829 to 1861, only Benjamin R. Curtis of Massachusetts was a Whig (though one of the Democrats, John McLean of Ohio, had turned Republican by 1857).

Taney himself, it is true, scrupulously avoided any appearance of involvement in politics. He never endorsed political candidates, for instance, and unlike John Marshall he never engaged in newspaper controversy. In this respect he stands as a contrast to McLean, whose political maneuvers and hankering for the presidency became something of an embarrassment to the Court.[60] Yet Taney was no less political-minded than McLean and no more disposed to hold his tongue on subjects that mattered, if he could somehow speak within the bounds of his judicial duties. In one extraordinary display of partisanship bursting through restraint, he disqualified himself from a case involving the Bank of the United States but then wrote a long commentary, amounting to a dissenting opinion, and had it printed as an "appendix" to the official report.[61]

Where slavery was concerned, Taney certainly gave every indication of being an intense partisan, rather than a prophet of judicial self-restraint.* In *Prigg v. Pennsylvania* and *Groves v. Slaughter*, he took positions extremely defensive of slavery, and in *Strader v. Graham* he added a proslavery dictum to a ruling that the Court lacked jurisdiction.[62] His colleague Peter V. Daniel of Virginia was a brooding proslavery fanatic, and the other southern justices in 1857—James M. Wayne of Georgia, John Catron of Tennessee, and John A. Campbell of Alabama—were all unreserved defenders of slavery and slaveholding rights in the territories. Among the four northern justices, no one expected self-restraint from McLean on slavery or any other issue, and Curtis, though conservative in temperament and politics, was nevertheless accustomed to speaking his mind. Judicial self-restraint on slavery questions probably appealed most strongly to Samuel Nelson of New York and Robert C. Grier of Pennsylvania, because as northern Democrats they were subject to the usual cross-pressures of party and section. In their general outlook, however, both men fitted the "doughface" pattern, and some unpleasant experiences on circuit duty resulting from abolitionist resistance to the Fugitive Slave Law no doubt reinforced the natural tendencies of both to be, if not proslavery, at least grimly anti-antislavery.[63]

The Taney Court, like all courts, sometimes avoided deciding an issue laid before it, but this was the rare exception rather than the rule and unlikely to occur with respect to issues of great popular concern about which the justices themselves had formed strong opinions. In dealing with slavery, Taney and his colleagues showed a consistent disposition to meet the issue head-on and settle it conclusively.[64] Any failure to do so resulted from the diversity and vehemence of their views, and not from any sense of restraint. The Dred Scott decision therefore represented no "aberration"—no sharp break with a Taney Court tradition of judicial self-restraint—because that tradition is itself largely illusive.

*For discussion of the curious myth that Taney was privately an opponent of slavery, see below, p. 560n.

The Dred Scott case, when it came before the Supreme Court, presented three issues that had been much debated in courtrooms, legislative halls, political meetings, and newspapers throughout the country: (1) Negro citizenship; (2) the status of slaves who had been held on free soil; and (3) the constitutionality of federal legislation prohibiting slavery in the territories. Because of certain technical complications, the Court had an unusual number of choices. It could dispose of the case by deciding the first issue alone, the second alone, the first and second together, the second and third together, or all three together. Taney, as the Court's official spokesman, chose to decide all three. But when people talk about the great "blunder in statecraft" or the "self-inflicted wound," they appear to mean specifically that Taney should have avoided deciding the *third* issue, and the Court, as we shall see, came close to doing just that by settling for a decision limited to the second and least controversial of the three issues.

To have followed such a strategy of "self-restraint," however, would have been rather like deciding *McCulloch v. Maryland* without considering the constitutionality of the Bank of the United States. It would have been inconsistent with the tradition of judicial power and with the Court's assigned role as final arbiter of constitutional questions. It would have been, in the circumstances and in short, an aberration.

II

A DECADE OF LITIGATION

❧ 9 ❧

Dred Scott and His Travels

Gateway to the trans-Mississippi West, St. Louis in 1830 was a flourishing river port that attracted many Americans on the move. Among the newcomers that year were Peter Blow and his wife Elizabeth, together with their three daughters, four sons, and six slaves. One of the sons would eventually become a member of Congress, but one of the slaves is far better remembered.

In coming to St. Louis, Blow had joined the urban movement as well as the westward movement. Once the owner of many acres in his native Virginia and more recently an Alabama planter, he was ready, at the age of fifty-three, to try something other than farming. Accordingly, he set himself up as proprietor of a boarding house called the Jefferson Hotel. Patrons were readily available in a town with many single men and transients, but accumulating unpaid bills indicate that the venture proved less than successful. Elizabeth Blow soon fell victim to a lingering disease and died in the summer of 1831. Early the next year, Peter Blow gave up hotel-keeping and moved his family into another house. His own health failed in the months that followed, and he died on June 23, 1832.[1]

In the records of the 1830 census, Blow appears as the owner of five male slaves and one female slave. Evidently, he sold one of the five before he died, for the inventory of his estate lists only four males and one female. After his death, and probably during the year 1833, a second slave, named Sam, was sold for $500 to meet creditors' claims against the estate. None of the other four Blow slaves were sold at this time. Meanwhile, Dr. John Emerson of St. Louis had been trying to obtain an appointment as assistant surgeon in the United States Army. In December 1833, Emerson received his commission and reported for duty at Fort Armstrong in Illinois. He took with him a Negro slave who had previously been the property of Peter Blow and who is known in history as Dred Scott. But which of the two slaves had Emerson purchased—the one that Blow himself apparently sold, or the one sold after Blow's death? Was Dred Scott always so named, or did he live more than half of his life as Sam and then somehow acquire a new name after entering Emerson's service? Historians are divided on the subject, and so is the evidence. Neither side has been able to prove its case beyond doubt. But the only facts that matter are indisputable: John Emerson bought one of Peter Blow's slaves, and that slave was the plaintiff in *Dred Scott v. Sandford*.[2]

Whatever name he originally wore, Dred Scott had apparently been with the Blows since his childhood or early youth. Probably born in Virginia around the beginning of the century, he had a very dark skin and may have been no more than five feet tall. He could neither read nor write and on legal documents made his "mark" in lieu of a signature. He has also been called shiftless, but this characterization seems to be derived from reminiscence of dubious reliability. In contrast, a onetime governor of Missouri is quoted as recalling that "Scott was a very much respected Negro." A St. Louis newspaper article, published in 1857 and evidently based on a personal interview, described the by then famous slave as "illiterate but not ignorant," with a "strong common sense" that had been sharpened by his many travels. Such contemporary traces of the man Dred Scott are so scarce, however, that he remains a very indistinct figure. Little if anything can be said with authority about his personality, his quality as a worker, or his relations with various owners and employers. One would especially like to know how much of the initiative was Dred's own in the eleven-year legal contest that began in 1846. He has usually been regarded as more of a pawn than a player, but there are hints of a stronger spirit, determined to be free.[3]

Certainly the most curious feature of Dred Scott's personal history is his close association with the Blows long after he ceased to be in their service. Either the first or second slave to be sold when troubles struck the Blow household in the years from 1831 to 1833, he scarcely appears to have been a family favorite. Yet the Blows and their in-laws were his principal supporters throughout the series of court actions from 1846 to 1857. The contrast may simply reflect differences within the family. Dred was sold to Emerson either by Peter Blow or (as Sam) by Blow's oldest daughter, Elizabeth. Perhaps the sale distressed some of the younger children and especially the third son, Taylor. To a boy suddenly orphaned at the age of twelve, it may have meant the loss of a good friend at a bad time. At any rate, it was Taylor Blow who later became Dred Scott's most loyal sponsor in the long fight for freedom.[4]

One version of Scott's relationship with the Blows has won more acceptance than it deserves. By 1846, so the story goes, Dred had been virtually abandoned by his owner and was living, together with his wife and child, on the charity of the Blow family. The latter therefore underwrote his lawsuit in order to free themselves from the burden of supporting slaves that belonged to someone else. This cynical explanation does not square with the facts, however. Its chronology is defective, and its logic outruns common sense. Dred was not subsisting on handouts from the Blows when his suit for freedom got under way in 1846.[5] Perhaps at a later time he did become dependent on their generosity, but there was little reason for the Blows to expect that such dependence would cease if Dred were freed. On the contrary, by supporting his legal efforts to escape from slavery, they were accepting added responsibility for his welfare. The record is clear that Taylor Blow continued to be Dred Scott's benefactor after the slave was finally manumitted and until the day of his death.[6] Moreover, it was Taylor Blow who in 1867 had Scott's body removed from an abandoned cemetery to another resting place.[7] No strong antislavery commitment inspired this loyalty; for Blow's sympathies during the Civil War were with the South. His benevolence seems to have sprung wholly from a personal affection extending back to his boyhood, and this may reveal something of Dred Scott's character as well as Taylor Blow's.

It is uncertain how Dred felt about being sold to Dr. Emerson.

According to one story, he was so unhappy that he ran away and hid for a time in a swamp near St. Louis; but according to another, he begged Emerson to buy him after having been badly whipped by Peter Blow.[8] Nor can much be said about the slave's life with his new master in the years that followed. The details of their relationship are almost entirely lacking, and it is not even known whether they liked or disliked each other. What proved to be important, however, was where they traveled together, and of that there is some record.

John Emerson is just a name sometimes mentioned in history books, and he never knew that his undistinguished career would carry him to even that modicum of fame. But from the scant data available something of the man himself emerges. His best talent, it appears, was largely wasted, while his principal eccentricity gave him a tragicomic 'quality. One suspects that in some ways he may have been a rascal, but there is not enough evidence to prove it. Emerson obviously possessed a rare ability to make friends and put them to use. Temperamentally, he was perhaps better suited for politics than for medicine, and at a later time he might have found more opportunity to capitalize on his skill as a lobbyist. Instead, he spent some nine years of his short life as an assistant surgeon in the United States Army. During that period, if Emerson's own words are taken at face value, he must have been one of the sickest doctors ever kept on active military duty. There was always method in his illness, however; for he seldom wrote to the Surgeon General without requesting a transfer or a leave of absence. The number and variety of his self-diagnosed ailments would be hilarious if it were not for his early death at about forty years of age.

Emerson was probably a native of Pennsylvania and about as old as Dred Scott, having been born either in 1802 or in 1803. He studied medicine for two years at the University of Pennsylvania and received his degree in 1824.[9] Of his early practice little is known, although he apparently lived for a time somewhere in the South. By 1831, he had settled in St. Louis. When the regular medical officer at nearby Jefferson Barracks became ill in the fall of 1832, Emerson was hired as his temporary replacement at $100 per month, the quartermaster's office certifying that "no competent physician could be ob-

tained . . . at a lower rate."[10] The arrangement proved highly satisfactory on both sides. General Henry Atkinson and many of the
troops had just returned to the comforts of a permanent army post
after fighting in the Black Hawk War, and they were no doubt in an
appreciative mood. Emerson, for his part, found military life and regular pay so congenial that he decided to apply for a commission.

Not many medical officers were needed, however, in an American army that numbered only about six thousand men. Clearly, it
would take something more than a mere application to obtain an appointment, and Emerson accordingly marshaled some influential support. Thirteen members of the Missouri legislature signed a letter
recommending him. So did most of the officers at Jefferson Barracks,
including General Atkinson and Lieutenant Albert Sidney Johnston.
Senator Thomas Hart Benton wrote two notes in his behalf to the
secretary of war. The campaign lasted for a year or more before it
ended successfully and Assistant Surgeon Emerson set out with his
slave for Fort Armstrong.[11]

For Dred Scott, life as a personal servant at an army post was
probably not arduous, but his owner must have found this first assignment disillusioning. Situated in lightly settled country some two
hundred miles north of St. Louis, Fort Armstrong lacked the amenities of Jefferson Barracks. Within two months of his arrival, Emerson
asked for leave of absence, explaining that he desperately needed
treatment of a "syphiloid disease" contracted during a recent visit to
Philadelphia. This request he subsequently canceled when his condition improved, but in 1835 the War Department began to receive letters from varous persons urging that Emerson be transferred to the
arsenal in St. Louis. Swiftly apprised that such maneuvering was improper, he apologized for enlisting the aid of friends and reiterated
the request for transfer to St. Louis. He now suffered from a "slight
disease" in his left foot which prevented him from wearing a shoe and
might require surgery. Unsuccessful, he tried again in January 1836,
citing a quarrel with one of the company commanders as his reason
for wanting to leave Fort Armstrong.[12] His various afflictions did not
prevent Emerson from taking up land speculation on a modest scale.
He entered several small acreages close to the fort in Illinois and

bought a claim to an entire section directly across the Mississippi near what is now Davenport, Iowa. Such claims were extralegal arrangements among settlers on public land not yet open to entry, the purpose being to circumvent the federal auction system and enable claimants to acquire their tracts eventually at the minimum price of $1.25 an acre. In order to improve his claim, Emerson built a log cabin on it, with Dred probably doing much of the work.[13]

In 1836, when the Army decided to vacate Fort Armstrong, Emerson found himself transferred at last, but in the wrong direction. His new station was to be Fort Snelling, located on the west bank of the upper Mississippi River near the later site of St. Paul, Minnesota. Then a part of Wisconsin Territory and shifted to Iowa Territory in 1838, the region lay within the boundaries of the Louisiana Purchase. Thus Dred Scott, who had been held as a slave in a free state for more than two years, was now taken into an area where slavery was forbidden by the Missouri Compromise.

At Fort Snelling, with its garrison of one company, Scott soon met Harriet Robinson, a slave girl of perhaps half his age who belonged to the resident Indian agent, Major Lawrence Taliaferro. The Major either sold Harriet to Emerson or gave her to Dred for a wife, and, as local justice of the peace, he himself performed the ceremony uniting them. This marriage of Dred and Harriet Scott lasted until his death more than twenty years later. Of the four children apparently born to them, two sons died in infancy, but two daughters became parties in the suit for freedom.[14]

One winter at Fort Snelling was enough for Emerson. In the spring of 1837, he wrote to the Surgeon General complaining that the cold weather had crippled him with rheumatism and requesting transfer to St. Louis or six months' leave beginning the next autumn. This time the response from Washington was favorable. Ordered to Jefferson Barracks in October, the happy doctor hurried off on his trip down the Mississippi, traveling part of the way by canoe because of low water. He left his two slaves and many of his personal possessions behind him at Fort Snelling, expecting to send for them later. Bad news greeted him at Jefferson Barracks, however. Newer orders had been prepared directing him to report for duty at Fort Jesup in western Louisiana.[15]

Emerson reached Fort Jesup on November 22, 1837, and found it unsatisfactory. Two days later, he sent off a request for transfer back to Fort Snelling, which he now suddenly looked upon as just about the "best post" in the country. Several more importunate letters followed during the next month. The damp climate of Louisiana had revived an old liver disorder. Rheumatism was attacking his "muscles of respiration," and he could scarcely breathe. He did not have a moment free of pain. Yet, somehow, the wretched invalid managed to carry on a courtship and make his way to the altar on February 6, 1838.[16] His bride was Eliza Irene Sanford, twenty-three-year-old daughter of Alexander Sanford, a Virginia manufacturer who had moved to St. Louis. Miss Sanford, usually called Irene rather than Eliza, was described at the time of her death many years afterward as "a cultivated woman of unusual beauty." She had come to Fort Jesup for a visit with her sister, whose husband, Captain Henry Bainbridge, was stationed there.[17] Emerson, as a married man, now had more use for servants. Soon after the wedding, he apparently sent for Dred and Harriet Scott, who were still at Fort Snelling, hired out to one or more of its officers. That the two slaves did make the long journey to Louisiana seems fairly certain. They traveled in the spring of 1838 and no doubt by steamboat, but of how the trip was managed no details are known.[18]

Meanwhile, Emerson's honeymoon euphoria was wearing off, and he resumed his efforts to escape from Fort Jesup. After several letters to the Surgeon General rehearsing the effects of a baneful climate on his delicate health, he began to add other reasons for wanting a transfer northward. Writing on July 10, 1838, he explained that legal difficulties had arisen concerning his Iowa land claim. Then his next words seem to leap from the page: "Even one of my negroes in Saint Louis has sued me for his freedom."[19] No record of this suit has been found, and the Scotts were presumably still with Emerson at Fort Jesup. Yet, since the traces of their movements are exceedingly faint, it is not impossible that the slave in question was Dred, making an early and abortive attempt to secure his freedom.[20]

Again the Surgeon General proved accommodating, perhaps in the hope of reducing his correspondence. By September, Emerson was on his way back to Fort Snelling. Mrs. Emerson accompanied him, and so apparently did the Scotts, contrary to what most accounts say on the subject. That is, Dred was taken not just once but twice into territory supposedly closed to slavery by the Missouri Compromise. The travelers arrived at St. Louis on September 21, 1838, and three days later, Emerson wrote to the Surgeon General informing him that low water would slow the rest of their journey. He booked passage on the *Gypsy*, a small stern-wheeler of light draft that crept cautiously up the Mississippi, reaching Fort Snelling on October 21.

Another man who boarded the *Gypsy* at St. Louis was the Reverend Alfred Brunson, a Methodist missionary to the Indians. In his autobiography published many years later, Brunson recalled that the nine-hundred-mile trip to Fort Snelling took four weeks because of the low water and the supply-laden barge in tow behind the little steamboat. "Among the passengers," he added, "were Dr. Emerson and his wife, having with them their servants, Dred Scott and his family, who belonged to this lady. On the upward trip one of Dred's children, a girl, was born."[21] The Scotts gave their baby Mrs. Emerson's first name, Eliza. Her birth occurred when the *Gypsy* was north of the northern boundary of Missouri—that is, indisputably in free territory. This fact later added another complication to the Dred Scott case. In one respect, Brunson's statement contradicts the standard account; for most writers have assumed that Eliza was born on a *downstream* run of the *Gypsy*, but the available evidence tends to confirm the accuracy of the missionary's recollection.[22]

Immediately upon his arrival at Fort Snelling, Emerson got involved in a squabble with the medical officer whom he was replacing, the latter accusing him of using underhanded methods to obtain the transfer. A more spectacular quarrel the following year is not as well authenticated, but it may throw some light on the doctor's second departure from the fort. According to a story told many years afterward, Emerson asked the quartermaster to provide Dred with a stove and, upon being refused, became angry and abusive. The quartermaster, a small man, responded by striking Emerson, a large man, with enough force to bruise his nose and break his glasses. Emerson left the scene but soon returned brandishing two pistols. His adversary fled, and the post commander placed Emerson under arrest.

Whether as an outgrowth of this incident or not, Fort Snelling before long had a new medical officer. In the spring of 1840, orders arrived transferring Assistant Surgeon Emerson to Florida, where the Seminole War was still in progress.[23]

The Emersons and their slaves took passage on a steamboat to St. Louis in May or early June. Mrs. Emerson did not accompany her husband when he continued on to Florida. Instead, she settled down to await his return on her father's estate near the city. The Scotts remained behind with her and may have been employed by Sanford or hired out as servants. At this time, after an absence of nearly seven years, Dred probably renewed his connections with the Blow family, showing off his family and giving a full account of his army adventures.

Emerson's tour of duty in Florida lasted more than two years. He complained frequently of illness, adding remittent fever to his list of disorders. Before twelve months had passed, he began writing requests for transfer to St. Louis, Fort Snelling, or "any cold climate." Then, on August 18, 1842, Emerson dashed off an angry letter to the Surgeon General's office, protesting against a new assignment in Florida while two of his juniors were being sent to Washington for duty. Furthermore, he needed some free time for medical study in Philadelphia so that he could take the examination required for promotion. "I now most respectfully ask," he concluded, "for permission to attend the medical lectures this winter or a post to which my place on the Army Register entitles me." For his long-suffering superiors, this outburst must have been the last straw. Taking advantage of an order for reduction of medical staff, and ignoring seniority, they awarded him an honorable dismissal from the service. Five weeks after writing the letter, Dr. Emerson found himself suddenly returned to civilian life.[24]

Upon arriving home in St. Louis, Emerson was soon discouraged about the prospect of building up a private practice there. His best hope, it seemed, was to get back into the Army. So once again he mobilized friends and acquaintances for a campaign of letter-writing to the Secretary of War. In the spring of 1843, still awaiting an answer from Washington, Emerson moved to Davenport, a new town near his land claim in Iowa Territory. There he advertised his professional services, purchased two town lots, and started construction of a brick house. At this point, with his wife now expecting a child, Emerson's health began to fail in earnest. He survived for only a month after the birth of his daughter, Henrietta. On December 29, 1843, he signed a will prepared to his order and then died sometime during that same night. The recorded cause of death was consumption, but this may have been a polite cover for the late stages of syphilis.[25]

Emerson's will deserves close attention because of the confusion surrounding its later effect on the Dred Scott case. Except for one minor bequest, he left his entire estate to his wife "during the term of her natural life without impeachment of waste," and after that to his daughter, Henrietta. He directed his wife to educate their daughter and support her until she reached the age of twenty-one. He also authorized Irene Emerson to sell all or any part of his land and tenements and to use the proceeds for her own and Henrietta's maintenance.[26] From these provisions, it is obvious that Emerson, contrary to what some historians have written, did not simply leave his property "in trust" for his daughter. The will made Mrs. Emerson the holder of an estate for life, with Henrietta designated as remainderman. At law, a life estate does have some characteristics of trusteeship, but it is essentially a limited inheritance, and in this instance the heiress was vested with broad authority, including the right to invade the principal of the estate. It is therefore misleading, if not inaccurate, to describe Mrs. Emerson's legal status under her husband's will as that of a trustee.[27]

As executors of his will, Emerson named a friend in Davenport and his wife's brother, John F. A. Sanford of St. Louis. Sanford was a businessman of some prominence whose marriage to Emily Chouteau had linked him with one of the city's oldest families. By neglecting to meet certain legal requirements, he failed to qualify as executor in Iowa, but it is not clear that he was ever informed of the fact.[28] In Missouri, where the inventory of Emerson's estate listed only nineteen acres of land and some furniture, the administrator appointed by the court was Mrs. Emerson's father, Alexander Sanford. There is no evidence that John Sanford ever participated in the process of executing his brother-in-law's will. Although probate records do not give the date, settlement of the estate in Iowa was probably accomplished without unusual delay, since the provisions of the will were simple enough. But the elder Sanford dawdled over his responsibilities in Missouri and had not yet filed a final report when he died in 1848. No successor was appointed, and Mrs. Emerson assumed full control of her husband's property. This seems clear from the fact that she herself sold some of his land in both states. The estate, in short, had apparently been settled by 1850 and without any known formal assistance from John Sanford. Thus there would appear to be no legal connection between the provisions of Emerson's will and Sanford's later involvement in the Dred Scott case. Still, it is possible that he *thought* himself responsible, as executor, for supervision of the Emerson estate during his sister's lifetime.[29]

Emerson's slaves were not mentioned in the Missouri inventory of his estate, and the Iowa inventory, which may have listed them, has disappeared. It is unlikely that he took the Scotts with him to Davenport in the spring of 1843; for not only was slaveholding prohibited there, but, in addition, the Emersons had little need for servants, since they lived at a hotel while work proceeded on their new house. At this time, perhaps, or shortly after their owner's death, Dred and Harriet were apparently turned over on loan to Mrs. Emerson's brother-in-law, Captain Bainbridge, who was transferred to Jefferson Barracks from Florida in 1843. It appears that Dred may have been in Bainbridge's service continuously until 1846. If so, he accompanied the Captain to Fort Jesup in 1844 and then into Texas after its annexation the following year. Whether Harriet and Eliza were with him during this period is uncertain. Bainbridge was a graduate of West Point who later received two promotions for bravery in the Mexican War. Dred remembered him as a "good man." The slender evidence suggests that Bainbridge kept Dred with him at Corpus Christi until about February 1846 and sent him back home after General Zachary Taylor received orders to advance from the Nueces River to the Rio Grande. At any rate, Dred Scott was in St. Louis for sure by March, when Mrs. Emerson hired him and Harriet out to a Samuel Russell. A few weeks later, the Scotts took the first step in their suits for freedom.[30]

∽ 10 ∾

Versus Emerson

U pon returning from Texas, Dred Scott tried to buy his own and his family's freedom from Mrs. Emerson, but she refused. This, at least, is what he apparently told a newspaper reporter many years later. If true, the story leaves unanswered the question of why his mistress rejected the opportunity to get rid of an allegedly "shiftless" and by then middle-aged slave for whom she obviously had no personal use. Perhaps Mrs. Emerson doubted her legal right to sell the Scotts, although that seems unlikely in view of the broad authority that she had been given and was exercising under her husband's will. Perhaps the terms supposedly offered by Scott (partial payment with security for the remainder) were unsatisfactory; or, at the moment, it may just have seemed financially more advantageous to keep the slaves and hire them out.[1]

On April 6, 1846, Dred and Harriet Scott filed petitions in the Missouri circuit court at St. Louis, summarizing the circumstances of their residence on free soil and requesting permission to bring suit against Irene Emerson in order to establish their right to freedom. The judge promptly granted them leave to sue, and on the same day the Scotts filed declarations initiating actions of trespass for assault and false imprisonment. Dred's complaint—and Harriet's was similar—stated that on April 4, Mrs. Emerson had "beat, bruised and ill-treated him" and had then imprisoned him for twelve hours. The

declaration also averred that Dred was a "free person" held in slavery
by the defendant, and it claimed damages of ten dollars. Thus, during
the early stages of the legal battle, there were two suits against Mrs.
Emerson, proceeding in tandem through the Missouri courts.[2]

In these preliminaries, the attorney representing Dred and Harriet Scott followed a course carefully prescribed by statute. Missouri
slave law, modeled after that of Virginia and Kentucky, had always included a chapter on suits for freedom.[3] By 1845, when the newest of
several revisions was in force, the statute contained some interesting
contradictions. It still provided that the opening petition should be
"for leave to sue as a poor person," while the privilege originally
implied in this phrase was swept away by a requirement that the petitioner give security for costs.[4] In addition, the law of 1845 specified a
suit for damages as the proper legal action and then declared that no
damages should be recovered.[5] But this peculiarity merely points up
the indirectness of the whole procedure. A suit for freedom took the
conventional form of a suit for damages in which it was understood
that the alleged acts of the defendant were lawful chastisement of a
slave by his master but constituted assault and false imprisonment if
the plaintiff were indeed a free man. Thus, the jury could not reach a
verdict without first deciding on the validity of the plaintiff's claim to
freedom. This legal indirection meant that the suit for damages might
be brought against some person other than the actual owner, if such
person had held and treated the plaintiff as a slave. That is, A could
conceivably win his freedom from B by suing C. The later confusion
about who really owned the Scotts was therefore not as important as
it has sometimes seemed.[6]

Just how the Scott suits got started, and who provided the original initiative, remains a mystery. It seems utterly clear, however, that
the motives of the people involved were straightforward and personal.[7] There is no evidence of underlying political purposes, or of an
intent to contrive a test case. Besides, the central question raised in
the suit—whether extended residence on free soil liberated a slave—
was not an issue in American politics and had already been tested
many times in the Missouri courts, with consistent results. Another
explanation, only faintly supported by evidence, is that Dred brought

suit at the urging of one or two lawyers who hoped to make considerable money from the case. In the words of one historian, "their main object was to pave the way for a suit against the Emerson estate for the twelve years' wages to which Scott would be entitled should the courts declare that he had been illegally held as a slave since 1834."[8] However, any attorney familiar with the legal precedents would have known that the chances of obtaining such a judgment were exceedingly remote. Seldom did a successful plaintiff in a freedom suit win compensation for services rendered before the institution of the suit, and then only when the court was convinced that the defendant had not acted in good faith.[9]

The possibility that Dred Scott himself conceived the idea of going to court should not be discounted entirely. From his travels, he had no doubt gained some measure of self-reliance, as well as a fund of practical knowledge, and suits for freedom occurred often enough to be common talk among St. Louis slaves. What seems most likely is that the decision to take legal action emerged from discussions with old friends like the Blows and new acquaintances whose sympathies he managed to enlist. The number of lawyers involved in the Scott suits suggests that their services may have been donated or performed for nominal fees.[10]

Once the subject of a suit for freedom was raised, anyone familiar with Missouri law could have told the Scotts that they had a very strong case. Again and again, the highest court of the state had ruled that a master who took his slave to reside in a state or territory where slavery was prohibited thereby emancipated him. To be sure, military service at an army post was somewhat different from taking up residence, but the court had even disposed of this special problem in *Rachel v. Walker* (1836). Rachel had been held in slavery by an officer at Fort Snelling and at Prairie du Chien on the Wisconsin side of the Mississippi. The decision in her favor acknowledged that the defendant had been required to stay at those posts but then added: "No authority of law or the government compelled him to keep the plaintiff there as a slave." Judge Mathias McGirk also expressed annoyance at having to reaffirm a ruling already made many times. "It seems," he declared, "that the ingenuity of counsel and the interest of those disposed to deal in slave property, will never admit anything to be settled in regard to this question." [11]

The Judge's complaint turned out to be a prophecy. Unfortunately for Dred and Harriet Scott, their suits were to make only slow progress in the face of determined opposition from Mrs. Emerson and the men handling her case. Meanwhile, the climate of opinion in Missouri was already beginning to change, and judicial attitudes were bound to change with it. In the end, the Scotts as suitors for freedom would become casualties of the sectional conflict.

Mrs. Emerson's pleas of not guilty were filed by her attorney on November 19, 1846. Owing to a crowded docket, however, it was June 30 of the following year when the suits finally came to trial. Then justice momentarily became swift, as verdicts were returned on the same day. Since Harriet's case was always a repetition of Dred's, it will be sufficient to describe the proceedings in *Scott v. Emerson*, with the understanding that everything said applies also to *Harriet v. Emerson*.

The "Old Courthouse" in St. Louis, now one of the city's major historical landmarks, was new and still only partly completed in 1847. There Judge Alexander Hamilton presided over Dred Scott's first legal contest for freedom. A native of Philadelphia, Hamilton was young, as judges go, and a newcomer to the bench. Which of Dred's attorneys spoke for him at the trial is not clear, but it seems most likely to have been Samuel Mansfield Bay, formerly attorney general of Missouri. Mrs. Emerson was represented by George W. Goode, a Virginian of strong proslavery sentiments. [12]

The task for the Scott attorneys seemed fairly simple. They needed only to prove that Dred had been taken to reside on free soil and that he was now claimed or held as a slave by Mrs. Emerson. Witnesses who had known him at Forts Armstrong and Snelling established the first point beyond dispute. For the rest, his counsel relied primarily on the testimony of Samuel Russell, who declared that he had hired the Scotts from Mrs. Emerson, paying the money to her father, Alexander Sanford. On cross-examination, however, Russell acknowledged that his wife had made all the arrangements. He himself knew nothing about it, other than what his wife had told

him, and he had done nothing except pay the hiring money to Sanford. Henry T. Blow also testified that his father, Peter Blow, had
sold Dred to Dr. Emerson, but this was not to the point. None of the
testimony proved what everyone knew to be true—that Mrs. Emerson now owned Dred Scott. With this defect in mind, the jury returned a verdict for the defendant.[13]

The decision produced the absurd effect of allowing Mrs. Emerson to keep her slaves simply because no one had proved that they
were her slaves. Clearly, justice had been thwarted by a technical
weakness in the presentation of Scott's case. One of his attorneys
promptly moved for a new trial, arguing that Russell's testimony had
been a surprise and that the facts in question could readily be established. At the same time—that is, on July 1, 1847—petitions were
filed to institute a new pair of suits by Dred and Harriet against Alexander Sanford, Samuel Russell, and Irene Emerson. The obvious purpose here was to close the technical loophole by naming as defen-
dants all three of the persons directly involved in holding the Scotts
as slaves.

Dred and Harriet each now had two cases before the circuit
court, with Mrs. Emerson named as a defendant in all of them. On
July 31, Judge Hamilton ordered an end to this duplication. The
Scotts, he said, must choose one pair of suits or the other. But the
term of court soon ran out, and not until November 1847 did the
Scotts elect to pursue the original cases. On December 2, Hamilton
granted the motions for retrial, whereupon the other two suits
(against Sanford, Russell, and Emerson) were withdrawn. At this
point, however, Mrs. Emerson's counsel introduced a further complication by filing a bill of exceptions to the order for a new trial. Thus
Dred's case—and Harriet's too—was suddenly transferred on writ of
error to the supreme court of Missouri.[14]

By 1848, the firm of Alexander P. Field and David N. Hall was
in charge of the Scott suits, while Goode continued to act for Mrs.
Emerson. Field was an expert trial lawyer with a notorious political
past. For two decades he had been a prominent figure in Illinois politics, starting out as a leader of the proslavery faction in the legislature
and precipitating a bitter constitutional battle over his tenure as sec-

retary of state. More recently, he had been a territorial official in Wisconsin. He had the reputation of being a winner in the courtroom, with a special flair for damage suits.[15]

The supreme court considered Mrs. Emerson's appeal in April 1848 and handed down a decision two months later. This time, the technicalities of the law operated in Dred's favor. Since a new trial had already been ordered, said Judge William Scott for the court, there was no final judgment upon which a writ of error could lie. Furthermore, "Granting a new trial cannot be assigned for error."[16] As usual, Dred's case and Harriet's were treated together with duplicate results. But they had won nothing more than the right to make a new beginning in their quest for freedom.

By this time it had become clear that the determination of the Scotts to be free was matched by that of Mrs. Emerson to retain possession of her slaves. The legal maneuvers of defense counsel revealed an intent to win by any means available and had thus far blocked a court decision on the merits of the case. Indeed, the zeal of the Emerson side has a bitter flavor. As one historian suggests, bad feeling may have developed between the Blows and the Emerson-Sanford family, and no doubt all participants were caught up in "the spirit of combat which a court trial inevitably generates."[17]

In 1847, if not earlier, a second daughter was born to the Scotts and given the name Lizzie.[18] Her future, as well as that of her sister Eliza, would be determined by the outcome of the new trials. During the first two years of litigation, Dred and Harriet had continued to work for the Russells on hire from Mrs. Emerson.[19] Then, on March 14, 1848, George Goode appeared before Judge Hamilton to present his client's motion that the Scotts be taken in charge by the sheriff and hired out. The cynical nature of the Emerson defense becomes especially evident here; for according to Goode's argument before the state supreme court just a few weeks later, Dred's counsel had failed to prove that Mrs. Emerson was "in any manner connected with his being held in slavery." Judge Hamilton granted the motion, since Missouri law provided for just such action in freedom cases. But to whom the Scotts were then hired is not indicated in the record.[20]

By court order Mrs. Emerson was thus relieved of responsibility for the Scotts during the pending litigation, but without compromising her claim to them. She would eventually receive their accumulated earnings if a verdict were returned in her favor. The arrangement was probably made to suit the young widow's new plans. Her father, Alexander Sanford, died in 1848. Either that same year or the next, Irene Emerson left St. Louis for Springfield, Massachusetts, to live with another of her sisters, Mrs. James Barnes, whose husband was an engineer and executive in several eastern railroad companies.[21] At this point, John Sanford apparently took over the supervision of his sister's affairs in St. Louis and hired new counsel for the second trial. George Goode gave way to Hugh A. Garland and his law partner, Lyman D. Norris. Garland was a highly respected attorney with a background as interesting as that of his opposite number, Alexander Field. He had been a professor of Greek, a member of the Virginia legislature, and clerk of the national House of Representatives. Along with his legal practice, he was at this time writing a biography of John Randolph which would be published in 1850.[22]

After the Missouri supreme court dismissed Mrs. Emerson's writ of error in June 1848, more than a year and a half elapsed before the second trial was held. (Again, it will be sufficient to follow Dred's case, with Harriet's understood as a duplicate in every respect.) Twice the case was set for trial and then not called—in February and May 1849. The reasons for this double postponement are not known. Further delay ensued when St. Louis was swept by a disastrous fire and badly stricken by a cholera epidemic that year.[23]

The case finally came to trial on January 12, 1850, with Judge Hamilton again presiding. This time, testimony of Mrs. Russell clearly established that the Scotts had been hired from Mrs. Emerson. The defense accordingly changed its strategy, arguing that at Forts Armstrong and Snelling, Emerson had been under military jurisdiction and therefore not subject to laws of the civil government prohibiting slavery. This argument ignored the precedent of *Rachel v. Walker*. Besides, as Scott's counsel pointed out, it did not cover the fact that Emerson had left his slaves at Fort Snelling in the service of other persons after he was ordered to a different post. The decisive moment came when Judge Hamilton complied with a request that he instruct the jury in terms highly favorable to the plaintiff. The verdict that followed as a matter of course made Dred Scott nominally a free man.[24]

But the men acting for Mrs. Emerson were by no means ready to give up the struggle. After a vain effort to secure still another trial, they took the appropriate legal steps for carrying an appeal to the state supreme court. At this time, the opposing attorneys signed a stipulation that the decision of the high court in Dred's case would apply also to Harriet, since the law in both suits was "identical."[25] Briefs were filed in March 1850, but the supreme court put off consideration of the case to the October term. Further postponements then followed, and a decision that might have been reached as early as 1848 was in fact not handed down until 1852. This long delay, stemming from the technical flaw in Samuel Russell's testimony at the first trial, proved to be crucial because of new influences that came to bear on the judiciary during the interval. Down until 1850, the Scott case attracted little attention beyond the circle of those persons directly involved in the litigation. It had no political implications, and the legal precedents seemed to be all in Scott's favor. These circumstances were already beginning to change, however, and during the next two years his prospects were adversely affected by the recent course of national politics, by a peculiar crisis in Missouri politics, and by a decision of the United States Supreme Court.

II

The Scott suits for freedom had begun with the filing of petitions on April 6, 1846. War with Mexico followed a month later, and on August 8 David Wilmot introduced his famous Proviso, designed to prohibit slavery in any territory that might be acquired as a result of the conflict. Although the slavery problem had been far from dormant during the preceding decade, Wilmot's proposal inaugurated a new and more ominous phase of the sectional controversy. The presidential election of 1848, as we have seen, was the first one to be dominated by the slavery issue, and the long congressional struggle culminating in the Compromise of 1850 left a bitter aftertaste in both sections. Northern dissatisfaction centered primarily on the Fugitive Slave Act, while southern resentment was mixed with a general sense of apprehension and of vulnerability to antislavery assaults. Slaveholders regarded the Wilmot Proviso as an outrageous attempt to deprive them of their rightful share in the spoils of conquest. More than that, they were becoming convinced that any congressional restriction on slavery in the territories was a judgment on the morality of the institution and therefore degrading to the South. Feeding their anger and fear were the increasing manifestations of northern hostility in editorials, sermons, legislative resolutions, and fugitive slave "rescues." Southern attitudes accordingly hardened into a grim defensiveness, and, by 1850, the public mood of the slaveholding states was uncongenial to suits for freedom.

Geography and history made Missourians especially sensitive to the rising temperature of the sectional quarrel over slavery. Their state was in an exposed position, bordered on three sides by free territory, and many of them remembered Missouri's bitter struggle for statehood thirty years earlier. Furthermore, Missouri was unlike most other slaveholding states in having an articulate antislavery minority, whose presence and utterances heightened the feeling of insecurity among slave-owners in the state. The slavery issue caused discord within both political parties, but the sharper cleavage appeared in the ranks of the Missouri Democrats. Their longtime leader, Senator Thomas Hart Benton, had alienated many members of the party by his fierce hostility to John C. Calhoun, his opposition to the annexation of Texas, and his moderate views on the slavery question. Benton's enemies in the state legislature seized the opportunity to embarrass him. Early in 1849, they secured passage of the so-called Jackson Resolutions, which embraced Calhoun's extreme proslavery doctrines and instructed Missouri's two senators to "act in conformity" with them. Benton, with re-election in mind, came roaring home to vindicate himself in a lusty speech-making tour, but the old warrior's political future was obviously uncertain. At the polls in August 1850, pro-Benton Democrats captured only about one-third of the seats in the state legislature. The Whigs gained a plurality, while the anti-Benton Democrats emerged holding the balance of power. With election of a senator thus depending on negotiations between any two of these three groups, the situation was ripe for political intrigue.[26]

There is reason to believe that the real author of the Jackson Resolutions was Judge William B. Napton of the state supreme court.[27] Another member of the court, James H. Birch, denounced Benton from the stump in 1849, and, after a venomous exchange of personalities, he brought suit for libel against the senator.[28] Both Napton and Birch were more than willing to use their judicial power in the anti-Benton and proslavery interest. The Dred Scott case offered an opportunity to do so. On October 25, 1850, Edward Bates received inside information on their intentions from the third supreme court judge, John F. Ryland. A pro-Benton man, but uncombative by nature, Ryland confided that his colleagues were preparing to overrule the previous court decisions and reject Scott's claim to freedom. He, Ryland, intended to write a dissenting opinion.[29] Bates, a respected but somewhat passive leader of Missouri Whiggery, was like Benton a moderate on the slavery issue. In Ryland's disclosures he read signs of a plot to fuse the Whigs and anti-Benton Democrats, with the Whigs receiving the senatorship in exchange for swallowing the proslavery doctrine of the Jackson Resolutions. Much speculation centered on Henry S. Geyer, a well-known lawyer and Whig elder statesman whose pronounced southern sympathies made him acceptable to some of the anti-Benton men.

In this charged political atmosphere, the supreme court judges discussed the drafting of their Dred Scott decision. Birch, an aggressive partisan, wanted to declare the Missouri Compromise unconstitutional, but Napton thought it unnecessary to go that far. Meanwhile, under pressure from his colleagues, Ryland's opposition dissolved, and he agreed to concur in a ruling that under Missouri law Dred remained a slave. Napton was chosen to write the opinion of the court. For months, however, he put off the task, insisting that he must have certain law books not available at the state library. As a consequence, the history of the Dred Scott case took another curious turn.[30] While Napton procrastinated, the new state legislature convened. In January 1851, after a two-week deadlock, it elected Geyer to the Senate seat that Benton had occupied for thirty years. The downfall of "Old Bullion" was viewed with regret by many Missourians and may have influenced another election held later in the same year. A recent amendment to the state constitution had changed the supreme court from an appointive to an elective body. All three of the incumbents became candidates to succeed themselves, but only Ryland, still labeled a Benton Democrat, survived the contest at the polls in September. Birch and Napton were swept from office, the latter without having delivered his Dred Scott opinion. Thus the case would have to be considered again by a reorganized court.[31]

Still another event affecting Dred Scott's future had taken place in January 1851, when the Supreme Court of the United States handed down its decision in *Strader v. Graham*.[32] This Kentucky case, as we have seen, involved some slave musicians who were taken briefly into Ohio for performances and later fled from Kentucky to Canada. It was a suit, not for freedom by the slaves themselves, but for damages by their owner against several men who had allegedly aided the escape. Defense counsel argued that the Negroes had been liberated by virtue of the Northwest Ordinance as soon as they set foot on Ohio soil, and that their subsequent flight was therefore one of free men rather than slaves. The Kentucky Court of Appeals rejected this argument in rendering a decision for the slave-owner, whereupon the case was carried to the United States Supreme Court on a writ of error.[33] Chief Justice Taney, speaking for a unanimous Court, dismissed the case for lack of jurisdiction. The Northwest Ordinance, he declared, no longer had any force in Ohio, having been superseded by the constitution and laws of that state. Consequently, the case did not present a federal question under the Judiciary Act of 1789 and so could not be reviewed by the Supreme Court. In short, the decision of the highest Kentucky court was conclusive.

The *decision* of the Taney Court in the *Strader* case, being simply a refusal to accept jurisdiction, did not impinge significantly upon Dred Scott's cause before the high court of Missouri. Indeed, it was irrelevant unless the Missouri judges decided against him and he attempted an appeal to the United States Supreme Court. Even then, the two cases would be far from parallel. For Scott's claim to freedom rested upon several years of residence on free soil, rather than a brief

visit, and residence not only in a free state but in free federal territory. The Missouri Compromise restriction had certainly been operative in the Fort Snelling region during the years from 1836 to 1840.
So the *Scott* case, unlike the *Strader* case, clearly involved a right
claimed under the federal Constitution, and the Supreme Court
could not justifiably refuse to hear it on jurisdictional grounds.*

So much for the *Strader decision*, but Taney's *opinion* announc-
ing the decision was a different matter. In it, he managed to cover
much of the substantive ground that presumably lay beyond the
Court's jurisdiction. Taney, in fact, endorsed the main line of reasoning by which the Kentucky court had arrived at its decision in favor of
the slaveholder. Namely, whatever effect the laws of Ohio might have
had upon the status of the slaves while they were in Ohio, their condition after returning in bondage to Kentucky "depended altogether
upon the laws of that State and could not be influenced by the laws of
Ohio." This placed a federal stamp of approval on the doctrine of
reversion, but what of Dred Scott's claim to freedom under the Missouri Compromise, based on his residence at Fort Snelling? Did the
same rule of comity likewise govern the relationship between federal
territorial law and state law? To this problem Taney also addressed
himself in a passage that was patently extrajudicial. Before concluding that the Northwest Ordinance had been superseded in Ohio, he
considered the hypothetical effect of a hypothetically contrary conclusion. "The ordinance in question, if still in force," he declared, "could
have no more operation than the laws of Ohio in the State of Kentucky."[34]

Taney's *Strader* opinion, if accepted as precedent, would have a
controlling effect on the future disposition of any similar cases in the
United States Supreme Court. It amounted to a declaration of judicial
self-restraint, promising noninterference by the federal judiciary with
state court decisions on the subject. This meant, however, that the effect of the opinion on a case being heard *in a state court* was permissive rather than controlling. It confirmed the principle of reversion,
but left the state to decide whether it would apply the principle of

*Taney took the opposite view in his Dred Scott opinion, but he was plainly wrong.
See below, pp. 386–87.

reattachment. Taney's remarks, even if relevant to Dred Scott's case, indicated neither that Scott was free nor that he was still a slave but only that his condition depended solely on Missouri law. And the law expounded by the Missouri supreme court had been consistently favorable to suits for freedom like his, involving long-term residence on free soil. Technically, therefore, the *Strader* opinion ought not to have prejudiced Scott's cause, but its timing and psychological effect worked to the advantage of the other side.

The Missouri precedents for the Dred Scott case had been set by liberal-minded judges who were predisposed to favor freedom and whose opinions seemed to reflect the older view of enlightened southerners that slavery was, at best, a necessary evil. In addition, these opinions embodied the belief that taking a slave to reside in a free state or in free territory worked his emancipation, that such emancipation was permanent, and that the courts of Missouri were obligated to recognize and enforce the external law that had made him free.[35] By 1850, however, the climate of opinion no longer encouraged and scarcely permitted a bias in favor of freedom, and the judges were, for the most part, a different breed of men. With slavery now under bitter attack, its defenders regarded the old liberalism as a display of weakness. An opinion delivered by Napton in 1847 had set the new tone. It was unsound policy, he declared, for a slaveholding state to encourage the increase of free Negroes, whose presence tended "only to dissatisfy and corrupt those of their own race and color remaining in a state of servitude."[36] Coming in this context, the *Strader* opinion assured Missourians that they were under no legal compulsion to enforce the laws of another jurisdiction hostile to slavery, and that they were entirely free to consult their own self-interest in disposing of suits for freedom relying on such laws. Thus Taney's extrajudicial pronouncement gave a green light to judicial reaction in Missouri.

The two new state supreme court judges elected, along with Ryland, in September 1851 were William Scott and Hamilton R. Gamble. This was the same Judge Scott who, during a previous term of service, had spoken for the court when it dismissed Mrs. Emerson's writ of error in 1848. As an ardent proslavery Democrat, how-

ever, he was prepared to take up where Napton had left off and overrule the Missouri precedents favorable to Dred Scott's cause.
Gamble, on the other hand, was a Whig, and having received the
largest popular vote, he became the presiding judge of the court. Fifteen years earlier, he had represented the slaveholding army officer
in *Rachel v. Walker*, and some of his arguments were now being
echoed by Mrs. Emerson's counsel. But Gamble was also the
brother-in-law of Edward Bates and a member of the Whig faction
that opposed collaboration with the proslavery Democrats. His presence on the court, together with the pro-Benton label still worn by
Ryland, probably made Dred Scott's prospects seem brighter than
they really were.[37]

Soon after the new court convened in the autumn of 1851, Alexander P. Field drew its attention to the Dred Scott case by resubmitting the original briefs filed for each side in 1850. He took this step, it
appears, without consulting Mrs. Emerson's attorneys. One of the latter, Lyman D. Norris, was at work on a supplementary brief when he
learned that the case had been turned over to Judge Scott for preparation of the court's opinion. Norris thereupon hastily obtained permission to file his brief in its unfinished form. The fact that Scott had
been chosen to write the opinion clearly indicated that the decision
would be in Mrs. Emerson's favor. Thus the new brief was actually a
superfluous effort in a cause already won, but its contents are instruc-
tive as evidence of the striking changes that occurred in the historical
context of the case.[38]

For one thing, Norris now relied more heavily on *Strader v.
Graham* than on the military jurisdiction argument that had been the
burden of the earlier Emerson brief. This shifted the emphasis from
denying that Dred Scott had become free while on free soil to denying that any alleged change of status remained operative after his return to Missouri. Obviously taking a cue from Taney, Norris contended that the court "ought not, either in comity, equity or reason,
to consider, interpret and enforce foreign constitutions and laws,
which . . . work the forfeiture of the property of our citizens." But
the most significant feature of the brief was its open appeal to the political passions of the day. Norris denounced "higher law dem-

agogues" and the "black vomit" of antislavery agitation. He quoted
Napton on the threat to slavery posed by free Negroes. He even cast
doubt, in passing, on the constitutionality of the Missouri Compromise.

On March 22, 1852, Judge Scott finally announced the decision
of the court. With Ryland concurring, he found that Dred Scott was
still a slave and ordered the judgment of the lower court reversed.
His accompanying opinion had much in common with the Norris brief
and probably followed the line of reasoning previously marked out by
Napton, with whom he was in close communication. As a legal document the opinion dealt essentially with the problem of comity or
conflict of laws:

> Every State has the right of determining how far, in a spirit of
> comity, it will respect the laws of other States. Those laws have no
> intrinsic right to be enforced beyond the limits of the State for
> which they were enacted. The respect allowed them will depend
> altogether on their conformity to the policy of our institutions. No
> State is bound to carry into effect enactments conceived in a spirit
> hostile to that which pervades her own laws.

Comity, Scott declared, was therefore a matter of judicial discretion,
to be "controlled by circumstances." But at this point the necessity
of demonstrating that changed circumstances dictated the overthrow
of precedent turned a legal explication into a political tract:

> Times are not now as they were when the former decisions on this
> subject were made. Since then not only individuals but States
> have been possessed with a dark and fell spirit in relation to slav-
> ery, whose gratification is sought in the pursuit of measures,
> whose inevitable consequences must be the overthrow and de-
> struction of our government. Under such circumstances it does
> not behoove the State of Missouri to show the least countenance to
> any measure which might gratify this spirit. . . . Although we
> may, for our own sakes, regret that the avarice and hard-heart-
> edness of the progenitors of those who are now so sensitive on the
> subject, ever introduced the institution among us, yet we will not
> go to them to learn law, morality or religion on the subject.

After this outburst, there followed a homily on slavery as a civilizing force that had raised the American Negro far above the "miserable " African. "We are almost persuaded," Scott concluded, "that the introduction of slavery amongst us was, in the providence of God, who makes the evil passions of men subservient to His own glory, a means of placing that unhappy race within the pale of civilized nations."[39]

On that pious note ended the six-year effort to establish Dred Scott's right to freedom under the laws and in the courts of Missouri. The decision, moreover, was reached by a two-to-one vote; for Judge Gamble entered a dissenting opinion. His argument was almost entirely an appeal to the principle of *stare decisis*. Without actually contesting Judge Scott's conclusion that the extending of comity was optional, he maintained, in effect that Missouri had already exercised her option by choosing to enforce the laws of other jurisdictions against slaveholding. "I regard the question," he said, "as conclusively settled by repeated adjudications of this court." Furthermore, those earlier cases had been decided "when the public mind was tranquil," and they embodied principles that had not changed with the changing times.[40]

As Gamble plainly implied, his colleagues had subordinated the rights of the parties in the case to the public issues associated with it. Their decision, rendered nominally against Dred Scott, was primarily an expression of mounting southern anger and an act of retaliation against antislavery words and deeds. Judge Scott's convincing legal analysis of the nature of comity carried him only to a reassertion of state sovereignty. Beyond that, he deserted the judicial path, lined as it was with disagreeable precedents, and followed a political route to the proslavery position from which he delivered his opinion.* For the first time, but not the last, a court had used the Dred Scott case as a means of determining public policy.

* Judge Scott did not make it clear whether he regarded Dred's years in Illinois and at Fort Snelling as constituting residence or mere sojourning, but the language of his opinion was broad enough to cover both and make it out of line with virtually all other southern decisions on the subject. See above, p. 60.[41]

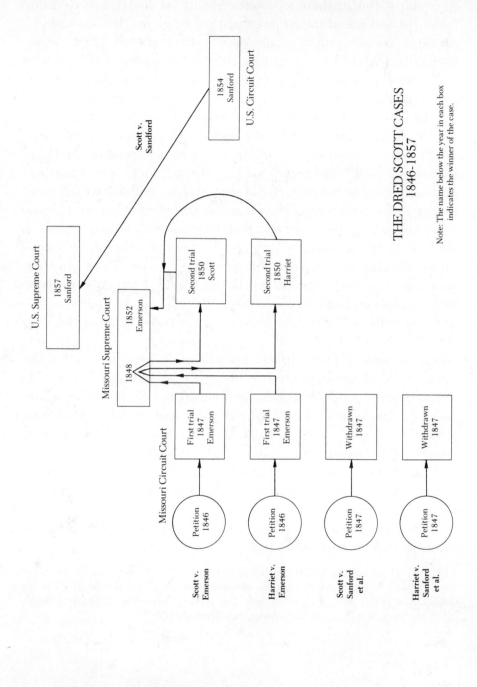

THE DRED SCOTT CASES
1846-1857

Note: The name below the year in each box
indicates the winner of the case.

Versus Sandford

Proceedings in *Dred Scott v. Emerson* did not end with the decision of the Missouri supreme court announced on March 22, 1852. The case was then remanded to the trial court for final action in the form of a judgment implementing the decision. In addition, the Emerson attorneys filed a motion calling for termination of the sheriff's custody of the Scotts and for payment to Mrs. Emerson of the wages earned by them during the preceding four years. These appeared to be merely formalities, but in the Dred Scott case anomaly had almost become the rule. On June 29, Judge Alexander Hamilton denied the Emerson motion, thus retaining Dred and his family in public custody. Furthermore, he put off rendering the final judgment ordered by the higher court. Instead, according to an entry in the circuit court record for January 25, 1854, the case was "continued by consent, awaiting decision of Supreme Court of the United States."[1]

The only satisfactory explanation of Judge Hamilton's action on June 29, 1852, is that he had already been privately informed of an intention to carry Dred Scott's cause to the federal Supreme Court. This does not necessarily mean, however, that the precise strategy for further litigation had been worked out at that early date. From the fact that another sixteen months passed before new court action was initiated, one might well infer that the Scott forces were for a time perplexed about how to proceed. On the other hand, the delay may

have resulted primarily from the need to find new counsel in place of
Alexander P. Field and David N. Hall. Hall had died in the spring of
1851, and, apparently not long afterward, Field moved to Louisiana,
where he remained for the rest of his life. It is possible that Field's
departure from St. Louis preceded the decision of the Missouri supreme court in March 1852. If not, his plans for leaving were so far
advanced that he could no longer represent Dred Scott.[2]

What requires explanation at this point is why something did not
happen. By all logic, the next move in behalf of Dred Scott should
have been an appeal directly to the United States Supreme Court, as
provided for in Section 25 of the Judiciary Act of 1789. The failure to
take such action was one of those decisive choices that determine the
course of subsequent events. Perhaps the change of counsel made the
difference. That is, if Field and Hall had continued in charge of the
case, they might possibly have elected to proceed with an appeal. But
the paramount *reason* for not appealing may have been the expectation that the Supreme Court, with *Strader v. Graham* in mind, would
refuse to accept jurisdiction. To the extent that the Chief Justice
spoke for the Court, this fear was well grounded. Five years later, at
the very close of his historic opinion in *Dred Scott v. Sandford*, Taney
declared:

> If the plaintiff supposed that this judgment of the Supreme Court
> of the State was erroneous, and that this court had jurisdiction to
> revise and reverse it, the only mode by which he could legally
> bring it before this court was by writ of error directed to the
> Supreme Court of the State, requiring it to transmit the record of
> this court. If this had been done, it is too plain for argument that
> the writ must have been dismissed for want of jurisdiction in this
> court. The case of *Strader et al. v. Graham* is directly in point;
> and, indeed, independent of any decision, the language of the
> 25th section of the Act of 1789 is too clear and precise to admit of
> controversy.[3]

In short, an appeal was the only proper way to have proceeded in
1852, and it would have been useless.

It was one of Taney's characteristics that his language often
tended to become most dogmatic when his argument became most

dubious. He sometimes used a phrase such as "too plain for argument" to introduce an assertion flagrantly contrary to fact. The *Strader* decision had turned on the Court's finding that the Northwest Ordinance was no longer operative in Ohio and that accordingly there was no federal question at issue to justify review of the state court decision. But Dred Scott claimed his freedom by virtue of an operative federal law, and the claim had been denied by the Missouri court. These circumstances plainly qualified his case for appeal under Section 25 of the Judiciary Act of 1789, and Taney's emphatic pronouncement to the contrary was preposterous.[4] The *Strader* case had not been a suit for freedom. It had not involved actual resistance on free soil. It had not, in the Court's judgment, raised a federal question. Indeed, it had not produced adjudication of the central issue in *Dred Scott v. Emerson*—that is, whether residence in free *federal* territory at the will of his master worked the permanent emancipation of a slave. Taney, to be sure, had made some extrajudicial remarks on the subject, and he apparently assumed in 1857 that the whole of his *Strader* opinion, including the dicta, had been written into the law of the land. A majority of his colleagues proved willing to accept this assumption, but they regarded the *Strader* opinion as precedent for a decision against Dred Scott *on the merits*. This is clear from the opinion of Justice Nelson in 1857, drafted with the understanding that he was speaking for the Court. Taney took a more extreme position, however. He insisted that the Judiciary Act had not authorized—and that the *Strader* precedent would have forbidden—even *acceptance of jurisdiction* by the Court in *Dred Scott v. Emerson*. That the other justices would have acquiesced in such a denial of access to the Court seems unlikely.

Yet the fear that an appeal would be dismissed for lack of jurisdiction, though perhaps mistaken, may have been the determining factor in the failure to initiate such an appeal. If so, Taney's freewheeling *Strader* opinion takes on added historical significance as the principal reason why the Dred Scott case was not pressed to a final decision in 1852 or shortly thereafter. It is very doubtful that Dred himself could have fared any better by undertaking an appeal; for the Court, if it had accepted jurisdiction, would in all probability have upheld the Missouri court decision. But whatever the outcome, it would have marked the end of Dred's legal fight for freedom. In other words, if *Dred Scott v. Emerson* had been reviewed by the United States Supreme Court, there would have been no *Dred Scott v. Sandford,* which was simply the alternative way of getting the case before that same Supreme Court. The crucial difference was that the two major issues in the *Sandford* case—Negro citizenship and the constitutionality of the Missouri Compromise restriction—did not appear on the face of the record in the *Emerson* case and would have been beyond the scope of federal court review.[5] Thus a Supreme Court decision in *Dred Scott v. Emerson* would have been narrowly based and comparatively uncontroversial. In that event, unless Taney had been able to find another peg on which to hang his sweeping and inflammatory opinion of 1857, the great consequences attributed to the Dred Scott decision would have been unknown to history.

Between June 1852 and November 1853, Dred Scott acquired new legal counsel, allegedly became the property of a new owner, and instituted a new suit for freedom in the federal circuit court. Just how these changes were related to each other is far from clear, however, and the motives of several men involved in the case are difficult to explain. From beginning to end, *Dred Scott v. Emerson* had been a bona fide suit between private parties, with neither side having any purpose except to win its case. The only politically motivated behavior had been that of certain judges on the Missouri supreme court. In contrast, some aspects of *Dred Scott v. Sandford* compel consideration of the possibility that it was designed, at least in part, as a test case for political purposes.

Since 1851, Charles Edmund LaBeaume, brother-in-law of Henry T. Blow, had been hiring Dred and Harriet Scott from the sheriff.[6] LaBeaume, himself a lawyer, consulted another local attorney, Roswell M. Field, about the Scott case. He apparently told Field that the Scotts had recently been sold by Mrs. Emerson (now Mrs. Calvin C. Chaffee) to her brother, John F. A. Sanford. Furthermore, Sanford was now a resident of New York City, although his business affairs still brought him frequently to St. Louis. Field therefore recommended a suit in federal court under the diverse-citizenship clause and agreed to serve as counsel. For this version of how the new case got started, the principal authority is Field himself, in a letter written just a year later.[7]

If Field's explanation seemed entirely satisfactory, there would be little mystery about the origins of *Dred Scott v. Sandford*. Even before the case reached its conclusion in 1857, however, there were rumors and charges that Sanford's ownership of the Scotts had been contrived for the sole purpose of making a federal suit possible. Attorneys for both sides publicly denied that the case was fabricated, but the suspicion has persisted.[8] In many historical accounts, the transfer of the Scotts to Sanford is labeled a "fictitious sale"—meaning, apparently, that it was nominal.[9] More recently, historians have been disposed to accept the conclusion of one scholar that there was no transfer at all, that Sanford never owned the Scotts but instead exercised control over them in his capacity as an executor of John Emerson's will.[10] But if this is true, then Sanford's behavior becomes all the more curious. Why, if he was not the owner, did he allow himself to be sued without making any effort to disclaim ownership?

At the same time, there is also something puzzling about the strategy of the Dred Scott forces. The earlier suit against Mrs. Emerson had been undertaken with bright prospects of success, but the action against Sanford was a different matter. Scott could not obtain a hearing in federal court unless he were accepted there as a citizen of Missouri. Beyond that barrier loomed the discouraging precedent of *Strader v. Graham* and the proslavery record of the Supreme Court. As one historian has concluded, "only Scott's most naive supporters could have hoped for a favorable outcome."[11] Why, then, was such an unpromising battle ever begun? The Scotts themselves, it appears, would have been far better served if the money and energy expended in further litigation had been directed instead toward purchasing their freedom.

Contemporary suspicion about the origins of the case was voiced by both sides in the sectional controversy. One version made Sanford a tool of abolitionist intrigue; the other pictured him as the key figure in a carefully planned judicial assault on the constitutionality of the Missouri Compromise. Thus the argument became a triangular one.

Dred Scott v. Sandford was either a genuine suit, or a counterfeit designed for abolitionist purposes, or part of a proslavery plot that succeeded. The task confronting the historian, then, is one of trying to determine the motives of the persons involved in the suit and the extent to which any cooperation between the opposing parties was collusive. Previous efforts have been obfuscated by the question of ownership, which is almost a red herring and yet has received so much attention that it can hardly be ignored.

The chief reason for believing that Sanford actually did own the Scotts in 1853 is the repeated acknowledgment of such ownership by his counsel during the course of the trial. In fact, as part of his formal plea of not guilty to the nominal complaint of assault and false imprisonment, Sanford declared that the slaves were his "lawful property."[12] On the other hand, those historians who emphatically deny that Sanford was the owner submit two principal reasons for doing so. First, no bill of sale or any other legal record of the alleged transaction between Mrs. Chaffee and her brother has ever been found. This does not mean however, that such a document never existed, and besides, a transfer of slaves, unlike one of real property, could have been as informal as the principals desired. In sum, the lack of documentary proof falls short of constituting disproof. The second consideration probably carries more weight. Sanford died on May 5, 1857, two months after the Supreme Court decision in his favor, and his probate papers contain no mention of the Scotts. Moreover, just three weeks later, Dred and his family were manumitted by Taylor Blow, who had recently acquired them *from the Chaffees*. Thus, if Sanford owned the Scotts in 1853, he must have returned them to his sister at some time before his death in 1857.[13] Again, there is no record of such a transfer, which, again, may have been made informally, but two unrecorded transactions do tend to stretch belief. The facts therefore discourage certitude. Sanford may have owned the Scotts as he said; there is reason to suspect, but no evidence to prove, that he did not.[14]

In an alternative explanation now widely accepted, Vincent C. Hopkins maintains that Mrs. Emerson lost control of Dred Scott and his family when she married Calvin Chaffee in 1850. "By her marriage, according to the Laws of Missouri," Hopkins writes, "she could no longer act in any capacity in regard to her first husband's estate, which had been left in trust for her daughter, Henrietta Emerson." He then cites two Missouri statutes declaring that no married woman could act as guardian of a minor's estate or serve as an executrix or administratix. "As a matter of fact," he continues, "her duties, so far as Emerson's Missouri possessions were concerned, had, since the death of her father, who had been named administrator in Missouri, and her departure for the east, completely devolved on her brother."[15]

The logical flaw in this explanation is obvious enough. If, as a consequence of their father's death in 1848 and her own departure soon thereafter, Mrs. Emerson's duties had already "completely devolved" on John Sanford, then her marriage in 1850 did not change matters at all. Moreover, if Mrs. Emerson lost all control of the estate by her remarriage in 1850, how could she have transferred the Scotts to Taylor Blow in 1857?[16] Hopkins has, in fact, misread John Emerson's will, and the Missouri laws that he cites are not relevant. Emerson's primary heir was his wife, not their daughter. His will, as we have seen, made Irene Emerson neither a trustee nor an executrix but the virtual owner of his estate for life, with no restriction on remarriage. Although a life heir does owe certain obligations to the remainderman, it is inconceivable that the Missouri statutes could have been interpreted as absolutely depriving Mrs. Emerson-Chaffee of her lawful property. It is also difficult to understand how control of the Emerson estate could have "devolved" on Sanford, who had not qualified as an executor in Iowa and had never been appointed administrator in Missouri. To be sure, Sanford may have been under the erroneous impression that he was an executor or that he had succeeded his father as administrator in Missouri.[17] The best explanation may be simply that no one knew for sure who legally owned the Scotts. But two other possibilities are no less credible: that Sanford did actually become their owner, or that he continued after 1850 to act as his sister's agent, even permitting himself to be sued in her behalf.

Anyway, it makes little difference whether Sanford was acting as owner, agent, or executor when he accepted the role of defendant. For one thing, the "validity" of the case did not depend upon the source of his authority over the Scotts but merely upon whether he had exercised such authority.[18] It has already been shown that in a suit for freedom, the matter at issue was not primarily the owner's title to his slave property but rather the right of *anyone* to treat the plaintiff as a slave. Thus the owner or any other person holding the Scotts as slaves was an appropriate target for legal action in the form of a damage suit.[19] Moreover, solving the problem of ownership would not in itself solve the problem of Sanford's motives; for we would still need to know why he acquired the Scotts, or why he misrepresented himself as their owner. In neither case would an ulterior purpose be any more assumable than personal convenience, consideration for his sister, or some other private reason.

Therefore, 'the fact that Sanford's convenient acknowledgment of ownership made a federal suit possible, while raising the question of collusion, does not constitute evidence of it.[20] The filing of an "agreed statement of facts," signed by opposing counsel, also contributes to the appearance of coziness, but this may have been simply an effort to limit the time and costs of the trial. What aroused the most contemporary suspicion about Sanford's conduct was the revelation in 1857 of his family tie with Mrs. Chaffee and her earlier role in the case; for Calvin Chaffee by that time had taken a seat in Congress as an emphatic opponent of slavery. Many historians ever since have jumbled the chronology and portrayed Sanford as the tool of his "abolitionist" brother-in-law. But Chaffee in 1853 was still a physician in private practice and had not yet entered politics (he served two terms in Congress, from 1855 to 1859). There is no evidence to connect him or his wife with the litigation getting under way in Missouri. Indeed, it is doubtful that Chaffee even knew of the Scotts' existence in 1853.[21] Neither does it seem credible that Sanford, himself a slaveholder and the real manager of his sister's defense in the Missouri courts, had undergone such a complete change of heart by 1853. He retained the same attorney, Hugh Garland, who had won the earlier case and no doubt expected to win again. Nothing in Garland's strategy suggests mere token resistance to the new Scott suit. The idea that Sanford was a cardboard defendant, secretly in league with the other side, does not have enough substance to be taken seriously.

On the other hand, both before and after the Supreme Court decision in 1857, there were charges in the antislavery press that the case had been fabricated by proslavery interests.[22] But this implied that the Scott forces, by initiating the suit, wittingly played into the hands of the enemy, which was absurd. The men behind Dred Scott's federal suit were generally the same ones who had supported him in the Missouri courts, with the exception of his new counsel. Roswell M. Field (not related to Scott's previous attorney, Alexander P. Field) is remembered not only for his part in the Dred Scott case but as the father of journalist-poet Eugene Field.[23] A native of Vermont, he was probably stronger in his antislavery convictions than any of the other lawyers who represented the Scotts. In view of the odds against success, one may question the wisdom of undertaking the suit, but not the honesty of its purpose. Field appears to have been determined that Dred Scott should obtain a hearing before the nation's highest tribunal. The worst that can be said is that he and his associates failed to look beyond that goal to the possible consequences of submitting such an issue to a hostile Supreme Court.

What remains is the possibility that the suit, while genuine enough on the Scott side, was exploited for proslavery purposes by the defense. One New York Republican newspaper asserted that Sanford, a Democrat, had "consented to place himself in the attitude of a defendant after enduring an amount of importunity, badgering, and worrying, from persons having no other than a political interest in the case."[24] This explanation seems to fit Sanford's curious willingness to be sued, but it breaks down completely when one examines the manner in which his case was conducted. The strategy of defense counsel in the courtroom, as we shall see, was aimed at winning a favorable verdict and not at testing the constitutionality of the Missouri Compromise restriction or at any other major political issue.

Thus the odor of conspiracy detected in *Dred Scott v. Sandford* proves to be extremely elusive, and certain puzzling things about its origin do not add up to a "fabricated case." Unless more positive documentary evidence is discovered, the suspicion of a political plot should probably be laid aside. No doubt both sides became increasingly aware of the broader implications of the case as it progressed, but private purposes are enough to explain their actions in the beginning. At stake, after all, was the freedom of four human beings, together with their property value as slaves and their accumulated wages. In addition, one sees here the resumption of an old, hard-fought battle, with the opposing forces in agreement that it should be carried swiftly to a final decision.

II

Dred Scott v. Sandford was a suit for freedom in the customary form of an action of trespass.[25] The declaration filed for Scott on November 2, 1853, asserted that he was a citizen of Missouri. It complained that on the preceding January 1, Sanford had assaulted and wrongfully imprisoned Scott himself, his wife Harriet, and their two children, Eliza and Lizzie. The damages claimed on these three counts totaled $9000. LaBeaume and Taylor Blow provided the bond for costs. A summons was promptly issued and served personally on Sanford, who had come to St. Louis for business reasons.[26]

The United States circuit court for the district of Missouri had no permanent home in St. Louis. It moved from one rented hall to another, and by 1854 had been pushed into "a small back room over a Main Street store."[27] There the Dred Scott case was tried before Judge Robert W. Wells, a Virginian who had previously been attorney general of Missouri. Wells, according to one of his contemporaries, was something of a cold fish, with a shrill voice and awkward manner. A slaveholder who nevertheless regarded slavery as a barrier to progress, he was apparently free of the intense prejudice that had permeated the decision of the Missouri supreme court.[28]

At the next term, in April 1854, Sanford filed a plea in abatement challenging the court's jurisdiction on the grounds that Scott, as a Negro descended from slaves of "pure African blood," was not in fact a citizen of Missouri. This move, if successful, would have foreclosed any testing of the Missouri Compromise. It therefore seems incompatible with the notion of a proslavery plot. However,

Judge Wells upheld Scott's demurrer to the plea, ruling that for the purpose of bringing suit in a federal court, citizenship implied nothing more than residence in the designated state and the legal capacity to own property.[29] In his ruling, it should be noted, Wells limited himself to interpreting just the diverse-citizenship clause in Article Three, Section Two, of the Constitution. The question of whether free Negroes qualified as citizens under this clause had not been settled by a federal court, the only jurisdiction in which it could arise. In a number of state court cases, the general subject of Negro citizenship had been raised under Article Four, Section Two, which declares that "the citizens of each state shall be entitled to all privileges and immunities of citizens in the several states." The decisions in these cases were generally against Negro citizenship.* However, Wells made it clear that his ruling did not extend to the privileges-and-immunities clause or define citizenship in all its aspects. By implication, he adopted the view that the meaning of the word "citizen" might vary with its context. A free Negro, he held, was *enough of a citizen* to be covered by the diverse-citizenship clause, whatever his status otherwise. This was by no means the first time that citizenship had been recognized for jurisdictional purposes only. In fact, the Wells ruling about Negroes bore a remarkable resemblance to conclusions already reached by the Taney Court in dealing with corporations.†

As constitutional interpretation the ruling was probably sound, and as a practical matter, it was eminently sensible. There is little evidence that the framers of the Constitution intended to exclude native-born free Negroes from a privilege extended even to aliens of every race.[30] Such exclusion, aside from its patent injustice, would have been legally troublesome in a number of ways. For one thing, the definition of "Negro" varied from state to state but ordinarily embraced most persons of mixed ancestry from predominantly black to predominantly white. So, in a given case, the jurisdiction of a federal

---

* See above, p. 68.

† Especially in *Louisville, Cincinnati and Charleston Railroad v. Letson* (1844). See above, p. 72.

court might depend upon verification of the race of a great-grand-mother of one of the parties. Moreover, as Wells himself later observed, such exclusion would not only deny a privilege but confer a special immunity; for if a Negro could not sue, neither could he be sued, under the diverse-citizenship clause.[31]

Among the puzzling features of defense strategy is the limited nature of this plea to the court's jurisdiction. It did not even canvass the entire question of Scott's claim to citizenship, which might also have been challenged on the ground that he was a *slave*. This, to be sure, would have had the bizarre effect of raising as a jurisdictional question the very substance of the cause brought before the court. Yet the assumption that Scott was free until proved otherwise, with which the trial proceeded, had less foundation than an assumption that he was a slave; for he had been adjudged a slave by the highest court of Missouri. Taney subsequently indicated that such a challenge would have been proper and sound. Curiously, however, *Scott v. Emerson* went unmentioned until after the demurrer had been sustained, at which point a brief and vague summary was appended to the agreed statement of facts. The record of the earlier litigation could have been put to additional use by defense counsel. Aside from the question of citizenship, objection might have been made to hearing *Scott v. Sandford* when virtually the same case, having been remanded to a state trial court for final judgment, was still pending there. This vulnerable spot in the plaintiff's armor likewise remained unexploited until Taney delivered his opinion.[32]

Having failed to obtain dismissal of the suit on jurisdictional grounds, Sanford entered a plea of not guilty to the charges in Scott's declaration. Did he have any other choice at this time? Did he, by pleading over, acknowledge the court's jurisdiction and thus waive the right to reopen the subject later? These questions would produce controversy bordering on confusion when the case came before the Supreme Court. The issue was especially important because of its potential bearing on the Fugitive Slave Law. The Wells ruling, as Field soon realized, would mean that an alleged fugitive might claim citizenship in the state where he was apprehended and secure a federal trial before a friendly jury. His right to do so, being derived straight from the Constitution, would presumably override the act of 1850 with its provisions for summary hearing and *ex parte* testimony.[33] On a matter of such obvious consequence, a mere district judge like Wells was unlikely to have the final word.

Sanford's plea, claiming the Scotts as his lawful slaves, asserted that he had "gently laid his hands upon them and restrained them of their liberty as he had a right to do." The replication of the plaintiff, in turn, denied that such right existed.[34] Thus, according to the custom in suits for freedom, there was no contest over the alleged trespass itself, even though it may have been a fiction. Whether Sanford had committed assault and false imprisonment depended entirely upon whether the Scotts were free persons or slaves. At this point in the proceedings, opposing counsel filed their "Agreed Statement of Facts," an inaccurate summary of the Scott family's life and travels with Dr. Emerson. The document has misled many unwary historians, but for the immediate legal purpose it was adequate and fair.[35]

The case came to trial on May 15, 1854. Neither side called any witnesses or introduced additional evidence. Arguments of counsel were based entirely on the Agreed Statement. By this time the struggle over the Kansas-Nebraska bill, which repealed the slavery restriction of the Missouri Compromise, was approaching its angry climax in Congress. Yet, significantly, Sanford's attorney did not seize the opportunity to challenge the constitutionality of the restriction. Instead, he relied on the line of reasoning that had been successful before the Missouri supreme court. Judge Wells instructed the jury that the law was with the defendant, and the jury accordingly returned a verdict in Sanford's favor.[36] Later, Wells expressed a personal wish that it could have been otherwise. If Scott, he added, had been declared free under Illinois law *in Illinois*, the decision would have had full effect in Missouri. But Missouri possessed the same power to declare him a slave in Missouri under *its* laws.[37] So Wells plainly made comity the controlling consideration, taking his cue from *Strader v. Graham* and the decision of the supreme court of Missouri in *Scott v. Emerson.*

The verdict posed an odd technical problem that went unnoticed at the time. According to the decision of the court, Dred Scott was a slave and had always been a slave. This meant that he was never a citizen of Missouri and therefore had no right to bring suit in the first place. Having sent the case to a jury and received a verdict, Judge Wells apparently did not consider a last-minute dismissal of the suit for want of jurisdiction. Yet this is precisely what he should have done in the official judgment of the Supreme Court as subsequently rendered by Chief Justice Taney.[38]

After an unsuccessful motion for a new trial, Field filed a bill of exceptions, the first step in taking the case to the Supreme Court on a writ of error.[39] This had obviously been expected from the start, whichever side won, and the expectation may account for the almost perfunctory nature of the proceedings in the circuit court.

III

The trial had attracted little attention locally or elsewhere. A brief account in the St. Louis *Herald* concluded with these words: "Dred is, of course, poor and without any powerful friends. But no doubt he will find at the bar of the Supreme Court some able and generous advocate, who will do all he can to establish his right to go free."[40] The Scott forces did indeed now face the urgent task of recruiting a suitable attorney to argue their case before the Supreme Court, and they must either raise the money for his fee or else find someone willing to donate his services.

Their first effort was to publish a twelve-page pamphlet containing a record of the recent trial. The preface, dated the Fourth of July for symbolic effect, was attributed to Dred Scott himself. It summarized the background of the case, varying in some details from the Agreed Statement of Facts, and then closed with an appeal for help:

> I have no money to pay anybody at Washington to speak for me. My fellow-men, can any of you help me in my day of trial? Will nobody speak for me at Washington, even without hope of other reward than the blessings of a poor black man and his family? I do not know. I can only pray that some good heart will be moved by pity to do that for me which I cannot do for myself; and that if the right is on my side it may be so declared by the high court to which I have appealed.[41]

The months went by, however, and no champion for Dred Scott came forward. Finally, on Christmas Eve 1854, Field wrote to Montgomery Blair suggesting that he or some other lawyer in Washington might serve "the cause of humanity" by taking up the case. Blair, after consulting his family and certain friends, agreed to act as Scott's attorney without fee.[42] He also enlisted the aid of Gamaliel Bailey, abolitionist editor of the *National Era*, who promised to raise the money for court costs and incidental expenses.[43]

Montgomery Blair was the oldest son of Francis Preston Blair, who had come out of Kentucky in 1830 to edit the Washington *Globe* and become a prominent member of Andrew Jackson's "kitchen cabinet." By adhering to the Van Buren-Benton wing of Jacksonian Democracy during the 1840s, the elder Blair had incurred the enmity of many southern Democrats and made himself unacceptable to James K. Polk, who forced his retirement from party journalism. Blair and his sons had supported the Free Soil ticket in 1848, and their opposition to the Kansas-Nebraska Act in 1854 was drawing them into the new political coalition that would soon adopt the name Republican.

For many years, Montgomery Blair had practiced law in St. Louis and served as a political lieutenant of his father's old friend, Thomas Hart Benton. His younger brother, Francis Preston, Jr., had followed him to Missouri and in 1854 was a leader of the Benton Democrats in the state legislature. Montgomery now lived in Blair House on Pennsylvania Avenue, having moved to Washington in 1853. His wife was the daughter of the late Levi Woodbury of New Hampshire, member of Jackson's cabinet and for five years, until his death in 1851, an associate justice of the Supreme Court. Across the avenue, another son of New Hampshire was still trying to patch up cracks in the Democratic party. When Congress created a court of claims in 1855, President Franklin Pierce named Montgomery Blair as its solicitor general. Soon after his arrival, Blair had begun to practice before the Supreme Court. He also remodeled Blair House, given to him by his father, and made it a gathering place of Washington society.

Thus, at the age of forty-one, Blair was a man of considerable social and professional standing in the national capital. He still regarded himself as a citizen of Missouri and gave that as one reason for accepting the Dred Scott case. His knowledge of Missouri law made him especially qualified to handle the appeal. Blair was tall and lean, with a military bearing acquired as a cadet at West Point. Like Abraham Lincoln, he had an awkward manner, a high-pitched voice, and an aversion to windy oratory. Unlike Lincoln, he had no streak of playfulness in his nature, no disposition to court an audience by amusing it. His legal arguments, always compact and precise, were presented with an almost religious earnestness. His intellectual interest extended beyond law and politics to history, literature, and art. Years later, when he had become Lincoln's postmaster general, one observer judged him to be the "best read man" in the cabinet. A one-time slaveholder and no admirer of abolitionism, Blair was nevertheless utterly dedicated to the free-soil cause. In the Dred Scott case he may have seen an opportunity to enhance his own reputation and strike a blow against Benton's enemies in Missouri, but his decision to participate was also prompted by strong convictions.[44]

Yet Blair, for all of his merits, appeared to be overmatched against the opposing counsel. The quality of the two attorneys retained by Sanford indicates that the potential importance of the Dred Scott case had at last been recognized in certain political circles. One of them was Henry S. Geyer, the man who had unseated Benton. Geyer's career in the Senate was proving to be undistinguished, but he had few peers at the Missouri bar and was earning a high reputation in Washington's legal community. With Geyer pitted against Blair, the case continued to echo the din of Missouri politics. The other counsel for Sanford stood even higher in national repute. Reverdy Johnson of Maryland, former senator and attorney general under Taylor, was probably the most respected constitutional lawyer in the country. An old friend of the Chief Justice and veteran of many famous court battles, Johnson added luster to any legal cause that he undertook, and his name made opposing attorneys apprehensive. Facing such a formidable team, Blair tried several times to enlist the services of another lawyer, but without success. He therefore prepared to argue the case alone.[45]

Meanwhile, the record of *Dred Scott v. Sandford* had been officially received by the Supreme Court on December 30, 1854.[46] This late arrival placed the case far down on the docket, and to no one's surprise, it was continued to the next term. The delay meant that the case would probably be heard during the early stages of a presidential campaign.

THE TANEY COURT IN 1857

JUSTICE	BORN	TERM OF SERVICE	STATE	PARTY	PREVIOUS JUDICIAL EXPERIENCE	PREVIOUS POLITICAL CAREER
John McLean	1785	1829–61	Ohio	Rep.	Ohio supreme court	Congressman U.S. Postmaster General
James M. Wayne	1790	1835–67	Ga.	Dem.	State judge	State legislator Mayor of Savannah Congressman
Roger B. Taney	1777	1836–64	Md.	Dem.		State legislator Md. Attorney General U.S. Attorney General Secretary of Treasury
John Catron	1786	1837–65	Tenn.	Dem.	Tenn. supreme court, CJ	
Peter V. Daniel	1784	1841–60	Va.	Dem.	U.S. district judge	State legislator Privy Councillor Lieutenant Governor
Samuel Nelson	1792	1845–73	N.Y.	Dem.	State judge N.Y. supreme court, CJ	Postmaster
Robert C. Grier	1794	1846–70	Penn.	Dem.	State judge	
Benjamin R. Curtis	1809	1851–57	Mass.	Whig		State legislator
John A. Campbell	1811	1853–61	Ala.	Dem.		State legislator

Before the Supreme Court

For more than a year after it was docketed, the Dred Scott case awaited the attention of the Supreme Court. During that time the revolutionary effects of the Kansas-Nebraska Act became increasingly evident. Kansas itself appeared to be on the verge of civil war. Open hostilities between proslavery and free-state forces in the territory were narrowly averted in December 1855, just as the Court was beginning its new term. Meanwhile, the anti-Nebraska movement, already triumphant in many northern states, was approaching the final phase of transformation into a permanent political party. At a meeting scheduled for February 22 in Pittsburgh, Republican leaders planned to lay the foundation of a national organization. Kansas would obviously be the principal issue in the coming presidential election. Franklin Pierce fortified this expectation and confirmed his reputation as a doughface by endorsing the legitimacy of the proslavery legislature. The new thirty-fourth Congress, bogged down for two months in a partisan and sectional struggle over the speakership of the House, would likewise soon find itself preoccupied with the Kansas problem. The newspapers of the nation were already rehearsing every argument on the subject. And the Kansas controversy inevitably produced another round of angry debate on the constitutional power of Congress over slavery in the territories. Experience of recent years indicated that this issue and related ones were beyond the reach of legislative compromise. The possibility of judicial intervention inspired hope in some quarters, partly because it had never been tried. Thus the historical context of the Dred Scott decision was being prepared.[1]

Yet the public was still unaware of the case. It received no advance publicity in the press. Even the Washington correspondent of the *Missouri Republican* (St. Louis), though he mentioned other matters pending before the Supreme Court, said nothing about *Dred Scott*.[2] This lack of interest seems peculiar in retrospect, but it is easily explained. In almost ten years of litigation, Dred Scott's legal struggle for freedom had never yet elicited any extended argument or judicial pronouncement on the constitutionality of the Missouri Compromise restriction. The explosive political implications of the case and its potential bearing on the sectional conflict remained hidden from public view.

On February 7, 1856, with the Supreme Court nearly ready to hear the case, Montgomery Blair filed his brief for the plaintiff in error.[3] This ten-page document has several curious and perhaps revealing features. In the first place, Blair devoted only four pages to the primary task of arguing for *reversal* of the circuit court's decision against Scott's right to freedom. The remainder of the brief was a *defense* of the circuit court's ruling (on the plea in abatement) that free Negroes were citizens to the extent of being qualified to bring suit in a federal court. That is, Blair gave more attention to defending ground already won than to mounting the attack necessary for victory. As strategy for the plaintiff, it was rather odd, to say the least. There were, after all, good reasons for believing that the jurisdictional question as presented in the plea in abatement would not come before the Supreme Court at all. Scott, as the plaintiff, was not complaining against the lower court's ruling on the plea, since it had been in his favor. Sanford, after the plea was rejected, had pleaded over to the merits, thus waiving, it could be argued, all right to reopen the question of jurisdiction. Yet Blair did not mention these technical considerations favorable to his client. Instead, he devoted more than half of his brief to the subject of Negro citizenship, as though it were certain that the subject *would* come before the Court, certain that the jurisdictional question *would* be reviewed. In pursuing this course, it seems, he was making an unwise and unnecessary concession to the opposition.

In preparing the brief, Blair was obviously influenced by a letter he had recently received from Roswell Field. If the ruling of Judge Wells on the plea in abatement were allowed to stand, Field wrote, the resulting constitutional right of black men to sue in federal courts would probably make the Fugitive Slave Law "of little value" to southern masters. Significantly, Field expressed doubt that the jurisdictional question of Negro citizenship would come before the Supreme Court, and yet he thought it "very desirable" to obtain the Court's opinion on the subject.[4] Blair, although not an abolitionist, was apparently enough of an antislavery man to virtually invite such an opinion in his brief, a course of action that could scarcely benefit his client. Dred Scott, out of sight back in St. Louis, was becoming more clearly a pawn in the political game.[5]

It might be thought that Blair, with some foreknowledge of defense strategy, was merely anticipating an effort to reopen the jurisdictional question. But then one must ask why he did not also anticipate the argument of defense counsel against the constitutionality of the Missouri Compromise restriction. Indeed, the most striking feature of his four-page argument on the merits is that it claimed freedom for Dred Scott *solely* on the ground that he had been "emancipated by his master's having taken him to reside in the State of Illinois." Blair made no mention whatsoever of Scott's residence at Fort Snelling. Thus, he avoided the territorial issue entirely, perhaps seeing no advantage either to his client or to the Republican cause in having it tested.[6]

In this part of his brief, Blair drew heavily on Judge Gamble's dissenting opinion in *Scott v. Emerson*, whereas the verdict of the lower federal court had followed the majority opinion of Judge Scott in that case. Gamble had demonstrated that precedents in Missouri and elsewhere were generally on Dred's side (assuming that he was a resident rather than a sojourner in Illinois and at Fort Snelling). Judge Scott, *inter alia*, had cited Taney's opinion in *Strader v. Graham* as authority for reversing the earlier Missouri decisions. Blair

discreetly omitted reference to the *Strader* precedent but made it all
the more relevant with his strategy of concentrating on Dred's residence in Illinois.*

If Henry S. Geyer or Reverdy Johnson filed a brief, it has apparently not been preserved. Our knowledge of the case presented
for the defense is therefore limited to fragmentary newspaper reports
of the oral arguments, seasoned with gossip and speculation. Argument before the Court began on February 11, 1856, and extended
over four days. Blair spoke first, followed by Geyer and Johnson, with
Blair then closing for the plaintiff.[7] Newspaper accounts indicate that
defense counsel reiterated the arguments previously used in Sanford's
behalf, including the plea to jurisdiction that a Negro was not a citizen. In addition, both Geyer and Johnson advanced to new ground by
attacking the constitutionality of the Missouri Compromise restriction. Thus, in February 1856, the Dred Scott case and the major political issue of the day had finally converged. From this point on, Sanford became merely the nominal defendant. Stricken with mental
illness, he would be in an asylum before the end of the year. Reverdy
Johnson had taken up the case at the suggestion of a "southern gentleman," and appropriately so; for the real client that he and Geyer
now represented was the slaveholding South.[8]

During the latter part of February, the Court apparently conferred twice on the case without making much progress toward a
decision. Then it recessed for the entire month of March so that the
justices could spend some time on their circuits. Not until April 5 was
the next conference held, and three more followed it within a week.[9]

Meanwhile, a few newspapers had awakened to the potential significance of *Dred Scott v. Sandford*. The first was the Washington
Evening Star, which on February 12 declared: "The public of Washington do not seem to be aware that one of the most important cases
ever brought up for adjudication by the Supreme Court is now being
tried before that august tribunal." The *National Era* said about the

---

*Blair also undertook to discredit a second reason for the decision of the federal dis-
trict court—namely, that the relevant clause in the Illinois constitution, providing for
emancipation of persons held illegally in slavery, was "penal" in nature and therefore
not entitled to enforcement by other states.

same thing some days later, and Horace Greeley reported that the Court would soon decide "a most important case, involving the validity (in its day) of the Missouri restriction."[10] Greeley was spending the winter in Washington and supplying his New York *Tribune* with editorial correspondence in such biting style that it had recently earned him a caning at the hands of an Arkansas congressman. He talked with one man who had heard the argument of the case and found Blair's performance unimpressive. "Able counsel would have volunteered in behalf of Freedom," Greeley complained, "had they had the least intimation that they were wanted." After this one brief comment on the case, however, Greeley did not again mention it in his dispatches to the *Tribune.* His silence may have been dictated by the fear that any publicity given the Supreme Court at this time would enhance the reputation of Justice John McLean in free-soil circles. McLean had begun to emerge as a serious contender for the Republican presidential nomination, and Greeley was strongly opposed to his candidacy.[11]

But the *Tribune's* regular man in Washington held different views. James E. Harvey, a North Carolinian who signed his correspondence "Index," had been a McLean supporter for many years, and he soon realized that the Dred Scott case offered a rare opportunity for judicial heroics.[12] More than any other reporter, Harvey speculated in print about what the Court might decide, apparently mixing a good deal of gossip with some information obtained directly from McLean.[13] The five southern justices, he suspected, were planning to issue a narrowly based decision in order to prevent minority opinions upholding the constitutionality of the Missouri Compromise. He became increasingly confident, however, that their efforts at evasion would not succeed. Displaying only a perfunctory interest in the fate of Dred Scott, Harvey encouraged his readers to expect a rousing dissent from McLean, one that would make the Justice an antislavery hero on the eve of the Republican national convention.[14]

At this point, however, Harvey's fears were sounder than his hopes. When the Court resumed its conferences in April, Congress was passing through another rancorous debate over Kansas, and there were ominous signs of more violence in the territory itself. The justices accordingly seemed disposed to be prudent. In a letter to his uncle on April 8, Justice Benjamin R. Curtis confided: "The Court will not decide the question of the Missouri Compromise line—a majority of the judges being of opinion that it is not necessary to do so."[15] This probably meant either that jurisdiction would be denied or that the decision of the circuit court would be upheld as it stood, but Curtis did not say which choice was likely.

From other evidence it appears that the Court was divided on the question of jurisdiction, and more particularly on the technical problem of whether the plea in abatement was subject to review. Four justices were aligned on each side of this issue, with Samuel Nelson leaning toward the affirmative but uncertain about it and reluctant to cast a deciding vote.[16] On May 12, the Court ordered that the case be reargued in the next term with special attention to two questions: (1) Was the plea in abatement properly before the Supreme Court? (2) If so, had the circuit court ruled correctly on the plea—that is, did a Negro have a right as a citizen to bring suit in a federal court?[17]

Some observers were convinced, however, that the postponement was dictated by political considerations, and charges to that effect echoed through Republican rhetoric for several years. Harvey complained bitterly that the "artful dodgers" in black robes had deferred action in order to prevent a vindication of the Missouri Compromise. He had in mind, of course, the promised dissent from McLean.[18] Indeed, it was suspected in some quarters that the primary purpose of the postponement had been to spike McLean's presidential ambitions. Yet McLean himself apparently offered no objection to the order for reargument of the case.[19] Abraham Lincoln, on the other hand, later accused the Court of delaying its decision in order to conceal the proslavery intentions of the Democratic party until after the presidential election.[20] This was part of his famous conspiracy charge in the House-Divided speech, but there is no evidence to support his reading of judicial motives. What does seem likely, however, is that some justices, at least, were reluctant to render such a controversial decision on the eve of a major political campaign.

II

Only a few newspapers had thus far given the Dred Scott case anything more than routine attention, and it was soon completely overshadowed by a cluster of sensational events. During seven days in May, Senator Charles Sumner delivered his most famous philippic against the slave power; Congressman Preston F. Brooks of South Carolina responded with a physical assault on Sumner; proslavery Kansans carried out a raid on the free-state stronghold of Lawrence, and John Brown retaliated with cold-blooded murder on Pottawatomie Creek. Against this background of violence, the presidential campaign got under way.

Democrats assembled in Cincinnati on June 2 for their national convention and nominated James Buchanan on a platform endorsing popular sovereignty in ambiguous terms while bypassing the constitutional issue of congressional power over slavery in the territories. The Republicans, meeting two weeks later in Philadelphia, expressly affirmed the existence of such power, and of course many southern spokesmen categorically denied it. Yet the issue was not clearly drawn between the parties in the campaign. The election did not become explicitly a referendum on the question laid before the Supreme Court in the Dred Scott case.

McLean had strong support at the Republican convention, receiving about 35 per cent of the votes on a first informal ballot. The new party preferred younger, more colorful leadership, however, and its presidential nomination went, as expected, to the western adventurer, John C. Frémont. With Millard Fillmore already nominated by the American party, there were three contestants in the field. Kansas was inevitably the principal issue of the campaign, and from the South came threats of secession in the event of a Republican victory. "If Frémont is elected there will be a revolution," predicted the governor of Virginia.[21] Buchanan's election by a narrow margin in November left the Republicans disappointed but not discouraged. Their candidate had carried eleven free states, and they set their eyes confidently on the next test of strength in 1860. On the other hand, the fact that Buchanan and Fillmore together had received 70 per cent of the popular vote could be interpreted as a mandate for conservatism on the slavery issue. When the Supreme Court convened for its new term in December 1856, the atmosphere was one of a storm weathered, of tensions relaxed, of a reprieve granted to the nation.

But sectional and partisan animosities were quickly revived by the retiring president, Franklin Pierce, in his final annual message. Half of this extraordinary document was an intemperate denunciation of the party that had lost the recent election. Pierce still suffered keenly from the unique humiliation of being denied renomination after having led his party to an overwhelming victory four years earlier. He now hailed the outcome of the election as a personal vindication and as an emphatic condemnation of the antislavery movement, upon which he placed the entire blame for sectional discord. The American people had refused to be led down "this path of evil"; the Republican party had failed in its efforts "to usurp the control of the Government of the United States."[22] As for the Missouri Compromise restriction, Pierce continued, it was already "a mere nullity . . . a monument of error . . . a dead letter in law" at the time of its repeal.

> In the progress of constitutional inquiry and reflection it had now at length come to be seen clearly that Congress does not possess constitutional power to impose restrictions of this character upon any present or future State of the Union. In a long series of decisions, on the fullest argument and after the most deliberate consideration, the Supreme Court of the United States had finally determined this point in every form under which the question could arise, whether as affecting public or private rights—in questions of the public domain, of religion, of navigation, and of servitude.[23]

These words may be susceptible of more than one construction, but at their most obvious they amounted to an executive pronouncement on what had latterly become the paramount issue in the Dred Scott case.[24]

There was an immediate flurry of angry replies from Republicans in Congress and especially in the Senate, where John P. Hale of New Hampshire and Lyman Trumbull of Illinois took the lead in denouncing the President's message. Southerners were by no means silent, but they seemed content to leave rebuttal primarily in the hands of northern Democrats like Lewis Cass of Michigan and George E. Pugh of Ohio. The debate had been going strong for two weeks when reargument of the Dred Scott case got under way on December 15, and it ranged over much of the ground that the Court would cover. For instance, Trumbull cited John Marshall's decision in *American Insurance Company v. Canter* as judicial authority for congressional power to prohibit slavery in the territories. Cass and Pugh responded with exceedingly narrow interpretations of the territory clause and of Marshall's opinion, presenting arguments remarkably similar to those later used by Taney.[25]

The running debate in Congress was well covered by the press, and the discussion spilled over into private conversations of Washington society. There were renewed expressions of hope for a judicial settlement of the central issue. Obviously, postponement of the Dred Scott case had not defused it. Every one of the nine justices must have realized by this time that the Court had an explosive package on its hands. The conflict over slavery had not subsided since the election, and, indeed, the southern mood was darkened further by reports of slave revolts in several states. Many more people were now aware of what might be at stake in one Negro's suit for freedom. The reargument, when it began on December 15, drew a large audience that included "many distinguished jurists and members of Congress."[26]

III

At first it appeared that Montgomery Blair would again be Scott's only counsel, but at the last moment he acquired the limited assistance of George T. Curtis, who agreed to present a defense of congressional power in the territories. Curtis, like his brother Justice Benjamin R. Curtis, had been a supporter of Daniel Webster and was associated in the public mind with enforcement of the Fugitive Slave Act in Massachusetts. So he seemed even further removed than Blair from the mainstream of the antislavery movement. Now that the political implications of the case were widely recognized, it became more noticeable that Dred Scott had no prominent champion of freedom in his corner. This state of affairs inspired some comment and controversy at the time, and the failure of antislavery radicals to take an earlier interest in the case remains something of a puzzle. Yet Scott himself was better off with relatively conservative counsel, for his hope of freedom depended upon the Court's rising above political and sectional considerations.[27]

Again the Court heard some twelve hours of argument extending over four days. Blair led off alone, with Geyer and Johnson following, and Blair then used up another two hours on the final day, leaving only one hour for Curtis. The performances of Johnson and Curtis won most of the public acclaim, in part, perhaps, because they concentrated more heavily on the territorial issue. There was some grumbling in Republican circles that Blair should have allotted more time to his associate.[28]

The technical question of whether the plea in abatement was before the court, supposedly the moot issue that had prompted the order for reargument, received only brief attention, and that from just two of the counsel. Blair predictably maintained that Sanford, by pleading over to the merits, had waived any further right to raise the question of jurisdiction. Among the precedents that he cited were several rulings by the Taney Court itself.[29] Geyer, in turn, emphasized the limited nature of federal jurisdiction in civil suits brought under the Judiciary Act of 1789. Scott's averment, he argued, must be without defect or there could be no jurisdiction. Not even an uncontested averment could give jurisdiction if it were defective. Thus, everything depended on the soundness of the circuit court's decision on the plea in abatement. "If that was erroneous," said Geyer, "it was error to proceed further, and the defendant's pleading over could not give jurisdiction."[30]

The matter at issue here was virtually a second jurisdictional question grafted onto the first—namely, did the Supreme Court have jurisdiction over the jurisdictional question that had been presented to the lower federal court? A negative answer, which Blair desired, would leave standing the decision by Judge Wells confirming Scott's right to bring suit and accepting jurisdiction. This would presumably mean that the Court must proceed directly to a consideration of Scott's claim to freedom, bypassing the entire subject of Negro citizenship. On the other hand, an affirmative answer, for which Geyer argued, would reopen the basic jurisdictional question of whether a Negro was a citizen to the extent of being able to bring suit under the Judiciary Act of 1789. This latter, more important issue, which might or might not be adjudicated, had likewise been made a subject of special interest in the Court's order for reargument.

Blair spoke for more than an hour on the citizenship question, going over much the same ground that he had covered in February. His argument was perceptive and cogent, deserving of more praise than it received. He demonstrated that the word "citizen" had been used frequently in both state and federal law to mean "inhabitant" or "free inhabitant." He pointed to the mingling of these terms in the fourth Article of Confederation, which provided that the "free inhabitants" of each state should be entitled to all the privileges and immunities of "free citizens" in the other states; and he reminded the Court that two efforts to exclude non-white persons from this guarantee had been defeated by votes of eight to two. The Constitution, to be sure, spoke only of "citizens" in its version of the privileges-and-immunities clause. But this verbal change, Blair insisted, implied no change in substance, no intention to exclude free Negroes; for it had been made without the objections and debate that would surely have greeted any effort at such exclusion. Blair also distinguished between "civil rights," and "political functions" such as voting, officeholding, and jury service—functions from which various classes of citizens were excluded. Political disabilities, in short, did not deprive free Negroes of citizenship, and neither did the social discrimination which made them "a caste in society"; for the color line, like other lesser social distinctions, belonged in the category of "manners and customs," while it was "unknown to the law." At the very least, Blair argued, free Negroes were "*quasi* citizens," possessing the right to own property, carry on business, and seek redress in the courts.

Even if they were excluded, as some state courts had mistakenly held, from the protection of the privileges-and-immunities clause in Article Four, Section Two, of the Constitution, this did not impair their rights under Article Three, Section Two (the diverse-citizenship clause), which had been exercised "without question." Indeed, the Chief Justice himself, in *LeGrand v. Darnall*, had once brought suit for a client against a Negro under the diverse-citizenship provision. Thus Blair's last line of defense was the concept of limited citizenship that Judge Wells had adopted in ruling against Sanford's plea in abatement.[31]

Geyer's treatment of the citizenship question was briefer and less coherent than Blair's, but it contained the elements of a clever argument. He began, significantly, by asserting that parties in a federal suit must be able to prove their national as well as their state citizenship: "Citizens within the meaning of art. 3, sec. 2, are citizens of the United States who are citizens of the States in which they respectively reside"—so ran his brief. Citizens of the United States, Geyer continued, were either born to that status or they had acquired it by naturalization under some federal law or treaty. But Dred Scott, admittedly, was by birth a slave rather than a citizen, and he had never been naturalized. Therefore, even if his travels with Emerson had made him a free man, they had not made him a citizen of the United States. "The power of naturalization is exclusively vested in Congress," Geyer declared. "A slave, who is not a citizen, can not become such by virtue of a deed of manumission or other discharge from bondage."[32] What seemed to be emerging here was a distinction between free-born free Negroes and slave-born free Negroes, with the latter more obviously excluded from United States citizenship. Geyer failed to clinch his argument, however. Instead, he obscured it by mixing in statements and citations to the effect that *all* free blacks were excluded from citizenship. Nevertheless, in shifting the focus from state to federal citizenship, he anticipated the line of reasoning that Taney would follow.

Reverdy Johnson contributed little to the debate, and George T. Curtis said nothing at all on the subject of Negro citizenship. The contest lay between Blair and Geyer, with Blair having the better of it except in the matter of federal citizenship as presented by Geyer. The exception proved to be critically important.

It was likewise Blair and Geyer, primarily, who dealt with the question of whether Dred Scott's two-year stay in Illinois had worked his emancipation. Geyer, for the negative, merely reiterated two familiar arguments: (1) Emerson, as an army officer at a military installation in Illinois, had been a sojourner rather than a resident of the state, and as such he had not forfeited ownership of his slave; (2) whether free or not under Illinois law, Scott's status after his return to Missouri was determined by Missouri law as interpreted by the highest court of that state (the doctrine of reversion).[33]

Blair's treatment of the subject showed more originality and indicated that he had given the case much additional study since the first round of arguments in February. For one thing, he now came to grips with the *Strader* case and put his finger accurately on the fallacy of regarding it as a controlling precedent. To wit, the Supreme Court had refused to accept jurisdiction in that case on the ground that it involved no federal question. This ruling therefore affirmed only the *finality*, and not the *legal soundness*, of the decision rendered in the supreme court of Kentucky. No such jurisdictional question arose in *Dred Scott v. Sandford*, where federal jurisdiction was original and depended upon the character of the parties rather than the nature of the law to be applied. Blair did not go so far, however, as to pin the *dictum* label on Taney's opinion in the *Strader* case.[34]

As for the military sojourner argument, Blair neatly inverted it by pointing to the lack of any evidence in the record "that Dr. Emerson had or claimed a residence elsewhere whilst he was living at these [military] posts." And he reminded the Taney Court that according to one of its own decisions, "where a person lives is taken *prima facie* to be his domicil."[35]

Blair's principal task, of course was to discredit the majority opinion in *Scott v. Emerson*, which had in turn largely governed the decision of the federal circuit court in *Dred Scott v. Sandford*. First he minimized the legal weight of the opinion, and then he attacked the substance of its argument. "The decision of the supreme court of Missouri," he declared, "is of no weight at all, beyond what is due to the research, reason and authority which the opinion accompanying the judgment displays, or which may be due to the character of the court which pronounces it."[36]

> It is only upon questions arising upon a local law of real property, or on the construction of the statutes of a State, that the exposition given by the supreme court of a State is adopted by the courts of the United States . . . whereas, in this case, no such statute or local law is involved. But the question depends on general principles of law; and the courts of the United States, whilst they will respectfully consider the decisions of the State court, decide such questions according to their own judgment of the law.[37]

But if *Scott v. Emerson* deserved no special consideration, its logic might still be compelling. Was there a sound legal basis for the doctrine of reattachment—that Dred Scott, even if temporarily freed by Illinois law, had resumed the status of slavery when he went back to Missouri with his master? Not at all, said Blair. The decision of the Missouri supreme court had been made in defiance of longstanding Missouri precedent and for admittedly political reasons. The cases cited as authority were not relevant.[38] Furthermore, the Missouri court had been wrong in viewing the enforcement of Illinois antislavery law as a forfeiture of property. Emancipation in cases like Scott's was not a penalty imposed upon the slaveholder, but rather a recognition of the legal effect produced by the master's voluntary act of taking his slave to reside in a free state. Thus no "penal" justice was involved, and the obligations of interstate comity were binding on Missouri.

Blair acknowledged that a sovereign state might put some limits on this obligation by refusing to enforce laws of other states that it found repugnant. But Missouri, he argued, had never manifested hostility to suits for freedom. On the contrary, its code of laws made such suits "favored actions," no matter where a plaintiff had acquired this asserted right to freedom. The same was true, he added of all the other slaveholding states in the Union.[39]

Aside from the question of whether Emerson, as an army officer, had been a resident or merely a sojourner during his two years in Illi-

nois, this was the fundamental matter at issue—the nature and operation of interstate comity. The general principles, as set forth by Story
in his *Conflict of Laws* and endorsed by Taney in *Bank of Augusta v.
Earle,* were not in dispute. A state law had extraterritorial force
within the boundaries of another state only with the latter's consent.
Such consent might be assumed, however. "In the silence of any positive rule, affirming or denying, or restraining the operation of foreign
laws," Taney had echoed Story in 1839, "courts of justice presume the
tacit adoption of them by their own government, unless they are
repugnant to its policy, or prejudicial to its interests."[40] The critical
importance of the Story-Taney exception is obvious. Presumably a
"positive rule" would have to come from a state legislature, but the
Chief Justice had plainly indicated that "courts of justice" might on
their own responsibility find a foreign law to be "repugnant" or "prejudicial." And that was precisely what the supreme court of Missouri
had done in *Scott v. Emerson.* Thus, in spite of Blair's able argument,
the weight of judicial precedent seemed to be on Sanford's side,
unless Missouri law authorizing suits for freedom constituted a "positive rule" on the subject (as Blair contended), or unless it should be
held that interstate relations involving slavery were not governed by
the established rules of comity.

As for Dred Scott's claim to freedom by virtue of his residence at
Fort Snelling, there was no compelling legal reason why it should not
have been argued on the same ground. The federal law prohibiting
slavery north of 36° 30′ was municipal rather than national in character. It could scarcely have any more extraterritorial force than the law
of a sovereign state like Illinois. Inside Missouri, the prohibition was
as "foreign" as the law of Illinois and therefore just as unenforceable
without Missouri's consent. Such, at least, had been the reasoning of
Judge Scott in the state supreme court, and it accorded with Taney's
dictum in *Strader v. Graham.*[41]

Curiously, however, both Geyer and Johnson neglected this line
of defense, which might have benefited their client but not the slaveholding South in any significant way. Instead, they relied wholly on
the argument that Dred Scott had remained a slave during his years
at Fort Snelling because the federal law forbidding slavery in that

region was unconstitutional. The constitutionality of the Missouri
Compromise restriction, it will be remembered, had never been at
issue in the earlier deliberations of three courts that heard the case.
Neither had it received any special mention in the Supreme Court's
order for reargument. Yet this constitutional question, the only subject taken up by all four counsel, was now plainly the center of attention. With Dred Scott's private cause converted into a public issue,
the courtroom of highest justice had become a political arena.

In challenging congressional power over slavery in the territories, counsel for Sanford were forced to rely heavily on theoretical
assertion, since the weight of precedent and established practice was
against them. Scott's lawyers, for the same reason, were more disposed to recite the historical record. The argument of Geyer and
Johnson rested largely upon a narrow interpretation of the territory
clause and a broad appeal to the principle of state equality. In response, Blair and Curtis maintained that broad construction of the
territory clause had been intended by the framers of the Constitution,
implemented repeatedly by Congress, confirmed by the Supreme
Court, and accepted virtually without question by the American people for half a century. Instead of attempting to summarize the entire
debate on the subject, it may be more illuminating to abstract a few
significant exchanges of argument:

Geyer-Johnson: The word "territory" as used in the Constitution
means nothing more than "land." A clause intended merely to provide for disposal of soil cannot endow Congress with "supreme, universal and unlimited power" over the persons and property of territorial inhabitants. *Blair-Curtis:* The clause in question comprises two
distinct powers, originating in two separate proposals by Madison at
the Constitutional Convention. One is the power to dispose of public
lands and other federal property. The other is the power, in
Madison's words, to "institute temporary governments," rephrased to
read: "make all needful rules respecting the territory" (not respecting
merely *disposal* of the territory, for that would be tautological). The
fact that the territory clause is combined with the clause providing for
admission of new states, the two constituting a separate section of

Article Four, indicates that the framers were dealing with the problem of government, as well as the disposal of soil, in the western territories. The authority to "make all needful rules" is therefore a plenary legislative power, limited only by specific constitutional restrictions such as those set forth in the First Amendment.[42]

Geyer-Johnson: The power of Congress to institute temporary municipal governments in the territories is acknowledged. But it is an implied power, rather than an expressly enumerated one, and arises out of necessity. Only legislation that is necessary for the establishment of a temporary government can be constitutionally justified, and a law prohibiting slavery does not fall within that category. *Blair-Curtis:* The question of whether any particular piece of legislation is "needful" cannot be settled by judicial action. It is, instead, a political question, and aggrieved persons must seek political remedies. Slavery has been a subject of legislation wherever legislative power exists and is as much so in the territories as in the states.

Blair-Curtis: Southerners like John C. Calhoun have frequently acknowledged the power of Congress to prohibit slavery in the territories. They accepted the Missouri Compromise line, for example, and later proposed extending it to the Pacific. *Geyer-Johnson:* The Missouri Compromise was a "compromise of principle necessary to the existence of the Union," and the Supreme Court has never upheld its constitutionality. The measure is therefore no final authority for a court of justice.

Geyer-Johnson: The Missouri Compromise restriction violates the spirit of the Constitution by disparaging the domestic institutions of certain states and denying their citizens equal access to western territories. *Blair-Curtis:* The law excludes no citizen from any territory, and southerners have in fact emigrated to free territories in large numbers. Instead, the law forbids the holding of a kind of property that can be legally held in certain states. To find it unconstitutional would be to make the constitutionality of federal legislation dependent on the variable property laws of the states. The law in question does not affect the states, either in their "equality or dignity, or in any other respect," for the states have no rights, legislative or otherwise, in the territories.

Geyer-Johnson: The restriction is unconstitutional because the power to prohibit slavery is not expressly conferred on Congress by the Constitution. *Blair-Curtis:* The restriction is a valid exercise of the legislative power because it is nowhere expressly forbidden in the Constitution.

For all its dry legal content, the debate in the crowded little courtroom was also at times intensely political, especially on the part of Geyer and Johnson. Their case argument turned frequently into general vindication of the South and slavery—an institution, said Johnson, that would last "for all time." In the background all the while, like an orchestral accompaniment to the arguments of counsel, were the echoes of acrimonious congressional debate on the same subject in the same building, while incoming reports of slave insurrections, planned or in progress, heightened the sense of urgency with which many Americans watched the judicial proceedings.

IV

Thus the second round of arguments ended, and although further delay ensued, it seemed almost certain that a decision would be handed down before the end of the term. In summary, the Court had a series of four questions before it, presumably to be answered in the following order:

1. *Was the plea in abatement before the Court?* On this question, the justices themselves were badly divided; for although the common law rule of pleading seemed to support a negative answer, it was by no means clear that the rule applied within the federal court system. A negative answer, desired by Scott's counsel, would leave standing the lower court's ruling against the plea, and the Supreme Court would move directly to consideration of the merits of the case—that is, to questions 3 and 4. An affirmative answer would lead the Court to a review of the lower court ruling and to a decision on the second question.

2. *Was Dred Scott a citizen of Missouri and thus capable of bringing such a suit in a federal court?* Here, precedent and logic

seemed to favor slightly the limited affirmative answer previously returned by the lower court—namely, that a free Negro was a citizen,
at least to the extent of being able to sue under the diverse-
citizenship clause. A negative answer to this question would presumably conclude the action in Sanford's favor with an order directing the
lower court to dismiss the case for lack of jurisdiction. An affirmative
answer would carry the Court on to a consideration of the case on its
merits.

3. *Was Scott free as a consequence of his residence in Illinois?*
Much depended here upon whether Scott's residence at Forts
Armstrong and Snelling was regarded as mere sojourn or as the
equivalent of domicile. Yet, even if the latter, more reasonable view
were to prevail, the sweeping character of Judge Scott's pronouncement in *Scott v. Emerson,* together with the *Strader* "precedent" and
established judicial doctrine on interstate comity, gave the advantage

THE QUESTIONS BEFORE THE COURT

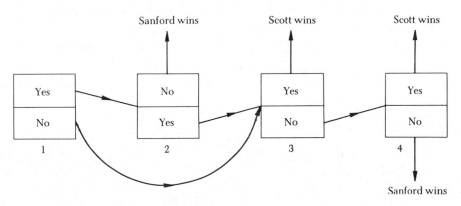

1. Is the plea in abatement before the court?
2. Is a Negro a citizen?
3. Did Scott become free in Illinois?
4. Did Scott become free at Fort Snelling by virtue of the Missouri Compromise?

to Sanford. An affirmative answer would, of course, mean victory for Scott. A negative answer, which seemed more likely, would necessitate consideration of question 4.

4. *Was Scott free as a consequence of his residence at Fort Snelling?* Insofar as the answer depended upon a decision regarding the constitutionality of the Missouri Compromise restriction, the weight of history and practice appeared to be on Scott's side. However, the same principles of reversion and reattachment with which the defense had responded to question 3 were arguably applicable here as the basis for a decision in Sanford's favor.

Given the makeup of the Court, a decision against Scott seemed almost certain, but the political magnitude of the case depended upon the way in which that decision was reached. One simple solution would have been to answer question 1 in the affirmative and question 2 in the negative, thereby reversing the lower court's ruling against the plea in abatement and causing the case to be dismissed for want of jurisdiction. Excluding free Negroes from citizenship would no doubt arouse anger in abolitionist circles, but not among the great majority of northerners who equated black skins with natural inferiority. The Court, however, was so evenly divided on the status of the plea in abatement that an effective decision probably could not be reached in this manner.

Another solution, equally simple and even less controversial, was also available. The Court could merely uphold the decision of the lower court, using the *Strader* doctrine as the basis for returning negative answers to both question 3 and question 4. It was toward this strategy of self-restraint that a majority of the justices, with some reluctance, began to move.

∽ 13 ∽

Voices in Confusion

B y Christmas 1856, Dred Scott's name was probably familiar to most Americans who followed the course of national affairs. Major newspapers throughout the country carried summaries of the four-day reargument, though only a few added editorial comment. The "great case," as Alexander H. Stephens now labeled it, received some attention on the floor of Congress and a good deal more in the private discussions of Washington politicians.[1]

Contrary to some expectations of a prompt decision, another delay of many weeks set in. The principal reason, it appears, was the prolonged absence of one justice and an accompanying reluctance to dispose of such an important case without the full Court present. Justice Daniel's wife suffered a horrible death on January 3 when her clothing caught fire, and the grief-stricken man did not attend another session until the middle of February. Accordingly, it was on February 14 that the Court held its first conference of the term on the Dred Scott case.[2]

As the first conference proceeded, two things became clear. First, Nelson had come over to the side of the four justices who held that the plea in abatement, embracing the question of Negro citizenship, was not before the Court; or at least he now believed that this jurisdictional problem need not and should not figure in the decision. Second, only the five southern justices were willing to invalidate the

305

Missouri Compromise restriction. Curtis and McLean took the opposite view, while Nelson and Grier preferred simply to uphold the
circuit court's decision.[3] The prospect of having such a momentous
pronouncement supported by just the bare majority of a court divided
along sectional lines could not fail to inspire misgivings. At any rate,
the relatively innocuous strategy of Nelson and Grier won approval.
Nelson was appointed to write the opinion of the Court, in which six
other justices would presumably concur. This would mean no decision on the citizenship issue or on the power of Congress to prohibit
slavery in the territories.

As a way of settling the contest between Dred Scott and John
Sanford, such a course of action was technically unexceptionable. A
majority of the justices now believed that they could not or should
not review the jurisdictional question of Negro citizenship, and the
territorial issue was not even a part of the record forwarded from the
lower court with the writ of error. Yet the claims of Scott and Sanford
were no longer primary matters of concern. The sectional debate over
the constitutionality of the Missouri Compromise restriction had dominated the reargument of the case, and the public now generally expected a decision on this issue.

The very setting and atmosphere in which they deliberated
tended to press the justices toward a broader decision. Here, it
seemed, was an opportunity for judicial statesmanship. By acting
boldly, the Court might be able to dispose of a dangerous public issue
and perhaps save the nation from disaster. In addition, some of the
southern justices may have been subjected to sectional pressures of a
more definite kind; for here also was an opportunity to rescue the
South officially from the discrimination and insult discernible in federal laws hostile to slavery.[4] From the few hints available, it is impossible to determine the amount of such pressure or to say just how it
was applied. The Chief Justice would have resisted any intrusion
upon his rigorous sense of propriety, but some of his colleagues were
perhaps more accessible. For example, Alexander H. Stephens informed his brother on December 15 that he was urging the Court to a
prompt decision, with the full expectation that it would settle the territorial issue in the South's favor. A likely object of Stephens's influ-

ence was his fellow Georgian, Justice Wayne, and Wayne proved to be the pivotal figure in an abrupt reversal of the strategy first adopted by the Court's majority.[5]

There was also pressure, direct but characteristically subtle, from the President-elect. James Buchanan, fussing with the problem of what to say about the territorial issue in his inaugural address, wrote to his old friend Justice Catron on February 3. Ostensibly, he wanted merely to know whether the Court would hand down a decision before Inauguration Day, so that he could take it into account. Catron replied that the Court had as yet taken no action on the case, but he thought that Buchanan was entitled to the information, and he would try to obtain it. The implications of this exchange were plain enough. Only a decision on the constitutionality of the Missouri Compromise restriction could be of any importance to Buchanan in preparing his inaugural. The new President saw himself as the country's peace-maker, but he had no formula for peace. Like the Democratic plat-form, his campaign pronouncements on the territorial issue had been equivocal, and Congress showed no signs of producing a satisfactory solution. Perhaps instead there could be a solution made acceptable by the fact that it came from a satisfactory source. A Supreme Court decision firmly supported by the President would no doubt settle the troublesome constitutional arguments and abate the sectional storm.

Catron wrote again on February 10 with what must have been disappointing news. The Dred Scott case, he revealed, would be decided in a conference on Saturday, the fourteenth, but not in a way to help Buchanan with his inaugural; for the Court would probably not pass judgment on the power of Congress over slavery in the terri-tories.[6] The assignment of the majority opinion to Nelson soon con-firmed Catron's prediction.

Nelson set to work promptly, perhaps on the weekend of Febru-ary 14–15, and produced a short opinion of about five thousand words.[7] This, the Dred Scott decision that almost was, began with an equitable summary of the opposing views on the plea in abatement. Tactfully, as the spokesman of the Court, Nelson left the issue open, saying only: "In the view we have taken of the case, it will not be nec-essary to pass on this question." Turning then to the merits of the

case, he began, significantly, by assuming that Dred had been taken from Missouri into Illinois "with a view to a temporary residence."*
He then reasoned his way from the accepted definition of comity to the principle of reversion, with the resulting conclusion that Dred Scott's status when he brought suit depended entirely on the law of Missouri as previously determined by the highest court of that state in *Scott v. Emerson*. "The laws of each [state]," he declared, "have no extraterritorial operation within the jurisdiction of another, except such as may be voluntarily conceded by her laws or courts of justice." If Scott became free at Fort Armstrong, he did so because Illinois refused to recognize and enforce the slave law of Missouri. Once he returned to Missouri, the situation was reversed. "Has the law of Illinois any greater force within the jurisdiction of Missouri than the laws of the latter within the former? Certainly not. They stand upon equal footing." For the same reasons, Nelson continued, Scott did not become free by virtue of the Missouri Compromise restriction during his residence at Fort Snelling. A territorial law of Congress had no extraterritorial force superior to that of a state law. Taney had made this clear in *Strader v. Graham*, declaring that the Northwest Ordinance, if still in force, "could have no more operation than the laws of Ohio, in the State of Kentucky." Thus Missouri law likewise controlled Scott's status after his return to that state from Fort Snelling. Nelson's logic, as we shall see, was by no means impeccable, and his conclusions rested upon more than one dubious assumption. Still, it appeared that his opinion, as the official opinion of the Court would affect only a relatively few Negroes, and he had made effective use of the Chief Justice's own words to demonstrate that there was no need to consider the constitutionality of the Missouri Compromise restriction.

II

The ink was scarcely dry on Nelson's draft, however, before the Court majority reversed itself and decided to take hold of the thornier

---

*For discussion of this point and a more extensive treatment of the Nelson opinion, see below, pp. 390–94.

problems that he had so carefully avoided. On the motion of Wayne, it was agreed that Taney should write the opinion of the Court, covering all the questions arising in the case. This change occurred after February 14 but apparently no later than February 19; for on the latter date, Catron wrote again to Buchanan, indicating that the Court *would* render a decision on the constitutionality of the Missouri Compromise restriction. The inaugural address, he added, might therefore include a passage leaving the whole matter with the "appropriate tribunal" and declining to "express any opinion on the subject."[8] Wayne justified his crucial motion with the argument that public expectation had made it the Court's duty to decide the larger issues in the case.[9] But Catron offered a different explanation in his letter to Buchanan. The Court majority, he asserted, had been "forced up" to its change of plan by the determination of Curtis and McLean to present extensive dissenting opinions discussing all aspects of the case. Justice Grier said about the same thing in a letter written to Buchanan four days later. This evidence has been enough to convince many historians that the willfulness of the two dissenting justices compelled the shift from Nelson's supposedly innocuous treatment of the case to Taney's broader and more inflammatory opinion.[10] The explanation is appealingly simple but not entirely satisfactory.

For one thing, the statements of Catron and Grier amount to second-hand information that is unsupported by any contemporary testimony from Curtis and McLean themselves, or from any of the other four southern justices who were supposedly "forced up" to changing their plans by the two dissenters. It appears that Curtis in later years may have denied the accuracy of the Catron-Grier explanation and insisted that his opinion had been a response to that of the Chief Justice. As for the four southern justices, only Campbell among them ever wrote out an account of the last-minute change of strategy, and he said nothing about pressure from the dissenters.[11]

Furthermore, as Allan Nevins has asked, what purpose could have inspired the allegedly perverse determination of McLean and Curtis to discuss issues that the other seven justices were allegedly willing to keep silent about? After all, the power to regulate slavery in the territories, frequently exercised by Congress, would have re-

mained judicially unimpaired in the Nelson opinion. Why force the
issue and thereby run the risk of provoking a decision far more unfavorable to the cause of freedom? There were some northern radicals,
to be sure, who desired such a decision for its incendiary effects, but
McLean, a conservative Republican, can scarcely be fitted into that
kind of role, and Curtis even less so. [12]

One answer, offered by the historian Frank H. Hodder, is that
both men were motivated by self-interest. McLean still believed that
an eloquent dissent might lift him into contention for the Republican
presidential nomination. Curtis, having decided to retire from the
Court and resume his Boston law practice, was eager to rehabilitate
his reputation in that city, where he had made himself highly unpopular by upholding the rights of slaveholders under the Fugitive
Slave Act. For the most part, however, these are merely Hodder's
conjectures. There is no evidence, for instance, that Curtis's decision
to retire from the Court preceded his decision to dissent in the Dred
Scott case. As for McLean, he did indeed continue to dream of the
presidency, even though he would be seventy-five years old when the
next campaign got under way. But whether these pathetic whispers of
hope for 1860 actually governed his judicial conduct in 1857 is a different question. Furthermore, one may well suspect bias in a historical explanation that attributes selfish personal motives only to the two
dissenting justices. [13]

The principal mistake of many historians has been their assumption that the five southern justices were all willing at first to let Nelson speak for them, and that only McLean and Curtis insisted on discussing the territorial question. The majority never came to such
complete agreement, however, and multiple opinions, as we have
seen, were common in the Taney Court. Wayne prepared a separate
Dred Scott opinion that undoubtedly dealt with the Missouri Compromise, since he laid it aside as unnecessary when Taney replaced
Nelson as spokesman for the Court. There is also evidence that Daniel intended to file his own opinion, and the same may have been true
of Taney and Campbell. [14] Thus what seems to have been in prospect
was a debate carried on over Nelson's head. Dissenting *and* concur-

ring justices would be arguing the paramount issue of the decade, while the subject was avoided in the official "opinion of the Court." The Court majority, it appears, had maneuvered themselves into an absurd situation, and their abrupt change of plan was, among other things, a way of getting out.

But the best explanation may well be the most obvious one. That is, the change of plan did spell victory for those justices who had wanted all along to issue an emphatically pro-southern decision. Here, the conspicuous figure was Wayne. He made the key motion in conference and later claimed that the initiative had been his alone. Yet one should not discard the possibility that Taney played a more important part than is visible on the surface. Behind his mask of judicial propriety, the Chief Justice had become privately a bitter sectionalist, seething with anger at "Northern insult and Northern aggression." His ostensibly passive role in the conferences is inconsistent with the temper of the opinion that he ultimately delivered. It seems unlikely that Wayne offered his motion shifting the opinion of the Court to Taney without first sounding him out. Furthermore, Wayne specified that the Chief Justice should cover *all* the major issues raised in the case. This is highly significant, for it meant including the question of Negro citizenship, which a majority of the justices had supposedly waved aside, but which Taney was anxious to discuss, as his opinion subsequently revealed. In short, the voice was Wayne's but the hand may have been the hand of Taney. Physically weak but still a man of strong will, the Chief Justice wrote the opinion that he had wanted to write all along.[15]

There remained the problem that a five-man decision on the territorial issue would be of dubious effect and might damage the Court's prestige. Accordingly, pressure was brought to bear on Grier, the one likely recruit among the four northern justices. Although privately disposed to regard the Missouri Compromise restriction as unconstitutional, Grier had nevertheless preferred to join Nelson in bypassing the question. Catron, in his letter of February 19 and again four days later, urged Buchanan to help bring his fellow Pennsylvanian into line.[16] Buchanan promptly wrote to Grier, who promptly

conferred with Taney and Wayne. They had little difficulty complet-
ing the work of persuasion. On February 23, Grier replied to Buchanan in a long letter that ended as follows:

> I am anxious that it should not appear that the line of latitude
> should mark the line of division in the court. I feel also that the
> opinion of the majority will fail of much of its effect if founded on
> clashing and inconsistent arguments. On conversation with the
> chief justice, I have agreed to *concur with him.* Brother Wayne
> and myself will also use our endeavors to get brothers Daniel and
> Campbell and Catron to do the same. . . . But I fear some rather
> extreme views may be thrown out by some of our southern
> brethren. There will therefore be six, if not *seven* (perhaps Nelson
> will remain neutral), who will decide the compromise law of 1820
> to be of *non-effect.* But the opinions will not be delivered before
> Friday the 6th of March. We will not let any others of our
> brethren know anything about *the cause of our anxiety* to produce
> this result, and though contrary to our usual practice, we have
> thought due to you to state to you in candor and confidence the
> real state of the matter.[17]

From this letter several interesting facts emerge. Catron and
Grier were, for the moment at least, unaware of each other's correspondence with Buchanan. Each thought that the other needed persuading—Grier, to join the majority in a decision against the constitutionality of the Missouri Compromise restriction; Catron, to agree
with Taney in the reasons given for that decision. It is also obvious
that Grier, fearing the "extreme views" of some southern justices
while at the same time preparing to concur with Taney, had no clear
idea of the kind of opinion that the latter intended to write. In the
end, neither Grier nor Catron gave the Chief Justice total support.

Buchanan, whose intervention had undoubtedly contributed to
the turn of events, was now assured of the judicial rescue that he so
desperately desired. Knowing, however, that it would not occur until
after his inauguration, he could only prepare to follow the advice of
Catron. On March 4, a bright spring day, the new President took the
oath of office administered by the aged Chief Justice. The two men
held a brief conversation during one pause in the ceremonies, and the

exchange did not go unnoticed among the attending crowd. For some hostile onlookers, the incident assumed a sinister meaning as they listened to a passage in the inaugural address. Near the beginning, Buchanan celebrated American devotion to the principle of self-government, as exhibited in the recent presidential election. After a tempestuous contest, all was now calm. "The voice of the majority, speaking in the manner prescribed by the Constitution, was heard, and instant submission followed." Fortunately, Congress had determined that the same principle of majority rule should prevail in the territories, where the people were left perfectly free (by the Kansas-Nebraska Act) to deal with the institution of slavery in their own way, subject only to the Constitution. There was, to be sure, a minor problem still awaiting solution:

> A difference of opinion has arisen in regard to the point of time when the people of a Territory shall decide this question for themselves.
>
> This is, happily, a matter of but little practical importance. Besides, it is a judicial question, which legitimately belongs to the Supreme Court of the United States, before whom it is now pending, and will, it is understood, be speedily and finally settled. To their decision, in common with all good citizens, I shall cheerfully submit, whatever this may be.[18]

These disingenuous words were made to seem all too pat by the issuance of the Dred Scott decision just two days later. In antislavery circles, remembrance of the little chat preceding the inaugural soon blossomed into a tale of high-level intrigue. Taney, it was said, had revealed the substance of the forthcoming decision to Buchanan, who had then and there altered his text to make use of the information.[19] Many years afterward the ironic truth would come to light—that no such revelation was necessary because the President already knew, and the Chief Justice knew that he knew, what the Court would decide.

So runs the standard modern account of Buchanan's involvement in the Dred Scott case. But there is something more to puzzle over—a conspicuous discrepancy that has somehow escaped the attention of historians.

Both Catron and Grier had plainly informed Buchanan that the Court would rule on the constitutionality of the Missouri Compromise restriction—that is, on the power of *Congress* to prohibit slavery in the territories. This was the question that had received so much attention in the reargument of the case, and in the political arena it was the chief issue between Republicans and southern defenders of slavery. In his inaugural, however, Buchanan addressed himself to a different problem entirely. He proclaimed the imminent judicial settlement of the intraparty disagreement, largely between northern and southern Democrats, over the meaning of popular sovereignty.* That is, he predicted a ruling on the power of a *territorial legislature* to prohibit slavery. Now, since Dred Scott had laid no claim to freedom by virtue of a territorial law, this issue was not present in his suit and had never been argued by counsel. Neither had it been associated with the case in any newspaper commentary. What, then, had led Buchanan to think that the Court would settle the question?

One justice, and only one, actually answered the question that Buchanan had so ostentatiously turned over to the Court. That was Taney, who slipped into his opinion a few lines on the power of a territorial legislature over slavery. Although there is no evidence of any secret communication between the two men, one must at least consider the possibility that before Inauguration Day Buchanan saw a draft of the Taney opinion or received information in detail about its content. If so, the tale of intrigue was not entirely off the mark. The alternative explanation, no less difficult to believe, is that Buchanan not only misunderstood the significance of the Dred Scott case but somehow misread the explicit statements of Catron and Grier.[20]

III

On March 5, Taney absented himself from that day's session of the Court, no doubt in order to put the finishing touches on his opinion. The work must have taxed his strength to the limit. Justice Curtis, in a letter to his uncle on February 27, remarked: "Our aged Chief Jus-

*See above, pp. 197–98.

tice, who will be eighty years old in a few days, and who grows more feeble in body, but retains his alacrity and force of mind wonderfully, is not able to write much."[21] Besides the actual writing, a certain amount of preparatory reading would have been necessary, together with the labor of searching out the appropriate citations. Yet barely two weeks had passed since the decision that Taney should replace Nelson as spokesman for the Court majority. Previously, to be sure, he may very well have been drafting his own concurring opinion, and it is not impossible that Wayne, having written an opinion which he no longer intended to file, made it available to the Chief Justice, with whom he was in complete agreement.* Nevertheless, Taney did not finish the work to his own satisfaction by March 6. The opinion that he delivered on that date would have to be revised before it went into the record.

Taney led off the reading of opinions in a crowded courtroom on March 6. Already fatigued from the work of composition, he spoke in a low voice that became almost inaudible before the end of his two hours. To Republicans in the audience, this subdued presentation seemed appropriate for such a shameful decision. Nelson and Catron followed the Chief Justice with their relatively brief opinions. McLean and Curtis, the two dissenters, were heard the next day, taking up about five hours. The remaining justices filed their opinions without reading them from the bench.[22] In the explosion of editorial comment that ensued, Taney's "opinion of the Court" naturally received the most attention. It was caught in a crossfire of lavish Democratic praise and furious Republican denunciation, although its contents were but imperfectly known. Whereas McLean and Curtis promptly released the full texts of their opinions for newspaper publication, the Chief Justice withheld his manuscript for revision. The public had access only to a summary of the opinion, taken down in court by an Associated Press reporter and printed in major newspapers throughout the country.[23] This gave Republicans a definite advantage in the war of words. Taney found the situation embarrassing, and he nursed his resentment of the action taken by the two dis-

* On this subject there is further discussion below, pp. 389–90.

senters, which seemed not only improper and disrespectful but deliberately intended to encourage the violent partisan outcry against the
decision.

As weeks passed, and Taney's full opinion did not appear in
print, the word spread that he was undertaking extensive revisions.
The rumor had reached McLean by the end of March, and he wrote
to Montgomery Blair: "Can it be true that the opinion of the court has
been modified in the Dred Scott case? This, it appears to me, to be
unusual, if not improper."[24] At about the same time, James Harvey
investigated the matter and reported his findings to McLean: "There
are strong surmises about the manipulation to which the majority
opinions have been subjected. . . . Last week, they had not been
filed and were inaccessible. Taney's had been twice copied for revision, and an application from the *Intelligencer* to publish was refused,
owing to non-completion."[25]

The rumor worried Justice Curtis especially, for his dissent had
been keyed to Taney's opinion at many points. On April 2, he wrote
to William T. Carroll, Clerk of the Supreme Court, asking for a copy
of the opinion whenever it should be available in printed form. Carroll replied four days later that he had been directed not to give anyone a copy of the opinion before it was published officially in Howard's *Reports*. The directive had been issued by the Chief Justice with
the concurrence of Daniel and Wayne, the only other justices remaining in Washington after the close of the term, and it was obviously
aimed at Curtis. Taney's written confirmation of the order bore the
same date as Carroll's reply to Curtis (April 6). One sentence revealed
the anger that motivated him: "I have observed that the opinion of
the Court has been greatly misunderstood and grossly misrepresented in publications in the newspapers." Curtis promptly addressed
a second letter to the Clerk, repeating his request for a copy of the
opinion and expressing doubt that the directive extended to members
of the Court. It included everyone, Carroll replied. He had checked
again with the Chief Justice to make sure.[26]

Curtis then wrote to Taney for an explanation, saying that he did
not suppose the Chief Justice intended to deny him access to the
opinion of the Court. Taney responded with a hostile letter implying
that Curtis wanted the opinion for use by partisan critics of the Court.

"It would seem from your letter to me," he wrote, "that you suppose you are entitled to demand it as a right, being one of the members of the tribunal. This would undoubtedly be the case if you wished it to aid you in the discharge of your official duties. But I understood you as not desiring or intending it for that purpose. On the contrary, you announced from the Bench that you regarded this opinion as extrajudicial—and not binding upon you or anyone else."[27] Thus Taney made it plain that he resented the content of Curtis's dissenting opinion, as well as its early release for publication.

Stung by Taney's words, Curtis unwisely elected to continue the futile quarrel. In a letter dated May 13, he protested the impugnment of his motives, questioned the authority of three justices to impose such a restriction without first consulting their colleagues, and suggested that it was a violation of the rules of the Court to withhold an opinion for so long a time.* He reasserted his own official right to examine an opinion of the Court that, according to reports, had been "materially altered" since its oral delivery.

The Chief Justice fumed for nearly a month before firing off an eleven-page answer. Meanwhile, the whole argument became academic with the official publication of the Dred Scott decision late in May. He had no desire, Taney wrote on June 11, to continue the "unpleasant correspondence" that Curtis had been "pleased to commence," but certain statements could not be "passed by without notice." Having published his own opinion without consulting the Court, Curtis had no right to share in the disposition of the opinion of the Court, especially when his avowed object was to "impair its authority and discredit it as a judicial decision." This was the first time in history that a partisan attack upon a decision of the Supreme Court had been started by the publication of a dissenting opinion. As for the report that he, Taney, had substantially altered his opinion, it was utterly untrue:

> There is not one historical fact, nor one principle of constitutional
> law, or common law, or chancery law, or statute law in the printed

---

*The Supreme Court's Rule 25 (in force since 1834) declared: "All opinions delivered by the court shall, immediately upon the delivery thereof, be delivered over to the clerk to be recorded."[28]

opinion which was not distinctly announced and maintained from
the Bench; nor is there any one historical fact, or principle, or
point of law, which was affirmed in the opinion from the Bench,
omitted or modified, or in any degree altered, in the printed
opinion.

What had been added, Taney continued in an incredible passage,
were certain proofs and authorities to support historical facts and legal
principles asserted in his oral opinion but denied in the dissenting
opinions. "And until the Court heard them denied, it had not thought
it necessary to refer to proofs and authorities to support them—
regarding the historical facts and the principles of law which were
stated in the opinion as too well established to be open to dispute."
Here, covered over with a good deal of self-righteous indignation, was
the plain acknowledgment that the Taney revisions were indeed rebuttal to certain parts of the dissenting opinions.

A few days later, Taney confided to a close friend: "When I saw
you I thought Mr. Justice Curtis would not answer my [first] letter.
You thought otherwise, and that his letter would be in the tone of a
demagogue. You were right and I have received from him just such a
letter as you predicted. . . It was of a character that made it proper
to reply to it." Taney added that he expected Curtis to answer again.
"But every attempt to justify what cannot be justified, can only
plunge one in further difficulties. Yet he cannot feel comfortable in
his present position."[29]

Curtis did write still another letter, to which Taney responded
with a short acknowledgment that brought the exchange to a close.
And Curtis did feel uncomfortable about the dispute—so uncomfortable that by September he had submitted his resignation from the
Court.[30] His had been the initial blunder that provoked the quarrel,
but thereafter Taney was the aggressor. Personal spite is visible in
Taney's treatment of his colleague from Massachusetts, a state that he
detested.* After all, Justice McLean had also sinned against judicial
propriety by rushing his opinion into print, and yet there is no indication that the Chief Justice ever censured him for doing so. Such

* See below, pp. 554, 560.

antics had come to be expected from McLean, however, and he was armored with age and seniority. Curtis, on the other hand, was one of the Court's newest and youngest members—in Taney's eyes, a veritable whippersnapper and a typical product of New England hypocrisy.

In virtually forcing his younger associate off the bench, the Chief Justice was undoubtedly venting his hostility to the antislavery movement and his resentment of the personal abuse to which he had been subjected since the announcement of the Dred Scott decision. At the same time, he obviously derived a certain amount of pleasure from the quarrel with Curtis, and he found it invigorating to be at the center of a public controversy. He was an old warhorse given a whiff of political gunsmoke and remembering the excitement of former battles. To Franklin Pierce he wrote in August:

> You see I am passing through another conflict, much like the one which followed the removal of the deposits, and the war is waged upon me in the same spirit and by many of the same men who distinguished themselves on that occasion by the unscrupulous means to which they resorted.
>
> At my time of life when my end must be near, I should have enjoyed to find that the irritating strifes of this world were over, and that I was about to depart in peace with all men and all men in peace with me. Yet perhaps it is best as it is. The mind is less apt to feel the torpor of age when it is thus forced into action by public duties.[31]

When he finally acquired a copy of Taney's published opinion, Curtis compared it with his recollection of the oral version, which he had heard twice—first in conference and then again on March 6. He concluded that "upwards of eighteen pages" had been added. "No one can read them," he declared, "without perceiving that they are *in reply* to my opinion."[32] Thus Curtis maintained that about one-third of the published opinion was new material introduced as rebuttal, whereas Taney insisted emphatically that he had made no significant changes or additions. Which man's reckoning is more trustworthy? How much did Taney change his opinion after delivering it from the bench? For the most part, historians have merely recorded the disagreement, without attempting to settle it.

Unfortunately, the opinion that Taney read from the bench was not preserved, and the newspaper summary is inadequate for systematic comparison with the published version.[33] There are, nevertheless, some indications of the extent to which he revised the original document. For one thing, the Chief Justice read his opinion on March 6 in two hours or a little more, but at his measured pace, the published version (containing about 23,000 words) would have required at least three hours for reading. If so, the opinion was ultimately expanded about 50 per cent, making it some eighteen pages longer, as Curtis calculated.

This conclusion is partly confirmed by more definite evidence in the National Archives, where two different sets of page proofs of the Taney opinion have been preserved. Handwritten additions to the proofs constitute about eight pages of the version finally published.[34] The three most lengthy additions are as follows:

1. Five paragraphs (19 Howard 428–430) supplementing a passage of three paragraphs in which Taney defended the right of the Court to examine the facts in the case after having upheld the plea in abatement. All eight paragraphs are plainly rebuttal to the assertion of Curtis (and McLean) that much of Taney's opinion was without authority.[35]

2. Fifteen paragraphs (19 Howard 442–446) in which Taney attempted to reconcile his views on the territory clause with those of John Marshall in *American Insurance Company v. Canter*. This was likewise rebuttal, but primarily to McLean rather than Curtis.[36]

3. Three paragraphs (19 Howard 453–454) near the end of the opinion, denouncing the manner in which the case had been brought before the Supreme Court. This introduced a new question that had not been argued by counsel.[37]

Now, if Taney added eight pages *after* the document had been set in type, it is not difficult to believe that he had expanded the original manuscript by as much as ten pages *before* he sent it to the printer. It therefore appears that Curtis was substantially correct in his critique of the published opinion. Taney's denial of having made any significant changes, though perhaps not untruthful according to his own peculiar lights, must be labeled inaccurate. The so-called opinion of the Court included a considerable amount of material that few if any of the other justices heard or read before its publication. And much of this new material was rebuttal to the dissenting opinions of Curtis and McLean. Another complication is thereby added to an already labyrinthine case, and especially to the question that has fascinated and confused several generations of historians and legal scholars: *What did the Court actually decide?*

What the Court Decided

O nly one thing was absolutely certain. Dred Scott had lost his eleven-year legal battle for freedom in the last court of appeal. Seven of the nine justices agreed that at law he was still a slave. Beyond that simple fact, the results of the contest were far from clear. In his "opinion of the Court," Chief Justice Taney had emphatically excluded Negroes from citizenship and denied Congress the power to prohibit slavery in the territories. But were these declarations part of the *ratio decidendi* and therefore authoritative? Concerning the first, there was doubt that it had the support of a majority of the justices, while the second was promptly challenged with the label, *"obiter dictum."*

The perplexities of the Dred Scott decision were partly inherent in the case as it came before the Supreme Court and partly a result of the manner in which the Court handled the case. Confusing enough in itself was the double-layered jurisdictional problem presented by the plea in abatement. But in addition there was the peculiar circularity of relationship between the jurisdictional question and the merits of the case, for the latter could be subsumed entirely under the former. And then the complications were multiplied by the number and variety of concurring opinions, as well as by the widespread doubt that Taney, in some of his principal conclusions, actually spoke for a majority of the Court.

Accordingly, it is not surprising that efforts at clarification by several generations of scholars have, in some respects, only added new layers of confusion. Although one more such attempt can scarcely make things much worse, the record discourages any hope of a dazzling success. Some years ago, a young history teacher set out to discover what was decided in the Dred Scott case by examining the specialized scholarly literature on the subject. The report of his adventures is one of the best essays ever written about the decision, but it ended on a wry note. "After protracted wanderings in the Dred Scott labyrinth," he declared, ". . . the teacher is tempted to conclude that the only sensible way of handling the Dred Scott case in class is to ask—hurriedly—if there are any questions on the reading assignments which cover the subject, pray that there will be none, and then pass rapidly on to the Lincoln-Douglas debates."[1]

From one point of view, of course, there is nothing to puzzle over. What the Court decided was what the designated opinion of the Court announced as having been decided. To wit:

1. The ruling of the circuit court on the plea in abatement was subject to review by the Supreme Court.

2. Negroes were not citizens of the United States and therefore had no right to bring suit in a federal court under the diverse citizenship clause of the Constitution.

Consequently the circuit court had been wrong in its ruling on the plea in abatement and should not have accepted jurisdiction of the case.

3. Dred Scott, a slave, had not become a free man during his residence at Fort Snelling; for the Missouri Compromise restriction under which he claimed freedom was unconstitutional because Congress had no power to prohibit slavery in the federal territories.

4. Scott was not free as a result of his residence in Illinois; for his status, after his return to Missouri, depended entirely upon the law of that state as determined in *Scott v. Emerson.*

Consequently, Scott was still a slave, therefore not a citizen and therefore incapable of bringing suit in a federal court under the diverse-citizenship clause.

5. For these reasons, the suit must be returned to the circuit

court with instructions that it be dismissed for want of jurisdiction.

For the most part, however, historians have been unwilling to accept Taney's opinion as a definitive statement of what the Court decided. Instead, they have examined all of the opinions and endeavored, in effect, to count the "votes" of the justices on each of the major issues. This calculation of box scores began with contemporary critics of the decision and has continued ever since, with a variety of results that is in itself indicative of the difficulties involved.[2] The most common summing-up appears to be as presented in the box score that follows.

BOX SCORE

1. Four justices held that the plea in abatement was properly before the Court (Taney, Wayne, Daniel, and Curtis).

2. Three justices held that a Negro could not be a citizen of the United States (Taney, Wayne, and Daniel).

3. Six justices held that the Missouri Compromise restriction was invalid (Taney, Wayne, Grier, Daniel, Campbell, and Catron).

4. Seven justices held that the laws of Missouri determined Scott's status as a slave after his return to that state from Illinois (Taney, Wayne, Nelson, Grier, Daniel, Campbell, and Catron).

5. Seven justices held that Scott was still a slave, though there were differences on what the final judgment of the Court should be (same as in number 4).[3]

From these tabulations it has been easy enough to infer that "there was no judicial decision on the question of Negro citizenship."[4] For Taney's pronouncement on this issue appears to have been extrajudicial (because only a minority of justices thought that it was before the Court), and, in any case, only two other justices explicitly endorsed his ruling. From the tabulations it has also been possible to argue that there was no effective decision on the constitutionality of the Missouri Compromise restriction. The reasoning is that three of the six justices making up the majority on this question

(Taney, Wayne, and Daniel) had no right to consider the merits of the case after having declared that the circuit court lacked jurisdiction from the beginning.[5] By such logic, the decision of the Court has sometimes been reduced to what was contained in Nelson's opinion— namely, that Dred Scott remained a slave because his status was governed by the laws of Missouri. James Bradley Thayer, in preparing his *Cases on Constitutional Law* (1895), included Nelson's opinion rather than Taney's because it alone was limited "to grounds agreed upon by a majority of the court."[6] There are other scholars who have come to about the same conclusion, but it is a conclusion based on dubious reasoning and not in accord with historical realities.[7]

The most obvious flaw in the whole argument is that it proves self-destructive and leads ultimately to an absurdity. If, because of their stand on the Negro citizenship or jurisdictional question, three of the six justices invalidating the Missouri Compromise restriction actually had no right to consider the issue, then the same three obviously had no right to consider the other major substantive issue— that is, the effect of Missouri law upon Scott's status after his return from Illinois. To put it another way, if the three justices listed in item 2 of the box score must be subtracted from the total of six in item 3, then they must also be subtracted from the total of seven in item 4. Nelson's opinion is then not a bit more valid than Taney's. This would leave us with *nothing* decided by the Court except the judgment itself—that Scott, for some reason or other, was still a slave.

The absurdity results from the mistake of confusing the logic of individual justices with the decision-making of the Court. And the confusion begins with a false assumption that any justice who favors dismissal on jurisdictional grounds is automatically disqualified, *even against his will*, from considering the merits of the case. But this is true only if his views on jurisdiction are shared by a majority of the Court, in which case *all* the justices would be equally barred from proceeding authoritatively to the merits.[8] Jurisdiction is decided upon by the Court, not by individual justices, and if the Court decides to accept jurisdiction, then all members, whatever their views on the jurisdictional question, have the right to join in reviewing the case on its merits. As a matter of personal consistency, a justice may decline to participate in consideration of the merits after having opposed acceptance of jurisdiction. Taney had done so, for example, in *Rhode Island v. Massachusetts* (1838, 1846).[9] But the point is that this was his own voluntary choice. There was no rule of the Court, then or later, compelling such a choice.* Thus, whatever personal inconsistency may be attributed to Taney, there is no basis for arguing that he had no right to go to the merits and examine the constitutionality of the Missouri Compromise restriction, *unless* one accepts that his ruling on Negro citizenship (in spite of the box score) was authoritative. In short, critics of the Dred Scott decision cannot have it both ways. Either the Court did rule authoritatively against Negro citizenship, or else it did legitimately consider and settle the substantive issues in the case without indulging in dicta. It cannot have done *neither;* presumably it must have done *one or the other;* but what greatly complicates matters is the possibility that it may have managed to do *both.*

The way in which most of the box scores have been compiled is, in fact, open to question. They rest squarely on the assumption that, at each major point in the case, only those justices *expressly agreeing* with Taney are to be counted on his side. This means that justices not committing themselves on a certain issue are counted with the opposition. Yet, since Taney's opinion was the authorized opinion of the Court, it seems more reasonable to regard only those justices *explicitly disagreeing* with him as constituting the opposition. Such was the view of Judge Woodbury Davis of the Maine supreme court. Speaking of Taney's opinion, Davis said: "I do not perceive why the other members of the court should not be regarded as concurring in it, ex-

---

* In a case decided by the Supreme Court almost a century later, Justice John Marshall Harlan, "concurring in part and dissenting in part," concluded that the lower federal court had lacked jurisdiction. "Accordingly," he wrote, "I would vacate the judgment below and remand the case to the Court of Appeals with directions to dismiss the petition for lack of jurisdiction." Then at the end of his opinion he added: "The Court having decided, however, that the Court of Appeals had jurisdiction, I concur with the Court on the merits." Justice Felix Frankfurter, agreeing with Harlan on the jurisdictional question, preferred not to express views on the merits. At the same time, Frankfurter acknowledged that there were "exceptional situations" where it was "proper for a dissenter to go to the merits when a majority of the Court removes from the case threshold objections of procedure and jurisdiction." It is plain that for both men the choice was one that each justice must make for himself.[10]

cept upon those points which they have expressly disclaimed." The mandate to the circuit court, he pointed out, "could not have issued, except by order of a majority of the court," and that mandate directed the case to be dismissed for want of jurisdiction.[11] Consequently, there is another way to count the votes of individual justices:

COUNTER BOX SCORE

1. Two justices denied that the plea in abatement was properly before the Court (Catron and McLean).

2. Two justices held that Negroes were eligible for United States citizenship (McLean and Curtis).

3. Two justices upheld the validity of the Missouri Compromise restriction (McLean and Curtis).

4. Two justices held that Scott had become free in Illinois and remained so after his return to Missouri (McLean and Curtis).

5. Two justices favored reversing the decision of the circuit court and ordering a new trial (McLean and Curtis).

From this tabulation one can draw the conclusion that the official "opinion of the Court," since it never at any one point encountered explicit dissent from more than two justices, was authoritative on all the major questions presented by the case. What the Court decided was what Taney announced as decided. So much for the conclusiveness of box scores. Their meaning is derived less from the raw data than from the manipulation of the data by the respective scorekeepers.

The question of what the Court decided actually presents two distinct problems, with the second contingent on the first: (1) When Taney reviewed and reversed the ruling of the circuit court on the plea in abatement, thereby denying citizenship to Negroes, did he speak for a majority of the Supreme Court? If he did, and *only* if he did, the second problem arises. (2) Was it then legally possible for him and the Court to review the facts of the case and render judgment on whether Dred Scott had become a free man by virtue of Illinois law or the Missouri Compromise restriction?

The belief that Taney did not have a majority with him in his determination to review the plea in abatement stems not only from the box-score method but also from knowledge of what went on in conferences preceding the decision. At first, it will be remembered, the Court had been evenly divided on this technical question, with Nelson undecided but leaning toward Taney's side. Then, after the reargument, Nelson ostensibly switched to the other side, thus producing an anti-Taney majority, and as a consequence he was momentarily designated to write the opinion of the Court. But here a subtle distinction becomes important. From his published opinion it is plain that Nelson remained undecided about the plea in abatement, having concluded only that it would be better for the Court to by-pass an issue on which it was so badly divided.[12] Thus the anti-Taney group, with the addition of Nelson, became a negative majority only on the question of whether the Court should, as a matter of judicial strategy, consider the plea in abatement, and not on the question of whether it had the authority to do so.

The decision against taking up the plea in abatement, arrived at in conference on February 14, 1857, is therefore less conclusive than it has been made to appear.[13] Furthermore, the decisions reached at that time did not stand. Taney replaced Nelson as official spokesman for the Court majority, which, by approving Wayne's motion, instructed the Chief Justice to write an opinion covering *all* the questions arising in the case.[14] Since Taney could not have been expected to repudiate his own views on the subject, this development suggests that the majority against consideration of the plea in abatement lasted only a few days.

But of course the only legitimate basis for a determination of what the Court decided is the official record of the Court, rather than the unofficial reports and recollections of what occurred in conference. According to that record, four justices (Taney, Wayne, Daniel, and Curtis) expressly maintained that the plea in abatement was properly before the Court, while two justices (Catron and McLean) expressly argued that it was not. What of the other three?

Nelson summarized the opposing arguments and then left the question moot, but his phrasing suggests that he was still leaning to

Taney's side.[15] Grier concurred with Nelson "on the questions discussed by him," but he also concurred with Taney on several points, including the judgment that "the record shows a *prima facie* case of jurisdiction, requiring the court to decide all questions properly arising in it."[16] This seems to place Grier on Taney's side; certainly he cannot be counted as an opponent of Taney on the jurisdictional question. Campbell's treatment of the issue is the most puzzling of all. We have his own later statements counting himself among the anti-Taney group and insisting that the group constituted a five-man majority (including Nelson and Grier) that determined the question by declining jurisdiction.[17] In his concurring opinion, Campbell originally wrote: "My opinion in this case is not affected by the plea to the jurisdiction (for reasons stated in the opinion of Justice Catron)." By associating himself with Catron, he plainly embraced the view that the plea in abatement was not properly before the Court. But then, when the opinion was in page proof, he struck out the words enclosed in parentheses, leaving a statement of considerable ambiguity.[18] With this revision, Campbell accommodated his opinion in some degree to that of the Chief Justice. That is, he avoided an explicit dissent from Taney's holding on the plea in abatement.[19]

So a survey of the individual opinions does not indicate that Taney was speaking only for a minority of the Court when he declared, "The plea in abatement is necessarily under consideration." Indeed, the contrary seems true when we consider the words of Grier. But another interesting point must be noted. The Chief Justice devoted some twenty-four pages of his opinion to the question of Negro citizenship, all of which was extrajudicial if he had not carried a majority with him on the plea in abatement. And yet the cry of *obiter dictum* has seldom been raised against those twenty-four pages. Among the justices, only Catron did so, and in a private letter rather than in his official opinion.[20]

But for the confusion caused by the plea in abatement, Taney probably would have had little trouble getting the support of a clear-cut majority for his ruling against Negro citizenship. As it was, only two justices (Wayne and Daniel) expressly endorsed the ruling, and two others (McLean and Curtis) expressly dissented from it. The four remaining justices offered no opinions on the issue of Negro citizenship itself. If the historian decides (or, for the sake of argument, assumes), that the technical question posed by the plea in abatement was settled in Taney's favor, he then has two choices before him. He can conclude that the Court *did* rule against Negro citizenship, since only a minority of justices explicitly dissented on this point from the opinion of the Court, or he can conclude that the Court *did not* so rule, since only a minority explicitly endorsed the opinion.

Scholars have generally preferred the second option, and yet there is reason to believe that a majority of the Court took the opposite view. We have been asking how many justices agreed with Taney's ruling against Negro citizenship. Now, instead, let us ask how many justices *thought* that the Court had ruled against Negro citizenship. The answer is "at least five," and this number includes the two dissenters, McLean and Curtis, both of whom obviously realized, as so many historians have not, that only if the Court did so rule was there any basis for asserting that the decision on the Missouri Compromise was extrajudicial. More than one scholar has noted with some puzzlement that this evidence contradicts the standard box score. "How was it," one of them asks, "if only three of the judges held that no Negro could be a citizen, that five of the judges could, in their opinions, speak of this question as having been 'decided' by the Court?"[21] The simplest explanation of the discrepancy would seem to be that on this point, at least, the standard box score is unreliable.

In summary, the opinion of the Court declared that Negroes were not citizens; this ruling was neither expressly endorsed nor expressly challenged by a majority of justices; but a majority did apparently regard the ruling as authoritative. Thus, on balance, the evidence seems to support the unorthodox view that Taney's ruling was indeed the Court's decision on the subject of Negro citizenship.

If the Court did authoritatively decide that Negroes were not citizens, then we must seriously consider the possibility that it had no right to proceed further and examine the facts of the case. Instead, critics have argued, the case at that point should have been returned to the circuit court with the order that it be dismissed for lack of jurisdiction. And here it is well to underscore a point that has escaped scholarly notice. This argument applies with equal force to *all* discussion of the merits. If the ruling on the Missouri Compromise was *obiter dictum*, so too was the ruling on interstate comity. The argument, in short, does not allow the substitution of Nelson's opinion for that of Taney as the opinion of the Court, whatever the comparative logical integrity of the two opinions.

The Republican cry of *obiter dictum*, raised in 1857 and inspired by the two dissenting justices, has echoed persistently down through the years. In popular thought the phrase is still vaguely associated with the Dred Scott decision. But the words themselves are somewhat misleading, and the charge no longer carries much conviction in the face of scholarly judgment to the contrary.

In the first place, one must consider the meaning of the phrase "*obiter dictum.*" Ordinarily, it is used to describe an opinion offered more or less in passing on some point of law that is not at issue in the case before the court. Very often, the point is one that has not been argued by counsel or discussed in conference.* These criteria obviously do not fit the Court's ruling on the Missouri Compromise restriction. McLean, Curtis, and others like them were in fact accusing the Court of indulging in another kind of extrajudicial behavior—that of reviewing the Dred Scott case on its merits after having decided that the federal courts had no jurisdiction.†

---

* Definitions vary, of course, and "*obiter dictum*" (or simply "*dictum*") is often used more broadly to indicate any part of an opinion not essential to the decision reached. This could include points argued by counsel and far from gratuitous or irrelevant—indeed, everything not clearly within the "holding" or *ratio decidendi*. A Wisconsin judge in the later nineteenth century proposed to distinguish between two kinds of *dicta*, saying: "An expression of opinion upon a point involved in a case, argued by counsel and deliberately passed upon by the court, though not essential to the disposition of the case, if a *dictum*, should be considered a *judicial dictum* as distinguished from a mere *obiter dictum*, i.e., an expression originating alone with the judge writing the opinion, as an argument or illustration."[22] That part of Taney's opinion dealing with the Missouri Compromise restriction could perhaps be labeled a "*judicial dictum*" because the decision could have been reached without it. But the determination of what parts of an opinion constitute *dicta* are made by the Court itself in later decisions, not by newspaper editors, political leaders, or other public critics.

† This is the same criticism leveled by McLean (with good reason, in my opinion) against Taney's opinion in *Strader v. Graham*. See below, pp. 385, 660. As a matter of

What the accusation ignores or rejects is Taney's contention that throughout the whole of his opinion he was canvassing the question of jurisdiction. In effect, his line of reasoning took advantage of the peculiar circularity that had characterized the case from the moment it entered the federal court. That is, in order to bring suit, Dred Scott had to affirm that he was a citizen of Missouri, which meant assuming that he was a free man. But if it should be determined from the facts that he remained a slave, this would mean that he was never a citizen and had no right to bring suit in the first place. Thus Taney, after having held that Scott could not be a citizen because he was a Negro, proposed to demonstrate also that Scott could not be a citizen because he was still a slave. He therefore proceeded to examine the facts of the case. In doing so, he was not, technically, turning to the case on its merits, but rather was still pursuing the question of jurisdiction and "fortifying his decision" on it.[24]

That a judicial opinion may legitimately offer more than one reason for reaching a decision is well established. And such reinforcement, it can be argued, was especially appropriate in the Dred Scott case because of the confusion surrounding the plea in abatement. At any rate, the question now under consideration is what the Court decided, not whether its decision was sound. In this instance, a conclusive answer seems to emerge from the record. The mandate to the circuit court, it must be remembered, ordered dismissal of the suit for want of jurisdiction. One must assume that this mandate had the support of a majority of the Supreme Court. But how was that majority formed?

Four justices explicitly held that the circuit court had lacked jurisdiction, but their reasons varied—because Scott was a Negro (Daniel), because Scott was a slave (Campbell), and for both reasons (Taney and Wayne). Three justices explicitly favored a decision on the merits (Nelson for affirming the lower court's decision; McLean and Curtis for reversing it). Grier explicitly indicated a willingness either

---

convenience and brevity, "*dictum*" is often employed to describe this kind of extrajudicial behavior. It is worth noting, however, that neither McLean nor Curtis used the term. McLean declared that the Court's rulings on the merits were "of no authority." Curtis said that they were "not binding."[23]

JUDGMENTS FAVORED BY INDIVIDUAL JUSTICES

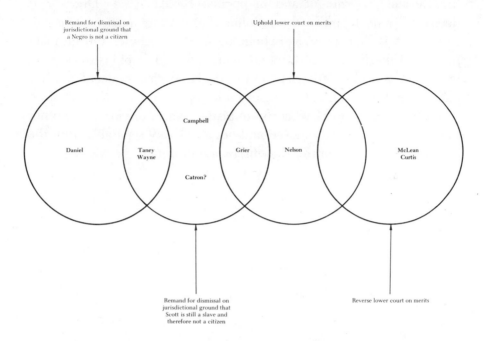

to deny jurisdiction or to affirm the previous judgment, thus supporting both Taney and Nelson. Catron said nothing explicitly on the subject, but his final sentence permits placing him with Campbell.[25]
Thus the majority supporting disposal of the case on jurisdictional
grounds reached agreement along the two different routes marked
out by Taney, and in order to speak for the majority, it was necessary
for him to demonstrate that Scott was doubly not a citizen—that is,
both because he was a Negro and because he was a slave.

It therefore appears that none of the major rulings in Taney's
opinion can be pushed aside as unauthoritative. The charge that one
of them was extrajudicial does not stand up under close scrutiny, and
the evidence indicates that in each of the rulings he did present the
opinion of the Court. On this latter point, something further must be
said, however. The whole argument over "what the Court really
decided" has been in one respect merely an academic exercise. For
there can be no doubt that Taney's opinion was accepted as the

opinion of the Court by its critics as well as its defenders. In all branches of government and in popular thought, the "Dred Scott decision" came to mean the opinion of the Chief Justice. The evidence of this linkage is overwhelming, and it includes the ultimate passage of the Fourteenth Amendment. As a matter of historical reality, the Court decided what Taney declared that it decided. This places only the stamp of legitimacy on his opinion, however. Whether it was based on sound law, accurate history, and valid logic is another question, still to be considered and not absolutely separable from the moral problem inherent in the enslavement of men.

∽ 15 ∽

The Opinion of the Court:
Negroes and Citizenship

Historians have been preoccupied with counting noses to determine "what the Court really decided" in the Dred Scott case and with evaluating the charge of *obiter dictum* leveled against the Court's most important pronouncement. Scholarly interest, in short, has centered on the question of how much—or how little—of Taney's opinion was authoritative. Systematic analysis of the opinion itself is remarkably scarce and largely limited to contemporary critiques published in 1857 or soon thereafter.

"Here was a situation," David M. Potter has written, "in which the chief justice advanced some highly vulnerable arguments about the citizenship of Negroes and about the power of Congress over the territories. But for decades, historians passed over these flaws with a minimum of analysis, while devoting elaborate emphasis to the claim that Taney had no right to rule on a question on which they would clearly have been delighted to have him rule if only he had ruled differently."[1] Precisely so. The alleged illegitimacy of Taney's broader opinion would scarcely have been a significant issue if he had *upheld* the constitutionality of the Missouri Compromise restriction. Neither the Republicans who first raised the cry of *obiter dictum* nor the scholars who later gave it so much attention were primarily concerned about abuse of judicial power. Underlying all the partisan wrath and scholarly fuss about the scope of Taney's opinion there has

always been a more fundamental conviction that the Dred Scott decision was egregiously wrong or at least exceedingly unwise.

But, for Republicans in 1857, there was little to be gained from
showing merely that the decision was wrong. Right or wrong, decisions of the Supreme Court are law, and few Republicans were prepared to advocate open defiance of the law, however bad it might be.
Better, then, to concentrate on the argument that much of Taney's
opinion was not authoritative; for thus defiance of the opinion would
not be defiance of the law.*

Many historians likewise seem to regard the decision as wrong,
but their emphasis is usually upon its presumably disastrous consequences, which presumably could have been avoided if the Court had
adhered to its original intention of handing down a narrow decision,
with Nelson as its spokesman. Thus the major blame comes to rest on
the justice or justices who brought about the shift from Nelson to
Taney, and fixing this responsibility has received more scholarly attention than the quality of Taney's opinion.[2] Yet the extent of congressional power over slavery in the territories was a constitutional
issue that had agitated the country for more than a decade. The issue
was legitimately presented to the Supreme Court in the Dred Scott
case, and it had been argued extensively by counsel. The Court, in
disposing of the question, did what it had been urged and was expected to do, indeed, what the modern Court is expected to do as a
matter of course. To have settled for the Nelson opinion would have
been an act of political prudence but of judicial abdication. Historians
who deplore the shift from Nelson to Taney are really saying that,
given the makeup of the Court, a broad decision was bound to be a
wrong decision; therefore, a narrow decision, evading the major
issue, was in retrospect the right strategy.

Inherent, then, in all adverse comment on the authoritativeness
and wisdom of the broader decision is a judgment on the intrinsic
merit of Taney's opinion. If scholars make the judgment explicit, they
usually mingle it with an assessment of consequences, and they seldom give much space to validating the judgment by close examination

* See below, pp. 438–39.

of the opinion. And yet the Taney opinion *is*, for all practical purposes, *the* Dred Scott decision and therefore a historical document of prime importance. Consequences attributed to the decision are actually consequences of the opinion. Likewise, it was because of Taney's opinion that the Dred Scott decision constituted a landmark in the history of judicial review, injected a new meaning into the phrase "due process of law," and cast the Supreme Court in a new role as the arbiter of current political controversy. Furthermore, the opinion can be read as a sectional credo no less revealing than Lincoln's House-Divided address or a series of Greeley editorials. It is not only a statement of southern assumptions and arguments but also an expression of the southern mood—fearful, angry, and defiant—in the late stages of national crisis.

II

The fifty-five pages of Taney's opinion, as printed in Howard's *Reports,* were apportioned approximately as follows:

1. Introductory summary of the litigation   1 page
2. Plea in abatement   3 pages
3. Negro citizenship   24 pages
4. Propriety of reviewing facts of the case   4 pages
5. Territorial question   21 pages
6. Comity question (Scott in Illinois)   1 page
7. Criticism of suit as improper   1 page

The amount of attention given to the territorial issue was to be expected. More surprising in the above table are the number of pages devoted to proving that Negroes were not citizens and, in contrast, the brevity of the argument on the comity question. But to Taney, a Marylander, the status of free Negroes was a matter of critical importance, and on the comity issue he was apparently allowing for the more elaborate treatment by Nelson.*

Introductory summary. In this routine passage, which otherwise

---

*This is no doubt why Taney ordered that Nelson's opinion be placed third in the official publication, right after Wayne's.

requires no comment, Taney made the categorical statement that he was speaking for the Court. After explaining that the Court had twice heard argument in the case, he declared: "I now proceed to deliver its opinion."[3] This assertion is not challenged by any of the other eight justices in their separate opinions.

Plea in abatement. Taney, in deciding that the plea was before the Court, based his ruling on the limited nature of federal court jurisdiction and on the inclusiveness of appellate review by writ of error. The principal argument of Montgomery Blair, echoed by Justices Catron and McLean, had been that Sanford, by pleading over to the merits after failing in his plea to jurisdiction, waived his right to raise the jurisdictional issue again. McLean, accusing the Chief Justice of "sharp practice," also argued that it was unfair to make the plaintiff-in-error defend himself on points already decided in his favor.[4] Taney insisted, however, that the principle of waiver had been drawn from the common law of England and the various states, which did not govern pleadings in the courts of the United States.[5] The difference lay in the "peculiar and limited jurisdiction" of the federal courts, where, unlike pleadings under the common law, a plaintiff must show his right to bring suit by explicitly averring his citizenship in a state different from that of the defendant. Thus, "the record, when it comes before the appellate court, must show, affirmatively, that the inferior court had authority, under the Constitution, to hear and determine the case." If the averment of citizenship was challenged by a plea in abatement, that challenge likewise became a part of the record. And a writ of error "always brings up to the superior court the whole record of the proceedings in the court below."

On this technical question, Taney had the support not only of Wayne and Daniel but also of Curtis, whose argument was even more forceful. Among other things, it demonstrated that under the law of Congress regulating appellate procedure, lower federal courts were not intended to be "the final judges of their own jurisdiction in civil cases." The first duty of the Supreme Court, Curtis declared, is "to take care that neither the Circuit Court nor this court shall use the judicial power of the United States in a case to which the Constitution and laws of the United States have not extended that power."[6]

Whether Taney actually spoke for a majority of the Court on the plea in abatement is a problem that has already been discussed. The question here is as to the soundness of his ruling, and Taney's argument, reinforced by that of Curtis, seems convincing. There is no escaping the fact that a writ of error brought the *whole record* of the case to the Supreme Court for review. Neither is there much doubt that the Court in subsequent years generally agreed with Taney and Curtis concerning its duty to examine the jurisdiction of the lower court whenever such jurisdiction was not plain and unchallenged on the face of the record.[7] Furthermore, as Curtis insisted, it is doubtful that Sanford's pleading over to the merits actually constituted a waiver of the jurisdictional issue; for waiver implies consent, and Sanford had no choice but to plead over. Thus, if Taney's ruling put Dred Scott to the extra trouble and hazard of proving his citizenship a second time, the opposite ruling would have worked a greater injustice to Sanford by denying him all access to the Supreme Court on the jurisdictional question.[8]

But the issue involves something more than the technicalities of pleading. It also raises a question about the role of the Supreme Court in the American judicial system. The Court's primary function is not to see that justice is done to individuals such as Dred Scott and John Sanford, but rather, in the process of deciding a limited number of cases, to lay down the general lines of interpretation for the instruction of other federal courts and, to some degree, of state courts as well. Thus the rulings of the Supreme Court affect the disposition of countless cases that it never hears, and the Constitution, laws, and treaties of the United States are interpreted and applied with some consistency throughout the nation. The question of whether a Negro could be a citizen was clearly the kind of legal question that deserved the Court's attention. It was not a matter that could be left permanently to the decision of a lower federal court. Taney's determination to review the plea in abatement therefore appears to have been not only technically sound but in accordance with the broader functional responsibilities of his Court.

III

To the Negro citizenship issue, then, Taney devoted some 44 per cent of his entire opinion, and he did it largely on his own initiative. A majority of his colleagues probably would have been content to by-pass the question, and there was no significant public clamor for its resolution. Unlike the territorial issue, it was not a storm center of political controversy. Furthermore, in insisting upon consideration of the citizenship question, however appropriate it may have been to do so, Taney produced a large amount of technical confusion that seriously weakened the force of his ruling on the Missouri Compromise. Why, one must ask, did he persist in such strategy?

For one thing, Taney was seizing an opportunity to reaffirm what he had written twenty-five years earlier about the status of Negroes in American society. As Jackson's attorney general, it will be remembered, he had prepared an official (but unpublished) opinion declaring that the African race was a "degraded class" not intended to be embraced in any provisions of the Constitution except those dealing with slavery.* This doctrine went far beyond the issue raised by the Dred Scott case; for it excluded Negroes, whether free or slave, from all rights guaranteed in the Constitution (and by logical extension, presumably from all rights guaranteed in amendments to the Constitution). Yet Taney found that he could use the Dred Scott case to vindicate his extreme views at length and graft them authoritatively onto American constitutional law.

But there was more involved than personal conviction and consistency. Free Negroes, as a category, had not been objects of great concern during the first years of the American republic. Laws excluding them from the suffrage and from other privileges, like laws discriminating against women, reflected the dominant view of the order of creation and were not drafted as solutions to pressing social problems. Long before 1857, however, free Negroes had become a serious social problem in the South, where they were regarded as a disturbing element among the slave population. At the same time, south-

* See above, p. 70.

erners had grown increasingly sensitive about any suggestion of federal interference with their slave system or their racial arrangements. Taney may or may not have realized, as Roswell Field did, that the ruling of Judge Wells upholding Dred Scott's right to bring suit in a federal court posed a potential threat to the Fugitive Slave Law. But in any case, he was determined to meet every threat to southern stability by separating the Negro race absolutely from the federal Constitution and all the rights that it bestowed, thus leaving the states in complete control of black men, whether free or slave. The breadth with which he treated the issue of Negro citizenship reveals the true purpose of Taney's Dred Scott opinion—to launch a sweeping counterattack on the antislavery movement and to reinforce the bastions of slavery at every rampart and parapet.

The question before the Court, it should be borne in mind, was whether Dred Scott, if he were a free Negro, could be regarded as a citizen of *Missouri*, at least to the extent of being eligible to bring suit in a federal court under the diverse-citizenship clause. Judge Wells, in the circuit court, had held that any resident capable of owning property was to this extent a citizen. Another obvious criterion might have been whether free Negroes were citizens of Missouri to the extent of being able to bring suit in the courts of that state, which they most certainly were. For Taney, however, it was not enough to settle such a limited issue, and in his opening paragraph he redefined the whole problem:

> The question is simply this: Can a negro, whose ancestors were imported into this country and sold as slaves, become a member of the political community formed and brought into existence by the Constitution of the United States, and as such become entitled to all the rights, and privileges, and immunities, guarantied by that instrument to the citizen. One of which rights is the privilege of suing in a court of the United States in the cases specified in the Constitution.[9]

The difference between the two approaches is startling. Taney in this passage shifted the ground of inquiry from state citizenship to federal citizenship, and he made the right to bring suit in federal courts dependent upon the confirmation of all rights enjoyed under the federal Constitution. The effect was to prejudice Scott's cause and at the same time clear the way for the broad conclusions that Taney was determined to reach.

But while the purpose is clear, the argument as one reads it soon becomes confusing. Having asserted that the question was whether a Negro of slave ancestry could be a member of the "political community" created by the federal Constitution, Taney proceeded to complicate matters with a restatement. The issue before the Court, he wrote, was "whether the descendants of such slaves, when they shall be emancipated, or who are born of parents who had become free before their birth, are *citizens of a State,* in the sense in which the word 'citizen' is used in the Constitution of the United States."[10] So now it appeared to be a question of state rather than federal citizenship.

After these two introductory paragraphs that defined the issue in somewhat contradictory terms, Taney, for no logical reason, abruptly turned aside to consider a troublesome parallel. The American Indian, though not generally included in the "political community" of the United States and, indeed, "under subjection to the white race," had nevertheless in some instances been admitted to federal citizenship. Why, then, should not freed slaves and their descendants be eligible for the same kind of elevation? But the Indian tribes, said the Chief Justice, were in law equivalent to foreign nations, and when the federal government extended citizenship to an Indian, it did so by virtue of its constitutional authority to naturalize foreigners. Taney took no notice of the paradox by which American aborigines could be naturalized, while a race transplanted from Africa could not.[11]

With this mixed bag of preliminaries behind him, the Chief Justice announced that he was ready to "examine the case as presented by the pleadings." What came next illustrates his tendency to use tautology for emphasis:

> The words "people of the United States" and "citizens" are synonymous terms, and mean the same thing. They both describe the political body who, according to our republican institutions,

> form the sovereignty, and who hold the power and conduct the
> Government through their representatives. They are what we fa-
> miliarly call the "sovereign people," and every citizen is one of
> this people, and a constituent member of this sovereignty.

The gross inaccuracy of the final clause will be readily apparent. A
large majority of American citizens—namely, women and children—
were not members of the sovereign people in the sense of holding
power and conducting the government through their representatives.
Moreover, when the Constitution was first put into effect, many adult
male citizens had been barred from constituent membership by property and religious qualifications for voting. Citizenship and sovereign
power were far from synonymous.[12]

For the third time in two pages, Taney stated the question under
consideration, returning to his original emphasis on national citizenship:

> The question before us is, whether the class of persons described
> in the plea in abatement compose a portion of this people, and are
> constituent members of this sovereignty. We think they are not,
> and that they are not included, and were not intended to be in-
> cluded under the word "citizens" in the Constitution, and can
> therefore claim none of the rights and privileges which that in-
> strument provides for and secures to citizens of the United States.
> On the contrary, they were at that time considered as a subordi-
> nate and inferior class of beings, who had been subjugated by the
> dominant race, and, whether emancipated or not, yet remained
> subject to their authority, and had no rights or privileges but such
> as those who held the power and the Government might choose to
> grant them.[13]

Here we are introduced to one of the fundamental assumptions underlying Taney's argument, summed up in the words "whether emancipated or not." All blacks, according to his view, stood on the same
ground. Emancipation made no difference. The status of the free
Negro was fixed forever by the fact that he or his ancestors had once
been enslaved. This assumption led him a little later to the most
egregious sentence in his whole opinion.

At this point, Taney seemed to realize the need for some definition of the relationship between state and national citizenship. The two must not be confounded, he declared. "It does not by any means follow, because he has all the rights and privileges of a citizen of a State, that he must be a citizen of the United States." Thus Taney rejected the theory that state citizenship was primary, with federal citizenship derived from it. In this respect he may have been on sounder ground than Justice Curtis, who insisted that every native-born citizen of a state was automatically a citizen of the United States.[14] But now observe where Taney's mind jumped in his very next sentence:

> He may have all of the rights and privileges of the citizen of a
> State, and yet not be entitled to the rights and privileges of a citi
> zen in any other State.

It would be difficult to formulate a more categorical contradiction of a specific clause of the Constitution, in this case, the one that declares: "The citizens of each state shall be entitled to all privileges and immunities of citizens in the several states."[15] From the argument that state and federal citizenship were independent of each other, Taney had shifted to the proposition that state citizenship had no value outside the boundaries of the state.

Before the adoption of the Constitution, Taney continued, every state had the right "to confer on whomsoever it pleased the character of a citizen." But this character "was confined to the boundaries of the State, and gave him no rights or privileges in other States beyond those secured to him by the laws of nations and the comity of States." What changes were wrought, then, by adoption of the Constitution? None, as far as the rights of a state were concerned. It could still confer citizenship upon any class of person, even an alien.

> Yet he would not be a citizen in the sense in which that word is
> used in the Constitution of the United States, nor entitled to sue
> as such in one of its courts, nor to the privileges and immunities of
> a citizen in the other States. The rights which he would acquire
> would be restricted to the State which gave them.

Nevertheless, the Constitution did make a significant change, Taney declared:

> It gave to each citizen rights and privileges outside of his State which he did not before possess, and placed him in every other State upon a perfect equality with its own citizens as to rights of person and rights of property; it made him a citizen of the United States.

In these passages, the Chief Justice displayed an astonishing obliviousness to the Articles of Confederation and a cavalier disregard for the precise wording of the Constitution.[16]

Taney wrote of the privileges-and-immunities clause of the Constitution as though it were something brand new, giving a citizen rights "which he did not before possess." He had forgotten that the clause was actually derived from the fourth Article of Confederation, which declared: "The free inhabitants of each of these states, paupers, vagabonds and fugitives from justice excepted, shall be entitled to all privileges and immunities of free citizens in the several states." There was method in his historical inaccuracy, however; for Taney was determined to associate this clause and other interstate guarantees with United States citizenship. And national citizenship, in his view, did not exist under the Articles. It was created by the Constitution. His purpose was clearly revealed when he undertook, for the fourth time, to state the question before the Court. It was, he asserted, whether a single state, by endowing a Negro with citizenship, could thereby "make him a citizen of the United States, and endue him with the full rights of citizenship in every other State without their consent." The Court, he continued, had decided that an affirmative answer to this question could not be maintained. "And if it cannot, the plaintiff in error could not be a citizen of the State of Missouri, within the meaning of the Constitution of the United States, and, consequently, was not entitled to sue in its courts."[17] The crucial phrase here, already used twice before, was "within the meaning of the Constitution." Out of his own will and imagination, Taney had fashioned *two different kinds of state citizenship*. One, existing under the Articles and continuing under the Constitution, was entirely within the control of the states, but it qualified no one for the extraterritorial rights and privileges guaranteed by the Constitution. The second kind of state citizenship, created by the Constitution, embraced only those persons who were also citizens of the United States, and they alone were covered by the privileges-and-immunities clause or had the right to bring suit under the diverse-citizenship clause. In effect, Taney arbitrarily amended both of these clauses as follows.

who are also citizens of the United States
The citizens of each state ∧ shall be entitled to all the privileges and immunities of citizens in the several states.

The judicial power shall extend . . . to controversies . . . be-
the United States residing in different states.
tween citizens of different states.

By conjuring up a special kind of state citizenship that was "within the meaning of the Constitution," Taney converted the question of whether Dred Scott was a citizen of Missouri into the question of whether he was a citizen of the United States. For, as he used the phrase, state citizenship "within the meaning of the Constitution" was virtually synonymous with federal citizenship. In addition, Taney demonstrated to his own satisfaction that no state could, by virtue of laws passed after the adoption of the Constitution, admit any new classes of persons to citizenship of the kind that enjoyed the protection of that instrument. Only Congress could do so, under its exclusive power over naturalization. So any state laws conferring state citizenship on Negroes after 1789 were irrelevant. They could not and did not make such persons citizens "within the meaning of the Constitution."

IV

But what about the status of free Negroes before 1789? The Chief Justice acknowledged that "every person, and every class and description of persons, who were at the time of the adoption of the Constitution recognized as citizens in the several States, became also citizens of this new political body." This would seem to mean that some blacks, recognized as citizens by their states at the time of the Revolution, acquired national citizenship in 1789. Not so, however. State citizenship, according to Taney, came into existence with the Declaration of Independence, and it embraced those people "whose rights and liberties had been outraged by the English Government; and who declared their independence, and assumed the powers of government to defend their rights by force of arms." Thus Taney's increasingly rambling and repetitious argument returned to a familiar groove. State citizenship before 1789, like national citizenship after that date, was to be defined in terms equating it with the exercise of political sovereignty.

Having earlier concluded that Negroes had never been citizens of the United States because they were not a part of the sovereign people who made the Constitution, Taney now asserted that Negroes were not state citizens at the time of the Revolution (no matter what the states themselves may have said about it) because they did not belong to the sovereign people for whom the Declaration of Independence was written. The basic reasons were the same, and so again Taney's argument became repetitious. "It is difficult at this day," he wrote, to realize the state of public opinion in relation to that unfortunate race, which prevailed in the civilized and enlightened portions of the world at the time of the Declaration of Independence, and when the Constitution of the United States was framed and adopted."

> They had for more than a century before been regarded as beings of an inferior order, and altogether unfit to associate with the white race, either in social or political relations; and so far inferior, that they had no rights which the white man was bound to respect; and that the negro might justly and lawfully be reduced to slavery for his benefit. He was bought and sold, and treated as an ordinary article of merchandise and traffic, whenever a profit could be made by it. This opinion was at that time fixed and universal in the civilized portion of the white race.[18]

One clause in the above paragraph has, of course, become memorable. It inspired an outburst of anger and recrimination that in the end redounded to Taney's advantage. His statement that Negroes "had no rights which the white man was bound to respect" was part of his analysis of the state of public opinion at the time of the founding of the Republic. He did not declare that such a view still prevailed in 1857; indeed, on the contrary, he implied that public opinion had changed over the years. His critics have been accused of lifting the statement from its historical context and presenting it as Taney's own view of the Negro's status in 1857. The effect is to exonerate the Chief Justice on this point and to picture him as the victim of Republican misrepresentation. "By the brazen propagation of this lie the country was long deceived," writes one constitutional historian, "and the prejudices and passions aroused against the Court and its decision were due far more to Taney's alleged statement than to the point of law decided by him."[19] Yet the Republican editors who flaunted Taney's explosive words without explaining their context, thereby distorting their literal meaning, were perhaps not entirely wrong in regarding the clause as a fair representation of the tenor of the entire decision. For if Negroes in 1789 had no rights that white men were bound to respect, and if, as Taney maintained, they had acquired no rights since that time "within the meaning of the Constitution," then their condition remained substantially unchanged, from the viewpoint of a federal judge. In 1857, they still had no rights under the Constitution that a white man was bound to respect.

Moreover, the furor over this one unpleasant clause has diverted attention from the whole argument of the paragraph in which it appears. Defenders of the Chief Justice have assumed that the clause becomes far less objectionable when it is read in context and understood to be merely part of a "historical narrative." But what about the honesty and accuracy of this historical narrative, which, after all, was to be the basis for a legal judgment? Did the generation of the Founding Fathers really believe that a *free* Negro had *no* rights which a white man was bound to respect? Does the notorious clause really cease to be outrageous when it is read in context?

The question under consideration at this point, as formulated by Taney himself, was whether *free Negroes* possessed *state citizenship* in the period from *1776 to 1789*. Yet the Chief Justice persisted in his refusal to regard free Negroes as a category of persons distinct from Negro slaves. Thus, in asserting that "the negro might justly and lawfully be reduced to slavery," he was talking about what could be done to blacks in Africa. Punishment for crime aside, free Negroes in the United States could not lawfully be hunted down and reduced to slavery in the African manner. In fact, some states defined the practice as kidnapping and made it punishable accordingly. Likewise, Taney was thinking of slaves when he declared that the Negro had no rights which the white man was bound to respect. Even then, the statement was not absolutely true, for slaves had some rights at law before 1789, and as a summary of the status of free Negroes in the 1780s, it was plainly a falsehood. A list of the Negro's legal rights at that time would be at least as long as a list of his legal disabilities. In some respects, such as property rights, a black man's status was superior to that of a married white woman, and it was certainly far above that of a slave. He could marry, enter into contracts, purchase real estate, bequeathe property, and, most pertinently, seek redress in the courts. The effect of Taney's statement was to place Negroes of the 1780s—even free Negroes—on the same level, legally, as domestic animals. As "historical narrative," it was a gross perversion of the facts.

Just as he failed to concentrate on free Negroes as a class, although they were presumably the subject of his inquiry, so Taney also refused to confine his attention to the relevant period of time, 1776–89, for determining whether free Negroes were state citizens before the Constitution went into effect. For example, he referred to the universality of slavery in the thirteen colonies with no mention, at this point, of post-Revolutionary abolition in several states. He cited two colonial laws, both forbidding miscegenation, and several state laws passed in the nineteenth century which excluded Negroes from certain privileges. The latter citations were obviously irrelevant to the matter at hand, and Taney's logic was peculiar, to say the least. Having earlier held that no state law passed after 1789 could make a Negro a citizen "within the meaning of the Constitution," he now cited state laws passed after 1789 as part of his proof that Negroes were not citizens before the adoption of the Constitution. The only proof offered from the appropriate period consisted of a Massachusetts law of 1786 forbidding miscegenation and a Connecticut law of 1774 requiring Negroes to have a pass when they traveled. He also examined Connecticut legislation abolishing slavery and outlawing the slave trade to show that it was not inspired by humanitarian motives or accompanied by any indication that Connecticut intended to place emancipated slaves "upon a level with its citizens." Thus he unloaded the burden of proving his point by declaring the absence of evidence to the contrary.[20]

Seldom did Taney stick to the subject of state citizenship. Instead of examining state laws and constitutions of the Confederation period to see whether the word "citizen" was used in such a way as to include or exclude free Negroes, he merely cited various discriminatory acts as evidence that Negroes were regarded as "beings of an inferior order and altogether unfit to associate with the white race." But this line of argument begged the question. It asserted that Negroes could not have been citizens in the 1780s because they were considered inferior, but then other categories of people were likewise regarded as inferior. The real question was whether Negroes were considered *too inferior* to be citizens, something that Taney's evidence failed to show.[21]

More than anything else, Taney cited laws against interracial marriage as proof of the Negro's "inferior and subject condition." Such legislation did, of course, spring from the dominant assumption of black inferiority and did contribute to the social degradation of the Negro. But in legal terms, it can scarcely be regarded as having marked the limits of citizenship. For miscegenation laws placed restrictions on both white and black races, with punishments for both parties when a violation occurred. The fact that laws of this kind remained common and in force long after the ratification of the Fourteenth Amendment is perhaps the best indication that Americans never associated them with citizenship.

In the midst of his citations of colonial and state laws discriminating against the Negro, Taney also discussed the Declaration of Independence and the Constitution. Both documents seem irrelevant to an examination of *state* citizenship before 1789, which, he had already asserted, was entirely within the control of the states themselves. But Taney's purpose was to show that the public attitude toward Negroes in the early years of American independence made it impossible to believe that they could have been regarded as citizens. In addition, there are indications that he sometimes simply lost track of the specific point that he was pursuing.*

The language of the Declaration of Independence, said Taney, was "conclusive" on the subject. Then he proceeded to argue that the language did not really mean what it plainly said. Jefferson's self-evident truths "would seem to embrace the whole human family," but it was "too clear for dispute that the enslaved African race were not intended to be included." Otherwise, "the conduct of the distinguished men who framed the Declaration of Independence would have been utterly and flagrantly inconsistent with the principles they asserted." The framers, Taney continued, were in fact honorable men whose language was neither intended nor understood by contemporaries to embrace the black race, "which was never thought of or spoken of except as property."[23] The Chief Justice, it should be noted, ignored the obvious fact that the opening generalizations in the Declaration were statements of aspiration for mankind, not descriptions of its condition. Yet, even if it is true that the words "all men are created equal" were written and endorsed with fingers crossed for slavery, Taney was manifestly up to his old trick of lumping free Negroes with slaves. The result in this instance was a false syllogism: Slaves could not have been embraced in the philosophy of the Declaration; all slaves are Negroes; therefore, all Negroes are excluded from the rights enumerated in the Declaration. Only if the minor premise were reversible would the syllogism be valid. What seems "too clear for dispute" is that the language of the Declaration of Independence is utterly inconclusive as an indication of whether free Negroes were or were not state citizens prior to the adoption of the Constitution.

*For example, after citing the two colonial laws forbidding miscegenation, Taney declared that reference to such historical fact was necessary "in order to determine whether the general terms used in the Constitution of the United States, as to the rights of man and the rights of the people, was intended to include them, or to give to them or their posterity the benefit of any of its provisions." This was a question raised and answered in an earlier passage. His present purpose was supposedly "to determine who were citizens of the several States when the Constitution was adopted."[22]

As for the Constitution, it used the terms "people of the United States" and "citizens of the several States" without defining them because, said Taney, these words were "so well understood that no further description or definition was necessary." Then he continued:

> But there are two clauses in the Constitution which point directly and specifically to the negro race as a separate class of persons, and show clearly that they were not regarded as a portion of the people or citizens of the Government then formed.

The clauses to which he referred were those dealing with the African slave trade and the recovery of fugitive slaves. "And these two provisions show conclusively," he declared, "that neither the description of persons therein referred to, nor their descendants, were embraced in any of the other provisions of the Constitution." Now, although the purposes of both clauses were perfectly clear, neither was in fact phrased in such a way as to refer exclusively to Negro slaves.* And there was certainly nothing in them affecting the *descendants* of slaves, unless those descendants were slaves themselves. The Fugitive Slave Law, for example, had no legal bearing on the legal status of free Negroes. Except in the strange thinking of Roger B. Taney, who brushed free Negroes aside with the casual remark that they were few in number at the time of the Constitutional Convention and were in any case "regarded as part of the slave population rather than the free."[24]

Thus Taney revealed again his determination to treat emancipation as legally meaningless and to mix free Negroes with slaves in one legal category based on race. But his very words were belied by a third provision of the Constitution that he conveniently ignored. Article One, Section Two, apportioned representation and direct taxation among the states according to the number of "free persons" in each, plus three-fifths of the number of slaves. Here, then, was a clause of the Constitution that plainly separated slaves from free Negroes, and more than that, it appeared to make the latter a part of the "people" upon whom the federal government was to be founded. It is

---

* See above, pp. 24–25.

therefore perhaps significant that Taney preferred to overlook this clause. It was *never mentioned* in his whole opinion.

Up to this point, Taney had insisted that attitudes toward the Negro and his enslavement were uniform throughout the country. Now, however, he suddenly felt constrained to acknowledge the progress of abolition in northern states during and after the Revolution, and to explain that progress in terms that would suit his own argument:

> But this change had not been produced by any change of opinion in relation to this race; but because it was discovered, from experience, that slave labor was unsuited to the climate and productions of these States; for some of the States, where it had ceased or nearly ceased to exist, were actively engaged in the slave trade. . . . And this traffic was openly carried on, and fortunes accumulated by it, without reproach from the people of the States where they resided. And it can hardly be supposed that, in the States where it was then countenanced in its worst form—that is, in the seizure and transportation—the people could have regarded those who were emancipated as entitled to equal rights with themselves.[25]

The historical inaccuracy of this passage should perhaps be attributed to a combination of ignorance and willfulness. Appeals to conscience were prevalent in the early abolition movement, and there is no reason to believe that they were any more rhetorical than the appeals to interest that often accompanied them. To be sure, the limited investment in slavery made it easier to consult conscience in the northern states, but Taney was not content to make such an observation. He would concede no humanitarian motives whatsoever to antislavery men. Similarly, he overreached himself in asserting that northern slavetraders carried on their business "without reproach from other residents of their states." Here, in fact, a substantial commercial interest eventually yielded to the mounting cries of conscience, though not without resistance.

But Taney's fundamental error was his flat assertion that abolition in the North did not reflect any change of attitude toward the black race. Evidence to the contrary is overwhelming. In the intellec-

tual ferment of the Revolutionary period, as we have seen, efforts at
national self-definition brought many Americans face to face with the
anomaly of slavery in civilized society and compelled them to scruti-
nize, as never before, the assumptions underlying the institution. The
fact that they did not then and there embrace interracial equality is
no measure of the amount of change that did take place. The Revolution, according to Winthrop D. Jordan, was actually a "critical turning
point" in the history of white thought about slavery as an institution
and about the Negro as a man.[26]

V

Taney had now demonstrated to his own satisfaction (1) that Negroes
were not state citizens before 1789; (2) that the protection of the Constitution did not extend to Negroes, whom it recognized neither as
citizens of the United States nor even as state citizens within its use of
the term; and (3) that no state had the power to make Negroes state
citizens "within the meaning of the Constitution." Yet Taney's argument rambled on as though he could not find his way to a conclusion.

Aware of the inadequacy of his legislative citations, Taney said
that it would be impossible to enumerate all the state laws revealing
the "inferior and subject condition" of the black race. Instead, he
found it "sufficient" to cite a footnote in the 1848 edition of Kent's
Commentaries to the effect that "in no part of the country, except
Maine, did the African race, in point of fact, participate equally with
the whites in the exercise of civil and political rights."[27] Here one of
Taney's many inconsistencies becomes especially noticeable. Repeatedly, when it served his purpose, he asserted or implied that the
status of the Negro had improved significantly since 1789.[28] Yet he
also maintained that Negroes were in an "inferior and subject condition . . . at the time the Constitution was adopted and long afterwards." How long afterwards? Well, his citation of Kent indicated
that as late as 1848 their condition had not changed, except in Maine.
This leaves only nine years between 1848 and 1857 for the improvement in racial feeling that Taney sometimes pretends to see. But the
trend of those years was rather in the opposite direction—toward a
worsening of the Negro's status—as Lincoln would soon argue and

historians would later demonstrate.[29] Thus nothing is left except Taney in flat contradiction of himself.

But the citation of Kent's *Commentaries* deserves particular notice primarily because of what it reveals about Taney's basic strategy and purpose. There is no disputing Kent's statement that Negroes did not "participate equally with the whites in the exercise of civil and political rights." The conclusion that Taney drew, however, was that if the Negro did not participate equally he could not have been intended to participate at all. The strategy of the argument was to limit the alternatives to the two extremes, allowing no middle-ground choice. Negroes had equal rights with white men in *all* respects or in *none*. And Taney rightly assumed that most Americans of his time, if restricted to such a choice, would answer "None." His purpose was to exclude Negroes from all rights guaranteed in the Constitution, including several that were more crucial to southern security than the right to maintain a civil suit in a federal court.

It was at this point in his opinion that Taney let the sectional cat out of the bag. The slaveholding states, he declared, would never have accepted the Constitution if free Negroes had been embraced in the word "citizens."

> For if they were . . . entitled to the privileges and immunities of citizens, it would exempt them from the operation of the special laws and from the police regulations which they considered to be necessary for their own safety. It would give to persons of the negro race . . . the right to enter every other State whenever they pleased, . . . to go where they pleased at every hour of the day or night without molestation, . . . and it would give them the full liberty of speech in public and in private upon all subjects upon which its own citizens might speak; to hold public meetings upon political affairs, and to keep and carry arms wherever they went. And all of this would be done in the face of the subject race of the same color, both free and slaves, and inevitably producing discontent and insubordination among them, and endangering the peace and safety of the State.[30]

Obviously, Taney was reading southern apprehensions of the 1850s back into the minds of southerners in 1787, forgetting his earlier assertion that free Negroes were then so few in number that they "were not even in the minds of the framers of the Constitution." What the Chief Justice feared, then, was that if the Negro were recognized as a citizen under the diverse-citizenship clause, he would have a firm basis for claiming the rights of a citizen under the privileges-and-immunities clause, and there lay a more serious threat to southern security.

Taney, it should be noted, repeatedly shifted the focus from the diverse-citizenship clause, where it belonged, to the privileges-and-immunities clause, which was irrelevant to the case. He ignored Judge Wells's simple formula for determining citizenship under the former clause (residence and the capacity to own property) and instead persisted in treating the word "citizen" as one of fixed and precise meaning, regardless of context. This was directly contrary to the Taney Court's interpretation when the citizenship of corporations, rather than the citizenship of Negroes, had been the issue. As pointed out on a previous page, Taney in 1839 had ruled that corporations were not entitled to the rights and protections of citizenship under the privileges-and-immunities clause. Five years later, however, the Court had declared a corporation to be "within the meaning of the law, a citizen of the state which created it, and where its business is done, for all the purposes of suing and being sued."[31] Citizenship at least to the extent of having access to federal courts for interstate suits—this was exactly the status that Judge Wells had accorded to Dred Scott in the circuit court, but Taney would have none of it.

Still not sure that he had closed every possible avenue to Negro citizenship, the Chief Justice returned to the subject of naturalization. The framers of the Constitution, he asserted, "took from the several States the power of naturalization, and confined that power exclusively to the Federal Government." But again Taney was misstating the facts. The pertinent clause of the Constitution confers on Congress the power "to establish an uniform rule of naturalization, and uniform laws on the subject of bankruptcies throughout the United States." There is nothing in the wording of either part of the clause that tells us the grant of power was intended to be exclusive. Supreme power, yes, but in the absence of its exercise by Congress, a state might conceivably exercise concurrent power in the field. This was precisely the interpretation given to the bankruptcy clause by the Marshall Court in 1819. On the other hand, two years earlier the Court had held congressional power over naturalization to be exclusive.[32] It might easily have decided the other way with no significant effect, since Congress had already enacted a naturalization law. But the point is that the exclusiveness of the naturalization power and the nonexclusiveness of the bankruptcy power were determined by the Supreme Court *some thirty years after the framing of the Constitution*. Yet Taney used the exclusiveness of the naturalization power as proof that *in 1787* "no state was willing to permit another State to determine who should or should not be . . . entitled to demand equal rights and privileges with their own people, within their own territories." Thus we are carried back to the beginning of the argument, with the Chief Justice once more concluding that no state "can give any right of citizenship outside of its own territory."[33]

Yet something new was also added, for Taney insisted that the power of naturalization extended only to "persons born in a foreign country under a foreign government."[34] The federal government had no power to "raise to the rank of a citizen anyone born in the United States, who, from birth or parentage, by the laws of the country, belongs to an inferior and subordinate class." Taney, it will be remembered, had already excepted Indians from this dictum. They could be "naturalized," while neither the states nor the federal government could confer citizenship on Negroes "within the meaning of the Constitution." At the same time, no category of foreigners, including black foreigners, was constitutionally incapable of being naturalized.* What this meant, though Taney never explicitly said so, was that *American Negroes, free and slave, were the only people on the face of the earth who (saving a constitutional amendment) were forever ineligible for American citizenship.*

At this late stage, Taney's attention was somehow finally drawn to the clause in the Articles of Confederation that he had previously contradicted. Earlier, he had asserted that the privileges-and-immunities clause of the Constitution gave each citizen rights "outside

---

*To be sure, Congress by statute had limited naturalization to white persons, but, as Taney acknowledged, it had the power to do otherwise.

of his State which he did not before possess." Now, without going back to correct his error, he noted that the Articles contained a "similar" clause, using, however, the words "free inhabitants" instead of "citizens" at one point. This terminology would, he conceded, "in the generality of its terms . . . certainly include one of the African race who had been manumitted."

> But no example, we think, can be found of his admission to all the privileges of citizenship in any State of the Union after these Articles were formed. . . . And, notwithstanding the generality of the words "free inhabitants," it is very clear that, according to their accepted meaning in that day, they did not include the African race, whether free or not.[35]

Black inhabitants, even if free, were not free inhabitants, and the fact that some rights had been denied them meant that they had no rights at all. So much for the logic of white justice, and so much for the plain meaning of plain words.

But why did Taney find everything so "very clear"? Because, he said, in another part of the Articles providing for requisition of armed forces, each state's quota was to be in proportion to its "white inhabitants."

> Words could hardly have been used which more strongly mark the line of distinction between the citizen and the subject—the free and the subjugated races. The latter were not even counted when the inhabitants of a State were to be embodied in proportion to its numbers for the general defense. And it cannot for a moment be supposed, that a class of persons thus separated and rejected from those who formed the sovereignty of the States, were yet intended to be included under the words "free inhabitants," in the preceding article.[36]

What Taney refused to consider in his own evidence was the possibility that when the framers of the Articles meant white inhabitants only, they said "white inhabitants." The use of the word "white" in this passage strengthens the case for the universal meaning of "free inhabitants" in the other passage. Furthermore, here again Taney ignored the provision of the Constitution that included free Negroes (and even slaves to a considerable extent) in the apportionment of representation. The very same argument that debased Negroes under the Articles could only elevate them under the Constitution.

Having demonstrated to his own satisfaction that the privileges-and-immunities clause of the Articles could not possibly have been intended to include free Negroes, the Chief Justice concluded that the clause was "the same in principle with that inserted in the Constitution." Then he reversed himself and proceeded to argue that the change from "free inhabitants" to "citizens" was significant—that "this alteration in words would hardly have been made unless a different meaning was intended to be conveyed, or a possible doubt removed." The word "citizen," Taney continued, obviously excluded unnaturalized foreigners and also "every description of persons who were not fully recognized as citizens in the several States."[37] But elsewhere Taney had already insisted that recognition of citizenship by a state did not necessarily mean state citizenship "within the meaning of the Constitution." So his whole argument here actually led nowhere. He succeeded only in demonstrating the obvious—that the Constitution, by using the word "citizens," excludes noncitizens from the protection of the privileges-and-immunities clause. Dred Scott, however, claimed to *be* a citizen. That was the issue, and nothing in the clause itself provided the definition of citizenship necessary to settle the issue.

One other statement in this passage illustrates Taney's chronic inability to get the facts straight. Speaking of the privileges-and-immunities clause, he said that by the intention of the framers, "this privilege was about to be placed under the protection of the general government, and the words expounded by its tribunals, and all power in relation to it taken from the State and its courts." Now there is no evidence whatever that federal courts were intended to be the sole interpreters and enforcers of the privileges-and-immunities clause. The clause did provide the basis for the appeal of decisions from state courts to the Supreme Court. But it did not prevent state courts from interpreting the clause in decisions that might be intermediate or might be final if there were no appeal to the Supreme Court. Furthermore, state courts *had* actually set forth interpretations of the clause in a number of significant decisions before 1857, and Taney, just a few pages earlier in his opinion, *had cited* one of them to show that Negroes were not regarded as citizens![38]

The difficulties involved in attempting a thorough critique of Taney's opinion become painfully obvious in this discussion of his four paragraphs on the privileges-and-immunities clauses. Multiple errors and logical confusion in the opinion militate against brevity and simplicity in the critique. The entire passage is more or less an afterthought and almost a *non sequitur*. Most of its argument is beside the point. It contains cavalier misstatements of fact and misreadings of documentary evidence. It contains internal contradictions as well as contradictions of statements made in other parts of the opinion. Textual criticism of such a text can scarcely avoid taking on some of the diffuseness and exasperating redundancy of the text itself. Yet no brief, neat summary or sampling could fully reveal the character of this remarkable document.

VI

Still not ready to leave the subject, Taney next turned to federal legislation for evidence that Negroes were never intended to be citizens. He cited three laws, ignoring others that did not suit his purpose. First there was the act of 1790 regulating naturalization and confining that privilege to aliens of the white race. With some eccentric reasoning that included another digression on Indians, he arrived at the conclusion that the racial restriction in the law "followed out the line of division which the Constitution has drawn between the citizen race . . . and the African race."[39] Actually, of course, there is no racial line of division in the Constitution, but only a line between "free persons" and "other persons." No doubt Taney was right in maintaining that the naturalization statute accurately reflected the racial attitudes of its time. But he was presiding over a court of law, not a survey of public opinion, and the act of 1790 in no way clarified or affected the status of free American Negroes. In fact, it could be regarded as expressing a determination to have *no more* Negro citizens besides those already present in the United States. Having meandered back to the subject of naturalization, Taney in this passage repeated his earlier assertion that Congress had no power to naturalize any member of the African race "imported into or born in this country." This was dictum and purely arbitrary, reflecting the apprehensions of a slaveholding society but lacking any basis in law. The text of the Constitution places no limitations on the power of Congress to make any non-citizen a citizen of the United States.

The second federal law cited by Taney was the act passed in 1792 requiring enrollment in the militia of every "free able-bodied white male citizen." But this phrasing tended to contradict his whole argument, as Taney himself inadvertently made clear. "The word 'white,' " he wrote, "is evidently used to exclude the African race, and the word 'citizen' to exclude unnaturalized foreigners." Exactly! If free Negroes were nowhere at that time considered to be citizens, as Taney insisted, the word "white" would have been unnecessary. The word "citizen" should have been enough to exclude both aliens *and* Negroes.

The third law cited by Taney is something else again; for it restricted employment on American ships to "citizens of the United States" and "persons of color, natives of the United States." Here, the phraseology did indeed plainly imply that Negroes were not part of the national citizenry. But this statute was enacted in 1813, and Taney had already undercut its value by stressing the fact that the other two laws were passed soon after the drafting of the Constitution when many of the framers were sitting in Congress. Elsewhere, Taney insisted that the Constitution "must be construed now as it was understood at the time of its adoption." A law passed in 1813 was hardly best evidence of what the word "citizen" meant in 1789.[40]

From his three carefully selected acts of Congress, Taney turned to the policies of the federal executive branch. In 1821, he said, Attorney General William Wirt had ruled that "free persons of color were not citizens." Quite recently, he added, that ruling had been confirmed by Attorney General Caleb Cushing, with the result that Negroes could not obtain passports as citizens of the United States.[41] For whatever it might be worth, the general tendency of federal executive rulings had indeed been unfavorable to Negro citizenship. Yet

Taney, playing the advocate instead of the judge, persisted in over-stating his case. He misrepresented Wirt's opinion, which, by impli-cation, actually left room for Negroes to become United States citi-zens through equality of treatment by their own states. As for passports, they had sometimes been issued and sometimes been de-nied to Negroes. In any case, the opinions of the attorneys general carried no authority of a judicial nature. Their status was that of learned argument, not precedent.

Much of the remainder of Taney's discussion of Negro citizenship was rebuttal to points raised by Montgomery Blair in his argument. For one thing, Blair had referred to the case of *LeGrand v. Darnall* (1829) in which a former slave was one of the parties in a federal suit under the diverse-citizenship clause, and in which Taney himself was one of the attorneys. The Chief Justice did not quarrel with the facts but took refuge in a technicality, asserting quite correctly that the question of Darnell's race was not raised until too late in the litigation to affect the Court's jurisdiction.[42]

Moreover, Blair had maintained that a person might be a citizen under the diverse-citizenship clause without being necessarily en-titled to all the protection given under the privileges-and-immunities clause, and that such recognition of citizenship would not militate against laws regulating the activities of free Negroes under the state police power. This argument was in line with the ruling made by Judge Wells in the circuit court and with several state court decisions, such as *Ely v. Thompson* and *State v. Manuel.** But Taney, who con-sistently ignored the relevant but embarrassing fact that free Negroes had access to state courts, was likewise unwilling to discuss the possi-bility of a limited citizenship for Negroes that included the right to bring suit in federal courts. Instead, he responded as though Blair had been talking about the privileges-and-immunities clause. If the clause protected free Negroes, he declared, it protected them as fully as it protected white persons against discriminatory state laws. This would mean that a black recognized as a citizen in a northern state could enter a southern state and be exempt from all its laws regulat-

* See above, pp. 67, 277.

ing black behavior. So he returned to his *argumentum ad horrendum* and pursued it to the familiar conclusion that the consequences which would follow such an interpretation made it "absolutely certain that the African race were not included under the name of citizens of a State . . . in the contemplation of the framers of the Constitution."[43]

Taney began the conclusion of this part of his opinion with a repetition of his pronouncement excluding Negroes, free and slave, from all rights and protections guaranteed in the Constitution:

> The only two provisions which point to them and include them,
> treat them as property, and make it the duty of the Government
> to protect it; no other power, in relation to this race, is to be found
> in the Constitution; and as it is a Government of special, delegated
> powers, no authority beyond these two provisions can be constitu-
> tionally exercised. The Government of the United States had no
> right to interfere for any other purpose but that of protecting the
> rights of the owner, leaving it altogether with the several States to
> deal with this race, whether emancipated or not, as each State
> may think justice, humanity, and the interests and safety of society
> require. The States evidently intended to reserve this power ex-
> clusively to themselves.[44]

There, in one paragraph, is the proslavery Constitution, with "property" substituted for "persons," with free Negroes undifferentiated from slaves, with all antislavery "interference" proscribed and proslavery interference required. From the implied recognition of slavery in the Constitution and from the limited protection extended to the institution in the fugitive-slave clause, Taney derived a racial categorization, permanent and inflexible, that appears nowhere on the face of the document and is clearly belied in the provision for apportionment of representation and direct taxes. In holding that free Negroes had no rights under the Constitution, Taney denied them status not only as citizens but as persons. For instance, a Negro would not need to be a citizen to claim the protection of the Fifth Amendment, which declares that no *person* shall be deprived of life, liberty, or property without due process of law. Whether the Fugitive Slave Law of 1850 violated this and other procedural guarantees is a matter of controversy, but the point is that Taney proposed to settle the issue simply by excluding Negroes as a race from all constitutional rights, even those extended to *persons*. This is one more manifestation of his resolve to plug every loophole in the southern defense.

"No one, we presume, supposes," Taney continued, "that any change in public opinion or feeling, in relation to this unfortunate race . . . should induce the court to give to the words of the Constitution a more liberal construction in their favor than they were intended to bear when the instrument was framed and adopted." To do so, he added in a statement dripping with unconscious irony, "would abrogate the judicial character of this court, and make it the mere reflex of the popular opinion or passion of the day."[45] The disingenuousness of this passage is too evident. Taney had repeatedly used evidence of unfavorable treatment of the Negro since 1789 to bulwark his argument, including a very recent opinion of the attorney general. But he rejected as irrelevant any evidence of more favorable treatment after that date.

Summing up, Taney cited "the language of the Declaration of Independence and of the Articles of Confederation" (in both instances, he insisted that the language did not mean what it said). He cited the "plain words of the Constitution" (which he made plain by virtual judicial amendment); the laws of Congress and state legislatures (actually, an unrepresentative selection of such laws, frequently misinterpreted); and the "uniform action" of the executive department (rendered uniform by ignoring every exception). All of these things, "concurring together," led to the same conclusion. "And," he declared in his best *ex cathedra* tone, "if anything in relation to the construction of the Constitution can be regarded as settled, it is that which we now give to the word 'citizen' and the word 'people.' "

> And upon a full and careful consideration of the subject, the court is of opinion that, upon the facts stated in the plea in abatement, Dred Scott was not a citizen of Missouri within the meaning of the Constitution of the United States, and not entitled as such to sue in its courts; and, consequently, that the Circuit Court had no jurisdiction of the case, and that the judgment on the plea in abatement is erroneous.[46]

∽ 16 ∽

The Opinion of the Court:
Slavery in the Territories

Taney had devoted the first half of his opinion to overturning the lower court's ruling against the plea in abatement—that is, to sustaining the contention that Negroes were not citizens. At this point, according to his critics, the Chief Justice could and should have remanded the case to the lower court with instructions to dismiss it for want of jurisdiction. Instead, he proceeded to take up the substantive issue of whether Dred Scott had become free by virtue of his residence in Illinois or at Fort Snelling. Taney justified his procedure in a four-page passage, nearly half of which is known to have been added as rebuttal to Justice Curtis after the early publication of the latter's dissenting opinion. This impropriety aside, Taney's argument seems the more impressive of the two:

Curtis: The Court majority, by sustaining the plea in abatement, had held that this was a case to which the judicial power of the United States did not extend. The Court had no power to consider any other jurisdictional question not raised by the plea in abatement. In examining the merits of the case after having denied federal jurisdiction, the Court had exceeded its authority. *Taney:* The plea in abatement was a plea to the jurisdiction of the federal circuit court, *not* to the jurisdiction of the Supreme Court. It was the duty of the Supreme Court to correct any and all errors made in the lower tribunal, and it must take notice of a want of jurisdiction appearing on the record, whether or not such want had been specified in a plea in abatement. Waiving the whole question of Negro citizenship, the so-called merits of the case still presented a jurisdictional problem; for if Scott was and always had been a slave, he obviously had never been a citizen with a right to sue in a federal court. So the lower court had made two major errors, both of which must be corrected: (1) It should have dismissed the case for lack of jurisdiction on the grounds presented in the plea in abatement. (2) Failing that, having at the end of the trial determined that Scott remained a slave, instead of awarding the verdict to the defendant, it should *then* have dismissed the suit for lack of jurisdiction. And therefore Taney, in pursuing the question of whether Scott had become free in Illinois or Wisconsin Territory, was technically not going to the merits but offering a second reason for dismissal on jurisdictional grounds.[1]

Of course the legal justification for continuing on, whatever may be said of its soundness, was not Taney's real reason for doing so. He was, in fact, determined to rule on the constitutionality of the Missouri Compromise restriction, and his strategy clearly reflected that determination. There were, he asserted, two questions requiring attention. First, was Dred Scott free by reason of his stay in federal territory where slavery had been forbidden? Second, was he free by reason of his removal into a free state? "We proceed," said Taney, "to examine the first question." But Scott's residence in Illinois, it will be remembered, had preceded his residence at Fort Snelling. Taney, significantly, was taking up the two questions in reverse chronological order, thereby confronting immediately the issue of congressional power in the territories. In this way he avoided a serious problem. For if he had first considered the effect of Scott's residence in Illinois, it would have been difficult to explain why the same reasoning should not apply to Scott's residence in the federal territory, making it unnecessary to examine the constitutionality of the Missouri Compromise restriction. This was precisely how Justice Nelson had fashioned his opinion. But Taney, with a different purpose in mind, adopted a strategy that carried him directly to the territorial issue and the storm center of controversy.[2]

II

The Chief Justice began his discussion of the territorial question by dismissing as irrelevant the one clause of the Constitution in which the word "territory" appears—the part of Article Four, Section Three, authorizing Congress "to dispose of and make all needful rules and regulations respecting the territory or other property belonging to the United States." An exceedingly narrow interpretation of this passage, developed by certain Democratic spokesmen, had been echoed in Senator Geyer's argument as counsel for Sanford. The gist of the interpretation was that the territory clause referred only to ownership and disposal of public land, that it conferred no power to govern the territories, and that such power must be implied from some other part of the Constitution. Taney likewise proposed to limit severely the scope of the clause, but he did so in his own unique way.

Ten pages of rambling, repetitious prose were devoted to the singular argument that the territory clause, whatever power it conferred, affected only the land already owned or claimed by the United States in 1789. In all areas subsequently acquired, such as Louisiana, the clause simply had no force of any kind. "It was a special provision for a known and particular territory, and to meet a present emergency, and nothing more." The purpose of the clause, Taney declared, was "to transfer to the new Government the property then held in common by the States . . . before their league [meaning the Articles of Confederation] was dissolved." The word "territory" meant land; the words "other property" meant movable property such as ships, arms, and munitions inherited by the new government. All of this the Chief Justice deduced from the language of the clause itself. He quoted no framers of the Constitution, cited no court decisions in support of his bizarre explication.[3]

It is difficult to take the passage seriously. Of course the framers of the Constitution had the existing western territory particularly in mind when they approved Article Four, Section Three. It might also be said that they had existing states specifically in mind when they approved the interstate commerce clause, and they had no notion of encompassing railroad transportation across the continent, airplane flights to Hawaii, or radio transmissions from California. To say that future acquisitions of territory could not be regulated under the territory clause because the framers were thinking only of territory already acquired was absurd. Such a principle, generally applied, would have made the Constitution useless long ago. Besides, what evidence exists indicates that some of the framers probably did have later acquisitions in mind. The mouth of the Mississippi, for instance, had already become a coveted place by 1787.[4]

Taney, who was not often satisfied to say a thing just once, called attention in one sentence to the "language used in the clause" and also to its "somewhat unusual phraseology." It did not speak, he continued, "of *any* territory, nor of *territories*, but . . . only [of] the Territory of the United States— that is . . . a Territory then in existence, and then known or claimed as the Territory of the United States." What the Chief Justice overlooked was the fact that in August 1787, when the Constitutional Convention began to consider the subject, *there was just one* "Territory of the United States." It had been created a month or so earlier by the Northwest Ordinance, and it did not include all western lands but only those north of the Ohio River. The words "other property belonging to the United States" presumably referred to land not yet organized as a territory—to land south of the Ohio, much of which had not yet even been ceded to the United States by the states claiming it. The context allows no other meaning; for the whole of Article Four, Section Three, it should be remembered, dealt with the admission of new states and the administration of the transappalachian West. To insist, as Taney did, that "other property" here meant "ships, arms, and munitions" was nonsense.

As for the authority to "make all needful rules and regulations respecting the territory," this was associated, said Taney, with the power to dispose of public lands, not the general power to govern. "They are not the words usually employed by statesmen, when they mean to give the powers of sovereignty," he declared.

> The words "rules and regulations" are usually employed in the Constitution in speaking of some particular specified power which it means to confer on the Government, and not, as we have seen, when granting general powers of legislation. As, for example, ". . . the particular and specific power to regulate commerce"; "to

establish an uniform rule of naturalization"; "to coin money and regulate the value thereof." And to construe the words of which we are speaking as a general and unlimited grant of sovereignty over territories which the Government might afterwards acquire, is to use them in a sense and for a purpose for which they were not used in any other part of the instrument. But if confined to a particular territory, in which a government and laws had already been established, but which would require some alterations to adapt it to the new Government, the words are peculiarly applicable and appropriate for that purpose.[5]

Here is another manifestation of the logical slippage (such as from "free Negro" to "slave") that Taney, whether by calculation or instinct, often used to advantage. His purpose was to demonstrate that "rules" and "regulations" are relatively weak words not associated with the exercise of sovereignty. But faced with the fact that the word "regulate" is sometimes used to invest Congress with plenary power (as in the commerce clause), he shifted his discussion from the force or strength of the words themselves to the breadth of the context in which they appear. The fallacy embodied in the first sentence of the above passage is obvious and egregious. With the exception of the necessary-and-proper clause, there *are* no provisions of the Constitution that grant "general powers of legislation." Every delegated power is in some way a "specified power," whether or not the words "rules and regulations" are employed. Thus the power "to establish an uniform rule of naturalization" is no more "particular" or "specified" (and no less plenary) than the power "to promote the progress of science and useful arts by securing for limited times to authors and inventors the exclusive right to their respective writings and discoveries." Similarly, the authority to "make all needful rules and regulations respecting the territory," a broad and untrammeled grant of power if there ever was one, is the precise equivalent of authority to "pass all necessary laws respecting the territory."[6] Of course the power was "particular" in the sense that legislation for a territory would be limited in its operation to the area of the territory, and that was a good reason for using "rules and regulations," rather than "laws," to designate such legislation.[7]

The weakness of Taney's argument, however, results less from its logical inconsistency than from its incompatibility with the context of historical events. For the new United States in the 1780s, the two principal western problems (aside from defense against the Indians) were land disposal and government. The first had been dealt with in the Land Ordinance of 1785; the second, in the Northwest Ordinance of July 13, 1787, with its roots going back to 1784. In the Convention on August 18, 1787, James Madison proposed additions to the emerging Constitution empowering Congress "to dispose of the unappropriated lands of the United States" and also "to institute temporary governments for new States arising therein."[8] It was these proposals that were converted into the territory clause, and the parallel between what had already been done under the Articles and what was authorized under the Constitution is plain enough. Madison and the other framers expected Congress to continue exercising the same kind of power in the western territory that had produced the two ordinances, and this included the power to forbid slavery. Then, in 1789, the Northwest Ordinance was re-enacted by a Congress that included many of the framers, and there was no resistance on constitutional grounds.* The conclusion is inescapable that the territory clause simply confirmed the exercise of power in the territories equivalent to that previously exercised in the famous ordinances. Nor is there any reason to agree with Taney that such power was limited to land already belonging to the United States; for that argument, strictly speaking, would have excluded most of the Southwest, which was still unceded.

What the Chief Justice managed to do with his eccentric interpretation of the territory clause was to clear the way for invalidating the Missouri Compromise restriction without challenging the legitimacy of the more venerable Northwest Ordinance. Here again, Taney constructed his own peculiar version of American history to serve his judicial purpose. Under the Articles of Confederation, he asserted, "there was no Government of the United States in existence." Instead, there were "thirteen separate, sovereign, independent

* See above, pp. 83–84.

States, which had entered into a league or confederation for their mutual protection and advantage. . . . But this Confederation had none of the attributes of sovereignty. . . . It was little more than a congress of ambassadors, authorized to represent separate nations, in matters in which they had a common concern."[9] Apparently, Taney did not regard the power to declare war, or the power to make peace, or the power to enter into treaties, or the power to fix the value of coins, or the power to regulate all relations with the Indians, or the power to establish post offices, or the power to grant letters of marque and reprisal, or the power to settle all disputes between two or more states, as constituting an "attribute of sovereignty."

> It was this Congress [Taney continued] that accepted the cession from Virginia. They had no power to accept it under the Articles of Confederation. But they had an undoubted right, as independent sovereignties, to accept any cession of territory for their common benefit, which all of them assented to.

Note the verbal slippage here from "Congress" to "they" to "independent sovereignties." The Northwest Ordinance, including the prohibition against slavery, was not the work of a United States government created by the Articles of Confederation, but rather the work of the independent sovereign states acting through the agency of Congress. "We do not question the power of the States, by agreement among themselves, to pass this ordinance, nor its obligatory force in the Territory," Taney declared. For the states "had a right to establish any form of government they pleased, by compact or treaty among themselves."[10] In short, the Articles Congress, usually pictured as a relatively weak body, actually possessed virtually unlimited authority, according to the Chief Justice, because, being too weak to be classified as a government, it constituted collective state sovereignty in action. But this theory assumed *unanimous* action by the thirteen "independent sovereignties"; Taney conveniently ignored the fact that the Ordinance of 1787 was passed by the vote of only eight of the thirteen states. It was not something "which all of them assented to."

The Northwest Ordinance, according to Taney, was an act of

"despotic and unlimited power over persons and property" which was nevertheless legitimate because it had been exercised by the "confederated States" in their "common property." Such unlimited power was not, however, vested in Congress by the territory clause of the Constitution; for the new federal government was one of strictly limited powers. But then by what authority did the new government in 1789 re-enact the Northwest Ordinance? Not by authority of the territory clause, said Taney. Instead, the law of 1789 merely acknowledged that by the Ordinance of 1787, the states in their separate sovereign capacities had determined "the purposes to which the land in this territory was to be applied, and the form of government and principles of jurisprudence which were to prevail there."[11] So the act of 1789 was no exercise of power at all, but merely an acceptance of a decision previously made.

Thus, in Taney's phantasmal history of the United States, the Congress under the Articles was not only mightier than the Congress established by the Constitution; it was capable of wielding "despotic and unlimited power." Furthermore, the Articles Congress could govern the western territory in any way that it chose, including the exclusion of slavery, even though the Articles themselves did not authorize it; whereas a Constitutional Congress possessed no explicitly granted power to govern the territories, in spite of the territory clause because that referred only to land disposal.

At this point, Taney inserted about four pages of rebuttal to McLean, denying that there was any conflict between his opinion and that of John Marshall in *American Insurance Company v. Canter* (1828). "Florida," Marshall had declared, "continues to be a territory of the United States, governed by virtue of that clause in the constitution which empowers congress 'to make all needful rules and regulations respecting the territory or other property belonging to the United States.' " This sentence plainly conflicted with Taney's argument that the territory clause did not apply to *any* area acquired after 1789. But Taney simply ignored the sentence and concentrated instead on Marshall's supplementary acknowledgment (made in the interest of consensus) that the right of Congress to govern the territories might be derived from any of several sources. One of these was the "inevitable consequence of the right to acquire territory." Whatever the source of the power, Marshall had added, the possession of it was "unquestioned."[12] Taney agreed. The power itself was indeed unquestionable, but then he closed the question that Marshall had left open. The power to govern the territories was not conferred in the territory clause but could be implied from the right to acquire territory, which in turn would have to be implied from some other power expressly delegated. Double implication was preferred to a plain reading of the Constitution.

Thus Taney took advantage of Marshall's ambiguity to obscure the fact that he was in sharp disagreement with Marshall about the meaning of the territory clause. But another sentence in Marshall's opinion was even more troublesome. Speaking of the territories, he declared: "In legislating for them, Congress exercises the combined powers of the general, and of a state government." Since no one questioned the power of a state to prohibit slavery, it would seem that Marshall had clearly acknowledged the power of Congress to prohibit slavery in the territories. Not so, said Taney, for Marshall's statement applied only to legislation regarding the territorial judiciary, which was the matter at issue in the *American Insurance Company* case. But it is obvious to anyone reading the passage that the sentence quoted above was Marshall's generalization about congressional power in the territories, *from which* he drew his specific conclusion about organization of the judiciary. Taney's interpretation is untenable.[13]

III

Having cast aside both the judicial decision and the clause of the Constitution that seemed most relevant to his subject, the Chief Justice then unveiled his own explanation of the source and limits of federal power in the territories. The power to govern, he had already said, proceeded from the power to acquire. The latter, one might think, would be derived from the power to make war and enter into treaties. Instead, Taney declared that the power to acquire territory stemmed solely from the power to admit new states into the Union. This was a kind of reasoning analogous to pumping water uphill, but what strikes one most forcibly is the sharp contrast between Taney's strangulated interpretation of the territory clause and his expansive use of the state-making clause.

These two clauses, it will be remembered, lie side by side in the Constitution, comprising the whole of Article Four, Section Three, and there can be no doubt that in the minds of the framers they were closely linked. Yet the territory clause, according to Taney, applied only to land already held by the central government in 1789. The statehood clause, in contrast, applied as well to all land that might in the future be acquired by the United States. More than that, the statehood clause was the *sole authority* for any such future acquisitions. Thus a judicial decision can arbitrarily shrink one passage of the Constitution and expand another.[14]

Next, Taney attempted to strengthen his argument with another excursion into American history. The power exercised by the Confederation Congress in acquiring western territory and establishing a government there had been viewed, he said, "with great jealousy by the leading statesmen of the day." As his only documentation he offered a passage from *The Federalist*, 38, describing it as follows.

> Mr. Madison . . . speaks of the acquisition of the Northwestern Territory by the confederated States, by the cession from Virginia, and the establishment of a government there, as an exercise of power not warranted by the Articles of Confederation and dangerous to the liberties of the people. And he urges the adoption of the Constitution as a security and safeguard against such an exercise of power.[15]

The facts are, of course, that until the cession of western lands had begun, the Articles of Confederation could not even begin to function, and the need for some kind of government in the ceded territory was generally acknowledged. There is no evidence of any "great jealousy" among leading statesmen about congressional assumption of authority over the West. On the contrary, Madison asserted categorically that no blame had been whispered in the matter and that he himself intended no censure of Congress, which "could not have done

STANDARD INTERPRETATION

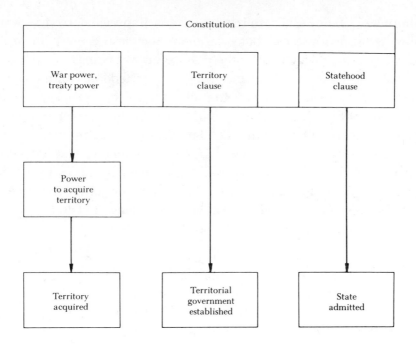

TANEY INTERPRETATION

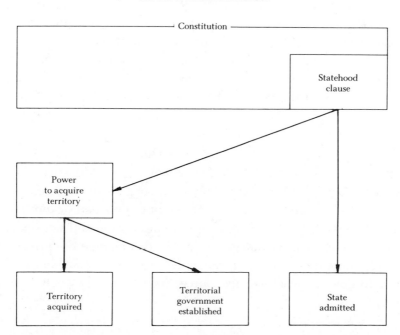

otherwise." Taney's generalization is thus impeached by the testimony of his own witness, but even more notable is the way in which he misread the very intent of the passage he was citing.

Madison expressed no misgivings about federal control of the western territories. It was he, after all, who had first proposed in the Convention that Congress be authorized to "institute temporary government" there. In *Federalist* 38, he was using the problem of the West to illustrate a more general argument—namely, that a government granted too little power could be driven by necessity to the dangerous habit of assuming power. The members of the Confederation Congress, he maintained, had had little choice but to accept the state cessions and provide government for the West.

> The public interest, the necessity of the case, imposed upon them the task of overleaping their constitutional limits. But is not the fact an alarming proof of the danger resulting from a government which does not possess regular powers commensurate to its objects? A dissolution or usurpation is the dreadful dilemma to which it is continually exposed.

Plainly, Madison's words offered no support to the concept of implied power. The Constitution, in his view, removed a potential source of danger by *expressly* vesting in Congress the authority to govern western territory until it was ready for statehood. Taney, in emasculating the territory clause and in insisting that the power to govern the West could be justified only by double implication, was contradicting almost everything that Madison had said on the subject in the Convention and in *The Federalist*.

In some fifteen printed pages the Chief Justice had made but scant progress toward his goal of invalidating the Missouri Compromise restriction. He had first denied that Congress possessed any delegated power to govern the territories but then had acknowledged that such power nevertheless existed by implication and as a matter of necessity. Just what advantage he saw in this change of derivation is not clear, for the key question remained virtually untouched: Did the power to govern, whatever its source, include the power to exclude slavery?

For one thing, it was obvious that the necessities of government in a territory could not be provided by Congress within the limits of the powers delegated in Article One, Section Eight. On the contrary, what a frontier community needed primarily was the means of social control ordinarily associated with police powers reserved to the states. Taney, try as he might, could not set aside the factual accuracy of John Marshall's assertion that in legislating for the territories Congress exercised the "combined powers" of the federal and state governments. Thus, to say that the Constitution did not explicitly empower Congress to exclude slavery from the territories was in itself virtually meaningless; for the same was true of a great many powers that Congress necessarily exercised in the territories.* Strict construction, whatever its utility elsewhere as a curb on congressional authority, simply would not work in the context of the territorial system.

Furthermore, too much emphasis upon the meagerness of federal power in the territories might be disadvantageous to the proslavery cause. Events in Kansas were demonstrating that mere "nonintervention" would no longer encourage the expansion of slavery. Some measure of positive protection seemed necessary, and Taney intended that the slaveholder's constitutional right to such protection should receive judicial confirmation. In short, while the power to prohibit slavery in the territories must be nullified, the power to protect it must be not only affirmed but converted into an obligation.

Most important of all, perhaps, strict construction has always been a relatively weak foundation for the assertion of judicial power. It is essentially a negative concept, giving the impression of mustiness and narrow-mindedness, and it is highly susceptible to the erosion of time. Something more potent was needed to obliterate a legislative power that had been routinely exercised for two-thirds of a century. So Taney began moving toward the conclusion that excluding slavery from the territories was not only unauthorized by the Constitution but positively forbidden by it.

*Such as provision for the arrest, trial, and punishment of criminals; enforcement of contracts; probating of wills; solemnizing of marriages; and Congress passed territorial laws forbidding fornication, dueling, and gambling—so why not laws forbidding slavery?

The Chief Justice therefore turned his attention to rights of the people living in the territories. He apparently believed that he had strengthened those rights by deriving the power of territorial government indirectly from the statehood clause, rather than directly from the territory clause. This presumably made it more evident that the Constitution conferred no authority to establish permanent colonies in the West or to treat the people there as "mere colonists, dependent upon the will of the general government."[16] Instead, persons migrating to federal territory retained all the rights guaranteed to them by the Constitution and were in this respect "on the same footing" with residents of the various states. The Constitution, that is, followed the flag promptly and absolutely into newly acquired territory.

For example, said Taney, no one would contend that Congress, in legislating for the territories, could abridge the personal liberties protected by the First Amendment. Neither could it deny a territorial population the right to bear arms, or the right to trial by jury, or exemption from compulsory self-incrimination. Similarly, the rights of private property were guarded against congressional invasion by the due-process clause of the Fifth Amendment. "And," Taney continued, "an act of Congress which deprives a citizen of the United States of his liberty or property, merely because he came himself or brought his property into a particular Territory of the United States, and who had committed no offense against the laws, could hardly be dignified with the name of due process of law."[17]

With this emphatic assertion of the principle of "substantive due process," Taney had arrived at the climax of his argument but seemed unaware of the fact. Surprisingly, he did not proceed straightway to the conclusion that the Missouri Compromise restriction was in violation of the Fifth Amendment and therefore void. Instead, he went on giving examples of what Congress could not do in governing the territories. And throughout the remainder of his opinion, he said nothing more at all about the due-process clause.

"The powers over person and property of which we speak," continued the Chief Justice, "are not only not granted to Congress, but are in express terms denied, and they are forbidden to exercise them. And this prohibition is not confined to the States, but the words are general, and extend to the whole territory over which the Constitution gives it power to legislate, including those portions of it remaining under territorial government, as well as that covered by States."[18] Then, in a digression of only two sentences, Taney struck a fierce judicial blow at the Douglas version of popular sovereignty:

> And if Congress itself cannot do this—if it is beyond the powers conferred on the Federal Government—it will be admitted, we presume, that it could not authorize a territorial government to exercise them. It could confer no power on any local government, established by its authority, to violate the provisions of the Constitution.[19]

The reasoning here may well have been sound, granting the premises upon which it rested, but whether a territorial legislature could constitutionally forbid slavery was a question that had never arisen in the Dred Scott case.* Whatever may be said about the rest of Taney's opinion, this passage was *obiter dictum,* pure and simple. It exemplifies, however, his determination to provide slavery with comprehensive judicial reinforcement.

IV

Taney had used some nineteen printed pages (or about one-third of his entire opinion) to arrive at a position that could have been reached in two or three sentences—namely, that the Bill of Rights and other constitutional limitations on the power of Congress were operative in the territories as well as in the states.[20] Next, however, he moved with extraordinary haste through the crucial part of his argument to a conclusion based largely upon a few flat assertions. First, he denied that there was any difference between slave property and other kinds of property. He also dismissed the law of nations as being of any authority on the subject. Then there followed a paragraph of summary that requires not only quotation in full but a certain amount of commentary. For convenience, each sentence is numbered:

* See above, p. 314, and below, pp. 510, 517.

[1]Now, as we have already said in an earlier part of this opinion, upon a different point, the right of property in a slave is distinctly and expressly affirmed in the Constitution. [2]The right to traffic in it, like an ordinary article of merchandise and property, was guarantied to the citizens of the United States, in every State that might desire it, for twenty years. [3]And the Government in express terms is pledged to protect it in all future time, if the slave escapes from his owner. [4]This is done in plain words—too plain to be misunderstood. [5]And no word can be found in the Constitution which gives Congress a greater power over slave property, or which entitles property of that kind to less protection than property of any other description. [6]The only power conferred is the power coupled with the duty of guarding and protecting the owner in his rights.[21]

Since the Constitution uses neither the word "slavery" nor the word "property" in connection with Negroes, the first sentence is manifestly untrue. Whatever implications may have been understood by the framers, nothing is *expressly* affirmed about slavery as a property right. The second and third sentences constitute the whole of Taney's proof for his assertion in sentence number one, and both are stated in misleading terms. The Constitution permitted, but did not guarantee, continuation of the African slave trade for twenty years. Even this temporary immunity applied only to the original thirteen states. Hence, insofar as the slave-trade clause did recognize a "right of property" in slaves, it likewise acknowledged the power of Congress to extinguish that right, eventually in the original states and immediately in the rest of the national domain.* As for the fugitive-slave clause, it appears in the section of the Constitution devoted to interstate comity and from its text alone could have been interpreted as an obligation laid solely on the individual states (as with the rendition of fugitives from justice). There is no express "pledge" of assistance from the central government in the recovery of fugitive slaves. If the clause required such intervention, it did so only by implication.† The fourth sentence, coming after emphatic use of the words

* See above, pp. 23–24.
† See above, pp. 25, 46–47.

"express" and "expressly," is one of those superfluous reiterations that weaken credibility. It exemplifies Taney's habit of strengthening a dubious argument by declaring it to be an incontestable argument. The fifth sentence, restating the principle of the unexceptionalness and equality of slave property, seems incompatible with the fugitive-slave and slave-trade clauses, which, if they treat slaves as property, treat them as a unique and specially favored kind of property. The sixth sentence may or may not have been intended merely as an elaboration of sentence number three, on the fugitive-slave clause, but the effect of its broad phrasing was to endorse subsequent southern demands for a comprehensive federal slave code in the territories.

Together, the fifth and sixth sentences of this summary paragraph constituted a return to the strict-construction approach with which Taney had begun his discussion of the Missouri Compromise restriction. After affirming that slaves were recognized as property by the Constitution, he did not, as one might expect, invoke the due-process clause in defense of property rights against congressional interference. Instead, he contented himself with holding that Congress had been delegated no power to treat property in slaves differently from other property. This is not the broad construction of the negative or restraining clauses of the Constitution with which we associate later use of the due-process clause. Nevertheless, he was now ready to make his historic pronouncement:

> Upon these considerations, it is the opinion of the court that the Act of Congress which prohibited a citizen from holding and owning property of this kind in the territory of the United States north of the line therein mentioned, is not warranted by the Constitution, and is therefore void; and that neither Dred Scott himself, nor any of his family, were made free by being carried into this territory; even if they had been carried there by the owner, with the intention of becoming a permanent resident.*

*This final clause was Taney's only reference to the important question of whether Dred Scott's half-dozen years in free territory constituted "temporary" or "permanent" residence. Taney, by implication, took the view that it was temporary, ignoring a long tradition of southern jurisprudence to the contrary. See above, pp. 54–55, 252–53.

"Upon these considerations . . ." What, precisely, did the Chief Justice mean? Was he referring to the preceding paragraph or to the preceding twenty pages? Did the "considerations" include, for instance, his earlier reference to the due-process clause? If so, it is strange that he should have been so unexplicit about it. For, in spite of a general impression to the contrary, Taney never did specifically declare the Missouri Compromise restriction to be a violation of the Fifth Amendment.[22] He did not even say more generally that it was "forbidden" by the Constitution. Instead, he merely held that it was "not warranted by the Constitution," thus concluding on a vague note of strict construction.

Taney's contribution to the development of substantive due process was therefore meager and somewhat obscure. He did, to be sure, endorse the southern version of the doctrine (stressing property rather than liberty) but then seemed to draw back from making full use of it in arriving at his final judgment. Certainly the few lines that he devoted to the subject barely scratched its surface. For one thing, he ignored the abolitionist contention that the "liberty" aspect of the due-process clause made slavery illegal in the federal territories. The clause, after all, did extend its protection to every "person" in the United States, and were not slaves invariably referred to as "persons" in the Constitution?[23] How, then, could it be denied that a slave was a person who had been deprived of his liberty without due process of law? Perhaps with this counter-argument in mind, the Chief Justice consistently spoke of the rights of "citizens" in the territories, rather than the rights of "persons" there.

Taney, moreover, said nothing to justify use of the due-process clause as a restraint upon legislative power—that is, as a limitation upon the substance of law and not merely upon the manner of its enforcement. He said nothing, in spite of the fact that "due process," a concept derived from Magna Carta, had traditionally meant a guarantee of proper procedure in law enforcement, thus constituting a restraint primarily upon the executive function. It is true that the "substantive" version of due process had been broached in a few state court cases and in a variety of extrajudicial constitutional discussions. But only once previously had the subject received even passing mention in a decision of the Taney Court.[24]

Most important of all, Taney never came to grips with the question of whether the mere prohibition of slavery in a federal territory actually constituted deprivation of property. A slaveholder, after all, was in no danger of losing his human "property" *unless he deliberately violated the law,* and even Taney, with somewhat muddled logic, had virtually acknowledged that a lawbreaker's property rights might be more limited than those of a law-abiding citizen.[25] For example, an anti-gambling law of Illinois Territory ordered the seizure of "all monies exhibited for the purpose of alluring persons to bet."[26] Did such a forfeiture differ from the emancipation of a slave taken into a territory where slavery had been made illegal by federal law? Furthermore, as Justice Curtis pointed out in his dissenting opinion, forfeiture through emancipation had been a common penalty, even in certain slaveholding states, for the illegal importation of slaves. And apparently no one, he added, had ever supposed that such laws were in conflict with Magna Carta or with the due-process clauses of state constitutions. The same could be said of federal laws suppressing the African slave trade. Did their emancipation provisions constitute deprivation of property without due process of law? "If so," Curtis asked, "what becomes of the laws prohibiting the slave trade? If not, how can a similar regulation respecting a Territory violate the 5th Amendment of the Constitution?"[27]

But even if it were conceded that emancipation of a slave on account of his having resided in free territory constituted deprivation of property without due process of law, this would not be the same as conceding the unconstitutionality of the Missouri Compromise restriction. For the latter merely declared slavery "forever prohibited" north of 36° 30'. Like the Northwest Ordinance, it provided no means of enforcement, specified no penalties for violators. The law could have been enforced, for example, by assessing a fine and ordering removal of slaves from the territory in question to any of the slaveholding states—a sanction that would scarcely have amounted to deprivation of property. Thus emancipation was not inherent in the Missouri Compromise restriction itself, but rather in the remedy that had come to be accepted as standard practice and to be embodied in both state and federal statutes. So, even putting aside all other objections, perhaps the most that Taney could have maintained was that federal enforcement of emancipation as a sanction violated the due process clause. This would have been enough to deny Dred Scott his freedom, but not enough to overthrow the Missouri Compromise restriction and other such laws.

We are accustomed to having "due process of law" interpreted so broadly as to be relevant in almost any contingency, but such was not the case in 1857, when the words had barely begun to acquire a substantive implication. Perhaps Taney was so tentative and sketchy in his use of the clause because he realized how inadequate it was as a basis for nullifying congressional power to prohibit slavery in the territories.

Thus, neither strict construction of congressional power in the territories (from whatever source that power might be derived) nor a broad, substantive construction of the due-process clause provided a sufficient basis for invalidating the Missouri Compromise restriction. Taney also tried to bolster his argument with some brief references to Calhoun's "common-property" doctrine, in which the federal government appears as a mere agent or trustee for the true joint-owners of the territories—the sovereign states. But again his language was not precise enough to indicate how much, if any, of his conclusion rested upon the principle of state equality and the extrajurisdictional force of states' rights.[28]

Here, then, was the historic first instance of judicial invalidation of a major federal statute, with an argument weak in its law, logic, history, and factual accuracy. Taney had directed much of his effort at constriction of the territory clause, and to no purpose; for he did not then deny the power of Congress to provide territorial government but instead converted it from a delegated to an implied power. Next, having perhaps realized the difficulty of applying strict construction to an implied power, he shifted from the strategy of demonstrating that Congress lacked constitutional authority over slavery in the territories to the strategy of demonstrating that the exercise of such power was forbidden by the due-process clause. Running into difficulties here too, he turned back again toward his original strict construction approach. But he never said specifically why the Missouri Compromise restriction was unconstitutional.

V

After disposing of Dred Scott's claim to freedom based on his residence at Fort Snelling, Taney still needed to consider the claim based on Scott's two years in Illinois. Here, the Chief Justice merely cited his opinion in *Strader v. Graham* as controlling precedent, ignoring all the differences between it and the Dred Scott case and insisting that everything he had said in that opinion was authoritative:

> The slaves had been taken from Kentucky to Ohio, with the consent of the owner, and afterwards brought back to Kentucky. And this court held that their *status* or condition, as free or slave, depended upon the laws of Kentucky, when they were brought back into that State, and not of Ohio; and that this court had no jurisdiction to revise the judgment of a State court upon its own laws. This was the point directly before the court, and the decision that this court had not jurisdiction, turned upon it, as will be seen by the report of the case.
>
> So in this case. As Scott was a slave when taken into the State of Illinois by his owner, and was there held as such, and brought back in that character, his *status*, as free or slave, depended on the laws of Missouri, and not of Illinois.[29]

Taney, it will be noted, first restated the doctrine of reversion, and then, perhaps in answer to Justice McLean,* he declared that enunciation of the doctrine in the *Strader* case had been a necessary preliminary to reaching the decision that the Supreme Court had no jurisdiction. But this was demonstrably untrue.

Let us begin with the statement that the Supreme Court "had no jurisdiction to revise the judgment of a state court upon its own laws." Taken by itself as a fundamental proposition, the statement is absurd. Revising the judgments of state courts upon their own laws was precisely the work often required of the Supreme Court under Section 25 of the Judiciary Act of 1789, as exemplified in *McCulloch v. Maryland, Cohens v. Virginia*, and many other leading decisions. The judgment of the Kentucky court in the *Strader* case was indeed im-

---

* McLean, in both his *Strader* and his *Dred Scott* opinions labeled most of Taney's *Strader* opinion *obiter dictum*.

mune from such revision, but *only* because there was no federal question to give the Supreme Court jurisdiction. Taney, however, with that clever fallaciousness that may have been instinctive, simply transposed cause and effect in order to justify his *Strader* dictum. That is, in reality the decision of the state court proved to be final because the Supreme Court discovered that it had no jurisdiction; but in Taney's looking-glass world, the Supreme Court had no jurisdiction because the state court's decision was final.

Still, whatever the value of the *Strader* decision as precedent, the doctrine of reversion could stand firmly by itself, based as it was upon the principle of state sovereignty and the authority of Story's *Conflict of Laws*. Taney, it appears, did not carry the subject further because he regarded Nelson's opinion, which was limited to the comity issue, as a kind of supplement to his own. There remained, to be sure, the contention of Blair that even if Scott's status did depend entirely upon the laws of Missouri, those laws favored his freedom. Taney responded to this argument with one long sentence rejecting it out of hand. In effect, he held that *Scott v. Emerson* was now the "settled" law of Missouri on the subject.[30]

The Chief Justice concluded his opinion with a denunciation of the manner in which the case had come before the Supreme Court. Dred Scott, he said, had brought a similar suit in the Missouri courts, had carried it to the state supreme court, and had lost it there. After that, Scott's only legal recourse was to take the case directly to the United States Supreme Court by writ of error. If he had done so, the writ would have been dismissed for want of jurisdiction—because of the *Strader* precedent and because "the language of the 25th section of the Act of 1789 is too clear and precise to admit of controversy."* The plaintiff, Taney continued, did not "pursue the mode prescribed by law" but instead turned to the federal court system and as a consequence was now bringing before the Supreme Court "the same case from the Circuit Court, which the law would not have permitted him to bring directly from the State court."

> And if this court takes jurisdiction in this form, the result . . . is
> in every respect substantially the same as if it had, in open viola-

*The validity of this conclusion has been criticized above, pp. 268–69.

tion of law, entertained jurisdiction over the judgment of the State court. . . . It would ill become this court to sanction such an attempt to evade the law, or to exercise an appellate power in this circuitous way which it is forbidden to exercise in the direct and regular and invariable forms of judicial proceedings.[31]

The verbal escalation in this passage is striking enough, and the implication, when fully realized, is nothing less than astonishing.

"The law," said Taney, "would not have permitted" Scott to bring his suit up directly from the state court. But further than that, the Supreme Court would have been "in open violation of law" if it had entertained jurisdiction in such an appeal. Still further, it was actually "forbidden" to exercise its appellate power in this manner. Now, what "law," precisely, did Taney have in mind? Not his own words in *Strader v. Graham*, one would think; for even if one grants that they were authoritative, there is nothing illegal about a court's reviewing and even reversing its previous decisions. Was he referring, then, to the Judiciary Act of 1789? If so, it all came to the same thing; for that statute was phrased in the language of authorization, rather than of prohibition, and only the peculiar gloss of *Strader* could give it the meaning and force indicated by Taney. The circular effect of the whole argument is fascinating. The Court was "forbidden by law" to accept jurisdiction in any case resembling *Strader v. Graham*. Forbidden by what law? Why, by the Judiciary Act of 1789 as interpreted in *Strader v. Graham*. A few years later, there would be much discussion in Congress of adding an "unamendable amendment" to the Constitution. Here, in a sense, was an effort to make a court decision unreviewable.

According to Taney, then, the federal courts generally had no power to hear *Scott v. Sandford* because it was an illegitimate substitute for appealing *Scott v. Emerson;* but at the same time, the Supreme Court would have had no power (indeed, was "forbidden") to hear *Scott v. Emerson.* For Dred Scott, then, there *was* no legitimate access to the Supreme Court, even though his claim to freedom rested in part on federal law.

These paragraphs under discussion, coming just before the judgment, had not been a part of the opinion read orally on March 6. Taney added them later to the page proof. His complaint, considered

by itself, was well founded; for *Scott v. Sandford* did amount to taking an appeal from the highest court of Missouri to a lower federal
court. But the full import of this passage becomes clear only when
one remembers how Taney disposed of the case before him. Holding
that Scott was not a citizen of Missouri and therefore without right to
bring suit in a federal court, the Chief Justice reversed the decision of
the circuit court (made in Sanford's favor on the merits) and ordered
that court instead to dismiss the case for "want of jurisdiction."[32] The
denial of citizenship rested in turn on two conclusions—that no Negro
could be a citizen and that Scott could not have been a citizen at the
time of bringing suit because he was then still a slave. But now, as an
afterthought, Taney was introducing another reason for refusing jurisdiction, one that seemed to take priority over the question of citizenship—namely, the very manner in which the case had reached the
Supreme Court. In fact, if the Court were to accept jurisdiction in the
case, according to Taney, it would be acting "in open violation of
law." If these paragraphs had been placed at the beginning of Taney's
opinion, he could scarcely have justified going any further; for in a
sense they converted everything else he said into dicta.*

   The excessiveness of the argument and language in this curious
addendum may be explained in part by the fact that the paragraphs
were written in the midst of public reaction to the decision as announced in Taney's oral opinion on March 6. The abuse heaped upon
him would have severely tested anyone's self-restraint. It would be a
mistake to conclude, however, that passion entered the Dred Scott
affair at this point. For the fierceness of the northern outcry against
Taney's opinion was no more intense than the passionateness with
which it had been written. As a historical document, it can be fully
understood only if one senses the anger that simmered just below the
surface of its flat judicial prose.

* This is in terms of Taney's own reasoning. As far as the decision of the Court is concerned, this was new matter, not considered, apparently, by the rest of the Court majority. Consequently, it is these paragraphs themselves that may perhaps be considered *obiter*.

Concurrence and Dissent

E xcept, perhaps, for the dissent of Justice Curtis, which won wide acceptance in Republican circles as the official rejoinder to Taney, none of the other opinions delivered in the Dred Scott case had a significant effect on the course of events. Yet each in its own way reveals something about the nature of the sectional conflict, and, taken together, they exemplify the subtle variations possible in American constitutional thought.

Of the four other southerners on the Court, only from Justice Wayne did Taney receive total support. And Wayne announced that because of his unqualified concurrence with the Chief Justice, he would neither read nor file the opinion he had written at a time when it had seemed "necessary and proper . . . to do so." He contented himself instead with a brief disquisition on the Court's right to review all aspects of the case.[1]

The interesting question to be asked about Wayne's unused opinion is whether it served in any significant degree as the basis for Taney's opinion. Wayne it was who had proposed that Taney replace Nelson in writing the opinion of the Court, and the withdrawal of his own opinion suggests that he believed its argument would be adequately covered by the Chief Justice. Taney had only a few weeks in which to prepare his opinion, and this at a time when, being "feeble in body," according to Justice Curtis, he was "not able to write much."[2] It therefore seems possible that Wayne handed over his draft to Taney, and that the latter made some use of it. The theory advanced a quarter of a century ago that Wayne was the virtual author of Taney's opinion has never gained much acceptance, but perhaps it is not totally wrong.[3]

The order in which the opinions were published in Howard's *Reports* did not follow the order of their oral delivery on March 6 and 7, but rather was carefully specified by Taney.[4] Thus, after Wayne's outright concurrence came the Nelson opinion, presumably because it supplemented that of the Chief Justice with a more extensive treatment of the issue presented by Scott's residence in Illinois. As we have seen in an earlier chapter, Nelson, writing what he thought was to be the opinion of the Court, avoided the two big issues of Negro citizenship and the constitutionality of the Missouri Compromise restriction. So only in a very limited way could it be regarded as a "concurring" opinion. Yet Taney was obviously pleased with what amounted to an emphatic reaffirmation of his *Strader* opinion.

Nelson's opinion asserted once again the principle that comity was subordinate to state sovereignty. The law of one state had extrajurisdictional effect inside the boundaries of another state only with the latter's consent. And, Nelson added, the same thing was true of a federal territorial law, as the Chief Justice had "authoritatively declared" in the *Strader* decision. Thus, in cases involving slavery and a conflict of laws, the law of the forum state must prevail. Dred Scott's status therefore depended entirely on the law of Missouri, which in turn had been conclusively determined by the highest court of that state in its most recent (and hence currently definitive) decisions on the subject.[5]

Taking its basic doctrine directly from the work of Joseph Story, the Nelson opinion has been treated gently by most historians and seems at first glance to reflect a cool neutralism in the midst of sectional bitterness. Upon closer scrutiny such an impression quickly dissolves, however. Within the limits that he had set for himself, Nelson leaned toward slavery at every opportunity.

For one thing, while supposedly avoiding the whole controversy over the validity of the Missouri Compromise restriction, Nelson nevertheless volunteered the following remark in passing: "Many of the most eminent statesmen and jurists of the country entertain the opinion that this provision . . . was not authorized by any power under the Constitution."[6] These were virtually his only words on the subject, and the effect accordingly was halfway endorsement of the pro-slavery doctrine. Remembering that Nelson wrote as official spokesman for the Court, only to be replaced by Taney at almost the last minute, one can readily imagine the confusion and excitement that might well have been inspired by this provocative but inconclusive judicial pronouncement on the most inflamed public issue of the age.

Another passage aptly illustrates the deceptive appearance of evenhandedness with which Nelson weighed the claims of freedom and slavery. He had just rejected the idea that the Missouri Compromise restriction, simply because it was federal law, "possessed some superior virtue and effect, extraterritorially and within the State of Missouri, beyond that of the laws of Illinois." He then continued:

> The consequences of any such construction are apparent. If Congress possesses the power, under the Constitution, to abolish slavery in a Territory, it must necessarily possess the like power to establish it. . . . It is a power, if it exists at all, over the whole subject; and then, upon the process of reasoning which seeks to extend its influence beyond the Territory, and within the limits of a State, if Congress should establish, instead of abolish, slavery, we do not see but that, if a slave should be removed from the territory into a free State, his status would accompany him, and continue, notwithstanding its laws against slavery. The laws of the free State, according to the argument, would be displaced, and the Act of Congress, in its effect, be substituted in their place.[7]

The sophistry here is in the imperfection of Nelson's analogy, and that imperfection resulted from his false assumption of an exact equivalence between slavery and freedom. But whereas the power to prohibit slavery implied the power to emancipate, the power to establish slavery did not imply the power to enslave. And slavery, unlike freedom, could never be universal within any jurisdiction because along with slaves there must always be masters, who are by definition free. An American "free state" in the 1850s was one in which freedom was universal and slavery was totally forbidden. There *were* no equivalent "slave states" where slavery was universal and freedom totally forbidden. Instead, there were only states where slaveholding was permitted (but not required) and where slavery and freedom existed side by side. The Dred Scott case involved a slave's being taken into a federal territory and becoming free by virtue of its antislavery law, then returning to a slaveholding state, where his status was open to question because both freedom and slavery were legally possible there. Nelson's analogy, to be sound, would have had to involve a free person's entering a federal territory and becoming a slave by force of its proslavery law, then returning to a free state and remaining a slave there in spite of its antislavery law. All of this was legally impossible and almost inconceivable. In short, the entire analogy breaks down under detailed analysis and thus becomes invalid as argument.

There are still other features of Nelson's opinion that betray his proslavery bias. Responding to the assertion that earlier decisions of the Missouri supreme court lent consistent support to Dred Scott's cause, he had declared that the later decisions (beginning with *Scott v. Emerson*) took precedence and were now authoritative.[8] Not satisfied to leave it at that, however, he then proceeded to muddy his argument by maintaining that there was "no discrepancy between the earlier and the present cases upon this subject." But how could there be "no discrepancy" when the earlier Missouri cases—eight of them—had all been decided in favor of the slave? Because, said Nelson, most of those cases had involved removal to a free state "with a view to permanent residence," and Dred Scott's did not. What this amounted to was shifting the ground of his opinion by endorsing and emphasizing the old argument of defense counsel that Emerson, as an army officer, had never been other than a temporary resident in Illinois and the federal territory.

Nelson, however, could not just ignore the embarrassing precedent of *Rachel v. Walker*, in which the Missouri supreme court had freed a slave held, like Dred Scott, in free territory by an army officer. After first categorically denying *any* discrepancy between the earlier and later cases, he then had to admit that the *Rachel* decision constituted a major exception, having been "departed from in the case before us." But, he continued, the later Missouri decisions (especially *Scott v. Emerson*) were "in conformity with those in all the slave states bordering on the free," also with Story's *Conflict of Laws* and with the British case of *The Slave Grace*.[9] With this change of direction, Nelson was well launched into a display of the art of begging the question. He had presumably set out to argue that Dred Scott's case was different from those eight Missouri precedents because it involved temporary rather than permanent residence on free soil. The critical question, then, was whether army service over an extended period at a single post constituted temporary or permanent residence. Faced, however, with the fact that the one relevant Missouri decision ran counter to his own judgment, Nelson dropped the matter as abruptly as he had taken it up and began to quote authorities that supported his views on comity rather than on the army service question. Then, very near the end of his opinion, he returned to the subject of residence and, without the slightest reference to the *Rachel* case, declared:

> We regard the facts as set forth in the agreed case as decisive. The removal of Dr. Emerson from Missouri to the military posts was in the discharge of his duties as surgeon in the army, and under the orders of his Government. He was liable at any moment to be recalled. . . . In such a case, the officer goes to his post for a temporary purpose, to remain there for an uncertain time, and not for the purpose of fixing his permanent abode. The question we think too plain to require argument.[10]

This was the same Nelson who, on an earlier page of the same opinion had said, "It belongs to the sovereign State of Missouri to determine by her laws the question of slavery within her jurisdiction, subject only to such limitations as may be found in the Federal Constitution."[11] But Missouri law on the subject of army officers taking slaves into free states was still embodied in *Rachel v. Walker*, which Nelson's opinion, if it had been the opinion of the Court, would presumably have overruled. Apparently the law of the forum state need not prevail if it favored freedom instead of slavery.[12]

And precisely what did Nelson mean when he said that the question of slavery belonged to the separate states, "subject only to such limitations as may be found in the Federal Constitution"? (Taney had made approximately the same statement in *Strader v. Graham.*)[13] As a minimum, he was referring to the recovery of fugitive slaves, but the possible maximum of such limitations on state power was not easy to visualize. That it might well extend to the legitimizing of slavery in the free states would soon be suggested by Abraham Lincoln.[14] That Nelson had more than the minimum in mind is indicated by the curiously marginal and vaguely menacing comment with which he concluded his opinion:

> A question has been alluded to, on the argument, namely: the right of the master with his slave of transit into or through a free State, on business or commercial pursuits, or in the exercise of a Federal right, or the discharge of a Federal duty, being a citizen of the United States, which is not before us. This question depends upon different considerations and principles from the one in hand, and turns upon the rights and privileges secured to a common citizen of the republic under the Constitution of the United States. When that question arises, we shall be prepared to decide it.[15]

These words, which may have been comment on a case then in the New York courts,* would have had much greater impact if they had come at the conclusion of the official decision in *Dred Scott v. Sandford;* for they plainly cast doubt on the power of free states to forbid or restrict any entry of slaves that might be defined as "temporary." And we have seen that the Nelson opinion, if it had been the official one, would have emphatically confirmed the right of an army officer to take a slave into a free state for an unlimited period of time. Remembering also that Nelson did at least cast doubt on the power of Congress to exclude slavery from the territories, one suspects that his opinion, though less controversial than Taney's, would nevertheless have aroused considerable anger throughout the North if it had been presented as the opinion of the Court.

Lemmon v. the People (1852–60). See below, pp. 444–45.

II

Grier, like Wayne, really wrote no opinion. In just a few sentences that appeared fourth in Howard's *Reports*, he concurred with Nelson's opinion and with Taney's ruling against the constitutionality of the Missouri Compromise restriction. As we have seen, he also lent welcome support to Taney on the issue of the plea in abatement by finding a *"prima facie* case of jurisdiction" which required the Court to decide all questions "properly arising" in the record.[16]

Taney perhaps set the Nelson and Grier documents close to his own in order to stress the bisectional nature of the Court's decision. After Grier's statement he placed the remaining opinions of southern justices—Daniel, Campbell, and Catron. Of the three, only Daniel supported Taney on the plea in abatement. Campbell announced that he was ignoring the issue. Catron flatly disagreed with the Chief Justice, though without the censoriousness that appeared in his oral presentation on March 6. Privately, he maintained that the entire section of Taney's opinion dealing with Negro citizenship was dictum.[17]

Daniel was the only one of the three to discuss the question of Negro citizenship, and he reached the same conclusion as Taney but by a shorter and straighter path: A slave, being "strictly property," could not be a citizen. Emancipation did not automatically convert a slave into a citizen, for the conferring of citizenship was an act of sovereignty which no slave-owner or other individual could perform. State governments might bestow civil and political privileges upon anyone they chose, but "they could not add to or change in any respect the class of persons to whom alone the character of citizen of the United States appertained at the time of the adoption of the Federal Constitution." And the African in 1787 was not a party to the social compact, was, indeed, not "politically a person" at all. Daniel, like Taney, had achieved the result he desired by misreading the Constitution in such a way as to make "state citizenship" mean "United States citizenship—no blacks admitted."[18]

Like Taney also, Daniel was determined to proceed to the merits of the case even though he had already decided against Scott on jurisdictional grounds. He offered no technical justification for doing so, however, but instead bluntly asserted that questions of such "primary interest and magnitude," having been elaborately discussed in argument of counsel, should be considered and, if possible, "finally put to rest."

In considering the case on its merits, the three southern justices, unlike Taney, began with the issues presented by Scott's residence in Illinois. Catron was content merely to concur with Nelson, but not until he had in one sentence increased the confusion about the meaning of Nelson's opinion. Referring to the effect of Illinois law on Scott's status, he wrote: "Unless the master becomes an inhabitant of that State, the slaves he takes there do not acquire their freedom; and if they return with their master to the slave State of his domicil, they cannot assert their freedom after their return."[19] The phrase "slave State of his domicil" signifies an assumption of merely temporary residence for Scott in Illinois and thereby makes the second half of the sentence superfluous. For if a slave did not become free according to the laws of the free state while living within its jurisdiction, what possible basis could there be for claiming freedom under the laws of the slave state to which he returned? Catron, like Nelson, was muddling two issues—the legal nature of Scott's residence in Illinois, and the legal effect in Missouri of Scott's residence in Illinois. It appears, however, that instead of endorsing the new proslavery radicalism of *Scott v. Emerson*, he was reaffirming the principles of the old tacit agreement between the sections. Domiciling a slave in a free state worked his emancipation. Temporary residence did not (thus he rejected the doctrine of *Commonwealth v. Aves*). But if a slave after returning home should nevertheless claim freedom on the basis of temporary residence in a free state, the principles of reversion and reattachment made that claim invalid.

Justice Campbell's half-dozen pages on the subject are likewise somewhat puzzling. First he declared that he did not "impugn the authority" of those cases in which southern courts had upheld a slave's claim to freedom on the ground of his having had "actual domicil" within a free state. Then he denied that the record showed any evidence of such domicile on the part of John Emerson and Dred Scott. Like Catron, he seemed to be endorsing the principles of the old tacit agreement. Now, since Dred Scott's case had been built upon the assumption of domicile (or its equivalent) in Illinois, and since no one had argued that mere temporary residence there would have worked his emancipation under Illinois law of the 1830s, Campbell's next step logically should have been to reinforce his conclusion that Scott's residence had been of the temporary kind. Instead, he launched into a display of legal and historical learning intended to demonstrate (1) that the *Somerset* decision was defective as precedent because it did not rest on any positive law against slavery; and (2) that the *Grace* decision was the one directly applicable to the Scott case.[20]

For southerners, it had become almost a reflex action to attack the *Somerset* tradition whenever the opportunity arose, but Campbell, by stressing the absence of positive antislavery law in England, only underlined a major weakness of the *Grace* decision as a guiding precedent in the Dred Scott case. That is, Illinois law, as Montgomery Blair had pointed out in argument, *did* positively forbid slavery and specify emancipation as the consequence of violation.[21] Antislavery law was accordingly more potent in Illinois than it had been in England at the time of the *Somerset* and *Grace* decisions. More potent, but also in certain respects more restricted. And here was what made the *Grace* case largely irrelevant in *Dred Scott* argument—not the positive force of Illinois antislavery law but rather the established exceptions to that law allowing transit and sojourn with one's slaves. Grace and her mistress, it should be remembered, were merely visitors to England for a period of one year. Nevertheless, Lord Stowell had acknowledged that the status of the slave was changed by English law during that time. Grace became free within "a sort of parenthesis," only to have her slave status *reattach* itself when she returned to Antigua. But since temporary residence in Illinois would not have changed a slave's status in the 1830s, there was no reason to invoke the principle of reattachment if Dred Scott's residence in Illinois was regarded as temporary; and at the same time there was little legal basis in the *Grace* case or in American precedent for invoking the principle if his residence was regarded as equivalent to domicile.

It is therefore difficult to determine just what Campbell intended when he declared that there was "no distinguishable difference" between the *Grace* and *Dred Scott* cases. Taken literally, it would have amounted to conceding more than Scott's lawyers had claimed—that even temporary residence on free soil temporarily freed a slave. Campbell, however, was probably concentrating on the Antigua end of the *Grace* decision, and with reference not so much to the principle of reattachment as to the associated principle of reversion—that the law of the forum state prevailed. Such appears to have been the import of the rather peevish summary with which he closed discussion of the comity issue:

> The complaint here, in my opinion, amounts to this: that the judicial tribunals of Missouri have not denounced as odious the Constitution and laws under which they are organized, and have not superseded them on their own private authority, for the purpose of applying the laws of Illinois, or those passed by Congress for Minnesota, in their stead.[22]

This outburst, virtually impeaching the conduct of the Missouri supreme court in all of the relevant decisions preceding *Scott v. Emerson*, revealed the intensity of feeling with which most of the justices wrote their opinions.

Justice Daniel, with a mind completely closed on the slavery issue, likewise attacked what he called the "vaunted" *Somerset* decision, rejoicing somewhat inaccurately that it had been "overruled by the lucid and able opinion of Lord Stowell in the more recent case of *The Slave Grace*."[23] In sharp contrast to his restrictive view of state sovereignty where definition of citizenship was concerned, Daniel declared that with respect to slavery and the tenure of property generally, the states of the Union were "entirely separate, and absolutely independent of each other." But then, saying not a word about Missouri law or Illinois law in relation to Dred Scott, he quoted extensively from a marginally relevant Virginia case involving a slave set free under Ohio law while temporarily resident with her master in that state.[24] Furthermore, he referred to Scott's stay in Illinois as "commorancy," a term that covers sojourning as well as more established residence. All of this suggests that he too regarded the Scott case as one of temporary rather than permanent residence.

Thus, in their treatment of interstate comity and the conflict of laws, as related to slavery, Daniel and Campbell only compounded the difficulty of discerning just what, if anything, the Court majority contributed to the law of the subject. Dred Scott's suit had been based upon an assumption of permanent residence in Illinois, while the principal decisions cited against him, such as *Grace* and *Strader*, dealt with instances of temporary residence. Obviously John Emerson's tour of duty in Illinois constituted a borderline case, but *Rachel v. Walker* provided strong Missouri precedent in Scott's favor. Southern courts for some time had been using the *Grace* doctrines of reversion and reattachment, largely as a basis for turning aside claims to freedom arising out of temporary residence on free soil. Beginning with *Scott v. Emerson*, however, the Missouri supreme court applied the *Grace* principles to all suits for freedom based upon residence in free territory, no matter how permanent that residence might have been. That is, the court wiped out the distinction between domicile and sojourn, making it irrelevant in Missouri. Against this background, the stand taken by the Supreme Court majority in *Dred Scott v. Sandford* was fraught with confusion. On the one hand, five of the justices indicated a belief that Scott's residence in Illinois was temporary, though only Nelson said so clearly. On the other hand, the opinion of the Court as delivered by Taney merely reaffirmed the principle of reversion and thereby left standing the extremist doctrine of *Scott v. Emerson* as the final word on the subject. Thus there was no authoritative ruling on whether Scott's residence in Illinois was temporary or permanent, and none on whether it made any difference one way or the other.

In their treatments of the territorial questions, Daniel, Campbell, and Catron traveled different paths to the same conclusion that the Missouri Compromise restriction was unconstitutional. Daniel, the most passionate of the three in his devotion to slavery, relied partly upon the "common-property" doctrine associated with Calhoun, declaring that Congress as mere agent or trustee could not discriminate against part of the American people in its administration of the territories. Like Taney he insisted that the territory clause referred to the disposal of land and "did not extend to the personal or

political rights of citizens or settlers."[25] He went beyond the Chief
Justice, however, in asserting that the antislavery clause of the
Northwest Ordinance was "*ab initio* void," and that the Constitution,
by giving slavery special protection, placed it on higher ground than
any other kind of property. But Daniel's extremism revealed itself
most clearly in the intemperateness of his language, which impugned
the motives, intelligence, and patriotism of persons supporting congressional power over slavery in the territories.[26]

Campbell agreed substantially with Taney and Daniel in minimizing the scope and force of the territory clause by associating it almost exclusively with disposal of the public domain.[27] He relied heavily upon argument by analogy, stressing American hostility to British
imperialism during the era of the Revolution. Parliament, he said,
had claimed supreme legislative power co-extensive with dominion
over crown lands. Americans had acknowledged British supremacy in
the matter of land titles, while insisting that political power must rest
on consent of the people. In other words, the distinction between
land disposal, as a function of central authority, and government, as
an exercise of local right, had been inherent in the very nature of the
Revolution. And the Founding Fathers, having just rebelled against
the British colonial system, could not possibly have intended that the
territory clause should be used to establish an American colonial system. Thus Campbell equated the Missouri Compromise restriction
with British tyranny. His argument, as a consequence, was based less
upon the Calhoun principle of equal rights for all states within the
territories than upon the Douglas principle of territorial self-government.[28] He was the only justice besides Taney who said anything
touching on the problem of whether a territorial legislature had the
constitutional authority to prohibit slavery. But unlike the Chief Justice, he concluded that it was a political question: "How much municipal power may be exercised by the people of the Territory, before
their admission to the Union, the courts of justice cannot decide."[29]

Campbell made no use of the due-process clause and very little
of the common-property doctrine. His principal emphasis was upon
strict construction and a resulting absence of federal power. He insisted, for example, that the defining of what constituted property was

a prerogative belonging exclusively to the states, and that the United
States government must accordingly accept all such definitions without discriminating against any one of them.[30] It was settled judicial
doctrine, he declared, that the federal government could exercise "no
power over the subject of slavery within the States, nor control the
intermigration of slaves, other than fugitives, among the States."[31]
This meant that a master might take his slave anywhere in the Union
without fear of federal interference. Only the sovereign authority of a
state could place any impediment in his path. The question, then,
was whether Congress could exercise such "municipal sovereignty" in
the territories to deny those rights of the master which, within the
states of the Union, it was bound to observe and protect. Simply ignoring John Marshall's statement in *American Insurance Company v.
Canter,* Campbell concluded that the territory clause provided no
basis for these "enormous pretensions."[32]

Justice Catron was something of a maverick among the southern
majority in the Dred Scott case, and it is little wonder that Taney
caused his opinion to be published seventh, just ahead of the two dis-
sents. Catron, as we have seen, declared flatly that the Court had no
right to review the plea in abatement, adding privately that Taney's
entire treatment of Negro citizenship was dictum. He also rejected
Taney's narrow construction of the territory clause, maintaining that
the clause *did* vest Congress with the power to govern in the territories. "It is due to myself to say," he wrote protestingly, "that it is
asking much of a judge, who has for nearly twenty years been exercising jurisdiction, from the western Missouri line to the Rocky Moun-
tains, and, on this understanding of the Constitution, inflicting the extreme penalty of death for crimes committed where the direct
legislation of Congress was the only rule, to agree that he had been
all the while acting in mistake, and as an usurper." It was now too
late, he thought, to call congressional power into question, especially
since the Supreme Court itself had confirmed that power in *Cross v.
Harrison* just three years earlier.[33]

In Catron's view, however, the power to govern did not, of and
by itself, include the power to prohibit slavery. What determined the
extent of congressional authority within the original United States, he

maintained, were the terms of the land cessions made by the states. Thus, slavery was legally abolished in the Old Northwest because Virginia assented to the Ordinance of 1787, an "engagement" which Congress could not break. But south of the Ohio River, "Congress had no more power to legislate slavery out from the North Carolina and Georgia cessions, than it had power to legislate slavery in, north of the Ohio."[34]

Beyond the Mississippi, Catron proceeded, congressional authority was limited by the terms of the Louisiana Purchase. There, under Spain and France, slavery had been lawful, and the treaty with France had guaranteed inhabitants "the free enjoyment of their liberty, property, and the religion which they profess."[35] Congress had no power to repeal this guarantee, which stood "protected by the Constitution." The Missouri Compromise restriction was therefore void.[36] Catron's view that the treaty of 1803 laid a permanent restriction on the legislative power of Congress was neither original with him nor sound constitutional law. Advanced without much success during the Missouri controversy, the argument would have elevated treaties above statutes virtually to the level of the Constitution. In effect, this would have meant investing the President and two-thirds of the Senate with the power of amendment, and it would have made the Supreme Court the enforcer of international agreements against the two collateral branches of the federal government. In decisions handed down after the Civil War, the Court upheld the power of Congress to alter or override a treaty.[37]

Not satisfied, however, with declaring the Missouri Compromise restriction to be an invalid violation of the Louisiana treaty, Catron also invoked the common-property doctrine as a second reason for its invalidity. The point, he said, was "not that citizens of the United States shall have equal privileges in the Territories, but the citizen of each State shall come there in right of his State, and enjoy the common property. He secures his equality through the equality of his State, by virtue of that great fundamental condition of the Union— the equality of the States."[38] Catron then moved on to the *argumentum ad horrendum* for northerners that "if Congress could prohibit one species of property, lawful throughout Louisiana when it was acquired, and lawful in the State from whence it was brought, so Congress might exclude any or all property." Thus the northern farmer might have been kept out of Louisiana Territory by bans on horses and cattle; the northern mechanic, by prohibitions against tools and machines. The Missouri Compromise restriction, he concluded, was therefore doubly void—as an invasion of the treaty with France and as a violation of the "most leading feature of the Constitution . . . which secures to the respective States and their citizens an entire equality of rights, privileges and immunities."[39]

As the chart on the next page indicates, the justices who ruled against the constitutionality of the Missouri Compromise restriction produced a variety of reasons for doing so and never agreed completely on any of them. Plainly, too much emphasis has been placed upon the due-process clause. Taney alone mentioned it, and how much his argument rested upon the clause is far from clear. The justices were closer to consensus on three other lines of reasoning: (1) a narrow interpretation of the territory clause, with Catron as the principal exception; (2) Calhoun's common-property doctrine, with Campbell something of an exception; and (3) the insistence that slavery was no different from other property and had the same rights attached to it, with Daniel going further and declaring that slavery was a kind of super-property given special status by the Constitution.

III

The dissenting justices, McLean and Curtis, submitted two of the three longest opinions, constituting about 44 per cent of the total judicial wordage. As a professional performance, the Curtis contribution was more thorough, scholarly, and polished. McLean's opinion, as a consequence, and also in view of his inveterate presidential aspiration, has been taken less seriously by historians.[40]

The two men disagreed with each other about whether the plea in abatement was before the Court. McLean, after insisting that it was not, went ahead and discussed the issue raised by the plea anyway. His argument lacked coherence, but he seemed to be reaffirming the conclusion of Judge Wells that any free person domiciled in a

SLAVERY IN THE TERRITORIES

	TANEY (WAYNE AND GRIER)	DANIEL	CAMPBELL	CATRON
Missouri Compromise restriction is unconstitutional	yes	yes	yes	yes
Extremely narrow interpretation of territory clause	yes	yes	yes	no
Common-property doctrine	refers to	relies on heavily	mentions	relies on partly
Slavery has same rights as other property	uses	has higher standing than other property	uses extensively	uses
Due-process clause	relies on to some extent	no mention	no mention	no mention
Missouri Compromise restriction violates treaty with France	no mention	no mention	no mention	yes
Ordinance of 1787	legal because of unanimous state consent	illegal	legal because of state and territorial consent	valid and unbreakable as a compact
Power of territorial legislature over slavery	denies	no mention	implies that it is a political question	no mention

state was a citizen of that state for purposes of suit in a federal court. In rebuttal to Taney's holding that no Negro could be a citizen, McLean pointed out that inhabitants of Louisiana, Florida, and the Mexican Cession, without exception as to race, had been guaranteed citizenship in the treaties of acquisition.[41]

Curtis, as we have seen, joined Taney in maintaining that the Court could and should review the plea in abatement.* But then, in an extended technical discussion, he proceeded to set strict limits on the Court's authority to review the question of jurisdiction and Dred Scott's claim to citizenship. In disagreement with Taney, he held that the Court was governed by the common-law rules of pleading; that it could examine no jurisdictional matter not appearing in the plea in abatement; and that the facts presented in the plea must "of themselves" constitute a negative of the averment of citizenship. This highly formalistic line of reasoning had the effect of disqualifying any *inference* drawn from the plea in abatement, as well as any direct evidence drawn from other parts of the record showing that Scott, at the time of filing suit, had been a *slave* and therefore not a citizen (as Taney maintained). The only question before the Court, Curtis insisted, was that raised literally by the plea in abatement—whether the fact of Scott's African ancestry and the fact that his parents had been slaves were "necessarily inconsistent with his own citizenship in the State of Missouri, within the meaning of the Constitution and laws of the United States."[43]

The phrasing here is important, for it indicated that Curtis did not intend to seek his answer in the constitution and laws of Missouri. Instead, he followed Taney in converting the question to one of na-

---

*Curtis demonstrated that (1) according to the Judiciary Act of 1789, lower federal courts were not intended to be final judges of their own jurisdiction; (2) even if neither party in a suit raised the question of jurisdiction, the Court must determine whether the record showed the case to be one reached by the judicial power of the United States; (3) Sanford had no choice but pleading over to the merits after having lost his plea to jurisdiction; for since the decision on the latter was not a final judgment, it could not have been tested in the Supreme Court by writ of error; and (4) the question of whether error might be assigned by a defendant did not arise under the rules of the Court, and, in any case, a writ of error opened the entire record to inspection by the appellate court.[42] See above, pp. 338–39.

tional citizenship, citing an opinion of the Marshall Court to the effect that "a citizen of the United States, residing in any State of the Union, is, for purposes of jurisdiction, a citizen of that State."[44] This formula superficially resembles the subsequent Fourteenth Amendment in its definition of the relationship between federal and state citizenship, although its scope was narrowly restricted to the determination of jurisdiction. Taney had used a similar line of reasoning as a bridge back to the general racial attitudes of the Founding Fathers, only to find the evidence so conflicting that he had been driven to the dubious strategy of proclaiming two distinct kinds of state citizenship. In Curtis's clever and complicated treatment, however, the formula became a bridge connecting the law of Missouri to the law of those states that had been most favorable toward Negro citizenship.

The Curtis argument ran as follows:

1. According to the Marshall Court formula, nothing in the law of Missouri could deprive Dred Scott of his rights under the diverse-citizenship clause, provided that he was a citizen of the United States and a resident of Missouri at the time of bringing suit.

2. Since his residence had not been controverted, the only question was whether Scott's African ancestry and slave parentage made him ineligible for United States citizenship.

3. If *any* person of such background could be a United States citizen, Scott had the right to claim citizenship too, since no other reason for excluding him had been advanced in the plea in abatement.

4. United States citizenship antedated the Constitution, having originated under the Confederation government. This was indicated by the language of Article Two, Section Four, referring to "a citizen of the United States at the time of the adoption of the Constitution."

5. But the Confederation was a government of severely limited authority and had been delegated no power "to act on any question of citizenship, or to make any rules in respect thereto." The matter was left entirely in the hands of the states, and thus United States citizenship was synonymous with state citizenship in 1789.

6. Under the Confederation government, free Negroes in five states, being recognized as citizens of their respective states, were also citizens of the United States.*

7. The fourth of the Articles of Confederation in fact included free Negroes among those persons who, "by reason of their citizenship in certain States, were entitled to the privileges and immunities of general citizenship of the United States."

8. There was nothing in the Constitution which, *proprio vigore*, deprived any class of persons of citizenship possessed at the time of its adoption.

9. The Constitution in fact neither defined citizenship nor invested Congress with any authority to do so, except in regard to naturalization of aliens. Instead, all relevant clauses of the Constitution pointed to the necessary conclusion that "those persons born within the several States, who, by force of their respective constitutions and laws, are citizens of the State, are thereby citizens of the United States."

10. The plea in abatement therefore showed no facts inconsistent with Dred Scott's being a United States citizen or a resident of Missouri, entitled to bring suit in federal court.[45]

What all of this demonstrated, it should be noted, was not the citizenship of Dred Scott but merely the absence of any disproof of citizenship within the narrow confines of the plea in abatement. Other parts of the record showed clearly that Scott had *not* been born free within a state that recognized Negroes as citizens. The validity of Curtis's conclusion thus depended upon the validity of his technical argument (strenuously contested by Taney) that the Court could not pursue the question of jurisdiction beyond what appeared on the face of the plea in abatement.

Furthermore, Curtis's argument, although it seems enlightened in comparison with Taney's, was racially conservative and of limited scope. It asserted only that free Negroes born in states recognizing

*The states named by Curtis were New Hampshire, Massachusetts, New York, New Jersey (all by their constitutions), and North Carolina (by court decision in *State v. Manuel*, 1838).

them as citizens were also citizens of the United States* and that every such person was entitled to sue in federal courts as a citizen of the state in which he or she resided. Thus, a free Negro born in Massachusetts would not forfeit his United States citizenship by moving permanently to South Carolina, and a free Negro born in South Carolina would not acquire United States citizenship by moving permanently to Massachusetts. Each state, according to Curtis, had the power to say which members of its native-born population were citizens of the United States. No state could confer such citizenship on one of its residents born elsewhere.†

Curtis, in addition, spelled out a restricted meaning of citizenship, denying emphatically that it meant civil equality. It was for each state to decide "what civil rights shall be enjoyed by its citizens, and whether all shall enjoy the same, or how they may be gained or lost." As for the privileges-and-immunities clause, so feared by southerners when associated with the idea of Negro citizenship, it did not bestow any specific rights. "Privileges and immunities which belong to certain citizens of a State, by reason of the operation of causes other than mere citizenship, are not conferred." Clearly, except for guaranteeing some free Negroes access to the federal courts, the Curtis interpretation of the Constitution would have entailed no significant change in the discriminatory racial arrangements of the time.[46]

Having confirmed Dred Scott's capacity to bring suit against Sanford in a federal court, the two dissenting justices then proceeded to the merits of the case, while denying the right of the Court majority to do so, and indicating an unwillingness to be bound by those parts of the majority opinion that were, in their view, "of no authority."[47] The two men dealt with the substantive issues in different order, but their arguments, as a matter of convenience, can be treated together under three major headings.

---

*This was more or less in line with the opinion of Attorney General William Wirt in 1821. See above, p. 69.

† The point here, of course, is the doctrine of *jus soli*—that citizenship depends on place of birth. Dred Scott, born in Virginia, obviously did not fall within Curtis's favored group, but this fact did not appear in the plea in abatement, which relied on the assumption that *no* Negro could be a citizen of the United States.

1. *Congressional power over slavery in the territories and specifically, the constitutionality of the Missouri Compromise restriction.* Here, both McLean and Curtis assumed the Republican position of interpreting the territory clause broadly as an express and plenary delegation of power to govern. They struck effectively, each in his own way, at the Court majority's view that the clause referred only to land and that the framers of the Constitution made no provision for temporary government of western territory, in spite of the obvious need for it and in spite of the conspicuous example of the Northwest Ordinance. Curtis, in particular, probed the weakness of this argument with an irony that was all the more effective because of its judicial coolness:

> That Congress has some power to institute temporary governments over the Territory, I believe all agree; and, if it be admitted that the necessity of some power to govern the Territory of the United States could not and did not escape the attention of the Convention and the people, and the necessity is so great that, in the absence of any express grant, it is strong enough to raise an implication of the existence of that power, it would seem to follow that it is also strong enough to afford material aid in construing an express grant of power respecting that Territory; and that they who maintain the existence of the power, without finding any words at all in which it is conveyed, should be willing to receive a reasonable interpretation of language of the Constitution manifestly intended to relate to the Territory, and to convey to Congress some authority concerning it.[48]

Curtis also disposed expertly of Taney's dubious contention that the territory clause had been designed only for land already in the possession of the United States when the Constitution was written. He showed that this intent would have been inconsistent with the framers' expectation of cessions from North Carolina and Georgia, as well as with their realization that further territorial acquisitions might some day be made by treaty. Such a clipped-off interpretation of part of a constitution intended to last indefinitely was contrary, he declared, not only to the language but also to the "nature and purpose of the instrument."[49] Both Curtis and McLean likewise made short

work of Taney's ill-advised argument that the phrase "rules and regulations" had a weaker, more limited meaning then the word "laws."
The prime exhibit here was the commerce clause, by virtue of which,
Curtis pointed out, Congress "regulated" the conduct of American
citizens as far away as China, having "established judicatures with
power to inflict even capital punishment within that country."[50]

Of course, all of Taney's straining had come to nothing because
he had been compelled to acknowledge that Congress *did* have the
power to organize and govern the territories. Curtis's assessment was
crisp and apt: "I confess myself unable to perceive any difference
whatever between my own opinion of the general extent of the power
of Congress and the opinion of the majority of the court, save that I
consider it derivable from the express language of the Constitution,
while they hold it to be silently implied from the power to acquire
territory.[51]

The crucial question, then, seemed to be whether slavery was
somehow exempt from this acknowledged authority, contrary to the
established practice of more than half a century. If so, Curtis declared, the exemption should derive from a specific provision of the
Constitution, and not from "abstract political reasoning" which,
though it might well guide legislation, had no legal force in a judicial
proceeding. Among such extrajudicial generalizations, Curtis included the southern common-property doctrine, along with the pop-
ular-sovereignty doctrine embraced by many northern Democrats
and the radical antislavery argument that Congress possessed the
power to forbid, but not the power to protect, slavery in the territories.[52]

Curtis could find just one specific provision of the Constitution
alleged to have been violated by the Missouri Compromise restriction. That was the due-process clause of the Fifth Amendment. But
the due-process clause, after all, had been "borrowed from Magna
Charta," and the principle "existed in every political community in
America in 1787." Why, then, had no one discovered at the time that
the antislavery provision of the Northwest Ordinance violated Magna
Carta? Furthermore, congressional legislation forbidding slavery in a
territory did not result in forfeit of property except as a consequence

of disobedience to the law, and this kind of sanction had been common even in the slave states themselves.[53]

Both McLean and Curtis also took time to refute the assertion that the Missouri Compromise restriction was invalid because it violated the terms of the treaty with France for the purchase of Louisiana. Curtis in fact devoted several pages to demolishing an argument that scarcely deserved so much attention. Citing an opinion of John Marshall, he maintained that the treaty provision in question was a temporary guarantee extended only to French inhabitants of Louisiana in 1803. But in any case, where was the basis for elevating the treaty power of president and Senate, with its dependence on the cooperation of foreign governments, above the legislative power of Congress? "I am not aware it has ever been considered," Curtis wrote, "that the Constitution has placed our country in this helpless condition."[54]

2. *The effect of taking a slave into a jurisdiction where slavery was forbidden.* Here, the nature of Emerson's residence in Illinois and at Fort Snelling was crucial. The Court majority, as we have seen, apparently assumed that it was temporary; McLean and Curtis found it sufficiently permanent to be classed with domicile.[55] Neither the justices then nor historians later seem to have been fully aware of the fact, but the two sides were thus arguing from different premises and, to a considerable extent, talking past each other. Arguments and citations of the majority demonstrating that residence other than permanent in a free state or territory left a slave's status unchanged were met by the two dissenters with arguments and citations demonstrating that residence other than temporary made him forever free.

Both Curtis and McLean emphatically reaffirmed the principle that slavery was entirely a creation of municipal law and had no existence where such law did not give it positive protection. This was the *Somerset* tradition, of course, and it applied to temporary as well as permanent residence in the sense that even right of transit depended ultimately upon positive law of the transit state. The *Somerset* principle had the effect of denying a slaveholder any legal sanction in the control of his slave, while protecting the latter against any use of physical force. It made the slave virtually free while he remained within the jurisdiction, but it did not in any formal way terminate the relationship between master and slave. This left open the question of the slave's status if he departed the jurisdiction.[56]

But in some American jurisdictions, said McLean and Curtis, echoing Montgomery Blair, there was also such a thing as positive antislavery law, which *did* operate with a force sufficient to change the status of a slave brought within its reach. This, according to Curtis, was conspicuously the case with the Missouri Compromise restriction and other federal legislation forbidding slavery in the territories. "It is not simply that slavery is not recognized and cannot be aided by the municipal law. It is recognized for the purpose of being absolutely prohibited, and declared incapable of existing within the Territory, save in the instance of a fugitive slave." The effect was to dissolve completely the old relationship and "terminate the rights of the master." Curtis apparently believed that such a transformation occurred only as a result of more or less permanent residence in a free territory, but McLean seemed vaguely in favor of applying the principle to sojourners as well.[57]

Curtis added, however, that in his opinion certain features of the Dred Scott case made it unnecessary to settle the question of domicile. For one thing, John Emerson had gone to Fort Snelling not only as a citizen but "in a public capacity in the service of the same sovereignty which made the laws." Was it possible, then, to deny that the United States could "govern their own servants, residing on their own territory, over which the United States had the exclusive control?" But Curtis laid even heavier emphasis on the fact that at Fort Snelling Dred Scott had, with Emerson's consent, taken a wife. The validity of the marriage could not be contested (since slavery had had no status in Wisconsin Territory), and according to international law it commanded recognition in other jurisdictions. Further than that, Curtis declared, any law of Missouri having the effect of annulling such a lawful marriage would be an impairment of the obligation of contract, forbidden to states by the Constitution. As a consequence, "the consent of the master that his slave, residing in a country which does not tolerate slavery, may enter into a lawful contract of marriage, attended with the civil rights and duties which belong to that condi-

tion, is an effectual act of emancipation. And the law does not enable
Dr. Emerson, or anyone claiming under him, to assert a title to the
married persons as slaves, and thus destroy the obligation of the contract of marriage, and bastardize their issue, and reduce them to
slavery."[58]

3. *The effect on Dred Scott's status of his return to Missouri, and
the extent to which the law of Missouri, as interpreted by the supreme
court of Missouri, was binding on the Supreme Court of the United
States.* Both dissenting justices maintained that the emancipation of
Scott, by virtue of his residence in a free state and a free territory,
had been absolute and irrevocable. They thus rejected the principle
of reattachment, and McLean perceptively noted that the principle
had not been directly asserted by the Missouri supreme court in *Scott
v. Emerson*. Instead, Judge William Scott had asserted the doctrine of
reversion in an extreme form, ruling that Dred Scott's status depended entirely on Missouri law, and that Missouri would no longer
enforce foreign law against its own citizens.[59]

McLean and Curtis responded to this refusal of comity by denying that *Scott v. Emerson* had become the law of Missouri on the subject and that the Court must accept it as such. International law, they
said, required Missouri to recognize Dred Scott's change of status
under the laws of Wisconsin Territory; for international law, as part of
the common law, had been incorporated into the law of Missouri and
could be displaced only by statute, not by mere judicial decision. Besides, *Scott v. Emerson* was a sharp departure from well-established
judicial opinion in Missouri, and the Supreme Court had repeatedly
held that, in reviewing state court decisions, it was not compelled to
take the most recent decision as the rule. "I do not feel at liberty,"
said Curtis, "to surrender my own convictions of what the law
requires, to the authority of the decision in 15 Missouri Reports."[60]

Curtis, with his habitual thoroughness, even anticipated Taney's
parting complaint about the manner in which the case had reached
the Supreme Court. Some reliance, he said, had "been placed on the
fact that the decision in the Supreme Court of Missouri was between
these parties, and the suit there was abandoned to obtain another trial
in the courts of the United States." But he cited two recent cases in

which the Taney Court had not only permitted the same procedure but also virtually overruled the state court decisions—in one instance, unanimously.[61]

If the two dissenting opinions seem more convincing than the opinions of the Court majority, it is not merely because they were, by modern standards, on the right side. Curtis and McLean, in spite of their differing styles, displayed a fundamental agreement on the major issues that contrasted sharply with the heterogeneity of the majority's reasoning. They were in many respects the sound constitutional conservatives, following established precedent along a well-beaten path to their conclusions. Taney and his southern colleagues were the radical innovators—invalidating, for the first time in history, a major piece of federal legislation; denying to Congress a power that it had exercised for two-thirds of a century; sustaining the abrupt departure from precedent in *Scott v. Emerson;* and, in Taney's case, infusing the due-process clause with substantive meaning. And even though McLean did indulge his weakness for playing to the antislavery gallery, the southern justices were by far the more idiosyncratic and polemical.

Curtis's opinion, especially when read head-on against Taney's, is very impressive. One cannot entirely suppress the suspicion that the intense hostility displayed by the Chief Justice in the aftermath of the decision was partly inspired by the realization that he had been badly beaten in the argument by his much younger colleague from Massachusetts.

III

CONSEQUENCES AND ECHOES

❦ 18 ❦

The Judges Judged

T he first wave of public comment on the Dred Scott decision
was in response to the newspaper summaries of the oral
opinions delivered on March 6 and 7, 1857. Soon thereafter, the two dissenters filed their written opinions and released copies
to the press. Thus antislavery elements for a time had better documentary ammunition along with the eruptive force of their moral outrage.

The fierceness of the attack upon the decision was reminiscent of
the uprising against the Kansas-Nebraska bill three years earlier.
Horace Greeley's New York *Tribune* set the pace with editorials almost every day denouncing this "atrocious," this "wicked," this "abominable" judgment, which was no better than what might be obtained in any "Washington bar-room"—denouncing also the "cunning
chief" whose "collation of false statements and shallow sophistries"
revealed a "detestable hypocrisy" and a "mean and skulking cowardice."[1] The *Tribune* invective, though never surpassed, was matched
by scores of Republican newspapers across the North, such as the
Chicago *Democratic-Press*, which expressed a "feeling of shame and
loathing" for "this once illustrious tribunal, toiling meekly and pa-
tiently through this dirty job"; and the Chicago *Tribune*, which declared: "We scarcely know how to express our detestation of its inhuman dicta, or to fathom the wicked consequences which may flow
from it."[2]

But this time the defending hosts had the special advantage of being able to appeal to the sanctity of the judicial system, thereby invoking their own brand of moral imperative. "The decision is right, and the argument unanswerable, we presume," said the Louisville *Democrat*, "but whether or not, what this tribunal decides the Constitution to be, that it is; and all patriotic men will acquiesce." The New Orleans *Picayune* spoke in worshipful tones of the Supreme Court— that "august and incorruptible body, which, elevated above the turmoils of party, has so adjudged the vexed question of the times as to rebuke faction, confirm and strengthen the doubting, give the loftiest mind support to patriotism, and consolidate the Union—be it reverently hoped—for all time." More forthright was the *Constitutionalist* of Augusta, Georgia, which declared: "Southern opinion upon the subject of southern slavery . . . is now the supreme law of the land . . . and opposition to southern opinion upon this subject is now opposition to the Constitution, and morally treason against the Government."[3]

Many Democratic editors in the North were equally emphatic, including James Gordon Bennett, whose New York *Herald* had supported Frémont during the recent presidential contest but then had swung back into the Buchanan camp. "The supreme law is expounded by the supreme authority," said the *Herald* on March 8, "and disobedience is rebellion, treason, and revolution." The decision was now the supreme law of the land, a New Hampshire newspaper declared. "It is practically the constitution itself. . . . Resistance to that decision is therefore resistance to the constitution—to the government—to the Union itself."[4]

Of all political groups, northern Democrats stood to gain the most from a subsidence of the slavery controversy, and some of them pretended to believe that the Dred Scott decision would have such a happy effect. The Washington *Union*, official organ of the Buchanan administration, repeatedly asserted that the decision would have a "salutary influence" and would restore "harmony and fraternal concord throughout the country." Sectionalism, it predicted, would henceforth "cease to be a dangerous element in our political contests."[5] The New York *Journal of Commerce*, calling the decision an "authoritative and final settlement of grievous sectional issues," hailed it as "almost the greatest political boon which has been vouchsafed to us since the foundation of the Republic."[6]

As prophecy, such sanguine pronouncements carried little conviction, but as an element of political strategy they were clever enough. The Dred Scott decision was a potential threat to the survival of the Republican party, and much depended upon the degree of skill with which Democrats exploited it. Of course the most obvious point to be made was the doctrinal effect of the decision. Labeling it "the funeral sermon of Black Republicanism," the Philadelphia *Pennsylvanian* proclaimed: "It sweeps away every plank of their platform, and crushes into nothingness the whole theory upon which their party is founded." The phrasing varied from editor to editor in the refreshing manner of nineteenth-century American journalism, but the message was the same. New York *Herald:* "at a single blow, shivers the anti-slavery platform of the late great Northern Republican party into atoms." New Orleans *Picayune:* "puts the whole basis of the Black Republican organization under the ban of the law." Augusta *Constitutionalist:* "crushes the life out of that miserable political organization."[7]

But it is doubtful that many persons really expected the dynamic new Republican party to crawl away and die just because its cardinal principle had been declared unconstitutional. Thanks to the comprehensiveness of Taney's proslavery zeal, party leaders would have no serious difficulty coping with the theoretical implications of his opinion. The greater danger lay in the excessiveness of much Republican reaction to the decision; for this could destroy the party's moderate image in the North and push it closer to a fatal association with abolitionism in the public mind. The status of Republicanism as a major party depended heavily on maintenance of the distinction between it and the radicalism of the abolitionists. Criticism of the Supreme Court which seemed to denigrate it as an institution placed the critic on treacherous ground by tending to blur this distinction. Garrisonians, after all, were detested and feared in the North less for their denunciation of slavery than for their attacks on the Constitution.[8]

Thus, along with many Democratic claims of vindication in the decision, shrewder party spokesmen emphasized the nonpartisan, sacerdotal character of the Court and pictured its assailants as dangerous men verging on outlawry and blasphemy. The Republicans must go out of business or accept the role of revolutionaries, a New England editor insisted; for there were now only two categories—loyal citizens and Garrisonians. The issue, echoed a Pennsylvania newspaper, was "submission to the laws of the land, or open rebellion." The New York *Journal of Commerce* told its readers that Republicanism was "only another name for revolution and anarchy," while the Richmond *Enquirer*, seeing evidence of an "epidemic of apoplexy" in radical antislavery circles, predicted, "All the insane asylums in Yankeedom will be inadequate for the accommodation of its victims." Some kind of rhetorical climax on the subject was reached in the editorial column of the Davenport *Iowa State Democrat:* "These daring libellers will next ascend to the Throne of the Supreme Ruler of the Universe and accuse God of partiality. . . . They have the audacity of the devil. . . . They hate, the Constitution, the Bible, and God. . . . Where they will stop in their blasphemies and their treasons no mortal can tell."[9]

A windfall in mid-March further strengthened the Democratic case; for at this point the public learned that the real owner of Dred Scott was probably not John F. A. Sanford but his sister Irene, the wife of a prominent Massachusetts Republican. The revelation apparently first appeared in the Springfield *Argus*, Democratic organ in the city where the onetime wife and widow of John Emerson now lived with her second husband, Congressman Calvin C. Chaffee. Republican embarrassment was acute as Democrats relentlessly exploited their advantage with comments like this one by the *Argus:* "All the long years of servitude through which this family has been doomed to labor . . . has this hypocrite kept their ownership by his family from the public, while he has profited, not only by their labor, but on the other hand by his extraordinary professions of love for the poor Negro."[10]

Chaffee, meanwhile, was responding to the exposé with an emphatic disclaimer. "In the case of Dred Scott," he wrote to the

Springfield *Republican*, "the defendant was and is the only person who had or has any power in the matter, and neither myself nor any member of my family were consulted in relation to, or even knew of the existence of the suit till after it was noticed for trial, when we learned it in an accidental way."[11] Presumably, there being no "trial," in the ordinary sense of the word, before the Supreme Court, this meant that Chaffee and his wife had known about the case since 1854 but denied having any association with it or any control over Sanford's course of action.

Events soon conspired to impair the credibility of this disclaimer, however. John Sanford, confined to an asylum, died on May 5, and just three weeks later out in Missouri, Taylor Blow manumitted Dred Scott and his family, having received title to them by quitclaim from the Chaffees.'[12] Estates are never settled so swiftly; therefore the one thing clear is that Irene Chaffee did not recover possession of the Scotts by bequest from her brother.[13] There are several possible explanations of the mysterious transaction, and the Chaffees' use of quitclaim suggests that they themselves may have been unsure of their legal interest in the slaves.[14] But Democratic editors naturally preferred to believe that Congressman Chaffee had acknowledged himself a slave-owner and a liar. Certainly the Dred Scott affair took on a peculiar odor with the revelations of the Chaffee role, and nothing contributed more to the suspicion that it was a contrived case, got up to serve the same Republican purpose as "bleeding Kansas."[15] The suspicion, as we have seen, was probably mistaken, but historians ever since have had difficulty putting the idea of a conspiracy aside.[16]

A new surge of public interest in Dred Scott's case during late May and early June, 1857, resulted partly from the news of his manumission and the curious circumstances surrounding it, but also from publication of the official version of the decision in Howard's *Reports*. The Supreme Court reporter in 1857 received an annual salary of $1300, supplemented by profits from sales of the *Reports* and occasional pamphlet editions of individual cases. For Benjamin C. Howard, the Dred Scott decision thus constituted "a kind of windfall," which his friend the Chief Justice was anxious to protect.[17] This was

one reason Taney objected to the early release of the McLean and
Curtis opinions.[18] Competitive publication could not be prevented,
however. Arrangements were soon being made to print 20,000 copies
of the decision for senatorial distribution. Howard protested and received an indemnity of $1500, but that was about the extent of his
good fortune.[19] His own pamphlet edition, published by D. Appleton
and Company, did not become a best seller. In August 1858 he
learned that there had been "no sales" during the previous six months
and, indeed, an increase of stock owing to returns.[20] By no means did
this reflect a lack of public interest in the decision. Howard's expectations were blighted by just too much cheap competition, such as the
twenty-five-cent pamphlet rushed into print by the New York
Tribune, containing the Taney and Curtis opinions in full, plus summaries of the others.[21] Most remarkable, however, was the extensive
newspaper coverage in a day when only a few major journals exceeded four pages. Such publication was likely to be selective on a
partisan basis, but the *National Intelligencer*, for example, undertook
to print all of the opinions, beginning on May 29 and filling about 150
columns by the time it finished. The justices themselves were well
aware that newspapers provided the widest circulation of their opinions, and Catron in particular was worried about not getting enough
coverage.[22]

For the official version in Howard's *Reports*, Taney took over the
reporter's duty of supplying a headnote, perhaps because he had
been annoyed by editorial comments to the effect that his opinion was
not really the opinion of the Court. An unusually elaborate affair, covering some three pages, the headnote ignored concurring opinions to
concentrate exclusively on that of the Chief Justice.[23]

Although the newspaper press was the primary medium for documentary publication and public discussion of the Dred Scott decision, there were other channels of information and criticism. Some of
the more zealous antislavery clergy, for example, did not hesitate to
raise the subject in their churches. Montgomery Blair heard John
McLean's opinion read from a pulpit on the first Sunday after it was
read in court.[24] One of the most notable performances was a series of
sermons denouncing slavery and the Supreme Court by George B.

Cheever, pastor of the Church of the Puritans in New York City. The equal of William Lloyd Garrison and Wendell Phillips in vituperative power, Cheever preached resistance even to the extreme of revolution if necessary, declaring that when sin and the Devil usurped power, it was the duty of everyone to disobey, and that "such a government ought to be put out of existence, as a piracy against mankind."[25] Cheever was also associated with Henry Ward Beecher and several other Congregationalist ministers in the editing of *The Independent,* a radical church weekly that equaled the New York *Tribune* in the fierceness of its attacks on the Dred Scott decision, which it called a "vain attempt to change the law by the power of Judges who have achieved only their own infamy." The decision was a "deliberate, willful perversion, for a particular purpose," the paper said. "If the people obey this decision, they disobey God."[26]

The decision also received the attention of many official church organizations, notably the annual district conferences of the Methodist Episcopal Church, North. For example, the committee on slavery of the Providence Conference, meeting on April 1, denounced the Taney opinion as an effort at "nationalizing slavery." The New Hampshire Conference rejected the decision as contrary to religion, justice, and the Constitution. Such condemnation echoed through other religious meetings across the North and provided further basis for the already widespread conservative protest against the mixing of clergy in politics.[27]

II

After full publication of the decision in Howard's *Reports,* the discussion became more substantive and technical, with members of the legal profession now offering their expert commentary, first in letters to editors and public speeches, then in magazine articles, pamphlets, and books. The best of these critiques were much cooler in tone than the general run of editorial comment and all the more effective as a consequence. Such was the case, for example, with an article in *The Law Reporter* for June 1857 written by two young Bostonians, John Lowell and Horace Gray. Lowell, then editor of the *Reporter,* later became a federal judge; Gray's distinguished judicial career would include twenty-one years on the United States Supreme Court. Their review was essentially an endorsement of the Curtis opinion, but they were respectful in their disagreement with Taney, calling his opinion "unworthy of the reputation of that great magistrate . . . to whose grasp of mind, logical power, keen discrimination, and judicial wisdom, the people have been accustomed to look, with a confidence rarely disappointed." This, it scarcely need be said, was not the language of Horace Greeley and other such Republican critics of the decision. Instead, Lowell and Gray anticipated the "aberration" view of Taney's conduct popularized in the twentieth century by Charles Evans Hughes. Yet, aside from the absence of personal abuse, their conclusions were very much like those of the New York *Tribune.* [28]

The Christian Examiner in July presented another careful examination of the decision, one that was highly critical and yet seldom denunciatory. It was especially perceptive on the subject of race, finding in Taney's opinion the fundamental, false assumption that "the slave States as a class hold as property the black race as a class, and so are injured by this [36° 30'] restriction.[29] A harsher tone pervaded the review of the case published by the *North American Review* in its October issue, but the author, a Boston lawyer named Timothy Farrar, relied on sarcasm rather than vituperation. On the issue of the plea in abatement, for instance, he concluded: "Four judges are of one opinion; two of the opposite; two will give no opinion, and one is divided." Farrar's depreciative estimate of the decision extended to his expectations of its influence. He saw nothing very dangerous in Taney's overextended argument. "But for its effect on the character of the court," he wrote, "the world will probably move on very much as it did before."[30]

All three of these articles exemplified a general tendency of contemporary criticism and later scholarship to spend much time on questions associated with the legitimacy of the decision or of large parts of it—whether the Chief Justice really spoke for a majority of the Court, what the Court really decided, how the justices aligned themselves on each specific issue, and whether the invalidation of the Missouri Compromise restriction was dictum. Here, Farrar was the most excessive, declaring that the decision was of no authority on any of the three major questions (citizenship, comity, and the Missouri Compromise), and that for a court to decide a case not within its jurisdiction was "in every just sense of the word, *usurpation.*"[31]

Although most of the critiques were general in nature, the *New Englander* (later the *Yale Review*) chose to specialize. Its August issue carried one article undertaking to demonstrate that Justice Daniel had been wrong in his interpretation of Roman law, and another analyzing that part of Taney's opinion dealing with Negro citizenship. The latter piece, by W. A. Learned, was particularly effective in exposing the historical and logical weaknesses of the Taney argument. Learned called attention, for example, to the Chief Justice's habit of lumping free Negroes with slaves when defining their status, and he had a keen eye for the instances in which Taney seemed to draw the very opposite inference from that indicated by the facts.[32]

Pamphlet commentaries on the decision also began to appear soon after publication of the Howard volume. George T. Curtis's argument in the case dealing solely with the territorial question, was thus circulated and, along with his brother's dissenting opinion, provided prime ammunition for Republican editors and orators. One of the ablest critiques in pamphlet form came out of Louisville, with the author identified only as "A Kentucky Lawyer." He was apparently the first, for example, to point out the aimlessness of Taney's distinction between original territories and those later acquired, since the limitations on Congress were precisely the same in each case. Especially perceptive were his remarks on Taney's use of the due-process clause, for he showed that the crucial question here was not whether slaves constituted property but whether prohibition constituted deprivation.[33]

The rousing effect of the Dred Scott decision on a considerable segment of the public consciousness is well illustrated by the fact that the longest critique produced in 1857 was the work of a seventy-five-year-old man already stricken with cancer. Thomas Hart Benton, moreover, was running a race with death in an effort to finish his monumental sixteen-volume *Abridgment of the Debates in Congress.* Yet the old political warhorse, smelling far too much essence of Calhoun in Taney's opinion, turned aside to write "with incredible speed" a book of 130 pages (plus a 62-page appendix) which a modern biographer has labeled "one of the most meticulous, thoroughly documented, and closely reasoned pieces of historical research ever done on a single subject of constitutional law."[34]

Benton concentrated entirely on the territorial aspect of the decision. Everything wrong in it stemmed, he said, from the Court's assumption that the Constitution extended automatically to new territories as soon as they were acquired, carrying protection of slavery with it. That was Calhoun doctrine, which Daniel Webster had ridiculed in 1849 and Henry Clay had demolished during the great debates of the year following. Benton agreed with Taney that the territory clause referred only to disposal of public land and that nothing in the Constitution expressly endowed Congress with power to govern a territory. But then the theories of the two men parted company. Benton viewed congressional authority in the territories as legitimate and confirmed by long usage. But it was derived straight from the inherent sovereign power of the federal government, without reference to the Constitution. That document, he insisted, embraced only the states, and none of its limitations extended to the territories, except when Congress so provided by positive enactment. Benton's doctrine, no less extreme in its way than Calhoun's, gained considerable support later in the century, but was eventually rejected by the Supreme Court. In 1857, it had too much of an imperial flavor to win many adherents.[35]

Other books treating the case soon followed Benton's. The decision came just in time, for example, to receive extensive attention in the first volume of one of the most remarkable works ever published on the subject of slavery—John Codman Hurd's 1400-page work, *The Law of Freedom and Bondage in the United States.* Hurd was a thoroughgoing legal positivist who rigorously distinguished law from ethics, recognized the existence and underlying force of natural law but insisted that it had no legal authority, and regarded jurisprudence as strictly the study of positive law, defined in Austinian terms as the command of a superior to a subordinate.[36] The thoroughness of his research, the clarity of his organization, and the density of his prose reminded a contemporary reviewer of "those masterpieces of German scholarship which are the achievement of a lifetime and the wonder of an age."[37] These qualities, together with Hurd's cool detachment and the obliqueness of his approach (being interested in the case only as it fitted into his general treatment of slavery and law) furnish a sharp contrast to the flaming denunciations that issued from the Republican press. Hurd's treatise did not so much attack the Dred Scott decision as pass over it like a glacier, with devastating effect. For example, he exposed the weakness and circularity of Taney's argument that the Constitution recognized slaves as property and that such recognition was co-extensive with federal authority.[38] And he also exposed the inconsistency of denying congressional authority over "rights and obligations incident to the status of persons in the Territories," while at the same time asserting federal executive and judicial authority over the same subjects.[39] The course of events soon overtook Hurd's monumental work, however, and rendered it largely obsolete except for historians, who, with a few exceptions, have given the two volumes only passing attention.

From the foregoing discussion it must not be inferred that there were no articles, pamphlets, or books written in support of the Dred Scott decision, but the literature of defense was less impressive in both volume and quality. This fact is not surprising. The Court had put the ball in the antislavery court, so to speak, and the best defense for a decision allegedly already complete and perfect was not further supportive argument but rather obeisance to the Court—"the gravest, the most learned, and most august tribunal in America and perhaps in the world."[40]

Such was the emphasis of Caleb Cushing, recently attorney general under Pierce, in a speech delivered at Newburyport, Massachusetts, on October 31 and circulated as a broadside. Not satisfied with describing the Chief Justice as "the very incarnation of judicial purity, integrity, science, and wisdom," the orotund Cushing also declared that Taney was "infirm of body, but with a mind which seems to beam out the clearer from its frail earthly shrine as if it had already half shaken off the dust of mortality and begun to stand as it were transfigured into the celestial glory and beauty of immortality."[41] This was an eloquent way of saying that the man had one foot in the grave, but Taney liked it and thanked Cushing for his kind words at a time when "evil passions" ruled the hour. "I ought to be thankful," Taney continued, "for the abuse that has been lavished on me when it calls out such a defender and defense. What they have said, I do not know, as I do not read the newspapers in which they are published, or the anonymous letters which they frequently send to me—and I have thought all along that this wrath and fury was strong proof that I was right."[42]

Earlier in the year, Taney had also received from Samuel Nott a copy of his pamphlet, "Slavery and the Remedy," in a new edition containing a favorable commentary on the Dred Scott decision. Taney's letter of acknowledgment to the Massachusetts clergyman is the most revealing recorded statement of his attitude toward the Negro—"this weak and credulous race," as he put it, whose life in slavery was "usually cheerful and contented," and for whom a general and sudden emancipation would mean "absolute ruin." Many slaves had been freed in Maryland, Taney wrote. "And in the greater number of cases that have come under my observation, freedom has been a serious misfortune to the manumitted slave." He himself had freed his own slaves more than thirty years past. "And I am glad to say that none of those whom I manumitted disappointed my expectations, but have shown by their conduct that they were worthy of freedom, and knew how to use it." If Taney noticed the glaring discrepancy in his words, he offered no explanation of it.[43]

III

The views of the Court majority in the Dred Scott case seemed to confer a certain amount of high legal sanction upon the thriving racist anthropology of the day which defined the black race as a distinct and lower species of mankind, the product of a separate creation. Thus, in 1859, one of the leading popularizers of the theory of polygenesis, Dr. John H. Van Evrie of New York, published a pamphlet edition of the Dred Scott decision with an introductory essay in which he declared that it was a document second in importance to the Declara-

tion of Independence. The decision "fixed the *status* of the subordinate race *forever*," he said, and, being in accord with nature, could
"never perish." It "must be accepted and sustained by the northern
masses, or there must be disunion."[44]

The racist implications of the decision were fiercely denounced
in radical antislavery circles. For the free Negro community especially, this "judicial incarnation of wolfishness," as Frederick Douglass
called it, seems to have inspired a sudden shift to a higher level of
militancy. Words of defiance rang out at numerous protest meetings,
and it was as a response to the Dred Scott decision that black abolitionists organized a celebration of "Crispus Attucks Day" on March 5,
1858, in Boston's cradle of liberty, Faneuil Hall. This spectacular
meeting honoring the Negro killed in the Boston Massacre was "a
feast of sight and sound," repeated every year until ratification of the
Fifteenth Amendment in 1870.[45]

Many white critics of the decision likewise deplored its repres-
sive effect on free Negroes. The *Whig and Courier* of Bangor, Maine,
called it a "monstrous doctrine" which denied colored citizens of the
state "the ordinary justice which the meanest individual of any other
race of foreign people may obtain among us."[46] And the heading of an
editorial in the *Independent* read: "The Decision of the Supreme
Court is the Moral Assassination of a Race and Cannot be Obeyed."[47]
But throughout most of the North such voices were in a minority.
Taney's ruling against Negro citizenship carried nothing like the same
emotional charge as his ruling against the Missouri Compromise restriction. Complaints about it, such as those just quoted, exposed
Republicanism to counterattack at one of its most vulnerable points—
namely, the degree to which an enemy of slavery was a friend of the
Negro.

The dilemma confronting Republicans was this: The record of
racial discrimination throughout most of the North laid them open to
charges of hypocrisy in their expressions of sympathy for the slave;
but any words or actions tending to vindicate themselves of the
charge laid them open to another and more dangerous one of advocating racial equality. In short, whenever discussion shifted from slavery
to race, Republicans were in trouble, and the first half of Taney's

Dred Scott opinion was concerned with race. Complaints about it were answered with variations on the theme of the mote and the beam. "Ye hypocrites," said the Louisville *Democrat* to the northern states generally, "reform yourselves, before you preach to us." If the Negro was a citizen, why were so many of his rights trampled upon? How could a citizen be excluded from school, jury service, and the polls—indeed, from entire states? Had not the Topeka constitution, drafted by ardent antislavery forces in Kansas, proposed to bar Negroes from the state?[48]

This tender spot was probed, of course, not only by proslavery southerners but by antislavery militants, black and white, who pointed out that the Dred Scott decision, as it applied to free Negroes, had a majoritarian ring that transcended sectional lines. "While the cruel slave driver lacerates the black man's mortal body, we of the North flay the spirit," declared Susan B. Anthony just as the Civil War was beginning. "Judge Taney's decision, infamous as it is, is but the reflection of the spirit and practice of the American people, North as well as South."[49]

In its primary effect, the decision meant the exclusion of most Negroes from access to the federal courts in civil cases, but the potential ramifications were far more numerous and complex than anyone realized at the time. For one thing, there was the problem of definition. Could an Ohio quadroon, white according to the law of his state, bring a federal suit against a white man in Tennessee, where quadroons were legally black? Could the Tennessean sue the quadroon? Would the same definition apply in the federal courts of both states? Clearly, either Congress or the Supreme Court would some day have to say who was and who was not a Negro.[50]

Meanwhile, the executive branch of the federal government, which, over the years, had not been entirely consistent about it, could now proceed with authority to deny Negroes all privileges associated with United States citizenship, such as passports for travel abroad and eligibility for pre-emption of federal land. In addition, the Dred Scott decision lent the semblance of constitutionality more emphatically to various forms of racial discrimination authorized or permitted by Congress, such as exclusion of Negroes from employment in the postal service and the black code operating in the District of Columbia.[51]

The decision likewise lent support to various discriminatory laws of state governments, southern and northern (such as those prohibiting Negro immigration), and it encouraged further assaults upon the already limited freedom and security of the nonslave black population. In Arkansas, for instance, a proposal to enslave all free Negroes who did not leave the state within a year had recently failed, owing in part to constitutional scruples. The Dred Scott decision "breathed new life" into the movement, and the legislature passed the expulsion act in 1859, with the result that most free Negroes hastily fled the state. Several other southern states came close to following the Arkansas example, especially in the aftermath of the Harpers Ferry raid, but none other went so far as to put expulsion into effect.[52]

At the same time, the decision posed a threat to black suffrage in the few states allowing it, for the franchise was in each case limited to United States citizens. Had Taney's opinion, then, made Negro voting unconstitutional? The legislature of Maine laid this question before the state supreme court, which returned a negative reply based primarily on the dissenting opinion of Justice Curtis.[53] There were other indications that the Dred Scott decision, insofar as it impinged on state law in New England, would probably go unenforced. Curtis himself had learned some years earlier that legal positivism was no match for puritan conscience.[54]

IV

There was, in fact, a strong reaction to the decision in a number of state legislatures during the spring of 1857, one that has received only passing notice from historians but was especially conspicuous at a time when Congress had withdrawn into its biennial nine-month cocoon.* The decision evoked such a response partly because of its legal implications at the state level and partly because of its provocative

*The thirty-fourth Congress had adjourned on March 3, 1857; the thirty-fifth Congress, though elected largely in the autumn of 1856, would not convene until December 7, 1857.

relevance wherever politicians were gathered, but also because of the peculiar functional relationship between state and national governments in the American federal system of the mid-nineteenth century. Perhaps the key factor was the constitutional provision endowing state legislatures with the power and responsibility of electing United States senators. This arrangement apparently encouraged the notion that, whereas members of the House represented their constituents directly, members of the Senate represented their states as corporate entities and were in some degree responsible to them. At any rate, state legislatures had developed the custom of expressing themselves on national issues by telling their senators what to do. The common form was a resolution "instructing" the state's two senators (and sometimes "requesting" its representatives) to follow a certain course on the floor of Congress. Passage of such a resolution was often preceded by extensive committee work and floor debate. Sometimes it was inspired by a recommendation from the governor, whose annual message frequently included a section dealing with national affairs.[55]

Thus, Governor Alexander H. Holley of Connecticut was following custom when he sent a message to the legislature in May 1857 attacking the Dred Scott decision as tending to nationalize slavery and place free blacks in a condition of "outlawry." The legislature responded with denunciatory resolutions, as well as with bills declaring free any slave brought into the state and defining state citizenship in such a way as to include Negroes.[56] The Maine legislature had already taken similar action. It passed resolutions asserting that the decision was "not binding in law or conscience" and that the Supreme Court should be "reconstituted." The laws of Maine (a state with fewer than 1500 blacks in a total population exceeding half a million) were already free of racial discrimination and scarcely needed improvement in that respect; but the legislature did accompany its Dred Scott resolutions with two new antislavery laws—one providing for the emancipation of any slave carried into the state by his master and the other putting the legal services of county attorneys at the disposal of accused fugitive slaves.[57]

There was a flurry of such retaliatory action also in New Hampshire, New York, Pennsylvania, Ohio, and several other states. The

general pattern included resolutions protesting the Dred Scott decision and legislation that was not only antislavery (denial of sojourners'
rights) but also in some degree pro-Negro (protection against wrongful capture under the Fugitive Slave Act; express conferral or confirmation of Negro citizenship).[58] Indeed, for a time it appeared that the
free black population in the North might profit substantially from the
reaction to the decision, but the reaction itself had repercussions
which, though significant, have largely escaped attention. What happened in New York may serve as an illustration.

In 1857, New York was the only state outside New England extending suffrage to Negroes, but it subjected them to a special property qualification that limited their participation. Efforts to erase this
discriminatory provision had failed repeatedly. Now, however, the
safely Republican legislature seemed ready to act. The appropriate
resolution, introduced in the state Senate on January 13, 1857, was
passed (21 to 5) on March 3 and sent on to the Assembly, which formally received it on March 5, the day before Taney announced the
Dred Scott decision in Washington. The resolution progressed to passage in the Assembly (65 to 38) on March 25, during those first weeks
of public reaction to the decision. Inevitably, it came to be regarded
as a prominent feature of that response.[59]

Meanwhile, a special joint committee had been created to consider "the serious and alarming doctrines" of the Dred Scott decision.
The report submitted on April 9 was a diatribe which began by asserting that the decision jeopardized the sovereignty of the state, the constitutional rights and morals of her citizens, agricultural and commercial prosperity, the security of free labor, and the educational system.
More than that: "The decision . . . will bring slavery within our
borders against our will, with all its unhallowed, demoralizing, and
blighting influences." The committee recommended passage of several resolutions and an "act to secure freedom to all persons in this
state." Its report closed with a states' rights quotation from the
Virginia and Kentucky resolutions of 1798.[60]

The committee's resolutions, after some juggling back and forth
between Senate and Assembly, were approved in both chambers on
April 18, the final day of the session. (Leading the hopeless Demo-

cratic resistance in the Senate was Daniel E. Sickles, already elected
to sit in the next Congress. Within two years, Sickles would be on
trial in Washington for murdering a nephew of Chief Justice Taney.
Four years after that adventure, he would command the Union left at
Gettysburg and lose one of his legs in the battle.)[61] One of the
resolutions declared that the Supreme Court had sacrificed the confidence and respect of the people of New York. Another announced:
"That this State will not allow slavery within her borders in any form
or under any pretence, or for any time, however short."[62] The "act to
secure freedom" got lost in the closing legislative bustle, but the successful suffrage resolution was regarded everywhere as part of the
anti-*Dred-Scott* package.

Amendment of the New York constitution required approval by
two different legislatures and by the electorate in referendum. The
proposed suffrage amendment would enfranchise perhaps as many
Negroes as those already authorized to vote in six states.[63] Its preliminary success at this point lent substance to the charge that critics of
the Dred Scott decision were advocates of racial equality. Thus, the
New Orleans *Picayune* discussed the New York legislation under the
headline, "New York Negrophilism," and ridiculed the effort to
"make fellow citizens . . . of all the motley mass of native born
loafers of the African complexion."[64] Democrats in the state were
quick to exploit the racial theme, and in the fall election, with Know-
Nothing help, they defeated the Republicans by some 18,000 votes.[65]
"Last year's vast Republican majority is gone like last year's snow,"
wrote George Templeton Strong in his diary.[66] The equal suffrage
amendment was submitted in 1860 to the same New York electorate
that gave Lincoln a 50,000-vote majority. It was defeated by twice
that margin, which seems to mean that at least 40 per cent of the
state's Republicans voted against it. "The black baby of Negro suffrage
was thought too ugly to exhibit on so grand an occasion," Frederick
Douglass bitterly complained.[67]

In Ohio, there was an even clearer sequence of advance and retreat on the racial front. The Ohio legislature, likewise Republican in
1857, passed resolutions condemning the Dred Scott decision,

together with laws to prevent slaveholding and kidnapping in the state (meaning prohibition of sojourning and increased interference with enforcement of the Fugitive Slave Act). Ohio, too, held an election in 1857 and a much more important one than the contest in New York; for both the legislature and the governorship were at stake. The Republican state convention denounced *Dred Scott* as "anti-constitutional, anti-republican, anti-democratic, incompatible with State rights and destructive of personal security." The Democrats, in response, stressed the white supremacy aspects of the decision. For instance, they assembled quotations from various radical Republican statements and published them as the "Congo Creed." Although Salmon P. Chase won re-election as governor by a very narrow margin, the Democrats captured control of the legislature. They then not only repealed some of the antislavery legislation of the previous session but, citing the Dred Scott decision, they also passed the so-called visible admixture law, which, in effect, disfranchised persons of mixed blood between white and mulatto.[68]

These Republican setbacks in New York and Ohio elections of 1857 cannot be attributed solely, perhaps not even primarily, to a racist backlash against the more radical attacks on the Dred Scott decision. Aside from the historic tendency of majority parties to lose ground in off-year elections, the financial panic that began in late summer no doubt disposed many men to vote for a change of management. Ohio Republicans were further handicapped by an embezzlement of public funds in the Chase administration.[69] Nevertheless, the remarkable capacity of the Democratic party (unlike the Federalists and Whigs) to survive through years of adversity, when it was divided, defeated, and tainted with treason, may have been owing in part to a deepset feeling that it was "right" on the race question. No one can say for sure that large numbers of northern votes were determined or heavily influenced in the late 1850s by vigorous Democratic appeals to racism, but Republicans plainly believed that such was the case. Abraham Lincoln had come to that bitter conclusion after the defeat of Frémont in 1856. Speaking at Chicago, just six days before the Dred Scott decision, he complained, "We were constantly charged with seeking an amalgamation of the white and black races; and thousands turned from us, not believing the charge (no one believed it) but *fearing* to face it themselves."[70]

But Lincoln himself increasingly evinced the same fear. His first public comment on *Dred Scott* had a schizoid quality. With elaborate but moving metaphor he argued, in direct contradiction of Taney, that the condition of the Negro in America had worsened over the years and "never appeared so hopeless" as in the 1850s:

> All the powers of earth seem rapidly combining against him. Mammon is after him; ambition follows, and philosophy follows, and the Theology of the day is fast joining the cry. They have him in his prison house; they have searched his person, and left no prying instrument with him. One after another they have closed the heavy iron doors upon him, and now they have him, as it were, bolted in with a lock of a hundred keys, which can never be unlocked without the concurrence of every key; the keys in the hands of a hundred different men, and they scattered to a hundred different and distant places; and they stand musing as to what invention, in all the dominions of mind and matter, can be produced to make the impossibility of his escape more complete than it is.[71]

Yet, almost in the next breath, his sympathies in the matter seemed to shift abruptly from the black race to the white, and he used his strongest language ever on the subject when he said that there was a "natural disgust in the minds of nearly all white people, to the idea of an indiscriminate amalgamation of the white and black races." Douglas, he added, was misrepresenting opposition to the Dred Scott decision in the hope of "being able to appropriate the benefit of this disgust to himself."[72]

It was at about this time that Lincoln began to use census statistics to show miscegenation as a by-product of slavery, and it was at this point that he introduced the rhetorical flourish of disclaiming any wish to have a Negro woman either for a slave or for a wife.[73] A year later, under heavy pounding from Douglas, he would awkwardly back off from criticizing the first half of Taney's opinion and declare emphatically his opposition to Negro citizenship.[74] Various other Republican leaders joined in the scramble to dissociate themselves from the unpopular doctrine of racial equality, and some, it appears, even took up the cause of colonization for that purpose.[75] Too many Republican politicians, Horace Greeley complained, thought that "they must be as harsh, and cruel, and tyrannical, toward the unfortunate blacks as possible, in order to prove themselves 'the white man's party.' "[76]

V

Thus reaction to the Dred Scott decision does not appear to have produced any significant gains for the free Negro community or any significant number of new adherents for the Republican party. Critics of the decision laid themselves open to the charge of having joined Garrison not only in his anti-constitutionalism but also in his racial equalitarianism. The race question tended to unite Democrats and divide Republicans, whereas the slavery question tended to divide Democrats and unite Republicans, who could agree especially in opposing further extension of the institution on both pro-Negro and anti-Negro grounds. Republican politicians therefore concentrated their attacks on the second half of Taney's opinion, which, after all, was the part that struck directly at the foundations of their party.

To be sure, the invalidation of a law already substantially repealed seemed unlikely to make any great difference in the territories themselves, but Republicans could point with alarm to certain broader implications of the decision. Slavery, previously considered legal only where authorized by positive local law, had been made legal throughout the country, except where forbidden by positive local law. In other words, slavery, once local, was now national; and freedom, once national, was now local. Worse, however, was the ominous possibility that the power of local law to prohibit slavery had been seriously impaired and would be further eroded. In its report on the Dred Scott decision, the joint committee of the New York legislature declared:

> It follows as a direct consequence of this doctrine, that a master
> may take his slave into a free State without dissolving the relation

of master and slave; and your committee cannot but be alarmed and shocked at the apprehension that some future decision of the pro-slavery majority of the supreme court will authorise a slave driver, as threatened by the devotees of slavery, to call the roll of his manacled gang at the foot of the monument on Bunker Hill, reared and consecrated to freedom.[77]

This protest that *Dred Scott* constituted a long step toward the nationalization of slavery rang out many times throughout the North before Lincoln took it up in his House-Divided speech of June 16, 1858. It was a dramatic way of holding the emphasis of the discussion to slavery, rather than race, and of countering the emotional impact of the "racial equality" outcry coming from the Democrats. Historians, made overly wise by hindsight, have been disposed to regard the charge as more or less empty political rhetoric, ignoring the fact that even unrealistic fears may be utterly real. Actually, slavery had *already* been nationalized in various ways beyond the minimal requirements of the Constitution, and northern fear of further nationalization in the wake of the Dred Scott decision was, in the circumstances, no more unjustified than southern fear concerning the ultimate intentions of the Republican party.[78]

Even so, further expansion of federal protection for the rights of slavery within the free states did not follow directly from the decision. It was at most a potential danger. Meanwhile, the Republican party faced the immediate problem of having had its principal objective pronounced unconstitutional. "With all of your outrage, what are you going to *do* about it?" the Democrats gleefully demanded. Republican editors and other spokesmen frequently replied, "We intend to get the decision overruled."[79] This answer could only aggravate southern fear of the presidential appointing power's falling into the hands of a Republican, and such a reversal obviously could not be achieved for a number of years, even under the most favorable circumstances. It did not solve the problem of how Republicans could reject the decision without defying the law. But Taney, by trying to cover too much ground in his defense of slavery, provided them with the solution. The opportunity to challenge the legitimacy of the decision was, in the words of David M. Potter, a "psychological godsend."[80]

Accordingly, *"obiter dictum"* became the Republican battle cry in the war upon the Dred Scott decision. The Court's invalidation of the Missouri Compromise restriction should some day be formally overruled, but until then it could simply be ignored as without authority. Both dissenting justices had said so, and their views were emphatically endorsed in the professional criticism of the case emanating from the northern bar. Historians of the next half-century would generally echo those same views. And, as we shall see, the decision would be virtually nullified by disregard in the administration of Abraham Lincoln. The *obiter dictum* argument served Republican needs not only by vindicating the legality of the party platform but also by pulling discussion away from the race issue in *Dred Scott.* Indeed, since the argument rested necessarily on the assumption that the Court had refused to accept jurisdiction in the case, it amounted to a silent acknowledgment that Taney's ruling against Negro citizenship was authoritative.*

The widespread fascination, then and later, with the *obiter dictum* argument, which had the effect of pruning the authoritativeness of a single decision, has partly obscured the fact that some Republicans went further and set forth a narrow definition of the Court's authority generally, vis-à-vis the other branches of government. This was, after all, the first time that the American people had to consider the meaning and consequences of judicial review actually exerted at the level of federal law.† And the matter centrally at issue, it should be noted, was not the power of judicial review but rather the range of that power.

Over the years between the *Marbury* and *Dred Scott* cases, judicial review had won substantial acceptance in theory and practice (though primarily in respect to state law) as a necessary element of American constitutional government. Thus Taney in 1857, unlike

---

*Except for those contemporaries and later historians who, by counting votes of individual justices, arrived at the conclusion that virtually nothing in Taney's opinion was authoritative. See above, pp. 324–25.

†*Marbury v. Madison* had been in a sense self-liquidating. It required no enforcement by the executive branch and did not in any significant way inhibit the power of the legislative branch. See above, pp. 222–23.

John Marshall in 1803, felt no need to justify exercise of the power and said nothing whatever on the subject.* The critical question was not whether the Supreme Court could declare a law of Congress unconstitutional, but rather, what were the total effects of such a declaration. What did it mean beyond the judgment that Dred Scott was still a slave? Did the decision, as the New Hampshire editor asserted, immediately become part of the supreme law of the land and thus fully binding on all federal and state officials? Must members of Congress, sworn to protect the Constitution, now refrain from passing any new legislation discriminating against slavery in the territories? Must the President, similarly sworn and also charged to "take care that the laws be faithfully executed," lend prompt enforcement to the decision wherever it was applicable (such as in Minnesota Territory)? If Congress, in defiance of the decision, were to re-enact the Missouri Compromise restriction, was it the President's sworn duty to veto the measure? Must the two dissenting justices, McLean and Curtis, apply the decision in their circuit courts? Would a refusal to do so constitute an impeachable offense?

It was one thing to say that the Supreme Court might refuse to enforce a law plainly in conflict with a specific provision of the Constitution. It was another thing to say that the Court was the final, authoritative arbiter of all questions involving interpretation of the Constitution. The distinction is between the institution of judicial review, narrowly defined, and the doctrine of judicial supremacy or judicial sovereignty, which did not become settled American dogma until the twentieth century.[82] The issue had been debated many times before William Cullen Bryant's New York *Evening Post* on March 14, 1857, accused the Supreme Court of "judicial impertinence" in assuming the power to "act as the interpreter of the Constitution for the other branches of the government." Thomas Jefferson and Andrew Jackson

---

*Two years later in *Ableman v. Booth*, where it was not relevant to the issues before the Court, Taney affirmed the power, perhaps in answer to Republican comment on *Dred Scott*: "And as the Constitution is the fundamental and supreme law, if it appears that an act of Congress is not pursuant to, and within the limits of, the power assigned to the Federal Government, it is the duty of the courts of the United States to declare it unconstitutional and void."[81]

were but the two most prominent names on a long list of American statesmen who had insisted that Congress and the President were co-equals with the Court in this respect. Taney himself had taken precisely the same position as attorney general under Jackson, declaring:

> Whatever may be the force of the decision of the Supreme Court in binding the parties and settling their rights in the particular case before them, I am not prepared to admit that a construction given to the constitution by the Supreme Court in deciding in any one or more cases fixes of itself irrevokably and permanently its construction in that particular and binds the states and the Legislative and executive branches of the General government, forever afterwards to conform to it and adopt it in every other case as the true reading of the instrument although all of them may unite in believing it erroneous.[83]

Needless to say, the substantive tendency of the Court's decisions has always strongly influenced judgments about the proper limits of its authority. Twentieth-century conservatives and liberals, for instance, virtually traded places on the issue within a single generation. Similarly, Democratic hostility to judicial power in the days of John Marshall had substantially diminished during the tenure of his eminently Democratic successor. The ease with which attitudes could change is well illustrated in the following comment on federal legislation nullifying the Court's decision in the famous *Wheeling Bridge* case: "If the law settled by the highest judicial tribunal be not the accepted law of the land, and is liable to review by demagogues in Congress, of their own motion or by the inspiration of worse ones out of doors, the Court of last resort becomes but a mockery."[84] The author of this statement was James E. Harvey, correspondent "Index" of the New York *Tribune,* and the date was February 17, 1856, the very month in which the Court first heard argument in the Dred Scott case. But Harvey was talking about a decision rendered by his friend Justice McLean, with Taney among the dissenters. A year later, after announcement of the Dred Scott decision, the *Tribune* denounced Democratic efforts to clothe the Court with papal infallibility, declaring: "It has come to a pretty pass, indeed, if this Court, created by people, is to be considered as entirely above popular criticism, as incapable of error, as utterly irresponsible. If this were so, we might as well give up the executive and legislative branches of the Government at once."[85] Abraham Lincoln would say very much the same thing at his inauguration in 1861.

Lincoln, significantly, made no use of the *obiter dictum* argument in criticizing the Dred Scott decision, perhaps because it did not fit into his political strategy. Instead, he followed the Jefferson-Jackson line of limiting the scope and denying the finality of the decision, but he did so with a sophisticated realism that amounted to neither a full acceptance nor a complete rejection of the doctrine of judicial supremacy. In his first public comment on the case, he conceded the Supreme Court some measure of pre-eminence as constitutional authority. Republicans, he said, thought that "its decisions on Constitutional questions, when fully settled, should control, not only the particular cases decided, but the general policy of the country, subject to be disturbed only by amendments of the Constitution as provided in that instrument itself." The phrase "when fully settled" controls the rest of the sentence, and Lincoln insisted that this condition had not yet been met in the Dred Scott case:

> If this important decision had been made by the unanimous concurrence of the judges, and without any apparent partisan bias, and in accordance with legal public expectation, and with the steady practice of the departments throughout our history, and had been in no part, based on assumed historical facts which are not really true; or, if wanting in some of these, it had been before the court more than once, and had there been affirmed and re-affirmed through a course of years, it then might be . . . factious, nay, even revolutionary, to not acquiesce in it as a precedent.
>
> But when, as it is true we find it wanting in all these claims to the public confidence, it is not resistance, it is not factious, it is not even disrespectful, to treat it as not having yet quite established a settled doctrine for the country.[86]

Thus the Dred Scott decision as of June 1857, according to Lincoln, was in an intermediate phase between promulgation and legitimation. Its doctrines were not yet the accepted law of the land and not compelling as a "political rule." The Republicans, knowing that the Court had more than once overruled its own previous decisions, intended to work for such a reversal in this case. Neither was the decision, at its present stage, binding on the coordinate branches of the federal government. "If I were in Congress," Lincoln said a year later, "and a vote should come up on a question whether slavery should be prohibited in a new territory, in spite of that Dred Scott decision, I would vote that it should."[87]

Lincoln regarded the unqualified doctrine of judicial supremacy as incompatible with the principle of self-government and would say so emphatically at the very moment of entering the presidency. Meanwhile, the great advocate of popular sovereignty, Stephen A. Douglas, for his own political reasons, was paying solemn lip service to judicial supremacy and describing the conflict raging over Taney's opinion as a "naked issue between the friends and the enemies of the Constitution."[88] It would not be far wrong to say that the meaning of the Dred Scott decision became the heart of the matter in the famous debates of 1858.

VI

The ultimate judging of judicial decisions is by judges themselves in subsequent decisions, as they reaffirm, refine, modify, or discard previous definitions, interpretations, and rulings. If the Civil War had not intervened, some of the issues presented by the Dred Scott case presumably would have come before the Supreme Court again—first, because clarification was needed on a number of points, and second, because of a strong disposition among northern judges, state and federal, to defy Taney's decision. There was the question, for instance, of whether the Court's ruling against congressional power to prohibit slavery in the territories applied with equal force to the territorial legislatures. If, as Taney believed, it did so apply, the Douglas version of popular sovereignty had no more constitutional basis than the Republican doctrine of free soil.

More likely to come before the Court at an early date was the question, cryptically mentioned by Justice Nelson in the closing paragraph of his opinion, of a slaveholder's right to take a slave temporarily into a free state for a visit or in transit. In addition to various state laws against "sojourning" that might have been tested for constitutionality, there were several cases in state courts that could have been vehicles for presenting the problem to the Supreme Court.

Anderson v. Poindexter, decided in May 1857 during the aftermath of the Dred Scott decision, was a rare example of a court's turning the law of slavery to an antislavery purpose. It involved an effort to collect on notes signed by a Kentucky slave in payment for his freedom, the slave having, with the consent of his master, crossed over into Ohio both before and after the agreement was reached. The Ohio supreme court held that the notes were void because Kentucky law did not allow a slave to make a contract, but that under Ohio law he was nevertheless free as a consequence of having entered Ohio with his master's permission. The effect of this decision was to destroy the right of sojourning in the state and to reject the principle of reattachment.[89] But only a few hundred dollars were at stake, and this was obviously not a good test of sojourners' rights from the slaveholding point of view. Anderson v. Poindexter was not appealed to the United States Supreme Court.

A much more striking case was Lemmon v. The People. In 1852, the owner of eight slaves had them brought by sea from Virginia to New York City in order to send them on a coasting vessel to Texas. During their stopover, however, they were freed by writ of habeas corpus, and the ensuing litigation was to last nearly eight years. New York's emancipation law of 1827 had provided for the liberation of any slave brought into the state by his master, except that temporary visits of up to nine months were permitted. That exception had been repealed in 1841, and the lower state courts in disposing of the Lemmon case took the view that the prohibition, being now absolute, allowed no right of transit however brief. Here, then, was a test of whether slaveholders had any rights whatever within a free state, aside from provisions for the recovery of fugitives; and here, some antislavery leaders feared, there might be the basis for a "second Dred Scott decision" extending federal protection to temporary slaveholding in the free states and constituting another long step toward nationalization of slavery. It does in fact seem very likely that a majority of the Taney Court justices would have rendered a proslavery decision if they had gotten their hands on the case. But *Lemmon v. The People* was not decided by the highest court of New York until March 1860, which affirmed the lower court ruling. Before it could be carried further, the case had lost most of its meaning in the onrushing secession crisis.[90]

Taney's ruling against Negro citizenship likewise called for further judicial interpretation and invited judicial resistance. The supreme court of Maine, as we have seen, advised state officials virtually to ignore the ruling in performing their duties. There is also some evidence of defiance from John McLean on the circuit court bench. In May 1857, according to newspaper reports, McLean and his associate, Judge Thomas Drummond, refused to apply the Dred Scott decision in a suit at Chicago, even though the plaintiff was admittedly black. For one thing, they pointed out, there was nothing in the record to indicate that this Negro had ever been a slave or that he was descended from slaves. But in addition, they seem to have reasserted the definition of citizenship offered by Judge Wells and overruled by Taney—namely, free status and domicile in a state.[91]

It appears that another case arising the next year in the Indiana district of McLean's circuit again presented the question of whether the Dred Scott decision excluded all Negroes from citizenship or only those of slave ancestry like Scott. The court chose the narrower interpretation. This, like the problem of whether persons of mixed blood came under Taney's ban, was no minor matter; for it would often no doubt be difficult to prove that a Negro was descended from slaves. Newspaper reports of the Indiana decision reached Taney in Washington and helped crystallize his resolve to write a "supplement" to the Dred Scott decision for use, as he said, "if the questions come before the Court again in my lifetime."[92]

This curious document, dated September 1858 and running to about half the length of Taney's published Dred Scott opinion, is concerned exclusively with the racial aspect of that opinion. Its stated purpose, in fact, was to reinforce the assertion that Negroes in 1787 had been regarded as "beings of an inferior order," possessing "no rights which the white man was bound to respect." Taney began by rejecting the distinction reportedly drawn in the Indiana decision. "The Supreme Court," he said, "did not decide the case upon the ground that the slavery of the ancestor affixed a mark of inferiority," but rather upon the "opinions then entertained by the white race universally . . . in relation to the powers and rights which they might justly and morally exercise over the African or negro race."[93] In short, his Dred Scott opinion authorized "no distinction between persons of the negro race, whether their ancestors were held in slavery or not."

Taney then devoted most of his paper to demonstrating that the racial attitudes of colonial America reflected those of the mother country. Pointing to the notorious *Asiento* and related agreements whereby three British monarchs participated personally in the slave trade with Spanish colonies from 1713 to 1750, he concluded: "It is impossible to read these treaties, and not feel convinced that . . . the English government and people acknowledged no rights in the negro race which they were bound to respect. . . . The British law regarded them as absolute property, to be traded in like any other merchandise."[94]

Thus Taney was plainly determined to defend the most controversial passage of his Dred Scott opinion as a statement of unpleasant but verifiable historical fact. It will be remembered that in the aftermath of the decision he had been quoted in some antislavery newspapers as having said, "Negroes have no rights which a white man is bound to respect." This misrepresentation was promptly exposed by the Democratic press and has been, as we have already noted, a source of scholarly sympathy for Taney ever since. For instance, George T. Curtis, counsel for Dred Scott, declared in his *Constitutional History of the United States*:

> The calumniators of the chief-justice entirely ignored the fact that
> he spoke of a past state of opinion and feeling, and imputed to him
> as his personal opinion the atrocious sentiment that a negro has no
> right which a white man is bound to respect. The slander had its

effect, and it is probable that there are multitudes at this day who believe it.[95]

Taney, it has been pointed out over and over again, was not in this passage making a ruling about Negro rights in 1857; he was not expressing his own personal view; but instead he was talking about the racial attitudes of the founding fathers and their generation, which presumably no longer prevailed. His language was "simply that of historical narration."[96] He "distinctly recognized the change which has taken place," said a Philadelphia newspaper in the summer of 1857.[97] But did he really? Several sentences in his "supplement" are most revealing. After his long disquisition on English racial attitudes and their transplantation in the American colonies, he concluded:

> Indeed, so deep was this impression made on the white race in this country, that it appears to be indelible. For, amid all the changes in public opinion and legislation which have since taken place, the line of division between the two races, marking the superiority of the one and the inferiority of the other, is as plain now as it was in the days of the *assiento*.[98]

So apparently there had been no change from the "atrocious sentiment" of 1787. If the free Negro of 1857 could claim a single right not possessed in 1787, Taney never mentioned it. In the shift from "had no rights" to "have no rights" there appears to have been verbal inaccuracy with little corruption of meaning.

The effort expended by the eighty-one-year-old Chief Justice on this gratuitous supplementary opinion indicates the intensity of his feeling on the subject of the Dred Scott case. As he brought the paper to a conclusion, not even his abiding sense of judicial dignity could resist the temptation to say something in response to the antislavery censure of the preceding eighteen months. "I have seen and heard," he wrote, "of various comments and reviews . . . adverse to the decision of the Court. But I have seen none that I think it worth while to reply to, for they are founded upon misrepresentations and perversions of the points decided by the Court. It would be a waste of time to expose these perversions and misrepresentations. For if they were exposed, they would nevertheless be repeated, and new ones invented to support them. . . . They cannot mislead the judgment of any one who is in search of truth, and will read the opinion; and I have no desire to waste time and throw away arguments upon those who evidently act upon the principle that the end will justify the means."[99]

∾ 19 ∾

The Lecompton Connection

The comprehensiveness of Taney's Dred Scott opinion astonished friend as well as foe. "It covers every question regarding slavery and settles it in favor of the South," said the Augusta (Georgia) *Constitutionalist*.[1] In officially confirming the legal rectitude of the proslavery argument, the decision provided southerners with an offset to the moral advantage of the antislavery community. Now, more than ever, self-righteous appeals to conscience could be met with self-righteous appeals to the Constitution. In this respect, judicial vindication nourished the confidence of the South and perhaps made it somewhat more inflexible.

Yet the tangible significance of the decision was far from clear in the spring and summer of 1857. It had no immediate legal effect of any importance except on the status of free Negroes. Unlike the Fugitive Slave and Kansas-Nebraska acts, it provoked no turbulent aftermath, presented no problem of enforcement, inspired no political upheaval. Whether the Court's action had shifted the sectional balance of power remained to be seen, but the Charleston *Mercury*, that quintessential voice of southern extremism, found little cause for rejoicing. The South, it declared, had won another "victory more fatal, perhaps, than, defeat," for the antislavery forces seemed always to "rise up stronger after each struggle." And nothing had really been gained. "For the practical attainment of our rights, and their actual enforcement and security, the Dred Scott decision is just so many idle words."[2]

In thus belittling the practical value of an overwhelmingly favorable decision from the highest court in the land, the editors of the *Mercury* were no doubt pursuing their own secessionist course. Still, that does not detract from the accuracy of their perception that southern security depended less on the letter of the law than on the power and purposes of the northern majority. True security required a subsidence of the antislavery crusade, but early naïve expressions of hope that the Dred Scott decision would put slavery agitation "forever at rest"[3] were quickly smothered by the furious outburst of Republican denunciation. Together, the decision and the outcry against it had the net effect of convincing many southerners that their cause was hopelessly in the right.

For southern leaders, the Dred Scott decision was in some ways like an enormous check that could not be cashed. The sense of having won a victory without substance proved increasingly irritating, and many of them, as we shall see, were eventually driven to the self-contradiction of demanding federal intervention for the protection of slavery in the territories. The demand resulted only belatedly and indirectly from the Dred Scott case, however, and was provoked by certain later developments. Furthermore, it never came before Congress as a formal proposal. In short, the southern desire for concrete benefits from the Dred Scott decision inspired some heated argument but did not in itself lead to a legislative crisis.

The Republican response to the decision was likewise ambivalent and more conspicuously so; for it combined furious anger at the import of the decision with half-suppressed delight at its contemplated political effects. An energetic new governor, John W. Geary, had imposed a truce in Kansas during the autumn of 1856, and the territory remained relatively peaceful thereafter for the better part of a year. Announcement of the Court's decision thus came opportunely for the recently defeated Republican party, providing a new stimulus for political rhetoric at a time when Kansas seemed to have run out of "outrages."[4]

The partisan benefits harvested from the Dred Scott decision by

Republican leaders tend to reinforce doubts about the substance of the Republican argument. In particular, few historians have been disposed to take seriously the Republican charge that the decision was part of a conspiracy aimed at legalizing slavery in every part of the union. The extravagant language frequently used in leveling the charge has further impaired its credibility. For example, William Cullen Bryant's New York *Evening Post* declared that the conspiracy was one of a "most treasonable character" that had already "changed the very blood of the constitution." The Chicago *Tribune* echoed the word "conspiracy" and, like many other Republican newspapers, envisoned frightful consequences. "Chicago," it said, "may become a slave market and . . . men, women and children may be sold off the block in our streets, in defiance of our local laws."[5]

The idea of a slave-power conspiracy to nationalize slavery had originated with abolitionists many years earlier. Gaining strength from the Dred Scott decision, it would be exploited by hundreds of Republican editors and speakers over a period of fifteen months before Abraham Lincoln, on a warm June evening in 1858, made it the central theme of his opening speech in the senatorial campaign. This "absurd bogey," as Allan Nevins has called it, aptly serves to exemplify the "paranoid style" in American politics.[6] Unless one defines "conspiracy" so loosely as to mean little more than "tendency," evidence of an antebellum conspiracy to legalize slavery throughout the United States is virtually nonexistent. There were no conferences held, no organizations formed, no plots laid for the achievement of such a purpose.* But the disposition to see conspiracy behind unpleasant trends and unwelcome events is so common, and the cry "conspiracy" so often proves effective as strategy, that a certain amount of paranoid style must probably be regarded as one of the normalities of American life.

Given the behavior of Pierce, Douglas, Buchanan, and Taney, it is scarcely surprising that some Republicans should have suspected or half-suspected a monstrous plot and that other Republicans should

*A different matter is disunion conspiracy, which in some degree did exist. Here, the principal question is whether secession can be explained primarily or even substantially in conspiratorial terms.

have seen the advantages of pretending to do so. Moreover, the absence of a conspiracy in no way discounts the presence of a conspicuous tendency. There was nothing paranoid in Republican perception
of a decade-long trend toward expansion of the domain of slavery; for
by 1857 the law of the land appeared to have fully incorporated the
doctrine of John C. Calhoun that only the sovereign power of a state
government could prohibit slavery or even lay restrictions upon it. Indeed, there were now serious doubts about the capacity of state sovereignty to override the property rights of a slaveholder as set forth in
Taney's Dred Scott opinion. "Can a Free State Constitution prevent
slavery?" asked the Indianapolis *State Journal.* "In other words, can a
slaveholder, defying our State Constitution, bring his slaves here in
Indiana and hold them?"[7]

The reply of many Republican leaders was that the Taney doctrine, carried to its logical conclusion, made slavery legal everywhere
throughout the country. "The Constitution of the United States is the
paramount law of every State," said Senator James R. Doolittle of
Wisconsin, "and if that recognizes slaves as property, as horses are
property, no State constitution or State law can abolish it, or prohibit
its introduction." Senator James Harlan of Iowa agreed. In the United
States, he declared, private property was an "original right," anterior
to constitutions and laws, commanding protection but immune to annihilation. "If it be true that the title to private property cannot be
violated without an act of tyranny practiced by the Government on its
people, and that the title to slave property must be placed and maintained on the same basis, then it becomes inviolable and can be maintained everywhere."[8] Lincoln later adopted precisely the same argument. Again and again throughout the campaign of 1858 he warned
that there would probably soon be a second Dred Scott decision
"declaring that the Constitution of the United States does not permit
a *state* to exclude slavery from its limits."[9]

It is easy enough to read the folly of this prediction from the fact
that it never materialized. Yet there is such a thing as a self-defeating
prophecy, and the failure of the prediction, as Richard H. Sewell has
suggested, may be "better explained by the rush of events and the
resistance of the Republican party than by judicial wisdom or res-

traint."[10] In other words, the very force of Republican opposition no doubt helped prevent the realization of Republican apprehensions, and the early onset of the Civil War probably closed off certain potential legal consequences of the Dred Scott decision before they had time to emerge. What needs to be considered especially is the possibility that subsequent judicial decisions would have chipped away at state control over slavery without actually destroying it. Court action might have guaranteed sojourning rights in free states, for instance, and laws providing for manumission of slaves held illegally in free states might have been invalidated, either as violations of the due-process clause or as invasions of vested property rights in general.

This is not mere speculation. On November 17, 1857, the Washington *Union* carried an article setting forth the argument that emancipation in the northern states had been an outrageous attack on property rights and that state laws prohibiting slavery were unconstitutional, particularly insofar as they exacted forfeiture of slave property. If it signifies nothing else, such a pronouncement, published in the official organ of the Buchanan administration, indicates the unsettling effect of the Dred Scott decision and the scope of proslavery implication that could be drawn from it.[11] The judicial power of the United States had been cast into the sectional balance on the side of slavery, and it seemed unlikely that the Supreme Court, having taken this decisive step, would refrain from further intervention when the opportunity presented itself. In 1859, the Chief Justice handed down the decision of a unanimous Court in the sensational case of *Ableman v. Booth*, upholding the constitutionality of the Fugitive Slave Law and overruling the defiance of federal authority by the supreme court of Wisconsin. Although Taney was on much more solid ground here than in the Dred Scott case, radical antislavery elements flew to the attack once again, filling the air with denunciations of "judicial tyranny."[12]

Republican hostility to the Supreme Court thus remained strong throughout the final years of the sectional crisis, and it was given sober expression in Lincoln's first inaugural. Yet, despite all the denunciation of the Court on the floor of Congress, as well as in newspapers, sermons, and political speeches, there was no significant effort to curb judicial power. In the 1820s, for instance, and again in the late 1860s, bills were introduced to limit the tenure of justices, to make them removable by Congress, to require more than a majority vote in certain kinds of cases, to narrow the scope of judicial review, and to provide for the review of Supreme Court decisions by some other body, such as the Senate or a special commission.[13] But Republicans in Congress sponsored no such measures during the period from 1857 to 1861. At this time of suffering so much abuse and loss of prestige, the Court was free of formal congressional attacks on its authority. The extent to which the Dred Scott decision undermined the Court as an institution has in fact been greatly exaggerated.[14] For all their outrage at the "judicial Vatican," as one senator called it, Republicans for the most part wanted to change only the membership and conduct of the Court, not its structure and functions. "We shall reorganize the court, and thus reform its political sentiments and practices," said William H. Seward in 1858. The means of doing so were simple and easy, he added—"namely, to take the government out of unjust and unfaithful hands, and commit it to those which will be just and faithful."[15]

In short, the Republican remedy for the Dred Scott decision was to win the election of 1860, change the personnel of the Court, and have the decision reversed. According to Lincoln, a Republican victory at the polls would be enough in itself to prevent further proslavery onslaughts by the existing Court. "It is my opinion," he said in the Galesburg debate, "that the Dred Scott decision, as it is, never would have been made in its present form if the party that made it had not been sustained previously by the elections. My own opinion is, that the new Dred Scott decision, deciding against the right of the people of the States to exclude slavery, will never be made, if that party is not sustained by the elections."[16]

When the great Republican triumph of 1860 followed so soon thereafter, it was only natural to look back on the decision of 1857 as one of the critical factors in the political revolution. No one could have been more emphatic about it than Charles Warren, historian of the Supreme Court. "It may fairly be said," he wrote, "that Chief Justice Taney elected Abraham Lincoln to the Presidency."[17] But what

Warren had in mind primarily was the effect of the Dred Scott decision, not upon the strength of Republicanism but rather upon the unity of the Democratic party.

II

At this point, we must begin to come to grips with one of the most familiar stories in American political history—how the Dred Scott decision and Lincoln's shrewd exploitation of it in the Freeport debate compelled Douglas to take a stand that alienated the South, disrupted the Democratic party, and thus cleared the way for a Republican victory in 1860. The supporting evidence seems at first glance to carry conviction. Taney's opinion, as we have seen, did declare that since Congress had no power to prohibit slavery in the territories, it could not authorize a territorial government to do so. This was dictum, of course, but it seemed a logical corollary to his major conclusion. Furthermore, Douglas, in an effort to salvage the principle of popular sovereignty, did undercut the Taney dictum with his own "Freeport doctrine," and southern Democrats did reject that doctrine so vehemently as to split their party along sectional lines.

But when the chronology of these developments is examined in detail, some curious discrepancies emerge to view. The Dred Scott decision did not at first split the Democrats but instead drew them closer together in defense of the Supreme Court against Republican censure. Northern Democrats had little difficulty accepting the whole of Taney's opinion, aside from his brief dictum on popular sovereignty. They strongly approved of his ruling against Negro citizenship, and, having long maintained that congressional regulation of slavery in the territories was bad policy, they now found it easy to acquiesce in the verdict that such regulation was also unconstitutional.[18] The Democrats, in short, did not, as a direct result of the Dred Scott decision, suffer the kind of acute internal disagreement over slavery which had racked their party in 1846–50 and in 1854, and which was about to do so again in 1858. To be sure, there remained a "difference of opinion," as James Buchanan had phrased it in his inaugural, about "the point of time" when a territorial government could establish or

prohibit slavery. Southerners insisted that Taney had settled the issue
in their favor, and the President agreed.[19] But for northern Democrats, acquiescence meant renouncing the Cass-Douglas version of
popular sovereignty in favor of Calhounism, and this would have
placed them at a serious disadvantage in their unremitting struggle
with the Republicans.

Douglas faced up to the problem in a major political address at
Springfield on June 12, 1857. The question was whether Taney's dictum had put an end to the evasive strategy of the Benjamin formula,
whereby northern and southern Democrats had allegedly agreed to
disagree about the power of territorial legislatures over slavery.*
Seeking to undercut Taney's dictum without expressly repudiating it,
Douglas in effect carried an appeal from the formalities of constitutional law to the ineluctable realities of American political life. Acknowledging that the right to take slaves into a territory was fully
guaranteed by the Constitution and could not be alienated by act of
Congress, he added:

> It necessarily remains a barren and a worthless right, unless sus-
> tained, protected and enforced by appropriate police regulations
> and local legislation, prescribing adequate remedies for its viola-
> tion. These regulations and remedies must necessarily depend en-
> tirely upon the will and wishes of the people of the Territory, as
> they can only be prescribed by the local Legislatures. Hence the
> great principle of popular sovereignty and self-government is sus-
> tained and firmly established by the authority of this decision.[20]

Here was the essence of the "Freeport doctrine" articulated more
than a year in advance of the Freeport debate. Perhaps better designated the principle of "residual popular sovereignty," it amounted to
little more than a special application of the truism that unpopular law
is difficult to enforce.[21] Douglas had used the argument in 1850 to
minimize the historical significance of the Northwest Ordinance.
More recently, it had been taken up by several southern congressmen who wanted to demonstrate that granting their section its consti-

* See above, pp. 199–201.

tutional rights did not mean forcing slavery on an unwilling people. Thus Lawrence O. Branch of North Carolina declared on December 18, 1856: "Every one knows that if the majority of the Legislature are opposed to slavery, there are a multitude of ways in which the slaveholder may be harassed and kept out by hostile legislation, and by a failure to provide remedies for the protection of his rights. Practically, the institution can only be introduced and sustained where the majority are willing to tolerate it." Similar statements were made at about the same time by Samuel A. Smith of Tennessee and James L. Orr of South Carolina, soon to become Speaker of the House.[22]

Douglas, however, had discreetly avoided such argument during the campaign year 1856, asserting repeatedly instead that the extent of territorial power over slavery must be left to judicial determination. Thus he virtually pledged to accept a Supreme Court decision on the constitutionality of his "great principle," and in resorting to the doctrine of residual popular sovereignty at Springfield, he appeared to be reneging on that pledge. One therefore might expect to find the Springfield speech bitterly attacked in the southern press, but, on the contrary, it was generally praised. The Washington *Union*, which would lead the attack on the Freeport doctrine in 1858, said that the speech came from "one of the most powerful and original minds of the country," and that it deserved unqualified commendation for its "lucid statements, vigorous thoughts, and powerful arguments."[23]

In 1857, then, the Dred Scott decision did not cause any kind of crisis within the Democratic party, and Douglas, echoing the recent remarks of several southern congressmen, enunciated the principle of residual popular sovereignty without incurring southern censure. Yet, in 1858, Douglas came under fierce southern attack for saying virtually the same thing he had said at Springfield in 1857. And by 1859, southern insistence upon full acknowledgment of slaveholding rights under the Dred Scott decision was widening an already dangerous breach in the Democratic party. Clearly, the Dred Scott decision by itself did not have a convulsive effect on sectional politics, but it became one of the elements in an explosive compound. More particularly, in order to understand how the decision contributed to the disruption of the Union, one must study the complexities of its relationship to a new crisis arising in Congress over the Lecompton constitution for Kansas.

III

The struggle for Kansas entered a new phase in February 1857 when the proslavery territorial legislature, convinced that there was no hope of an enabling act from Congress, initiated a statehood movement of its own. Over the veto of Governor Geary, it passed legislation providing for a census in March, an election of delegates in June, and a constitutional convention to meet in September. The free-state forces, now a majority of the population by a wide margin, decided to boycott the election, predicting with good reason that the census-taking would be grossly unfair. Their stubbornness played into the hands of the proslavery faction, which readily undertook to exploit the last advantage it would ever have in Kansas.[24]

Meanwhile, Buchanan had entered the presidency and appointed Robert J. Walker to succeed Geary as governor of Kansas. Walker was a Pennsylvanian who had moved to Mississippi as a young man and become a slaveholder, land speculator, railroad promoter, United States senator, and secretary of the treasury in the Polk administration.[25] In his view, Kansas was bound to be a free state, and only if the Democrats accepted that fact could it be saved from Republicanism.* Ostensibly with Buchanan's full support, he set out with the intention of guaranteeing honest elections in Kansas, inducing the free-staters to participate in the regular electoral process, and making sure that the constitution to be drafted by the forthcoming convention was submitted to a popular vote.

Walker arrived in Kansas at the end of May and promptly began courting the good will of free-state leaders. In his "inaugural address" and other public statements, he declared that Kansas was climatically unsuited for slavery and predicted that a constitution not submitted to the people would probably be rejected by Congress.[27] The free-

---

*Walker estimated that the Democrats outnumbered the Republicans in Kansas two to one, but he thought that more than half of them were free-staters.[26]

staters were difficult to convince, however. They persisted in their
resolve to stay away from the polls on June 15, and a constitutional
convention of strictly proslavery sentiment was elected as a consequence.

Walker's pronouncements circulated quickly to all parts of the
country and fell harshly on the ears of many southerners. Perhaps
even more offensive than the words he had uttered were the reports
of his fraternizing with Jim Lane, Charles Robinson, and other radical
antislavery men who for several years had been openly defying federal authority in Kansas. By midsummer, Walker was the target of a
fierce southern attack that frequently extended to Buchanan himself.
At first some Democratic newspapers were disposed to defend the administration and give Walker the benefit of the doubt. But opposition
editors, now often trying to outdo the Democrats in devotion to
southern rights, seized the opportunity to associate their political
rivals with sectional appeasement and the surrender of Kansas to abolitionism. Thus the Mobile *Advertiser*, a leading organ of the American party in Alabama, seemed primarily interested in embarrassing its
Democratic competitor, the Mobile *Register*, by demonstrating that
Walker's policies were those of the administration and the Democratic party. Southerners, it declared, had been "cheated and sacri-
fied by the men whom they placed in power." Buchanan, who never
should have been trusted, was now revealing his free-soil proclivities,
and southern Democrats must soon choose between duty to party and
duty to the South.[28] Similarly, the Charleston *Courier*, which claimed
to be neutral in politics, denounced Walker as a "political Judas" who
was violating the principle of nonintervention and endorsing the
"odious principle of squatter sovereignty" in his insistence upon submission of the forthcoming constitution to the voters of Kansas. "The
victory was ours," said the *Courier*, "and, in the very moment of frui-
tion, Gov. Walker has wrested it from our grasp, by false doctrine
and heresy, mean truckling to rebels . . . and insolent threats of
Congressional and Executive interference, in the very teeth of the
principle of the Kansas-Nebraska act."[29]

Southern Democrats, and especially those in the Deep South,
were no less angered by Walker's behavior. Judge Thomas W.

Thomas of Georgia expressed the feelings of many when he wrote to Alexander H. Stephens: "I have just read Walker's inaugural in Kansas and if the document I have seen is genuine it is clear Buchanan has turned traitor. . . . It stands there and glares upon us. *We are betrayed.* . . . Our victory is turned to ashes on our lips, and before God I will never say well done to the traitor or to his master who lives in the White House."[30] The temper of local southern Democratic leaders like Thomas was not improved by the knowledge that the Americans intended to exploit the Walker issue in approaching state elections. Almost overnight, the new governor of Kansas had become political poison in the South. Stephens, Robert Toombs, Jefferson Davis, Robert M. T. Hunter, and many other high-ranking southern Democrats hastened to dissociate themselves from him. State conventions of the party in Georgia and Mississippi passed resolutions vehemently condemning him and demanding his recall. "The southern Democracy cannot and will not carry Gov. Walker on their backs," one editor declared.[31]

At the same time, many Democratic editors and politicians refrained from public attacks on the President, hoping that he could be persuaded or coerced into disavowing Walker's conduct. In the early weeks of the controversy, however, it appeared that Buchanan would stand firm against such southern pressure. The Washington *Union* stoutly defended Walker and condemned the Georgia and Mississippi resolutions as secessionist in spirit.[32] Buchanan himself, while making no public statements on the subject, assured Walker in July: "On the question of submitting the constitution to the *bona fide* resident settlers of Kansas, I am willing to stand or fall."[33] Senator Toombs, watching developments from his home in Georgia, had no doubt that the President intended to sustain Walker "and thereby ruin himself and his administration."[34] His apprehensions were shared by many other southern Democrats, and Buchanan did not dispel them until late in the year. In November, the Mobile *Advertiser* would still be insisting that Walker had full presidential support and that the South had been "cheated—swindled—outraged."[35]

Because of what happened later, it is often forgotten that in the summer of 1857, Douglas still commanded much respect in the

South, while Buchanan had become an object of suspicion and animosity. Douglas's speech at Springfield on June 12 came at a strategic time—some two weeks after Walker's inflammatory inaugural and just three days before the election in Kansas. His brief remarks on the subject amounted to a rose-colored endorsement of the arrangements for the election and a dismissal of free-state complaints about the unfairness of the apportionment of delegates. For southerners, this was a welcome contrast to the pronouncements of Walker. It no doubt helps explain why there were no strong southern objections to Douglas's accompanying statements about the Dred Scott decision. Buchanan, in his inaugural, had embraced the southern version of popular sovereignty, while Douglas was still trying to salvage *his* version in the face of the Dred Scott decision. The President, in short, was sounder, from the southern point of view, in his attitude toward *Dred Scott*, but Douglas appeared to be sounder on Kansas. That the latter counted for much more seems obvious from southern behavior in the summer of 1857.[36]

The constitutional convention, packed with proslavery men, assembled in early September at Lecompton, the territorial capital, but the delegates quickly decided to adjourn until after the legislative election in October. They were unwilling to proceed without knowing the results of that contest, which promised to mark a new departure in Kansas politics; for Walker had at last persuaded the free-state element to participate in the voting. The election returns first indicated a proslavery victory, but Walker threw out a large number of fraudulent votes in two counties, giving the free-state forces control of the territorial legislature. Southerners were furious when they learned of his action. Kansas, which for several years had been governed by a legal but unrepresentative proslavery legislature and an extralegal antislavery legislature, now had a legally elected proslavery constitutional convention and a legally elected antislavery legislature.[37]

The convention reassembled on October 19 and drafted a proslavery constitution, although the delegates knew from the results of the recent election that it would surely be defeated in a popular vote. Accordingly, they first decided to send the document directly to Washington, without allowing a referendum of any kind. Such a move would have been too brazen to win much support except from the more militant southerners, and so the outcome, paradoxically, might well have been a speedy rejection, by President and Congress, of this last proslavery effort in Kansas, and thus a defusing of the entire issue. Unfortunately, however, the moderate wing of the convention succeeded in putting through a compromise that was less straightforward and proved to be far more dangerous.

The tone of the constitution was set in the first section of an article devoted entirely to slavery. Probably reflecting the influence of the Dred Scott decision, it proclaimed: "The right of property is before and higher than any constitutional sanction, and the right of the owner of a slave to such slave and its increase is the same and as inviolable as the right of the owner of any property whatever." Here, embedded in a prospective state constitution was the proslavery version of the "higher law" doctrine.[38] Other sections of the article spelled out in some detail the establishment of slavery in Kansas. The compromise adopted by the convention lay, not in the body of the constitution, but rather in an accompanying provision for a limited referendum on December 21. Voters were offered a choice between the "Constitution with slavery" and the "Constitution without slavery," but the decision could affect only the further introduction of slaves into Kansas. Thus "without slavery" actually meant *with* slavery to some extent. About two hundred slaves already held within the territory would continue in bondage, and so too would any children born to them. More important, the fundamental law of Kansas would be that of a slave state, and it could not be amended for seven years.[39] Furthermore, the convention denied Governor Walker any role in the statemaking process, placing administration of the referendum completely under the control of its own presiding officer, an Illinois politician named John Calhoun. This arrangement strengthened the conviction of free-staters that the Lecompton movement was a fraud from beginning to end, and they accordingly determined to boycott the election. It appeared that the constitution "with slavery" would triumph by default.

IV

By mid-November, a week after the convention finished its work, the substance of the Lecompton constitution was known throughout much of the country, and the outlines of another fierce sectional controversy had begun to emerge. Many northern Democrats joined the Republicans in condemning the "Lecompton swindle," while southerners, though not without considerable doubt and some open dissent, showed a strong disposition to close ranks in militant support of the document. Up to this point, Walker still did not know where he stood with the administration, but recent rumors from the East were not encouraging. He therefore set out for Washington to clarify his status and argue against acceptance of the constitution. En route, he conferred with Douglas in Chicago and found him sympathetic, but by then it was already clear that the President would not heed his advice. Buchanan, after wavering for nearly half a year, had come down firmly on the southern side. In what may have been the most important single presidential decision of the 1850s, he resolved to support the Lecompton constitution.

The Lecompton controversy, being the last sectional crisis to end in compromise, could be said to mark the close of the antebellum era in national politics. Today, one has difficulty understanding the intensity of feeling manifested during the struggle; for nothing truly crucial appears to have been at stake, and the whole affair in fact seems infused with a certain madness. Kansas, whatever the manner and terms of her admission, was plainly destined to be a free state. The patterns of migration had settled the matter. "I regard this battle as already fought; it is over," said William H. Seward on the floor of the Senate in February 1858, and most southerners knew that he was right. Yet the Lecompton issue aroused Republicans to a new pitch of anger and apprehension, inspired a renewal of the secession movement in the South, and caused a disastrous split in the Democratic party. One explanation frequently offered is that too many men, North and South, had by 1857 "entered the sphere of hysteric emotions," with each section fearfully imputing aggressive designs to the other, so that "every proposal became a plot and every act a menace."[40] Yet there is little basis for belief that the decision-makers were more irrational in 1857–58 than at other times of crisis in history. More often than not, their actions sprang from calculation rather than impulse. The irrationality was in the historical circumstances for which they were only partly responsible. The madness lay in two centuries of rationalizing slavery.

The South, while realizing that any victory for slavery in Kansas would be temporary, was nevertheless anxious to test whether a slave state could ever again be admitted to the Union, now that an antislavery party had become predominant in the North. There had been no such admission, after all, since the introduction of the Wilmot Proviso. This test, it should be remembered, came right on the heels of another one that had greatly aggravated the southern sense of insecurity—namely, Republican reaction to the Dred Scott decision. The South's apparently foolish advocacy of the Lecompton constitution was simply another chapter in its perpetual quest for reassurance.

Republicans, at the same time, were not about to settle for assurances that Kansas was bound to end up as a free state; for why should slavery, even on a token and temporary basis, be installed among a population overwhelmingly opposed to it? Besides, with the proslavery faction controlling the constitutional referendum and the election of the first state legislature, there was no telling how long the will of the majority would be thwarted by election frauds. Kansas, admitted under the Lecompton constitution, seemed likely to become once again the scene of civil war. Furthermore, to Republicans, the "Lecompton fraud" was no isolated outrage but part of an ominous pattern. Indeed, it looked very much like the first major step along the route marked out by Taney in the Dred Scott decision. Slavery, having been forced into the territories, would now be forced upon a new state and eventually upon all the old ones.

Between southerners and Republicans stood the northern Democrats, pulled in different directions by party loyalty and sectional feeling. Having dutifully accepted and defended the Dred Scott decision, they could not at the moment carry much more proslavery weight. It seems incredible that Buchanan did not realize how much damage he would cause in the northern wing of his party by sponsoring the Lecompton constitution. This blindness, according to one biographer, is simply explained. "He was a legalist. He based his decision on the legality of the Kansas document." More convincing, perhaps, is the evidence that Buchanan gave in to southern pressure, partly out of sympathy and partly out of fear.[41] But in addition, it appears that the President chose to take a calculated risk, tempted by the apparent opportunity to remove forever from national politics the dangerous problem of Kansas. "When once admitted into the Union, whether with or without slavery," he said, "the excitement beyond her own limits will speedily pass away."[42] In a sense, he succeeded, even though the Lecompton constitution failed; for Kansas did cease to be a dangerous public issue after the spring of 1858. The price of that success proved to be high, however, and the subsidence of the Kansas problem only cleared the way for a venomous intraparty quarrel over the meaning of the Dred Scott decision.

The most conspicuously anomalous behavior was that of Douglas in breaking with the administration and leading the revolt of anti-Lecompton Democrats. The Little Giant had long since come to be regarded as one of the managers of American politics—pragmatic and flexible, an architect of compromise and always a loyal party man. Now, suddenly, he appeared as a party insurgent and a doctrinaire, taking an inflexible stand on principle and in the end rejecting a compromise that satisfied even many of his fellow insurgents. Actually, he had grown more doctrinaire over a period of several years, yielding, as we have seen, to the fashion of constitutionalizing debate on slavery in the territories. Popular sovereignty, embraced originally as an expedient, had truly become his "great principle." Earlier in the year, the principle had been cast under a legal cloud by the Dred Scott decision, and now, he believed, it was being reduced to travesty in the Lecompton constitution.

Still, popular sovereignty in Kansas had been a mockery for the preceding three years, and Douglas had always put the blame primarily on the free-state forces while brushing aside charges that the established territorial government was founded on fraud. In his Springfield speech of June 12, 1857, he praised the call for a convention and said that if the free-staters refused to vote in the impending election, they and the national Republican party would be fully responsible for turning Kansas into a slave state. But just six months later, he came down emphatically on the free-state side and denied that the Lecompton convention had any legal status, except as a gathering of private citizens petitioning their government.[43] The change was sharp and sudden enough to be generally astonishing, and for a time it caused as much confusion in Republican ranks as it did among Democrats. No single event contributed more to the southern sense of alienation. "This defection of Douglas," wrote a South Carolinian, "has done more than all else to shake my confidence in Northern men on the slavery issue, for I have long regarded him as one of our safest and most reliable friends." A correpondent of the Charleston *Mercury* put it more succinctly: "If he proved false, whom can you trust?"[44] From this point on, the principal sectional issue within the Democratic party would be Douglas himself.

Relations between Buchanan and Douglas were already chilly in the fall of 1857 because the latter believed that he had been badly treated in the distribution of federal patronage.[45] The predominant influence on Douglas, however, appears to have been the surge of anti-Lecompton sentiment in Illinois and the knowledge that his seat in the Senate would be at stake in the legislative election of 1858. A defeat in that contest might well ruin his presidential chances in 1860, and the outlook was far from encouraging. The Republicans had captured the governorship in 1856 and now expected to reap additional gains from the new Kansas controversy. Illinois Democrats desperately needed to dissociate themselves from southern ultraism and, if possible, even steal some antislavery thunder from the Republicans. Douglas dramatically provided the means of doing so. His anti-Lecompton heroics, which to Buchanan and many southerners seemed unreasonable and disloyal, were a response to stark political necessity in Illinois. "You have adopted the only course that could save the Northern Democracy from annihilation at the next election," wrote one of his correspondents. "Had you gone the other way," said a second, "the Dem[ocratic] party in this State would have been routed horse, foot and dragoon. As it is, we can sustain ourselves as a party before the people." Douglas's strategy, according to a third, would have the effect of "*killing dead* the leaders of the abolition free soil party."[46] Viewed from Illinois, the anti-Lecompton revolt was not so much anti-southern as anti-Republican.

The critical decisions were made in late November 1857, shortly before the convening of the thirty-fifth Congress, and at a time when the nation was feeling the full effect of a sharp financial panic that had begun several months earlier. On November 17, a day or two after the content of the Lecompton constitution became known in the East, the Washington *Union* carried its bizarre article attacking emancipation in the northern states as a violation of property rights. Then, significantly just twenty-four hours later, the *Union* published an editorial praising the Lecompton constitution. It had been written by Attorney General Jeremiah S. Black and approved by Buchanan.[47] Walker arrived in Washington on November 25 and found the President deaf to all anti-Lecompton argument. Douglas, who had made up his mind soon after talking with Walker in Chicago, was no more successful in a conference at the White House on December 3. Confronting each other in an atmosphere of icy courtesy, he and Buchanan reached a historic parting of the ways. The latter's first annual message to Congress on December 8 included an outright endorsement of the work of the Lecompton convention, together with a casuistic explanation of how this endorsement could be squared with his earlier insistence that the constitution must be submitted to the people. Douglas announced his opposition that same day and the next afternoon threw down the gage to the administration in a speech that was "probably the most significant of his career."[48]

It was a hasty commencement of hostilities, one that made Douglas seem almost eager to quarrel with the President and the South. Speaking with characteristic vigor and aggressiveness, he denied the legitimacy of the Lecompton convention, labeled the referendum "a system of trickery and jugglery," declared that the free-staters had a right to abstain from voting if they wanted to, and virtually accused the administration of proposing to "force this constitution down the throats of the people of Kansas, in opposition to their wishes and in violation of our pledges." When he finished, there was a burst of applause, starting on the Republican side of the chamber and spreading to the crowded galleries.[49] Angrily, James Mason of Virginia demanded that the galleries be cleared. The tone of the ensuing struggle had thus been set. For southerners, the greatest offense of Douglas, like that of Walker before him, consisted not so much in disagreeing with Democrats as in pleasing Republicans by doing their work for them. "With indecent haste," a Mississippi editor later wrote, "Douglas placed himself at the head of the Black column and gave the word of command." Thereby, he became "stained with the dishonor of treachery without a parallel in the political history of the country."[50]

Douglas's anti-Lecompton revolt proved to be the crucial event that set the Democratic party on the path to disruption, but major changes of public opinion are never instantaneous or total. Not all southerners turned against the Illinois senator; many northern Democrats remained loyal to Buchanan; and the Republicans were for a time divided over how to deal with him. Everywhere there was much uncertainty about where his bold venture would lead.

Of course, when Douglas first spoke out on December 9, the Lecompton constitution was still out west in the hands of the convention president, awaiting results of the slavery-or-no-slavery referendum on December 21. Thus Buchanan had not yet made a formal recommendation, and Congress did not yet have a formal proposal to consider. Nevertheless, for almost two months both houses engaged prematurely in extensive and often rancorous debate on the subject.[51] Meanwhile, new complications were arising in Kansas, and they tended to increase the bitterness of the struggle.

Frederick P. Stanton, the territorial secretary of Kansas, who had become acting governor upon Walker's departure in mid-November, fully shared the latter's disapproval of the Lecompton constitution. Daringly, he called into special session the newly elected territorial legislature, which had a free-state majority because of Walker's intervention. On December 8, the day that Congress received Buchanan's annual message, Stanton sent a message of his own to the Kansas legislature recommending that it pass a law submitting the entire constitution to the voters. The legislature hastened to comply and set January 4 as the date of the referendum. Buchanan promptly dismissed Stanton for thus undercutting the administration but could not undo the deed. Both elections took place as scheduled, and the outcome in each instance was predictable. On December 21, as the free-staters persisted in their refusal to participate, 6226 votes were cast for the constitution *with* slavery (nearly half of them apparently fraudulent), and 569 for the constitution *without* slavery. On January 4, with the proslavery element now abstaining, there were 10,226 votes against the constitution as a whole, 138 for the constitution with slavery, and 24 for the constitution without slavery.[52]

What the majority of Kansans wanted was as a consequence made unmistakably clear, and Buchanan had been given one last chance to avoid the egregious blunder of hitching his presidential career to the Lecompton constitution. Instead, he transmitted that dubious document to Congress on February 2, 1858, with a special message recommending admission of Kansas as the sixteenth slaveholding state. Kansas at that moment, he declared, was already "as much a slave State as Georgia or South Carolina." Insisting that the Lecompton movement had been scrupulously legal from beginning to end, that submission of the slavery question was all he had ever meant to require, that the free-state faction was "in a state of rebellion against the government," and that the referendum of January 4 had no legal force, he promised "domestic peace" if the constitution were accepted and predicted that "disasters" might follow its rejection.

The President also argued that if the territorial majority really wanted to abolish slavery, they could do so most swiftly by securing prompt admission to statehood and then amending their constitution.* "To the people of Kansas," he asserted, "the only practical difference between admission or rejection depends simply upon the fact whether they can themselves more speedily change the present constitution . . . or frame a second constitution to be submitted to Congress hereafter. . . . the small difference of time one way or the other is of not the least importance when contrasted with the evils

---

*Buchanan maintained that the clause prohibiting amendment before 1864 was unenforceable.

which must necessarily result to the whole country from a revival of the slavery agitation."

Yet if the choice made so little difference to the future of Kansas, why did it make so much difference to Buchanan? Why was he determined to have his own way, whatever the cost? For one thing, he believed that he was defending law and order against virtual insurrection. But he also offered another explanation that revealed his sympathetic understanding of the psychology of southern militancy. "In considering this question," he said, "it should never be forgotten that in proportion to its insignificance . . . the rejection of the constitution will be so much the more keenly felt by the people of . . . the States of this Union, where slavery is recognized."[53] Thus, paradoxically, the very futility of the proslavery cause in Kansas made northern acceptance of the Lecompton constitution all the more important in the eyes of many southerners. For if the South had nothing material to gain from the admission of Kansas, then the Lecompton question became a meaningful test of how *little* could be expected from the North in the way of concessions. As a South Carolinian remarked, it would have been "dirt cheap" for the free states to yield.[54] Denying the South an admittedly empty victory seemed doubly hostile.

V

The thirty-fifth Congress was safely Democratic and under firm southern control. In the Senate, there were 37 Democrats, 20 Republicans, and 5 Native Americans (all southerners); in the House of Representatives, there were 128 Democrats, 92 Republicans, and 14 Native Americans (all southerners). Within the Democratic party, southerners outnumbered northerners 25 to 12 in the Senate, and 75 to 53 in the House. The South controlled the Democratic caucuses and thus the organization of Congress. In both houses, the presiding officers and most of the important committee chairmen were southerners. In the Senate, southern majorities dominated many of the principal committees. Republicans complained bitterly about the "sectional character" of committee organization, but to no avail. "The fact now stands clearly revealed to the gaze of mankind," said Henry

Wilson of Massachusetts, "that the present Democratic party, and the proslavery party of this country are the same."[55]

One of the exceptions to general southern dominance was that Douglas retained the chairmanship of the Senate committee on territories. This proved to be awkward for the administration, but not a serious impediment. Pro-Lecompton Democrats still had a four-to-three majority on the committee, and it soon became evident that in the Senate as a whole, only two or three Democrats would join the Douglas revolt. The House was a different matter. There, more than twenty northern Democrats, together with a handful of southern Americans, aligned themselves with the Republicans to form a narrow anti-Lecompton majority. In an important test vote on February 8, for example, the administration forces, led by Alexander H. Stephens, were outvoted, 114 to 111.[56]

The closeness of the contest in the House had an important effect on the course of events, for it encouraged administration leaders to believe that with extra effort they could drive the Lecompton constitution through Congress. Buchanan undertook to check the rebellion within his party by ruthless use of federal patronage, removing many postmasters and other appointees who persisted in their support of Douglas. These tactics greatly increased the rancor of the struggle. Thomas L. Harris of Illinois, leader of the anti-Lecompton Democrats in the House, thought that there was more "sullen hostility and bitterness" than he had ever seen before, even in 1850. "I assure you," he wrote to a political associate, "nothing avails here now but *submission to administration on southern dictation. A life of devotion to equal rights in every section . . . is nothing. We must vote to admit Kansas under the Lecompton Constitution, or we are Black Republicans, renegades, demagogues and all that.*"[57] These were words that might have been written by Douglas, who became increasingly convinced that the chief aim of the administration was his political destruction by orders coming out of the South. He emerged from the Lecompton controversy deeply resentful of the southern Democratic leadership, which sought to expel him from the party for one act of dissent in a long record of strenuous efforts to accommodate the South.[58]

The long and tedious congressional debate on the Lecompton question ranged over the whole turbulent history of territorial Kansas and recapitulated all the earlier phases of the slavery controversy, but it concentrated especially upon the technicalities of statemaking, which Congress had never seen fit to regularize. There were extended arguments, for example, on whether the Kansas-Nebraska Act had been in itself an enabling act; whether, in the absence of an enabling act, a constitution could be legitimized only by submission to the people; whether admission without submission would violate the principle of popular sovereignty; whether Kansas, since the completion of the Lecompton constitution, was still a territory or already an incipient state. The Dred Scott decision, though not directly relevant to the issue at hand, was obviously much on men's minds and came often into the debates on Kansas. In fact, Republicans frequently seized any opportunity to attack the decision, no matter what subject might be under discussion. Thus Hannibal Hamlin of Maine, in condemning southern domination of senatorial committees, associated it with judicial subservience to the slave power as exemplified in the Supreme Court's recent effort "to decide political questions . . . on an issue not before them." And perhaps the most savage denunciation of the decision to be heard on the floor of the House was delivered with complete irrelevance by Philemon Bliss of Ohio during a debate on filibustering in Nicaragua.[59]

In January, Senator John P. Hale of New Hampshire, who for years had been the harshest congressional critic of the Supreme Court, delivered a set speech lasting at least four hours and extending over two days, the first half of which dealt with the Lecompton constitution and the second half, with the Dred Scott decision. In his closing sentences, Hale explicitly connected the two. "Sir," he said, "you are now proposing to carry out this Dred Scott decision by forcing upon the people of Kansas a constitution against which they have remonstrated, and to which, there can be no shadow of doubt, a very large portion of them are opposed. . . . If you persevere in that attempt—I think, I hope the men of Kansas will fight. I hope they will resist to blood and to death."[60]

Several Republicans, including Senator James Harlan of Iowa

and Representative John A. Bingham of Ohio, pointed out the ideological connection between Taney's pronouncements on slaves as
property and the Lecompton passage declaring that property rights in
slaves were "before and higher than any constitutional sanction." To
accept the Lecompton constitution, said Bingham, would accordingly
mean affirming that "atrocious provision" and placing the stamp of
congressional approval on "the wild and guilty fantasy of property in
man."[61] Other Republicans in the course of speeches on Kansas took
time to challenge the legitimacy of the decision. One of these men
was the putative recent owner of Dred Scott, Calvin C. Chaffee of
Massachusetts, who simply denied that the Supreme Court had decided the question of slavery in the territories. "The *dictum* of the
Court is a very different affair from a *decision*," he asserted.[62] Still
others, including William P. Fessenden of Maine and Benjamin F.
Wade of Ohio, attacked the principle of judicial supremacy, denying
that the Supreme Court was the exclusive, final arbiter of constitutional questions. "No, sir," said Wade, "each department must act for
itself. I stand here, clothed with the same power, to proclaim what is
the Constitution upon the passage of any law that comes before us, as
that or any other court. . . . I beg of the Senate never to yield to this
arbitrary doctrine that the Supreme Court can bind the other departments of the Government."[63]

But the most sensational attack on the Supreme Court consisted
of several paragraphs in "an elaborate and picturesque but venomous"
anti-Lecompton speech delivered by William H. Seward on March
3.[64] The Dred Scott decision, Seward charged, had been manufactured by the Court at the instigation of the President, both forgetting
"that judicial usurpation is more odious and intolerable than any other
among the manifold practices of tyranny." The "whisperings" between Buchanan and Taney at the inauguration ceremony thus confirmed an agreement already reached to hang "the millstone of slavery" on the people of Kansas. The next day, "without even
exchanging their silken robes for courtiers' gowns," Seward continued, "the President received them as graciously as Charles I did
the judges who had, at his instance, subverted the statutes of English
liberty." Then, on the following day, the Court rendered its decision,

and the President, "having organized this formidable judicial battery at the Capitol," was now ready to begin the work of subduing Kansas through the "fraudulent" agency of the Lecompton convention.[65] Evidence not made public until much later lends some support, as we have seen, to Seward's charge of collusion between Buchanan and the Court,* but much of what he said was untrue or at least grossly inaccurate. To southerners, the speech, like that of Charles Sumner two years earlier, seemed doubly offensive because it had been prepared so carefully and was in fact put into print before being delivered. Reverdy Johnson, counsel in the case and a personal friend of the Chief Justice, promptly denounced the "mad and reckless" oratory of the New York senator, who, he said, had subjected the Supreme Court to "as calumnious an attack as ever dishonored human lips." Taney himself appears to have resented the speech deeply. He later told his official biographer that if Seward had been elected president in 1860, he, Taney, would have refused to administer the oath of office.[66]

Certainly this was one of the principal speeches contributing to Seward's reputation as a radical Republican. It was neither interrupted during delivery nor commented upon afterward. Southern senators listened in angry silence. "It was difficult, extremely difficult," said one of them later, "for us all to sit here and hear what was said, and observe the manner in which it was said, and repress the utterance of the indignation that boiled up within us."[67] Southerners did sometimes reply to attacks on the Supreme Court, and upon occasion they appealed to the Dred Scott decision as authority. For example, in defending the clause of the Lecompton constitution guaranteeing rights to slaves already held in Kansas, John A. Gilmer of North Carolina cited the decision as proof that new states had no right to confiscate slaves imported during the territorial period. This was an interesting but apparently unnoticed confirmation of the Republican argument that the Dred Scott decision by implication intruded on state sovereignty.[68]

The principal southern response came, however, from Judah P.

---

* See above, pp. 307, 311–14.

Benjamin of Louisiana, who spoke for several hours on March 11 in defense of Taney, the Court, and the Dred Scott decision. Taking issue especially with arguments of Fessenden and Collamer, he devoted about two-thirds of his speech to the main theoretical issue arising out of Taney's controversial opinion—that is, whether slavery in Anglo-American law was the rule or the exception, whether nothing but the positive law of a sovereign state could establish the institution (as Republicans insisted) or whether nothing but the positive law of a sovereign state could prohibit the institution (as many southerners now maintained). Thus, in the midst of debate on the Lecompton constitution, Benjamin's senatorial audience heard once again about the Royal African Company and the participation of the British crown in the slave trade; about the Asiento of 1713; about the famous *Somerset* case (in which Lord Mansfield, said Benjamin, yielded to the "spirit of fanaticism" and "subverted the common law of England by judicial legislation"); about the decision in the case of *The Slave Grace* by Lord Stowell ("a judge of resplendent genius" with "an intellect greater than Mansfield's"); about Justice Story's endorsement of the Stowell decision; about the clauses in the federal Constitution recognizing the right of property in slaves; and about the reaffirmation of that right by the Supreme Court in *Prigg v. Pennsylvania.*

Everywhere in the United States, according to Benjamin, slaves were property under common law and by virtue of the Constitution. A master taking a slave into a free state did not forfeit *title* to his property; he merely placed himself in a position of having no *"remedy* or *process* for the assertion of his title." This meant in effect that the law of a state liberating slaves brought illegally within its boundaries had no legal effect outside its boundaries. But Benjamin went further and declared that such liberation, like a refusal to protect patents and copyrights, constituted a violation of the "principles of eternal justice." Benjamin's speech, like the notorious Washington *Union* editorial of November 17, 1857, reveals certain proslavery potentialities of the Dred Scott decision which, because of the intervention of the Civil War, were never fully explored.[69]

VI

Those members of Congress who, as a group, said the least about the Dred Scott case were the northern Democrats, for whom it had been an embarrassment from the beginning. Douglas in particular displayed remarkable prudence whenever the subject arose, having apparently determined not to give the administration additional reason for charging him with apostasy. During debate on the Lecompton constitution in early February, Lyman Trumbull posed virtually the same question that Lincoln would ask at Freeport—namely, what remained of popular sovereignty in the wake of the Dred Scott decision? "Even those," he said, "who contended for this right of the people of a Territory to regulate the subject of slavery, have abandoned it, and now indorse the monstrous doctrine put forth by the Supreme Court, establishing slavery in all the Territories." Douglas made no denial but instead announced his unwillingness to discuss the matter at that time.[70]

A few days later, Fessenden returned to the question of the relationship between the Kansas-Nebraska Act and the Dred Scott decision. This time Douglas responded, but in such a way as to accommodate the southern version of popular sovereignty. "Was it necessary," Fessenden demanded, "to repeal the Missouri compromise in order to give the people of the Territory of Kansas a right to prohibit or establish slavery *by their State constitution* as they saw fit?" Yes, Douglas replied, because the word "forever" in the 36° 30' restriction seemed to "apply to a State as well as a Territory." In any case, he argued, the Kansas-Nebraska Act had repealed a statute later declared unconstitutional, and was that not a wise thing to do? As for the status of *territorial* power over slavery, Douglas retreated to the explanation that had proved so serviceable in 1856. The Kansas-Nebraska Act, he said, "conferred all the power which it was possible . . . to give to the people of a Territory under the Constitution of the United States on the subject of slavery."[71]

During the discussion, Benjamin also chimed in with *his* familiar explanation that northern and southern Democrats had agreed to disagree about territorial power over slavery, leaving the issue to the

Supreme Court. But of course there had been an important change since the articulation of this formula of evasion in 1856, for the Court had spoken on the subject. The issue, Benjamin went on to declare, had "been decided, in the Dred Scott case, in conformity with the views then entertained by gentlemen from the South." This amounted to saying that the Cass-Douglas version of popular sovereignty was now officially unconstitutional, and yet Douglas, significantly, entered no dissent to Benjamin's assertion. In fact, never once throughout the session of Congress did he reiterate the principle of residual popular sovereignty that had figured so prominently in his Springfield speech of June 12, 1857. In short, he avoided every opportunity in Congress to set forth the Freeport doctrine, reserving it, apparently, for use among his constituents in Illinois.

So Douglas, while cooperating with the Republicans in the fight against the Lecompton constitution, carefully dissociated himself from their attacks on the Dred Scott decision. But in his final anti-Lecompton speech on March 22, discretion gave way to anger at efforts to read him out of the Democratic party. He struck back at the administration by denouncing the November 17 editorial of the Washington *Union*, which he labeled "authoritative," and by linking it with the clause in the Lecompton constitution that placed property in slaves alongside other fundamental natural rights. Together, he said, they constituted a "fatal blow . . . at the sovereignty of the States of this Union." Then, in a remarkable anticipation of Lincoln's principal argument in the House-Divided speech, he continued:

> This attempt now to establish the doctrine that a free State has no power to prohibit slavery, that our emancipation acts were unconstitutional and void, that they were outrages on the rights of property, that slavery is national and not local, that it goes everywhere under the Constitution of the United States, and yet is higher than the Constitution . . . will not be tolerated.[72]

Douglas later insisted that he had attributed the doctrine only to the *Union* and not to Buchanan, but his use of the word "authoritative" indicated that he was talking about the whole pro-southern administration establishment that had marked him for political destruction.[73]

And without making any reference to the Dred Scott decision, he had come close to endorsing the Republican thesis of a conspiracy to nationalize slavery.

The next day, March 23, the Senate took final action on the proposal to admit Kansas with the Lecompton constitution. John J. Crittenden of Kentucky offered a substitute measure requiring that the constitution first be resubmitted to the voters of the territory. It failed, 34 to 24, and then the main bill was passed, 33 to 25. Four northern Democrats (including Douglas) and two southern Whig-Americans joined the Republicans in opposition.[74] Once again, however, the decisive contest took place in the House, where the course of events pointed up the fact that something more elemental and less definable than the future of Kansas was at stake. What each side wanted above all was the emotional satisfaction that comes with victory. By 1858, the long-festering sectional quarrel over slavery had become a self-sustaining social phenomenon, as much the creator as the creature of specific issues.

In the House, the floor manager for the Lecompton bill, as he had been for the Kansas-Nebraska bill four years earlier, was Alexander H. Stephens. It soon became clear, however, that the power tactics of 1854 were not going to succeed. Despite heavy administration pressure on the anti-Lecompton Democrats, most of them held firm. Stephens could not put together a majority, and he therefore resigned himself to settling for a partial victory through compromise. Anti-Lecompton Democrats with few exceptions were amenable, and on March 29 they apparently offered to support the measure if it were revised to assure Kansans of the right to amend their constitution at any time. This would have meant canceling the clause prohibiting amendment for seven years, a provision that Buchanan had already labeled unnecessary and unenforceable. Thus the administration, as David M. Potter has said, was presented with a "dazzling opportunity" to achieve almost everything it wanted. But southern militants compelled rejection of the offer, declaring that it amounted to unacceptable federal intervention in the affairs of a sovereign state.[75]

The insurgent Democrats then joined with the Republicans on April 1 to defeat the Lecompton bill, 120 to 112, by substituting the

Crittenden proposal for resubmission of the constitution to the Kansas electorate. Now called the "Crittenden-Montgomery" amendment, the substitute received unanimous Republican support, even though it could be said to embody the principle of popular sovereignty.[76] The Senate again rejected the Crittenden plan, however, and both houses agreed to the formation of a conference committee. Administration forces accordingly had one more chance to avoid the humiliation of total defeat. Their influence lay behind the committee's report of a compromise bill on April 23, although the measure was ostensibly the work of William H. English, a lukewarm anti-Lecompton Democrat from Indiana.

The "English compromise" was designed to give the administration and the South a procedural victory masking a substantive defeat. It proposed admission of Kansas with the Lecompton constitution intact, provided that the voters of the territory first approved the more or less standard grant of federal land specified for the new state. If the land grant were disapproved in the referendum, Kansas could not again be considered for admission until its population equaled the current federal ratio for one representative in Congress, something more than 90,000. In short, rejection of the land grant would mean the end of the Lecompton constitution and postponement of statehood for several years.[77]

There seemed to be little doubt that the Kansans, given such an opportunity, would bury the "Lecompton fraud" under an overwhelmingly negative vote. The primary effect, then, would be much the same as if the Crittenden-Montgomery substitute had passed. Yet nearly everyone who had voted for the Crittenden plan now voted against the English bill, and vice versa. The principal exception was a group of anti-Lecompton Democrats in the House who were coaxed and coerced back into the comfortable circle of party regularity. At last the administration forces had the majorities they needed. On the last day of April, the compromise passed the Senate, 31 to 22, and the House, 112 to 103.[78]

Douglas, after almost agreeing to support the English bill, had come down on the side of the opposition, thus convincing many southerners that he was still in league with the black Republicans.

Certainly there was merit in his view of the bill as a shabby piece of legislation that promised Kansas immediate admission as a slaveholding state but punished her with delay if she preferred to be a free state. Yet the measure did seem to constitute the kind of pragmatic adjustment of sectional disputes that he had so often promoted, and it did also seem likely to bring about a restoration of the party unity for which he had so often labored and sacrificed. Douglas as a bitter-ender on the antislavery side of an issue was an unfamiliar sight—and an ominous one for the South. Intransigence in Washington translated into expedience on the prairies of Illinois, however. Douglas apparently decided that accepting the English compromise would look too much like caving in under administration pressure. It would undercut his effort of recent years to appear as a man of principle, and it would dissolve the heroic anti-Lecompton image that had proved so popular throughout the North. With his contest for re-election drawing near, mail from home strongly reinforced the conclusion that he must "yield not one inch."[79]

The opposition of Douglas probably facilitated passage of the English bill, making it look more attractive to southern militants who had pledged themselves against anything bearing the slightest resemblance to resubmission. The compromise was in fact a blessing for such men, even for those aiming at disunion, because it enabled them to climb down from a shaky limb. Threats of secession were numerous and vehement during the controversy. Often their tone was that of a letter to Senator James H. Hammond from one of his South Carolinian constituents: "Save the Union, if you can. But rather than have Kansas refused admission under the Lecompton Constitution, let it perish in blood and fire."[80] The ultimatum "Lecompton or disunion" reverberated in the halls of Congress, in the southern press, and in southern legislatures.[81] With Alabama leading the way, contingent steps toward secession were officially taken by several states. Governor Joseph E. Brown of Georgia told Stephens in early February that rejection of the Lecompton constitution by Congress would make it his "imperative duty" to call a convention for determining Georgia's future relationship to the Union. "If Kansas is rejected," he added, "I think self respect will compel the Southern members of Congress

. . . to vacate their seats and return to their constituents."[82] The Memphis *Appeal* predicted that rejection of Kansas would create "a universal state of excitement in all the Southern States," such as had "never been paralleled by any previous agitation—not even the Missouri excitement." For such "an act of injustice" would demonstrate that the North intended "forever to exclude the South from her constitutional rights."[83]

At the same time, many southerners realized that the Lecompton bill, with its disreputable background, constituted a very dubious basis for a sectional ultimatum. The issue was not sufficiently clear-cut to make a good test case. "It does not describe the contingency," said the New Orleans *Picayune,* "in which revolution has been solemnly pronounced to be a settled and foregone determination in the South."[84] Governor Brown later acknowledged that an outright defeat of the Lecompton bill would have produced "great confusion in Georgia" and that "the democratic party of the state would have been divided and distracted."[85] In other words, outright defeat would have placed militant southerners in the position of having to choose between launching a secession movement that seemed likely to fail and backing down from their threats to a chorus of northern jeers. It is therefore not surprising that the English compromise should have been welcomed throughout the South with far more praise than its substance merited. There were dissenting voices, to be sure, and a good deal of hairsplitting explanation was necessary, but southern Democrats for the most part embraced the fiction that the English bill, in contrast with the allegedly abolitionist-inspired Crittenden-Montgomery amendment, provided a complete vindication of the rights of the South. "At once," wrote a Virginia editor, "we will secure a recognition of the Lecompton Constitution, a defeat of the Black Republican party . . . and an expulsion of the irritating issue from the halls of Congress."[86]

But of course just about everyone knew that the South had squandered another round of disunion threats to gain nothing more than the veneer of technical victory over real defeat. The English bill, in effect, killed the Lecompton constitution but turned the carcass over to the people of Kansas for final disposal. On August 2, they per-

formed the task convincingly by a vote of 11,300 to 1788.[87] The secession movement of 1858 and the alacrity with which it was abandoned
lent reinforcement to the widespread northern conviction that disunion maneuvers in the South were largely blackmail and bluff. Thus,
the *Ohio State Journal* at Columbus, which often spoke for Governor
Salmon P. Chase, said that defeat of the Lecompton bill had provided
a test and exposed the emptiness of "the miserable threats" of disunion. And the *Illinois State Journal* at Springfield, which often spoke
for Abraham Lincoln, said that "secession would be killed by ridicule,
as nullification was by force." As for the southern habit of threatening
to begin the process of secession by calling a state convention, that
had become "a dull practical joke." Nothing dangerous would happen
if "there were a convention sitting in every Southern State, all the
time, and each convention were to talk about dissolving the Union
eighteen hours per day."[88]

The English bill, although it put only a temporary damper on
talk of secession, did remove Kansas permanently from the center of
sectional controversy. Yet, being an ill-favored thing as compromises
go, it left an unusually large residue of dissatisfaction and bitterness.
This time, for example, efforts to repair the split in the Democratic
party proved unsuccessful. The administration continued its patronage reprisals against anti-Lecompton Democrats, and in Illinois it
sponsored the formation of a rival party organization to challenge
Douglas's leadership. On the Senate floor, Douglas angrily denounced this "conspiracy against the unity and integrity of the Democratic party . . . in Illinois." He left room for reconciliation, however, by pretending to believe that the leaders of the divisive
movement were acting without presidential authority.[89] At this point,
various peacemakers began working strenuously to patch up a truce,
and when Douglas departed from Washington after the adjournment
of Congress, there was good reason to believe that they were succeeding. "From what I learn," Buchanan wrote on June 30, "Douglas
has determined to come back to the party with a bound and to acquiesce cordially . . . in the English bill."[90] But the Little Giant, taking
the measure of northern political opinion on a roundabout journey

home to Illinois, found hostility to the administration running high
and made his decision accordingly. Given a hero's welcome by an enthusiastic crowd in Chicago on July 9, he responded with a slashing
attack on the Lecompton constitution and the English bill in a speech
that amounted to a renewal of civil war within the Democratic
party.[91]

Coming as a severe shock after persistent reports of a reconciliation, this Chicago speech was probably the point of no return in the
process of Douglas's alienation from the South. The Washington
Union declared that party forbearance in dealing with his "treason"
had ceased to be a virtue. "What was the object of the senator?" it
asked. "Did he wish to reopen the old wounds? . . . It was his place
to forget what passed last winter." Howell Cobb bitterly expressed
the administration view that Douglas had reneged on a promise,
resumed his abuse of the President, and thus placed himself beyond
reach of forgiveness. To treachery he had now added duplicity, said a
Georgia newspaper. "We believe," it asserted, "there is not a single
southern democratic press of any influence that countenances Senator
Douglas since the publication of his Chicago speech."[92]

Of course the South never approached unanimity on any major
issue, and Douglas continued to have supporters in every southern
state right down to 1860. One is nevertheless struck by the volume
and intensity of southern editorial attacks upon him in the period following the Chicago speech. No abolitionist had ever been more fiercely denounced, but then abolitionists could not be accused of treason
to the South. "Douglas was with us," the indictment ran, "until the
time of trial came; then he deceived and betrayed us."[93] Now he was
the South's worst enemy, guilty of "flagrant inconsistency and patent
double dealing," covered with the "odium of . . . detestable here-
sies" and the "filth of his defiant recreancy."[94] He could "never
regain his former standing with either the Southern or the National
Democracy," which had shaken off Douglasism like "a leprous hide."
Southern Democrats would give him what they had always given all
northern enemies—"war to the knife," and then: "Away with him to
the tomb which he is digging for his political corpse." A generation

must die out and new issues cover the past before he could purge the guilt of his vile alliance with the Republicans. "He must be forgotten before he can be forgiven."[95]

On all sides there had been tremendous emotional investment in the Lecompton struggle. The English compromise formally disposed of the Kansas issue but drained off little of its emotional content. Anger remained—and went in search of other issues. In retrospect it is now clear that the critical question facing the nation in the summer of 1858 was whether the Democratic party could pull itself together sufficiently to prevent a Republican victory in the next presidential election. The paramount issue keeping Democrats divided after the English compromise was the person of Stephen A. Douglas, accused party traitor with designs on the presidency. Southern hatred for him had taken on a life of its own and to a considerable extent had become implacable. Yet it could not feed indefinitely on the record of his past transgressions—not in view of the obvious practical need to close ranks against the Republicans. Additional reasons for continuing to anathematize him were therefore required, and so some eighteen months after its promulgation, the Dred Scott decision became a disruptive issue within the Democratic party. This new phase of the sectional conflict began with a question asked and answered at Freeport, Illinois, on August 27, 1858.

〜 20 〜

The Freeport Doctrine

The various connections between the Lecompton controversy and the Dred Scott decision, and their interlocking influence on the coming of the Civil War, are nowhere more plainly visible than in the history of the Lincoln-Douglas debates. For one thing, the split in the Democratic party, provoked by the Lecompton affair and sustained by differences over the meaning of the Dred Scott decision, may have had a critical influence on the crisis of 1860–61.[1] But in addition, it could be argued credibly that without the Lecompton constitution and Douglas's opposition to it, there would have been no Lincoln-Douglas debates; that the debates were in large part a discussion of the Dred Scott decision; that without the debates Lincoln would not have become a serious contender for the presidential nomination; that Seward, the likely nominee instead, might well have lost the election; and that without the election of a Republican president there would have been no secession crisis in the winter of 1860–61.

When Douglas recognized Lincoln as his official rival in 1858 and even agreed somewhat reluctantly to participate in a series of debates, he did so because the Republicans of Illinois had formally nominated Lincoln as their candidate for the Senate. Since United States senators were elected by state legislatures rather than by the people, this nomination was so unusual as to be almost without precedent in American history.[2] It resulted primarily from the intervention of Horace Greeley and certain other eastern Republicans into Illinois politics with the importunate suggestion that Douglas, because of his anti-Lecompton heroics, should be returned to the Senate unopposed. In many county conventions and then in their state convention at Springfield on June 16, Illinois Republicans curtly rejected the unwelcome advice by resolving that Lincoln was their "first and only choice . . . for the United States Senate, as the successor of Stephen A. Douglas."[3] Lincoln responded to the resolution with his carefully prepared House-Divided speech, and the memorable campaign of 1858 was under way.

Lincoln had actually begun his stalking of Douglas a year earlier when he spoke at Springfield on June 26, 1857, in reply to the address delivered by Douglas two weeks before. At that time, it will be remembered, the Little Giant's remarks on Kansas were so pleasing to southern Democrats that they entered no objection to his enunciation of the principle of residual popular sovereignty—that is, the Freeport doctrine. Lincoln devoted more than 80 per cent of the 1857 speech to severe criticism of the Dred Scott decision, but one finds certain interesting omissions. For one thing, he made no effort to exploit the inconsistency between Taney's opinion and the Cass-Douglas version of popular sovereignty. That is, he did not press the issue later embodied in his famous "Freeport question," even though Douglas had already volunteered the substance of *his* Freeport *answer*. Furthermore, nowhere in the speech did Lincoln assert or imply the existence of a conspiracy to nationalize slavery, even though the charge had already been made in many Republican editorials. Instead, he concentrated on defining, first, the nature and limits of judicial review, and then the nature and limits of Negro rights under the Declaration of Independence. His purpose in the first instance was to justify Republican opposition (distinguished from "resistance") to the Dred Scott decision. His purpose in the second instance was to reaffirm Republican idealism, while at the same time vindicating the party from Democratic charges that it favored absolute racial equality. The speech, in short, had a generally defensive tone. And insofar as Lincoln discussed the substance of Taney's opinion, he dealt almost entirely with the question of Negro citizenship, rather than the question of slavery in the territories. Politically, it was dubious strategy; for Republicans, as we have noted, were usually at a disadvantage when the subject shifted from slavery to race.

The House-Divided speech was notably different in style and content. Its staccato sentences and muscular phrasing produced a bold effect, and its argument seemed to move Lincoln toward the radical side of Republicanism. A house divided against itself, he said, could not stand; the government could not endure permanently half-slave and half-free; he did not expect the Union to be dissolved but expected rather that it would cease to be divided; slavery would either be put in course of ultimate extinction or be legalized everywhere in the United States; the tendency was in the latter direction and had been ever since passage of the Kansas-Nebraska Act; the Dred Scott decision was the last step but one in a plan for the nationalization of slavery designed by Douglas, Pierce, Taney, and Buchanan; coming next and probably soon, another judicial decision would declare that no state had the power to exclude slavery from its limits. "We shall *lie down* pleasantly dreaming that the people of *Missouri* are on the verge of making their State *free;* and we shall *awake* to the *reality*, instead, that the *Supreme* Court has made *Illinois* a *slave* State."[4]

The House-Divided speech had a specific practical purpose and embodied a well-calculated political strategy shaped in response to recent political developments. Since delivering his Springfield speech of 1857, Lincoln had watched the Lecompton controversy in all of its stages and had seen the emergence of Douglas as a spectacular party rebel, much admired even in certain Republican circles. If any sizable number of Illinois Republicans were captivated by the Little Giant's new antislavery image, his re-election to the Senate would be ensured. Somehow, then, Lincoln had to minimize the significance of the Lecompton split in the Democratic party and maximize the distance, in matters of principle, between Douglas and the Republican party. He therefore took up the charge already widely disseminated that Democratic leaders, including Douglas, were engaged in a plot to nationalize slavery. Douglas's primary function in the plot, one that he continued to perform in spite of his anti-Lecompton revolt, was the undermining of northern resistance to slavery by inculcating a doctrine of moral indifference under the deceptive label of "popular sovereignty." Accordingly, said Lincoln, when Douglas had won enough northerners to his enunciated philosophy of not caring whether slavery was "voted down or voted up," the scene would be fully set for the "second Dred Scott decision" holding slavery to be lawful everywhere in the Union.[5] What claim, then, could such a man have upon Republican support? How could he lead the fight against the conspiracy to nationalize slavery when he was himself a part of the conspiracy? "Our cause," Lincoln insisted, "must be intrusted to, and conducted by its own undoubted friends—those whose hands are free, whose hearts are in the work—who *do care* for the result."

Lincoln appears to have been interested in the conspiracy charge only to the extent that it could be directed against Douglas. This seems clear from the way in which he treated the Lecompton affair. Many Republicans, it will be remembered, had portrayed the Lecompton constitution as a sequel to the Dred Scott decision, providing strong confirmation of the existence of a slave-power conspiracy. But Lincoln obviously could not follow such a line of argument without weakening his case against Douglas. To put Douglas into the conspiracy, the Lecompton bill had to be left out. So Lincoln dismissed the Lecompton controversy as a "squabble" over the "*mere* question of *fact,* whether the Lecompton constitution was or was not . . . made by the people of Kansas." On the principle involved—namely, "the right of a people to make their own constitution"—Douglas and the Republicans, he said, had "never differed." Moreover, in identifying Buchanan as a leader of the conspiracy to nationalize slavery, Lincoln mentioned only the President's endorsement of the Dred Scott decision and said nothing about his efforts to make Kansas a slave state under the Lecompton constitution. Not surprisingly, then, Lincoln in the House-Divided speech made only passing reference to the conflict between Taney's Dred Scott opinion and the Douglas version of popular sovereignty.[6] The strategy of the speech, after all, was to emphasize the affinities, not the differences, between Douglas and the slaveholding South. In other words, the Freeport question did not really fit into Lincoln's battle plan.

II

Obviously, Lincoln had adopted the common political maneuver of shoving his opponent toward an extreme position in order to pre-empt the middle ground for himself. Douglas, in opening his campaign for re-election, proceeded to do the same thing. At Chicago, on July 9, as we have seen, he aggressively renewed his quarrel with the administration, thereby restaking his claim to some measure of antislavery support. Then he turned his attention to the "kind, amiable, and intelligent gentleman" who had been nominated to oppose him, stressing the radicalism of Lincoln's house-divided doctrine, the radicalism of his "crusade against the Supreme Court," and the radicalism of his views on race. Indeed, "race" was the key concept in Douglas's strategy, just as "conspiracy" was the key concept in Lincoln's strategy. Lincoln, said the Little Giant, "objects to the Dred Scott decision because it does not put the negro in the possession of the rights of citizenship on an equality with the white man. I am opposed to negro equality. . . . I am in favor of preserving not only the purity of the blood, but the purity of the government from any mixture or amalgamation with inferior races."[7]

In the course of the long and strenuous contest that followed, the two men never wandered far from the main lines of their argument, in which Lincoln tried to show that Douglas, an opportunist, was insidiously proslavery, and Douglas tried to show that Lincoln, a radical, was obnoxiously pro-Negro.* Lincoln took his stand on the proposition that the principles of the Declaration of Independence were meant to include all the races of man, but then, as a matter of politi-

* Major speeches of Lincoln and Douglas in which the Dred Scott decision received significant attention:[8]

June 12, 1857: Douglas at Springfield	Aug. 27, 1858: Freeport Debate
June 26, 1857: Lincoln at Springfield	Sept. 15, 1858: Jonesboro Debate
June 16, 1858: Lincoln at Springfield	Oct. 7, 1858: Galesburg Debate
July 9, 1858: Douglas at Chicago	Oct. 13, 1858: Quincy Debate
July 10, 1858: Lincoln at Chicago	Oct. 17, 1858: Alton Debate
July 17, 1858: Douglas at Springfield	Sept. 16, 1859: Lincoln at Columbus, O.
July 17, 1858: Lincoln at Springfield	Sept. 16, 1859: Lincoln at Wooster, O.
Aug. 21, 1858: Ottawa Debate	Feb. 20, 1860: Lincoln at New York

cal survival in the racist context of the time, he was driven to loading this bold statement with so many qualifications that in the end it seemed to mean little more than the right not to be a slave.[9] Douglas took his stand on popular sovereignty—"the great principle that every people ought to possess the right to form and regulate their own domestic institutions in their own way."[10] This doctrine too was in certain respects vulnerable. Lincoln based his criticism of it primarily on the broad moral ground that slavery and self-government were essentially incompatible. Douglas's "gur-reat pur-rinciple," he said, meant simply that "if one man would enslave another, no third man should object."[11]

In the heat of forensic battle, however, neither of these veteran campaigners hesitated to seize any advantage presenting itself or to exploit any weakness in his opponent's argument. And so with Douglas praising popular sovereignty and defending the Dred Scott decision, Lincoln was bound to raise the question of their incongruity, even though it did not fit his general strategy to do so. Speaking at Chicago on July 10 in reply to the Douglas speech of the previous evening, he asked: "What is popular sovereignty? . . . What has become of it? Can you get anybody to tell you now that the people of a territory have any authority to govern themselves, in regard to this mooted question of slavery, before they form a state constitution?" No, he continued, the Supreme Court, in a decision approved by Douglas, had denied that the territories could rightfully exclude slavery. "When that is so, how much is left of this vast matter of squatter sovereignty I should like to know?" A voice from the audience answered, "It has all gone."[12]

Here was the substance of the Freeport question, put rhetorically but forcefully almost seven weeks before the debate at Freeport. Douglas, in his speeches at Bloomington and Springfield on July 16 and 17, accordingly revived the concept of residual popular sovereignty, which he had not used in public since the preceding summer. "If the people of a territory want slavery they will have it," he declared, "and if they do not want it they will drive it out, and you cannot force it on them. Slavery cannot exist a day in the midst of an unfriendly people and unfriendly laws."[13] Thus, in speeches made six weeks before the debate at Freeport and given wide circulation, Douglas clearly set forth the Freeport doctrine of "unfriendly legislation," doing so in response to questions from his opponent.

Lincoln did not pursue the matter further in his reply to Douglas at Springfield or in the first of their seven formal debates, held at Ottawa on August 21. In other respects, however, the Dred Scott decision received considerable attention from both speakers at Ottawa— so much so that at one point an Irishman in the audience interrupted Lincoln with the shout: "Give us something besides Dred Scott!" Lincoln reiterated his conspiracy charge, for instance, and Douglas pronounced it an "infamous lie."* Douglas again declared that Lincoln opposed the Dred Scott decision primarily because it denied citizenship to Negroes; Lincoln responded with a disavowal of racial equality as emphatic as any that he later made in the southern part of the state. Douglas again spoke of Lincoln's "warfare on the Supreme Court"; Lincoln asked how Republican criticism of the Dred Scott decision was any worse than the Democratic party's continued repudiation (in its official platform) of the Supreme Court decision upholding the constitutionality of a national bank.[14]

During the Ottawa debate also, Douglas fired a volley of seven questions at Lincoln, who cautiously put off answering them until the next debate at Freeport six days later. Meanwhile, some of Lincoln's Republican advisers decided that he had kept himself too much on the defensive at Ottawa and must become more aggressive. "We must not be parrying all the while," one of them wrote. "We want the deadliest thrusts. Let us see blood follow any time he closes a sentence."[15] And so, as part of the strategy of taking the offensive, Lincoln not only answered Douglas's seven questions at Freeport, but then countered with four of his own.[16] The phrasing was Lincoln's in each instance, but the substance of the questions undoubtedly reflected advice from his political associates.[17] There is no contemporary evidence that Lincoln regarded any one question as more important than the others.[18] Two of them, the second and third, were

*Somewhat illogically, Lincoln included Douglas in the conspiracy but also quoted from the latter's speech criticizing the Washington *Union* to show that he too had made the charge.

directly related to the Dred Scott decision, but only the latter conformed to the campaign strategy adopted in the House-Divided
speech.

This third question pressed the issue of a conspiracy to nationalize slavery: "If the Supreme Court of the United States shall decide
that States can not exclude slavery from their limits, are you in favor
of acquiescing in, adopting and following such decision as a rule of political action?" Douglas, who had been insisting that any decision of
the Supreme Court must be accepted as the law of the land, pru-
dently chose to ridicule the query instead of answering it. "Such a
thing is not possible," he said. "It would be an act of moral treason
that no man on the bench would ever descend to." It "amazed" him
that anyone should ask such a question. A school boy would know
better than to do so. Lincoln might as well ask whether, if he stole a
horse, Douglas would sanction it.[19]

At Galesburg and Quincy in October, Lincoln renewed the question, noting that there had been no response except sneers and adding, "I had not propounded it without some reflection." The essence
of the Dred Scott decision, he declared, was compressed into one of
Taney's sentences—namely, "The right of property in a slave is distinctly and expressly affirmed in the Constitution." If this premise
were accepted as true, said Lincoln, and if it were combined with the
supremacy clause of the Constitution, the effect would be to construct
a syllogism with the inevitable conclusion that nothing in the constitution or laws of any state could "destroy the right of property in a
slave." Thus the logical basis for the second Dred Scott decision had
been fully laid.

But Douglas steadfastly refused to consider even the possibility
of a decision "so ridiculous" as to declare that Illinois and other free
states could not prohibit slavery within their own boundaries. The
only person of any consequence in America who ever put forth such
an argument, he said, was the author of the November 17 article in
the Washington *Union*, and he, Douglas, had been the first to denounce it "as revolutionary" on the floor of the Senate. "Mr. Lincoln
knows," Douglas continued, "that there is not a member of the Supreme Court who holds that doctrine; he knows that every one of

them, as shown by their opinions, holds the reverse." Lincoln emphatically disagreed. "I will thank Judge Douglas," he replied, "to lay
his finger upon the place in the entire opinions of the court where
any one of them . . . said that the States can exclude slavery."
Douglas did not respond to this challenge but simply reiterated his
refusal to answer the third Freeport question. "It is an insult to men's
understanding, and a gross calumny on the court," he angrily declared, "to presume in advance that it was going to degrade itself so
low as to make a decision known to be in direct violation of the constitution." There, in spite of some further needling by Lincoln, the matter rested.[20]

If the Lincoln-Douglas debates are viewed properly as a representative event in the struggle between Republicans and northern
Democrats for public favor within the free states, this vision of a "second Dred Scott decision" becomes a matter of considerable importance. For it was in some respects a rhetorical device used to express
a widespread and deepening suspicion of southern motives that had
begun to affect even Douglas's political outlook and behavior. This
growing northern hostility to the slaveholding South, as distinguished
from hostility to southern slavery, may be the key to Republican success in 1860, thus constituting the main causal connection between
the Dred Scott decision and the coming of the Civil War. If so, then
Lincoln's third query at Freeport is perhaps the most significant of
the lot.[21] But of course it was the second Freeport question that
seemed at the time to have the more visible consequences and that
became in the retrospect of history and folklore one of those decisive
moments on which destiny turns.*

* Second Freeport question and answer:
"Can the people of a United States Territory, in any lawful way, against the wish of
any citizen of the United States, exclude slavery from its limits prior to the formation
of a State Constitution?"

"I answer emphatically, as Mr. Lincoln has heard me answer a hundred times from
every stump in Illinois, that in my opinion the people of a territory can, by lawful
means, exclude slavery from their limits prior to the formation of a State Constitution.
. . . It matters not what way the Supreme Court may hereafter decide as to the abstract question whether slavery may or may not go into a territory under the constitution, the people have the lawful means to introduce it or exclude it as they please, for
the reason that slavery cannot exist a day or an hour anywhere, unless it is supported

Exploitation of Democratic disunity, though not included in Lincoln's original campaign strategy, inevitably became a part of his battleground tactics; for, in the give and take of the debates, scoring points off one's opponent at every opportunity seemed more important than maintaining logical consistency. So Lincoln, in his very first question at Freeport, probed a very tender spot by asking Douglas whether he would vote for the admission of Kansas before it acquired the requisite population specified in the English compromise. The Little Giant's affirmative answer added another count to the southern indictment of him because, in the words of a Georgia editor, it would "repudiate the principal feature of the English bill, which commended itself to the South."[23]

Once Lincoln decided to fire back some questions of his own at Freeport, it was almost automatic to include one pointing up the contradiction between the Dred Scott decision and the Douglas version of popular sovereignty. Republicans had been asking it in one way or another for more than a year: Congressional prohibition having been voided by the Supreme Court, could a territorial legislature legally prohibit slavery? Douglas, it is important to note, actually returned two answers—one a carefully phrased implication, the other an emphatic assertion. He implied that the Court had not yet decided the question of territorial power over slavery, thereby treating the relevant passage in Taney's opinion as dictum, rather than as part of the official decision. This maneuver left room for a possible revival of the old leave-it-to-the-Court formula that had served the Democratic party so well in the past. It was thus a strategy looking forward to the presidential contest of 1860.*

For the senatorial campaign in progress, however, and especially for an audience in northern Illinois, something more forceful was needed. So Douglas answered Lincoln's second question primarily by reiterating the principle of residual popular sovereignty, which at this

---

by local police regulations. Those police regulations can only be established by the local legislature, and if the people are opposed to slavery they will elect representatives to that body who will by unfriendly legislation effectually prevent the introduction of it into their midst."[22]

* See below, pp. 534, 537–38.

point became known as the "Freeport doctrine." But whatever practical wisdom there may have been in the argument that slavery could
never survive where it was not wanted, the constitutional foundations
of the Freeport doctrine were extremely weak. Lincoln, seeing an opportunity to score forensic points against his adversary, pursued the
matter vigorously in subsequent debates and speeches. He reminded
Illinoisans that Douglas, when asked the same question on the Senate
floor in 1856, had labeled it a judicial issue, which only the Supreme
Court could settle. Now that the Court had decided the question,
however, Douglas was shifting his ground, maintaining in effect that a
territorial legislature could nullify a judicially recognized constitutional right. "Why this," said Lincoln, "is a *monstrous* sort of talk.
. . . There has never been as outlandish or lawless a doctrine from
the mouth of any respectable man on earth." It was a doctrine, moreover, which would no less fully justify resistance to the Fugitive Slave
Law.

> I defy anybody to . . . show that there is an iota of difference be-
> tween the constitutional right to reclaim a fugitive, and the consti-
> tutional right to hold a slave, in a Territory, provided this Dred
> Scott decision is correct. I defy any man to make an argument that
> will justify unfriendly legislation to deprive a slaveholder of his
> right to hold his slave in a Territory, that will not equally . . . fur-
> nish an argument for nullifying the fugitive slave law. Why there
> is not such an Abolitionist in the nation as Douglas, after all.[24]

Furthermore, at Jonesboro on September 15, Lincoln added an
important corollary to the famous second Freeport question when he
confronted Douglas with this "fifth interrogatory":

> If the slaveholding citizens of a United States Territory should
> need and demand Congressional legislation for the protection of
> their slave property in such Territory, would you, as a member of
> Congress, vote for or against such legislation?

Douglas responded promptly by reaffirming the principle of nonintervention and in a later debate stated more explicitly that he would oppose any effort to establish a congressional slave code for the territories.[25]

With this Jonesboro question, Lincoln anticipated the most significant southern response to the Freeport doctrine. Indeed, even as
the Jonesboro debate took place, the Washington *Union* and the
Richmond *Enquirer* were arguing over whether Douglas had done
the South a service by pointing up the need for a territorial slave
code.[26] In general, however, the Freeport doctrine provoked no
great new explosion of southern anger—certainly nothing to compare
with southern reaction to Douglas's Chicago speech of July 17 and to
his earlier anti-Lecompton speeches in the Senate. Some newspapers
of the South took notice of the doctrine and condemned it; others
took notice and excused it; still others paid little attention to the doctrine at all.[27] But there is no evidence of any major change in southern attitudes toward Douglas as a direct consequence of his famous
answer to Lincoln's famous question at Freeport. Most of the southern editors who denounced the Freeport doctrine had been denouncing its author ever since he declared his opposition to the Lecompton
constitution. Moreover, some editors were angered at least as much
by his answer to Lincoln's *first* question at Freeport. The Mobile *Register*, for instance, complained that Douglas was running for re-
election on a platform of admitting Kansas immediately, in defiance of
the restrictive terms of the English compromise. In a long editorial on
September 26, a month after the Freeport debate, it demanded, "Is
the Conference Act to be Respected?"—arguing that if not, the South
should leave the Union. Clearly, the whole pattern of Douglas's behavior beginning in December 1857, and not the Freeport doctrine
alone, was what ruined his political standing in the South.[28]

III

The political issue debated most earnestly throughout the South during the summer and fall of 1858 was not the Freeport doctrine but
rather Douglas himself and his future in American politics. Although
outright supporters of the Little Giant were a small and dwindling
minority, southerners nevertheless differed sharply over what result
to hope for in the Illinois senatorial contest. A good many political
leaders and editors came to the same conclusion as that set forth in a

Louisiana newspaper. "No rational, thinking man of the South," it declared, "can desire for one single moment the election of a black Republican so rank and foul as Abraham Lincoln, over Stephen A. Douglas."[29] A journalist friend of Alexander H. Stephens agreed, adding this trenchant argument: "Douglas, with all his past objectionable conduct, and with all he may do in future, is *sound on niggers;* and I have not hesitated to express to any and every one . . . that I preferred him . . . to a crazy fanatic, who openly proclaims the equality of the black and white races, and advocates the abolishing of the Supreme Court for its decision in the Dred Scott Case."[30] The fire-eating Richmond *South* regarded Douglas as a traitor, but for reasons of political strategy thought that the administration should cease giving aid to his enemies in Illinois. "The question," it said, "is simply this—shall we, to gratify an impulse of resentment, or to perpetuate an extinct issue, deliberately drive Illinois, Indiana, New Jersey, and Pennsylvania under the banner of Black Republicanism; or should we rather agree to co-operate with Democrats from whom we differ on a particular point, in order to prevent the success of a party which aspires to the subjugation of the South?"[31]

At the same time, however, many southern leaders and spokesmen joined the Washington *Union* in professing a "serene indifference" to the outcome in Illinois, and some even argued that the interests of the South would be better served by a Republican victory. The *North Carolina Standard* (Raleigh) filled nearly two columns with an explanation of why it refused to choose between Douglas and Lincoln, even though the latter was "the embodiment to a Southern mind of all political depravity and infamy." A false friend such as Douglas, said a Mississippi newspaper, was "ten thousand times more to be feared than a thousand Lincolns." The Memphis *Avalanche* declared that it would be "degradation and craven cowardice for the Democratic party to lick the hand that chastised them, to caress the viper that stung them."[32]

Calculation as well as resentment inspired much of the unrelenting southern hostility to Douglas, however. Without him in the Senate, said the Columbia *Banner,* there would be "no intermediating nucleus for the disaffected and disappointed to rally to and thus form

a balance of power party that will stand as a temptation to concession." This was in some respects the southern counterpart of Lincoln's
argument on the Republican side, stressing the corruptive influence
of persons like Douglas who persisted in "groping for some middle
ground between the right and the wrong." But more of the calculation centered specifically on the next presidential election. Thus the
Mobile *Register*, which regarded Douglas as "the worst enemy of the
South and the most mischievous man now in the nation," feared that
a victory in 1858 and a triumphant return to the Senate would give
him a commanding position in the contest for this Democratic nomination. Southerners in 1860 would then face a repulsive choice between Douglas and a Republican. Better, therefore, to defeat him
now, when only a Senate seat was at stake.[33]

The insurgency of Douglas, together with the fact that Buchanan's advanced age made him an unlikely candidate for re-election, seemed to throw the presidential race wide open on the Democratic side. Through the ranks of southern party leaders especially
there ran the thrill of realization that if Douglas could be held off, one
of their number might well be nominated. The South, after all, was
now the dominant section within the Democratic party, and yet for
the past three elections it had acquiesced in the choice of a northern
candidate. According to Senator James L. Hammond of South Carolina, at least twenty southerners were hungering after the nomination. The list included Hammond himself, Vice President John C.
Breckinridge of Kentucky, Secretary of the Treasury Howell Cobb of
Georgia, Governor Henry A. Wise of Virginia, and Senators Robert
M. T. Hunter of Virginia, Andrew Johnson of Tennessee, Sam Houston of Texas, John Slidell of Louisiana, and Jefferson Davis of Mississippi.[34]

Davis, who had been seriously ill during the early months of
1858, spent the summer vacationing in New England upon the advice
of his physician. His recovery apparently began on the voyage northward to Boston; for he delivered an address of "impassioned elo-
quence" as part of a Fourth of July celebration at sea. In the months
that followed, he accepted a number of invitations to speak on civic
occasions and at Democratic party meetings. The Democrats of New

England were hopelessly outnumbered and largely a patronage organization. They listened sympathetically to Davis's defense of southern rights and applauded his attacks on antislavery fanaticism. He, in turn, endeavored to please his audiences by praising New England culture, appealing to the nation's heroic past, and stressing his love for the Union. On September 11 in Portland, a Saturday-night Democratic rally received him with a "perfect storm of applause," and Davis, in the course of his speech, took up the alleged "aggressions of the slave power," with special reference to the territorial question:

> The territory being the common property of States, equals in the Union . . . it is an abuse of terms to call aggression the migration into that territory of one of its joint owners, because carrying with him any species of property recognized by the constitution of the United States. The Federal government has no power to declare what is property anywhere. The power of each State cannot extend beyond its own limits. As a consequence, therefore, whatever is property in any of the States must be so considered in any of the territories of the United States until they reach to the dignity of community independence, when the subject matter will be entirely under the control of the people and be determined by their fundamental law. If the inhabitants of any territory should refuse to enact such laws and police regulations as would give security to their property or to his, it would be rendered more or less valueless, in proportion to the difficulty of holding it without such protection. In the case of property in the labor of man, or what is usually called slave property, the insecurity would be so great that the owner could not ordinarily retain it. Therefore, though the right would remain, the remedy being withheld, it would follow that the owner would be practically debarred by the circumstances of the case, from taking slave property into a territory where the sense of the inhabitants was opposed to its introduction. So much for the oft repeated fallacy of forcing slavery upon any community.[35]

Thus, fifteen days after the debate at Freeport, but without any knowledge of what had been said there, Jefferson Davis unmistakably subscribed to the Freeport doctrine of residual popular sovereignty, using it in the customary southern way as a message of reassurance to northerners fearing slave power expansionism. He stated the doctrine, to be sure, in its less abrasive, negative form, by envisaging a refusal to pass protective legislation for slavery, rather than an enactment of "unfriendly legislation." But this, as Allan Nevins has said, was a distinction without a difference. For Davis did more than acknowledge the power of a territorial legislature to override the constitutional rights of a slaveholder; he offered that acknowledgment in order to demonstrate the "fallacy" of believing that slavery could be forced on any community. The implication was clearly in harmony with Douglas's reply at Freeport.

It took several weeks for Davis's remarks at Portland to percolate through the newspaper exchanges and reach the eyes of interested readers in Washington, D.C., Illinois, and Mississippi. During the seventh and final debate at Alton on October 15, Douglas quoted the critical passage and asserted that it took the "same view" he himself had taken at Freeport. The Washington *States,* a new, pro-Douglas newspaper in the national capital, reprinted Davis's words under the heading: "The Identical Views of Senators Douglas and Davis." The Vicksburg *Whig* quoted from Douglas at Freeport and Davis at Portland, declaring that it could see no difference between the two. The Mobile *Register* agreed, complaining of "grave error and heresy on the part of the Mississippi Senator."[36]

Finding himself under heavy attack when he returned home to Mississippi in November, Davis retreated hastily into denial and virtual falsehood. His statement at Portland, he asserted, bore "no similitude" to the doctrine enunciated by Douglas in the Freeport debate.

> The difference between us is as wide as that of one who should assert the right to rob from him who admitted the power. It is true, as I stated it at that time, all property requires protection from the society in the midst of which it is held. This necessity does not confer a right to destroy, but rather creates an obligation to protect.[37]

Here, in an argument leading directly toward the southern demand for a territorial slave code, Davis reversed the reasoning of his utter-

ance at Portland and contradicted its stated purpose. Plainly, it was a
retreat, not so much from the words spoken at Portland, as from the
resulting appearance of ideological affiliation with the man who had
"dishonorably betrayed his principles and his party in the hour of
their sorest need and severest trial."[38] The *Missouri Republican*, leading Democratic newspaper in St. Louis, expressed the judgment of
many reasonable observers when it said: "His own definition of popular sovereignty is so nearly that given by Mr. Douglas that all perceive how unhappily Mr. Davis is employed in his lame attempts to
discriminate between the two."[39] During the next two years, in a
continuing effort to purge himself of this taint, the Mississippi senator
led the southern attack on Douglas in Congress. Historians have often
said that the Freeport doctrine made Douglas unacceptable in the
South, but if the behavior of Jefferson Davis is any indication, it
would be more accurate to turn the statement around and say that
Douglas made the Freeport doctrine unacceptable in the South.

IV

If United States senators had been elected then as now by popular
vote, instead of by state legislatures, history might well record that
Lincoln defeated Douglas in a close contest. But the Illinois Democrats, having more holdover senate seats and a slight advantage in the
legislative apportionment, won narrow control of both houses at
Springfield and a joint majority of 54 to 46.[40] By that margin, Douglas.
was re-elected on January 6, 1859. The party also won five out of the
nine congressional races, thereby holding its own against the Republicans in the House of Representatives. These victors were all Douglas
Democrats. The pro-administration ticket, which had no purpose
other than to draw strength away from the Little Giant, polled only a
wretched 2 per cent of the popular vote. Thus Buchanan as well as
Lincoln was defeated in the Illinois election, and Douglas himself
spoke of his triumph as being over "the combined forces of the Abolitionists and the federal office holders."[41]

Elsewhere, the midterm congressional elections added up to disaster for the northern wing of the Democratic party. Its fifty-three

seats in the House of Representatives were reduced to thirty-one. This remnant, moreover, included at least a dozen anti-Lecompton Democrats, a majority of whom refused even to caucus with their party. The heaviest losses were sustained in New York and Pennsylvania, but what seems most significant is the pattern of voter shifts in the four states of the lower North that Buchanan had carried in 1856—namely, New Jersey, Pennsylvania, Indiana, and Illinois. In the thirty-fifth Congress their fifty House seats were filled by twenty-nine Democrats and twenty-one Republicans. When the thirty-sixth Congress assembled in December 1859, the four-state delegation would include five pro-administration Democrats, eleven anti-Lecompton Democrats, thirty-two Republicans, and two Americans. Thus, after 1858, the odds appeared to favor a Republican victory in the next presidential election, and the expectation of it increasingly affected political behavior, North and South.[42]

The Democrats also lost some ground in the southern congressional elections, many of which were not held until 1859. Perhaps our best measure of the over-all Democratic decline is the fact that, whereas the party had elected James L. Orr as speaker in 1857 with 128 votes, its caucus nominee in the speakership contest of 1859–60 never received more than eighty-eight votes. The Senate, of course, was less susceptible to sudden large changes in membership and remained a Democratic stronghold. Even so, the Republicans gained four seats in 1858–59, bringing their total to twenty-four. On a percentage basis, this was as great an increase as the one they achieved in the House.[43]

Some Democratic losses in the North probably resulted from fusion of Republican and Know Nothing forces that had supported separate tickets in 1856, thus allowing Democratic candidates to win with pluralities. Other losses in 1858 have been attributed to party infighting, especially over patronage.[44] Still, even with such qualifications, the election results seem to indicate a strong northern reaction against the administration and its Kansas policy. Of the fifty-three northern Democrats in the House of Representatives, twenty-six had been consistently pro-Lecompton, and eleven had been consistently anti-Lecompton to the extent of opposing even the English compro-

mise. Twenty-three of the twenty-six loyalists sought re-election, but
only six were successful (three of them in New York City). Of the
eleven insurgents, four did not run for re-election but were replaced
by anti-Lecompton Democrats; seven sought re-election, and six did
so successfully, even though three of them were denied renomination
by their regular party organizations. Thus, 86 per cent of the insurgents and only 26 per cent of the loyalists running for re-election
won the approval of the voters. Put in other terms, ten of the eleven
insurgent seats were filled with anti-Lecompton men, while eighteen
of the loyalists seats were lost to Republicans or anti-Lecompton
Democrats. The meaning of these figures was plain enough to Buchanan, who, with his eye especially on Pennsylvania, remarked,
"Well, we have met the enemy . . . and we are theirs."[45]

The election returns of 1858 therefore reflected two important
political changes growing out of the Lecompton controversy. One
was the split in the Democratic party—a split not strictly along sectional lines, but having a definite sectional tendency nonetheless. The
other was a substantial decline of Democratic strength at the polls in
certain crucial northern states—a decline which, if not reversed,
could mean nothing other than the election of a Republican president
in 1860.

Rumors of a reconciliation between Douglas and Buchanan
began to circulate soon after the results of the Illinois election were
known. The Washington *Union* sullenly acknowledged such a possibility, declaring: "It is for the belligerent minority to choose the relations that shall subsist between themselves and the party which they
have wounded, outraged, and insulted; but who are capable of even
yet forgiving and forgetting. . . . The relations must be positive one
way or the other. There must be either peace or war."[46] At the same
time, there were some conciliatory gestures from the Douglas camp,
although in private the Little Giant reportedly said of Buchanan, "He
made the war; and by God! he shall make peace if peace is to be
made at all.'[47] All doubt ended with a dramatic renewal of hostilities
on December 9. The news flashed out of Washington that the Democratic senatorial caucus was removing Douglas from the chairmanship
of the committee on territories, a position he had held for eleven

years. It was a petty act of revenge, obviously carrying the stamp of administration approval, and it set the tone of a rancorous session.[48]

The blow fell when Douglas himself was far away. Needing a rest after the strenuous contest with Lincoln and preferring not to resume his seat in the Senate until the Illinois legislature had formally re-elected him,* he traveled back to Washington by a circuitous water route, via New Orleans, Havana, and New York City. His reception in the South was predictably mixed. Large crowds turned out to greet him in the major river ports along the way; he made speeches in St. Louis, Memphis, and New Orleans; there were welcoming delegations, military escorts, and at least one illumination celebrating his arrival. Yet the public figures coming forward to associate themselves with his visit were for the most part former Whigs and political has-beens or outsiders.[49] From the power structure of the southern Democratic party there was little but hostility, some of it venomous. The legislature of Mississippi ostentatiously ignored his passage along the border of the state, and the Jackson *Mississippian* suggested that if this "degenerate politician" were to be lynched, "there would be a strong array of irresistible facts in the case, to extenuate the act."[50]

Douglas in the South, like Jefferson Davis in New England, tried to make his views as palatable as possible. He reiterated the Freeport doctrine, but in its milder, negative form. Slave property in a federal territory had the same standing as other property, he said. "If the people of a Territory are in favor of slavery they will make laws to protect it; if opposed to slavery they will not make those laws and you cannot compel them to do it."[51] There was no talk about "unfriendly legislation." This minor retreat would not be enough, however, to satisfy administration leaders and southern Democrats in Washington.

Knowing that the restoration of party unity depended on a subsidence of the slavery controversy, Douglas hoped that with Kansas no longer a burning issue, public interest might be shifted to territorial expansion. In each of his speeches he therefore rang the changes of Manifest Destiny, declaring that the bigger the country became, the better it could perform its God-given historical role. The acquisi-

* Douglas's re-election was not certain, for there were rumors that the administration would be able to control enough Democratic legislators to prevent it.

tion of Cuba was inevitable, he assured his New Orleans audience, because the island belonged "naturally" to the American continent and guarded the mouth of the Mississippi River. Central America, too, he suggested, would eventually become a part of the United States. On the very same day, December 6, 1858, James Buchanan in his annual message proposed a renewal of negotiations with Spain for the purchase of Cuba. Here, then, was the cause that might have served to restore peace within the Democratic party if peace had really been desired.[52]

Stopping over in Cuba, as if to punctuate his theme of expansionism, Douglas landed at New York shortly before New Year's Day, and from there on his journey became something of a triumphal procession. The New York common council organized a huge public reception. In Philadelphia, despite a heavy snowfall, there were fireworks, a salute of cannon, a torchlight parade, and a dinner at Independence Hall. In Baltimore, the spirit of celebration reached its peak with the arrival of a telegram from Springfield saying that the legislature had re-elected him. To the Buchanan administration and the southern Democrats, watching with jaundiced eyes, this all must have seemed a little too much like the return of a victorious Caesar or Bonaparte. Official Washington gave the Little Giant a cold reception. When he took his seat in the Senate on January 10, most of his colleagues ungraciously ignored him. When the Douglases staged a "grand ball" at their residence in early February, issuing some 1200 invitations, every member of the cabinet sent his regrets. The President, meanwhile, continued to operate his "guillotine" by making anti-Douglas appointments in Illinois. Douglas, moreover, quickly fell into a series of personal quarrels, first with Senators George W. Jones of Iowa and John Slidell of Louisiana, and then with Senator Graham N. Fitch of Indiana. All three were staunch administration supporters, and in the case of Fitch, the adversaries not only exchanged formal notes but appointed intermediaries, before reaching an awkward, unfriendly adjustment. These incidents lent credence to talk of a plot to force Douglas into a duel. "The war of the roses," wrote a New York *Times* correspondent, "is evidently just beginning."[53]

In the face of such hostility, Douglas displayed considerable restraint. He made no public protest about his removal from the chairmanship of the committee on territories; he attended party caucuses
and supported Buchanan's policy on Cuba; he refrained from raising
the issue embodied in his Freeport doctrine. As this second session of
the thirty-fifth Congress moved toward adjournment, the feud within
the Democratic party continued to sputter viciously, but it had not
erupted into a major confrontation.

V

It was John P. Hale, the radical Republican from New Hampshire,
who set off a sharp debate between Douglas and various southern
Democrats. During consideration of an appropriation bill on February
22, Hale offered an amendment repealing the section of the English
compromise that prohibited Kansas from again seeking admission to
statehood until her population had reached 93,420. Just ten days earlier, the House of Representatives had passed a bill previously approved by the Senate for the admission of Oregon, with most of the
opposition coming from Republicans while southern Democrats voted
heavily in the affirmative. Oregon's population amounted to about
half that of Kansas, but it was firmly in Democratic control; it had already elected two Democratic senators; and it seemed likely to provide three electoral votes for the Democratic column in the approaching presidential election. The discrimination against Kansas, now
securely Republican, seemed all the more indefensible as a consequence. Hale's amendment, which had little chance of passage, was a
gesture of protest and also an apple of discord tossed among the
Democrats.[54]

Douglas could not suppress the urge to define his position.
While deploring injection of the Kansas issue into debate on an appropriation measure, he nevertheless virtually repeated his answer to
Lincoln's first question at Freeport. Since the population of Kansas
had been considered large enough for her admission under the Lecompton constitution, it was large enough for her admission with any

other properly framed constitution. If the Hale amendment came to a vote, he would support it. By this time it was late in the evening, however, and the Senate chose to adjourn.[55]

Historians for the most part have failed to note that the critically important debate of the following day, February 23, almost never got started. In fact, a few seconds made all the difference. There is little reason to believe that administration and southern leaders decided overnight to press a quarrel with Douglas over Kansas. They knew that the continuing movement of new settlers into the territory would soon make a moot issue of the controversial population requirement. The Kansas question had obviously lost much of its explosive force, and the general inclination of the Senate was to dispose of the Hale amendment as quickly as possible and get on with the appropriation bill. After some brief remarks by two or three senators on the twenty-third, there came a pause in the discussion. Vice President Breckinridge promptly ordered the pending roll call on the amendment to begin. The clerk, after calling one name and receiving a response, was interrupted by Albert Gallatin Brown of Mississippi, who insisted that he had claimed the floor. Breckinridge at first suggested that Brown was too late, but then changed his mind and recognized him. In so doing, he opened a floodgate.[56]

More radical than Jefferson Davis, his bitter rival for leadership of the Democratic party in Mississippi, Brown was at the same time personally friendly toward Douglas, having supported him for President in 1856, applauded his victory over Lincoln, and opposed his deposition as committee chairman. Brown, a man of plebeian origins, had never been a member of the Senate's "inner circle."[57] In opening fire on the Little Giant at this point, he was acting, not as the agent of a vindictive administration, but rather as an independent voice of southern political extremism. He began by denouncing Hale's proposed amendment but soon transferred his attention to the more general theme of southern rights in the federal territories. The Constitution, as expounded by the Supreme Court, required the protection of slave property in the territories, he maintained. This meant "*adequate* protection, *sufficient* protection," and if not provided by the

territorial government, it must be provided by Congress. "We demand it and we mean to have it," Brown said. If the protection were
denied, he would recommend secession.[58]

The debate that followed lasted ten hours or more and constituted a milestone in the history of the slavery controversy; for at this
point the more theoretical implications of the Dred Scott decision replaced the practical problem of territorial Kansas as the storm center
of sectional conflict. Thomas L. Clingman of North Carolina summed
up the character of the new departure in national politics when he
complained, "We are debating imaginary issues. . . . There is no bill
pending under which this discussion can rise."[59] His words were appropriate for the entire period of two and one-half years between
enactment of the English compromise in May 1858 and the beginning
of secession in November 1860. The crisis of the Union in its final
stages sprang from the contest for the presidency and not from any
controversy over proposed legislation in Congress. The sectional conflict had become an independent emotional force, capable of self-
propulsion and of synthesizing its own specific issues to feed upon.

Douglas responded immediately to Brown's attack and was answered in turn by Jefferson Davis, who spoke frequently during the
debate. Other senators taking prominent part in the effort at giant-
killing were James Mason and Robert M. T. Hunter of Virginia,
James S. Green of Missouri (who had replaced Douglas as chairman
of the committee on territories), and William Bigler of Pennsylvania.
Douglas received help from his two anti-Lecompton colleagues,
David C. Broderick of California and Charles E. Stuart of Michigan,
as well as from George E. Pugh of Ohio. The Republicans sat back
and listened for the first seven hours or so, then joined in and prolonged the discussion.

Still backing away from the starkness of his "unfriendly legislation" formula, Douglas argued that slave property in the territories
was entitled to the same amount of protection given other kinds of
property, and no more; that the extent to which a territorial government might interfere with any property right, including slaveholding,
was a judicial question; and that congressional imposition of a slave
code in the territories would be a violation of the principle of nonin-

tervention. Douglas, in his answer to the second Freeport question, had already implied that the limits of territorial power remained judicially undetermined, thus ignoring Taney's dictum on the subject. But he had then gone on to declare that it did not matter *what* the Supreme Court might "hereafter decide"; that if the people of a territory wanted to exclude slavery, they would find the legal means of doing so. His southern critics were therefore little impressed when he now revived the familiar refrain, "Take it to the Supreme Court of the United States." For he was recommending a cure that he had already labeled futile.[60]

Davis and Brown replied that judicial remedies alone would not be sufficient to protect slave property against a hostile territorial legislature and thus echoed part of the Douglas pronouncement at Freeport. They agreed with his diagnosis but refused to accept his conclusion that nothing further could be done. "What the Government owes to person and property is adequate protection," Davis insisted. "If . . . constitutional rights are violated by the inhabitants of a Territory, or anybody else, it is the duty of Congress to interpose, with whatever power it possesses, to make that protection adequate." As for nonintervention, a "shadowy and fleeting" concept, it meant nothing more than the constitutional inability of Congress either to establish or to prohibit slavery in the territories. It in no way affected the "obligation of the United States to protect its citizens in their constitutional rights." Thus Congress could not establish slavery in the territories but must protect it there. This distinction between *establishing* and *protecting* enabled southerners to turn the meaning of "nonintervention" inside out for the benefit of slavery, without making any concessions to antislavery. As Brown bluntly phrased it, "Our understanding of the doctrine of nonintervention was, that you were not to intervene against us."[61]

With some justification, Douglas could now claim to be defending the principle of nonintervention against Republican and southern interventionists alike. But the theoretical question primarily at issue was whether an interpretation of the Constitution by the Supreme Court became as binding on Congress as the Constitution itself—the very question that Lincoln had raised during the debates in discussing Republican criticism of the Dred Scott decision. Douglas, who had then piously affirmed the sanctity and finality of Supreme Court decisions, now found himself resisting an extreme southern version of the doctrine of judicial supremacy. Pressed hard by Davis on the constitutional duty of Congress as "trustee of the owners of the Territory," he returned a categorical answer: "I will vote against any law by Congress attempting to interfere with a regulation made by the Territories, with respect to any kind of property whatever, whether horses, mules, negroes, or anything else."[62]

Even more emphatic was George E. Pugh, who had supported the Lecompton bill and voted for the English compromise. Vigorously denying that the principle of popular sovereignty had been ruled unconstitutional, he declared: "The court decided no such thing. . . . In the whole Dred Scott case there was no act of a Territorial Legislature before them in any shape or form." The question had not been argued by counsel and had been mentioned only by the Chief Justice. "This is the first time I ever heard," Pugh said, "in a case where nine judges pronounce their opinions *seriatim,* that because one of them in illustration collaterally makes a reference, that becomes the decision of the court." And to southern insistence on a federal slave code for the territories, he responded, "Never; while I live, never! I consider it a monstrous demand."*

The oratory died away at last, and the Senate then rejected Hale's amendment, 27 to 19, as Douglas and Broderick joined the Republican minority. What the long day's debate clearly revealed was the persistence of an irrepressible conflict within the Democratic party. Ostensibly, it had now become a conflict over the meaning of the Dred Scott decision, with each side crying "Never!" to the other's interpretation. Behind it, however, lay the bitter memory of the Lecompton struggle, and just ahead loomed the contest for the presidency. Southerners in large numbers had already announced what they would do if a Republican were elected to that office. Now the debate of February 23 made it plain that southern Democratic leaders

---

*Pugh supported the Lecompton constitution in a speech on March 16, 1858, but voted against it on instructions from the Ohio legislature. He voted against the Crittenden amendment.[63]

would not accept Douglas as the nominee of their party. A prime purpose of the slave code issue was to demonstrate his unacceptability.
As Douglas himself complained, the southerners neither hoped nor
attempted to get a territorial slave code enacted into law. What they
wanted instead was to make it a test of party loyalty and a plank in the
Democratic platform. If they succeeded, Douglas would no doubt be
driven into another revolt; if they failed, there would be adequate
reason for a southern withdrawal from the national convention. Either
way, the demand for congressional protection of slavery in the territories promised to disrupt the Democratic party.

Despite the relative weakness of his following in Congress, there
was mounting evidence that a majority of northern Democrats would
support Douglas, even in the face of Buchanan's determined hostility.
Their motives are easy enough to understand, for the alternative appeared to be political extinction. The lesson of the recent elections
could scarcely be clearer. "We are not in a condition to carry another
ounce of Southern weight," said a Douglas leader in Illinois.[64] Yet, at
a time when they were losing desperately needed ground to the
Republicans in nearly every free state, the northern Democrats were
called upon to shoulder the additional burden of endorsing a slave
code for the territories. The political insensitivity of the southern
demand is difficult to explain.

The South, though increasingly a minority section, had continued to exercise enormous power in national politics. Southerners,
at the beginning of the Buchanan administration, dominated the Supreme Court, dominated presidential counsels, and, through the
caucus system, controlled both houses of Congress. This had all been
possible because of a kind of holding-company arrangement, in which
the South was the majority section within the Democratic party, and
the Democrats were the majority party of the nation. Thus the critical
task of southerners endeavoring to protect slavery within the confines
of the Union was to maintain the majority status of the Democratic
party. In the past, this had meant tolerating some measure of internal
sectional disagreement and camouflaging it at election time with
vague or ambiguous planks in the party platform. Good sense would
seem to have required a continuation of such strategy in the late

1850s. What southern Democrats needed most of all from their northern allies were election victories. What they demanded instead was orthodoxy, as they themselves defined it.

Part of the southern power advantage had already been sacrificed in the struggle for the Lecompton constitution, which, even if successful, would have been admittedly an "empty victory," except as a "point of honour."[65] Now, with strong encouragement from the White House, southern Democratic leaders in Congress turned their backs on political reality by embracing the hopeless and useless cause of a territorial slave code—not with any serious legislative intent but rather as a litmus test for party loyalty. They did so, moreover, hoping to destroy the political effectiveness of the one man who might be able to avert defeat in 1860 and thus prevent a further deterioration of southern power.

In studying southern motives at this point, it is difficult to distinguish calculation from miscalculation, and both, in turn, from irrationality. Certainly there were avowed secessionists working openly to disrupt the Democratic party and welcoming the likelihood of a Republican presidential victory as the best means of achieving disunion. Covertly or subconsciously allied with these bold spirits was a larger group of southerners who continued to describe secession as a last resort while conducting themselves in a way that tended to eliminate other choices. Their "conditional Unionism" with impossible conditions amounted to secessionism in the end. Jefferson Davis exemplifies the latter category, but whether he calculated or miscalculated the consequences of the slave code movement is difficult to determine. He may have done both in that agony of ambivalence with which some southern leaders contemplated the prospect of disunion. Warnings against pressing the demand for a territorial slave code were issued in great profusion, not only by Douglas and his supporters but also by many prominent southerners. For instance, both senators from South Carolina, James Chesnut and James H. Hammond, labeled the demand unwise. James L. Orr, retiring Speaker of the House of Representatives, called it "transparent and atrocious." Robert Toombs, already strongly committed to secession if a Republican should be elected President, acknowledged the theoretical soundness of the demand but then declared:

It is the very foolishness of folly to raise and make prominent such *issues now.* . . . Hostility to Douglas is the sole motive of movers of this mischief. I wish Douglas defeated at Charleston, but I do not want him and his friends crippled or driven off. Where are we to get as many or as good men in the North to supply their places?[66]

Yet, despite such strong misgivings, the Brown-Davis strategy prevailed, and it led in a straight line, as we shall see, to the rupture of the Democratic party at Charleston. The strategy, in effect, gave the suppression of internal dissent priority over the defeat of the Republican enemy—a decision justified with the argument that Douglas's "squatter sovereignty" was as bad as the Wilmot Proviso and perhaps even worse. "It adds insult to injury," said the Memphis *Avalanche,* "for it mocks and derides the just claim of the slaveholder. . . . It is a snare and a swindle, full of mean cunning, rank injustice and insolence."[67] This sense of being cheated out of their judicial victory rankled southerners deeply and no doubt helps account for the unreasoning persistence with which so many of them pursued the slave code issue. Like the fight to prevent resubmission of the Lecompton constitution, it became a "point of honor" to invest the Dred Scott decision with some semblance of political effectiveness. With Kansas pushed into the background, the struggle for southern rights now seemed concentrated in the effort to defend the decision, not only against direct attack but also against the erosive effect of the Freeport doctrine. "I insist," said one Republican senator, "that the Dred Scott decision . . . is the only Democratic platform that now exists. . . . It is the party test."[68]

Still, the thirty-fifth Congress adjourned soon after that one day of explosive debate on February 23, and nine months would elapse before its successor convened. Given the reluctance of many leading southerners to push the slave code issue, it seems possible that in the interval the anti-Douglas movement might have lost some of its force, if Douglas himself had not insisted on pursuing the argument in his usual combative manner.

Not Peace But a Sword

N ow fully determined to seek the presidential nomination, even
though he issued perfunctory disclaimers from time to time,
Stephen A. Douglas felt the irrepressible urge to strike back
at his southern critics and to define his own position in forceful terms.
"I do not intend to make peace with my enemies, nor to make a concession of one iota of principle," he confided to one of his Illinois lieu-
tenants. In several letters written for publication during the summer
of 1859, he declared his opposition, not only to a territorial slave code
but also to reopening the African slave trade, which some southern
radicals had begun to demand.[1] In August, he wrote a long, belligerent reply to a recent speech by William M. Gwin in which the California senator said that Douglas had been removed from his committee chairmanship in condemnation of the "absurd, monstrous, and
dangerous theory" enunciated at Freeport. Douglas quoted the hostile Washington *Union* in support of his questionable contention that
he had been giving voice to the Freeport doctrine ever since 1850,
and he offered a catalog of southerners who had endorsed the principle of territorial self-government, often in language resembling his at
Freeport. Why had there been no reprisals against those other men,
he asked, and why none against him until December 1858?[2]

But these communications all amounted to mere small-arms fire
before a cannonade. Soon after the adjournment of Congress,

Douglas had set to work preparing a comprehensive statement of his position on the territorial question. Arrangements were made to publish it in the September issue of *Harper's Magazine* under the title, "The Dividing Line Between Federal and Local Authority: Popular Sovereignty in the Territories."[3] Anyone who now plods through this often tedious article of some twenty thousand words is likely to wonder how it could have stirred up so much excitement in its day. Yet its publication may have been the most important political act of the year in the United States, if one excludes the Harpers Ferry raid as being essentially a nonpolitical act that had momentous political consequences. The spectacular senatorial debate of February 23 reverberated in newspaper editorials and public speeches throughout the spring and summer of 1859, but the Douglas essay produced an astonishing increase in the volume and intensity of the argument. "Never before," says Robert W. Johannsen, "had the question of slavery in the territories been so widely discussed by so many people."[4]

Harper's Magazine, besieged with Republican and southern proposals to answer Douglas, turned them all down, but newspaper columns and hastily printed pamphlets provided ample battleground for the clangorous war of words. Reverdy Johnson and George T. Curtis, two of the four attorneys in the Dred Scott case, published extensive commentaries. So did Horace Greeley. Buchanan requested his attorney general, Jeremiah S. Black, to prepare a rebuttal, and Black complied with such speed that his unsigned pamphlet appeared scarcely two weeks after publication of the *Harper's* essay. A restatement of standard proslavery doctrine, it was offensive in tone, heaping sarcasm and ridicule, not only on Douglas's argument but also on his literary style.[5]

Douglas, meanwhile, had begun a short speaking tour of Ohio, where the Democrats needed help in the biennial state election. At Wooster on September 16, he replied angrily to Black, calling the latter a "calumniator" who would "prostitute a high government office by writing deliberate falsehoods to mislead the American people."[6] Lincoln, who had followed his old adversary into Ohio, spoke at Columbus on the same day and devoted most of his time to a critique of the *Harper's* essay, which was, he said, "the most maturely considered" of Douglas's "explanations explanatory of explanations explained."[7] But the battle at this point was primarily between Douglas and the administration. Soon Black published an "Appendix" in answer to the Wooster speech. Douglas countered with another pamphlet. Black again replied, and Douglas, in still another pamphlet, had the final word.[8] By then it was past the middle of November, and public attention had long since shifted to John Brown, now convicted, sentenced, and awaiting execution at Charlestown, Virginia. Most people had, in any case, grown weary of the repetitious, ill-tempered exchange between Black and Douglas. It remained to be seen whether they might have silenced the territorial issue by talking it to death.

The question fundamentally at issue in the interminable debate was how the Dred Scott decision had affected the status of slavery in the territories. By denying Congress the power to pass prohibitory legislation, the decision seemed to outlaw the principal plank in the Republican platform. The Republicans therefore could not stop with denunciations of the decision as egregiously wrong. As we have seen, they were also compelled to argue that it had no binding effect on them, and they found two ways of doing so. Many insisted that the Court's invalidation of the 36° 30' restriction was *obiter dictum* and accordingly without legal force. Others, like Lincoln, relied on a narrow definition of judicial review, denying that any court decision could inhibit the political power of Congress.[9] Either way, the arguments amounted to theoretical nullification of the Dred Scott decision and tended to put Republicans on the sidelines in the great territorial debate of 1859–60.

The Democrats, on the other hand, were united in their praise of the Dred Scott decision. They agreed that it affirmed a slave holder's constitutional right to take his slaves into a territory. They also agreed with the diagnostic portion of the Freeport doctrine—that slavery depended upon the support of local law and that a territorial legislature, by withholding such support, could effectively exclude slavery from the territory. But at this point the consensus broke down into bitter conflict. The principal matters of difference were as follows:

1. Orthodox southerners maintained that the Dred Scott decision invalidated not only the Republican doctrine of congressional prohibition but also the Douglas version of popular sovereignty (which they labeled "squatter sovereignty"). That is, the decision denied territorial legislatures the power to prohibit slavery. They quoted the appropriate sentence in Taney's opinion as proof and reinforced it with the logical inference that a subordinate government could not exercise authority denied to the superior government. The Douglas Democrats replied that the Supreme Court had not yet ruled authoritatively on territorial power because the issue had not even arisen in the Dred Scott case (thus they treated the Taney statement on the subject as dictum.) As for the logical inference, they said, it was a legal question that must be settled by the Court and in the meantime remained open to argument.

2. According to Douglas, the action or nonaction of a territorial legislature regarding protection of slavery (or any other property right) was legislatively conclusive. Sometimes he added that a slaveholder dissatisfied with territorial laws affecting slavery could seek redress in the courts. Southerners of the Davis-Brown persuasion insisted that if adequate protection for slavery in the territories was not otherwise provided, Congress must assume the responsibility of doing so.

3. Douglas argued that the Democratic principle of nonintervention, now constitutionally reinforced by the Dred Scott decision, forbade congressional protection of slavery in the territories. Southerners replied that to treat slavery like other property, giving it adequate protection, would not constitute intervention, and they quoted Taney's opinion to show that the Court had ruled only against federal legislation *interfering* with a slaveholder's property rights, not against legislation *protecting* those rights.*

The arguments on both sides were studded with logical flaws and historical inconsistencies. Southerners, after many years of calling for a policy of congressional "nonintervention," had now reversed themselves and begun demanding congressional intervention, while pro-

---

* "The only power conferred is the power coupled with the duty of guarding and protecting the owner in his rights."[10]

testing their continued devotion to the principle of nonintervention. Efforts to rationalize this anomaly resulted in some remarkable hairsplitting. A Memphis editor, for instance, explained that the South did not expect Congress to "foster" slavery in the territories—only to "protect" it.[11] In spite of such verbal camouflage, the southern argument amounted to a brazen assertion that while antislavery legislation by Congress or a territorial legislature was constitutionally forbidden, proslavery legislation by one or the other was not only constitutionally permitted but constitutionally required. Such "one-legged sovereignty," said Douglas Democrats, was not only ridiculous but dangerous; for if Congress had the power to intervene in favor of slavery, it had the power to intervene against slavery."[12] Southern replies to this objection were sometimes cast in colorful analogies. "If you appoint an agent to sell your house, may he set fire to it?" asked one newspaper. "Congress," said another, "cannot legislate any particular religion into the Territories, nor can it legislate any particular religion out of the Territories; but Congress *can* certainly legislate for the protection of the 'meek and lowly followers of Jesus.' "[13]

The argument presented by Douglas was no less vulnerable to criticism, partly because he claimed a consistency that his record did not confirm, and partly because of his determination to justify constitutionally a policy that was sounder in practice than in theory. Having begun to defend his brand of popular sovereignty on constitutional grounds in 1856, he now undertook the more difficult enterprise of providing a constitutional defense for residual popular sovereignty—the Freeport doctrine—in the face of the Dred Scott decision. That slavery could not prosper against the will of the majority in any locality had been acknowledged as an extralegal fact of life by various southerners, including Jefferson Davis. But it was a different matter to have the acknowledgment thrown back at them as a constitutional principle by the man already widely accused of betraying the South. Furthermore, Douglas had previously resorted to the Freeport doctrine primarily as local campaign strategy in Illinois. The *Harper's* essay, published with so much flourish in the nation's leading magazine, seemed far more deliberately anti-southern—almost like a declaration of war.

What Douglas set out to prove in the essay was that territorial legislatures possessed the legal right to establish or prohibit slavery, even though Congress did not.* There were essentially two ways of arriving at such a conclusion, and Douglas with characteristic flexibility followed both. One way (let us call it Argument A) was to derive territorial power from congressional authority, in spite of the Dred Scott decision, by drawing a distinction between what Congress could itself *do* and what it could *authorize* other agencies of government to do.† The other way (Argument B) was to derive territorial power directly from the text of the Constitution or from the natural right of self-government, without any reference to congressional authority. Douglas gave primary attention to Argument B, and the crux of it was his assertion that in the early Republic, western territories had been regarded as incipient states, possessing as much control over their domestic affairs as the thirteen original states of the Union. In evidence, he quoted extensively from Jefferson's Ordinance of 1784, with its generous provisions for the erection of "additional states" in the West. He failed to mention that the ordinance had never been put into operation, and he completely ignored the highly paternalistic Ordinance of 1787, which hardly would have lent support to his case.

Ignoring, indeed, even the official title, "An Ordinance for the government of the Territory of the United States north-west of the River Ohio," Douglas maintained that the founders' generation had always used the word "states" to designate new political communities in the West and the word "territory" to designate public land in the West. The territory clause of the Constitution, he reiterated in harmony with Taney, accordingly had no bearing on the slavery question. Temporary governments in the West were created by Congress under its constitutional authority to admit "new states," and no state,

---

*At other times Douglas acknowledged that this was ultimately a judicial question, but in the *Harper's* essay he was, in effect, presenting the brief for his side of the argument.

† Congress, Douglas argued, could establish judicial and executive bodies, conferring upon them powers that Congress could not itself exercise. Similarly, "Congress may also confer upon the legislative department of the Territory certain legislative powers which it cannot itself exercise."[14]

however incipient, could be denied control over its own domestic institutions. This theory virtually identifying territorial power with state sovereignty was incompatible with the other line of argument already mentioned, in which Douglas distinguished between what Congress could do and what it could authorize. It also conflicted sharply with the attitude he had taken during the recent struggle over Kansas, when he had belittled territorial legislative power in order to deny the legitimacy of the Lecompton constitution.[15] Douglas was in fact never able to make up his mind entirely whether a territorial legislature could prohibit (or establish) slavery because Congress had the power to authorize it (Argument A) or because Congress lacked the power to prevent it (Argument B). His confusion proved to be an advantage, however; for critics found it impossible to pin him down.

Insofar as he based his case for territorial self-government on a lack of congressional power, Douglas could and did follow Taney's strict-constructionist line of reasoning against the constitutionality of the Missouri Compromise restriction. Yet at the same time he could scarcely ignore Taney's loose-constructionist use of the Fifth Amendment and his accompanying dictum declaring that powers expressly forbidden to Congress in the Constitution could not be conferred by Congress on a territorial legislature. Elsewhere, in contexts of political action, it was perhaps enough to deny the legal force of the dictum and offer to abide by a judicial disposition of the question whenever it did in fact come about. But in this essay, designed as a complete vindication of the doctrine of popular sovereignty, Douglas felt compelled to come to grips with the substance of the dictum and its potential effect on his "great principle."

The Taney dictum was an obstruction primarily to Argument A,* and Douglas might have dealt with it by pursuing Argument B to a logical conclusion. The Supreme Court in *Barron v. Baltimore* (1833) had declared that the Fifth Amendment constituted a restraint solely on the federal government and not on the states.[16] Thus, if the people of a territory, as Douglas maintained, possessed "every right,

---

*It was one thing to argue that Congress could confer powers *not delegated* to it to exercise; it would have been something else again to argue that Congress could confer powers that it was *expressly forbidden* to exercise.

privilege, and immunity, in respect to their internal polity and domestic relations," that the people of a state could "exercise under
their constitution and laws," then it would have been reasonable to
conclude that territorial government, like state government, did not
come within the purview of the Fifth Amendment.[17] Such a conclusion, however, would have involved Douglas in difficulties exposing
the fundamental weakness of Argument B.* In any case, he seems
never to have heard of *Barron v. Baltimore.*[18] Instead, he disposed of
the Taney dictum with a different line of argument—one that contradicted the *Barron* decision, misconstrued Taney's opinion, and ended
up ideologically in Republican territory. This section of the *Harper's*
essay, written by the most prominent political figure of the time and
constituting one of the most bizarre commentaries on the Dred Scott
decision, has received curiously little attention from historians, perhaps because it is too much of a tangle.[19]

Taney, in his Dred Scott opinion, never explicitly connected
slaveholding with the Fifth Amendment, but did so rather by unmistakable implication, first defining slaves as property and then talking
about property rights under the Fifth Amendment. Douglas took advantage of this indirection. He quoted several paragraphs in which
the Chief Justice rejected the view that congressional power in the
territories was uninhibited by the restraints of the Constitution and
Bill of Rights. No one would contend, said Taney, that Congress
could pass any law restricting religious freedom in a territory, or
abridging freedom of speech or of the press, or denying the right of
trial by jury, or depriving any person of life, liberty, or property
without due process of law.

> The powers over person and property of which we speak are not
> only not granted to Congress, but are in express terms denied.
> . . . And this prohibition is not confined to the States, but the
> words are general, and extend to the whole territory over which
> the Constitution gives it power to legislate, including those por-

---

* For one thing, the territories were not self-created like the states. They had no bills
of rights, except as *Congress* provided them in organic acts. The people of a state
were protected against their state governments by their state constitutions and bills of
rights.

tions of it remaining under territorial government, as well as that
covered by States.[20]

Beyond any question, Taney was talking in this passage about *federal*
powers exclusively, arguing that constitutional restrictions upon them
were just as effective in the territories as in the states. But Douglas
apparently misread the words "And this prohibition is not confined to
the States." And he built his case on the assumption (contrary to *Barron v. Baltimore*) that the federal Bill of Rights restrained state governments as well as the federal government—which was not the case
until the twentieth century, and then only by virtue of the Fourteenth Amendment.[21]

"Nothing can be more certain," Douglas wrote, "than that the
Court were here speaking only of *forbidden powers*, which were denied alike to Congress, to the State Legislatures, and to the Territorial Legislatures." From this fallacious beginning, he proceeded to
the remarkable conclusion that Taney, in calling attention to such forbidden powers, could not possibly have meant to include power over
slavery. Just why the Chief Justice would otherwise have introduced
the whole subject, he did not attempt to explain.

> If [said Douglas] this sweeping prohibition—this just but inexo-
> rable restriction upon the powers of government—Federal, State,
> and Territorial—shall ever be held to include the slavery question,
> . . . then, indeed, will the doctrine become firmly established
> that the principles of law applicable to African slavery are *uniform
> throughout the dominion of the United States.* . . . If it be said
> that Pennsylvania is a sovereign State, and therefore has a right to
> regulate the slavery question within her own limits to suit herself,
> it must be borne in mind that the sovereignty of Pennsylvania,
> like that of every other State, is limited by the Constitution. . . .
>
> The question recurs then, if the Constitution does establish
> slavery in Kansas or any other Territory beyond the power of the
> people to control it by law, how can the conclusion be resisted
> that slavery is established in like manner and by the same author-
> ity in all the States of the Union? And if it be the imperative duty
> of Congress to provide by law for the protection of slave property
> in the Territories . . . why is it not also the duty of Congress . . .

> to provide similar protection to slave property in all the States of
> the Union, when the Legislatures fail to furnish such protection?[22]

In short, if southern Democrats were right about the meaning of the
Dred Scott decision, then Republicans were right in viewing the
decision as a fateful step toward the nationalization of slavery. Douglas, as Judah P. Benjamin later charged on the Senate floor, had appropriated one of the principal arguments used by Lincoln in the
debates of 1858.

As if that were not aggravation enough for southerners, Douglas
also concurred with Republicans in insisting that slavery was solely a
creature of state law, recognized but in no way authorized by the federal Constitution, and having no claim to special protection from the
federal government except in the matter of fugitive slaves. Otherwise,
he concluded, supporting his case with carefully selected quotations
from Taney's opinion, slave property everywhere stood on the same
footing as other kinds of property and therefore was "dependent upon
the local authorities and laws for protection."[23]

With good reason, then, the Richmond *Enquirer* labeled the
Harper's essay "an incendiary document." Its reverberations, to be
sure, were momentarily drowned out in mid-October by news of the
John Brown raid on Harpers Ferry. But Brown's startling adventure
and Douglas's aggressive manifesto were both incorporated by many
southerners into a nightmarish vision of the southern future within
the Union. For the Harpers Ferry raid seemed to dramatize the rising, implacable strength of their enemies, while the *Harper's* essay
seemed to confirm the dwindling numbers and increasing unreliabil-
ity of their northern friends.[24]

II

The new thirty-sixth Congress assembled on December 5, 1859, a
few weeks after Douglas published his final rejoinder to the attorney
general and just three days after John Brown died on the gallows in
western Virginia. Less than five months ahead lay the Democratic national convention, scheduled to meet at Charleston, of all places. In
retrospect, it appears that there was only one way for the party to

keep the presidency out of Republican hands and thus prevent, or at
least postpone, a secession crisis. That was by uniting behind Douglas. Unity in support of any other candidate probably would not have
been enough; for Douglas alone, precisely because of his recent resistance to proslavery domination, stood much chance of winning electoral votes in the free states.

Some southerners read the situation accurately and denounced
the "folly" of pressing the slave code issue in order to "ruin Douglas"
as a presidential candidate. "Lecompton didn't kill him," said the
Louisville *Democrat*, "and now they must try what the intervention
humbug will do. If it kills the party, no matter, so it kills
Douglas. . . . Never was such a crusade got up against a man, and at
such party expense." [25] These were minority voices for the most part,
however, and the *Harper's* article made it more difficult than ever to
continue supporting Douglas in the South. It was asking a great deal
of southern Democrats to realize that his conduct, however offensive
it might seem, was designed to save them and the party from the
consequences of a Republican victory. Certainly it was asking too
much of Buchanan, whose vindictiveness toward Douglas had become
an obsession, blinding him to the desperate need for party solidarity
at a time of supreme national peril.

Any lingering hope that the President might take the initiative in
a last effort at reconciliation was dispelled by his third annual message
of December 17. Buchanan's previous messages, concentrated as they
were on the Lecompton struggle, had contained only passing references to the Dred Scott case. Now, significantly, almost three years
after the Court's decision, he proceeded to "congratulate" the American people on the "final settlement . . . of the question of slavery in
the Territories." He followed with an explanation of the decision that
was bound to please southerners:

> The right has been established of every citizen to take his property
> of any kind, including slaves, into the common Territories belong-
> ing equally to all the States of the Confederacy, and to have it pro-
> tected there under the Federal Constitution. Neither Congress
> nor a Territorial legislature nor any human power has any author-

ity to annul or impair this vested right. . . . It is a striking proof of the sense of justice which is inherent in our people that the property in slaves has never been disturbed, to my knowledge, in any of the Territories. . . . Had any such attempt been made, the judiciary would doubtless have afforded an adequate remedy. Should they fail to do this hereafter, it will then be time enough to strengthen their hands by further legislation. Had it been decided that either Congress or the Territorial legislature possess the power to annul or impair the right to property in slaves, the evil would have been intolerable. In the latter event there would be a struggle for a majority of the members of the legislature at each successive election, and the sacred rights of property held under the Federal Constitution would depend for the time being on the result. The agitation would thus be rendered incessant whilst the Territorial condition remained, and its baneful influence would keep alive a dangerous excitement among the people of the several States.

Thus has the status of a Territory during the intermediate period from its first settlement until it shall become a State been irrevocably fixed by the final decision of the Supreme Court. Fortunate has this been for the prosperity of the Territories, as well as the tranquillity of the States.[26]

Here, straight from a Pennsylvanian in the White House, was proslavery doctrine pure enough to have satisfied John C. Calhoun, including even a perfunctory acknowledgment that the territories belonged to the states, rather than to the nation. Here was the Dred Scott decision stamped "irrevocable" and Taney's dictum on territorial power accepted as authoritative. Here was a lumping of Douglas's popular sovereignty with Republicanism as not only in violation of the Constitution but also "evil" and "intolerable" in its practical effect. And here was a flat endorsement of the southern demand for congressional protection of slavery in the territories whenever such protection should be needed.

Buchanan, it is true, did seem to leave some room for negotiation by suggesting that congressional intervention might never be necessary because the territorial governments and the federal judiciary could probably be relied upon to protect the slaveholder's "sacred rights of property." But even this narrow opening in the over-cast of mutual hostility was largely an illusion. For one thing, the President knew very well that territorial attacks on slavery had al-ready begun in a deliberate effort to test the status of Taney's dictum and the constitutionality of popular sovereignty. Early in 1858, with the Lecompton controversy raging in Congress, the new free-state legislature of Kansas had boldly repealed several of the territorial laws protecting slavery. One year later, perhaps at the instigation of an edi-torial in the Chicago *Press and Tribune*, the legislature set about test-ing Douglas's Freeport doctrine by enacting a bill abolishing slavery completely.[27] A dramatic announcement of this action punctuated the great one-day debate in the Senate on February 23, 1859.[28] Although a pocket veto by the territorial governor prevented the measure from becoming law, there would plainly be enough antislavery strength to override a veto when the effort was made again in 1860. A similar movement had begun in Nebraska Territory, despite the fact that there were no slaves in residence there.[29] So much, then, for de-pending on territorial protection of slavery. As for judicial protection, that, southerners knew, had already been undercut by Douglas, for the Freeport doctrine was *post-judicial* in its denial of southern con-stitutional rights. Residual popular sovereignty amounted to what remained of territorial power *after, and in spite of,* judicial interven-tion.

The question really at issue, in any case, was not whether Congress should enact protective legislation but whether the south-ern right to have such legislation should be established as Democratic dogma and imposed as a test of party loyalty, thus presumably closing off Douglas's path to the presidential nomination. Southern and ad-ministration leaders were determined to use their numerical advan-tage in the Senate as a kind of preliminary convention caucus to strengthen their hands against the Little Giant at Charleston. It did not matter that the question appeared to be almost entirely aca-demic—that the slave code recently adopted in New Mexico was as meaningless as the antislavery legislation proposed in Kansas and Nebraska—for sectional anger, having overrun the sectional issues, even within the Democratic party, had become an independent, ex-plosive force, now more cause than effect.

The mood of the new Congress was set by the Harpers Ferry raid and its aftermath, which sent a "wave of indignation, hatred, and fear" sweeping across the whole South.[30] To many southerners the irrepressible conflict for the first time seemed actually at hand. Most Republicans, dismayed and put on the defensive, hastened to dissociate their kind of antislavery from John Brown's violent activism. Yet the affair lent no encouragement to the restoration of Democratic solidarity. Rather, it reinforced the southern sense of being isolated in a hostile world and seemed to call more for sectional than party unity. Besides, another recent act of violence, overshadowed by the melodrama of Harpers Ferry, had pointed up the fierceness of enmities within the Democratic party. David Broderick of California, a vehement ally of Douglas in the Lecompton struggle, did not return to his seat in the Senate. He had been killed in a duel with a leader of the proslavery faction in his state. His last words reportedly were, "I die because I was opposed to a corrupt administration and the extension of slavery."[31]

The defection of Douglas taught many southerners not to depend any longer on the help of northern political allies, and the Harpers Ferry raid intensified the old southern fear of servile rebellion. At about the same time, a different kind of menace arose in the form of an antislavery book written by a nonslaveholding North Carolinian. Hinton Rowan Helper's *The Impending Crisis of the South*, published in 1857, exploited class divisions and struck at white solidarity by condemning slavery as an economic curse for the plain folk of the South. "No dogma of the southern creed was held more sacrosanct," says David M. Potter, "than the tenet that race transcended class and, indeed, extinguished it. . . . And no form of attack—not even the appeal for a slave insurrection—found the South more vulnerable than did an appeal to the nonslaveholders to reject the slave system."[32] Savagely denounced in the South as the "incendiary, insurrectionary" work of a "renegade" and "scoundrel," the book was obviously a propaganda windfall for the Republican party. By late 1859, plans were well advanced to print 100,000 copies of an abridged version for use in the approaching presidential campaign. Sixty-eight Republican members of Congress had given the project their written endorsement.[33]

One of the sixty-eight was John Sherman of Ohio, whom the Republican caucus nominated for speaker. The midterm elections had given the Republicans a plurality in the House of Representatives, but they needed ten additional votes for a majority. Sherman's association with the Helper book prevented him from making up the deficiency among anti-Lecompton Democrats or southern Americans. In his best showing he still fell three votes short of victory. Efforts to unite the anti-Republican majority, strenuously supported by Douglas, likewise ended in failure. The contest dragged on through December and to the end of January. Congress could transact no business, but it *could* engage in acrimonious debate, and frayed tempers were not improved by the inability of members to draw any compensation. Seething hostility often expressed itself in open discourtesy and insult—especially on the floor of the House, which more than once seemed likely to become the scene of a murderous brawl. Charles Sumner, back in his Senate seat after three and one-half years of almost unremitting absenteeism, was a conspicuous reminder that oratorical excess could easily lead to physical violence, even within the walls of the Capitol. In both houses many men armed themselves and fingered their weapons nervously when debate became heated. Senator James H. Hammond, with grim hyperbole, said that the only members not carrying a revolver and a knife were those carrying two revolvers. Some southern radicals favored withdrawing from Congress if Sherman was elected speaker. There was also talk of forcibly preventing Sherman from taking the chair. The governor of South Carolina promised to send a regiment in support of such a move, and there were reports that Governor Henry A. Wise of Virginia was ready to seize Washington if fighting should break out.[34]

Finally, on January 30, the Republicans shifted their support from Sherman to the less controversial William Pennington of New Jersey and elected him two days later. For southerners it was a defeat softened by the knowledge that the radical wing of the Republican party had been thwarted.* "We have whipped out Sherman and the

*Pennington, a former Whig now somewhat loosely associated with Republicanism, had not endorsed the Helper book. It is interesting to speculate on the possible consequences of a Sherman victory. There might have been some effort at resistance, but

Helperites," said Robert Toombs. "Seward died hard but he is slain."[35] At the same time, Douglas Democrats could take some encouragement from the fact that one of their number, John A. McClernand of Illinois, received the votes of most southern Democrats in a last-minute effort to head off Pennington.[36] Perhaps this signified that the South, however reluctantly, would accept Douglas as their only effective shield against Republicanism. As if to discountenance any such hopes before they could take root, Jefferson Davis arose in the Senate on February 2 and offered a series of resolutions designed to put Douglas in his place as a party heretic.

Of course the senatorial debate on slavery in the territories had been resumed many weeks earlier. Among southerners there was obviously a determination to strike back at the *Harper's* essay. On December 7, for example, the intemperate Alfred Iverson of Georgia launched into a series of speeches attacking not only the Republicans but Douglas and northern Democrats generally. The latter, he declared, were "as rotten as the Black Republicans" on the "vital question" of the day.[37] These remarks were ostensibly part of debate on a resolution concerning the Harpers Ferry raid. Then in mid-December, as a platform from which to answer Iverson, George E. Pugh offered a resolution looking toward repeal of the clause in the Utah and New Mexico acts reserving for Congress the right to disallow territorial legislation. A standard feature of organic acts until 1854, disallowance had been omitted from the Kansas-Nebraska Act in deference to the principle of nonintervention. Pugh was merely proposing to make that omission more nearly uniform throughout the territorial system.* Since the Utah and New Mexico governments had passed laws for the protection of slavery, the resolution seemed designed to forestall a Republican effort at disallowance. But Pugh justified it on grounds of nonintervention in terms that amounted to "waving a red flag in the faces of those who advocated a federal slave code."[38]

The Pugh resolution furnished the principal basis for senatorial

---

it probably would have failed, casting disrepute on secessionism generally and perhaps, like a small earthquake, taking off some of the strain.

*In legal terms, it seems likely that Congress retained the inherent power to disallow territorial laws, whether specified in the organic act or not.

debate on slavery in the month that followed. With Broderick dead,
Charles E. Stuart retired, and Douglas frequently absent because of
recurring illness, Pugh now became the chief spokesman for the
Douglas position. Under interrogation, he insisted that the authority
of a territorial government came from "the will of the people," thus
reaffirming the legality of residual popular sovereignty—that is, the
lawful right of a territorial population to exclude slavery, in spite of
the Dred Scott decision. This, of course, was a reply to the southern
inferential argument that what Congress could not do, Congress
could not authorize territorial legislatures to do; and a reply also to
the distinction between "right" and "power" with which Jefferson
Davis and other southerners sought to cover up their own flirtations
with the Freeport doctrine.

But Douglas, it will be remembered, had really given two answers to Lincoln's second question at Freeport, and ever since the
close of the senatorial contest he had been disposed to softpedal the
doctrine of unfriendly legislation, emphasizing instead the argument
that the Supreme Court had not yet decided the question of territorial power over slavery. Pugh followed this strategy in the debate on
his resolution and once again was bolder than Douglas in rejecting
Taney's dictum on territorial power, which, he said, conflicted with
other parts of the Taney opinion. Pugh also cited the passage in Justice Campbell's opinion that seemed to contradict the Taney dictum,
and he suggested that Taney's opinion was no more than nominally
the opinion of the Court. In passing, he even cast doubt on the propriety of Taney's decision to review the plea in abatement.[39]

Such talk from a fellow Democrat was gall and wormwood to
southerners whose territorial doctrine now depended heavily on the
content of Taney's opinion, and not merely on the letter of the
Court's decision in the Dred Scott case. The running debate on the
Pugh resolution became exceptionally heated during the second
week of January. Iverson plunged into another denunciation of the
Douglas Democrats, calling for the formation of a southern confederacy and promising swift retribution to any "abolition army" that
might attempt to preserve the Union by force. "By the Eternal," he
exclaimed, "we should hang them up like dogs to the trees of our

forests." Douglas, responding to this and other attacks, announced that he would wait until they were finished and then "fire at the lump." The phrase had a ring of contempt and provoked furious rejoinders from Davis, Green, and Clement C. Clay of Alabama. Albert Gallatin Brown added fuel to the fire with resolutions instructing the committee on territories to include positive protection of slavery in all future territorial legislation.[40]

The southern leadership in the Senate still had no desire to press for immediate legislation, however. What they wanted instead was an anti-Douglas platform for Charleston, phrased in such a way as to maximize southern solidarity. On February 2, 1860, Jefferson Davis supplied the need with a set of resolutions that sounded like "Calhoun brought up to date."[41] Endorsed by the President, approved with some minor revisions by the Democratic caucus, and reintroduced on March 1, they became the focus of sectional debate over slavery for the rest of the session. The critical resolutions were those numbered four to six, as follows:

> 4. That neither Congress nor a Territorial Legislature, whether by direct legislation or legislation of an indirect and unfriendly character, possesses power to annul or impair the constitutional right of any citizen of the United States to take his slave property into the common Territories, and there hold and enjoy the same while the territorial condition remains.

> 5. That if experience should at any time prove that the judiciary and executive authority do not possess means to insure adequate protection to constitutional rights in a Territory, and if the territorial government shall fail or refuse to provide the necessary remedies for that purpose, it will be the duty of Congress to supply such deficiency.

> 6. That the inhabitants of a Territory of the United States, when they rightfully form a constitution to be admitted as a State into the Union, may then, for the first time . . . decide for themselves whether slavery as a domestic institution shall be maintained or prohibited within their jurisdiction. . . .[42]

The sixth resolution, it will be seen, amounted to the barren southern version of popular sovereignty; the fourth reaffirmed the Dred Scott decision, with Taney's dictum included and the Freeport doctrine expressly rejected. Both were unacceptable to Douglas Democrats. The fifth resolution, on the other hand, stated the case for congressional intervention in terms so contingent and bland that not even Pugh opposed it when the resolutions finally came to a vote late in May.* Viewed as planks for the Democratic platform, the resolutions had the effect of excluding Douglas without embarrassing certain senators, such as Gwin of California and William Bigler of Pennsylvania, who were reluctant to appear as open advocates of a federal slave code. Davis himself insisted that all talk of a "slave code" was misrepresentation. The South, he said, wanted only the assurance of remedial legislation if local conditions in a territory should make it necessary.[44]

The fifth resolution was nevertheless already something of a farce by the time it came to a vote; for in February, the Kansas legislature had passed a bill prohibiting slavery and then repassed it over the veto of Governor Samuel Medary. The time for congressional intervention had therefore arrived, said the Jackson *Mississippian.* "We invoke the guardians of the people's rights at Washington to come at once to the rescue."[45] Albert Gallatin Brown promptly introduced a bill to "punish offenses against slave property" in Kansas, but it was referred to the Senate committee on territories and remained buried there.[46] During debate in May after the breakup of the Charleston convention, Judah P. Benjamin acknowledged that legislation for the protection of slavery in Kansas would be a waste of time. "We want a recognition of our right, because it is denied," he said, "but we do not want to exercise it now, because there is no occasion for exercising it now."[47]

*All of the Davis resolutions were approved *seriatim* on May 24 and 25; Douglas was again absent on account of illness. The Pugh and Brown resolutions never came to a vote.[43]

III

The interminable debate in the Senate over a right to be claimed but not exercised was echoed in the House of Representatives, in newspaper columns, in many state legislatures, and in the local and state conventions of the Democratic party which were at work choosing delegates to send to Charleston. With Illinois leading the way, the conventions in the Old Northwest lined up unanimously behind Douglas. Although his support in the other northern states was less solid, it became increasingly clear that he had no pre-eminent rival for the presidential nomination and could expect to receive a majority of the votes on the first ballot.[48] But a convention rule dating back to 1832 required a two-thirds majority to nominate, and that was a different matter. Douglas would need some southern help to win; yet the state conventions in the South, one by one, turned their faces against his candidacy and endorsed the principles of the Davis resolutions. The Alabama Democrats went further and instructed their delegates to withdraw from the national convention if a satisfactory platform were not adopted.[49]

So the Charleston convention assembled on April 23 in a condition of virtual stalemate, the Douglas delegates being numerous enough to dictate a platform but not to nominate their candidate. Hindsight accordingly encourages us to believe that the disruption of the convention was more or less inevitable from the start, but to the participants themselves other possibilities seemed open for a time. Southerners had reason to believe that by holding out firmly against Douglas they could force him to withdraw from the contest. His name had been withdrawn at a critical moment in the 1856 convention, and there were rumors that his floor manager carried conditional authorization to do so again.[50] Douglas men, at the same time, could see two ways of increasing their percentage of the total vote. By making concessions on the platform they might recruit some moderate southerners to their ranks. On the other hand, by rejecting demands for an explicitly proslavery platform they might provoke enough southern walkouts to leave themselves a two-thirds majority of the delegates remaining in the hall.

In the circumstances, the order of business became extremely important, and the Democratic party had no fixed precedent on the subject. The national conventions of 1848 and 1852 had nominated candidates before adopting platforms; the convention of 1856 had reversed the procedure. At Charleston, the delegates in a rare moment of consensus voted almost unanimously to construct their platform first.[51] The decision seemed to fit a variety of strategies. It suited the Douglas cohorts, for example, and also the proslavery militants who wanted a southern defeat as the provocation for a southern walkout. The acquiescence of southern moderates and northern doughfaces is more difficult to understand. On all sides, however, there appears to have been an urgent desire for a swift and conclusive showdown between the hostile forces in the convention. One vote on the platform would perhaps be enough, whereas the business of nomination might drag on through scores of ballots.

And so the Democratic party came to its breaking point over the issue of slavery in the territories, as affected by the Dred Scott decision—an issue that had lost much of its practical significance while becoming ever more intensely charged with symbolic meaning and emotional force. The platform committee consisted of thirty-three members, one from each state. The delegates from Oregon and California joined the fifteen southerners to present a majority report denying territorial power over slavery and calling for federal protection of the institution whenever it might be needed. The minority report discreetly reaffirmed the bland Cincinnati platform of 1856 and referred the question of territorial power to the Supreme Court. There was no insistence on the Douglas version of popular sovereignty, no reiteration of the Freeport doctrine.

The crisis came when these reports were presented to the convention. An anti-Douglas tirade by the Alabama fire-eater, William L. Yancey, and an angry rebuttal by Pugh, set the tone for the ensuing struggle. The Douglas forces, with their superior numbers, proceeded to adopt the minority report. As one last gesture of compromise, however, they eliminated the resolution referring the territorial question to the Supreme Court. This left a platform that said nothing about slavery beyond reaffirming the Cincinnati platform. It was an inoffensive rejection of southern demands, but a rejection none the less, and when the voting ended, the Alabama delegation announced its withdrawal from the convention, followed by the delegates from Mississippi, Louisiana, South Carolina, Florida, Texas, and Arkansas. The Georgia delegates took their departure the next day.[52] With the exception of Arkansas, these were the same states that, after Lincoln's election, would secede from the Union and form the Southern Confederacy. Their delegations withdrew from the convention, it should be emphasized, rather than accept the party platform of 1856 and out of implacable hostility to the man whom they had supported overwhelmingly for the nomination just four years earlier.* Such was the revolutionary change of attitude in the Deep South, wrought primarily by the Lecompton controversy, the Dred Scott decision, and the Harpers Ferry raid.

The withdrawal of fifty-one southern delegates cast a pall of gloom over the rest of the proceedings, and it brought Douglas no closer to success. With the New York delegation deserting him momentarily, the convention voted to require a two-thirds majority of its entire membership for the presidential and vice-presidential nominations. This questionable decision had the effect of allowing the seceders to vote silently against the Little Giant. As a consequence, the fifty-seven ballots that followed were plainly a waste of time, and Douglas in fact never even received two-thirds of the votes cast, let alone two-thirds of the whole number in the convention. Finally, on the tenth day of the convention, the delegates approved a proposal that they adjourn and reassemble at Baltimore on June 18.[53]

There followed an interval of consultation, planning, and maneuver in preparation for resumption of the struggle at Baltimore. Meanwhile, the Republican convention assembled at Chicago in mid-May and surprised everyone by nominating Abraham Lincoln instead of the odds-on favorite, William H. Seward. A week earlier, delegates from the Whig-American remnant had likewise gathered in convention and undertaken to "save the country . . . by ignoring all the

---

*Until the withdrawal of his name at Cincinnati in 1856, Douglas received all the votes of South Carolina, Alabama, Mississippi, Florida, Texas, and Arkansas, as well as 7 out of 10 votes from Georgia. Only Louisiana supported Buchanan.

rugged issues of the day."[54] Calling themselves the "Constitutional Union Party," they nominated the elderly Tennessee Whig, John Bell, on a platform of having no platform other than "the Constitution of the Country, the Union of the States, and the Enforcement of the Laws."

Congress continued in session, and the Senate resumed its long-winded discussion of the Davis resolutions. Douglas, still the target of furious southern attack, defended himself for three hours on May 15; then, sick and exhausted, he had to stop and finish up the next day. Davis was likewise ill but hastened to reply, displaying "the face of a corpse, the form of a skeleton," with "haggard, sunken, weary eye" and "thin white wrinkled lips clasped close upon the teeth in anguish."[55] He too extended his speech into a second day, and then it became a running exchange between the two ailing men. Toombs, Hale, Benjamin, Pugh, and others took their oratorical turns. The arguments, the quotations, the historical summaries were all familiar. Nothing new remained to be said.[56]

The central point at issue was still the meaning of the Dred Scott decision. Republicans continued to deny its legitimacy. It was a "perfectly monstrous" idea, said Hale, that the solemn convictions of the people of the free states could be set aside by "this snap judgment, in this suit, brought by a man who the Court decided was not competent to bring any suit at all."[57] Douglas Democrats continued to circumscribe the decision, acknowledging its force as applied to congressional power but denying that it had settled the question of territorial power. They promised, however, to acquiesce in any future judicial ruling on the latter subject. Southerners continued to insist that the Dred Scott decision had settled all outstanding territorial issues in their favor—that both the Republicans and the Douglas Democrats were trying to cheat them of a clear-cut victory in the courts. Douglas, said Benjamin, had solemnly agreed in 1856 to abide by a judicial decision on territorial power and had then violated that agreement during his debates with Lincoln. The Freeport doctrine, Toombs declared, turned judicial remedy into a farce; it meant "heads you win, tails we lose." Reiterating the demand for congressional protection of slavery in the territories, he added, "If the dissolution of the

Union be the cost of protection, I say, let it come, and the sooner the better." Nothing in the Senate debate justified any hope of a reconciliation at Baltimore.[58]

At Baltimore, before the platform struggle could be renewed, a crisis arose over the status of the Charleston bolters, most of whom now wanted to reclaim their seats. After several days of confusion and tension while the credentials committee pondered the problem, the convention voted to readmit about two-thirds of the bolters seeking reinstatement, but it awarded the Alabama and Louisiana seats to contesting Douglas delegations. Scarcely an overwhelming victory for the Little Giant, the decision nevertheless precipitated another walkout. This time, with the Virginians taking the lead, about one-third of the delegates withdrew from the floor. Caleb Cushing resigned as presiding officer and marched out with them. The shocked but resolute delegates remaining in the hall then nominated Douglas for the presidency.[59] The seceders hastened to convene elsewhere in Baltimore, placing Cushing in the chair and declaring themselves to be the true national convention of the Democratic party. As their candidate for the presidency, they nominated Vice President John C. Breckinridge of Kentucky, after which Yancey unlimbered his oratorical talents and for several hours pronounced a radical benediction on the proceedings.[60]

As a party platform, the Breckinridge convention simply adopted the majority report of the resolutions committee at Charleston, with its denial of territorial power over slavery and its demand for federal protection whenever needed. The Douglas convention had left itself at Charleston with a mere reaffirmation of the Cincinnati platform. During the Baltimore proceedings, however, an additional resolution was proposed by one of the new Douglas delegates from Louisiana:

> That it is in accordance with the interpretation of the Cincinnati platform, that during the existence of the Territorial Governments the measure of restriction, whatever it may be, imposed by the Federal Constitution on the power of the Territorial Legislature over the subject of the domestic relations, as the same has been or shall hereafter be finally determined by the Supreme Court of the United States, should be respected by all good citizens, and en-

forced with promptness and fidelity by every branch of the General Government.[61]

This diffuse formulation, highly praised by one of the leading Douglas managers and approved almost unanimously, surrendered much of what Douglas had presumably been contending for. It acknowledged that popular sovereignty might be unconstitutional and that the Supreme Court might already have declared it so. More than that, the resolution virtually embraced the principle of congressional intervention, declaring that "every branch" of the federal government must enforce whatever judicial determination there had been, or might be, regarding slavery in the territories.

The Douglas and Breckinridge platforms were very nearly identical, except in their interpretations of the Dred Scott decision, and by no means diametrically opposed even on that subject. The bolters had bolted at Charleston after failing to get everything they wanted in the platform, and at Baltimore after failing to get everything they wanted in the reseating of delegates. Back of all this intransigence there was an *ad hominem* determination. When it came to the test, a majority of Democrats from the Deep South preferred to break up their party rather than accept the nomination of Douglas, just as they had already resolved to break up the Union rather than accept the election of a Republican president. In this respect the Democratic conventions were rehearsals for secession.

The Republicans in their platform discreetly refrained from making any direct attack on the Supreme Court, but they repudiated the Dred Scott decision without mentioning it by name. One plank denounced the "new dogma" that the Constitution of its own force carried slavery into the territories, labeling it "a dangerous political heresy . . . revolutionary in its tendency, and subversive of the peace and harmony of the country." Another plank, drawn from the platform of 1856, defiantly reasserted that the "normal condition" of the territories was freedom and denied "the authority of Congress, of a territorial legislature, or of any individuals, to give legal existence to slavery in any territory of the United States." When it came to prescribing a course of action, however, the Republican phrasing seemed uncharacteristically tentative and mild. Whereas the platform of 1856 had labeled slavery a "relic of barbarism" and demanded "positive legislation" prohibiting it in the territories, the document approved in 1860 merely called for congressional prohibition "whenever such legislation is necessary."[62]

This modulation undoubtedly reflected a desire to broaden the appeal of Republicanism and dissociate the party from the radicalism of John Brown, but it signified no general retreat from the principles of 1856 and certainly no concession to the Douglas brand of popular sovereignty, which was dismissed elsewhere in the platform as a "deception and fraud."[63] The "when necessary" formula will be recognized as a qualification already added to the southern demand for congressional protection of slavery in the territories. Thus the Republicans and the southern militants now both took the position that territorial legislatures could decide the question of slavery as long as they decided it in the right way. Otherwise, Congress must intervene. This was what George E. Pugh had called "one-legged sovereignty."

The new Republican flexibility on the territorial issue was an expression, not of timidity but rather of confidence—a confidence springing from the realization that in practical terms the struggle against slavery in the territories had already been won, and also from the expectation that the Republican party would soon take possession of the federal government. A fierce doctrinairism is one of the modes of powerlessness. The Republicans could afford to speak more softly because they expected soon to be carrying a very big stick. Southerners, certainly, derived no comfort from the relatively moderate tone of the Chicago platform. They viewed it as mere "crafty tactics" of dissimulation aimed at gathering northern conservative votes and lulling southern apprehensions.[64]

The fact was that slavery in the territories as affected by the Dred Scott decision, although it continued to be a prime subject of controversy throughout the presidential campaign and during the secession crisis that followed, had long since ceased to be a critical national problem. With the future of Kansas as a free state actually determined in 1858, it is difficult to visualize a major sectional crisis arising thereafter out of any territorial or statehood struggles in Congress. Instead, the paramount problem already facing the American people by the late spring of 1860 was how the rest of the nation would respond to the likely secession of more than a few southern states in the likely event of a Republican presidential victory.

Secession and coercion had been discussed often enough in newspaper editorials and legislative debates. Along with their frequent threats of disunion, southerners had sometimes demanded to know whether northerners thought they could hold the South in the Union by force, perhaps adding some graphic description of what would happen to any army so foolish as to try. Republican leaders, while insisting that secession was tantamount to rebellion and utterly impermissible, were generally reluctant to say just how they would go about preventing it. Thus the Chicago platform declared;

> . . . we hold in abhorrence all schemes for disunion, come from whatever source they may; and we congratulate the country that no Republican member of Congress has uttered or countenanced the threats of disunion so often made by Democratic members, without rebuke and with applause from their political associates; and we denounce those threats of disunion, in case of a popular overthrow of their ascendancy, as denying the vital principles of a free government, and as an avowal of contemplated treason, which it is the imperative duty of an indignant People sternly to rebuke and forever silence.[65]

The emphatic tone of the passage is somewhat dissipated by the ambiguity of its final clause, which can be read as merely calling for a Republican victory at the polls or as proposing coercive measures against secession. Nevertheless, this was the only platform statement by any political party on the real issue facing the nation, and it could hardly be characterized as a retreat from the Republican principles of 1856. The degree of Republican radicalism on slavery now mattered less than the degree of Republican militancy toward secession. Lincoln, for instance, had been nominated in part because he seemed less radical than Seward. What mattered most in the winter and spring of 1861, however, was that he proved to be more militant than Seward.

IV

The nomination of Lincoln astonished most of the country, but his election in November took no one by surprise. Separately, neither Breckinridge nor Bell nor Douglas had any chance of winning, and efforts to form an anti-Republican coalition succeeded in only a few states.[66] The best hope was that Lincoln might somehow be denied an electoral majority, whereupon the election would be cast into the House of Representatives. Few southerners were sanguine, however. "The result of the Presidential struggle is no longer one of much doubt or uncertainty," said the Columbia *South Carolinian* more than three months before election day. "Take State by State, and make whatever calculations we may, . . . and we can arrive at no other conclusion than that Lincoln is to be the next President of the United States."[67]

Their early recognition of the likelihood of defeat gave southerners abundant time before the election to consider what a Republican presidency would mean for the South and what ought to be done about it. On both questions there was disagreement along a wide spectrum, for the southern consensus on slavery never translated into a consensus on disunion. In the Deep South, however, the emotional advantage was on the side of the immediate secessionists, who predicted the disruption, sooner or later, of slaveholding society if the southern people submitted meekly to Republican rule.

As president, Lincoln would of course appoint Republicans to territorial offices, thereby further discouraging slaveholders from exercising their rights under the Dred Scott decision. In cataloguing the reasons for withdrawing from the Union, secessionists did usually list the "exclusion of the South from the common territory," but they gave it surprisingly little emphasis. In the South Carolina "Declaration of Causes of Secession," for example, twenty times more space was devoted to the fugitive slave problem than to the territorial issue.[68]

The stated purpose of the Republican party from its inception had been to prevent the extension of slavery, and the election of Lincoln practically converted the purpose into an accomplished fact. Whether the South could have learned to live with that fact is an academic question; for a majority of southerners read much more in the outcome of the election than a mere confirmation of their defeat in the territorial struggle. Believing that Republicanism was a stealthier, more devious version of abolitionism, they saw Lincoln's victory as the beginning of a revolution and in some respects a declaration of war by the North on the South. The full consequences of the revolution might be slow in coming, but the message of the election took effect immediately and seemed plain enough to many southerners, including Thomas L. Clingman of North Carolina. "It is not," said he, ". . . merely that a dangerous man has been elected to the Presidency of the United States."

> We know that under our complicated system that might very well occur by accident, and he be powerless; but I assert that the President-elect has been elected *because he was known to be a dangerous man.* He avows the principle that is known as the "irrepressible conflict." He declares that it is the purpose of the North to make war upon my section until its social system has been destroyed. . . . That declaration of war is dangerous because it has been indorsed by a majority of the votes of the free States in the late election.[69]

Southern political leaders and editors favoring secession, or leaning toward it, developed a scenario for the future of the South under Republican rule, addressing themselves especially to the argument that disunion should not be embraced until the Lincoln administration had committed some kind of overt act against the South. Of course, said the scenarists, there would be no such overt act in the beginning. Instead, the Republicans would set about consolidating their power in the North and insidiously dividing the South. Their energy and public appeal further enhanced by capture of the presidency, they would regain control of the House of Representatives and, with the admission of additional free states, soon become masters of the Senate. Furthermore, it was only a matter of time until the presidential power of appointment would place an antislavery majority on the Supreme Court. Then, in full command of all departments of the federal government, the Republicans could "plunder the

South" with a protective tariff, repeal or emasculate the Fugitive Slave Law, abolish slavery in the territories, and prohibit the interstate slave trade. The South, at the same time, would be losing its ability to resist such aggression. Federal offices would furnish the basis for a southern abolitionist party. Then, said the Charleston *Mercury,* "the contest for slavery will no longer be one between the North and the South. It will be in the South, between the people of the South." Then, said the New Orleans *Delta,* "the armies of our enemies will be recruited from our own forces." Meanwhile, the slaveholding South would be shrinking in size, as the continued loss of slaves converted Missouri, Kentucky, Maryland, and Delaware into free states. And everywhere the uninhibited circulation of abolitionist propaganda and the emboldened invasions of abolitionist agitators would inspire chronic servile rebellion and thus destroy slave society from within.[70]

Indeed, many southerners were convinced that the work of destruction had already begun. In the midst of the presidential campaign, with apprehensions aroused by John Brown still keenly felt, a new wave of fear swept through the South. From here and there came reports of slaves in revolt, of conspiracies uncovered just in time, of abolitionist agitators caught and hung. The wildest rumors emanated from Texas, where a gigantic plot allegedly called for wholesale poisoning and arson as the first step in a general uprising. Skeptics insisted that this was largely campaign propaganda in behalf of Breckinridge and secession, but the reports were amplified in the southern press and widely believed to the verge of hysteria. The Charleston *Mercury,* for instance, solemnly declared on October 11 that twenty towns in Texas had been burned down by abolitionists during the preceding year. From Mississippi, the brother of Attorney General Joseph Holt wrote of "almost daily conflagrations" in the Deep South and of slaves supplied with knives and pistols by emissaries from the North. "This army of assassins," he said, "must number thousands and they have at their command strichnine and arsenic in such quantities as show that special factories have been established to meet their demand." Roger B. Taney was just one of many southerners who feared that the announcement of Lincoln's election would be the signal for a general slave rebellion. Others thought that it might all begin on Inauguration Day. But in any case, the full terror lay somewhere ahead. "If such things come upon us," said a Georgia newspaper, "with only the *prospect* of an Abolition ruler, what will be our condition when he is *actually in power?*" [71]

With the election of Lincoln, because of what that election seemed to signify, the sectional conflict had far overrun the issue of slavery in the territories. Then the secession movement began, precipitating a new national crisis and presenting a set of new national issues even more remote from the territorial question. Yet in the final efforts to save the Union by engineering another great compromise, the territorial question, despite its questionable relevance, once again became the center of attention. Its hypnotic influence was apparently still as strong as ever. Compromise leaders seemed pathetically convinced that if they could somehow solve this most troublesome of old problems, all the terrible new ones would go away.

The major sectional crises of the past had been susceptible of compromise in Congress because they had arisen in Congress and were more or less within congressional control. The crisis of 1860–61 was of an entirely different order; for it resulted from a decision of the American people at the polls, and that decision could not in itself be reversed or modified by congressional action. Compromise leaders could only try to cushion the shock of Lincoln's election by securing legislation that would in some degree meet southern demands for security and sectional parity within the Union. They had to contend, moreover, not only with the momentum of a secession movement briskly in progress but also with growing sentiment in the North against any concessions extorted by the threat of disunion. Congress, in short, had little control over the crisis of 1860–61, but historical tradition and public expectation required that it go through the familiar motions of legislative compromise.

Public attention was directed primarily to the Senate, which, after all, had long been the matrix of sectional compromise, and the Senate responded in the spirit of 1850 by creating a special Committee of Thirteen to consider remedies for the "agitated and distracted condition of the country." It seemed entirely appropriate that the

leader of the committee (though not its official chairman) should be
John J. Crittenden of Kentucky, who held the seat once occupied by
Henry Clay. Crittenden, moreover, was ready with his own "omnibus" of Union-saving measures.[72] Consisting of six constitutional
amendments and four supplementary resolutions, it was largely proslavery in character. It promised to settle once and for all the longstanding argument over whether slavery was an institution sanctioned
by the federal Constitution or strictly a creature of state and local law.
The words "slave" and "slavery," never used in the Constitution itself, appeared fifteen times in the text of the six amendments.

Thus the Crittenden package, unlike those of 1820 and 1850, did
not constitute a real compromise. Instead, it was a weight to be
placed on one side of the sectional balance as a means of restoring the
equilibrium allegedly destroyed by the election of 1860. It was in a
sense the price to be paid by Republicans for proceeding with the inauguration of Abraham Lincoln.

The most critical item in the package was a constitutional amendment restoring and extending the Missouri Compromise line:

> In all the territory of the United States now held, or hereafter
> acquired, situate north of latitude 36°, 30', slavery or involuntary
> servitude, except as a punishment for crime, is prohibited while
> such territory shall remain under territorial government. In all the
> territory south of said line of latitude, slavery of the African race is
> hereby recognized as existing, and shall not be interfered with by
> Congress, but shall be protected as property by all the depart-
> ments of the territorial government during its continuance.

Here, Crittenden proposed to revive a territorial solution that had
been dead and officially buried for a number of years—a solution that
antislavery men had long been unwilling to accept and that southerners had grown accustomed to denouncing in retrospect as a gross
injustice to their section.[73]

Other amendments forbade abolition of slavery on federal property within slaveholding states; forbade abolition in the District of
Columbia as long as slavery continued to exist in Virginia or Maryland; prohibited federal interference with interstate transportation of

slaves; and required Congress to provide for the compensation of any slaveholder who was prevented by force or intimidation from recovering a fugitive slave. Crittenden's sixth and final amendment, designed to place a double lock on southern security, provided that the other five amendments should never be subject to future amendment. It extended the same immunity to the three-fifths clause and the fugitive-slave clause. It also forbade any amendment authorizing Congress to "abolish or interfere" with slavery in states where it was permitted by law.[74] As a consequence, all parts of the Constitution relating directly to slavery would have been made unamendable—a privileged status accorded to no other clause of the Constitution, except the guarantee of equal state representation in the Senate.*

The Crittenden omnibus was defeated in the Committee of Thirteen and defeated again when brought independently to the floor of the Senate. Adopted with some modifications by the Washington Peace Conference in February and presented to Congress on the eve of adjournment, it was also rejected in that version by both houses.[75] This utter failure of the Crittenden plan, so starkly different from the success of compromise in 1850, dramatically epitomized the progress of sectional alienation during the intervening decade. Many historians have probed for the causes and pondered the consequences of the failure. Yet it retains elements of paradox and mystery that defy easy explanation. What does seem eminently clear is that the plan failed primarily because of overwhelming Republican opposition and that the principal sticking point was the amendment restoring and extending the 36° 30′ line.

The hostility of Republicans is not difficult to understand; for in their view, as an Indiana editor expressed it, the so-called Crittenden compromise was "no compromise at all, but a total surrender."[76] Furthermore, in the beginning many Republicans were convinced that secession was a bluff and unlikely to proceed very far. When events proved them wrong, their skepticism turned to anger at being

---

*Article Five made two clauses unamendable before 1808 (foreign slave trade and prohibition on direct taxes) and declared that no state without its own consent could be deprived of "its equal suffrage in the Senate." This left such deprivation technically possible by amendment but practically impossible.

coerced into making concessions, and they accordingly became more militant as the crisis became more palpable. Lincoln persuaded himself that the matter truly at issue was the viability of self-government and its core principle, majority rule. "No compromise, by public servants, could, in this case, be a cure," he subsequently told Congress; "not that compromises are not often proper, but that no popular government can long survive a marked precedent, that those who carry an election can only save the government from immediate destruction by giving up the main point upon which the people gave the election."[77]

Historians, while giving much attention to Republican motives in the defeat of compromise, have not with any thoroughness examined southern attitudes toward the Crittenden plan or calculated its prospects of success as a deterrent to disunion. The plan, after all, scarcely touched some of the worst southern apprehensions arising from the election of Lincoln. It offered no more than partial protection against the surge of Republican *power*, which was what southerners feared the most. Also, it is difficult to believe that anyone in the South or North seriously expected the plan to succeed. The six proposed amendments, even if passed by the required two-thirds majority in the Senate and House of Representatives, would then have had to win the approval of fifty-two legislative chambers in twenty-six states before becoming a part of the Constitution. The odds against such an achievement were forbidding enough in themselves, and the progress of secession made them enormous. By February 1, seven states had seceded and only twenty-seven remained in the Union. Yet the number required for ratification could not be reduced below twenty-six without acknowledging secession as a legal right and an accomplished fact—something that most Republicans and many northern Democrats were fiercely unwilling to do. All of which meant that the opposition of two states—say, Maine and Vermont—would have been sufficient to block ratification of the Crittenden amendments.[78]

In any case, the effort to secure ratification would have extended over many months, while the new Confederacy forged ahead in establishing itself as an independent nation. For there is little reason to believe that the seceded states would have renounced secession in anticipation of ratification. Meanwhile, the mounting crisis at Fort Sumter would have required attention. That is, the urgent problem of secession could not have been dissolved by the dim prospects of this inadequate, slow-motion solution to the problem of slavery. One suspects that many supporters of the Crittenden plan were simply going through the motions of what they knew to be a hopeless imitation of the Compromise of 1850.

It can of course be argued that passage of the Crittenden plan by Congress would have improved the atmosphere sufficiently to arrest the secession movement and lay the groundwork for negotiation of a peaceable reconstruction of the Union.[79] Yet the Republicans did in fact make some gestures toward compromise. They cooperated in the organization of three new territories (Nevada, Colorado, and Dakota) without attempting to prevent slavery in any of them.* They also refrained from renewing their efforts of the previous session to disallow the slave code in New Mexico, and some of them even displayed a willingness to admit the territory as a nominal slave state.[80] Most notable of all, with much Republican help and Lincoln's approval, both houses of Congress passed the "Corwin amendment," which was that part of the Crittenden plan forbidding any amendment authorizing Congress to interfere with slavery in the states.[81] These, said Douglas, were "startling, tremendous facts" that should be accepted as "evidence of a salutary change in public opinion at the North," but southern leaders treated them as "a mere bagatelle."[82]

Whatever its potential value in the struggle to save the Union, Crittenden's compromise plan was presumably shattered by adamant Republican resistance to the first of his six amendments, the one proposing to revive and extend the 36° 30′ line. On this point, the President-elect declared himself "inflexible" and urged members of Congress to "entertain no proposition for a compromise in regard to the *extension* of slavery."[83] In the circumstances, such intransigence

---

*By doing so, Douglas insisted, the Republicans had abandoned their platform and come over to popular sovereignty; but the Republicans, with the administration about to come into their control, had no fear that slavery would flourish in any of the three territories, and they were acting in accordance with the 1860 platform, which called for prohibitory legislation if it should prove "necessary."

seemed irrational and unconscionable to supporters of compromise. "What," asked a Douglas newspaper in upper New York, "would the North lose, then, by this Compromise line? Nothing. What would the South gain by it? We answer again, nothing. . . . The only real difference is of little practical importance. The quarrel, after all, is about an unsubstantial right—a mere abstraction."[84]

Obviously, however, this was an argument that could have been directed with equal relevance to the South. In fact, what perhaps needs explaining above all else is the extent to which southerners insisted upon the 36° 30' amendment as a *sine qua non* of a compromise. For in a way, the amendment appeared to be a substantial concession to antislavery sentiment, rather than to the slaveholding interest. That is, it virtually nullified the Dred Scott decision in three-fourths of the existing western territory and imposed the Republican principle of federal exclusion there. So this, it appeared, was an opportunity for advocates of free soil to gain back much of what had been lost in the 1850s. Yet Republican members of Congress were united in their opposition to the amendment, while a great many southerners, especially in the border states, regarded it as the most essential element in a compromise program that just might satisfy the minimal demands of the Deep South and thus prepare the way for a swift reconstruction of the Union.[85]

One may with good reason doubt that the momentum of secession could have been arrested by congressional approval of a constitutional amendment which had little practical significance and was unlikely ever to be ratified.* Yet there is also good reason to consider why this worn-out solution to a disappearing problem should have become laden with so much hope in the winter of 1860–61 and why it should have been rejected with so much passion. The answer ob-

*The assumption of some historians that the Crittenden compromise as a whole had "overwhelming" popular support in all sections of the country is based largely upon contemporary assertions to that effect and illustrates the weakness of the documentary method. James Ford Rhodes, for example, wrote: "No doubt can now exist, and but little could have existed in January 1861, that if it had been submitted to the people it would have carried the Northern States by a great majority; that it would have obtained the vote of almost every man in the border States; and that it would have received the preponderating voice of all the cotton States but South Carolina."[86]

viously lies, not in what the amendment was designed to accomplish but rather in what it was assumed to signify. Secession had begun in response to the election of Lincoln. Southern fear of Republican power could be substantially diminished only by a substantial renunciation of Republican purpose. "The crisis," said Albert Gallatin Brown, "can only be met in one way effectually, . . . and that is, for the northern people to review and reverse their whole policy upon the subject of slavery."[87] Lincoln himself had long since concluded that these were the real terms demanded by the South. At Cooper Institute in February 1860, after asking what would satisfy the southern people, he had replied, "This and this only: cease to call slavery *wrong*, and join them in calling it *right*. . . . The whole atmosphere must be disinfected from all taint of opposition to slavery, before they will cease to believe that all their troubles proceed from us."[88] By the terms of Crittenden's 36° 30' amendment, in contrast with the old Missouri Compromise restriction, slavery would have been not merely permitted in part of the federal territory but given positive constitutional protection there.* Thus Republican acceptance of the amendment would have constituted at least a partial renunciation of the Republican purpose—a signal of semi-surrender to southern demands. In this perspective, it appears that both sides may have understood clearly what southerners were asking and Republicans refusing in 1861, understood the critical symbolic meaning of their last, ostensibly empty, quarrel over slavery in the territories.

*It should be noted, however, that Crittenden's 36° 30' amendment did not authorize congressional enforcement, but merely declared that Congress must not interfere with slavery south of the line, charging territorial authorities with the work of protection. This left open the whole question of the Freeport doctrine—what Congress should do if the territorial government failed to do its duty. The amendment therefore suited Douglas more than it did Davis.

∞ 22 ∞

Reasons Why

In August 1860, Stephen A. Douglas carried his campaign for the presidency from New England down into Virginia, where it became primarily a crusade against the secession movement already taking shape in the South. Privately he had already resigned himself to the likelihood of defeat, but Douglas men in the doubtful states were still making vigorous efforts to save the day. One such effort in Maryland was a newspaper's publication of an anonymous report that Roger B. Taney favored the election of Douglas. Close friends knew that Taney's sympathies in fact lay elsewhere, and a Maryland congressman urged him to issue or authorize a public statement contradicting the report.

The reply of the eighty-three-year-old Chief Justice was characteristic. After asserting that physical weakness required him to be brief, he wrote a long letter explaining why he could not follow his friend's advice. It would be "unseemly" for him to answer an anonymous communication in a newspaper. A denial would only give the report notoriety, and more than that, "It would naturally be regarded as a mere pretext on my part . . . for entering into the political campaign." This in turn would make him a subject of discussion "among all the small-fry politicians." He had always scrupulously avoided any such open involvement in politics under the firm conviction that it would "destroy the usefulness of the Supreme Court":

I never speak upon political issues of the day in public, nor in mixed companies; nor do I enter into any argument, or ever express an opinion to friends who I know differ from me, or who I think may be so inconsiderate as to repeat what I say, in a way to involve my name in public discussions as one who is taking part in the canvass, and supporting or opposing a particular candidate. To my intimate and confidential friends, *as you know*, I speak freely and without reserve. And I do this because I know them well enough to be quite sure that they understand the nature of these conversations and guard them as you have done.[1]

A man so discreet in his conversation was bound to be doubly cautious about what he said in writing. Even if the bulk of Taney's incoming and outgoing correspondence had been preserved, it would probably yield only occasional glimpses of his private thoughts on politics and the sectional conflict. Yet the jurist had never ceased to be a Democrat and a southerner. Beneath the surface of aloofness and propriety, unquenched by physical infirmity, burned the embers of strong conviction and Jacksonian combativeness. It was the flame, not the heat, that had disappeared.

Taney watched the progress of the presidential campaign with great anxiety. "I am accustomed," he declared, "to look over papers on every side of this mixed-up and confused election."[2] By mid-October, the results of several important gubernatorial contests had clearly foreshadowed a Lincoln victory, and Taney's deepening pessimism, about to be vindicated, became apocalyptic. The very fact that he now unburdened himself on paper, even in a letter to his son-in-law, is a measure of the intensity of his feeling. "I have not the slightest hope of New York," he wrote, "and am by no means sure of the entire South for Breckinridge, not even of Virginia." What disheartened him was the strategy of the Breckinridge forces, whom he regarded as the only real defenders of the Constitution. In his opinion, they had sacrificed principle, weakened themselves, and divided the South by adopting the "wild and absurd" policy of fusion with the Bell and Douglas parties.

"I am satisfied," Taney continued, "that there are true men enough in the free states to have elected Breckinridge. But how could

they be expected to quarrel with their neighbors for Southern rights
while the South was everywhere quarreling among themselves . . .
at a moment when the knife of the assassin is at their throats." He
agreed with his son-in-law that the South faced an imminent danger
(unspecified but apparently a widespread slave insurrection), and he
thought that it might not wait for Lincoln's inauguration but "burst
out into the first flush of victory and excitement upon the news of his
election." The southern states, he complained, were doing nothing to
guard against this threat, and as for secession, "their own divisions
make such a project absurd and impracticable." Then followed
Taney's vision of an ugly future:

> My thoughts have been constantly turned to the fearful state of
> things in which we have been living for months past. I am old
> enough to remember the horrors of St. Domingo, and a few days
> will determine whether anything like it is to be visited upon any
> portion of our own Southern countrymen. I can only pray that it
> may be averted and that my fears may prove to be nothing more
> than the timidity of an old man.[3]

On December 3, with Lincoln president-elect and the secession
winter settling on Washington, members of the Supreme Court went
about their usual business of opening a new term. They even paid
their customary courtesy visit to the White House. There is no evidence that James Buchanan sought Taney's advice during this period,
but their general attitudes toward the impending national emergency
were similar. Both men placed the blame for the crisis on northern
antislavery agitators, and both regarded secession as an illegal act but
maintained that the federal government had no power to suppress it
by force of arms.

Buchanan's views were presented to Congress and the nation in
his last annual message.[4] It was about two months later that Taney, in
the midst of a busy court schedule, took time to put his thoughts on
paper. By then, secession had become a reality in six states. The purpose of this memorandum is not indicated. It may never have progressed beyond the rough draft, only part of which appears to be ex-
tant. What survives is a manuscript of eight consecutive pages, with

neither a beginning nor an ending, acquired by the Library of Congress in 1929. The fragment contains many interlineations and stricken passages; and the handwriting is often illegible. Enough can be deciphered, however, to follow the main line of its argument.[5]

The fragment begins with Taney arguing that slavery had a firm legal foundation in the international law of Europe as it existed during the long epoch of the African slave trade. Europe, he concluded, was "therefore estopped from denying our right to an institution which it built up here for its own benefit." As for the free states of the Union, they were doubly obligated to respect the institution of slavery because they also "bound themselves by the social compact of the Constitution to uphold it." Indeed, at the Constitutional Convention, "the Northern States proposed to withhold the power to abolish the slave trade before the year 1820, and the Southern states, who wished it abolished in 1800, yielded and agreed to 1808. And when the Constitution was published in Massachusetts, the paper printing it contained also an advertisement of a Negro for sale."*

Yet men were now violating their contractual obligation and appealing, said Taney, to a "higher law, which God discloses through their individual persons, commanding them to do acts which their forefathers considered perjury and theft." He attributed this "fanaticism against slavery" to radical individualism in religion and politics—the same doctrine, he added, that had produced the bloody excesses of the French Revolution.

Next, Taney traced the progress of "free state aggression" through the crises of 1820 and 1850; the passage of state laws defying the Fugitive Slave Act; the use of churches and schools for dissemination of antislavery propaganda; and the publication of a novel "well calculated to rouse the morbid thought of fanatics, which portrayed in pictures of exaggeration the evils of slavery." Finally, a party "educated by this means" was about to take possession of the federal government with all its patronage and power. The party had proclaimed an irrepressible conflict between free labor and slave labor, had con-

*These two pieces of historical misinformation so fascinated Taney that he repeated them on the very next page of his manuscript. The story of the Massachusetts advertisement also appears a third time along one of the margins.[6]

firmed its sectional character by nominating only northern men for high office, and had rejected all terms of conciliation offered by the slaveholding states. Its onward march to power left southerners convinced that Republicanism was "at best abolitionism in disguise only waiting for an opportunity."* This apprehension had already driven six states from the Union, and seven more were ready to leave unless they received "guarantees against wrongs for the future."

The South, Taney continued, was mistaken in claiming a constitutional right to secede; for secession was revolutionary and "only morally competent, like war, upon failure of justice." At the same time, federal laws could be enforced within a state only by its own citizens, and federal military power could enter a state only at the request of state officials. Was it possible, then, to talk about a choice between peace and war? Taney's answer was the last complete sentence in the fragment: "There is no rightful power to bring back by force the states into the Union."

These were the views of the Chief Justice who, on March 4, 1861, administered the oath of office to the incoming president, and his feelings on that occasion are not difficult to imagine. Taney must have listened unhappily to Abraham Lincoln's inaugural address, especially during several disagreeable moments when he found himself virtually the target of an attack on judicial review. After having acknowledged the binding effect of a judgment by the Supreme Court in any specific case brought before it, Lincoln, with *Dred Scott* obviously in mind, went on to declare: "If the policy of the government . . . is to be irrevocably fixed by decisions of the Supreme Court, the instant they are made, in ordinary litigation between parties, in personal actions, the people will have ceased to be their own rulers, having, to that extent, practically resigned their government into the hands of that eminent tribunal."[7] Horace Greeley's New York *Tribune* predictably applauded this passage, saying that it swept away "all the cobwebs of sophistry" that had been "woven over the public mind by the judgment in the case of Dred Scott."[8] For Taney, however, the passage could only have served to confirm his low opinion of

---

*Taney at first used the term "black republicanism" throughout the passage but then went back and struck out the adjective in every instance.

the new president. One wonders if the Chief Justice remembered that as Jackson's attorney general almost thirty years earlier, he himself had expressed views of judicial power very similar to those he now heard from Lincoln's lips.[9]

Soon Taney was watching his own state of Maryland become the scene of mob action, conspiracy, sabotage, and military repression. He saw the writ of habeas corpus suspended by presidential order, saw old friends arrested and held in prison without bail or trial.[10] The outpouring of northern passion after Fort Sumter appalled him. It amounted "almost to delirium," he declared in a letter to Franklin Pierce. Still, he hoped for the acceptance of peaceful separation, the only alternative to "military government and a reign of terror, preceded too by a civil war with all its horrors."[11]

Three months after Lincoln's inauguration, the Chief Justice clashed head on with the new administration and suffered defeat. His writ of habeas corpus ordering the release of a fellow Marylander, John Merryman, was defied by military authorities, and his sensational opinion declaring presidential suspension of the writ unconstitutional was in effect overruled by the attorney general.[12] This bitter experience convinced Taney that the President was establishing a military tyranny, and he clung to the conviction as long as he lived. In one letter, recalling George Washington's scrupulous respect for civil authority, he exclaimed, "How finely and nobly Washington's conduct contrasts with the military men of the present day, from the Lieutenant-General down."[13] As for the Supreme Court, he expressed doubt in 1863 that it would ever recover its constitutional authority and rank. "The supremacy of the military power over the civil seems to be established," he lamented, "and the public mind has acquiesced in it and sanctioned it."[14] In performing his wartime official duties, Taney consistently opposed the Lincoln administration at every opportunity. He even wrote out gratuitous opinions that were never called into use, holding several acts of the federal government unconstitutional.[15] His sympathies remained with the South, for which one of his sons-in-law was fighting. When the grandson of an old friend called upon him before leaving to join the Confederate army, the Chief Justice reportedly said: "The circumstances under which you are going are not unlike those under which your grandfather went into the Revolutionary War."[16]

II

What rivets attention in Taney's private views on the sectional crisis and Civil War is not so much the substance of his thought as the intensity of his feelings. A pro-southern bias could be read easily enough in his public record, but from all except a few close friends he concealed the fierceness of his hostility to the antislavery movement and to anyone who would temporize with it. This hostility, moreover, was not caused but merely aggravated by the flood of abuse that descended upon him after the Dred Scott decision. His attitudes were firmly set before that time, as he revealed in a letter to his son-in-law during the campaign of 1856:

> Passing events, which cast their shadows before them, have made me every day . . . more and more doubtful as to Buchanan's success. . . . And so far as the South is concerned, I think it matters very little if Buchanan is defeated, whether Fremont or Fillmore is chosen. But there will be no dissolution of the Union in either event. The Constitution will undoubtedly be trampled under foot, and the Union will be one of power and weakness, like the Union of England and Ireland, or Russia and Poland. But how can the Southern states divide, with any hope of success, when in almost every one of them there is a strong and powerful party, acting in concert with the Northern Know Nothings, and willing to hold power from the North, if they may be enabled thereby to obtain the honors and offices of the general government and domineer in their own states. . . . The South is doomed to sink to a state of inferiority, and the power of the North will be exercised to gratify their cupidity and their evil passions, without the slightest regard to the principles of the Constitution. There are many bold and brave men at the South who have no vassal feeling to the North. And they will probably stand to their arms if Fremont is elected, or further aggressions made under Fillmore. But what can they do, with a powerful enemy in their midst? I grieve over this condition of things, but it is my deliberate opinion that the South is

doomed, and that nothing but a firm united action, nearly unanimous in every state, can check Northern insult and Northern
aggression.[17]

Such, of course, had been the urgent message of Calhoun in his later
years—that southerners must unite as a people or die as a civilization
at the hands of an implacable enemy. Written shortly before the second round of arguments in the Dred Scott case, this letter would
have caused a sensation if it had somehow fallen into the hands of a
Republican editor.

The preceding year, 1855, had been one of great personal tragedy for Taney, and, according to his biographer Carl B. Swisher, the
ordeal may have seriously affected his judgment and sense of proportion thereafter. The Taneys were then accustomed to spending several months each summer at Old Point Comfort, the tip of the York
peninsula. In 1855, Taney's youngest daughter Alice, twenty-eight
years old, wanted instead to accompany her sister and brother-in-law
on their annual visit to Newport, Rhode Island, a favorite resort of
southerners seeking relief from the summer heat. Her father disliked
the idea. "I have not the slightest confidence," he said, "in [the] superior health of Newport over Old Point, and look upon it as nothing
more than that unfortunate feeling of inferiority in the South, which
believes everything in the North to be superior to what we have." He
gave his consent so grudgingly and with such strict financial conditions attached that Alice ended by going with her parents to Old
Point as usual.

Across the channel in Norfolk that summer there was an outbreak of yellow fever, and the Taneys found themselves trapped—
fearful that the disease would invade Old Point, but even more fearful
of mixing with possibly infected passengers on a boat back to Baltimore. So they stayed on and worried, as the epidemic spread to
other Virginia communities near by. Mrs. Taney appears to have suffered first a mild stroke and then a severe one. As Taney frantically
summoned a doctor from Baltimore, Alice suddenly fell ill with what
proved to be the dreaded yellow fever. Mother and daughter died
just a few hours apart on September 29–30.

Taney was prostrated with grief. "He says he shall not live," wrote a relative, "that he can never take his seat on the bench again. . . . He has been in tears like an infant, and he has given way to the most bitter self reproaches, for keeping his family at the Point in reliance on his own judgment that they were there free from danger." Soon, however, he began to recover, drawing strength from the conviction that the double tragedy was a chastisement by God, to which he must submit "with calmness and resignation." That helped him to smother any self-doubt about the soundness of his judgment and any guilty thought that his stubbornness and sectional prejudice had cost Alice her life. One of his first steps after regaining some strength of body and spirit was to sell the family house in Baltimore and establish himself permanently in Washington. Never again, it should be added, did he visit Old Point. Thus the year 1855 cut like an angry gash across Taney's personal life. "It is possible," says Swisher, "that the death of his wife and daughter and the breaking up of his home deprived him of the emotional reserves necessary to preserve the judicial balance for which he had hitherto received credit and led to the taking of more and more extreme positions."[18]

Yet it also seems possible that Taney's growing extremism in the late 1850s was primarily a response to ominous changes in the political environment—notably the rise of the Know-Nothings, whom he regarded as ugly bigots, and the rise of the Republicans, whom he regarded as dangerous fanatics. What needs to be emphasized in any case is that his Dred Scott opinion was written with an emotional commitment so intense that it made perception and logic utterly subservient. The extraordinary cumulation of error, inconsistency, and misrepresentation, dispensed with such pontifical self-assurance, becomes more understandable with the realization that the opinion was essentially visceral in origin—that law and history were distorted to serve a passionate purpose. Taney's real commitment, one must also emphasize, was not to slavery itself, for which he had no great affection, but rather to southern life and values, which seemed organically linked to the peculiar institution and unpreservable without it. He used the Dred Scott case to reinforce the institution of slavery at every possible point of attack, not because he had once been a slaveholder but because he remained, to the end of his life, a southern gentleman.*

The strong feelings that governed him were no doubt a mixture. Love for the South and pride in his own southern heritage mingled with emotions of a negative sort. One finds, to be sure, no evidence of the suppressed moral anxiety that some scholars have discovered as the eruptive source of mounting southern hysteria. The study of Taney's character and behavior contributes nothing to the "guilt thesis."[20] On the other hand, his private letters do lend support to recent emphasis on southern fears, especially the fear of slave uprisings. Indeed, by the late 1850s Taney had plainly been caught up in the pattern of reciprocating apprehension that C. Vann Woodward calls "paranoia" and "counterparanoia."[21]

Besides fear, there was indignation. The counterpart of Taney's love for the South was his growing hostility to its northern critics. He liked to single out Massachusetts, once the home of African slave-traders, but now the center of abolitionism as the epitome of northern selfishness and hypocrisy. Taney, above all in the late 1850s, was fiercely anti-antislavery. We must not be misled by his physical

---

*At the same time, one must put aside the curious notion that Taney was at heart an antislavery man—a notion that has a long history and retains surprising vitality. The Cincinnati *Enquirer* in 1857, condemning abusive attacks on the Chief Justice, declared: "Mr. Taney, personally, is opposed to slavery in principle and practice." Frank H. Hodder agreed in 1929. "Taney," he wrote, "was opposed to slavery. . . . The position that he took in the Dred Scott case was the result of a mistaken sense of duty and not of any partiality for slavery." Charles W. Smith, Jr., asserted in 1936 that Taney, like Jefferson, "believed slavery wrong and favored gradual emancipation." According to Walker Lewis, in a 1965 biography, "Slavery violated his conscience. His opposition to abolition was not because he wished to perpetuate slavery but because he believed the abolitionists misguided." In 1971, Robert M. Spector said of Taney: "From the standpoint of morality he hated slavery as much as any abolitionist." This legend of the antislavery Taney rests almost entirely upon two actions taken nearly forty years before the Dred Scott decision. In 1818, he served as defense attorney for an abolitionist minister and in the process denounced slavery as an evil that must in time be "gradually wiped away." Beginning the same year, Taney emancipated his own slaves to the number at least of eight. Whatever moral conviction may have encouraged these actions, it does not appear again in his public record or his private correspondence. His attitude on the bench was consistently and solicitously proslavery. By 1857 he had become as fanatical in his determination to protect the institution as Garrison was in his determination to destroy it.[19]

weakness or his gentle mien. Wrath, says an ancient Greek poet, is the last thing in a man to grow old. The Dred Scott opinion, defensive in substance but aggressive in temper, was the work of an *angry* southern gentleman.

From a study of Taney's private emotional responses to the sectional controversy, one can learn something about the coming of the Civil War. Like the Chief Justice, a majority of southerners had no significant economic stake in the institution of slavery, but they did have a vital stake in preservation of the southern social order and of southern self-respect. In the end, it may have been the assault on their self-respect—the very language of the antislavery crusade—that drove many southerners over the edge. Taney no doubt shared the sentiments of his colleague Justice Daniel, who, back in 1847, wrote to Martin Van Buren explaining southern opposition to the Wilmot Proviso. After discussing the constitutional aspects of the issue, he added:

> There is another aspect of this pretension now advanced, which exhibits it as fraught with dangers. . . . It is that view of the case which pretends to an insulting exclusiveness or superiority on the one hand, and denounces a degrading inequality or inferiority on the other; which says in effect to the Southern man, Avaunt! you are not my equal, and hence are to be excluded as carrying a moral taint with you. Here is at once the extinction of all fraternity, of all sympathy, of all endurance even; the creation of animosity fierce, implacable, undying.[22]

With increasing frequency and bitterness in the years that followed, southerners protested that they were being degraded by northern sanctimony. Taney's Dred Scott decision, like Daniel's letter, is a document of great revelatory value. In the very unreasonableness of its argument one finds a measure of southern desperation.

III

But the Dred Scott decision, aside from its revelatory significance, was also a public act that had important public consequences. The principal reason for the prominence of the decision in American historical writing is the belief that it became a major causal link between the general forces of national disruption and the final crisis of the Union in 1860–61. Scholars have tended to be emphatic in affirming the connection but vague about its mechanics. The Dred Scott case, we are told, "helped precipitate" or "did much to precipitate" or "helped to bring about" the Civil War.[23] But there is never much explanation of just how Taney's courtroom edict produced, or helped produce, disunion and armed conflict.

Of course the historian should take into account all discernible causal relationships, including those of such a general nature that they may be too vague to isolate and measure. Thus it is important to consider the ways in which the Dred Scott decision altered the formal argument over slavery; for secession, after all, was a highly formal public act as well as a highly emotional one. And no doubt the decision contributed heavily to the general accumulation of sectional animosity that made some kind of national crisis increasingly difficult to avoid. Taney's proslavery opinion lent credence to the fear of many northerners that an aggressive slave power was determined to extend its peculiar institution throughout the federal territories and perhaps even into the free states. At the same time, the fierce Republican attack on the decision confirmed many southerners in the fear that no amount of judicial vindication could protect their slaveholding society against increasing northern aggression.

Still, since there were many other causes of the hostility between North and South, it is difficult to imagine a dissipation of the gathering storm if only Justice Nelson had been allowed to speak for the Court, as originally planned, in his shorter and less controversial Dred Scott opinion. Most historians would probably agree that the sectional conflict over slavery was already deep-seated and pervasive before 1857. But what turned a chronic struggle into a secession crisis was the outcome of the presidential election in 1860. Accordingly, if one wishes to go beyond the unverifiable general impression or conviction that the Dred Scott decision, like *Uncle Tom's Cabin* and the Harpers Ferry raid, somehow helped to "bring about" the Civil War, it becomes necessary to test the accuracy of Charles Warren's assertion that Taney "elected Abraham Lincoln to the Presidency."[24]

There were two principal ways in which the Dred Scott decision could have had a critical influence on the election of 1860. One was by contributing significantly to the split in the Democratic party; the other was by contributing significantly to the growth of the Republican party. The disruption of the Democrats, because of its dramatic climax at Charleston and its association with the famous Lincoln-Douglas exchange at Freeport, has received the primary emphasis in historical writing. Yet, as we have seen, the Dred Scott decision did not at first place any serious strains on Democratic unity, and Douglas enunciated the Freeport doctrine in 1857 without incurring the slightest adverse criticism from southern Democrats.[25] Only after the Lecompton struggle had done its irreparable damage did the Dred Scott decision and the Freeport doctrine become, somewhat synthetically, a divisive influence within the party. Furthermore, the election statistics indicate that Lincoln would have won in 1860 even against a consolidated opposition; for he carried fifteen of the eighteen free states with popular majorities, and they were enough to give him an electoral majority.[26] The argument of certain historians that a reunited Democratic party (that is, a party approved and to some extent controlled by its southern wing) would somehow have attracted additional votes in the North remains a highly dubious speculation.[27] In summary, the Dred Scott decision was at most a secondary factor in the division of the Democratic party, and that division in any case probably did not determine the outcome of the presidential election.

There remains the question of whether the Dred Scott decision had a significant influence on the Republican upsurge that gave Lincoln 98 per cent of the northern electoral vote. The difference between defeat in 1856 and victory in 1860 was a half-million additional Republican voters in the free states, including 300,000 more than the party's proportionate share of the increase in the voting population. Approximately 70 per cent of the 300,000-vote gain was made in the five crucial free states that the Democrats had carried in 1856. The sixty-two electoral votes of New Jersey, Pennsylvania, Indiana, Illinois, and California had all gone to Buchanan in 1856; Lincoln won fifty-nine of them in 1860.[28]

This political revolution, moreover, was largely completed in the midterm elections of 1858, as the following table shows.[29] It therefore

REPUBLICAN PERCENTAGES OF THE POPULAR VOTE

	N.J.	PENN.	IND.	ILL.	COMBINED*
1856	28.5	32.0	40.1	40.2	35.4
1858	52.5 †	53.7	51.7	49.8	52.1
1860	48.2	56.1	51.1	50.7	52.7

*California, which had only four electoral votes, is omitted from the table because the mixing of Republican and anti-Lecompton votes in 1858 makes it impossible to measure Republican strength for that year. The Republicans carried 18.8 per cent of the state's vote in 1856 and 33 per cent in 1860.

† The New Jersey percentage for 1858 is somewhat inflated because in two congressional districts the Republicans supported anti-Lecompton Democrats.

seems chronologically sound to infer a causal connection between the Dred Scott decision and the Republican surge to power. Yet there are also considerations that militate against such an inference. For one thing, voting behavior in the late 1850s was affected by other influences besides the slavery issue. The economic depression that struck the country in 1857 undoubtedly had political repercussions, for instance, and it has been well demonstrated that many voters were not issue-oriented but tended rather to vote in ethnic-religious blocs.[30]

In addition, the Republican gains in the late 1850s can be explained to a large extent by the collapse of the Know-Nothing movement in the North and the resulting shift of many Whig-Americans into Republican ranks. The volume of shifting was particularly heavy in the states that had voted for Buchanan in 1856. Pennsylvania's sixteen strongest Know-Nothing counties, for example, gave Frémont only 12 per cent of their total vote in the presidential election of 1856 but gave the Republican ticket 54 per cent in 1858 and Lincoln 53 per cent in 1860. Throughout the northern tier of free states from New England to Wisconsin, this Republican absorption of political nativism had begun in 1856, when large numbers of Know-Nothings supported Frémont instead of Fillmore. Even the Fillmore men of the North and parts of the border states tended to be mildly antislavery in the Henry Clay tradition, and many of them were angered by the proslavery aggressiveness of southern Democrats. Edward Bates of St. Louis, for instance, campaigned for Fillmore in 1856 but became a leading Republican in 1860 and a member of Lincoln's cabinet in 1861. Although he was essentially an ultraconservative by Republican standards, Bates had nevertheless come to believe in the existence of a conspiracy to nationalize slavery.[31] This fact suggests that the Dred Scott decision may have had a strong influence on Bates's conversion to Republicanism. But was it a determining influence? And if so, was Bates in this respect a typical Whig-American? The evidence does not forbid an affirmative answer to either question. Yet there is also good reason to conclude that much of the Whig-American movement into Republican ranks was compelled by the lack of satisfactory alternatives and needed no additional stimulus such as the furor over the Dred Scott decision.

Aside from the knotty question of the relationship between *Dred Scott* and Republican absorption of the Fillmore vote, there is also the problem of distinguishing between the political effects of the Dred Scott decision and the political effects of the Lecompton controversy. It is essential to draw this distinction because both events took place during the two-year period of the Republican party's final surge to political dominance in the free states. One means of doing so is to examine the election results in seven northern states that held statewide elections in 1857 as well as in 1858. The pattern that emerges from such an examination is remarkably coherent. If the Dred Scott decision did enhance the chances of Republican victory in 1860, one would expect to find that it had a similar effect on the elections of 1857, when the shock of the decision was still new. Yet, as the following charts show, and as we have already noted in an earlier chapter, the Republicans generally lost ground that year. The exceptions were states—most notably, Pennsylvania—where the influx of Fillmore men offset other losses. For 1857, the Republican chart is affected one way by a general decline of party strength and the other way by the continuing recruitment of Whig-Americans in certain states. The Democratic chart is less ambiguous. It reveals a consistent pattern of Democratic gains in 1857, followed by declines in every state except Michigan and Iowa. In Pennsylvania, for instance, the Democrats captured the governorship in 1857, defeating the Republicans by more than forty thousand votes. A year later, the Democrats

REPUBLICAN PERCENTAGE
OF TOTAL VOTE

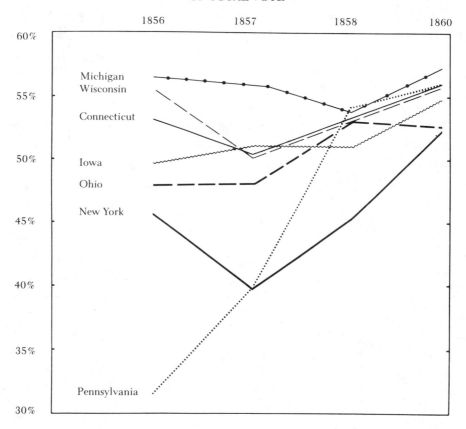

lost nearly all of their congressional seats and were outpolled by more than twenty-five thousand votes. And in Ohio, regarded as a safely Republican state, the race issue stirred up by the Dred Scott decision enabled the Democrats to win control of the legislature in 1857, but the Republicans rebounded strongly in 1858 after the Lecompton controversy. There is, in fact, no evidence that *Dred Scott* manufactured votes for Republicans anywhere. On the contrary, it is difficult to escape the impression that the decision, if it helped anyone, helped the Democrats and that the Lecompton struggle was the primary political influence in the final triumph of Republicanism.[32]

Perhaps what all this means is nothing more than that the Dred Scott decision and public reaction to it, like most relevant antecedent

DEMOCRATIC PERCENTAGE
OF TOTAL VOTE

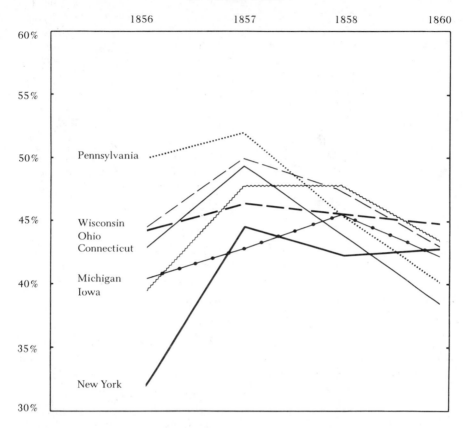

conditions of a historical event, does not by itself pass the rigorous *sine qua non* test for an efficacious or sufficient cause. Yet one should not overlook the strong possibility that northern reaction to the Lecompton controversy in 1858 was intensified by the fresh memory of Taney's proslavery ruling in 1857. A clustering of events in the late 1850s induced nightmarish visions of conspiracy among northerners and southerners alike. The Dred Scott decision by itself apparently caused no significant number of changes in political allegiance. Yet it was a conspicuous and perhaps an integral part of a configuration of events and conditions that did produce enough changes of allegiance to make a political revolution and enough intensity of feeling to make that revolution violent.

In the Stream of History

D red Scott, after his eleven-year struggle for freedom, lived only sixteen months as a free man. He and his family were transferred by the Chaffees to Taylor Blow in May 1857 and promptly manumitted. The Scotts remained in St. Louis, Dred working as a hotel porter and his wife Harriet, as a laundress. According to newspaper reports, Eliza and Lizzie ran away for a time but had returned home by 1858. A local newspaper described Scott as "a small, pleasant-looking negro," with a moustache and "imperial" beard, dressed in a suit of "seedy black," and looking "somewhat the worse for wear and tear." Missouri law required that Dred and Harriet post bond of $1000 for good behavior in order to continue living in the state. This they did on May 4, 1858, with Taylor Blow acting as security. Soon, however, Dred was stricken with consumption, and he died on September 17.* Press accounts of his death were generally brief, but some editors took time to reflect on the fame that had enveloped this obscure black man and on the significance of his day in court. "In ages yet to come," said the New York *Herald*, "Dred Scott and the decision which bears his name will be familiar words in the mouth of the ranting demagogue in rostrum and pulpit, and of the

---

*On the preceding day, at a town about a hundred and twenty miles away, Abraham Lincoln and Stephen A. Douglas resumed discussion of the Dred Scott decision in the fourth of their historic debates.[1]

student of political history." Scott was buried in the St. Louis Wesleyan Cemetery, which within a decade became a casualty of urban expansion and was abandoned. Taylor Blow, a convert to Catholicism, arranged for removal of the remains to Calvary Cemetery in 1867. Ninety years later, as part of a centennial observance of the Dred Scott decision, the grave was marked with a granite headstone provided by a granddaughter of Taylor Blow.[2] There appears to be no solid evidence of what happened to Dred's family after his death. It is said that Harriet and Eliza survived him only a few years. A woman claiming to be his other daughter, Lizzie, married Henry Madison of St. Louis, and several of her descendants attended the centennial observances in 1957.[3]

John F. A. Sanford, as we have seen, died in an insane asylum some two months after the handing down of the Dred Scott decision. His brother-in-law, Congressman Calvin C. Chaffee, perhaps because of the furor over his alleged ownership of the Scotts, chose not to run for re-election in 1858. He served for two years as librarian of the House of Representatives, then resumed the practice of medicine and engaged in lobbying and charity work. Chaffee died in 1896. Mrs. Chaffee, the Irene Emerson whom Scott had first sued for his freedom, lived until 1903, thus surviving her first husband by nearly sixty years.[4]

Several of the Missourians associated in one way or another with the Dred Scott case played prominent roles in the politics of the Civil War and Reconstruction. Henry T. Blow, Taylor's older brother, became a Republican in the late 1850s and helped hold Missouri loyal to the Union during the secession crisis. Lincoln appointed him minister to Venezuela, but he soon returned home to run for Congress. Serving two terms in the House of Representatives (1863–67), he was a member of the powerful Joint Committee on Reconstruction.* Charles D. Drake, onetime husband of Martha Blow, had lent some legal assistance to Dred Scott in getting the suit for freedom under way. A Democrat until 1861, Drake switched to the Republican party and

---

*Another member of this fifteen-man committee was Sanford's attorney before the Supreme Court, Reverdy Johnson, who was elected to the Senate during the Civil War as a Democrat from Maryland.

became the leader of its radical faction in Missouri, dominating the state's constitutional convention of 1865 and serving four years in the United States Senate during the critical years of Reconstruction. The Civil War governor of Missouri who resisted the radicals until his death in 1864 was Hamilton R. Gamble. As chief justice of the state supreme court in 1852, Gamble had dissented in the two-to-one decision that returned Dred Scott to slavery. And no one in wartime Washington watched Missouri affairs more closely than Scott's former attorney, Montgomery Blair, now postmaster general in the Lincoln administration; for his brother Frank Blair was one of the leaders in the struggle to keep the state out of radical hands.[5]

One of the new names in Missouri politics during the period of radical ascendancy was James Milton Turner, a Negro whose oratorical ability made him the acknowledged leader of the state's black population. From 1871 to 1878, he served as minister to Liberia, being the first Negro to hold a diplomatic appointment from the United States government. It appears that Turner may have been the person primarily responsible for a phantom Dred Scott who turns up briefly in the pages of popular history. In 1882, Turner was invited to participate in a ceremony at the Missouri Historical Society, the occasion being the presentation of an oil portrait of Dred Scott based upon a photograph taken in 1857. The donor was Mrs. Theron Barnum, whose late husband had employed Scott as a porter at Barnum's Hotel in St. Louis. Turner's "eulogy" revealed only in a vague way that he did not know how soon the famous slave had died after his manumission. Scott, he said, was probably between sixty-two and sixty-five years old at the time of his death and had been "for years at service in the family of the late Theron Barnum." Regarded thereafter as something of a local authority on the subject, Turner eventually began to embellish the story, remembering that after his return from Liberia in 1878 he had often talked with Dred Scott, who was by then an old man living on his reputation. Turner's pseudo-recollections were incorporated into an article published by the St. Louis *Globe-Democrat* in 1904. According to the reporter, Dred Scott died about twenty years after his liberation. For a time he had worked as a cook at Barnum's Hotel, and one of his fondest memories was preparing a meal for the Prince of Wales when that dignitary (the future Edward VII) made his American tour in 1860.[6]

Another person misled by Turner was the librarian of the Missouri Historical Society, Mary Louise Dalton. For a brief interval in 1907, it appeared to Miss Dalton that she had found some measure of confirmation. She interviewed Mrs. William T. Blow, a widow of Taylor Blow's youngest brother, from whose vague and flexible memory she extracted the assertion that Dred was worthless as a worker and had begged from the Blow family for twenty years after his manumission. Just a few weeks later, however, Miss Dalton made the not very difficult discovery that Dred Scott had actually died in 1858, and she did not allow that fact to be forgotten again. So perished the phantom ex-slave who had cooked a dinner for royalty and lived to a ripe old age. But even as one myth died, another, more durable one was in process of creation.

Miss Dalton had been lending research assistance to Frederick Trevor Hill as he prepared a chapter on the Dred Scott case for inclusion in his book *Decisive Battles of the Law.* Shortly after her interview with Mrs. Blow, she informed Hill that Dred was a "no-account nigger." This may have merely confirmed Hill in an impression already acquired, but at any rate he recorded in *Decisive Battles* that Dred Scott was "apparently a shiftless, incapable specimen of his race." Hill's essay, which could be labeled the first scholarly historical monograph about the Dred Scott case, no doubt influenced subsequent writing on the subject. Frank H. Hodder, for instance, was probably relying on Hill when he stated flatly in 1929 that "Scott was a shiftless negro." Hodder's article in turn, served as authority for Avery O. Craven, who likewise described Scott as "shiftless" in his important book, *The Coming of the Civil War* (1942). It is accordingly not surprising to find that the essay on Dred Scott in the *Dictionary of American Biography* (Volume XVI, published in 1935) calls him "shiftless and unreliable."[7]

Thus the image of Dred Scott as a good-for-nothing became entrenched as orthodox history, and to some extent it probably remains so, despite recent efforts at revision.* The image, like many other historical myths, may have some basis in historical reality, but there seems to be no better supporting evidence than the few oral remarks made a half-century after the event by an old woman with a demonstrably faulty memory.[9]

Most enduring of all Dred Scott myths, however, has been the notion that the case was an artificial one, contrived to bring about a judicial ruling on slavery that would serve partisan purposes. As we have seen, this charge was made in 1857 and publicly denied by counsel for both sides. Defense strategy throughout the litigation seems incompatible with the alleged collusion, and the more serious students of the case have given the charge little credence. Yet, in 1957, the *Atlantic Monthly* published a centennial article by a Yale professor of law in which readers were told that the suit was "fixed up" by Chaffee and Sanford (with Dred Scott promised his freedom beforehand whatever the verdict might be) and that this was therefore "one of those contrived 'test cases' lawyers delight in." And according to a more recent article in the *Family Encyclopedia of American History*, Mrs. Emerson, being opposed to slavery, gave her ready consent to the original suit, while Chaffee was from the beginning the chief architect of *Dred Scott v. Sandford.*[10]

What has been believed about the Dred Scott case is an important part of its history; for the network of such belief became in itself a discernible historical force, and no account of the case would be complete without some consideration of its later historical influence. *Dred Scott v. Sandford* was, of course, more than a passionately remembered historical event like John Brown's raid at Harpers Ferry. It was also an official public act never expressly recalled. Congress and the president had to come to grips with it. Judicial officers throughout the country had to consider its precedential effect. And for the Supreme Court the decision came to have a cluster of discrepant meanings. It was law to be cited, a lesson to be learned,

---

*The changing climate of racial opinion since the 1950s has made a difference, of course. For example, the Missouri Historical Society's *Bulletin* in 1948 carried an article that described Scott as "illiterate and somewhat stupid," whereas a textbook history of Missouri published in 1970 said that he was "well-mannered" and "intelligent."[8]

judicial vigor to be emulated, political imprudence to be regretted, but most of all, as time passed, it was an embarrassment—the Court's highly visible skeleton in a transparent closet.[11]

II

Taney's attempt to end the slavery controversy by judicial fiat "practically started a war," said a book on the Supreme Court published in 1961. And more than that, "The prestige of the Court . . . was dashed to the ground."[12] The allegedly ruinous effect of the Dred Scott decision on the prestige and power of the Supreme Court had been prophesied as early as 1848 by certain opponents of the Clayton Compromise.* Contemporary critics of the decision made similar predictions, and historical scholarship over the following century generally agreed that the predictions had proved to be accurate. Historians also tended to agree with Edward S. Corwin that the eclipse of judicial power resulting from the Dred Scott decision had its own "momentous" consequences. Corwin wrote in 1910:

> During neither the Civil War nor the period of Reconstruction, did the Supreme Court play anything like its due role of supervision, with the result that during the one period the military powers of the President underwent undue expansion, and during the other the legislative powers of Congress. The court itself was conscious of its weakness, yet notwithstanding its prudent disposition to remain in the background, at no time since Jefferson's first administration has its independence been in greater jeopardy than in the decade between 1860 and 1870; so slow and laborious was its task of recuperating its shattered reputation."[13]

In 1927, Charles Evans Hughes came to the same conclusion and coined a memorable phrase as he did so. The Dred Scott decision, he said, was the first of several "self-inflicted wounds" with which the Court seriously damaged its authority and reputation.[14]

This traditional interpretation was challenged in 1968 by Stanley I. Kutler, who argued that the Court's loss of prestige and power had

* See above, p. 150.

been greatly exaggerated. More recently, Kutler in turn has been accused of overstating his case, but he is clearly right in maintaining
that one must distinguish between public attitudes toward the Dred
Scott decision and its author on the one hand, *and* attitudes toward
the Court as a national institution on the other.[15]

The *Dred Scott* Court was no longer intact when the Civil War
began. Curtis resigned in 1858. Daniel died in 1860 and McLean, in
April 1861. After the attack on Fort Sumter, Campbell resigned to return to Alabama and serve the Confederacy. Of the three remaining
southern justices, Wayne and Catron quickly revealed themselves to
be staunch Unionists; so did Grier, who had provided the one northern vote against the constitutionality of the Missouri Compromise restriction. Taney alone remained unrepentant and unredeemed, as it
were, and Taney alone was responsible for *Ex parte Merryman*, a proceedings at chambers with which the rest of the Court had nothing to
do. The often venomous hostility of many radical Republicans followed the Chief Justice into his grave, but one should not make the
mistake of assuming that it was directed at the Supreme Court as a
whole.[16]

Soon after Lincoln's election there were reports in the press that
Taney had resigned or intended to resign so that Buchanan could appoint a Democratic successor. Wiser party heads advised against the
maneuver, and Taney in any case never gave it serious consideration.
Aside from the public outcry that surely would have greeted such a
move, the Chief Justice needed his salary to live on and support two
daughters, one of whom was a semi-invalid.[17] So he stayed on, an
isolated, decrepit figure in wartime Washington, still treated with respect and affection by professional associates but publicly detested as
a man who drew his pay from the federal government while lending
sympathy to its enemies. It seems likely that the Dred Scott decision
would have been at least partly forgiven if Taney had taken a Jacksonian stand against secession. Instead, as Senator Henry Wilson bitterly and accurately complained, he "never gave one cheering word
nor performed one act to protect or save" the Union.[18] The Chief Justice, in plain words, was a copperhead, and ever more emphatically
so as the war progressed. If it had been possible, he would have

struck down many of the administration's principal war measures, including conscription, emancipation, and the currency program.[19]

The fact that Taney remained chief justice until his death late in 1864, without any serious threat of removal, was testimony, perhaps, to the stability of the American constitutional system during its years of severest trial. Actually, his continuance in office may have given the Lincoln administration more freedom than it otherwise would have enjoyed; for a Supreme Court headed by Taney was a court without enough influence to restrain executive or congressional power.[20] Administration leaders nevertheless preferred to avoid direct confrontation with the Chief Justice, insofar as that was possible. For the most part, they simply ignored him. Thus, when Taney sent Lincoln a copy of his *Merryman* opinion, which closed by virtually accusing the President of usurpation, Lincoln made no direct reply, though both he and Attorney General Edward Bates later contradicted the opinion in official papers. And when Taney wrote Secretary of the Treasury Salmon P. Chase, complaining that a 3 per cent deduction from his salary for income tax was unconstitutional, he received no response of any kind.[21]

Congress likewise ignored the Dred Scott decision while defying its most memorable ruling. In June 1862, by overwhelming votes, the Senate and House passed a bill abolishing slavery in the federal territories, and Lincoln quickly signed it. Opponents of the measure raised various objections. One senator, for instance, suggested that it would interfere with the rights of Indian slaveholders and so constitute a violation of treaty obligations. But no one mentioned the Dred Scott decision throughout the debate. Although the press in general took little notice of this symbolic victory for the antebellum Republican party, the New York *Tribune* did publish a few paragraphs celebrating the end of a controversy which, it said, had begun with Jefferson's Ordinance of 1784. "Champions of Freedom and Justice for All," it exclaimed, "thank God that you have lived to see this day." But the *Tribune*, like Congress, said nothing about the Dred Scott decision.[22]

Attorney General Bates struck another blow at the decision in November of the same year when he issued an official opinion holding that free men of color born in the United States were citizens of

the United States. Near the end of the opinion, he took due note of
Dred Scott but dismissed it as irrelevant in several pages of opaque
argument. After insisting that Taney's ruling on the plea in abatement
applied only to full-blooded African negroes who were demonstrably
descended from slave ancestors, the attorney general continued:

> I raise no question upon the legal validity of the judgment in Scott
> *vs.* Sandford. I only insist that the judgment in that case is limited
> . . . to the plea in abatement; and, consequently, that whatever
> was said . . . respecting the legal merits of the case, and respect-
> ing any supposed legal disability resulting from the mere fact of
> color . . . was *"dehors the record,"* and of no authority as a judi-
> cial decision.[23]

One might easily read this passage as mistakenly classifying the citizenship question in *Dred Scott* with the merits of the case, but instead it appears that Bates was resorting to the familiar judicial strategy of "distinguishing" a precedent with such severity as to render it
inapplicable to the question at hand.

Naturally, Democrats were not disposed to accept the opinion of
a Republican attorney general as definitive. For instance, during discussion early in 1864 of a bill organizing Montana Territory, Senator
Reverdy Johnson insisted that Taney's *Dred Scott* ruling against
Negro citizenship was "conclusive" until reversed by the Supreme
Court itself. That set off a sharp exchange between Johnson and
Charles Sumner, who said that the Dred Scott decision had "dis-
graced the country" and ought to be "expelled from its jurisprudence," while Johnson responded with an eloquent defense of Taney
and the Court.[24]

Hostility to Taney and the Dred Scott decision was a sentiment
of the majority in the North during the Civil War. Hostility to the
Supreme Court as a whole, on the other hand, was confined to a
small though at times highly vocal minority that some historians have
taken much too seriously.[25] It is true that certain Republican newspapers, such as the New York *Tribune* and the Chicago *Tribune*, called
for measures remodeling or packing the Court, but their demands
had little effect on Capitol Hill.[26] In December 1861, John P. Hale of

New Hampshire, long the Senate's most inveterate critic of the Court, startled his colleagues with a resolution proposing: "That the Committee on the Judiciary be instructed to inquire into the expediency and propriety of abolishing the present Supreme Court of the United States, and establishing instead thereof another Supreme Court . . . which, in the opinion of Congress, will meet the requirements of the Constitution." In the brief debate that followed, no one came to Hale's support, and he found his proposal under heavy fire from three Republican senators. One of them declared that it was "not decorous" for members of Congress to attack a coordinate branch of the government and that undermining public confidence in the judiciary would lead straight to anarchy. The resolution was stifled in committee.[27]

Congress, at Lincoln's urging, passed a judicial reorganization act in 1862, but it was eminently moderate and designed primarily to bring the circuit court system into adjustment with recent population changes.[28] The Supreme Court, moreover, did nothing during the Civil War to invite Republican attack upon the structure of its authority. Presented only a few opportunities to review wartime legislation and executive orders, it generally upheld administration policies, or at least acquiesced in them. In *Ex parte Vallandigham* (1864), it even refused on technical grounds to hear a case involving issues similar to those in the Merryman affair.[29] Furthermore, Lincoln's appointees to the Court (five within three years) made it increasingly respectable in Republican eyes, the climax coming when Salmon P. Chase succeeded Taney as chief justice in December 1864.[30]

Taney's death on October 12, 1864, put an end to the anomaly of a nation's fighting a war with its highest judicial officer bound in sympathy to the enemy. "The temple of the man-stealers," said the Chicago *Tribune*, "has been rent from foundation to roof, and the ancient High Priest lies cold at the altar." In his diary, New Yorker George Templeton Strong wrote more pungently: "The Hon. old Roger B. Taney has earned the gratitude of his country by dying at last. Better late than never." By curious coincidence, Strong noted, death had occurred at the very time that Maryland voters were approving a new constitution providing for the abolition of slavery. Thus, "two ancient abuses and evils were perishing together."[31] The theme of "good riddance" was softened in many leading Republican newspapers by due acknowledgment of Taney's private virtues, professional skill, and good intentions, but all editorial comment led in the end to *Dred Scott.* "That decision itself, wrong as it was," said the New York *Times,* "did not spring from a corrupt or malignant heart. It came, we have the charity to believe, from a sincere desire to compose, rather than exacerbate, sectional discord. But yet it was nonetheless an act of supreme folly, and its shadow will ever rest on his memory."[32]

Despite such efforts at post-mortem restraint, Taney's death in the midst of a war still far from won did not drain away all of the animosity felt toward him and *Dred Scott.* In February 1865, for example, the *Atlantic Monthly* published a denunciatory essay asserting that he would be "most likely, after the traitor leaders, to be held in infamous remembrance" as the man who had done "more than any other individual . . . to extend the Slave Power." Where, except in the Dred Scott decision, the writer asked, could there be found "so monstrous a combination of ignorance, injustice, falsehood, and impiety"?[33]

Soon after the appearance of this diatribe, Lyman Trumbull reported from the Senate judiciary committee a routine bill, already passed by the House of Representatives, appropriating $1000 for a marble bust of Taney to be placed in the courtroom along with those of the other chief justices. First Charles Sumner and then several other radical Republicans angrily attacked the proposal to honor the author of the Dred Scott decision. That decision, Sumner declared, was "more thoroughly abominable than anything of the kind in the history of courts." Henry Wilson called it "the scoff and jeer of the patriotic hearts of America" and said that Taney had done "more than all other men . . . to plunge the nation into this bloody revolution." Benjamin F. Wade added that the people of his state, Ohio, "would pay $2,000 to hang this man in effigy rather than $1,000 for a bust to commemorate his merits." Again Taney's chief defender was Reverdy Johnson, who reminded critics of the Dred Scott decision that it had been rendered by at least six justices, not just one. But the radical attack was plainly a personal one upon Taney alone. Wayne, Catron, and Grier, having redeemed their *Dred Scott* complicity with their wartime loyalism, suffered no word of reproach. Sumner, in the course of his anti-Taney harangue, displayed only respect for the Court as an institution.[34]

So the notion that the Supreme Court, owing to its association with the Dred Scott decision, was in mortal danger during the Civil War, is largely fiction. Indeed, if one takes into account the fact that Taney was an exceptional case, and if one remembers too that the judiciary has always tended to play a somewhat subdued role in war time, it appears that the Civil War Court actually gained back much of the public respect sacrificed in 1857. In the postwar period, to be sure, Congress did take steps to curb or control the power of the Chase Court but only because the latter was displaying a degree of judicial activism that seemed to threaten the program of Radical Reconstruction.[35] Those congressional attacks on a Court that was dominated, after all, by Lincoln appointees can scarcely be attributed in any significant degree to a lingering resentment of the Dred Scott decision. They were part of the Reconstruction struggle for power. But *Dred Scott* continued to have great rhetorical value to Republicans as a point of departure, a basis of comparison, and a horrible example.

For instance, in December 1865, Thaddeus Stevens closed a militant speech in the House of Representatives by reiterating his condemnation of a familiar Democratic argument. "Sir," he said, "this doctrine of a white man's Government is as atrocious as the infamous sentiment that damned the late Chief Justice to everlasting fame; and, I fear, to everlasting fire."* The next year, when the Court in *Ex parte Milligan* seemed to threaten the developing program of military reconstruction, Republican editors and party leaders angrily compared the decision to *Dred Scott.* The new dictum, Stevens declared, was less infamous than Taney's but far more dangerous. "Like the Dred Scott decision," said the Cleveland *Herald*, "it is not a judicial opinion; it is a political act." And the Chicago *Tribune* predicted that it would "do much to revive the unfavorable impression of the tribu-

*Salmon P. Chase, now one of the judicial "brethren," was much more shocked by Stevens's disrespect for Taney than pleased by his defense of racial equality.[36]

nal, which rested on the public mind after the Dred Scott decision, and which has only been obliterated by the war because it has been supposed that the present Court is in sympathy with principles of liberty and the spirit of the age." Thus a rhetorical pattern was set. Thirty years later, John Marshall Harlan entered his lone protest against legalized segregation in *Plessy v. Ferguson* and added a prediction that the judgment rendered would in time "prove to be quite as pernicious as the decision made by this tribunal in the *Dred Scott case.*" And in 1935, when Franklin D. Roosevelt issued a public protest against the Court's invalidation of the NRA in *Schecter v. the United States,* he solemnized the occasion by declaring that this was "more important than any decision probably since the Dred Scott case."[37]

III

Dred Scott v. Sandford has been called "the most frequently overturned decision in history."[38] Of course the Thirteenth Amendment, ratified late in 1865, made Taney's opinion totally obsolete insofar as it had been concerned with the institution of slavery. But emancipation only magnified, without resolving, the other major issue treated in the opinion—the status of the free Negro population, now suddenly increased from half a million to nearly five million. There the overturning process proved to be far more complex and prolonged. To be sure, Taney's ruling against Negro citizenship was reversed soon enough—first by the Civil Rights Act of 1866 and then more conclusively by the Fourteenth Amendment, which passed Congress the same year and was ratified in 1868.* The opening sentence of the amendment declared: "All persons born or naturalized in the United States, and subject to the jurisdiction thereof, are citizens of the United States and of the State wherein they reside." This definition at least resolved the specific issue presented in the Dred Scott case. No

---

*The Civil Rights Act was based constitutionally on the Thirteenth Amendment. Reverdy Johnson argued in the Senate that statutory inclusion of Negroes as citizens was contrary to the Dred Scott decision.[39]

longer could Negroes be denied access to federal courts under the
diverse-citizenship clause. But what else did the confirmed possession
of citizenship imply? To be free and black in antebellum America had
actually meant being only partly free by white standards. Indeed, according to Taney, to be free and black in 1787 had meant having no
rights at all that a white man was bound to respect. What, then, did it
mean in the 1860s to be free, black, and a citizen? What rights did a
Negro now have that a white man was bound to respect?

The answer was provided piecemeal in the Civil Rights Acts of
1866 and 1875, in the Fourteenth and Fifteenth amendments, and in
certain other Reconstruction measures. Blacks were expressly guaranteed equal rights before the law and placed on a level of equality with
white persons in regard to contracts, litigation, property-holding, inheritance, and access to facilities used by the public (such as railroads,
inns, and theaters). In more indirect language, blacks were also made
eligible to vote and participate in jury service on the same terms as
white persons; their privileges and immunities as citizens of the
United States were protected against impairment by state governments; and they were presumably intended to be principal beneficiaries of the famous clause forbidding states to deprive any person of
life, liberty or property without due process of law.

Taken all together, and viewed against the background of the
predominant racial attitudes of the time, the Reconstruction program
constituted a blueprint for a social revolution of truly remarkable
proportions. But like the antislavery movement that accompanied the
birth of the Republic a century earlier, it was a revolution that became abortive. No doubt there were many reasons for the failure of
Radical Reconstruction. One of them was a widespread and tenacious
resistance to the interventional federalism aggressively embodied in
the program. That is, the employment of national power to prevent
white southerners from using their state governments to mistreat
black southerners not only offended racial sensitivities but also
clashed with traditional conceptions of the American federal system.
Among those leading the resistance to the expansion of national authority required by the Radical program was the federal Supreme
Court. In a series of decisions extending from the 1870s to the end of

the century, the Court virtually stripped the Negro of federal protection against private acts of oppression and against public discrimination indirectly imposed. It upheld laws and procedures that effectively disfranchised him and excluded him from jury service. It also placed a federal stamp of approval upon segregation as public policy.[40] So, although the principal rulings of the Dred Scott decision were, strictly speaking, overturned by the Thirteenth and Fourteenth amendments, the Court later breathed new life into Taney's racial doctrine and did not officially repudiate it until the middle of the twentieth century. In a broader sense, as federal judge John Minor Wisdom declared in 1968, it was *Brown v. Board of Education* that "erased *Dred Scott*"; for only after that landmark decision in 1954 were Negroes "no longer 'beings of an inferior race'—the *Dred Scott* article of faith."[41]

Yet the Supreme Court decisions of the late nineteenth century that contributed so heavily to the support of institutionalized racism were neither justified in racial terms nor primarily motivated by racial considerations. The Court, after all, was merely implementing the semi-tacit "Compromise of 1877," which returned the race problem to the states so that the American nation could get on with other matters, such as economic expansion, that seemed more important. "It was," says Loren Miller, "as easy for these men to tolerate the evils of the burgeoning Jim Crow system as it was for the Founding Fathers to accommodate themselves to the evils of human slavery. And for the same reason: both had blinded their eyes with visions of other goals."[42] One is therefore not surprised to find that in race-related decisions the Court made little use of the *Dred Scott* precedent, with its explicit racist doctrine. But *Dred Scott* had ranged over much other ground, as we have seen, and on a number of subjects it continued to be cited as authority. For example, in technical discussion of pleading procedures, there was occasional reference to Taney's ruling (or Curtis's comments) on the Sanford plea in abatement.[43] And perhaps no passage in the Dred Scott decision has been quoted more often by jurists than Taney's assertion that the Constitution was a changeless document, speaking "not only in the same words, but with the same meaning and intent with which it spoke when it came

from the hands of its framers."[44] Also, the Fourteenth Amendment
did not wipe out everything that Taney had said on the subject of citizenship. Insofar as his Dred Scott opinion supported the concept of
dual citizenship, it survived and was reinforced by Justice Samuel F.
Miller in the *Slaughterhouse Cases*.[45] As late as 1946, a Wisconsin
judge declared that Taney's holding on dual citizenship had "never
been overruled or modified."[46]

The Dred Scott decision was most influential as precedent, however, in cases calling for judicial elucidation of the source, nature, and
limits of congressional power in the territories. With the passing of
slavery, to be sure, territorial government had lost much of its prominence and explosiveness as a public issue, but the constitutional perplexities of the system became, if anything, more pronounced in its
later years, especially after the acquisition of an island empire in
1898.

As far as the *source* of congressional power was concerned, the
Court showed considerable respect for Taney's assertion that it
derived from the implied power to acquire territory, rather than from
the territorial clause in Article Four. In 1886, for instance, Justice
Miller depreciated the importance of the territory clause and said that
the power to govern arose from federal ownership of the land and
"the right of exclusive sovereignty which must exist in the National
Government, and can be found nowhere else."[47] Four years later, in
Mormon Church v. United States, Justice Joseph P. Bradley straddled
the issue in the Marshall manner, declaring: "The power of Congress
over the Territories of the United States is general and plenary, arising from and incidental to the right to acquire the Territory itself, and
from the power given by the Constitution to make all needful rules
and regulations respecting the Territory or other property belonging
to the United States." But then he went on to emphasize the power
of acquisition.[48] In 1901, Justice Henry B. Brown summed things up
vaguely but emphatically. "Whatever be the source of this power," he
said, "its uninterrupted exercise by Congress for a century, and the
repeated declarations of this court, have settled the law that the right
to acquire territory involves the right to govern and dispose of it. That
was stated by Chief Justice Taney in the *Dred Scott* case."[49] In later

years, however, the Court pushed aside the Taney interpretation. Chief Justice Harlan F. Stone declared in 1945: "It is no longer doubted that the United States may acquire territory by conquest or by treaty, and may govern it through the exercise of the power of Congress conferred by section 3 of Article IV of the Constitution."[50]

In defining the *nature* of congressional authority over the territories, the post-Civil-War Court ignored Taney's eccentric strict-constructionist argument and returned to the Marshall doctrine of plenary power. That is, it reaffirmed that Congress, in legislating for the territories, exercised the combined sovereign power of the federal government and a state government.* More than once, for instance, Justice Bradley linked the territories with the District of Columbia as areas "subject to the plenary legislation of Congress in every branch of municipal regulation."[51] But the Court at the same time agreed substantially with Taney (with Curtis and McLean too, for that matter) that congressional power in the territories was limited by the negative provisions of the Constitution. Congress, for example, might deviate from Article Three in establishing a territorial judicial system, but it could not impose *ex post facto* legislation anywhere—not in the territories any more than in the states.[52] This problem of constitutional *limits* arose in connection with anti-polygamy legislation directed primarily at Utah Territory and most notably in the *Insular Cases* of 1901, involving the status of the island possessions acquired three years earlier.

In opposing the Edmunds bill of 1882, a severe anti-polygamy measure, Senator George G. Vest of Missouri cited with lavish praise a passage in Taney's Dred Scott opinion. Vest, a former Confederate congressman, thought that "the highest judicial declaration . . . ever made by the Supreme Court of the United States was made by the late Chief Justice Taney when he declared that the Constitution of the national Government and the citizen walked into the Territories side by side." Taney, he said, had guaranteed the territorial citizen full protection of the Constitution in "letters of gold," such as the fol-

* See above, pp. 372–73.

lowing: "The Federal Government can exercise no power over his person or property beyond what that instrument confers, nor lawfully deny any right which it has reserved."[53]

The Edmunds Act and other anti-Mormon legislation was upheld in a number of Supreme Court decisions,[54] but after the acquisition of Hawaii, Puerto Rico, Guam, and the Philippines in 1898, Senator Vest returned to the theme of his earlier argument. He introduced a joint resolution declaring in part: "That under the Constitution of the United States no power is given to the Federal Government to acquire territory to be held and governed permanently as colonies." Again he relied heavily on the Dred Scott decision, quoting not only from Taney's opinion but also from the opinions of McLean and Curtis to show that on the issue of constitutional limitations, the Court had been unanimous.[55] Orville H. Platt of Connecticut was one of the Republican expansionists who attacked the Vest resolution. Insisting that the power to acquire territory was an inherent attribute of sovereignty, he rejected Taney's contention that no territory could be annexed to be held permanently as a colony.* The Dred Scott decision, Platt said, was "an unfortunate source to which to go for authority" because it had become "a hissing and a byword," and in any case, Taney's territorial pronouncement was "a mere dictum."[56]

In the *Insular Cases*, testing the constitutional status of the new island possessions, the Dred Scott decision received more attention as a precedent than at any other time before or after. It was cited and discussed by counsel on both sides, as well as by several of the justices. Delivering the nominal opinion of the Court in *Downes v. Bidwell*, Justice Henry B. Brown acknowledged that if Taney's Dred Scott opinion were taken at full value, it would be decisive in favor of the plaintiff. But then he went on to suggest that the Taney ruling on territories had been dictum, and he added that the Civil War had "produced such changes in judicial, as well as public sentiment, as to seriously impair the authority of that case."[57] This was perhaps as

*Taney, as we have seen on pages 373–75 above, derived the power to acquire territory from the power to admit new states; therefore, in his view, no territory could be annexed if it were not intended to become a state.

close as the Supreme Court ever came to declaring the Dred Scott decision totally overruled.* Brown was a Republican from Michigan. Justice Edward D. White, a Louisiana Democrat who had served in the Confederate army, objected to Brown's criticism of the Dred Scott decision, calling it "unwarranted." White, speaking for two of his colleagues, endorsed Taney's principle of constitutional limitation but nevertheless concurred in the pro-expansionist judgment of the Court as announced by Brown. He did so by inventing the distinction between "incorporated" and "unincorporated" territories which the Court later came to accept as true doctrine. In unincorporated territories, according to the White formula, the Constitution followed the American flag *ex proprio vigore* in some respects, but only by act of Congress in others. White thus circumvented *Dred Scott* while continuing to pay it lip service. But Chief Justice Melville W. Fuller, an Illinois Democrat speaking for himself and several other dissenting justices, quoted Taney as authority for his contention that legislation for the new territories was immediately subject to all the restraints of the Constitution.[59]

The use of *Dred Scott v. Sandford* in debate over the new American empire produced a curious mixture of anachronism and anomaly. Democrats praised this judicial relic of antebellum days, while Republicans once again dismissed it with the label *obiter dictum* and reasserted congressional supremacy in the territories. Thus far, it was very much like old times. But the Democrats were ostensibly quoting the Dred Scott decision *in support* of equal rights for the non-white populations of the new empire, whereas Republican expansionists were arguing *against* such equality. This seemed to be a reversal of their traditional roles. Actually, however, there was no basic conflict on the racial question. Both sides generally assumed that the island populations could not be assimilated into the American nation, but from that assumption they proceeded to different conclusions. The ex-

---

*Mr. Dooley, in his famous dissertation on the *Insular Cases*, translated Justice Brown as follows: "Again we take th' Dhred Scott decision. This is wan iv th' worst I iver r-read. If I cudden't write a betther wan with blindhers on, I'd leap off th' bench. This horrible fluke iv a decision throws a gr-reat, an almost dazzlin' light on th' case. I will turn it off."[58]

pansionists, in their hunger for empire, were willing to embrace the principle of colonialism; the anti-imperialists, in order to make empire all the more repulsive, were willing to argue that every constitutional right must extend to the territories. The triumph of imperialism amounted to a rejection or evasion of Taney's territorial doctrine, but it was in harmony with the racial theory of his Dred Scott opinion. Southerners were quick to exploit the analogy between Republican expansionist policies and their own domestic program of white supremacy. In the debates on the Vest resolution in 1899, for instance, a South Carolina senator congratulated Orville H. Platt on his acceptance of the southern racial philosophy. "The Senator from Connecticut," he said, "has most amply vindicated the South, perhaps unintentionally."[60]

IV

In the words of C. Vann Woodward, "At the very time that imperialism was sweeping the country, the doctrine of racism reached a crest of acceptability and popularity among respectable scholarly and intellectual circles."[61] The racial attitudes of the early twentieth century were one of several conditions favorable, as we shall see, to a restoration of Taney's reputation and even to some defense or at least extenuation of the Dred Scott decision.

The first book-length study of the decision since the 1850s appeared in 1909. The author was Elbert William R. Ewing, a southern lawyer who had already published a book on the coming of the Civil War entitled *Northern Rebellion and Southern Secession*. Ewing stoutly defended every part of Taney's Dred Scott opinion in a work that contains too much misinformation and special pleading to be taken very seriously as scholarship. Perhaps the most impressive chapter is one arguing that Taney, throughout his opinion, did indeed speak for a majority of the Court.[62] At about the same time, William E. Mikell, a South Carolinian who was professor of law at the University of Pennsylvania, published a long biographical essay on Taney, praising him as "the greatest *expounder* of the Constitution that ever sat on the Supreme Court bench." Mikell devoted more than thirty pages to the Dred Scott decision. Acknowledging that what Taney had said on the merits of the case was "technically dictum," he nevertheless regarded it as a minor and excusable error, and he found Taney's argument "unassailable in the logic with which it declared unconstitutional the aim and purpose of the Republican party."[63] Both Ewing and Mikell reserved their strongest language for the antislavery reaction to the Dred Scott decision, which they characterized with epithets such as "murderous roar," "partisan malice," and "open nullification." Both writers thus portrayed Taney as a man victimized by the same antislavery fanaticism which, they insisted, had plunged the nation into civil war.[64]

More influential than the one-sided writings of Mikell and Ewing was an article by Edward S. Corwin, published in the *American Historical Review* for October 1911. Corwin, then just beginning his distinguished career as a teacher and scholar in the field of American constitutional law, had no admiration for the substance of the Dred Scott decision, which he called "a gross abuse of trust by the body which rendered it." But at the same time he presented a strong case for the legitimacy of Taney's opinion, denying that any part of it was *obiter dictum*. The effect was to call in question the principal argument upon which critics of the decision had been relying for over half a century.[65]

Other defenses of Taney's Dred Scott opinion appeared from time to time. In 1927, an Oklahoma attorney named Horace H. Hagan published an article calling it the "most maligned" judicial decision in American history. Hagan's prose bubbled with anger at Seward, Lincoln, and other critics of the decision, whom he accused of "slanderous fabrication" and "outrageous calumnies," but like Corwin he offered an impressive rebuttal to the *obiter dictum* charge.[66] Twenty years later, Wallace Mendelson of the University of Tennessee began to publish a series of articles in which he argued that the Dred Scott decision "was undertaken only upon explicit invitation of Congress and did no more than give constitutional sanction to a position held long and persistently by most contemporary voters."[67]

Even the most eloquent defenses of *Dred Scott* nevertheless failed to carry conviction. It remained, in the orthodox view, a "ghastly error" and a "ruinous decision."[68] Yet the rehabilitation of Taney continued and was eminently successful. By the middle of the twentieth century he had come to be generally recognized as one of the nation's great Supreme Court justices. In fact, there has probably never been a sharper contrast between the reputation of an author and the reputation of his most famous work. It is a curious discrepancy and one that deserves some further examination.

Certain historiographical trends of the early twentieth century were conducive to an improvement in Taney's standing, partly because they tended to separate him from the Dred Scott decision. For instance, the so-called Progressive historians, notably Frederick Jackson Turner and Charles A. Beard, took a favorable view of Jacksonianism and its leaders, associating both with the democratic aspirations of their own age; and at the same time they reduced the slavery controversy to a matter of secondary importance in American history. Arthur M. Schlesinger, Jr., writing somewhat later but in the Progressive tradition, portrayed Taney as "an advanced radical Democrat" whose "judicial imperialism" led him into the anti-Jacksonian error of the Dred Scott decision.[69]

Meanwhile, the northern point of view (represented in the work of Hermann von Holst, James Schouler, and James Ford Rhodes) had ceased to dominate historical writing about the Civil War era. The younger generation of historians, professionally trained and more removed from the emotional heat of the conflict, included many southerners in the mainstream of its scholarship. Interpretation of the Civil War consequently took a turn that was in some degree pro-southern but more emphatically anti-abolitionist and anti-Republican. In scores of articles and books, the militant opponents of slavery from William Lloyd Garrison to Thaddeus Stevens became virtually the chief villains of their age—men who in their extremism precipitated an unnecessary war and in their vindictiveness imposed a tragically draconian peace.[70]

Hostility to abolitionism is especially apparent in the influential works of Charles Warren and Albert J. Beveridge. Without defending the Dred Scott decision, both went as far as Ewing and Mikell in treating Taney as a martyr to viciously unfair criticism. Furthermore,

Beveridge came to the conclusion that "the people had well-nigh no interest at all in the decision" and that most of the public excitement over it was synthetically manufactured by Republican leaders in order to save their party from disintegration.[71]

Likewise contributing to the rehabilitation of Taney was the publication in 1910 of the Catron and Grier letters informing Buchanan that the two dissenting justices had forced the Court majority to undertake a broad decision instead of the narrow one originally planned. As a consequence, much of the blame for the resulting judicial disaster could be shifted from Taney to Curtis and McLean. Frank H. Hodder thought that Curtis was the worst offender of the three, but McLean's notorious presidential ambitions made him the more obvious culprit. In 1927, Beveridge confided to Hodder: "Justice Holmes told me (but this is confidential, and you cannot use it unless you find it out some other way) that the tradition in the Court is that McLean stirred up the whole mess and that Curtis probably would not have peeped if McLean had not ripped and torn around so much and blew off so loudly."[72]

The work of reconstructing Taney's judicial reputation reached its climax during the 1930s. In September 1931, Chief Justice Charles Evans Hughes, son of an abolitionist minister, unveiled a bust of Taney at Frederick, Maryland, and praised him lavishly. It was unfortunate, Hughes said, that the estimate of Taney's career should have been so largely influenced by the Dred Scott decision, rather than by the whole of his "arduous service nobly rendered" and by his important contributions in many of the major categories of case law. Viewing the Dred Scott decision as a well-intentioned mistake, Hughes acknowledged that it had seriously impaired the prestige of the Court, but "chiefly because of the unbridled criticism induced by the temper of the times." Taney, he concluded, was a man of "invincible spirit" and a "great Chief Justice."[73]

Four years later, Carl B. Swisher published his sympathetic but not uncritical biography of Taney in which the Dred Scott decision, as one event in a long life and long judicial career, took up only one of twenty-seven chapters. Swisher did not encourage the myth that Taney was antislavery, and neither did he deny that a sectional purpose animated the latter's Dred Scott opinion. "First and foremost," he wrote, one must remember Taney's "devotion to the South . . . and his belief that, if the trend of events continued, the South was doomed." Swisher also recognized that Taney was at heart a secessionist who nevertheless considered secession impractical because of chronic southern disunity. Instead, the South's best hope seemed to lie in discrediting the antislavery crusade and thereby relieving the pressure of sectional conflict. Thus Taney and his southern colleagues on the Court "planned to defeat the abolitionists and avoid disaster." The purpose of the decision, in short, was to help protect the South and its culture from northern subjugation.[74]

The Swisher biography was followed the next year, 1936, by a laudatory study of Taney's jurisprudence. Charles W. Smith, Jr., in his *Roger B. Taney: Jacksonian Jurist,* declared that Taney "regarded slavery as an evil institution, but one which would have to be abolished gradually." On the bench, said Smith, Taney generally acted impartially in dealing with slavery. The Dred Scott opinion furnished evidence that Taney "was a firm believer in individual rights," and from the standpoint of technique it was "one of the best that he ever wrote." Admittedly a political mistake, it was nevertheless an effort "to save the Union by protecting property rights guaranteed in the Constitution."[75]

The Swisher and Smith books were published at a time of constitutional crisis over the Supreme Court's repeated invalidation of New Deal legislation. To some critics of the Court, Taney appeared as an attractive historical figure (setting aside the Dred Scott decision, of course) because of his association with the doctrine of judicial self-restraint. This was especially true in the case of Felix Frankfurter, the Harvard law professor who would soon be appointed to the "Roosevelt Court." During the presidential campaign of 1936, Frankfurter delivered a series of lectures later published as *The Commerce Clause Under Marshall, Taney and Waite.* He demonstrated that Taney, while disagreeing with Marshall in certain important respects, did not undertake "a wholesale reversal of Marshall's doctrines." He denied that Taney was an "agrarian" or a "localist" or a proslavery man "in any invidious sense." Eventually, Frankfurter hoped, it would become "intellectually disreputable" to see Taney predominantly as the judicial defender of slavery. "We do know," he said, "that Taney himself did not favor 'the peculiar institution,' and the probabilities are overwhelming that his deepest desire was to avoid disunion." Then, in an astonishing contribution to *Dred Scott* folklore, he continued:

> He [Taney] would probably have explained his policy on the Court in language not dissimilar to that of Lincoln's famous letter to Horace Greeley: "My paramount object in this struggle is to save the Union and is not either to save or to destroy slavery."

Frankfurter closed his lecture on Taney by placing the latter "second only to Marshall in the constitutional history of our country."[76]

Other scholars besides Hughes, Swisher, Smith, and Frankfurter contributed to the highly favorable estimate of Taney's career that was well established as historical orthodoxy by the end of the 1930s.[77] Later, as a consequence of the great revolution in civil rights, the abolitionist point of view regained respectability, and extenuation of the Dred Scott decision went out of fashion.[78] Yet Taney's reputation did not suffer severely, even though the climate of opinion had turned hostile again. In 1972, the *American Bar Association Journal* published the results of a poll in which sixty-five professors of law, political science, and history were asked to rate the performances of all members of the Supreme Court since its establishment in 1789. Taney's name appeared in the top category of twelve "great" justices, only four of whom served before 1900. One of the responding professors, a counsel for the American Civil Liberties Union, acknowledged that only with considerable hesitation had he voted to call the author of the Dred Scott decision a great jurist.[79]

Thus the twentieth-century rehabilitation of Roger B. Taney remains more or less intact. It rests primarily upon a proper appreciation of his entire judicial career, but it also draws strength from several dubious historical traditions that tend to mitigate his responsibility for the "disaster" of *Dred Scott.* These include repeated assertions that Taney was privately opposed to slavery; that the two dissenting justices forced the Court majority to render a broad decision; that Taney's Dred Scott opinion was an "aberration" from his ha-

bitual devotion to judicial self-restraint; and that the worst consequences of *Dred Scott* were produced, not so much by the substance
of the decision itself, as by the violent and unjust Republican attack
upon it.

V

In 1957, the year of the racial crisis in the schools of Little Rock, the
New York *Times* noted that the centenary of the Dred Scott decision
had arrived at a time when national unities were "again imperiled by
a Supreme Court judgment."[80] It was inevitable that *Brown v. Board
of Education*, the historic desegregation decision of 1954, should be
viewed as a kind of Dred Scott decision in reverse—with Negroes
now the beneficiaries instead of the victims of judicial activism, and
with sectional attitudes toward the Court directly contrary to what
they had been in 1857. This time, to be sure, wrote Fred Rodell of
the Yale Law School, the sectional controversy would not end in civil
war; for the American nation had "grown up a little since 1857." But
it had not grown up enough, he feared, to distinguish clearly and
treat separately the two basic issues in both the *Dred Scott* and the
Brown cases—namely, the status of the Negro in American life and
the amount of political power to be vested in the Supreme Court.[81]
Neither issue was resolved in the years that followed, as the racial
struggle continued and the Court under the leadership of Earl Warren carried judicial intervention in the making of public policy to a
new level of boldness and achievement. The Dred Scott decision accordingly lost none of its relevance. It had, in fact, long since become
a standard part of the nation's historical and legal vocabulary, being
the only court decision (said Rodell) that "every schoolboy" knew by
name.[82]

In 1974, *the American Bar Association Journal* invited its readers
to determine by ballot what "milestones" of legal history should be
celebrated in a proposed Bicentennial volume. The lawyers, judges,
and law professors taking part in the voting paid due respect to the
formative work of the Marshall Court but otherwise tended to be
present-minded in their selections. The twenty milestones chosen in-

cluded fourteen specific Supreme Court decisions, of which only *Dred Scott v. Sandford* was drawn from the 115 years between 1819 and 1935.[83] Furthermore, *Dred Scott* was the only milestone marking a conspicuous judicial failure. Rendered largely obsolete when the Civil War began, and having, in the words of Charles Evans Hughes, a "negligible influence" on modern constitutional jurisprudence, it nevertheless ranked fifth among the fourteen decisions selected as legal milestones. The balloting placed it right behind *Brown v. Board of Education* and ahead of every Marshall decision except *Marbury v. Madison.*[84]

The great importance thus attached to the Dred Scott decision by members of the American legal profession in the late twentieth century is extraordinary enough to inspire some reflection on the reasons for it. No doubt the heavy vote for *Dred Scott* was partly tribute to a familiar legend. No doubt it was inspired in some degree by exaggerated estimates of *Dred Scott* influence on the disruption of the Union, on the prestige of the Supreme Court, and on the emergence of substantive due process of law. No doubt it reflected the persistence of racial troubles in modern America and the central place of the Civil War in American historical consciousness. But in the long run, Taney's decision will probably be most significant as an epoch in the growth of American judicial power.

It was Alexis de Tocqueville who wrote long ago: "Scarcely any political question arises in the United States that is not resolved, sooner or later, into a judicial question."[85] But in Tocqueville's time and for more than a century thereafter, the political power of the judiciary was primarily a restraining force, reactive instead of innovative, holding legislation and executive action within constitutional bounds. The revolution that took place during the chief justiceship of Earl Warren was one in which the Supreme Court undertook to make public policy on a vast scale, and judicial activism as a consequence became the main channel of social change. Court decisions on desegregation, legislative apportionment, and the rights of accused persons had far-reaching effects and infused new meaning into the phrase, "government by judiciary." In 1967, two years before Warren's retirement, Adolf A. Berle opened a series of lectures at Columbia University with the startling statement that "ultimate legislative power in the United States has come to rest in the Supreme Court."[86]

The work of the Warren Court fairly dominated the list of "milestones" selected in 1974, and the leading Warren cases all involved judicial review of state rather than federal law. Yet the members of the American Bar Association in their balloting ignored *Fletcher v. Peck*, the earliest case in which the Court invalidated a state law on the ground that it conflicted with the federal Constitution. At the same time, they gave the largest number of votes to *Marbury v. Madison*, thereby placing it right next to the Declaration of Independence and the Constitution as an American legal landmark. This seems inconsistent, but the high rating of the *Marbury* decision reflected a clear understanding that the Warren Court, with all its bold action, had by no means tested the farthest limits of judicial power; for those limits depend upon the extent to which the Supreme Court achieves ascendancy, not over the state governments, but over Congress and the presidency. It remains to be seen whether Berle's pronouncement in 1967 was mere hyperbole or sound prophecy— whether the United States has or has not begun to replace representative government with the Platonic elitism of a "guardian democracy."[87] But the conduct of the Court in recent years suggests that we have yet to comprehend the full meaning of *Marbury v. Madison* and of the Dred Scott decision as well.[88] We have yet to glimpse the ultimate potential of judicial sovereignty, a theory of power set forth by John Marshall in 1803 but first put to significant use by his successor on March 6, 1857.

ABBREVIATIONS USED IN THE NOTES

AC	*Annals of the Congress of the United States*
AHA	American Historical Association
AHR	*American Historical Review*
CG	*Congressional Globe*
CWAL	Roy P. Basler et al., eds., *The Collected Works of Abraham Lincoln* (9 vols.; New Brunswick, N.J., 1953–55)
CWH	*Civil War History*
DSvS	*Dred Scott v. John F. A. Sandford,* 19 Howard 393 (1857)
JAH	*Journal of American History*
JNH	*Journal of Negro History*
JSH	*Journal of Southern History*
MDLC	Manuscript Division, Library of Congress
MVHR	*Mississippi Valley Historical Review*
MHS	Missouri Historical Society, St. Louis
NA	National Archives, Washington, D.C.

Notes

INTRODUCTION

1. New York *Tribune*, March 7, 1857.
2. Harry V. Jaffa, *Crisis of the House Divided: An Interpretation of the Issues in the Lincoln-Douglas Debates* (New York, 1959), 286.
3. The question of whether judicial review is a democratic institution has been argued at some length by legal scholars. For an excellent summary and critique of the debate, see Leonard W. Levy, *Judgments: Essays on American Constitutional History* (Chicago, 1972), 33–57.

CHAPTER 1

1. Gunnar Myrdal et al., *An American Dilemma: The Negro Problem and Modern Democracy* (New York, 1944), 85. Myrdal's interpretation had been anticipated by some crusaders against slavery. Thus, William Cullen Bryant's New York *Evening Post* of March 10, 1857, commenting on the Dred Scott decision, declared that race prejudice had scarcely existed, even in the days of the Founding Fathers. "It has grown," said the *Post*, "out of the institution of slavery, and not the institution of slavery out of the prejudice." For other discussion of the subject, see Oscar and Mary F. Handlin, "The Origins of the Southern Labor System," *William and Mary Quarterly*, 3rd Series, VII (1950), 199–222; Carl N. Degler, "Slavery and the Genesis of American Race Prejudice," *Comparative Studies in Society and History*, II (1959), 49–66; Louis Ruchames, "The Sources of Racial Thought in Colonial America," *JNH*, LII (1967), 268–72; Gary B. Nash, *Red, White, and Black: The Peoples of Early America* (Englewood Cliffs, N.J., 1974), 162–72.

2. George M. Fredrickson, *The Black Image in the White Mind: The Debate on Afro-American Character and Destiny, 1817–1914* (New York, 1971), xi, 47.

3. Winthrop D. Jordan, *White over Black: American Attitudes Toward the Negro, 1550–1812* (Chapel Hill, N.C., 1968; Baltimore, 1969), 66–67.

4. Degler, "Slavery and Race Prejudice," 51–52.

5. Kenneth M. Stampp, *The Peculiar Institution: Slavery in the Ante-Bellum South* (New York, 1956, 1964), 22–23.

6. Jordan, *White over Black*, 63–67, 147.

7. *DSvS*, 407.

8. By the ancient Roman rule of *partus sequitur ventrem*. Maryland for a time fixed status by male descent. John Codman Hurd, *The Law of Freedom and Bondage in the United States* (2 vols.; Boston, 1858, 1862), I, 249. Pages 228–311 of Volume I contain summaries of legislation related to slavery in the thirteen colonies. For an extensive discussion of the ramifications of the rule, see Thomas R. R. Cobb, *An Inquiry into the Law of Negro Slavery* (Philadelphia, 1858), 68–81. A useful summary of the colonial law of slavery is William M. Wiecek, "The Statutory Law of Slavery and Race in the Thirteen Mainland Colonies of British America," *William and Mary Quarterly*, 3rd Series, XXXIV (1977), 258–80.

9. The slave was usually defined as chattel or personal property but was treated as real estate for certain purposes, notably inheritance. Stampp, *Peculiar Institution*, 197; David Brion Davis, *The Problem of Slavery in Western Culture* (Ithaca, N.Y., 1966), 248–51.

10. John Hope Franklin, *From Slavery to Freedom: A History of American Negroes*, 3rd ed. (New York, 1967), 71–111. In New York, where slave conspiracies to revolt were not unknown, the code was more like those in the South.

11. New York allowed slaves to own personal property but not to contract legal marriages (a disability removed in 1809). See Edgar J. McManus, *A History of Negro Slavery in New York* (Syracuse, N.Y., 1966), 63, 65, 177–78. In New England, slaves had broader rights to testify and sue in courts. They could own property, and cohabiting slaves were required to marry according to the same rules governing white persons. Lorenzo Johnston Greene, *The Negro in Colonial New England* (New York, 1942, 1968), 177–79, 192–93. On northern slavery generally, see Edgar J. McManus, *Black Bondage in the North* (Syracuse, N.Y., 1973).

12. Jordan, *White over Black*, 134. The principal exceptions were the Quakers, among whom public opposition to slavery appeared in the late seventeenth century, and early, unsuccessful efforts to prohibit slavery in Georgia and Rhode Island.

13. Henry Steele Commager and Richard B. Morris, eds., *The Spirit of 'Seventy-Six: The Story of the American Revolution as Told by Participants* (2 vols.; Indianapolis, 1958), I, 20, 21, 24.

14. Quoted in Jordan, *White over Black*, 290. "How is it," asked Samuel Johnson, "that we hear the loudest *yelps* for liberty among the drivers of negroes?" See David Brion Davis, *The Problem of Slavery in the Age of Revolution, 1770–1823*

(Ithaca, N.Y., 1975), 273–84, for a discussion of "The Penalty for Being Inconsistent." On the paradox of slavery in a country dedicated to freedom, see Edmund S. Morgan, *American Slavery, American Freedom: The Ordeal of Virginia* (New York, 1975).

15. *CWAL*, III, 9–10, 112–13, 177, 216, 220, 237–38, 280, 296, 300–304. A third explanation, advanced by the Garrisonian abolitionists, was that the principles of the Declaration of Independence had been compromised in the Constitutional Convention and eventually betrayed in a series of surrenders to slavery. See Staughton Lynd, "The Abolitionist Critique of the United States Constitution," in Martin Duberman, ed., *The Antislavery Vanguard: New Essays on the Abolitionists* (Princeton, 1965), 209–39.

16. Donald L. Robinson, *Slavery in the Structure of American Politics, 1765–1820* (New York, 1971), 83–85; Jordan, *White over Black*, 430–35; Robert McColley, *Slavery and Jeffersonian Virginia*, 2nd ed. (Urbana, Ill., 1973), 136–37; John Chester Miller, *The Wolf by the Ears: Thomas Jefferson and Slavery* (New York, 1977), 27–29; Bernard Bailyn, *The Ideological Origins of the American Revolution* (Cambridge, Mass., 1967), 232–46; Duncan J. MacLeod, *Slavery, Race and the American Revolution* (Cambridge, England, 1974), 25–28.

17. W. E. Burghardt Du Bois, *The Suppression of the African Slave-Trade to the United States of America, 1638–1870* (New York, 1896), 14–15, 19, 23–25, 30, 33, 35–37, 71–74; Arthur Zilversmit, *The First Emancipation: The Abolition of Slavery in the North* (Chicago, 1967), 109–68; John H. Russell, *The Free Negro in Virginia, 1619–1865* (Baltimore, 1913), 59–60; Mary Stoughton Locke, *Anti-Slavery in America from the Introduction of African Slaves to the Prohibition of the Slave Trade, 1619–1808* (Boston, 1901), 74–75, 97–99; Benjamin Quarles, *The Negro in the American Revolution* (Chapel Hill, N.C., 1961), 51–67; Davis, *Slavery in the Age of Revolution*, 78–80; Robinson, *Slavery in American Politics*, 116–22; McManus, *Black Bondage*, 155–57; W. E. Hartgrove, "The Negro Soldier in the American Revolution," *JNH*, I (1916), 110–31. The antislavery achievements of the Revolutionary period are viewed differently by historians. Some emphasize how much change was wrought in one generation, whereas others stress how far the Revolutionary achievement fell short of the Revolutionary ideal. Compare Jordan, *White over Black*, 301–02, 308–11, with Robinson, *Slavery in American Politics*, 79–88, 133–34. On the exclusion of slavery from the Northwest Territory, see above, 76–82.

18. Du Bois, *Slave Trade*, 15, for example, attributes Virginia's opposition to the African slave trade primarily to fear of insurrection. By the beginning of the nineteenth century, Virginia's oversupply of slaves and worsening economy gave the state an economic stake in the closing of the foreign slave trade.

19. The phrase is Martin Duberman's in his *Antislavery Vanguard,* 396.

20. Including the populations of Vermont, Kentucky, and Tennessee, and counting New York and New Jersey with the free states, though they had not yet enacted abolition, one finds that the Census of 1790 records 1,968,154 persons living in the free states and 1,961,174 living in the slaveholding states.

21. Zilversmit, *First Emancipation*, 139–53. New Hampshire still had 150 slaves in 1790.

22. Max Farrand, ed., *The Records of the Federal Convention of 1787*, rev. ed. (4 vols.; New Haven, 1937), II, 10; Locke, *Anti-Slavery*, 120–21; John Alden, *The First South* (Baton Rouge, 1961), 10–11.

23. *Journals of the Continental Congress, 1774–1789* (34 vols.; Washington, D.C., 1904–37), IX, 800–802; Merrill Jensen, *The Articles of Confederation* (Madison, Wis., 1940), 145–50.

24. Farrand, *Records,* I, 542, 561, 593, 596; *Journals of the Continental Congress,* VI, 1099–1101; Robinson, *Slavery in American Politics,* 157n, 187–88.

25. *Ibid.*, 156–59. The three-fifths formula was adopted by Congress in 1783 as part of a proposed amendment to the Articles of Confederation, but the amendment was never ratified by the states.

26. Farrand, *Records,* I, 597; William M. Wiecek, *The Sources of Antislavery Constitutionalism in America, 1760–1848* (Ithaca, N.Y., 1977), 65–68.

27. Farrand, *Records,* III, 255. Approved on June 11, the federal ratio met a temporary setback on July 11, when it was defeated, six states to four. But the next day a proposal to link representation with direct taxation carried the three-fifths compromise to final victory, six to two, with two states divided. Maryland and Pennsylvania switched from opposition to support. *Ibid.,* I, 201, 594–97.

28. An example of the many abolitionist attacks on the federal ratio is in William Jay, *Miscellaneous Writings on Slavery* (Boston, 1853), 218–20. See also Albert F. Simpson, "The Political Significance of Slave Representation, 1787–1821," *JSH,* VII (1941), 315–42. In 1843 and 1844, the Massachusetts legislature proposed a constitutional amendment apportioning representatives and direct taxes according to the free population. It had not the slightest chance of success but stirred up a heated debate in Congress and provoked angry replies from some southern legislatures. See Herman V. Ames, ed., *State Documents on Federal Relations,* No. V, *Slavery and the Constitution, 1789–1845* (Philadelphia, 1904), 47–48.

29. The phrase is from one of the leading textbooks in American constitutional history, Alfred H. Kelly and Winfred A. Harbison, *The American Constitution, Its Origins and Development,* 4th ed. (New York, 1970), 132.

30. Farrand, *Records,* II, 417. In Convention debate and other discussion, Madison had no qualms about referring to slaves as property, and in *Federalist* 54 he presented an extensive argument demonstrating that they were both persons *and* property. The important distinction is between what he was willing to say otherwise and what he was willing to put *into the Constitution.*

31. Farrand, *Records,* III, 253.

32. In intersectional discussion, South Carolinians maintained that they were sacrificing two-fifths instead of gaining three-fifths. See remarks of Charles Pinckney (cousin of Charles C.) in the debates on the Missouri Compromise, Farrand, *Records,* III, 439–42.

33. For example, the remarks of Abraham Baldwin, Gouverneur Morris, John Rutledge, Rufus King, William Richardson Davie, and Pierce Butler in the Constitutional Convention, Farrand, *Records,* I, 475, 533, 534, 542, 562. The derivation was from John Locke, but perhaps not accurately so; see J. R. Pole,

Political Representation in England and the Origins of the American Republic (London, 1966), 24–26.

34. *Ibid.*, 354.

35. A different view is more common. Jordan, *White over Black*, 322, says of the three-fifths compromise: "It embodied more logic than has commonly been supposed. For the slave was, by social definition, both property and man, simultaneously partaking of the qualities of both; the three-fifths rule treated him accordingly, adding only a ludicrous fractional exactitude." Yet all arguments about the appropriate fraction had to do with the slave's productive power, as compared with white workers. Benjamin Harrison (father of William Henry Harrison) was apparently the first person to suggest a "fractional" compromise. At the end of July 1776, in discussion of the quotas of money to be requisitioned from the states, he proposed that "two slaves should be counted as one freeman," adding that "slaves did not do so much work as freemen" and that he "doubted if two effected more than one." See *Journals of the Continental Congress*, VI, 1100 (from notes made by Thomas Jefferson).

36. Article One, Section Nine, of the Constitution. By Article Five, this section was then made unamendable before 1808, thus giving slaveholders a double-layered guarantee. For the debate, see Farrand, *Records*, II, 364–65, 369–74, 414–17. John Rutledge of South Carolina, later an associate justice of the U.S. Supreme Court, declared: "If the Convention thinks that North Carolina, South Carolina, and Georgia will ever agree to the plan, unless their right to import slaves be untouched, the expectation is vain. The people of those States will never be such fools as to give up so important an interest."

37. *Ibid.*, II, 415, 416; III, 346. It is interesting to compare Spaight's explanation, offered in 1788, with the following explanation written by Roger B. Taney in 1861: "In the convention which formed the Constitution, a majority of Northern states or more particularly Massachusetts wished all power to abolish the slave trade to be prohibited until 1820, and it was only by the influence of the South that the power to prohibit it in 1808 was given. . . . The Northern states therefore continued the slave trade for their own benefit." From a fragmentary manuscript in the Roger B. Taney Papers, MDLC; and see above, 553–54. Thomas Jefferson, George Mason, and other Revolutionary Virginians indulged in similar fantasy when they insisted that Great Britain had forced slavery on the American colonies.

38. The compromise on the slave trade was part of a larger understanding in which southerners gave up their demands for restrictions on congressional power to pass navigation acts. Farrand, *Records*, II, 449–53; III, 210–13 (the latter passage is the account of Luther Martin of Maryland). see also Max Farrand, *The Framing of the Constitution of the United States* (New Haven, 1913), 149–52.

39. Legislation passed in 1807, effective January 1, 1808, U.S. Statutes at Large, II, 426–30. On the legislative history of the act, see Robinson, *Slavery in American Politics*, 324–38. Enforcement of the prohibition was incomplete right up to the Civil War, in spite of much supplementary legislation, including an act passed in 1820 declaring the foreign slave trade to be piracy. See Du Bois, *Slave Trade,*

and Warren S. Howard, *American Slavers and the Federal Law, 1837–1862* (Berkeley, 1963).

40. *DSvS*, 411.

41. Said James Wilson at the Pennsylvania ratifying convention: "I consider this as laying the foundation for banishing slavery out of this country." Farrand, *Records*, III, 161. See also the statement of Oliver Ellsworth, *ibid.*, 165.

42. Robinson, *Slavery in American Politics*, 227–28, 499. Robinson is mistaken, however, in his assertion that James Wilson in 1787 "apparently thought the word 'migration' referred to interstate commerce in slaves." Instead, Wilson obviously believed that "migration" and "importation" were used to differentiate between white immigrants and slaves. See Farrand, *Records*, III, 161. The clause became a lively issue during debates on the Alien Act in 1798, as well as during the Missouri controversy of 1819–21. See James Morton Smith, *Freedom's Fetters: The Alien and Sedition Laws and American Civil Liberties* (Ithaca, N.Y., 1956), 79–83.

43. Locke, *Anti-Slavery*, 138–39, 145–47. For Madison's comments in 1789 on the purpose of the tax, see Farrand, *Records*, III, 355–56.

44. Robinson, *Slavery in American Politics*, 228, also 501, where he declares: "This clause came closest to acknowledging the existence of slavery in America"; *DSvS*, 411.

45. Note the use of the word "service." Article One, Section Two, in dealing with the apportionment of direct taxes and representation, had originally referred to indentured servants as "persons bound to servitude for a term of years." However, Edmund Randolph of Virginia secured the replacement of "servitude" with "service," on the grounds, according to Madison, that the former expressed "the condition of slaves & the latter the obligations of free persons." Farrand, *Records*, II, 590, 607, 651. This interesting phraseological fact is pointed out in Richard Hildreth, *Despotism in America: An Inquiry into the Nature, Results, and Legal Basis of the Slave-Holding System in the United States* (Boston, 1854; New York, 1968), 233.

46. Farrand, *Records*, II, 443, 446; Robinson, *Slavery in American Politics*, 228–29.

47. In the fugitive-slave legislation of 1793 and 1850, and in *Prigg v. Pennsylvania*, 16 Peters 539 (1842).

48. It has been argued that provisions in Article One, Section Eight, for calling forth the militia to "suppress insurrections," and in Article Four, Section Four, for protecting states against "domestic violence," were primarily promises of federal intervention in case of slave uprisings. Gouverneur Morris did complain in the Convention that the northern states were pledged to "march their militia" to defend southerners against their slaves. Farrand, *Records*, II, 222. But see Robinson, *Slavery in American Politics*, 218n. It seems likely that troubles such as Shays' Rebellion were what the delegates had principally in mind.

49. On whether slaves were treated as property in the Constitution, for instance, compare Madison's statement in the Convention with his words in the Virginia ratifying convention, Farrand, *Records*, II, 417; III, 325–26.

50. *Ibid.*, II, 601, 628. Madison explained that the substitution of "under the laws thereof" for "legally" was made "in compliance with some who thought the term

(legal) equivocal, and favoring the idea that slavery was legal in a moral view."
One of the leading spokesmen for the view that slavery had no legal status except
under state law was Salmon P. Chase. See the discussion of his constitutional
theory in Eric Foner, *Free Soil, Free Labor, Free Men: The Ideology of the
Republican Party Before the Civil War* (New York, 1970), 75–77. My interpretation here differs from that in Wiecek, *Sources*, 80, where the revision is interpreted as intended "to recognize implicitly the moral legitimacy of slavery."

51.   *CWAL*, II, 492; *DSvS*, 451. However far off the mark Lincoln may have been,
he and most of his fellow Republicans appear to have believed sincerely that
"it had been the intention of the founding fathers to restrict slavery and divorce
the federal government from all connection with it." Foner, *Free Soil*, 84.

52.   Joseph Story, *Commentaries on the Constitution of the United States*, 5th ed. (2
vols.; Boston, 1891), I, 310, declares: "Contemporary construction is properly
resorted to, to illustrate and confirm, . . . it can never narrow down its true
limitations, it can never enlarge its natural boundaries." For a discussion of
meaning and intention in legal interpretation, see Charles A. Miller, *The Supreme Court and the Uses of History* (Cambridge, Mass., 1969; New York,
1972), 153–55.

53.   During debate on the Missouri question in 1820, Senator Jonathan Roberts of
Pennsylvania asked, "Why is a circumlocution of words used in that instrument,
to designate such persons, instead of one so appropriate as that of slaves? Either
[he continued] because it was considered as a painful word, or for the better
reason, that it was hoped the Constitution would survive a state of things where
the word would be applicable. In either case, emancipation must have been
looked to as a desirable event, and a righteous consummation of the promises of
the Revolution." *AC*, 16-1, col. 340. See also William W. Freehling, "The
Founding Fathers and Slavery," *AHR*, LXXVII (1972), 81–93. Charles A.
Miller, "Constitutional Law and the Rhetoric of Race," in Donald Fleming and
Bernard Bailyn, eds., *Perspectives in American History*, Volume V: *Law in
American History* (Cambridge, Mass., 1971), 154–57, contends that the word
"slavery" was generally avoided only where the institution of slavery was being
supported or acknowledged. The word was used straightforwardly, he says,
when "a positive moral good," such as the abolition of the institution, was being
implemented or discussed.

CHAPTER 2

1.   Francis Newton Thorpe, ed., *The Federal and State Constitutions, Colonial
Charters, and Other Organic Laws of the States, Territories, and Colonies Now
or Heretofore Forming the United States of America* (7 vols.; Washington, D.C.,
1909), 562–68 (Delaware, 1776), 777–85 (Georgia, 1777), 1686–1701 (Maryland,
1776), 1888–1911 (Massachusetts, 1780), 2451–53 (New Hampshire, 1776),
2594–98 (New Jersey, 1776), 2623–38 (New York, 1777), 2787–94 (North Carolina, 1776), 3081–92 (Pennsylvania, 1776), 3241–57 (South Carolina, 1776,
1778), 3812–19 (Virginia, 1776). See also Richard Hildreth, *Despotism in*

America: An Inquiry into the Nature, Results, and Legal Basis of the Slave-Holding System in the United States (Boston, 1854; New York, 1968), 221–26. The Articles of Confederation likewise made no reference to slavery.

2. Thomas R. R. Cobb, *An Inquiry into the Law of Negro Slavery in the United States of America* (Philadelphia, 1858), 5, citing *State v. Jones*, Walker Mississippi 83 (1820), and *The Antelope*, 10 Wheaton 66 (1825), in which John Marshall declared that slavery was contrary to natural law but in accordance with international law.

3. Arthur Zilversmit, *The First Emancipation: The Abolition of Slavery in the North* (Chicago, 1967). Abolition was achieved by judicial interpretation in Massachusetts. The powerful Council of Revision in New York did veto a 1785 bill for gradual emancipation, ostensibly because it included a provision denying suffrage to freedmen. New York, however, was not a typical state in its constitutional structure, being further removed from legislative supremacy. On the Council's action, see Edgar J. McManus, *A History of Negro Slavery in New York* (Syracuse, N.Y., 1966), 164–65.

4. Thorpe, *Constitutions*, 273–74, 283; Orville W. Taylor, *Negro Slavery in Arkansas* (Durham, N.C., 1958), 42–43.

5. John Codman Hurd, *The Law of Freedom and Bondage in the United States* (2 vols.; Boston, 1858, 1862), I, 234–41, 299–308, 310–11; Ralph Betts Flanders, *Plantation Slavery in Georgia* (Chapel Hill, N.C., 1933), 23. Some colonial legislation covered slaves and indentured servants together, such as a Virginia law of 1705. Daniel J. Flanigan, "The Criminal Law of Slavery and Freedom, 1800–1868," Ph.D. dissertation, Rice University, 1973, pp. 11, 418n, insists that the imitation of Virginia and South Carolina was by no means as complete as historians have generally believed.

6. *The Code of the State of Georgia*, prepared by R. H. Clark, T. R. R. Cobb, and D. Irwin (Atlanta, 1861), iii.

7. *Ibid.*, 263–67, 319–22, 367–74, 406–7, 512, 758–61, 875–82, 916–23.

8. Cobb, *Law of Slavery*, 91, 263, declared that "statutory enactments never extend to or include the slave . . . unless specifically named, or included by necessary implication." But even Cobb acknowledges some exceptions, and Flanigan, "Criminal Law of Slavery," 4–8, demonstrates that they were numerous.

9. *Ibid.*, 9–10, and the cases cited in notes 16–18, p. 418. Said the supreme court of North Carolina in 1818: "A man is liable for trespasses committed by his cattle . . . but he is not bound to keep his slaves confined, and if he were, it would be a monstrous thing to charge him with their depredations." *Campbell v. Staiert*, 2 Murphey 389, quoted in Helen Tunnicliff Catterall, *Judicial Cases Concerning American Slavery and the Negro* (5 vols.; Washington, D.C., 1926–37), II, 35. On the other hand, Arkansas by statute provided that "any person injured by the trespass of any slave shall have his action against the master for the damage he may have sustained." E. H. English, comp., *A Digest of the Statutes of Arkansas* (Little Rock, 1848), 379.

10. *Plumpton v. Cook*, 2 A. K. Marshall 450 (Ky., 1820), quoted by Jacob D. Wheeler in his *A Practical Treatise on the Law of Slavery, Being a Compilation of All the Decisions Made on That Subject in the Several Courts of the*

United States and State Courts (New York, 1837), 37. "In states where slaves were generally considered as personalty, they were treated as realty for purposes of inheritance. In Louisiana, where they were supposedly like real property, they retained many of the characteristics of 'chattels personal.' " Kenneth M. Stampp, *The Peculiar Institution: Slavery in the Ante-Bellum South* (New York, 1956, 1964), 197. In a given case, the classification could make all the difference. Thus in *Harper v. Destrehan*, 14 Martin 389 (La., 1824), quoted in Wheeler, *Law of Slavery*, 69–70, payment for a slave depended upon whether he was "moveable" property or not. The lower court had held in the affirmative, but its decision was reversed in the supreme court.

11. Cobb, *Law of Slavery;* Catterall, *Cases*. Only a small percentage of the cases in Catterall concerned free Negroes.

12. For example, Ulrich Bonnell Phillips, *American Negro Slavery* (New York, 1918), Chaps. 22–23; Stampp, *Peculiar Institution*, Chap. 5; C. Duncan Rice, *The Rise and Fall of Black Slavery* (New York, 1975), Chap. 3; Flanders, *Slavery in Georgia*, Chaps. 2, 10–11; Taylor, *Slavery in Arkansas*, Chaps. 12–13; Edgar J. McManus, *Black Bondage in the North* (Syracuse, N.Y., 1973), Chap. 5; Chase C. Mooney, *Slavery in Tennessee* (Bloomington, Ind., 1957), Chap. 1; Harrison Anthony Trexler, *Slavery in Missouri, 1804–1865* (Baltimore, 1914), Chap. 2.

13. Notably Flanigan, "Criminal Law of Slavery," and A. E. Keir Nash, "Negro Rights and Judicial Behavior in the Old South," Ph.D. dissertation, Harvard University, 1967, together with published articles of both men: Daniel J. Flanigan, "Criminal Procedure in Slave Trials in the Antebellum South," *JSH*, XL (1974), 537–64; A. E. Keir Nash, "A More Equitable Past? Southern Supreme Courts and the Protection of the Antebellum Negro," *North Carolina Law Review*, XLVIII (1970), 197–242; A. E. Keir Nash, "Fairness and Formalism in the Trials of Blacks in the State Supreme Courts of the Old South," *Virginia Law Review*, LVI (1970), 64–100. See also Michael S. Hindus, "Black Justice Under White Law: Criminal Prosecutions of Blacks in Antebellum South Carolina," *JAH*, LXIII (1976), 575–99. An earlier work is H. M. Henry, *The Police Control of the Slave in South Carolina* (Emory, Va., 1914).

14. Flanigan, "Criminal Law of Slavery," 18–19, 103.

15. *Ibid.*, 65–66, 406–12; Ulrich Bonnell Phillips, "Slave Crime in Virginia," *AHR*, XX (1915), 336–40. As Flanigan notes, there were economic reasons for resorting to transportation. When a slave was sentenced to death, the master received reimbursement from the state; a transported slave was sold to the benefit of the state.

16. Flanigan, "Criminal Law of Slavery," 12–19, 36; *Code of Georgia*, 1861, pp 686, 688. Hindus, "Black Justice," 590–91, finds that in South Carolina the mean number of lashes administered rose from 16.7 in the 1820s to 56.1 in the 1850s.

17. Flanigan, "Criminal Law of Slavery," 73–144, 145, 189; Nash, "Equitable Past," 203–13; Nash, "Fairness and Formalism," 76–89; Nash, "Negro Rights and Judicial Behavior," 110–57.

18. Hurd, *Law of Freedom and Bondage*, I, 232, 242, 297, 306; Flanigan, "Criminal

Law of Slavery," 147, 153. A South Carolina law of 1690 prescribed three months' imprisonment and a fine of £50 for the wanton, willful killing of a slave. By a law of 1740, the fine was increased to £700, with imprisonment for seven years only in the event of inability to pay the fine. The penalty for nonwillful killing was set at £350.

19. Hurd, *Law of Freedom and Bondage*, I, 296; II, 5, 83, 85, 97. The North Carolina law of 1774 imposed the death penalty only for the second offense of murdering a slave, punishment for the first conviction being one year in prison.

20. *Code of Georgia*, 1861, pp. 876–77.

21. Nash, "Equitable Past," 213–15, 219–20, 241–42. See also Flanigan, "Criminal Law of Slavery," 164–65, 171–76. Nash includes in his study eight appeals involving attacks on free Negroes, bringing the total of cases surveyed to fifty-five.

22. *Code of Georgia*, 1861, pp. 818, 877–82; Hurd, *Law of Freedom and Bondage*, II, 11, 173. It appears that such laws were not frequently invoked and that southern courts were often disposed to give freedom of speech priority. Social pressure and occasional mob action were apparently more effective deterrents to antislavery agitation in the South. See Clement Eaton, *The Freedom-of-Thought Struggle in the Old South*, rev. ed. (New York, 1964), 118–43.

23. Joseph Story, *Commentaries on the Conflict of Laws, Foreign and Domestic*, 5th ed. (Boston, 1857), 157–86. First published in 1834, Story's monumental work was immensely influential from the start.

24. *U.S. Statutes at Large*, II, 103. In Washington, the law of Maryland applied. Congress retroceded the Virginia portion of the District in 1846.

25. *U.S. v. King*, 26 Federal Cases, 786, 787; *Hickerson v. U.S.*, 30 Federal Cases 1087, 1088.

26. Letitia Woods Brown, *Free Negroes in the District of Columbia, 1790–1846* (New York, 1972), 14.

27. Charles R. Ritcheson, *Aftermath of Revolution: British Policy Toward the United States, 1783–1795* (New York, 1969, 1971), 70–75, 96–104, 336–37; Donald L. Robinson, *Slavery in the Structure of American Politics, 1765–1820* (New York, 1971), 347–61.

28. Samuel Flagg Bemis, *John Quincy Adams and the Foundations of American Foreign Policy* (New York, 1949), 231–32, 293; William Jay, *Miscellaneous Writings on Slavery* (Boston, 1853), 249–52.

29. Bemis, *Adams and Foreign Policy*, 416; John Spencer Bassett, *The Life of Andrew Jackson* (New York, 1911, 1925), 237–39; Jay, *Miscellaneous Writings*, 247–49. An account of the attack on the fort by the officer in charge is in *American State Papers* (38 vols.; Washington, D.C., 1834), *Foreign Relations*, IV, 559–61. The authorization, issued by Secretary of War William H. Crawford (of Georgia), had been anticipated by Generals Andrew Jackson and Edmund P. Gaines on the Florida border. The high mortality in the reduction of the fort resulted from the firing of hot shot into its powder magazine.

30. The vessels were the *Comet*, the *Encomium*, and the *Enterprise*. See Du Bois, *Slave Trade*, 292, and documents there cited; see also Jay, *Miscellaneous Writings*, 252–58. Andrew Stevenson of Virginia, American minister to Britain, informed Lord Palmerston that in the United States there was "no distinction in principle between property in persons and property in things."

31. *The Diplomatic and Official Papers of Daniel Webster While Secretary of State*
(New York, 1848), 83–94. Extensive contemporary accounts and documents are
printed in *McCargo v. New Orleans Insurance Co.*, 10 Robinson 202 (La.,
1845). See also Wilbur Devereux Jones, "The Influences of Slavery on the
Webster-Ashburton Negotiations," *JSH*, XXII (1956), 48–58; Howard Jones,
"The Peculiar Institution and National Honor: The Case of the *Creole* Slave
Revolt," *CWH*, XXI (1975), 28–50; Carl B. Swisher, *The Taney Period,
1836–1864*, Volume V of the Oliver Wendell Holmes Devise *History of the
Supreme Court of the United States* (New York, 1974), 197–99. Webster was
under pressure from President John Tyler (a Virginian), reported by the British
minister, Lord Ashburton, to be "very sore and testy about the *Creole.*"

32. *U.S. v. The Amistad*, 15 Peters 518 (1841); Swisher, *Taney Period*, 189–96;
Charles Grove Haines and Foster H. Sherwood, *The Role of the Supreme Court
in American Government and Politics, 1835–1864* (Berkelely, 1957), 98–110;
Christopher Martin, *The Amistad Affair* (New York, 1970). On both the *Creole*
and the *Amistad* affairs, see also Robert M. Cover, *Justice Accused: Antislavery
and the Judicial Process* (New Haven, 1975), 109–16, 287. John Quincy Adams
served as counsel for the *Amistad* Negroes, and his argument was afterward
circulated as an abolitionist tract. See Samuel Flagg Bemis, *John Quincy Adams
and the Union* (New York, 1956), 384–415.

33. *CG*, 31-1, p. 481.

34. *U.S. Statutes at Large*, I, 302–5; William R. Leslie, "A Study in the Origins of
Interstate Rendition: The Big Beaver Creek Murders," *AHR*, LVII (1951),
63–76; Thomas D. Morris, *Free Men All: The Personal Liberty Laws of the
North, 1780–1861* (Baltimore, 1974), 19–22.

35. The Taney Court ruled sixty-eight years later that a governor could not be
forced to perform his duty by writ of mandamus. *Kentucky v. Dennison*, 24
Howard 66 (1861); Swisher, *Taney Period*, 686–90.

36. *AC*, 2-2, cols. 630, 640, 860–61. The dissenters in the House were from seven
different states, including two southern.

37. Morris, *Free Men All*, 3–4.

38. On the personal liberty laws generally, see Morris, *Free Men All*, 3–4, and
especially the appendix, 219–22, with a list of laws passed between 1780 and
1861.

39. *Ibid.*, 35–40; *AC*, 15-1, cols. 259, 837–40, 1139, 1394.

40. *Johnson v. Tompkins et al.*, 13 Federal Cases 840, 852 (1833); Cover, *Justice Accused*, 163–64. Perhaps the first judicial use of the historical-necessity doctrine
was by William Tilghman, chief justice of the Pennsylvania supreme court in
Wright v. Deacon, 5 Sergeant and Rawle, 62, 63 (Penn., 1819): "It is well
known that our southern brethren would not have consented to become parties
to a constitution . . . unless their property in slaves had been secured." Cf.
Thomas Hart Benton, *Thirty Years View* (2 vols.; New York, 1854–56), 773: "A
right to recover slaves is not only authorized by the Constitution, but it is a
right without which there would have been no constitution." For similar assertions by southern political leaders, see Arthur Bestor, "State Sovereignty and
Slavery: A Reinterpretation of Proslavery Constitutional Doctrine, 1846–1860,"
Journal of the Illinois State Historical Society, LIV (1961), 131. See also Don-

ald M. Roper, "In Quest of Judicial Objectivity: The Marshall Court and the Legitimation of Slavery," *Stanford Law Review*, XXI (1969), 538.

41. *Prigg v. Pennsylvania*, 16 Peters 539, 611 (1842). Jefferson Davis quoted this passage in his resolutions of February 2, 1860 in the Senate. *CG*, 36-1, p. 658.

42. Hurd, *Law of Freedom and Bondage*, II, 439n.

43. On legal positivism and the fugitive-slave laws, see Cover, *Justice Accused*, 26–28, 159–74.

44. Story himself seems to have regarded his opinion as a well-struck blow in the cause of freedom; so says his son, William W. Story, *Life and Letters of Joseph Story* (2 vols.; Boston, 1851), II, 392–94. Swisher, *Taney Period*, 547, sees the Story opinion as essentially antislavery in nature.

45. 16 Peters 611–12. This was in accord with Story's interpretation of conflict of laws (see above, 56–57) and reasserted his ruling in *U.S. v. La Jeune Eugénia*, 26 Federal Cases 832 (1822), that slavery was contrary to natural law and to the law of nations. On the subject generally, see William R. Leslie, "The Influence of Joseph Story's Theory of the Conflict of Laws on Constitutional Nationalism," *MVHR*, XXXV (1948), 203–20.

46. Cobb, *Law of Slavery*, 67, says: "As all the negroes introduced into America were brought as slaves, the black color of the race raises the presumption of slavery, contrary to the principles of the common law, which would presume freedom until the contrary is shown. . . . In those States where slavery has been abolished, no such presumption would attach, except to persons proven to be fugitives from a slaveholding State." In his exception, Cobb begs the whole question at issue, for of course where a person is "proven" to be a fugitive, presumption of any kind is useless.

47. 16 Peters 627–28. It is very doubtful that Story carried the Court with him on federal exclusiveness. Two justices agreed with him and three disagreed. The seventh, Peter V. Daniel, also appears to have been in disagreement without specifically saying so. Yet Taney spoke of himself as opposing "my brethren of the majority" on this point. *Ibid.*, 632. See Joseph C. Burke, "What Did the Prigg Decision Really Decide?" *Pennsylvania Magazine of History and Biography*, XCIII (1969), 73–85.

48. Notably, Massachusetts and Vermont in 1843, Connecticut in 1844, Pennsylvania in 1847, and Rhode Island in 1848. Hurd, *Law of Freedom and Bondage*, II, 32, 39, 47, 50, 74; Morris, *Free Men All*, 109–26. In Ohio, a more stringent law forbidding any citizen of the state to participate in the recovery process failed of passage.

49. Although accurate figures are not available, it appears that the number of fugitives making their way into free states may not have averaged more than several hundred a year. See Allan Nevins, *The Emergence of Lincoln* (2 vols.; New York, 1950), II, 489.

50. Bestor, "State Sovereignty and Slavery," 130–31.

51. Larry Gara, "The Fugitive Slave Law: A Double Paradox," *CWH*, X (1964), 233.

52. 16 Peters 611. Bestor, "State Sovereignty and Slavery," 130, refers to the fugitive-slave clause as "the only provision of the Constitution that explicitly recognized the slaveowner's right of property in his slave," but of course there was no

such explicit recognition in the clause itself, only in the reading of the clause by federal officers—legislative, executive, and especially judicial.

53. See especially Calhoun's resolutions of December 27, 1837, in the Senate, *CG*, 25-2, p. 55; also Charles S. Sydnor, *The Development of Southern Sectionalism, 1819–1848* (Baton Rouge, 1948), 245.

54. The Garrisonian wing of abolitionism took the first view, with Wendell Phillips making the most eloquent case. Lysander Spooner and Richard Hildreth took the stand that slavery was unconstitutional. See Cover, *Justice Accused*, 149–58.

CHAPTER 3

1. From 1790 to 1820, the free black population of the South (not counting Missouri) increased 313 per cent, while that of the Northeast inceased 243 per cent. During those same years, the slave population of the Northeast was reduced from 40,000 to 18,000. These figures are no more than suggestive, however, because of various other influences on the size of the free black population in both regions—influences such as colonization, the selling of northern slaves in the South, the influx of refugees from Santo Domingo, and fugitivism, not to mention the dubiousness of census figures where free Negroes were concerned. For tables on the free black increase in the South, see Ira Berlin, *Slaves Without Masters: The Free Negro in the Antebellum South* (New York, 1974), 46–47.

2. Thomas R. R. Cobb, *An Inquiry into the Law of Negro Slavery* (Philadelphia, 1858), 279; Jacob D. Wheeler, *A Practical Treatise on the Law of Slavery, Being a Compilation of All the Decisions Made on That Subject in the Several Courts of the United States and State Courts* (New York, 1837), 386–88. In 1851, the North Carolina supreme court declared that "the power of the owner to give, and the capacity of the slave to receive, freedom, exist in nature, and therefore may be used in every case and every way, except those in which it is forbidden by law." *Thompson v. Newlin*, 8 Iredell Equity 32, 46, quoted in Helen Tunnicliff Catterall, *Judicial Cases Concerning American Slavery and the Negro* (5 vols.; Washington, D.C., 1926–37), II, 163. On the other hand, the Virginia supreme court held that manumission, because it raised property to the status of free persons, was an exercise of sovereign power delegated by the state. See John H. Russell, *The Free Negro in Virginia, 1619–1865* (Baltimore, 1913), 42–43, and cases cited there.

3. John Codman Hurd, *The Law of Freedom and Bondage in the United States* (2 vols.; Boston, 1858, 1862), I, 237, 241–42, 302; H. M. Henry, *The Police Control of the Slave in South Carolina* (Emory, Va., 1914), 168; John Hope Franklin, *The Free Negro in North Carolina, 1790–1860* (Chapel Hill, N.C., 1943), 20–21.

4. Berlin, *Slaves Without Masters*, 29; Benjamin Joseph Klebaner, "American Manumission Laws and the Responsibility for Supporting Slaves," *Virginia Magazine of History and Biography*, LXIII (1955), 443–46. Indebtedness of the slaveholder could also be a barrier to manumission.

5. From 1790 to 1810, the white population of the South increased 72.4 per cent; the slave population, 76.6 per cent; and the free black population, 232 per cent. Manumissions were heavily concentrated in the upper South. According to Russell, *Free Negro in Virginia*, 61, the free black population of Virginia more than doubled in the first two years after passage of the act of 1782.

6. Herbert Aptheker, *American Negro Slave Revolts* (New York, 1943), 219–26; Robert McColley, *Slavery and Jeffersonian Virginia*, 2nd ed. (Urbana, Ill., 1973), 107–13; and see the report of Governor James Monroe in Stanislaus Murray Hamilton, ed., *The Writings of James Monroe* (7 vols.; New York, 1898–1903), III, 234–43. "Unhappily," Monroe concluded, "while this class of people exists among us we can never count with certainty on its tranquil submission." It was Gabriel's plot that inspired Virginia's interest in colonization of Negroes abroad. The legislature on December 31, 1800, requested the governor to "correspond with the president of the United States on the subject of purchasing lands without the limits of the United States whither persons obnoxious to the laws or dangerous to the peace of society may be removed." See Russell, *Free Negro in Virginia*, 64–72.

7. Hurd, *Law of Freedom and Bondage*, II, 24, 87, 90, 92, 94, 96, 97, 99, 102, 107, 143, 145, 151, 158, 162, 165–66, 174, 191, 192, 194, 196, 199; Klebaner, "Manumission Laws," 448; Sumner Eliot Matison, "Manumission by Purchase," *JNH*, XXXIII (1948), 146–67; Joe Gray Taylor, *Negro Slavery in Louisiana* (Baton Rouge, 1963), 153–67; Marina Wikramanayake, *A World in Shadow: The Free Black in Antebellum South Carolina* (Columbia, S.C., 1973), 34–44; Chase C. Mooney, *Slavery in Tennessee* (Bloomington, Ind., 1957), 21–22, 80; James Curtis Ballagh, *A History of Slavery in Virginia* (Baltimore, 1902), 125–26.

8. *Preliminary Report on the Eighth Census, 1860* (Washington, D.C., 1862), 137. According to the report, there were 3018 manumissions in 1860, compared with 1467 in 1850.

9. Taylor, *Slavery in Louisiana*, 162–64; Orville W. Taylor, *Negro Slavery in Arkansas* (Durham, N.C., 1958), 239–40; James Hugo Johnston, *Race Relations in Virginia and Miscegenation in the South, 1776–1860* (Amherst, Mass., 1970), 217–29; Harrison Anthony Trexler, *Slavery in Missouri, 1804–1865* (Baltimore, 1914), 219–20; Franklin, *Free Negro in North Carolina*, 35. In most of the states of the Deep South, mulattoes constituted more than 70 per cent of the free colored population and only about 10 per cent of the slave population. *Eighth Census of the United States, Population* (Washington, D.C., 1864), xiii.

10. Russell, *Free Negro in Virginia*, 156; Berlin, *Slaves Without Masters*, 143–49; John Hope Franklin, "Slaves Virtually Free in Ante-Bellum North Carolina," *JNH*, XXVIII (1943), 284–310; Loren Schweninger, "The Free Slave Phenomenon: James P. Thomas and the Black Community in Ante-Bellum Nashville," *CWH*, XXII (1976), 293–307. With the exception of South Carolina, where it was prohibited, southern states generally recognized the right of a slaveholder to transfer slaves to another state or country for purposes of manumission. See Cobb, *Law of Slavery*, 290–91, and *Cox v. Williams*, 4 Iredell Equity 15 (N.C., 1845), quoted in Catterall, *Cases*, II, 114–16. The *Code of Georgia* for 1861, p. 372, declared: "Every master has the right of sending his slave to another State,

there to be manumitted." But it added: "He cannot direct this to be done by his executor or others after his death."

11. Several southern states prohibited importation of slaves for purposes of sale and declared that any so imported should be free. In Maryland and Virginia especially, these laws resulted in a number of manumissions. See Cobb, *Law of Slavery*, 307–8, and the following cases as summarized in Catterall, *Cases: Henderson v. Tom*, IV, 65; *Boisneuf v. Lewis*, IV, 55–56; *Hook v. Nanny Pagee and her children*, I, 121; *Garnett v. Sam and Phillis*, I, 128; *M'Michen v. Amos*, I, 144–45; *Hunter v. Fulcher*, I, 159; *Betty v. Horton*, I, 175.

12. 20 Howell State Trials 1. Mansfield's decision was delivered orally and not officially reported. For the problem of variant versions, see William M. Wiecek, "*Somerset*: Lord Mansfield and the Legitimacy of Slavery in the Anglo-American World," *University of Chicago Law Review*, XLII (1974), 141–46; David Brion Davis, *The Problem of Slavery in the Age of Revolution, 1770–1823* (Ithaca, N.Y., 1975), 472n, 476–77n; Jerome Nadelhaft, "The Somersett Case and Slavery: Myth, Reality, and Repercussions," *JNH*, LI (1966), 193–208.

13. Mansfield himself later declared that the *Somerset* decision went no further than that "the master cannot by force compel him to go out of the kingdom." Wiecek, "*Somerset*," 109.

14. *Ibid.*, 108.

15. See especially *Forbes v. Cochrane and Cockburn*, 127 English Reports (King's Bench, 1824), quoted in Wiecek, "*Somerset*," 110. One justice declared that slavery was "inconsistent with the genius of the English constitution." On blacks in England generally, see James Walvin, *Black and White: The Negro and English Society, 1555–1945* (London, 1973).

16. Richard Hildreth, *Despotism in America: An Inquiry into the Nature, Results, and Legal Basis of the Slave-Holding System in the United States* (Boston, 1854; New York, 1968), 200–218; Lysander Spooner, *The Unconstitutionality of Slavery* (Boston, 1845), 23–24.

17. *Butler et al. v. Delaplaine*, 7 Sergeant and Rawle 378, 383–84 (Penn., 1821); *Willard v. the People*, 4 Scammon 461, 472 (Ill., 1843); Kempes Y. Schnell, "Anti-Slavery Influence on the Status of Slaves in a Free State," *JNH*, L (1965), 260–62; Kempes Y. Schnell, "Court Cases Involving Slavery: A Study of the Application of Anti-Slavery Thought to Judicial Argument," Ph.D. dissertation, University of Michigan, 1955, 79–83; Anonymous, "American Slavery and the Conflict of Laws," *Columbia Law Review*, LXXI (1971), 87. A Pennsylvania law of 1780 (providing for gradual abolition) fixed six months as the maximum period for sojourn; a New York law of 1810 fixed nine months. Hurd, *Law of Freedom and Bondage*, II, 54, 69. Pierce Butler, member of the Constitutional Convention and a senator from South Carolina, kept a servant in Philadelphia for a number of years, and the slave was declared free by the federal circuit court presided over by Bushrod Washington, a nephew of George Washington. *Butler v. Hopper*, 4 Federal Cases 904 (1806).

18. Compare *Marie Louis v. Marot et al.*, 9 Louisiana 473 (1836), with *Lunsford v. Coquillon*, 2 Martin N.S. 401 (La., 1824).

19. *Harry et al. v. Decker and Hopkins*, 1 Walker 36, 42 (Miss., 1818): "Slavery is condemned by reason and the laws of nature. It . . . can only exist through municipal regulations"; *Griffith v. Fanny*, 1 Gilmer 143 (Va., 1820); *Rankin v. Lydia*, 2 A. K. Marshall 467, 470 (Ky., 1820): "a right existing by positive law of a muncipal character without foundation in the law of nature"; *Lewis v. Fullerton*, 1 Randolph 15 (Va., 1821); *Winny v. Whitesides*, 1 Missouri 472 (1824); *Bush's Representatives v. White*, 3 T. B. Monroe 100 (Ky., 1825); *Spotts v. Gillaspie*, 6 Randolph 566 (Va., 1828); *La Grange v. Chouteau*, 2 Missouri 20 (1828); *Hunter v. Fulcher*, 1 Leigh 189 (Va., 1829); *Blackmore and Hadley v. Phill*, 7 Yerger 452 (Tenn., 1835). For southern repudiation of the doctrine that slavery was contrary to natural law, see Cobb, *Law of Slavery*, 5–52; William Sumner Jenkins, *Pro-Slavery Thought in the Old South* (Chapel Hill, N.C., 1935), 121–45.

20. The Missouri cases are summarized in "Slavery and Conflict of Laws," 91. The most thorough study of slave transit and interstate comity is Paul Finkelman, "A More Perfect Union? Slavery, Comity, and Federalism, 1787–1861," Ph.D. dissertation, University of Chicago, 1976.

21. Schnell, "Status of Slaves," 270–71. As an "extreme case of such refusal," Schnell points to *Cleland et al. v. Waters et al.*, 16 Georgia 496 (1854) and 19 Georgia 35 (1855), but in this case freedom was *confirmed* to the slaves concerned as a result of emancipation by colonization in Africa. The court did denounce northern withdrawal of sojourners' rights, but it declared that slaves sent to live permanently in a free country became free.

22. Other such scholars besides Schnell are Robert M. Cover, *Justice Accused: Antislavery and the Judicial Process* (New Haven, 1975), 97: "Both by legislation and by judicial decision, the Southern approach described above was generally reversed in the last ten or fifteen years before the Civil War"; Wiecek, "*Somerset*," 137, likewise citing *Cleland v. Waters* as a culmination of the southern reaction; and "Slavery and Conflict of Laws," 96: "Faced with the growing conflict with the North, a number of southern states refused to recognize either the permanent freedom of Negroes born in free states or the emancipating effects of a slave's prolonged residence in a free state."

23. 9 California 147; William E. Franklin, "The Archy Case: The California Supreme Court Refuses to Free a Slave," *Pacific Historical Review*, XXXII (1963), 137–54.

24. Joseph Story, *Commentaries on the Conflict of Laws, Foreign and Domestic*, 5th ed. (Boston, 1857), 31–33. James Kent had previously said much the same thing in his *Commentaries on American Law* (4 vols.; New York, 1826–30; rev. ed., Philadelphia, 1889), II, 457: "There is no doubt of the truth of the general proposition, that the laws of a country have no binding force beyond its territorial limits; and their authority is admitted in other states, not *ex proprio vigore*, but *ex comitate*." New nations especially are likely to be jealous of their sovereignty. The Kent-Story doctrine is the nationalistic doctrine of a new nation, but as applied internally to interstate relations, it encouraged particularism.

25. *Commonwealth v. Aves*, 18 Pickering 193, 206–25 (Mass., 1836); Leonard W.

Levy, *The Law of the Commonwealth and Chief Justice Shaw* (Cambridge, Mass., 1957), 62–68; Finkelman, "A More Perfect Union," 106–22.

26. *Jackson v. Bulloch*, 12 Connecticut 38 (1837); Hurd, *Law of Freedom and Bondage*, II, 73; Schnell, "Status of Slaves," 268.

27. *Cleland v. Waters*, 19 Georgia 35, 42, Chief Justice Joseph H. Lumpkin.

28. *The Slave Grace*, 2 Haggard 94 (Admiralty, 1827).

29. *Somerset* obviously falls somewhere between typical domicile and typical sojourn. The slave had been kept in England for two years, with no indication of an early return to Virginia. Hurd, *Law of Freedom and Bondage*, I, 332, insists that the master had "done no act by which he acquired a domicil in England." But Cobb, *Law of Slavery*, 177, seems willing to regard it as a case in which the master did not adequately prove his intention of returning to Virginia. In this respect, the judgment of the court (but not all of its reasoning) is acceptable to Cobb as a southerner.

30. William W. Story, *Life and Letters of Joseph Story* (2 vols.; Boston, 1851), I, 558.

31. Wiecek, "*Somerset*," 137. Wiecek also writes: "In the accommodationist period of conflict of laws development, some of them [southern state supreme courts] had held that a slave taken into a free jurisdiction could not be reenslaved when returned to the domiciliary state." This is incorrect. Southern decisions in favor of emancipation assumed a *change* of domicile; thus the return was to the *former* domiciliary state. Wiecek cites *Lunsford v. Coquillon*, 2 Martin N.S. 401 (La., 1824), and *Hunter v. Fulcher*, 1 Leigh 172 (Va., 1829). But in the *Lunsford* case, the court found that the slave had been taken to Ohio with the intention of residing there. "It is this circumstance which governs the case," the court said. As for the *Hunter* case, it is irrelevant because it did not involve a slave's being taken into a free state.

32. "Slavery and Conflict of Laws," 97, citing *Davis v. Tingle*, 8 B. Monroe 539 (Ky., 1848), and *Collins v. America*, 9 B. Monroe 565 (Ky., 1849). The author quotes the "ground" of the *Collins* decision as follows: "If the laws and Courts of Ohio may determine the condition of the slave while in that State, they cannot, by their own force or power, determine what shall be his condition when he has gone beyond their territorial jurisdiction" (p. 571). Now, this was certainly *not* the ground of the decision. It was the ground for assuming the right to *make* the final decision. The ground of the decision was that the slave had been only temporarily in a free state. The confusion here results not only from the failure to discriminate between domicile and sojourn, but also from the failure to discriminate between the jurisdictional principle of reversion (set forth in the above quotation) and the substantive principle of reattachment.

33. Notably in *Graham v. Strader*, 5 B. Monroe 173 (Ky., 1844); *Maria v. Kirby*, 12 B. Monroe 542 (Ky., 1852); and *Ferry v. Street*, 14 B. Monroe 287 (Ky., 1854). In the *Maria* case, both the principle of reversion and the principle of reattachment were asserted (545, 548); in the *Ferry* case, a slave kept more than six months in Pennsylvania, while its sojourning law was in effect, was declared free.

34. *Graham v. Strader*, 5 B. Monroe 173 (Ky., 1844); *Strader v. Graham*, 7 B. Monroe 633 (Ky., 1847); *Strader v. Graham*, 10 Howard 82 (1850). The *Strader* case was not a suit for freedom. For discussion of its relation to the Dred Scott case, see above, 260–62, 268–69.

35. *Ibid.*, 94.

36. *Bank of Augusta v. Earle*, 13 Peters 519, 589 (1839).

37. Hurd, *Law of Freedom and Bondage*, II, 164.

38. *Josephine v. Poultney*, 1 Louisiana Annual 329 (1846); *Eugenie v. Préval et al.*, 2 Louisiana Annual 180 (1847); *Arsène v. Pignéguy*, 2 Louisiana Annual 620 (1847); *Lucy Brown v. Persifor F. Smith*, 8 Louisiana Annual 59 (1853) *Virginie and Celesie v. D. and C. Himel*, 10 Louisiana Annual 185 (1855).

39. 5 Louisiana Annual 696; 7 Louisiana Annual 80, 83. The court also discriminated between cases on the basis of whether the relevant events had occurred before or after enactment of the 1846 law, refusing to apply the law retroactively, but declaring "its provisions to be imperative in all cases occurring since its passage" (5 Louisiana Annual 696). Whether this imperative included cases of actual domicile on free soil was never put to a high court test. That is, in the only cases involving long-term residence that arose after 1846, the relevant events had occurred before 1846. What the court would have done if confronted with a case of domicile extending past 1846 cannot be said with certainty, but the quotation in the text suggests that it was prepared to enforce the law of 1846 only against slaves claiming freedom by virtue of temporary residence or sojourn on free soil.

40. *Mitchell v. Wells*, 37 Mississippi 235, 262. This case involved a slave freed by her owner-father in Ohio. From Ohio, she was trying to obtain the legacy he had left her and which had been denied her on the grounds that she was still a slave, Mississippi having by law forbidden the removal of slaves for the purpose of emancipation. The court held in effect that she was still a slave, but there was a vigorous dissent from one judge, and it is to be noted that the lower court had ruled in favor of the complainant. For a similar suit, likewise decided against the former slave, see *Henriette v. Heirs of Barnes*, 11 Louisiana Annual 453 (1856).

41. Wiecek, "*Somerset*," 137; *Lemmon v. The People*, 20 New York 562 (1860). See Hurd, *Law of Freedom and Bondage*, II, 360–66, and for further discussion of the case, see above, 444–45.

42. Henry Steele Commager, *Documents of American History*, 7th ed. (2 vols.; New York, 1963), I, 371–72.

43. Marion J. Russell, "American Slave Discontent in Records of the High Courts," *JNH*, XXXI (1946), 418–19.

44. Winthrop D. Jordan, *White over Black: American Attitudes Toward the Negro, 1550–1812* (Chapel Hill, N.C., 1968; Baltimore, 1969), 125–26; Berlin, *Slaves Without Masters*, 8–9; Russell, *Free Negro in Virginia*, 119; Jeffrey R. Brackett, *The Negro in Maryland, a Study of the Institution of Slavery* (Baltimore, 1889), 110–11n, 186–87, 196.

45. Franklin, *Free Negro in North Carolina*, 59.

46. *Code of Georgia*, 1861, p. 321.

47. *Ibid.*, 265–66, 878, 881, 919–22; Berlin, *Slaves Without Masters*, 96–97, 230–31; Russell, *Free Negro in Virginia*, 104, 143–45, 149. See also Duncan J.

MacLeod, *Slavery, Race and the American Revolution* (Cambridge, England, 1974), 164–67.

48. *Code of Georgia*, 1861, pp. 158, 920.

49. Berlin, *Slaves Without Masters*, 209–12.

50. Leon F. Litwack, *North of Slavery: The Negro in the Free States, 1790–1860* (Chicago, 1961), 64–186; Hurd, *Law of Freedom and Bondage,* II, 217; Richard C. Wade, "The Negro in Cincinnati, 1800–1830," *JNH*, XXXIX (1954), 43–57. See also Arthur Zilversmit, *The First Emancipation: The Abolition of Slavery in the North* (Chicago, 1967), 222–26; Eugene H. Berwanger, *The Frontier Against Slavery: Western Anti-Negro Prejudice and the Slavery Extension Controversy* (Urbana, Ill., 1967), *passim;* Norman Dwight Harris, *History of Negro Slavery in Illinois and of the Slavery Agitation in That State* (Chicago, 1906), 226–38; Emma Lou Thornbrough, *The Negro in Indiana, a Study of a Minority* (n.p., 1957), 55–73.

51. Litwack, *North of Slavery,* 31; Letitia Woods Brown, *Free Negroes in the District of Columbia, 1790–1846* (New York, 1972), 134–35, 140; Max Farrand, *The Legislation of Congress for the Government of the Organized Territories of the United States, 1789–1895* (Newark, N.J., 1896), 26, 34, 40.

52. Litwack, *North of Slavery,* 32, 53–57.

53. Articles of Confederation, IV; Constitution, I, 2, 3; II, 1; III, 2; IV, 2. Citizenship was defined in the Civil Rights Act of April 9, 1866, and again in the Fourteenth Amendment.

54. Hurd, *Law of Freedom and Bondage,* II, 270–341, has an extensive discussion of the subject. See also John S. Wise, *A Treatise on American Citizenship* (Northport, N.Y., 1906), 1–33.

55. Noah Webster associated citizenship with suffrage in his *An American Dictionary of the English Language* (2 vols.; New York, 1828): ". . . . A person, native or naturalized, who has the privilege of exercising the elective franchise, or the qualifications which enable him to vote for rulers, and to purchase and hold real estate." This definition was echoed about 1890, with special reference to the United States, by the compilers of the *Oxford English Dictionary,* who had apparently not heard of the Fourteenth Amendment.

56. One striking example of a woman's suing as a citizen in federal court is the litigation in the sensational Myra Gaines case, extending over more than a half-century. See Carl B. Swisher, *The Taney Period, 1836–1864,* Volume V of the Oliver Wendell Holmes Devise *History of the Supreme Court of the United States* (New York, 1974), 756–72, and the sources there cited. A law of Congress passed in 1855 declared: "Any woman who might lawfully be naturalized under the existing laws, married, or who shall be married to a citizen of the United States, shall be deemed and taken to be a citizen." *U.S. Statutes at Large,* X, 604.

57. *Journals of the Continental Congress, 1774–1789* (34 vols.; Washington, D.C., 1904–37), XI, 652.

58. *Ibid.,* XXIV, 223.

59. Hurd, *Law of Freedom and Bondage,* II, 4.

60. *U.S. Statutes at Large,* II, 205; *AC,* 8-1, col. 786.

61. Gordon E. Sherman, "Emancipation and Citizenship," *Yale Law Journal*, XV (1906), 267.
62. *Journals of the Continental Congress*, XI, 650–51; Donald L. Robinson, *Slavery in the Structure of American Politics, 1765–1820* (New York, 1971), 153–54.
63. *U.S. Statutes at Large*, I, 103, 414. Later revisions of the law retained the racial restriction. See Robinson, *Slavery in American Politics*, 253; and on the early colonization movement, Jordan, *White over Black*, 542–69.
64. Francis Newton Thorpe, ed., *The Federal and State Constitutions, Colonial Charters, and Other Organic Laws of the States, Territories, and Colonies Now or Heretofore Forming the United States of America* (7 vols.; Washington, D.C., 1909), 957–62, 1264–77, 3414–25.
65. *Ely v. Thompson et al.*, 3 A. K. Marshall 70, 73–75 (Ky., 1820); Hurd, *Law of Freedom and Bondage*, II, 14. The law in question, passed in 1798, had in fact been repealed.
66. *State v. Manuel*, 4 Devereux and Battle 20, 24–25, 37 (N.C., 1838).
67. *State v. Newsom*, 5 Iredell 250, 254–55 (N.C., 1844).
68. 1 Littell 326, 334 (Ky., 1822). Emphasis added.
69. Notably, *Amy v. Mills*, 1 Littell 326; *State v. Claiborne*, 1 Meigs 331 (Tenn., 1839); *State v. Newsom*, 5 Iredell 250 (N.C., 1844); *Pendleton v. the State*, 6 Arkansas 509 (1846); and the superior court decision of Chief Justice David Daggett, reviewed but neither upheld nor overturned by the state supreme court in *Crandall v. the State*, 10 Connecticut 339, 347 (1834).
70. Hurd, *Law of Freedom and Bondage*, II, 5, 16, 20, 78, 95–97, 117, 146, 158.
71. *AC*, 16-2, cols. 1228, 1237, 1239–40; Glover Moore, *The Missouri Controversy, 1819–1821* (Lexington, Ky., 1953), 129–69. The Missouri constitution, said Clay's compromise resolution, "shall never be construed to authorize the passage of any law . . . by which any citizen of either of the States in this Union shall be excluded from the enjoyment of any of the privileges and immunities to which such citizen is entitled under the Constitution of the United States." Samuel C. Allen received no support when he tried to eliminate ambiguity by replacing "citizen" with "free negro or mulatto." The compromise passed the House by a vote of 87 to 81.
72. *Official Opinions of the Attorneys General of the United States*, I, 506–9.
73. Philip M. Hamer, "Great Britain, the United States, and the Negro Seamen Acts, 1822–1848"; and "British Consuls and the Negro Seamen Acts, 1850–1860," *JSH*, I (1935), 3–28, 138–68; Henry, *Police Control*, 124–33; William W. Freehling, *Prelude to Civil War: The Nullification Controversy in South Carolina, 1816–1836* (New York, 1965), 111–16; Swisher, *Taney Period*, 378–82. Some states, instead of having Negroes arrested, required that they remain on board their ship while it was in port.
74. *Elkison v. Deliesseline*, 8 Federal Cases 493; *Opinions of Attorneys General*, I, 659–61.
75. Berrien to Andrew Jackson, March 25, 1831, in *Opinions of Attorneys General*, II, 426–42.
76. The opinion accompanies Taney's letter to Secretary of State Edward Livingston, May 28, 1832, Miscellaneous Letters, Department of State Papers, Na-

tional Archives. The supplement accompanies Taney's letter to Livingston, June 9, 1832. See Carl B. Swisher, *Roger B. Taney* (New York, 1935), 151–59; Marvin Laurence Winitsky, "The Jurisprudence of Roger B. Taney," Ph.D. dissertation, UCLA, 1973, pp. 92–94.

77. Opinions of the attorneys general were first published in 1843 when Taney was chief justice. It appears that he either suppressed the 1832 opinion or perhaps had never filed it. See Swisher, *Taney*, 152.

78. Hamer, "Negro Seamen Acts," 18–19, 24–26.

79. *House Reports*, 27 Congress, 3 session, No. 80 (Serial 426); *CG*, 27-3, p. 384. The committee was the committee on commerce; Robert C. Winthrop of Massachusetts was the chairman. The vote to table on March 2, 1843, was 86 to 59.

80. Hamer, "Negro Seamen Acts," 22–23; George F. Hoar, *Autobiography of Seventy Years* (2 vols.; New York, 1903), I, 24–27; Herman V. Ames, *State Documents on Federal Relations*, No. V (Philadelphia, 1904), 237–38.

81. On the abolitionist theory of paramount national citizenship, see Jacobus ten-Broek, *The Antislavery Origins of the Fourteenth Amendment* (Berkeley, 1951), 71–93; Howard Jay Graham, *Everyman's Constitution: Historical Essays on the Fourteenth Amendment, the "Conspiracy Theory," and American Constitutionalism* (Madison, Wis., 1968), 175–85.

82. See note 69 above.

83. For instance, in *Pendleton v. the State*, 6 Arkansas 509, 512 (1846), the court said: "The constitution was the work of the white race . . . and it could not have been intended to place a different race of people in all things upon terms of equality with themselves. . . . The two races differing as they do in complexion, habits, conformation and intellectual endowments, could not nor ever will live together upon terms of social or political equality. A higher than human power has so ordered it."

84. *Bank of Augusta v. Earle*, 13 Peters 519, 585–87. The argument was made by Daniel Webster, counsel for the Bank of the United States in an associated suit. See Swisher, *Taney Period*, 115–21; Maurice G. Baxter, *Daniel Webster and the Supreme Court* (n.p., 1966), 185–93.

85. *Louisville, Cincinnati and Charleston R.R. v. Letson*, 2 Howard 497, 555. Said Justice James M. Wayne in the opinion of the Court: "A corporation created by a State . . . and only suable there, though it may have members out of the State, seems to us to be a person, though an artificial one, inhabiting and belonging to that State, and therefore entitled, for the purpose of suing and being sued, to be deemed a citizen of that State." Later, the Court retreated from the *Letson* doctrine but created a fiction whereby corporations could continue to have access to federal courts. See Swisher, *Taney Period*, 464–70, and the review of the same by Don E. Fehrenbacher, *University of Chicago Law Review*, XLII (1974), 220–21.

86. *Le Grand v. Darnall*, 2 Peters 664 (1829). See above, 296, 362.

87. Catterall, *Cases*, III, 18n.

88. *Acts of the General Assembly of the State of South-Carolina Passed in December, 1844* (Columbia, S.C., 1845), 293–94; Hamer, "Negro Seamen Acts," 23–24.

CHAPTER 4

1. Julian P. Boyd, ed., *The Papers of Thomas Jefferson* (19 vols. to date; Princeton, 1950–), I, 353, 363, 383, 385n; Jack Ericson Eblen, *The First and Second United States Empires: Governors and Territorial Government, 1784–1912* (Pittsburgh, 1968), 18–19.
2. Thomas Donaldson, *The Public Domain, Its History with Statistics* (Washington, D.C., 1884), 61–62.
3. *Ibid.*, 63–64; Merrill Jensen, *The Articles of Confederation* (Madison, Wis., 1940, 1959), 228–31; Thomas Perkins Abernethy, *Western Lands and the American Revolution* (Charlottesville, Va., 1937; New York, 1959), 242–44.
4. Donaldson, *Public Domain*, 67–69; Jensen, *Articles of Confederation*, 235–38; Boyd, ed., *Jefferson Papers*, VI, 571–80.
5. *Ibid.*, 581–607. In the first stage, the territorial residents would organize their own temporary government, based on the constitution of one of the original states. In the second stage, they would frame their own constitution for a permanent government. The final step would be admission to full representation in Congress.
6. *Ibid.*, 603–4; John Chester Miller, *The Wolf by the Ears: Thomas Jefferson and Slavery* (New York, 1977), 26–29.
7. *Journals of the Continental Congress, 1774–1789* (34 vols.; Washington, D.C., 1904–37), XXVI, 247; Boyd, ed., *Jefferson Papers*, VI, 611–12; VII, 118; X, 58; Donald L. Robinson, *Slavery in the Structure of American Politics, 1765–1820* (New York, 1971).
8. Boyd, ed., *Jefferson Papers*, VI, 612–13, 615.
9. Eblen, *United States Empires*, 23–24, overstates the extent to which the Ordinance contemplated creation of an empire. The amendment, after all, applied only to the brief period before the residents of a territory organized their own temporary government.
10. *Journals of the Continental Congress*, XXVIII, 164–65, 239; Robert Ernst, *Rufus King, American Federalist* (Chapel Hill, N.C., 1968), 53–55. King's original proposal was for immediate abolition in the West, but the committee report returned to Jefferson's provision for abolition after 1800. This was apparently the first proposal of a fugitive-slave law at the national level.
11. Slavery was still entirely legal in New York and New Jersey, while gradual abolition laws had been enacted in Rhode Island, Connecticut, and Pennsylvania. See Arthur Zilversmit, *The First Emancipation: The Abolition of Slavery in the North* (Chicago, 1967).
12. Walter Clark, ed., *The State Records of North Carolina* (26 vols.; Goldsboro, N.C., 1886–1905), XXIV, 561–63.
13. On November 20, 1784, North Carolina repealed her offer of cession, but not for reasons connected with slavery as suggested by Robinson, *Slavery in American Politics*, 380. See North Carolina's statement of the reasons in Clark, ed., *Records of North Carolina*, 679, quoted in Payson Jackson Treat, *The National Land System, 1785–1820* (New York, 1910), 342. See also Thomas Perkins Abernethy, *From Frontier to Plantation in Tennessee* (Chapel Hill, N.C.), 67–70.

14. *Journals of the Continental Congress*, XXX, 251–55; Monroe to Jefferson, May 11, 1786, in Boyd, ed., *Jefferson Papers*, IX, 510–11; Eblen, *United States Empires*, 28–33.

15. *Journals of the Continental Congress*, XXXII, 281, 313. For earlier versions, see XXX, 402–6; XXXI, 669–73. A tacit understanding had probably developed earlier about limiting the scope of the proposed ordinance to the Northwest, that being the only part of the West that had been cleared of state claims.

16. *Ibid.*, XXXII, 339–40, 343. On the Ordinance of 1787 in general, see Jay A. Barrett, *Evolution of the Ordinance of 1787* (New York, 1891); Francis S. Philbrick, ed., *The Laws of Illinois Territory, 1809–1818* (Springfield, Ill., 1950), cccliv–ccclxxxvi; Eblen, *United States Empires*, 30–51; Robert F. Berkhofer, Jr., "The Republican Origins of the American Territorial System," in Allan G. Bogue et al., eds., *The West of the American People* (Itasca, Ill., 1970), 152–60. Robert F. Berkhofer, Jr., "Jefferson, the Ordinance of 1784, and the Origins of the American Territorial System," *William and Mary Quarterly*, 3rd Series, XXIX (1972), 231–62; and on the background of constitutional thought, see Arthur Bestor, "Constitutionalism and the Settlement of the West: The Attainment of Consensus, 1754–1784," in John Porter Bloom, ed., *The American Territorial System* (Athens, Ohio, 1973), 13–44.

17. *Journals of the Continental Congress*, XXXII, 343; Barrett, *Ordinance of 1787*, 76–80. The other two northern delegations present were New York and New Jersey. The strongest individual opposition to the Ordinance seems to have come from Abraham Yates of New York.

18. Staughton Lynd, "The Compromise of 1787," *Political Science Quarterly*, LXXXI (1966), 230–33. This article also appears in Lynd's *Class Conflict, Slavery, and the United States Constitution* (Indianapolis, 1967), 185–213.

19. The South Carolina cession of a twelve-mile strip of land in 1787 was not yet completed when the Northwest Ordinance was passed in July of that year. Treat, *Land System*, 355–56.

20. Lynd, "Compromise of 1787," 225. Robinson, *Slavery in American Politics*, 386, 391, 401, 402, generally endorses the Lynd thesis.

21. See above, 19–20. The irony is that if the South had had its way, each slave would have counted *five-fifths* in the apportionment of representation. Then, with no discrimination between slaves and free persons in the clause, the Constitution, by yielding *more* to slaveholders, would have contained *less* recognition of slavery.

22. Eblen, *United States Empires*, 39; Lynd, "Compromise of 1787," 230.

23. This was the contemporary explanation offered by William Grayson, member of Congress from Virginia. Edmund C. Burnett, ed., *Letters of Members of the Continental Congress* (8 vols.; Washington, D.C., 1921–36), VIII, 631–32.

24. Madison was not denouncing the Ordinance but rather arguing for the advantages of specific grants of power over implied powers. For the most extensive discussion, see Philbrick, *Laws of Illinois Territory*, lxiii–xciii, in which he maintains that the Articles of Confederation had been informally amended to include authority over the West.

25. *Ibid.*, ccli–cclii, cccxviii, ccclvii. See also Eblen, *United States Empires*, 49. The

territorial governor in the second stage was even more powerful than the royal colonial governor because he was not dependent on his constituents for his salary. But of course the promise of early statehood made the system fundamentally different from the British colonial system.

26. *Journals of the Continental Congress*, XXXIII, 599–602. As first governor of the territory, Congress chose its own presiding officer, Arthur St. Clair.

27. Max Farrand, ed., *The Records of the Federal Convention of 1787*, rev. ed. (4 vols.; New Haven, 1937), II, 321, 324.

28. *Ibid.*, 458–59, 465–66, 578, 602, 662. The committee of style changed the word "Legislature" to "Congress." There is some confusion in the record as to whether Maryland voted in the negative.

29. *AC*, 1-1, cols. 56, 660. The principal alteration was to make territorial officers appointive by the president instead of by Congress.

30. The nineteen included Oliver Ellsworth and Roger Sherman of Connecticut, Rufus King (who had moved from Massachusetts to New York), William Paterson of New Jersey, Robert Morris of Pennsylvania, James Madison of Virginia, and Pierce Butler of South Carolina. Eleven of the nineteen sat in the Senate. See Clinton Rossiter, *1787: The Grand Convention* (New York, 1966, 1968), 260.

31. Madison noted the absence of a provision for the admission of new states in the Articles of Confederation, and, in obvious reference to the Northwest Ordinance, spoke of the "assumption" of this power on the part of the Confederation Congress. From this, one might conclude that Madison inferred the power to re-enact the Ordinance from the statehood clause. However, he then took up the territory clause and said that it was "required by considerations similar to those which show the propriety" of the statehood clause. See also *Federalist* 38 and above, 367–76.

32. Philbrick, *Laws of Illinois Territory*, ccxxxvii–ccxlix; St. Clair to George Washington, May 1, 1790, in Clarence Edwin Carter, ed., *The Territorial Papers of the United States* (Washington, D.C., 1934–), II, 248, saying: "I have thought proper to explain the Article respecting Slaves as a prohibition to any future introduction of them, but not to extend to the liberation of those the People were already possessed of." Duncan J. MacLeod, *Slavery, Race and the American Revolution* (Cambridge, England, 1974), 48, places heavy emphasis upon a resolution reported by a committee to the Confederation Congress on September 25, 1788, declaring that the antislavery article of the Northwest Ordinance should not be construed as applying retroactively. However, it is by no means clear that this resolution actually received congressional approval, and if it did, no one appears to have been informed of the fact. No one discussing the problem thereafter ever mentioned the resolution. See *Journals of the Continental Congress*, XXXIV, 540–41; Philbrick, *Laws of Illinois Territory*, ccxli, n. 144; Bartholomew Tardiveau to St. Clair, June 30, 1789, in William Henry Smith, ed., *The St. Clair Papers: The Life and Public Services of Arthur St. Clair* (2 vols.; Cincinnati, 1882; New York, 1971), II, 117–19. It was clearly St. Clair, not Congress, who made the effective decision against retroactive enforcement. On the opposition of Judge George Turner, see Emma Lou Thornbrough, *The*

Negro in Indiana: A Study of a Minority (n.p., 1957), 6–7; J. P. Dunn, *Indiana: A Redemption from Slavery* (Boston, 1888), 223–24.

33. The French inhabitants were said to be protected in their slaveholding rights by the British treaty with France in 1763 and by conditions attached to the Virginia act of cession in 1784. The terms "free inhabitants" and "free male inhabitants" appear to have been used because the Ordinance had no antislavery provision until just before passage, at which time no one thought to remove the word "free," even though it had presumably become a redundancy. See Philbrick, *Laws of Illinois Territory*, ccxxiii–ccxl.

34. Smith, ed., *St. Clair Papers*, II, 331. See also Dunn, *Indiana*, 243–49, with a summary of William Wirt's argument on the subject in *Menard v. Aspasia*, 5 Peters 505.

35. Francis S. Philbrick, ed., *The Laws of Indiana Territory, 1801–1809* (Springfield, Ill., 1930), 42–43; Dunn, *Indiana*, 314–16. The governor was William Henry Harrison. Indenture could be for any duration, twenty to forty years being common. A few were for ninety years. Ostensibly indentures were arranged by mutual agreement, but the Negro who did not agree could be sold away in a slave state within sixty days.

36. Philbrick, *Laws of Indiana Territory*, 136–39, 203–4, 463–67, 523–26; Dunn, *Indiana*, 329–34, with some contemporary newspaper comment; Thornbrough, *Negro in Indiana*, 8–11, quoting an indenture binding Jacob, a sixteen-year-old Negro, to one Eli Hawkins for ninety years, after which, at the age of one hundred six, "said Jacob shall be free to all intents and purposes."

37   Philbrick, *Laws of Illinois Territory*, 5. The governor was Ninian Edwards, whose son of the same name would be Abraham Lincoln's brother-in-law. One of the judges was Jesse Thomas, later a United States senator and leading figure in the Missouri Compromise.

38. Illinois Constitution of 1818, Article Six, in Emil Joseph Verlie, ed., *Illinois Constitutions* (Springfield, Ill., 1919), 38–39; *AC*, 15-2, cols. 306–10. There were antislavery objections in Congress to the Illinois constitution. See above, 101.

39. For the exciting story of the contest over revision of the constitution, see Norman Dwight Harris, *History of Negro Slavery in Illinois and of the Slavery Agitation in That State* (Chicago, 1906), 27–49. Census reports showed 747 slaves in Illinois in 1830, and 331 in 1840. The indenture system was not fully erased in Illinois until it was omitted from the constitution of 1848.

40. *AC*, 1–2, cols. 942, 948, 951–52, 963–64, 1477–78, 1549, 1556, 2208–12, 2226–27. The relevant documents are also in Carter, ed., *Territorial Papers*, IV, 3–19.

41. There was anxiety about North Carolina because that state had earlier ceded her western lands and then rescinded the cession. See above, 78. Kentucky remained a part of Virginia until admitted as a state, never experiencing territorial status. In 1790, there were 12,430 slaves in Kentucky, about 17 per cent of the total population; in Tennessee, 3417 slaves, about 10 per cent of the total population.

42. There were some antislavery efforts in the Kentucky constitutional convention of

1792, especially by the Presbyterian leader David Rice. Mary Stoughton Locke, *Anti-Slavery in America from the Introduction of African Slaves to the Prohibition of the Slave Trade, 1619–1808* (Boston, 1901), 117–19.

43. Justice Campbell disputed this point in his Dred Scott opinion, however (*DSvS*, 505–6).

44. *AC*, 5-2, cols. 1306–12. The debate is summarized in Locke, *Anti-Slavery*, 160–62, and in Robinson, *Slavery in American Politics*, 387–92. Thacher (often spelled "Thatcher") represented the Maine district of Massachusetts from 1789 to 1801. Robinson implies that his motives were primarily political, but Thacher's devotion to antislavery seems to have been strong. He was one of the seven House members, for example, who voted against the fugitive-slave law in 1793. See the article by Robert E. Moody in *Dictionary of American Biography*, XVIII, 386–87.

45. *AC*, 5-2, cols. 656–70. The Quakers in this instance were complaining that some of their manumissions in North Carolina had been canceled by state officials. Such an "abominable tragedy," they declared in true Garrisonian style, had a "tendency to bring down the judgments of a righteous God upon our land." George Thacher was also involved in this debate.

46. *Ibid.*, 1307–8.

47. For example, at Galesburg, Oct. 7, 1858: "In legislating for new countries, where it does not exist, there is no just rule other than that of moral and abstract right!" *CWAL*, III, 222.

48. One Pennsylvania congressman did speak vaguely of the amendment as interfering with property rights, and the fact that Georgia still claimed the region cast some doubt upon the extent of congressional authority in the Yazoo strip, but there was no suggestion that slavery in the territories was constitutionally beyond the reach of Congress.

49. The Senate had previously passed the bill, 20 to 8, without any controversy on the slavery issue. In the House, after the defeat of the Thacher amendment, a section was added forbidding foreign slave trade in the territory. *AC*, 5-2, cols. 1312, 1314, 1318, and for the Senate, 515. A copy of the bill as passed is in Carter, ed., *Territorial Papers*, V, 18–22.

50. See above, 86. Arthur Zilversmit, *The First Emancipation: The Abolition of Slavery in the North* (Chicago, 1967), 113–15. In 1798, Gallatin had presented the controversial Quaker resolution and supported the Thacher antislavery proviso for Mississippi Territory. See notes 44 and 45 above.

51. On Jefferson and slavery, *inter alia*, see David Brion Davis, *The Problem of Slavery in the Age of Revolution, 1770–1823* (Ithaca, N.Y., 1975), 164–84; Miller, *Wolf by the Ears;* Winthrop D. Jordan, *White over Black: American Attitudes Toward the Negro, 1550–1812* (Chapel Hill, N.C., 1968; Baltimore, 1969), 429–81; William Cohen, "Thomas Jefferson and the Problem of Slavery," *JAH*, LVI (1969), 503–26; William W. Freehling, "The Founding Fathers and Slavery," *AHR*, LXXVII (1972), 81–93; Robert McColley, *Slavery and Jeffersonian Virginia*, 2nd ed. (Urbana, Ill., 1973), 124–32. It is worth noting that Noble E. Cunningham, Jr., *The Jeffersonian Republicans in Power* (Chapel Hill, N.C., 1963), covering Jefferson's two terms as president, contains no entry

for "slavery" in its index. For Jefferson's rationalization of his silence on slavery during his presidency, see the letter he wrote to George Logan, May 11, 1805, in Paul Leicester Ford, ed., *The Writings of Thomas Jefferson* (10 vols.; New York, 1892–99), VIII, 351–52.

52. Gallatin, like Jefferson, seems to have fallen silent on the slavery issue when his party came to power. Note how little attention a biographer gives to the subject in Raymond Walters, Jr., *Albert Gallatin, Jeffersonian Financier and Diplomat* (New York, 1957).

53. Quoted in Linda K. Kerber, *Federalists in Dissent: Imagery and Ideology in Jeffersonian America* (Ithaca, N.Y., 1970), 27n.

54. That Jefferson assumed Louisiana would be slaveholding territory seems plain enough. See his "Description of Louisiana," with a digest of laws that included a rigorous slave code, sent to Congress on November 14, 1803, presumably as an aid to the drafting of the organic act. *AC*, 8-1, cols. 1498–1578; Robinson, *Slavery in American Politics*, 399n.

55. Breckinridge, grandfather of Vice President John C. Breckinridge, had acted as front man for Jefferson in presenting the Kentucky Resolutions of 1798. Hillhouse was later one of the hardline Federalists at the Hartford Convention of 1814.

56. The official record is in *AC*, 8-1, cols. 240–42, 244. The record of the debate is in a journal kept by Senator William Plumer of New Hampshire. The relevant passages are in Everett S. Brown, ed., "The Senate Debate on the Breckinridge Bill for the Government of Louisiana, 1804," *AHR*, XXII (1917), 340–64. See also Everett S. Brown, *The Constitutional History of the Louisiana Purchase, 1803–1812* (Berkeley, 1920), 101–46.

57. *AC*, 8-1, cols. 241–42.

58. Some historians give the impression that the proposal amounted to abolition. See, for example, Robinson, *Slavery in American Politics*, 398; Kerber, *Federalists in Dissent*, 42.

59. A census in 1785 showed 16,500 slaves in Louisiana. The first U.S. census of the region in 1810 reported almost 38,000.

60. *AC*, 8-1, cols. 242, 244; Brown, ed., "Senate Debate," 351–56. A motion to change the word "citizen" to "person" failed, 13 to 14, according to Plumer.

61. *AC*, 8-1, cols. 256, 290, 1186, 1196–99, 1206–8, 1229–30, 1293–1300; Carter, *Territorial Papers*, IX, 202–13; Henry Adams, *History of the United States of America During the First Administration of Thomas Jefferson* (2 vols.; New York, 1903), II, 120–25; Brown, *Louisiana Purchase*, 141–42. Adams mistakenly gives the final vote in the House on the entire bill as 51 to 45. The Sloan amendment is cloaked in obscurity; there was no specific vote recorded by the Senate in rejecting it, or by the House in receding from it.

62. Brown, ed., "Senate Debate," 346, 351, 352, 362–63; Samuel Flagg Bemis, *John Quincy Adams and the Foundations of American Foreign Policy* (New York, 1949), 415–16; Charles Francis Adams, ed., *Memoris of John Quincy Adams* (12 vols.; Philadelphia, 1874–77), I, 286–89.

63. Brown, ed., "Senate Debate," 345–53; *AC*, 8-1, cols. 241–42, 244; J. Q. Adams, *Memoirs*, I, 293. Bradley, a distinguished figure in Vermont politics,

was one of the state's first two senators and served a total of sixteen years in that office.

64. Brown, ed., "Senate Debate," 349, 352. Jackson is best remembered for leading the fight against the Yazoo land frauds.

65. Besides Hillhouse and Bradley, Israel Smith of Vermont both participated in the discussion and voted for the second amendment, but Smith, like Bradley—and for similar reasons—voted against the first amendment. Antislavery statements made include the following: John Breckinridge, "I am against slavery"; Jesse Franklin of North Carolina, "Slavery is a dreadful evil"; Joseph Anderson of Tennessee, "It will prove a curse to us"; Samuel White of Delaware, " 'Tis our duty to prevent, as far as possible, the horrid evil of slavery." See Brown, ed., "Senate Debate," 345, 347, 354.

66. *Ibid.*, 348.

67. J. Q. Adams, *Memoirs*, I, 352, 353, 354, mentions the Orleans bill, but not the provisions affecting slavery. The same is true of Ehlen, *United States Empires*, 147; Brown, *Louisiana Purchase*, 160–61; and Max Farrand, *The Legislation of Congress for the Government of the Organized Territories of the United States* (Newark, N.J., 1896), 24, 59.

68. On February 16, there was a roll call in the Senate on a proposal to substitute a new bill, one that authorized the people of Orleans to draft their own frame of territorial government by means of a convention. It contained no concessions to or restrictions on slavery. Its few supporters were a strange mixture that included Adams, Hillhouse, Jackson, and Pickering. *AC*, 8-2, cols. 59–61. It is not clear whether final approval of the act took place on March 1 or 2. A House amendment presented to the Senate on March 1 was presumably concurred in before Jefferson signed the bill on March 2, but there is no record of the concurrence. *Ibid.*, 69.

69. *Ibid.*, 47, 48, 54, 59–61, 69, 1201, 1209–11. The act is in *U.S. Statutes at Large*, II, 322–23; and Carter, *Territorial Papers*, IX, 405–7. See also the letter of James Brown, U.S. Attorney in New Orleans, to Albert Gallatin, Dec. 11, 1805, *ibid.*, 548: "Our lawyers have unanimously expressed an opinion that the prohibitions against the importation of slaves contained in the Act of 1804 . . . are repealed by the Act of 1805."

70. *AC*, 8-2, cols. 68, 69, 1213, 1215; Carter, *Territorial Papers*, XIII, 87–89, 92–95. The bill as originally drafted provided for the swift movement of Louisiana to the second territorial stage, but this was eliminated in the revision, which was thus emphatically less democratic and somewhat less proslavery. As Carter explains, there is no record of the actual approval of the amendment by the Senate, neither in the Senate *Journal* nor in the *Annals* (p. 92n.).

71. Matthew Lyon to President James Madison, Washington, D.C., Jan. 26, 1810, in Carter, *Territorial Papers*, XIV, 365.

72. *Ibid.*, 357–64; *AC*, 11-2, col. 1253. Another bill met the same fate a year later. *AC*, 11-3, col. 486.

73. Carter, *Territorial Papers*, XIV, 552–59; *AC*, 12-1, cols. 242–43, 244, 1248, 1279, 1434; 14-1, cols. 362, 1358, 1362, 1893–94. Only seventeen members supported the Lacock motion.

74. *AC*, 16-1, col. 337, remarks of Jonathan Roberts. See also Glover Moore, *The Missouri Controversy, 1819–1821* (Lexington, Ky., 1953), 32.

75. *Ibid.*, 33, *AC*, 15 1, cols. 1672, 1675 76.

76. *AC*, 15-2, cols. 305–11; Moore, *Missouri Controversy*, 34, 281; Harris, *Slavery in Illinois*, 24–26.

77. This is especially true of textbooks and other general works but not of special studies, such as Moore, *Missouri Controversy*, and Lonnie J. White, *Politics on the Southwestern Frontier: Arkansas Territory, 1819–1836* (Memphis, 1964). See also William R. Johnson, "Prelude to the Missouri Compromise," *New York Historical Society Quarterly*, XLVIII (1964), 31–50.

78. *AC*, 15-2, cols. 251, 253, 273, 274, 279, 1166, 1193, 1215, 1217, 1222, 1235, 1237, 1272–74.

79. *Ibid.*, 1227–35.

80. *Ibid.*, 1184; 16-1, cols. 307, 320.

81. *DSvS*, 508–9.

82. See remarks of Felix Walker of North Carolina, Louis McLane of Delaware, and John Rhea of Tennessee in *AC*, 15-2, cols. 1226, 1230–33, 1280.

83. *Ibid.*, 1193, 1204–5, 1214, 1224.

84. *Ibid.*, 1222, 1235, 1237–39, 1272–74; White, *Southwestern Frontier*, 10–12. The motion to reconsider was carried by the vote of Speaker Henry Clay after a tie, 88 to 88. Part two of the Taylor amendment, by itself, would have done little to inhibit slavery in Arkansas, however. Taylor, who served ten successive terms in the House of Representatives from 1813 to 1833, was twice elected Speaker.

85. *AC*, 15-2, cols. 1279–82, 1283; White, *Southwestern Frontier*, 12–14.

86. *AC*, 15-2, cols. 272–73, 274, 1433–35, 1436–38. The Senate returned the Missouri bill a second time to the House, which again refused to concur in the Senate's deletion of the Tallmadge amendment. This time the vote was 78 to 66.

87. Moore, *Missouri Controversy*, 65–83. On early-nineteenth-century reform, see Clifford S. Griffin, *Their Brothers' Keepers: Moral Stewardship in the United States, 1800–1865* (New Brunswick, N.J., 1960); W. David Lewis, "The Reformer as Conservative: Protestant Counter-Subversion in the Early Republic," in Stanley Coben and Lorman Ratner, eds., *The Development of an American Culture* (Englewood Cliffs, N.J., 1970), 64–91. The colonization movement typified the conservative reformism of the period. In the words of David Brion Davis, it "suited the northeastern mercantile elites, such as the Boston Unitarians, who managed to reconcile both 'higher law' platitudes and a theoretical abhorrence of slavery with a genteel distaste for controversy" (*Slavery in the Age of Revolution*, 334).

88. Floyd Calvin Shoemaker *Missouri's Struggle for Statehood, 1804–1821* (Jefferson City, Mo., 1916), 81–113.

89. Moore, *Missouri Controversy*, 86.

90. *AC*, 16-1, cols. 424, 428–30, 457, 467–69, 849, 1455–57, 1540, 1553–55, 1572–73, 1576–77, 1586–88.

91. *Ibid.*, 1578–83. Kinsey had been born in Maryland.

92. Moore, *Missouri Controversy*, 111; Homer Carey Hockett, *The Critical Method*

in Historical Research and Writing (New York, 1955), 75. This means, of course, that Moore was essentially right.

93. *AC*, 16-1, cols. 428, 1587–88. The test vote on the compromise package was taken in the Senate on February 17. It passed, 24 to 20, with northerners contributing only four of the affirmative votes and all 20 of the negative ones. In the House, there was no vote on the Compromise as a whole. The test of northern willingness to compromise was on the motion to delete the antislavery clause from the Missouri bill. The vote was 90 to 87 for deletion with the North providing only 14 of the affirmative votes and all 87 of the negative ones. The Compromise, in short, succeeded because the admission of Missouri was supported almost unanimously by southerners, together with a small minority of northerners, making just enough to constitute a majority in each House. The Thomas amendment had an easier time of it, being supported almost unanimously by the North and by a bare majority of southerners.

94. *Ibid.*, 802, 1326–27, 1391. It is also worth noting that Alexander Smyth of Virginia denounced the House's antislavery proviso for Missouri as a violation of the due-process clause of the Fifth Amendment. *Ibid.*, 998.

95. Moore, *Missouri Controversy*, 122.

96. J. Q. Adams, *Memoirs*, V, 4–9, 14–15; Worthington Chauncey Ford, ed., *Writings of John Quincy Adams* (7 vols.; New York, 1913–17), VII, 1–2; Harry Ammon, *James Monroe: the Quest for National Identity* (New York, 1971), 449–61. Monroe, says Ammon, was determined to veto the Missouri bill if it passed with the Tallmadge amendment attached.

97. Jefferson to John Holmes, Apr. 22, 1820, in Ford, ed., *Writings of Jefferson*, X, 157–58; Madison to James Monroe, Feb. 23, 1820, in *Letters and Other Writings of James Madison* (4 vols.; Philadelphia, 1865), III, 167–69. See also Moore, *Missouri Controversy*, 252–56; Miller, *Wolf by the Ears*, 234–52.

98. The southern vote against the antislavery proviso in the Arkansas bill was 15 to 0 in the Senate; 59 to 1 and 73 to 1 on parts one and two in the House.

99. Jefferson to Hugh Nelson, Feb. 7, 1820, and to John Holmes, Apr. 22, 1820, in Ford, ed., *Writings of Jefferson*, X, 156–58.

100. *Ibid.*, 157–58.

101. *AC*, 16-1, col. 1025.

102. *Ibid.*, 259–75 (Smith speech), 279 (Ruggles), 335 (Barbour), 347 (Johnson); Moore, *Missouri Controversy*, 125–26.

103. See above, 68, 616, and Moore, *Missouri Controversy*, 129–69.

CHAPTER 5

1. Louis Filler, *The Crusade against Slavery, 1830–1860* (New York, 1960), 82.

2. *AC*, 17-1, col. 277.

3. *Register of Debates in Congress*, 24-1, cols. 1053–58, 4260–67, 4291–92, 4294; Orville W. Taylor, *Negro Slavery in Arkansas* (Durham, N.C., 1958), 44–45; Lonnie J. White, *Politics on the Southwestern Frontier: Arkansas Territory, 1819–1836* (Memphis, 1964), 192–99. Opposition to the admission of Arkansas

was not all the result of antislavery feeling. Some Whigs opposed it on purely partisan grounds, since Arkansas was sure to be one more Democratic state. Also, there were objections because Arkansas had framed a constitution without the blessing of a congressional enabling act. The admission of Arkansas was paired with that of Michigan, though the latter was delayed until 1837 by a dispute over its boundary with Ohio. One of the strongest supporters of the Adams antislavery amendment was a young Massachusetts congressman named Caleb Cushing, who delivered an impassioned speech on the subject. Twenty-one years later, the same Cushing would deliver one of the strongest public speeches in the North endorsing the Dred Scott decision.

4. P. J. Staudenraus, *The African Colonization Movement, 1816–1865* (New York, 1961), 169–87.

5. Samuel Flagg Bemis *John Quincy Adams and the Foundations of American Foreign Policy* (New York, 1949), 432–35.

6. *Register of Debates of Congress*, 18–2, cols. 623, 696–97; Robert Ernst, *Rufus King, American Federalist* (Chapel Hill, N.C., 1968), 392–93.

7. *Register of Debates in Congress*, 20-1, cols. 899– 925, 968–98, 1006–30, 1048–63, 1067–84, 1093–1122, 1458–86. See also William W. Freehling, *Prelude to Civil War: The Nullification Controversy in South Carolina, 1816–1836* (New York, 1966), 134–36. Freehling is mistaken in saying that the House voted in favor of reimbursement: The bill was tabled March 24; *House Journal, 20-1* (Serial 168), 442, 890.

8. On this subject, see *House Journal*, 20-1 (Serial 168), *passim;* Richard H. Brown, "The Missouri Crisis, Slavery, and the Politics of Jacksonianism," *South Atlantic Quarterly*, LXV (1966), 55–72.

9. *The Liberator* (Boston), Aug. 13, 1831. On immediatism, see especially David Brion Davis, "The Emergence of Immediatism in British and American Antislavery Thought," *MVHR*, XLIX (1962), 209–30; Anne C. Loveland, "Evangelicalism and 'Immediate Emancipation' in American Antislavery Thought," *JSH*, XXXII (1966), 172–88.

10. *AC*, 15-1, col. 1223.

11. Staudenraus, *African Colonization*, 139. Even some Quakers were persuaded to support colonization. And it should be noted in passing that one of the leaders of the movement was Francis Scott Key, brother-in-law of Roger B. Taney.

12. See George M. Fredrickson, *The Black Image in the White Mind: The Debate on Afro-American Character and Destiny, 1817–1914* (New York, 1971), 6–12.

13. Leonard L. Richards, *"Gentlemen of Property and Standing": Anti-Abolition Mobs in Jacksonian America* (New York, 1970), 30–31.

14. Russel B. Nye, *Fettered Freedom: Civil Liberties and the Slavery Controversy, 1830–1860*, 2nd ed. (East Lansing, Mich., 1963), 67–85; Clement Eaton, *The Freedom-of-Thought Struggle in the Old South*, rev. ed. (New York, 1964), 196–215.

15. *Ibid.*, 118–95; Nye, *Fettered Freedom*, 174–218.

16. *Ibid.*, 42–51; Charles M. Wiltse, *John C. Calhoun, Nullifier, 1829–1839* (Indianapolis, 1949), 278–86; Samuel Flagg Bemis, *John Quincy Adams and the Union* (New York, 1956), 334–40. The House rule of 1836 provided for auto-

matic tabling, without printing or reference. A standing rule adopted in 1840 provided that petitions on the subject of slavery should not be received at all. The Senate accomplished the same purpose by tabling motions to receive or not receive petitions.

17. According to the American Anti-Slavery Society, more than a half-million petitions were sent to Congress during the year 1837–38 alone. Nye, *Fettered Freedom*, 47.

18. *Register of Debates in Congress*, 24-1, 1966.

19. Richard K. Crallé, ed., *The Works of John C. Calhoun* (6 vols.; New York 1851–55, 1888), II, 629.

20. *CG*, 24-1, p. 82 (Jan. 7, 1836).

21. *Ibid.* 25-2, pp. 55, App. 61. Perhaps the most widely used argument was that interference with slavery in the District would be a violation of the agreements with Maryland and Virginia made when the land was ceded. For Daniel Webster's convincing rebuttal, see *CG*, 25-2, App. 64.

22. *CG*, 25-2, p. 98, App. 71; Wiltse, *Calhoun, Nullifier*, 372–73.

23. *CG*, 27-2, pp. 342–43, 344–46, 347; James Brewer Stewart, *Joshua R. Giddings and the Tactics of Radical Politics* (Cleveland, 1970), 70–76.

24. Nye, *Fettered Freedom*, 47. '

25. Charles Francis Adams, ed., *Memoirs of John Quincy Adams* (12 vols.; Philadelphia, 1874–77), V, 54; Bemis, *Adams and Foreign Policy*, 321, 339–40; David M. Pletcher, *The Diplomacy of Annexation: Texas, Oregon, and the Mexican War* (Columbia, Mo., 1973), 69.

26. Bemis, *Adams and the Union*, 338.

27. Much has been written about the annexation of Texas. See especially Justin H. Smith, *The Annexation of Texas* (New York, 1911); Joseph William Schmitz, *Texas Statecraft, 1836–1845* (San Antonio, 1941); Pletcher, *Diplomacy of Annexation*, 64–88, 113–207. Pletcher, it should be noted, believes that Houston was "never entirely sure whether he wanted annexation or independence" (p. 130).

28. The Clay and Van Buren letters are in the *National Intelligencer*, Apr. 27, 30, 1844. The Calhoun letter is in Calhoun, *Works*, V, 333–39. All three letters are printed conveniently together in abbreviated form in Arthur M. Schlesinger et al., eds., *History of American Presidential Elections, 1789–1968* (4 vols.; New York, 1971), I, 814–28.

29. *CG*, 28-1, App., 707; *The Writings and Speeches of Daniel Webster*, National ed. (18 vols.; Boston, 1903), II, 205.

30. *CG*, 31-1, p. 454.

31. *CG*, 28-2, pp. 191–94, 358–63, 372; Pletcher, *Diplomacy of Annexation*, 179–83; Charles Sellers, *James K. Polk, Continentalist, 1843–1846* (Princeton, 1966), 168–89, 205–8. See also Frederick Merk, *Slavery and the Annexation of Texas* (New York, 1972).

32. Antislavery forces fought also against the admission of Texas to statehood. Julius Rockwell of Massachusetts tried to add an antislavery amendment, declaring as he did so that a new question on slavery had been presented to the "consciences of men"—that is, the extension of slavery into a place where it had been abolished. This, he said, was for America an evil "darkening that national character

which she ought to hold up to all nations and ages of the world." His amendment was not brought to a vote. The joint resolution for admission of Texas was passed by the House, 141 to 56, on December 16, 1845, and by the Senate, 31 to 14, on December 22. *CG*, 29-1, pp. 64–65, 92.

33. *U.S. Statutes at Large*, V, 797–98. The "south of 36° 30′" clause was brought forward as an amendment by Milton Brown of Tennessee; the "north of 36° 30′" clause was added at the request of Stephen A. Douglas. Brown was probably responding to a proposal made by Thomas Hart Benton and others that Texas be admitted as a smaller slave state, with slavery forbidden in the rest of her territory, *CG*, 28-2, p. 193; Eric Foner, "The Wilmot Proviso Revisited," *JAH*, LVI (1969), 271; Thomas Hart Benton, *Thirty Years' View . . . 1820 to 1850* (2 vols.; New York, 1854–56, 1865), II, 632–33.

34. Don E. Fehrenbacher, "The Mexican War and the Conquest of California," in George H. Knoles, ed., *Essays and Assays: California History Reappraised* (n.p., 1973), 55–63; Pletcher, *Diplomacy of Annexation*, 422–23; Sellers, *Polk, Continentalist*, 421–23. James Buchanan, Polk's secretary of state, made a curiously obtuse proposal to inform other governments that the United States had no designs on New Mexico or California. The astonished Polk emphatically rejected the proposal and was supported by the rest of his cabinet. See Milo Milton Quaife, ed., *The Diary of James K. Polk* (4 vols.; Chicago, 1910), I, 396–99.

35. On the Proviso generally, see Charles Buxton Going, *David Wilmot, Free-Soiler* (New York, 1924), 94–226; Chaplain W. Morrison, *Democratic Politics and Sectionalism: The Wilmot Proviso Controversy* (Chapel Hill, N.C., 1967); Joseph G. Rayback, *Free Soil: The Election of 1848* (Lexington, Ky., 1970), 23–33; Foner, "Wilmot Proviso Revisited," 262–79.

36. *CG*, 29-1, p. 1217.

37. John Quincy Adams argued that the Proviso was unnecessary, as Morrison, *Democratic Politics*, 18–19, 21, 91, 95, repeatedly points out. But Morrison fails to add that Adams nevertheless voted for the Proviso at every opportunity and eventually changed his mind about its being superfluous. In the following session he voted against the $3 million bill with the Proviso deleted. *CG*, 29-1, pp. 1215–16; 29-2, pp. 425, 573.

38. Foner, "Wilmot Proviso Revisited," 277–78. See also Don E. Fehrenbacher, *Chicago Giant: A Biography of "Long John" Wentworth* (Madison, Wis., 1957), 69–70.

39. *CG*, 29-1, p. 1204; Sellers, *Polk, Continentalist*, 479. The vote was 108 to 43. The amendment was offered by James Thompson, like Wilmot a Pennsylvania Democrat. Actually, such an amendment had been added to an Oregon bill in the preceding session on the motion of Robert C. Winthrop of Massachusetts. The House had approved it, 85 to 56, on February 1, 1845 (*CG*, 28-2, p. 232).

40. According to Davis himself, he intended to allow just enough time for the Senate to accept the bill with the Proviso, and yet not enough for its return to the House; but he miscalculated. See Going, *Wilmot*, 102–4.

41. Salmon P. Chase was one of those who thought that a great opportunity had been missed. In 1847 he wrote to Charles Sumner: "Ten political lives of ten

John Davises, spent in earnest efforts in the best direction, could not compensate for this half-hour's mischief." See "Diary and Correspondence of Salmon P. Chase," AHA *Annual Report*, 1902, II, 124–25.

42. Morrison, *Democratic Politics*, 25–26. Wright himself was a somewhat diffident Proviso man, however. See John Arthur Garraty, *Silas Wright* (New York, 1949), 394–95. Brian George Joseph Walton, "James K. Polk and the Democratic Party in the Aftermath of the Wilmot Proviso," Ph.D. dissertation, Vanderbilt University, 1968, pp. 50–53, points out that the mid-term congressional elections extended over a period of fifteen months and argues that they were not a clear-cut rejection of Polk's policies.

43. *CG*, 29-2, pp. 166, 178–80; Charles M. Wiltse, *John C. Calhoun, Sectionalist, 1840–1850* (Indianapolis, 1951), 294–95; Robert W. Johannsen, *Stephen A. Douglas* (New York, 1973), 202. The antislavery article, as reported from the committee on territories by Stephen A. Douglas, did not mention the word "slavery," but simply extended to Oregon all the privileges and restrictions of the Northwest Ordinance.

44. *CG*, 29-2, pp. 187, 198; *Senate Journal*, 29-2 (Serial 492), 110, 129, 144, 181, 270. Committed and recommitted, the Oregon bill came up for consideration on the final day of the session and was tabled by the Senate.

45. *CG*, 29-2, p. 188, App., 244–47.

46. *Ibid.*, 352–55, and App., 314–18 and *passim*; Going, *Wilmot*, 159–81. Wilmot managed to have the Proviso read on February 1. It was more strongly worded than the 1846 version, applying to "any territory on the continent of America which shall hereafter be acquired" (*CG*, 29-2, p. 303). Because of technical barriers, the Proviso was not formally proposed even on February 8. Debate on it preceded its formal introduction.

47. *CG*, 29-2, p. 188.

48. *Ibid.*, 424–25. The *Globe* gives the vote on the bill itself as 115 to 105, but the official record in the *House Journal*, 29-2 (Serial 496), 349–50, says 115 to 106. Wilmot being absent, the Proviso was moved by Hannibal Hamlin of Maine. See H. Draper Hunt, *Hannibal Hamlin of Maine, Lincoln's First Vice-President* (Syracuse, N.Y., 1969), 39–40.

49. *Senate Journal*, 29-2 (Serial 492), 112, 194, 200, 268.

50. *CG*, 29-2, pp. 453–55.

51. The Senate rejected an effort to add the Proviso by a vote of 32 to 21. *Senate Journal*, 29-2 (Serial 492), 252–53.

52. David M. Potter, *The Impending Crisis, 1848–1861*, completed and edited by Don E. Fehrenbacher (New York, 1976), 61–62.

53. *Ibid.*, 69–72, 77–82; Morrison, *Democratic Politics*, 87–173; Holman Hamilton, "Election of 1848," in Schlesinger, ed., *Presidential Elections*, II, 865–918; Rayback, *Free Soil*, 131–310; Bruce I. Ambacher, "The Pennsylvania Origins of Popular Sovereignty," *Pennsylvania Magazine of History and Biography*, XCVIII (1974), 339–52. Curiously, the Democratic platform did use the phrase "sovereignty of the people," but in connection with European revolutions. On the failure of an effort to attach an anti-popular-sovereignty statement to the platform, see above, 152n.

54. Allan Nevins, "The Constitution, Slavery, and the Territories," in *The Gaspar G. Bacon Lectures on the Constitution of the United States, 1940–1950* (Boston, 1953), 120, 133; Robert R. Russel, *Critical Studies in Antebellum Sectionalism* (Westport, Conn., 1972), 53, 55, 57. Thomas Hart Benton, *Historical and Legal Examination of . . . the Dred Scott Case* (New York, 1857), 115–16, declared that as of August 1848, "the dogma of the unconstitutionality of the Missouri Compromise Act had not . . . been invented." According to Alfred H. Kelly and Winfred A. Harbison, *The American Constitution: Its Origins and Development*, 4th ed. (New York, 1970), 368, the doctrines discussed by Russel, together with several others, "made their appearance" during the period from 1846 to 1850. See also Andrew C. McLaughlin, *A Constitutional History of the United States* (New York, 1935), 512.

55. Wilmot himself said that Jefferson was the real author of the Proviso. Going, *Wilmot*, 107.

56. The idea that scarcely anyone in 1819–20 questioned the constitutionality of the Thomas amendment owes much to Benton, *Examination*, 95–100.

57. Nevins, "Constitution, Slavery, and the Territories," 105. Nevins misread the evidence in part because he relied on the text of Calhoun's 1837 resolutions, which, for strategic reasons, did not flatly declare prohibition of slavery in the territories to be unconstitutional. In his accompanying speeches, Calhoun did so declare. See above, 122–23.

58. Chase to James Gillespie Birney, April 2, 1844, in Dwight L. Dumond, ed., *Letters of James Gillespie Birney, 1831–1857* (2 vols.; New York, 1938), II, 805–6. See Jacobus tenBroek, *The Antislavery Origins of the Fourteenth Amendment* (Berkeley, 1951), 116 and *passim*. Some antislavery radicals insisted, in spite of the Marshall Court's decision to the contrary in *Barron v. Baltimore* (1833), that the Fifth Amendment operated as a restraint on the states as well as on the federal government, and that slavery was therefore illegal everywhere in the United States. The question of whether the Constitution was essentially a proslavery or antislavery document had the abolitionist movement split. Garrisonians said it was proslavery; political abolitionists like Birney and Gerrit Smith, that it was antislavery. Lysander Spooner was among the most extreme in arguing the latter. See his *The Unconstitutionality of Slavery* (Boston, 1845); Wendell Phillips, *The Constitution: A Proslavery Document* (New York 1844); Robert M. Cover, *Justice Accused: Antislavery and the Judicial Process* (New Haven, 1975), 149–58.

59. Cass to A. O. P. Nicholson, Dec. 24, 1847, in Schlesinger, ed., *Presidential Elections*, II, 906–12. During the Missouri controversy in 1820, Alexander Smyth of Virginia had said: "The clause obviously relates to the territory belonging to the United States, as property only"; and John Scott, delegate from Missouri, had argued: "The whole amount of the authority Congress could claim under this clause of the Constitution was to make rules and regulations for the surveying and disposing of the public lands." *AC*, 16-1, cols. 1003, 1502. The fullest exposition of the Cass doctrine is in his speech of January 21–22, 1850, in *CG*, 31-1, App., 58–74.

60. Just how much Cass was fishing for southern votes in the Nicholson letter is in-

dicated by the fact that he also paid his respects to the doctrine of "diffusion"—
the idea that expansion of slavery would ameliorate the institution. Embraced
by Jefferson, Madison, and other southern leaders, it reached its extreme in the
"drainhole" thesis of Robert J. Walker, justifying annexation of Texas as a means
of draining slavery (and Negroes) southward out of the United States. See
James P. Shenton, *Robert John Walker, a Politician from Jackson to Lincoln*
(New York, 1961), 38–39; Frederick Merk, "A Safety Valve Thesis and Texas
Annexation," *MVHR*, XLIX (1962), 413–36.

61. *CG*, 31-1, p. 398 (Feb. 20, 1850).
62. *National Intelligencer*, Dec. 22, 1847; Francis P. Weisenburger, *The Life of
      John McLean* (Columbus, Ohio, 1937), 118. Salmon P. Chase on March 10,
      1848, said that McLean was "emphatically right" on the free soil issue (letter to
      Joshua R. Giddings quoted in *ibid.*, 135).
63. Max Farrand, *The Legislation of Congress for the Government of the Organized
      Territories of the United States* (Newark, N.J., 1896), 41–43, 70; Howard Rob-
      erts Lamar, *Dakota Territory, 1861–1889* (New Haven, 1956), 14. The disallow-
      ance provision was included in the Utah and New Mexico organic acts of 1850,
      and Cass voted for both.
64. 1 Peters 511, 546. According to Cass, speaking in 1856, Marshall had not meant
      that Congress exercised *all* the powers of a state government in the territories
      but only "certain local powers." *CG*, 34-3, pp. 85–86.
65. *DSvS*, 540–41.
66. Stephen A. Douglas, "The Dividing Line Between Federal and Local Authority:
      Popular Sovereignty in the Territories," *Harper's Magazine*, XIX (Sept. 1859),
      519–37. This essay is most readily accessible in Harry V. Jaffa and Robert W.
      Johannsen, eds., *In the Name of the People: Speeches and Writings of Lincoln
      and Douglas in the Ohio Campaign of 1859* (Columbus, Ohio, 1959), 58–125.
67. See above, 585–86. Thomas Hart Benton maintained that the Constitution
      "was not made for the Territories and does not include them." *Examination*,
      129. He took a narrow view of the territory clause as referring only to land but
      believed that Congress governed the territories by right of sovereignty and own-
      ership, without reference to the Constitution. *Ibid.*, 35.
68. Of course, the discussion here is of general sectional tendencies only. Some
      southerners supported the Cass-Douglas version of popular sovereignty, and
      some northerners, such as James Buchanan, came round to the southern ver-
      sion. Gerald M. Capers, *Stephen A. Douglas, Defender of the Union* (Boston,
      1959), 48, says that popular sovereignty was "preferable to the Proviso, and at
      first acceptable to many southerners." See Buchanan's third annual message to
      Congress, Dec. 19, 1859, in James D. Richardson, *A Compilation of the Mes-
      sages and Papers of the Presidents* (11 vols.; Washington, 1913), IV, 3085–86.
69. Douglas, "Dividing Line." Douglas was not driven to such lengths, however,
      until after the Dred Scott decision.
70. Going, *Wilmot*, 282–84, gives some striking examples, one of them being that
      the slavery question "occupied a large place in the discussion of proposed reso-
      lutions of congratulation to France on the deposition of Louis Philippe."
71. *CG*, 30-1, pp. 136, 309, and for some of the debate, 804–5, 811–12, 871,

875–76, 879–80, 883. See R. Alton Lee, "Slavery and the Oregon Territorial Issue: Prelude to the Compromise of 1850," *Pacific Northwest Historical Quarterly*, LXIV (1973), 112–19.

72. *CG*, 30-1, App., 500–510. This debate on April 20, 1848, followed an outbreak of anti-abolitionist rioting in Washington, and Hale provocatively asked leave to introduce a bill plainly aimed at protecting the antislavery *National Era* from threatened destruction. Both Hale and the *Era* were accused of abetting a recent attempt to carry off nearly eighty slaves from the District. Foote, in his *Casket of Reminiscences* (Washington, D.C., 1872; New York, 1968), 76, declared: "These frantic and indecent words had scarcely been enunciated ere I became painfully sensible of the stupid and unbecoming nature of my conduct, and I would have really given worlds to recall all the nonsense I had uttered." See also Richard H. Sewell, *John P. Hale and the Politics of Abolition* (Cambridge, Mass., 1965), 112–18.

73. *CG*, 30-1, pp. 875–76; Polk, *Diary*, III, 501–5.

74. *Senate Journal*, 30-1 (Serial 502), 465, 467; *CG*, 30-1, pp. 927–28, 932. The two northern Democrats on the committee were both administration men; thus the Barnburners were unrepresented. The two northern Whigs were moderately antislavery. Samuel S. Phelps of Vermont supported the Clayton measure. John H. Clarke of Rhode Island opposed it but was too ill to take a very strong stand. *Ibid.*, 953, 992. Apparently, six of the eight committee members supported the bill; Clarke and Calhoun opposed it at least in part.

75. *CG*, 30-1, p. 988.

76. *Ibid.*, 1002–5, for the text of the Clayton bill. One explanation of the discrimination against New Mexico, offered by Clayton, who was something of a nativist, was that the population of those territories was too ignorant to govern itself. *Ibid.*, 988.

77. *Ibid.*, 950.

78. *Ibid.*, 988.

79. *Ibid.*, 988, 994, 998. Sidney Breese of Illinois, pp. 992–93, discussed the technical route of the case to the Supreme Court in a manner predictive of the Dred Scott case. See also Potter, *Impending Crisis*, 74–75.

80. All quoted in Charles Warren, *The Supreme Court in United States History*, rev. ed. (2 vols.; Boston, 1932), II, 209, 212–13. George P. Marsh of Vermont said that the Court itself "would become the defeated party."

81. *Senate Journal*, 30-1 (Serial 502), 502–3; Wiltse, *Calhoun, Sectionalist*, 352. Democrats, 26 to 8 in favor; Whigs, 14 to 7 against; southerners, 23 to 3 in favor; northerners, 19 to 10 against.

82. *House Journal*, 30-1 (Serial 513), 1124–25, 1155–56. The vote to table was 112–97. Northerners voted 104 to 21 in favor of tabling; southerners, 77 to 8 against. The motion to table was made, however, by Alexander H. Stephens, Georgia Whig. For his explanation, see *CG*, 30-1, App., 1103–7. The vote in favor of the House bill was 128 to 71.

83. *CG*, 30-1, p. 1060.

84. *Senate Journal*, 30-1 (Serial 502), 562–63. On the passage of the bill itself, with the amendment attached, Calhoun and James D. Westcott of Florida switched

to the negative. The southern straddle was well illustrated in some remarks of Senator Henry Johnson of Louisiana. The South, he said, "honestly held the opinion that Congress has no power to prohibit slavery." If the North insisted on the exercise of such power, it would mean "the degradation of the South, or the dissolution of the Union." Then, in the next breath, he declared: "If the Missouri Compromise was offered to the South in the spirit in which it was offered in 1820, she would accept it." Besides the striking inconsistency here, it is interesting to note the lack of understanding that in 1820, the 36° 30' line had been a concession made *by* the South *to* the North. *CG*, 30-1, p. 1061.

85. *Senate Journal*, 30-1 (Serial 502), 590; *House Journal*, 30-1 (Serial 513), 1245; Polk, *Diary*, IV, 61–62, 67–68, 70–76. Calhoun and Burt tried unsuccessfully to persuade Polk to veto the bill.

CHAPTER 6

1. Taylor gave some satisfaction to northerners by indicating a proper Whig attitude toward the presidential veto, which was interpreted to mean that he would not veto the Proviso if it were somehow to pass the House and Senate. On the campaign generally, see Holman Hamilton, *Zachary Taylor, Soldier in the White House* (Indianapolis, 1951), 38–133; Joseph G. Rayback, *Free Soil: The Election of 1848* (Lexington, Ky., 1970); Holman Hamilton, "Election of 1848," in Arthur M. Schlesinger et al., eds., *History of American Presidential Elections, 1789–1968* (4 vols.; New York, 1971), II, 865–918.

2. John Witherspoon Du Bose, *The Life and Times of William Lowndes Yancey* (2 vols.; Birmingham, Ala., 1892), I, 212–21; Milo Milton Quaife, *The Doctrine of Non-intervention with Slavery in the Territories* (Chicago, 1910), 74–76.

3. Charles Sellers, *James K. Polk, Continentalist, 1843–1846* (Princeton, 1966), 101–7; James C. N. Paul, *Rift in the Democracy* (Philadelphia, 1951; New York, 1961), 164–65. On the Free Soil party in general, see Frederick J. Blue, *The Free Soilers: Third Party Politics, 1848–1854* (Urbana, Ill., 1973).

4. Robert W. Johannsen, *Stephen A. Douglas* (New York, 1973), 244–46.

5. *CG*, 30-2, pp. 38, 39, 55–56, 71; David M. Potter, *The Impending Crisis, 1848–1861*, completed and edited by Don E. Fehrenbacher (New York, 1976), 84.

6. *CG*, 30-2, pp. 83–84; Don E. Fehrenbacher, *Chicago Giant: A Biography of "Long John" Wentworth* (Madison, Wis., 1957), 88–89; Charles M. Wiltse, *John C. Calhoun, Sectionalist, 1840–1850* (Indianapolis, 1951), 377–88.

7. The text is in the Washington *Union*, Feb. 4, 1849, and, in slightly variant form, in Richard K. Crallé, ed., *The Works of John C. Calhoun* (6 vols.; New York, 1851–55, 1888), VI, 290–313.

8. *Ibid.*, 312–13. "We have completely foiled Calhoun in his miserable attempt to form a Southern party," wrote the Georgia Whig leader Robert Toombs. The purpose of the movement, he declared, was "to disorganize the Southern Whigs and either to destroy Genl. Taylor in advance or compel him to throw himself in

the hands of a large section of the democracy at the South." Toombs to John J. Crittenden, Jan. 3, 22, 1849, in Ulrich Bonnell Phillips, ed., *The Correspondence of Robert Toombs, Alexander H. Stephens, and Howell Cobb,* AHA *Annual Report,* 1911, II, 139, 141.

9. Johannsen, *Douglas,* 242. The clause appears in the Iowa organic act of 1838, for instance (*U.S. Statutes at Large,* V, 239).

10. *CG,* 30-2, p. 561. According to Thomas Hart Benton, *Thirty Years' View . . . 1820 to 1850* (2 vols.; New York, 1854–56, 1865), II, 730, Calhoun was the "prompter" of the amendment in its final form (Walker had begun with a more innocuous version). Benton was there in the Senate, but his prejudice against Calhoun made him less than reliable as a witness. Walker himself said that he consulted with Henry S. Foote of Mississippi before modifying his amendment.

11. *CG,* 30-2, App., 273–74. The full debate extends over 253–309. William L. Dayton of New Jersey, later the first Republican vice-presidential nominee, was especially prominent in the debate on the northern side. Webster did acknowledge that Congress was bound by the basic principles of the Constitution in legislating for the territories. John M. Berrien of Georgia followed with the sensible argument that some parts of the Constitution extended over the territories and other parts did not. Among the former were private rights and those basic liberties that the American citizen took with him everywhere in the national domain (*ibid.,* 279–81). Berrien to some degree was anticipating the distinction between incorporated and unincorporated territories arrived at by the Supreme Court in the aftermath of the Spanish-American War. See above, 586.

12. Hermann E. von Holst, *The Constitutional and Political History of the United States* (8 vols.; Chicago, 1876–92), III, 445–46.

13. *CG,* 30-2, App., 273.

14. See above, 507–9. The outstanding treatment of this transformation is Arthur Bestor, "State Sovereignty and Slavery: A Reinterpretation of Proslavery Constitutional Doctrine, 1846–1860," *Journal of the Illinois State Historical Society,* LIV (1961), 117–80, especially 162–66.

15. *Senate Journal,* 30-2 (Serial 528), 314; *House Journal,* 30-2 (Serial 536), 539–40; *CG,* 30-2, pp. 605–9, 668; Johannsen, *Douglas,* 247–48.

16. *Senate Journal,* 30-2 (Serial 528), 140, 154, 158, 164, 259, 278–79, for a series of such resolutions; also the New York *Tribune,* July 23, 1849; and speech of John A. Bingham in House of Representatives, May 24, 1860, *CG,* 36-1, pp. 2311–12, quoting many resolutions passed by state legislatures between 1847 and 1850. Of course southern legislatures were also passing resolutions. One from North Carolina first declared that a law excluding slaveholders from the territories would be unconstitutional, but then it endorsed extension of the Missouri Compromise line "for the sake of preserving the peace and promoting the perpetuity of the Union." *Senate Journal,* 30-2, p. 278.

17. In private correspondence as early as December 13, 1848, John M. Clayton was promoting the direct-admission by-pass for both California and New Mexico. In the House of Representatives on February 7, 1849, William B. Preston of Virginia brought forward a bill to convert the entire Mexican cession into one state. Clayton became Taylor's secretary of state and Preston became his secre-

tary of the navy. See Hamilton, *Taylor in White House*, 142–43; *CG*, 30-2, p. 477; *Correspondence of Toombs, Stephens, and Cobb*, 147.

18. Hamilton, *Taylor in the White House*, 177–80; Cardinal Goodwin, *The Establishment of State Government in California, 1846–1850* (New York, 1914); William Henry Ellison, *A Self-Governing Dominion: California, 1849–1860* (Berkeley, 1950), 1–51; Theodore Grivas, *Military Governments in California, 1846–1850* (Glendale, Calif., 1963), 187–220.

19. James D. Richardson, ed., *Messages and Papers of the Presidents* (11 vols.; Washington, D.C., 1913), IV, 2545–46; Hamilton, *Taylor in the White House*, 224–25. The filibuster leader was Narcisco Lopez. See Robert Granville Caldwell, *The Lopez Expeditions to Cuba, 1848–1851* (Princeton, 1915).

20. Wiltse, *Calhoun, Sectionalist*, 398–99, 406–8; Avery O. Craven, *The Growth of Southern Nationalism, 1848–1861* (Baton Rouge, 1953), 62–63. On southern attitudes generally in 1849, see the works cited in Potter, *Impending Crisis*, 89n.

21. Hamilton, *Taylor in the White House*, 407. On the danger of secession in 1850, see Potter, *Impending Crisis*, 122–30.

22. *CG*, 31-1, pp. 2–189, *passim*, but especially 66, 138, 187–88. Cobb was elected on the sixty-third ballot with 102 votes out of 221, the Whig candidate getting 99. Cobb had received 103 votes on the first ballot. See Holman Hamilton, *Prologue to Conflict: The Crisis and Compromise of 1850* (Lexington, Ky., 1964), 41–42; Fehrenbacher, *Chicago Giant*, 93–96.

23. *CG*, 31-1, pp. 244–47. The growing Mormon population in the vicinity of Great Salt Lake had made it advisable to separate Utah from New Mexico. The Mormons had asked for admission as the state of "Deseret" with boundaries extending to the Pacific Ocean.

24. Robert W. Johannsen, ed., *The Letters of Stephen A. Douglas* (Urbana, Ill., 1961), 191. The Clay report is in *CG*, 31-1, pp. 944–48.

25. See the tables in Hamilton, *Prologue to Conflict*, 191–92. The closest vote was on the Texas bill, 30 to 20. Abstentions on the New Mexico and fugitive-slave bills were 23 and 21, respectively. The totals for all six votes combined were: yeas, 183; nays, 97; and not voting, 82. On Fillmore's role, see Robert J. Rayback, *Millard Fillmore* (Buffalo, 1959), 224–47.

26. Hamilton, *Prologue to Conflict*, 156–59, and tables at 195–200; *CG*, 31-1, pp. 1746–58, 1762–64, 1769–76, 1806–7, 1837; *House Journal*, 31-1 (Serial 566), 1372–73; Fehrenbacher, *Chicago Giant*, 101–2.

27. Holman Hamilton, " 'The Cave of the Winds' and the Compromise of 1850," *JSH*, XXIII (1957), 331–53, is the most thorough examination of the role of the House in the Compromise.

28. Hamilton, *Prologue to Conflict*, 191–92, 195–200; Hamilton, " 'Cave of the Winds,' " 348. Of course, the Texas bill cannot be separated out of the House's record because it was attached to the New Mexico bill.

29. Johannsen, *Douglas*, 296. Hamilton, " 'Cave of the Winds,' " 349, broadens the definition of compromiser in the House by counting "congressmen who cast affirmative ballots in four instances and either opposed or abstained in the fifth," but I am convinced that, since there were only two pro-northern and three pro-southern measures, no member who voted against any one of them can be clas-

sified as a supporter of compromise. But those antislavery men who abstained on the fugitive-slave bill, and those proslavery men who abstained on the District of Columbia bill, did not by that one action disqualify themselves from the category.

30. Potter, *Impending Crisis*, 90. Henry Clay is not included in the sixty-one because he did not return to the Senate in time to vote on any of the compromise measures except the District of Columbia bill. Even without him, however, Kentucky contributed six compromisers and Illinois, seven. Thus the lower Ohio Valley can be regarded as the valley of compromise. From these two states came Jesse Thomas, Henry Clay, Stephen A. Douglas, and John J. Crittenden. Eleven northern states contributed at least one of the sixty-one compromisers of 1850.

31. See, for example, the speech of Thomas L. Clingman of North Carolina on January 22, acknowledging the South's failure to win California as a slaveholding region and blaming "antislavery agitation" for it. *CG*, 31-1, p. 202.

32. *Ibid.*, 245; App., 274.

33. *CG*, 31-1, pp. 249, 1005–6.

34. *Ibid.*, 258.

35. *Ibid.* "Whilst you have been heaping outrage upon outrage, adding insult to insult," Brown continued, "our people have been calmly calculating the value of the Union." Cf. the remarks of Justice Peter V. Daniel in 1847, quoted above, 561.

36. *Ibid.*, 26 (Richard K. Meade). See also the belligerent statement of Robert Toombs, pp. 27–28.

37. *Ibid.*, 531.

38. *Ibid.*, 343, 398, 454, 528; App., 72–73; 151–52; Johannsen, 275–76. An exception among southerners was the maverick Sam Houston, a strong supporter of popular sovereignty.

39. Alexander H. Stephens pointed out this advantage to the South in a letter defending the Compromise, *Correspondence of Toombs, Stephens, and Cobb*, 283.

40. *CG*, 31-1, App., 919.

41. *Ibid.*, 916. The Clayton bill, said Henry S. Foote of Mississippi, "was a non-intervention bill. It simply proposed to establish a territorial government, leaving the question of slavery to be decided judicially. This bill does the same thing. The 'Clayton compromise bill' is adopted in it, so far as this matter is concerned, word for word, and letter for letter." *Ibid.*, 920.

42. *Ibid.*, 919 (John M. Berrien).

43. *Ibid.*, 917.

44. *CG*, 31-1, pp. 1003, 1044–45, 1074, 1083, 1134. The Davis amendment, first presented on May 15 and voted down on June 5, went through a number of revisions and in its final form was actually the handiwork of Thomas G. Pratt of Maryland.

45. The three were Webster, a Whig, and Daniel Sturgeon and George W. Jones, Democrats. *Ibid.*, 1134.

46. The Clayton compromise was worded to forbid legislation "respecting the prohi-

bition or establishment of African slavery." The Berrien amendment precisely captured its meaning. Davis, in a particularly candid moment, declared: "If non-intervention means that we shall not have protection for our property in slaves, then I always was, and always shall, be opposed to it." *CG*, 31-1, App., 919.

47. *CG*, 31-1, pp. 1134–35. Hale's amendment was objected to as out of order because it amounted to the Proviso, which had already been rejected. Hale was one of several free-soilers who voted against the Douglas motion. Presumably, he was still depending upon the operation of Mexican law to keep the territories free. If so, he apparently had more faith in the Supreme Court than in the territorial legislatures. It should be remembered that nearly all northern senators were under legislative instruction to vote against the introduction of slavery into the Southwest. Some of them alternated between voting their convictions and voting their instructions. Douglas was one of these. *Ibid.*, 1143; App., 911; Johannsen, *Douglas*, 252–54, 288.

48. *CG*, 31-1, pp. 1144–46.

49. *CG*, 31-1, App., 897–902. Hale's amendment as originally presented was technically defective, and he replaced it with the phrasing from the Clayton compromise.

50. *Ibid.*, 902–11; *U.S. Statutes at Large*, IX, 447, 453; Robert R. Russel, "What Was the Compromise of 1850?" *JSH*, XXII (1956), 293; reprinted in his *Critical Studies in Antebellum Sectionalism* (Westport, Conn., 1972), 15; and see above, 127.

51. *Ibid.*, 7, 15. Russel was quoting from George P. Garrison, *Westward Extension, 1841–1850* (New York, 1906), 331.

52. Alexander H. Stephens, *A Constitutional View of the Late War Between the States* (2 vols.; Philadelphia, 1868–70), II, 218–19. Russel, *Critical Studies*, 15n, calls this a "misleading passage."

53. *CG*, 31-1, App., 903 (Henry S. Foote).

54. *CG*, 31-1, p. 1216; App., 904, 907.

55. *CG*, 31-1, pp. 1120–21 (Cass); App., 903 (Foote; italics added). The one roll call on this date, June 15, shows Cass and Douglas not voting.

56. *CG*, 31-1, App., 1463–73.

57. Hamilton, *Prologue to Conflict*, 172–74, summarizes Russel's conclusions without any evaluation except general praise.

58. Russel, *Critical Studies*, 14, 16–18, 20.

59. In spite of the factor of Mexican antislavery law, the Utah and New Mexico measures were not similarly adaptable to the Proviso principle because the latter could not operate without federal intervention of some kind—notably, a court decision enforced by the executive branch; whereas the Calhoun doctrine could become operative solely as a result of private initiative on the part of slaveholders; and popular sovereignty, on the initiative of the territorial legislature.

60. *CG*, 31-1, p. 531.

61. *Population of the United States in 1860; Compiled from the Original Returns of the Eighth Census* (Washington, D.C., 1864), 572, 574–75.

62. Loomis Morton Ganaway, *New Mexico and the Sectional Controversy,*

1846–1861 (Albuquerque, 1944), 60–76. New Mexico also inherited systems of Indian slavery and peonage, but the code of 1859 was limited to African slavery. It was repealed in December 1861.

63. Potter, *Impending Crisis*, 143–44.
64. Stephens, *Constitutional View*, II, 676–77; Richard Harrison Shryock, *Georgia and the Union in 1850* (Philadelphia, 1926), 329–42.
65. Johannsen, ed., *Letters of Douglas*, 207.
66. *Ibid.*, 191. Extension of the Missouri Compromise line had at first been Douglas's preferred solution to the territorial problem, and in 1848 he had supported the Clayton compromise, which expressly forbade the territorial legislatures of New Mexico and California to establish or prohibit slavery. See his explanation of why he supported the Clayton proposal, *CG*, 31-1, p. 1115.
67. See, for example, his remarks in the Senate on June 3, 1850, *ibid.*, 1114–16.
68. *CG*, 31-1, App. 369–70 (Douglas speech of March 12–13, 1850). See also Douglas to Edward Coles, Feb. 18, 1854, in Johannsen, *Letters of Douglas*, 290–99.
69. *CG*, 32-2, pp. 1111–17; Johannsen, *Douglas*, 396–98. The Senate tabled the bill, 23 to 17, with southerners voting 19 to 2 for tabling.
70. The railroad interpretation, also called the "Hodder thesis," originated with the Kansas historian Frank H. Hodder in "Genesis of the Kansas-Nebraska Act," *Wisconsin State Historical Society Proceedings*, 1912, pp. 69–86; and "The Railroad Background of the Kansas-Nebraska Act," *MVHR*, XII (1925), 3-22. For a good brief bibliography of the subject, see Potter, *Impending Crisis*, 153n.
71. *Ibid.*, 168; Roy Franklin Nichols, "The Kansas-Nebraska Act: A Century of Historiography," *MVHR*, XLIII (1956), 187–212.
72. Johannsen, *Douglas*, 436–37. Douglas himself did try to get a Pacific railroad bill enacted at the next session. It passed the Senate but was not acted upon in the House. *CG*, 33-2, pp. 805–14; *House Journal*, 33-2 (Serial 776), 428. The House passed its own bill but then reconsidered and recommitted it. *Ibid.*, 225–31. See also Potter, *Impending Crisis*, 170–71.
73. *CG*, 33-1, pp. 115, 221–22, 239–40, 281–82 (text of the "Appeal," published first in newspapers on January 24, 1854). The text of the Kansas-Nebraska Act is in *U.S. Statutes at Large*, X, 277–90. In line with the principle of popular sovereignty, Congress omitted its customary reservation of the right to disallow territorial legislation. See also Johannsen, *Douglas*, 405–19; Potter, *Impending Crisis*, 160–65; Roy Franklin Nichols, *Blueprints for Leviathan: American Style* (New York, 1963), 94–99; Allan Nevins, *Ordeal of the Union* (2 vols.; New York, 1947), II, 93–113.
74. *CG*, 33-1, pp. 275–80; Johannsen, *Douglas*, 420–21.
75. Potter, *Impending Crisis*, 156–58. See also Harry V. Jaffa, *Crisis of the House Divided: An Interpretation of the Issues in the Lincoln-Douglas Debates* (New York, 1959), 133–46. On repeal efforts, see *CG*, 31-1, pp. 1736, 1772; Quaife, *Non-intervention*, 106–7.
76. In the Oregon territorial act of August 14, 1848, slavery had been doubly prohibited—first by subjecting the territory to "all conditions and restrictions and prohibitions" of the Northwest Ordinance; second by continuing in force the

legislation of the Oregon provisional government, which likewise prohibited
slavery. Over Washington Territory in 1853, Congress, without mention of the
Northwest Ordinance, extended "the laws now in force in said Territory of
Washington, by virtue of the legislation of Congress in reference to the Territory of Oregon, which have been enacted and passed subsequent to the first day
of September, eighteen hundred and forty-eight," together with the legislative
enactments of Oregon Territory until amended or repealed. The effect, it appears, was to exclude Washington Territory from the operation of the Oregon
territorial act and therefore from the restrictions of the Northwest Ordinance,
leaving slavery prohibited there only by the force of territorial law, which was
repealable by the territorial legislature. Thus, quietly, antislavery in Washington Territory was switched from the Proviso track to the popular sovereignty
track. The measure passed Congress without serious debate, in the Senate by a
voice vote, and in the House, 128 to 29, with no antislavery opposition. *CG*, 32-
2, pp. 555, 1020. Franklin Pierce, in his third annual message (Dec. 31, 1855),
claimed Washington Territory for popular sovereignty: "But the true principle
of leaving each State and Territory to regulate its own laws of labor according to
its own sense of right and expediency had acquired fast hold of the public judgment, to such a degree that by common consent it was observed in the organization of the Territory of Washington." Richardson, ed., *Messages and Papers*, IV,
2881. See also the speech of Congressman W. N. H. Smith of North Carolina in
1860, *CG*, 36-1, App., 277.

77.   Henry Barrett Learned, "The Relation of Philip Phillips to the Repeal of the
Missouri Compromise in 1854," *MVHR*, VIII (1922), 303–17; Quaife, *Non-inter-*
vention, 119. Robert R. Russel, "The Issues in the Congressional Struggle over
the Kansas-Nebraska Bill, 1854," *JSH*, XXIX (1963), 205, reprinted in Russel,
Critical Studies, 42–43, insists emphatically, as he did in the case of the Compromise of 1850, that popular sovereignty was understood by both northerners
and southerners to be established in the bill. "Under catechism," he writes,
"most of the Southern leaders admitted, although not all in unequivocal language, that under the bill the territorial legislatures would have the power to
exclude slavery. But some, notably Senators Toombs and Dixon, avoided making the unpleasant admission." Russel names ten southern senators as making
the acknowledgment, but his own citations, far from supporting his generalization, tend rather to contradict it. Only five of the ten were Democrats, and
yet this was a Democratic measure. Furthermore, the Democrats made it plain
that they believed Congress was restrained by the Constitution from investing
territorial legislatures with the power to prohibit slavery, whatever might be
implied to the contrary in the Kansas-Nebraska Act. One of the five, Andrew P.
Butler of South Carolina, declared: "I have, therefore, no idea that in the vote
which I shall give upon this bill, I will be committing myself to any such doctrine as that of the uncontrolled sovereignty of the people of the Territories."
The territorial legislatures, he said, were deputed "to pass such laws as may be
within their constitutional competency to pass, and nothing more." Albert Gallatin Brown, another of Russel's five Democratic senators, was unmistakably
clear on the subject: "The period is well fixed in my mind at which the right to

exclude slavery from a Territory attaches. It is when the Territory comes to form a State constitution for herself." Only two or three of the southern Whigs stated explicitly that territorial power to legislate on slavery had been included in the bill. The Democrats, instead, spoke of giving the territorial legislatures all the power within the constitutional authority of Congress to bestow. Such circumlocution marked the beginning of what I have called the Benjamin formula. See above, 199–201. Russel's insistence that there was neither ambiguity in the bill nor disagreement among its supporters about territorial power is especially surprising because most of his evidence is drawn from a heated debate inspired by the suspicions of two northern Democrats, Charles E. Stuart of Michigan and Isaac P. Walker of Wisconsin. *CG*, 33-1, 691; App. 231, 239–40, 285–89, 291–92, 303, 937–39.

78. See, for example, the remarks of John R. Franklin (Md.), Wiley P. Harris (Miss.), Davis Carpenter (N.Y.), William T. S. Barry (Miss.), and Augustus Drum (Pa.), *CG*, 33-1, App., 421, 549, 599, 618, 741.

79. For an example of the statement that the Dred Scott decision invalidated a law already repealed, see Don E. Fehrenbacher, *Prelude to Greatness: Lincoln in the 1850's* (Stanford, 1962), 51.

80. Avery Craven, *The Coming of the Civil War* (New York, 1942), was apparently the first book to point out this initial southern coolness toward the bill. See especially 348–57.

81. *Senate Journal*, 33-1 (Serial 689), 236–37, 413; *House Journal*, 33-1 (Serial 709), 872–924; Potter, *Impending Crisis*, 165–67; Johannsen, *Douglas*, 432–34. Gerald W. Wolff, "Party and Section: The Senate and the Kansas-Nebraska Bill," *CWH*, XVIII (1972), 293–311, reprinted in Robert P. Swierenga, ed., *Beyond the Civil War Synthesis: Political Essays of the Civil War Era* (Westport, Conn., 1975), 165–83, contains some useful information but reveals the limitations and Procrustean distortions of scale analysis. For instance, James C. Jones of Tennessee scores as a "moderate" and Judah P. Benjamin of Louisiana, as a "pro." They voted the same way on nine out of ten Senate roll calls in Wolff's scalogram. Their only disagreement was on a question of postponing consideration of the bill from a Friday to Monday! Furthermore, the Kansas-Nebraska issue does not lend itself very well to the Guttman scaling technique. The problem is that the measure was supported for different reasons in the North and in the South, and this tends to make the distinction between "moderate" and "pro" more or less meaningless. Wolff's selection of roll calls has the effect of scaling attitudes toward repeal of the 36° 30' restriction, rather than attitudes toward popular sovereignty. Only in this way could Albert Gallatin Brown emerge as a stronger supporter of the Kansas-Nebraska Act than Douglas or Cass. Wolff's conclusion is neither surprising nor exceptionable. He finds that "both party and sectional influences played a major role in determining the voting behavior of Senators on this issue." Of the two factors, he adds, sectionalism appears to have been the more potent. Perhaps more revealing than any of Wolff's figures are these: In the two houses combined, 193 voted with their parties and 71 against; 195 voted with their sections and 69 against. My assumption that the Kansas-Nebraska bill was essentially a Democratic, pro-southern mea-

sure is supported by the facts that it received 89 per cent of the southern votes in both houses and only 36 per cent of the northern votes; and that it received 72 per cent of the Democratic votes and only 27 per cent of the Whig votes.

CHAPTER 7

1. David M. Potter, *The Impending Crisis, 1848–1861*, completed and edited by Don E. Fehrenbacher (New York, 1976), 175.
2. Don E. Fehrenbacher, *Prelude to Greatness: Lincoln in the 1850's* (Stanford, 1962), 37–39.
3. The items listed in the Georgia platform were all matters within the control of professional politicians in Congress, but the election of a president was in the control of the people. On the importance of this distinction, see Don E. Fehrenbacher, "The Election of 1860," in Arthur S. Link, ed., *Crucial American Elections* (Philadelphia, 1973), 39.
4. *CG*, 29-2, p. 191 (Allen G. Thurman, Jan. 15, 1847).
5. The most thorough and perceptive examination of the subject is Eric Foner, *Free Soil, Free Labor, Free Men: The Ideology of the Republican Party before the Civil War* (New York, 1970), 11–39, but Foner defines the "free labor ideology" so broadly as virtually to include the entire economic, social, and religious ethic of the northern part of the Union.
6. *Ibid.*, 262. On the subject generally, see Eugene H. Berwanger, *The Frontier Against Slavery: Western Anti-Negro Prejudice and the Slavery Extension Controversy* (Urbana, Ill., 1967); V. Jacque Voegeli, *Free but Not Equal: The Midwest and the Negro During the Civil War* (Chicago, 1967), 1–12.
7. Lincoln used the argument frequently, saying of the territories in 1854, for example: "We want them for homes of free white people" (*CWAL*, II, 268; see also *CWAL* II, 363; III, 311, 312).
8. On the ambiguities in Republican attitudes, see especially Foner, *Free Soil*, 261–300.
9. Chicago *Tribune*, Jan. 31, 1856; Jeter Allen Isely, *Horace Greeley and the Republican Party, 1853–1861* (Princeton, 1947), 147–50. The congressman was Albert Rust, later a Confederate general.
10. David Donald, *Charles Sumner and the Coming of the Civil War* (New York, 1961), 289–311; Larry Gara, "Slavery and the Slave Power: A Crucial Distinction," *CWH*,, XV (1969), 5–18. In 1859, the Indiana Republican leader Caleb B. Smith wrote: "There is nothing that I so much desire as to see the insolence of the slave power rebuked and its pride and arrogance humbled." Quoted in Foner, *Free Soil*, 211.
11. Despite the shortcomings that critics have exposed in David Donald's essay, "Toward a Reconsideration of Abolitionists," in his *Lincoln Reconsidered: Essays on the Civil War Era*, 2nd ed. (New York, 1961), there remains good reason to qualify rather than reject his argument that the antislavery crusade was a means of self-fulfillment. No one reading Tilden G. Edelstein, *Strange Enthusiasm: A Life of Thomas Wentworth Higginson* (New Haven, 1968), for instance, is likely

to conclude that Donald was entirely wrong. For a brief bibliographical introduction to the subject, see James Brewer Stewart, *Holy Warriors: The Abolitionists and American Slavery* (New York, 1976), 207–8.

12. The historical literature on the Kansas struggle is copious. See especially James A. Rawley, *Race and Politics: "Bleeding Kansas" and the Coming of the Civil War* (Philadelphia, 1969); James C. Malin, *John Brown and the Legend of Fifty-Six* (Philadelphia, 1942); Samuel A. Johnson, *The Battle Cry of Freedom: The New England Emigrant Aid Company in the Kansas Crusade* (Lawrence, Kansas., 1954); Allan Nevins, *Ordeal of the Union* (2 vols.; New York, 1947), II, 301–16, 380–93, 431–37; Potter, *Impending Crisis*, 199–224.

13. Although it might have been much more serious, the Wakarusa War was limited to a few brawls and exchanges of shots over a period of about ten days in late November and early December 1856. Johnson, *Battle Cry*, 138–43.

14. *House Journal*, 34-1 (Serial 838), 8–446; Fred Harvey Harrington, "The First Northern Victory," *JSH*, V (1939), 186–205.

15. James D. Richardson, ed., *Messages and Papers of the Presidents* (11 vols.; Washington, D.C., 1913), IV, 2877–83; Carl B. Swisher, *The Taney Period, 1836–1864*, Volume V of the Oliver Wendell Holmes Devise *History of the Supreme Court of the United States* (New York, 1974), 722.

16. Richardson, ed., *Messages and Papers*, IV, 2885–93. *Senate Reports*, 34-1, No. 34 (Serial 836). Robert W. Johannsen, *Stephen A. Douglas* (New York, 1973), 492–93, says: "No longer satisfied merely to defend it as an expedient, or even as a moral right, he now sought a legal and constitutional basis for his position."

17. *Senate Reports*, 34-1, No. 34 (Serial 836), 2–4.

18. Speaking of slavery in the territories, Douglas said on March 14, two days after reading his report: "All men who agree with me deny the power of Congress either to extend or curtail it." *CG*, 34-1, p. 657.

19. Cass and Pierce are the two other most notable cases of northerners denying the power of Congress to prohibit slavery in the territories, but more important, perhaps, no Democrats any longer affirmed the power, as Douglas himself had formerly done, and as the Democratic party of Maine had done at its state convention in 1849: "*Resolved*, That the institution of human slavery is at variance with the theory of our Government, abhorrent to the common sentiment of mankind, and fraught with danger to all who come within the sphere of its influence; that the Federal Government possesses adequate power to inhibit its existence in the Territories of the Union; that the constitutionality of this power has been settled by judicial construction, by contemporaneous expositions, and by repeated acts of legislation. . . ." Quoted in *CG*, 36-1, p. 2312.

20. Quoted in Johannsen, *Douglas*, 493. Johannsen believes that Douglas weakened his case with his constitutional argument.

21. *CG*, 34-1, pp. 1–2, 58, 579–84. The protest was based upon a clause in the Illinois constitution providing that any person elected to the state supreme court should be ineligible for any other office during the course of his term. Trumbull had been elected to a nine-year term on the court in 1852 but had resigned in 1853. Senators viewed the resignation as erasing the disability, and some of them maintained that no state had any power to define eligibility for the United

States Senate. Southern senators, knowing Trumbull's antislavery position, nevertheless voted almost unanimously in his favor. Douglas took no part in the voting, but two northern Democrats especially close to him led the fight against Trumbull. They were George E. Pugh of Ohio and Charles E. Stuart of Michigan. On Trumbull, see Horace White, *The Life of Lyman Trumbull* (Boston, 1913); Mark M. Krug, *Lyman Trumbull: Conservative Radical* (New York, 1965). On the contesting of Trumbull's right to his seat, see Douglas to James W. Singleton, Mar. 5, 1856, in Robert W. Johannsen, ed., *The Letters of Stephen A. Douglas* (Urbana, Ill., 1961), 349.

22. *CG*, 34-1, pp. 652–54; App., 200–206.
23. Johannsen, *Douglas*, 496.
24. See Seward's speech of April 9, 1856, in *CG*, 34-1, App., 399–405, which his biographer calls "a formidable effort in a dubious cause." Glyndon G. Van Deusen, *William Henry Seward* (New York, 1967), 169.
25. *CG*, 34-1, p. 1092. No one "broke" the Missouri Compromise until the 36° 30′ restriction was repealed in 1854. Benjamin presumably referred to other northern antislavery efforts, or to the second Missouri controversy over exclusion of Negroes in the state constitution. Most Republicans, of course, did maintain that the territory clause gave Congress express authority to govern the territories. Benjamin, a former Whig, announced that he was joining the Democrats. *Ibid.*, 1096–97.
26. *Ibid.*, 1093.
27. *Ibid.*, 1097, 1100.
28. Just ten days later, for instance, Albert Gallatin Brown of Mississippi engaged in an argument with Cass over whether President Pierce supported the northern or southern construction of the Kansas-Nebraska Act. *CG*, 34-1, App., 520.
29. Arthur M. Schlesinger et al., eds., *History of American Presidential Elections, 1789–1968* (4 vols.; New York, 1971), II, 1037–38, 1045–47; Roy Franklin Nichols, The *Disruption of American Democracy* (New York, 1948), 7–18; Johannsen, *Douglas*, 505–20; Roy Franklin Nichols, *Franklin Pierce, Young Hickory of the Granite Hills*, 2nd ed. (Philadelphia, 1958), 450–56, 466–69; Philip Shriver Klein, *President James Buchanan* (University Park, Pa., 1962), 248–55.
30. In a speech at his Wheatland home, November 6, 1856, with the Pennsylvania and Indiana results already in and spelling victory, Buchanan interpreted the Cincinnati platform as recognizing "the right of a majority of the people of a Territory, when about to enter the Union as a State, to decide for themselves whether domestic slavery shall or shall not exist among them." Schlesinger, ed., *Presidential Elections*, II, 1065.
31. The Republican platform is in Schlesinger, ed., *Presidential Elections*, II, 1039–41. See also Allan Nevins, *Frémont, Pathmarker of the West* (New York, 1939), 421–58; Ruhl Jacob Bartlett, *John C. Frémont and the Republican Party* (Columbus, Ohio, 1930); Andrew Wallace Crandall, *The Early History of the Republican Party* (Boston, 1930), 154–88; Francis P. Weisenburger, *The Life of John McLean, a Politician on the United States Supreme Court* (Columbus, Ohio, 1937), 146–51; Richard H. Sewell, *Ballots for Freedom: Antislavery Politics in the United States, 1837–1860* (New York, 1976), 277–89.

32. *Senate Journal*, 34-1 (Serial 809), 401–2, 414; *CG*, 34-1, pp. 1439, 1506–7; App., 749–805; *Senate Reports*, 34-1, No. 198 (Serial 837), for Douglas's committee report accompanying the Toombs bill; William Y. Thompson, *Robert Toombs of Georgia* (Baton Rouge, 1966), 112–14.

33. *CG*, 34-1, App. 844, 851, 856. See also the remarks of Jacob Collamer of Vermont, *CG*, 34-1, pp. 1567–70.

34. *CG*, 34-1, App., 805; Rawley, *Race and Politics*, 153–56. For a summary of subsequent efforts in the same session to pass a Kansas bill, see Johannsen, *Douglas*, 527–28.

35. *CG*, 34-1, pp. 1369–75. Trumbull set off this particular debate by introducing a bill annexing Kansas Territory to Nebraska Territory.

36. Trumbull argued that the amendment was relevant because the convention would have discretionary power to adopt a state constitution and might not use it, thus leaving Kansas in its territorial stage. But George E. Pugh replied that Congress would be back in session when the convention acted and could deal then with any such contingency. *CG*, 34-1, App., 796–97.

37. *Ibid.*, 797–99, including statements by Cass and by Isaac Toucey of Connecticut. The latter insisted that interpretation of the Constitution was "exclusively for the judicial tribunals." Cass, unlike Douglas, expressed his belief that territorial legislatures did have the power to exclude slavery, but he added that it was in the end a constitutional question which could not be settled by legislation. See also the statement of William Bigler of Pennsylvania, *ibid.*, 843, which includes these words: "It is a question of what degree of law-making power it is competent for Congress to confer upon the people and Legislature of a Territory. It is a question of construing the Constitution, and, therefore, a judicial question, which I am not called upon to decide."

38. Potter, *Impending Crisis*, 271.

39. Wallace Mendelson, "Dred Scott's Case—Reconsidered," *Minnesota Law Review*, XXXVIII (1953), 16, 28. Mendelson, like a number of other scholars, depicts Lincoln as pledging himself in 1856 to support a judicial resolution of the territorial question. For a critique of this view, see Don E. Fehrenbacher, "Lincoln and Judicial Supremacy: A Note on the Galena Speech of July 23, 1856," *CWH*, XVI (1970), 197–204.

CHAPTER 8

1. Charles Grove Haines, *The American Doctrine of Judicial Supremacy* (Los Angeles, 1932; New York, 1959), 23.

2. Julius Goebel, Jr., *Antecedents and Beginnings to 1801*, Volume I of the Oliver Wendell Holmes Devise *History of the Supreme Court of the United States* (New York, 1971), 1.

3. *Ibid.*, 3–7; William E. Nelson, *Americanization of the Common Law: The Impact of Legal Change on Massachusetts Society, 1760–1830* (Cambridge, Mass., 1975), 8–10, 30. In *Guardians of the Poor v. Greene*, 5 Binney 554, 557–58 (Pa., 1813), Chief Justice William Tilghman declared: "Every country has its

common law. Ours is composed partly of the common law of England, and partly of our own usages. . . . It required time and experience to ascertain how much of the English law would be suitable to this country. By degrees, as circumstances demanded, we adopted the English usages, or substituted others better suited to our wants."

4. Lawrence M. Friedman, *A History of American Law* (New York, 1973), 16–18.

5. *Ibid.*, 17.

6. Goebel, *Antecedents*, 2; Julius Goebel, Jr., "Constitutional History and Constitutional Law," *Columbia Law Review*, XXXVIII (1938), 558–59; Haines, *Judicial Supremacy*, 206–8; Robert Kenneth Faulkner, *The Jurisprudence of John Marshall* (Princeton, 1968), 59–60.

7. Haines, *Judicial Supremacy*, 19–20; Nelson, *Americanization*, 16–18.

8. *Ibid.*, 14, 91.

9. Goebel, *Antecedents*, 57–83; Haines, *Judicial Supremacy*, 44–59. The case was *Winthrop v. Lechmere* (1727), for which see James Bradley Thayer, ed., *Cases on Constitutional Law* (2 vols.; Cambridge, Mass., 1895), I, 34–39. The quotation is from Clinton Rossiter, *Seedtime of the Republic: The Origin of the American Tradition of Political Liberty* (New York, 1953), 460n.

10. Gordon S. Wood, *The Creation of the American Republic, 1776–1787* (Chapel Hill, N.C., 1969), 403–9; Haines, *Judicial Supremacy*, 67–87; Francis Newton Thorpe, ed., *The Federal and State Constitutions, Colonial Charters, and Other Organic Laws of the States, Territories, and Colonies Now or Heretofore Forming the United States of America* (7 vols.; Washington, D.C., 1909), 564, 784, 798, 1905, 2452, 2596, 2791, 3087–88, 3254, 3263, 3817. On the state constitutions generally, see Elisha P. Douglass, *Rebels and Democrats: The Struggle for Equal Political Rights and Majority Rule during the American Revolution* (Chapel Hill, N.C., 1955); Fletcher M. Green, *Constitutional Development in the South Atlantic States, 1776–1860* (Chapel Hill, N.C., 1930), 47–141; Allan Nevins, *The American States During and After the Revolution, 1775–1789* (New York, 1924), 117–82.

11. Douglass, *Rebels and Democrats*, 162–213. For documents of the Massachusetts movement, see J. R. Pole, ed., *The Revolution in America, 1754–1788, Documents and Commentaries* (Stanford, 1970), 405–515; Oscar and Mary Handlin, eds., *The Popular Sources of Political Authority: Documents of the Massachusetts Constitution of 1780* (Cambridge, Mass., 1966).

12. Goebel, *Antecedents*, 125–42. The principal cases were *Rutgers v. Waddington* (N.Y., 1784); *Trevett v. Weeden* (R.I., 1786); and *Bayard v. Singleton* (N.C., 1787).

13. "An absolute or qualified negative in the executive upon the acts of the legislative body is admitted, by the ablest adepts in political science, to be an indispensable barrier against the encroachments of the latter upon the former. And it may, perhaps, with no less reason, be contended that the powers relating to impeachments are, as before intimated, an essential check in the hands of that body upon the encroachments of the executive." *The Federalist* 66.

14. Max Farrand, *The Records of the Federal Convention of 1787*, rev. ed. (4 vols.; New Haven, 1937), I, 97. On the attitudes of the framers toward judicial re-

view, see Charles A. Beard, *The Supreme Court and the Constitution* (New York, 1912). For a rebuttal to Beard, see Louis B. Boudin, *Government by Judiciary* (2 vols.; New York, 1932), I, 568–83.

15. For Hamilton's views, see especially *The Federalist* 78; For Madison's, see Jonathan Elliot, ed., *The Debates in the Several State Conventions on the Adoption of the Federal Constitution*, 2nd ed. (4 vols.; Washington, D.C., 1836), IV, 382–83; Edward S. Corwin, *Court over Constitution: A Study of Judicial Review as an Instrument of Popular Government* (Princeton, 1938), 31–33.

16. Edward S. Corwin, "The Constitution as Instrument and as Symbol," *American Political Science Review*, XXX (1936), 1072; Robert K. Carr, *The Supreme Court and Judicial Review* (New York, 1942), 54–55. On Calhoun, see *CG*, 30-2, App., 274 (Feb. 24, 1849).

17. Charles Warren, *The Supreme Court in United States History*, rev. ed. (2 vols.; Boston, 1932), I, 493. In circuit court, Justice Bushrod Washington held that the power was exclusively federal; Justices William Johnson and Henry Brockholst Livingston, that the states had concurrent power.

18. Farrand, *Records*, I, 21.

19. Article VI; Farrand, *Records*, I, 245; II, 22, 132, 183, 389. On the supremacy clause, see William Winslow Crosskey, *Politics and the Constitution in the History of the United States* (2 vols.; Chicago, 1953), II, 984–1002, where it is argued that judicial review of laws of Congress was not intended. See also Alexander M. Bickel, *The Least Dangerous Branch: The Supreme Court at the Bar of Politics* (Indianapolis, 1962), 8–14.

20. Article III, Section 2; *U.S. Statutes at Large*, I, 85–87. There is an excellent brief discussion in Alfred H. Kelly and Winfred A. Harbison, *The American Constitution, Its Origins and Development*, 4th ed. (New York, 1970), 137–41. On the Judiciary Act of 1789, see Goebel, *Antecedents*, 457–508.

21. Farrand, *Records*, I, 21, 97–98, 138–40; II, 73–80, 298; *The Federalist*, 78 (Hamilton); Elliot, *Debates*, II, 196 (Ellsworth); *ibid.*, 445–46 (Wilson). For John Marshall's statement in the Virginia ratifying convention that laws of Congress would be subject to judicial review, see Elliot, *Debates*, III, 553. Ellsworth, it should be noted, did not say that *federal* judges would invalidate unconstitutional state laws. He was discreetly vague on that point.

22. Corwin, "Instrument and Symbol," 1078, declares: "That the Framers anticipated some sort of judicial review of acts of Congress there can be little question. But it is equally without question that ideas generally current in 1787 were far from presaging the present vast role of the Court." And according to Bickel, *Least Dangerous Branch*, 15, "it is as clear as such matters can be that the Framers of the Constitution specifically, if tacitly, expected that the federal courts would assume a power—of whatever exact dimensions—to pass on the constitutionality of actions of the Congress and the President, as well as of the several states."

23. *Hayburn's Case*, 2 Dallas 409; Haines, *Judicial Supremacy* 173–79; Warren, *Supreme Court*, I, 69–82.

24. Bickel, *Least Dangerous Branch*, 29–31; Charles L. Black, Jr., *The People and the Court: Judicial Review in a Democracy* (New York, 1960), 34–55.

25. For a discussion of the theories of the effect of judicial review, see Corwin, *Court over Constitution*, 2–3.

26. Benjamin Hoadley, quoted in Learned Hand, *The Bill of Rights* (Cambridge, Mass., 1958), 8.

27. *The Federalist*, 78; Alexis de Tocqueville, *Democracy in America*, edited by Phillips Bradley (2 vols., Vintage; New York, 1945), I, 155–56; Warren, *Supreme Court*, I, 76, 118–21, 124, 156, 171–72, 275. John Rutledge was appointed between Jay and Ellsworth, but the Senate refused to give its approval.

28. *U.S. Statutes at Large*, II, 132, 156–67. Congress first repealed the Federalist Judiciary Act of 1801, which had relieved the justices of circuit duty, then passed a new act revising the system established in 1789. The constitutionality of both the repeal and the new act was tested in *Stuart v. Laird*, 1 Cranch 299 (1803).

29. *Marbury v. Madison*, 1 Cranch 137 (1803); Warren, *Supreme Court*, I, 231–68.

30. *Cohens v. Virginia*, 6 Wheaton 264 (1821). The Court had previously asserted its appellate jurisdiction over state court decisions in another Virginia case, *Martin v. Hunter's Lessee*, 1 Wheaton 304 (1816), but resistance in the state had continued, led by Judge Spencer Roane and encouraged by Thomas Jefferson. See Warren, *Supreme Court*, I, 443–53, 545–47, 554–59.

31. *Ware v. Hylton*, 3 Dallas 199 (1796); *Fletcher v. Peck*, 6 Cranch 87. On the latter, see C. Peter Magrath, *Yazoo: Law and Politics in the New Republic, the Case of Fletcher v. Peck* (Providence, 1966).

32. *Gibbons v. Ogden*, 9 Wheaton 1 (1824); *Osborn v. Bank of the United States*, 9 Wheaton 738 (1824); *Brown v. Maryland*, 12 Wheaton 419 (1827). In the *Brown* decision, Marshall set forth the "original package" doctrine to designate the exact point at which imported goods ceased to be a part of foreign commerce and came within state taxing power.

33. *Sturges v. Crowninshield*, 4 Wheaton 122 (1819). Marshall upheld the power of state governments to enact bankruptcy laws in the absence of federal legislation, but he declared this particular New York law to be in violation of the contract clause.

34. *Fletcher v. Peck*, 6 Cranch 87 (1810); *Dartmouth College v. Woodward*, 4 Wheaton 518 (1819); *Green v. Biddle*, 8 Wheaton 1 (1823). These three decisions held, respectively, that the contract clause covered state land grants, state charters of incorporation, and agreements between states. In *New Jersey v. Wilson*, 7 Cranch 164 (1812), the Court also held that the clause protected state grants of tax exemption. See Benjamin Fletcher Wright, Jr., *The Contract Clause of the Constitution* (Cambridge, Mass., 1938), 27–61; Francis Noel Stites, "The Dartmouth College Case, 1819," Ph.D. dissertation, Indiana University, 1968.

35. Donald G. Morgan, "Marshall, the Marshall Court, and the Constitution," in W. Melville Jones, ed., *Chief Justice John Marshall, A Reappraisal* (Ithaca, N.Y., 1956), 174–83; R. Kent Newmyer, *The Supreme Court under Marshall and Taney* (New York, 1968), 81–88. In what was perhaps the last truly notable decision of the Marshall Court, *Barron v. Baltimore*, 7 Peters 243 (1833), it held that the federal Bill of Rights was not a restriction on state governments.

36.   The quotation is from Max Lerner, *America as a Civilization* (New York, 1957),
      442.
37.   *Register of Debates in Congress*, 21-2, cols. 532, 542; Robert J. Steamer, *The
      Supreme Court in Crisis: A History of Conflict* (Amherst, Mass., 1971), 49. All
      but five of the fifty-one affirmative votes were from the South.
38.   Richard P. Longaker, "Andrew Jackson and the Judiciary," *Political Science
      Quarterly*, LXXI (1956), 341–64.
39.   In 1820, at the age of forty-three, Taney wrote: "As to my own health it is hardly
      worth complaining about. It has been so long bad I have got used to it." In
      1843, Justice John Catron said of Taney: "The Chief Justice is exceedingly
      frail—indeed he will hardly outlast the next three years, I think clearly not."
      Carl B. Swisher, *The Taney Period, 1836–1864*, Volume V of the Oliver Wen-
      dell Holmes Devise *History of the Supreme Court of the United States* (New
      York, 1974), 212, 258; Carl B. Swisher, *Roger B. Taney* (New York, 1936), 102;
      Samuel Tyler, *Memoir of Roger Brooke Taney, LL.D.*, 2nd ed. (Baltimore,
      1876), 509–10; Walker Lewis, *Without Fear or Favor: A Biography of Chief Jus-
      tice Roger Brooke Taney* (Boston, 1965), 258–60.
40.   Warren, *Supreme Court*, I, 694–95; Swisher, *Taney Period*, 17; J. F. Lee to
      Montgomery Blair, Aug. 31, 1861, Francis P. Blair Family Papers, MDLC. The
      statement about Taney's "apostolic manner" has been attributed both to William
      Wirt and William Pinkney.
41.   Swisher, *Taney*, 27, 43–44, 49–50, 52; Tyler, *Memoir of Taney*, 100–102,
      109–119 (containing Taney's account, dated 1856, of the writing of "The Star-
      Spangled Banner"); Warren, *Supreme Court*, II, 16.
42.   So Reverdy Johnson recalled in 1864. See his speech in *CG*, 38-1, p. 1363.
43.   Warren, *Supreme Court*, I, 653–55. Justice William Johnson was always un-
      happy with the Marshall system and dissented more often than any other
      member of the Court.
44.   *Charles River Bridge v. Warren Bridge*, 11 Peters 420; *New York v. Miln*, 11
      Peters 102; *Briscoe v. Bank of Kentucky*, 11 Peters 257. On the Taney Court
      generally, besides the works by Newmyer, Swisher, Tyler, and Lewis cited in
      notes 35 and 39, above, see Charles Grove Haines and Foster H. Sherwood,
      *The Role of the Supreme Court in American Government and Politics,
      1835–1864* (Berkeley, 1957); Bernard Schwartz, *From Confederation to Nation:
      The American Constitution, 1835–1877* (Baltimore, 1973), 1–37; Robert J. Har-
      ris, "Chief Justice Taney: Prophet of Reform and Reaction," in Leonard W.
      Levy, ed., *American Constitutional Law, Historical Essays* (New York, 1966),
      93–128; Marvin Laurence Winitsky, "The Jurisprudence of Roger B. Taney,"
      Ph.D. dissertation, UCLA, 1974. Winitsky's first chapter has been published as
      "Roger B. Taney: A Historiographical Inquiry," *Maryland Historical Magazine*,
      LXIX (1974), 1–26. On the *Charles River Bridge* case, see Stanley I. Kutler,
      Privilege and Creative Destruction: The Charles River Bridge Case (Philadel-
      phia, 1971).
45.   All cases had been argued before the Marshall Court and carried over. For evi-
      dence that Marshall was on the same side as Taney in the *Charles River Bridge*
      case, see Kutler, *Privilege*, 172–79.

46. *Ibid.*, 95–101; Gerald T. Dunne, *Justice Joseph Story and the Rise of the Supreme Court* (New York, 1970), 357–64, 426–27.

47. Newmyer, *Marshall and Taney*, 109–10.

48. *Louisville, Cincinnati and Charleston Railroad v. Letson*, 2 Howard 497 (1844); Swisher, *Taney Period*, 457–83; and see above, 72.

49. *New York v. Miln*, 11 Peters 102 (1837); *License Cases*, 5 Howard 504 (1847); *Passenger Cases*, 7 Howard 283 (1849); *Cooley v. Board of Wardens*, 12 Howard 299 (1852). Also *Holmes v. Jennison*, 14 Peters 540 (1840); *Groves v. Slaughter*, 15 Peters 449 (1841); *Prigg v. Pennsylvania*, 16 Peters 539 (1842).

50. *Charles River Bridge v. Warren Bridge*, 11 Peters 420 (1837); *Briscoe v. Bank of Kentucky*, 11 Peters 257 (1837); *Bank of Augusta v. Earle*, 13 Peters 519 (1839); *Bronson v. Kinzie*, 1 Howard 311 (1843); *Strader v. Graham*, 10 Howard 82 (1851); *Piqua Branch v. Knoop*, 16 Howard 369 (1853); *Ohio Life Insurance Company v. Debolt*, 16 Howard 416 (1854); *Dodge v. Woolsey*, 18 Howard 331 (1855). See also Kutler, *Privilege*, 133–54.

51. For example, *Swift v. Tyson*, 16 Peters 1 (1842); *Louisville, Cincinnati and Charleston Railroad v. Letson*, 2 Howard 497 (1844); *Genesee Chief v. Fitzhugh*, 12 Howard 443 (1851).

52. See, for example, Ben W. Palmer, *Marshall and Taney, Statesmen of the Law* (Minneapolis, 1939), 258–60; Bernard Schwartz, *A Basic History of the U.S. Supreme Court* (Princeton, 1968), 33–34; Schwartz, *Confederation to Nation*, 35–36.

53. Dean G. Acheson, "Roger Brooke Taney: Notes upon Judicial Self Restraint," *Illinois Law Review*, XXXI (1937), 705.

54. *Rhode Island v. Massachusetts*, 12 Peters 657, 752–54 (1838).

55. Schwartz, *Confederation to Nation*, 30–33. See also Lewis, *Without Fear or Favor*, 318–19; Leonard W. Levy, *Judgments: Essays on American Constitutional History* (Chicago, 1972), 20.

56. Charles W. Smith, Jr., *Roger B. Taney: Jacksonian Jurist* (Chapel Hill, N.C., 1936), 155, 173; Schwartz, *Confederation to Nation*, 30.

57. William E. Nelson, "Changing Conceptions of Judicial Review: The Evolution of Constitutional Theory in the States, 1790–1860," *University of Pennsylvania Law Review*, CXX (1972), 1166–85.

58. The literature on the political-questions doctrine is extensive, stimulated especially by the reapportionment decisions of the mid-twentieth century, notably *Colegrove v. Green*, 328 U.S. 549 (1946), and *Baker v. Carr*, 369 U.S. 186 (1962). See Charles Gordon Post, Jr., *The Supreme Court and Political Questions* (Baltimore, 1936); William M. Wiecek, *The Guarantee Clause of the U.S. Constitution* (Ithaca, N.Y., 1972), 270–89, and the works cited in notes 7, 9–13; Louis Henkin, "Is There a 'Political Question' Doctrine?" *Yale Law Journal*, LXXXV (1976), 597–625.

59. *Luther v. Borden*, 7 Howard 1 (1849); Swisher, *Taney Period*, 515–27; Marvin E. Gettleman, *The Dorr Rebellion, a Study in American Radicalism: 1833–1849* (New York, 1973), 174–99; George M. Dennison, *The Dorr War: Republicanism on Trial, 1831–1861* (Lexington, Ky., 1976), 141–92; Michael A. Conron, "Law, Politics, and Chief Justice Taney: A Reconsideration of the Luther v. Borden

Decision," *American Journal of Legal History*, XI (1967), 377–88; John S. Schuchman, "The Political Background of the Political-Question Doctrine: The Judges and the Dorr War," *ibid.*, XVI (1972), 111–25; Wiecek, *Guarantee Clause*, 111–29.

60. Francis P. Weisenburger, *The Life of John McLean, a Politician on the United States Supreme Court* (Columbus, Ohio, 1937), stresses McLean's political activity, somewhat to the neglect of his judicial career. On Marshall, see Gerald Gunther, ed., *John Marshall's Defense of McCulloch v. Maryland* (Stanford, 1969).

61. *Bank of the United States v. United States*, 2 Howard 711, 745–68 (1844). See the comment on Taney's conduct in John P. Frank, *Marble Palace: The Supreme Court in American Life* (New York, 1961), 83n.

62. *Prigg v. Pennsylvania*, 16 Peters 539, 627–28 (1842), and see above, 45, *Groves v. Slaughter*, 15 Peters 449, 508–9 (1841); *Strader v. Graham*, 10 Howard 82, 93–94, 97 (1850), and see above, 260–61, 268–69, 385–87. In the *Groves* case, as well as in the *License Cases*, 5 Howard 504 (1847), and the *Passenger Cases*, 7 Howard 283 (1849), Taney showed a determination to kill any suggestion that the commerce clause might be used as the basis for federal interference with the interstate slave trade. See the comment in Wiecek, *Guarantee Clause*, 133–34n.

63. Swisher, *Taney Period*, 69–70, 576–83, 585. Leon Friedman and Fred L. Israel, eds., *The Justices of the United States Supreme Court, 1789–1969: Their Lives and Major Opinions* (4 vols.; N.Y., 1969), I, 535–46, 601–11, 635–54, 737–49, 795–804; II, 817–29, 873–83, 895–908, 927–39, presents biographical essays by Frank Otto Gatell on McLean, Wayne, Taney, Catron, Daniel, Nelson, and Grier, and by William Gillette on Curtis and Campbell. See also Alexander A. Lawrence, *James Moore Wayne, Southern Unionist* (Chapel Hill, N.C., 1943); Henry G. Connor, *John Archibald Campbell* (Boston, 1920); Benjamin R. Curtis, ed., *A Memoir of Benjamin Robbins Curtis, LL.D.* (2 vols., Boston, 1879); Richard H. Leach, "Benjamin Robbins Curtis: Judicial Misfit," *New England Quarterly*, XXV (1952), 507–23; John P. Frank, *Justice Daniel Dissenting: A Biography of Peter V. Daniel, 1784–1860* (Cambridge, Mass., 1964), 243–47.

64. Lewis, *Without Fear or Favor*, 321–23, claims *Groves v. Slaughter* as one of Taney's self-restraint cases because the decision of the majority, written by Justice Smith Thompson of New York and concurred in by Taney, avoided answering the question whether a provision of the Mississippi constitution violated the commerce clause of the federal Constitution. But Taney, responding to some comment by McLean, spoke out on the sensitive point, and a reading of the report discloses, I think, more confusion and disagreement than self-restraint. On the Supreme Court and slavery generally, see William M. Wiecek, "Slavery and Abolition Before the United States Supreme Court, 1820–1860," *JAH*, LXV (1978), 34–59. For an example of quantitative misinformation, see John R. Schmidhauser, "Judicial Behavior and the Sectional Crisis of 1837–1860," *Journal of Politics*, XXIII (1961), 615–40, adapted with a co-author, David Gold, in John R. Schmidhauser, ed., *Constitutional Law in the Political Process* (Chi-

cago, 1963), 486–505. Schmidhauser prepared a scalogram of twenty-nine Taney Court decisions that were "deemed regionally divisive." Only five of these cases involved slavery, whereas twenty involved the status of corporations. Schmidhauser assumed that any pro-corporation decision was a pro-northern decision. Furthermore, he did not weight the decisions in any way. *Dred Scott* counted the same as any one of several obscure corporation cases. Schmidhauser also classified the majority decision in *Prigg v. Pennsylvania* as pro-northern, a questionable judgment that gave Daniel his only pro-northern vote on the scalogram. Taney emerges from this scholarly enterprise as a "neutral" on sectional issues, with twelve pro-northern votes—eleven in corporation cases and the twelfth in the case of the *Amistad*, which involved a Spanish vessel illegally engaged in the international slave trade.

CHAPTER 9

1. John A. Bryan, "The Blow Family and Their Slave Dred Scott," *Missouri Historical Society Bulletin*, IV (1948), 223–25; Estate of Peter Blow, Probate Court Records (No. 976), St. Louis.
2. Manuscript Returns for Missouri, Census of the United States for 1830, Population, NA; Peter Blow probate records; John Emerson Letters and Reports, 1833–43, Medical Officers File, RG 94, Old Military Records Division, NA.; Bryan, "Blow Family," 226–28; Vincent C. Hopkins, *Dred Scott's Case* (New York, 1951, 1967), 4–5, 7; Walter Ehrlich, "History of the Dred Scott Case Through the Decision of 1857," Ph.D. dissertation, Washington University, 1950, pp. 5–8. Bryan and Hopkins assert that Dred and Sam were the same man. Ehrlich argues that they were not. The case for Sam may be the stronger of the two, since there is documentary proof that he existed and was sold sometime between September 21, 1832, and February 7, 1834—the dates covered in the accounting of Peter Blow's estate. Furthermore, among the probate papers there is a summons dated August 8, 1833, directing Blow's oldest son and married daughter (Peter E. Blow and Charlotte Blow Charless) to appear before the county court regarding a suit by John Emerson against the executor of the Blow estate. Hopkins suggests that this action may be connected with the story later circulated that Dred tried to run away when he was sold to Emerson. Sam's alleged change of name has not been satisfactorily explained, though Bryan makes an imaginative effort to do so. He speculates that "Dred Scott" may have been a dialectal rendition of "Great Scott," referring to General Winfield Scott. The Peter Blow probate records list five slaves in the estate: Sam (sold for $500), Solomon (who died in 1833), William, Luke, and Hannah. Dred Scott is not mentioned, but he could have been that sixth slave listed in the census and presumably sold by Peter Blow himself shortly before his death. Ehrlich rests his case primarily on the fact that both Dred Scott and Henry T. Blow, under oath in 1846 and 1847, named Peter Blow as the person who sold Dred to Emerson. In addition, Erhlich produces evidence that Emerson paid $28 to Peter Blow on August 9, 1831. Whether or not this transaction had any-

thing to do with the sale of Dred, it does indicate that the two men were acquainted at that early date.

3. St. Louis *Evening News*, April 3, 1857; St. Louis *Globe-Democrat*, Jan. 10, 1886. An interview with Mrs. William T. Blow in 1907 (Dred Scott Collection, MHS) seems to be the principal basis for the belief that Scott was shiftless, but her memory was so confused that the notes taken by Mary Louise Dalton are almost worthless. Scott told the reporter in 1857 that the suits for freedom had given him a "heap of trouble" and that his own expenditures had been about $500 in cash, plus about the same amount in labor.

4. Besides Taylor Blow (1820–69), the following persons lent support to Dred Scott at one time or another: Henry Taylor Blow (1817–75), later a Republican congressman; C. Edmund LaBeaume, brother-in-law of another one of the Blow sons, Peter E. T. Blow (1814–66); Joseph Charless, Jr., husband of Charlotte Blow Charless (1810–1905); and Charles D. Drake, widower of Martha Blow Drake (1812–41). Drake, son of the famous physician Daniel Drake, became a United States senator and the Radical Republican leader in Reconstruction Missouri. Historians often confuse Taylor Blow with his brother Henry Taylor Blow. Taylor was their mother's maiden name, and she used it in naming several of her children.

5. See above, 249. Among the works that follow this interpretation are Avery O. Craven, *The Coming of the Civil War* (New York, 1942), 381–82; Allan Nevins, *The Emergence of Lincoln* (2 vols.; New York, 1950), I, 84; Walker Lewis, *Without Fear or Favor: A Biography of Chief Justice Roger Brooke Taney* (Boston, 1965), 382–83.

6. For example, it was Taylor Blow who signed as security on the $1000 bond for good behavior posted for Scott after his manumission in 1857. See above, 568. By Missouri law, any person emancipating a slave over forty-five years old was "held to support and maintain such slave." *Revised Statutes of the State of Missouri, 1854–55* (2 vols.; Jefferson City, Mo., 1856), II, 1479.

7. J. Hugo Grimm to Charles Van Ravenswaay, Oct. 29, 1946, citing 1867 records of Calvary Cemetery, Dred Scott Collection, MHS.

8. Hopkins, *Dred Scott's Case*, 4; John D. Lawson, ed., *American State Trials* (17 vols.; St. Louis, 1914–36), XIII, 220; Springfield (Mass.) *Republican*, Feb. 12, 1903 (obituary of Emerson's wife).

9. Charles E. Snyder, "John Emerson, Owner of Dred Scott," *Annals of Iowa*, 3rd Series, XXI (1937–39), 441. The records of the University of Pennsylvania, according to Snyder, give that state as Emerson's place of birth, but there is also a tradition that he was born in Ireland. The notation "Ireland" appears on one of the documents in the Emerson file, NA.

10. Major J. B. Brant to War Department, March 7, 1833; Emerson to Surgeon General, Nov. 24, 1837, Emerson file, NA.

11. The recommendations are in Emerson file, NA. Hopkins, *Dred Scott's Case*, 4, suggests that influence was also brought to bear through Emerson's wife, whose family had "army connections," but this is obviously wrong, since Emerson did not marry until 1838.

12. Emerson file, NA.

13. Snyder, "John Emerson," 442–44; Emerson to Surgeon General, July 10, 1838, Emerson file, NA. In this letter, Emerson said that the claim amounted to 640 acres, but according to Snyder it was only 320 acres.

14. Petition of Harriet Scott, April 6, 1846, typescript copy in Dred Scott Collection, MHS; "Auto-Biography of Maj. Lawrence Taliaferro (Written in 1864)," *Minnesota Historical Society Collections*, VI (1894), 235; St. Louis *Evening News*, April 3, 1857. Harriet's statement that she was bought by Emerson is contradicted only in Taliaferro's memoir. Dred Scott is himself apparently the authority for the assertion that he and Harriet had four children. The same newspaper article reports him as saying that an earlier wife had been sold away from him, presumably by Peter Blow.

15. Emerson file, NA; Ehrlich, "Dred Scott Case," 29–31.

16. Emerson file, NA: Ehrlich, "Dred Scott Case," 32–33.

17. Springfield (Mass.) *Republican*, Feb. 12, 1903; George W. Cullum, *Biographical Register of the Officers and Graduates of the U.S. Military Academy*, 3rd ed. (3 vols.; Boston, 1891), I, 273–74.

18. Harriet Scott later stated that she went from Fort Snelling to Fort Jesup after Emerson's marriage. A witness named Catherine Anderson testified in 1847 that she had known the Scotts at Fort Snelling and that they went to the Southwest in 1838, but she mistakenly named Fort Gibson (in Indian Territory) instead of Fort Jesup. Typescript copies of Missouri circuit court (St. Louis) records of *Scott v. Emerson* and *Harriet v. Emerson* (1846–57) in Dred Scott Collection, MHS. The Anderson testimony is published in Lawson, ed., *State Trials*, XIII, 229.

19. Emerson file, NA.

20. It is possible that Harriet and Dred were separated when they left Fort Snelling, she going to Louisiana and he to St. Louis, where he could have been placed in the charge of Mrs. Emerson's father. Or it is possible that Dred was sent to St. Louis sometime after arriving at Fort Jesup. The separation from his wife could have provoked a move toward seeking freedom. Curiously, there is a seven-page typewritten manuscript in the Thomas W. Chamberlin Collection, MHS, entitled "Dred Scott—Life of the Famous Fugitive and Missouri Litigant," and marked "Probably written by William Vincent Byars," which declares that *in 1838* Dred Scott was approached by two "nigger lawyers" (that is, men who handled freedom suits) named Burd and Risk, who persuaded him to sue and pleaded his case unsuccessfully in the circuit court. The designation of Scott as a "fugitive" is just the first of numerous inaccuracies in the piece, however.

21. Alfred Brunson, *A Western Pioneer* (2 vols.; Cincinnati, 1872–79), II, 125. Brunson's account, though written with full knowledge of the Dred Scott case, nevertheless seems credible because it differs from the published material available to him but corroborates details in archival material not available to him. See also the note following.

22. Historians have relied too heavily on the Agreed Statement of Facts, prepared by the opposing attorneys in 1854, for *Dred Scott v. Sandford*. This statement appears several times in the official record of the case and is printed in Lawson, ed., *State Trials*, XIII, 250–51; there is a photostatic copy of the original manu-

script in the Dred Scott Collection, MHS. Intended to get the legal facts straight, it contains a number of historical inaccuracies. Two sentences read as follows: "Eliza is about fourteen years old, and was born on board the steamboat Gipsey, north of the north line of the State of Missouri, and upon the river Mississippi. . . . In the year 1838, said Dr. Emerson removed the plaintiff and said Harriet and their said daughter Eliza from said Fort Snelling to the State of Missouri, where they have ever since resided." The contradiction here is obvious. Eliza was "removed" from Fort Snelling in 1838, having been born, presumably, on some previous steamboat trip, and yet is said to be only fourteen years old in 1854. In fact, Emerson left Fort Snelling in 1837, while the Scotts remained there about six months and departed in the spring of 1838. That Emerson returned to Fort Snelling in the autumn of 1838 and stayed there until 1840, is certain. That the Scotts returned with him is almost certain. In addition to Brunson's account of the trip, the petition filed by Harriet in 1846 declared that from Fort Jesup she was taken back to Fort Snelling. Dred stated at the same time that he had been with Emerson at Fort Snelling for about five years (that is, from early 1836 to 1840, with the sojourn at Fort Jesup omitted from his calculation). As for Eliza's birth, it occurred on one of three steamboat trips: downstream in the spring of 1838, upstream in the autumn of 1838, or downstream in 1840. The earliest of these three dates, confusedly implied in the Agreed Statement of Facts, is accepted by most historians, including Hopkins, *Dred Scott's Case*, 5–6. But the fact that Eliza was given Mrs. Emerson's first name suggests that she was born sometime after the Scotts first met their mistress—that is, on the second or third steamboat trip. Ehrlich, "Dred Scott Case," 38–39, declares that the child was born on the down-river trip to St. Louis in 1840, which would accord with the statement that she was fourteen years old in 1854. But after further study, Ehrlich came to a different conclusion. Independent examination of the evidence has led both of us to the conviction that Eliza was born on the trip from St. Louis to Fort Snelling in the autumn of 1838. Besides the recollection of Brunson, Thomas Gray, longtime captain of the *Gypsy* (often spelled "Gypsey"), later recalled that on one occasion he "carried to Fort Snelling that famous negro Dred Scott." St. Louis *Republican*, July 29, 1883. Thus the two pieces of collateral testimony actually placing Dred on the *Gypsy* both specify an *upstream* trip. In addition, the Missouri *Republican (St. Louis), Sept. 24, 25, 1838, announced the imminent departure of the Gypsy* for Galena, Dubuque, and St. Peter's (an early name for the Minnesota River). As stated in the text, it was on September 24 that Emerson wrote to the Surgeon General, indicating *his* imminent departure for Fort Snelling. But the historian doggedly determined to cull the inconsequential truth from the slender evidence can only throw up his hands at reading the following statement ghostwritten for Dred Scott in 1854: "Our oldest daughter, Eliza, was born while we were living in Wisconsin." See Lawson, ed. *State Trials*, XIII, 244. Lawson, p. 250, also provides a snippet of evidence that Eliza was actually sixteen years old in 1854.

23.   Emerson file, NA; W. H. C. Folsom, *Fifty Years in the Northwest* (St. Paul, 1888), 754–56.
24.   Emerson file, NA.

25. *Ibid.;* Snyder, "John Emerson," 452–55. Emerson complained of "syphiloid rheumatism" in December 1837, more than four years after his infection.
26. Estate of John Emerson, file no. 1914, Probate Court, St. Louis. This file includes an ancillary will, the original being in the Scott County Court House at Davenport, Iowa. Snyder, "John Emerson," 455–56, gives the entire text.
27. The provision concerning Henrietta's education and support probably constituted a special or precatory trust. Yet the restriction, it should be noted, was not on Mrs. Emerson's power to dispose of the property, but rather on the use to which the proceeds were put. For further discussion, see above, 272–73.
28. James W. Bollinger of Davenport to Mary Louise Dalton, Feb. 16, 1907, Dred Scott Collection, MHS.
29. Emerson probate file, St. Louis; Synder, "John Emerson," 455–56; Walter Ehrlich, "Was the Dred Scott Case Valid?" *JAH*, LV (1968), 260.
30. Cullum, *Biographical Register*, I, 273–74; Springfield (Mass.) *Republican*, Feb. 12, 1903; St. Louis *Evening News*, April 3, 1857; petitions of Dred and Harriet Scott, April 6, 1846, typescript copies in Dred Scott Collection, MHS. Evidence concerning the whereabouts of the Scotts from 1843 to 1846 is slight, recollective, and partly contradictory. Harriet's petition did not mention service with Bainbridge. Dred's petition stated that he was left in Bainbridge's charge when Emerson went to Florida (in 1840), but this seems inaccurate because Bainbridge was himself in Florida from 1840 to 1843. According to information provided at the time of Irene Emerson's death and probably originating with her, the Scotts were both taken by Bainbridge after Emerson's death, kept with him at army posts for four years, and then sent back to St. Louis. Dred himself apparently told a newspaper reporter in 1857 that he was with Bainbridge at Corpus Christi when the Mexican War began. Adeline Russell, testifying at the second circuit court trial in 1850, declared: "At the time I hired these negroes they were in the service of Col. Bainbridge." Lawson, *State Trials*, XIII, 234.

CHAPTER 10

1. St. Louis *Evening News*, April 3, 1857; Vincent C. Hopkins, *Dred Scott's Case* (New York, 1951, 1967), 20, n. 8. It seems unlikely that Emerson's will, because it specifically mentioned only his land and tenements, could have been interpreted to mean that his wife, while empowered to sell any or all of his real estate, was powerless to dispose of his other property. Indeed, the only chattels listed in the Missouri inventory of his estate (some pieces of furniture) had been sold in 1844. Nevertheless, Missouri, like other slaveholding states, did place certain restrictions on the disposal of slaves during probate, and Mrs. Emerson could have believed or been informed that it would be illegal to accept Dred's proposal. See Harrison Anthony Trexler, *Slavery in Missouri, 1804–1865* (Baltimore, 1914), 28–29, 60–62.
2. The Permanent Record Books of the Missouri circuit court in St. Louis contain summaries of the proceedings. Typescript copies of the surviving documents are

in the Dred Scott Collection, MHS. Some of the documents are printed in John D. Lawson, ed., *American State Trials* (17 vols.; St. Louis, 1914–36), XIII, 223–41. Harriet filed a separate suit, perhaps because her attorneys were taking into account a technical rule against joint actions in trespass. In *Violet and William v. Stephens*, 1 Littell Selected Cases 147, 148 (Ky., 1812), the court declared: "The rule is well established, that for an injury done two, where the wrong done one is no wrong to the other, they cannot join in an action, as in cases of trespass, assault and battery, etc." For a discussion of the technicality, see Duncan J. MacLeod, *Slavery, Race and the American Revolution* (Cambridge, England, 1974), 11–12.

3. *Laws of . . . the District of Louisiana, of the Territory of Louisiana, of the Territory of Missouri, and of the State of Missouri, up to the Year 1824* (2 vols.; Jefferson City, Mo., 1842), I, 96–97; *Laws of the State of Missouri, Revised and Digested* (2 vols.; St. Louis, 1825), I, 404–6; *Revised Statutes of the State of Missouri* (St. Louis, 1835), 284–86; Trexler, *Slavery in Missouri*, 59–60, 211–12.

4. *Revised Statutes of the State of Missouri* (St. Louis, 1845), 531–34. The petition was for the petitioner's benefit, said the court in *Tramell v. Adam*, 2 Missouri 155–57 (1829).

5. *Revised Statutes of Missouri* (1845), 531–34. Recovery of damages was authorized in the revision of 1824, but by 1835 it had been forbidden.

6. *Ibid.:* "The action . . . shall be instituted in the name of the petitioner, against the person holding him in slavery, or claiming him as a slave." See above, 273–74.

7. For a discussion of this problem, see Hopkins, *Dred Scott's Case*, 181–82; Walter Ehrlich, "The Origins of the Dred Scott Case," *JNH*, LIX (1974), 132–42. Hopkins finds "no evidence of a political cast," but more or less accepts the view that there was a "financial angle to the case." Ehrlich, p. 135, declares: "It can now be asserted with finality that the Dred Scott case originated not for mercenary or political reasons, but rather for the humanitarian purpose of obtaining freedom for the slaves involved, and absolutely nothing more."

8. Frederick Trevor Hill, *Decisive Battles of the Law* (New York, 1907), 117–18. Hill's source was probably the unsigned manuscript in the Thomas H. Chamberlin Collection, MHS, cited in note 20 for the preceding chapter. A similar story apparently originated with Mrs. Emerson. See Springfield (Mass.) *Republican*, Feb. 12, 1903.

9. *Tramell v. Adam*, 2 Missouri 155 (1829); *Paup v. Mingo*, 4 Leigh 163 (Va., 1833); *Ralph Gordon v. R. Duncan*, 3 Missouri 385 (1834); *Aleck v. Tevis*, 4 Dana 242 (Ky., 1836); *Hudgens v. Spencer*, 4 Dana 589 (Ky., 1836); *Henry v. Bollar*, 7 Leigh 19 (Va., 1836); *Thomas v. Beckman*, 1 Ben Monroe 29 (Ky., 1840); *Peter v. Hargrave*, 5 Grattan 12 (Va., 1848); *Dowrey v. Logan*, 12 Ben Monroe 236 (Ky., 1851); *Warfield v. Davis*, 14 Ben Monroe 33 (Ky., 1853). Some of these cases were decided after 1846, but they show the relative consistency of judicial interpretation. Compensation was often but not always awarded for service during the pendency of a suit. Compensation for earlier service might be required where a free person had been knowingly held in slavery, but

even then a statute of limitations might prevent full recovery, and the presumption was usually in favor of the alleged owner. In the *Hudgens* case, the court declared: "The question as to his right to freedom was sufficiently doubtful to authorize the presumption that he had been held in slavery in good faith; and that, therefore . . . he is not entitled to a decree for compensation for his services whilst he was detained . . . but that he is entitled to the amount due for his hire . . . during the pendency of this suit" (pp. 594–95).

10. In filing their petitions, the Scotts were represented by Francis B. Murdoch. Charles D. Drake and James R. Lackland took depositions in their behalf. Alexander P. Field, David N. Hall, and Samuel Mansfield Bay appeared for them in court when the trial stage was reached. Ehrlich, "Origins," 141, credits Murdoch with being the "originator of the Dred Scott case."

11. *Rachel v. Walker*, 4 Missouri 350, 352, 354. The other pertinent cases, all summarized in Helen Tunnicliff Catterall, *Judicial Cases concerning American Slavery and the Negro* (5 vols.; Washington, D.C., 1926–37), V, are: *Winny v. Whitesides*, 1 Missouri 472 (1824); *Merry v. Tiffin and Menard*, 1 Missouri 725 (1827); *La Grange v. Chouteau*, 2 Missouri 20 (1828); *Tramell v. Adam*, 2 Missouri 155 (1829); *Milly v. Smith*, 2 Missouri 171 (1829); *Vincent v. Duncan*, 2 Missouri 214 (1830); *Ralph v. Duncan*, 3 Missouri, 194 (1833); *Julia v. McKinney*, 3 Missouri 270 (1833); *Nancy v. Trammel*, 3 Missouri 306 (1834); *Nat v. Ruddle*, 3 Missouri 400 (1834); *Hay v. Dunky*, 3 Missouri 588 (1834); *Wilson v. Melvin*, 4 Missouri 592 (1837); *Randolph v. Alsey*, 8 Missouri 656 (1844).

12. Lawson, ed., *State Trials*, XIII, 224; Walter Ehrlich, "History of the Dred Scott Case Through the Decision of 1857," Ph.D. dissertation, Washington University, 1950, pp. 70–71.

13. Permanent Records, Missouri circuit court, St. Louis, Volume 18; Typescript copies of proceedings in Dred Scott Collection, MHS. The Russell and Blow testimony, as summarized in the court records, is printed in Lawson, ed., *State Trials*, XIII, 228. Blow's testimony does indicate that the family was already interested in Dred's case, and it also throw's doubt on the idea that Dred was "Sam."

14. Typescript copy of proceedings in Dred Scott Collection, MHS. Court records give two different dates for dismissal of the suits against Sanford, Russell, and Emerson: December 11, 1847, and February 29, 1848. Probably because of this uncertainty, Mrs. Emerson's first bill of exceptions was withdrawn in December. A second one was filed on March 4, 1848.

15. Frank E. Stevens, "Alexander Pope Field," *Journal of the Illinois State Historical Society*, IV (1911), 7–37. Field, on his mother's side, was a member of the well-known Pope family, being a nephew of the Illinois political leader, Nathaniel Pope, and a first cousin of the Civil War general, John Pope. He moved to New Orleans in the 1850s and became attorney general of Louisiana after the war.

16. *Emmerson v. Harriet (of color)*; *Emmerson v. Dred Scott (of color)*, 11 Missouri 413 (1848); Ehrlich, "Dred Scott Case," 85–87. Judge Scott cited one of his own earlier opinions wherein the technical problem was thoroughly examined: *Helm v. Bassett*, 9 Missouri 52 (1845).

17. Walker Lewis, *Without Fear or Favor: A Biography of Roger Brooke Taney* (Boston, 1965), 383.

18. The Agreed Statement of Facts drawn up in 1854 declared: "Lizzie is about seven years old, and was born . . . at the military post called Jefferson Barracks." But the Scotts were presumably not at Jefferson Barracks after March 1846 and were most probably there with Bainbridge in 1843 and 1844.

19. Deposition of Adeline Russell at second trial, Jan. 12, 1850, typescript copy, Dred Scott Collection, MHS.

20. Permanent Records, Missouri circuit court, St. Louis, Volume 18; typescript copy of proceedings in Dred Scott Collection, MHS; Ehrlich, "Dred Scott Case," 85. Hopkins, *Dred Scott's Case*, 14, says that the Scotts were hired to C. Edmund La Beaume, brother-in-law of Peter E. Blow, but according to the court record, this did not occur until 1851.

21. Ehrlich, "Dred Scott Case," 101–2, suggests that Mrs. Emerson moved to Massachusetts at some time after March 28, 1849, when she appeared in person before the recorder of deeds in St. Louis to sell some of her husband's land. This, however, does not take into account the possibility that she transacted the business on a return visit to St. Louis. According to the article published at the time of her death in the Springfield (Mass.) *Republican*, Feb. 12, 1903, she lived five years in St. Louis after the death of her husband in 1843. She married Calvin C. Chaffee in 1850. Barnes was a West Pointer who had resigned from the Army in 1836 to enter the more lucrative field of railroad construction. During the Civil War, he rose to the rank of major-general of volunteers. George W. Cullum, *Biographical Register of the Officers and Graduates of the U.S. Military Academy*, 3rd ed. (3 vols.; Boston, 1891), I, 423–24.

22. *Appleton's Encyclopedia of American Biography*, II, 605; Hopkins, *Dred Scott's Case*, 12–13.

23. Typescript copies of court proceedings, Dred Scott Collection, MHS; Ehrlich, "Dred Scott Case," 89–90.

24. Typescript copy of court proceedings, Dred Scott Collection, MHS. From the set of instructions accepted by Judge Hamilton, it appears that Mrs. Emerson's counsel also argued that she was acting as agent for her daughter.

25. *Ibid.*; also, Permanent Records, Missouri circuit court, St. Louis, Volume 19. The cases were not identical, of course, because Harriet had not been in Illinois for two years, as Dred had.

26. William Nisbet Chambers, *Old Bullion Benton, Senator from the New West: Thomas Hart Benton, 1782–1858* (Boston, 1956), 341–42, 344–52, 368–70.

27. Trexler, *Slavery in Missouri*, 152–53.

28. The suit did not come to trial until 1855, when Birch was awarded $5000 in damages; but the case was still in litigation when Benton died in 1858. Chambers, *Old Bullion Benton*, 346–47; Elbert B. Smith, *Magnificent Missourian: The Life of Thomas Hart Benton* (Philadelphia, 1958), 251.

29. Ms. Diary of Edward Bates, Oct. 26, 1850, MHS.

30. Ms. Diary of William B. Napton, p. 223, MHS. Napton was waiting for Haggard's *Reports* of British Admiralty cases, no doubt intending to cite Lord Stowell's opinion in the case of *The Slave Grace*.

31. Chambers, *Old Bullion Benton*, 374–75; John Vollmer Mering, *The Whig Party in Missouri* (Columbia, Mo., 1967), 173–76; Wilbert Henry Rosin, "Hamilton Rowan Gamble, Missouri's Civil War Governor," Ph.D. dissertation, University of Missouri, 1960, pp. 93–94.

32. *Strader v. Graham*, 10 Howard 82, 94. See above, 268–69.

33. *Graham v. Strader*, 5 Ben Monroe 173 (Ky. 1844); *Strader v. Graham*, 7 Ben Monroe 633 (Ky., 1847).

34. In a brief and overlooked concurring opinion, Justice John McLean noted that the question of jurisdiction, governed by the inoperative condition of the Northwest Ordinance in Ohio, was the only matter before the Court. Taney's other remarks about the Ordinance, he said, were "extrajudicial." *Strader v. Graham*, 10 Howard, 82, 97.

35. The two judges responsible for most of the opinions were Mathias McGirk and George Tompkins. Lyman D. Norris, attorney for Mrs. Emerson, called Tompkins "the great apostle of freedom."

36. *Charlotte v. Chouteau*, 11 Missouri 193, 200–201.

37. Ehrlich, "Dred Scott Case," 116; Rosin, "Gamble," 93–94.

38. Ehrlich, "Dred Scott Case," 119–24, 389–99. *Scott v. Emerson*, 15 Missouri 576, 577–81 (1852), contains most of the Norris brief. Ehrlich, in an appendix, reproduces the complete text of the manuscript version.

39. *Scott v. Emerson*, 15 Missouri 576, 582–87.

40. *Ibid.*, 587–92.

41. In fact, it seems quite clear that Judge Scott was waving aside the distinction between sojourning and domicile: "On almost three sides the State of Missouri is surrounded by free soil. If one of our slaves touch that soil, with his master's assent, he becomes entitled to his freedom. . . . If a master sends his slave to hunt his horses or cattle beyond the boundary, shall he thereby be liberated? But our courts, it is said, will not go so far. If not go the entire length, why go at all? The obligation to enforce to the proper degree, is as obligatory as to enforce any degree. Slavery is introduced by a continuance in the territory for six hours as well as for twelve months, and so far as our laws are concerned, the offense is as great in the one case as the other." *Ibid.*, 584–85.

CHAPTER 11

1. Permanent Record Books, Missouri circuit court, St. Louis, Volumes 22, 24. There were further continuances until March 18, 1857, when the court finally returned a verdict for Mrs. Emerson. *Ibid.*, Volume 26.

2. John D. Lawson, ed., *American State Trials* (17 vols.; St. Louis, 1914–36), XIII, 227. The date of Field's removal to Louisiana is unknown, but the St. Louis directory for 1850 was the last one to carry his name. According to William H. Herndon, at some time in the late 1850s he and Abraham Lincoln raised money by subscription for the release of a free Negro being held in jail in Louisiana and sent it to "Col. A. P. Field, a friend of ours in New Orleans, who applied it as directed, and it restored the prisoner to his overjoyed mother." Paul M. Angle, ed., *Herndon's Life of Lincoln* (Cleveland, 1949), 308–9.

3. *DSvS*, 453.
4. The section (*U.S. Statutes at Large*, I, 85–86) specified three circumstances in which an appeal could be taken from the highest court of a state to the Supreme Court of the United States. The third of these was "where is drawn in question the construction of any clause of the constitution, or of a treaty, or statute of, or commission held under the United States, and the decision is against the title, right, privilege, or exemption specially set up or claimed by either party, under such clause of the said constitution, treaty, statute or commission."
5. Citizenship was obviously not at issue in an alleged slave's suit for freedom in a state court. The question arose only when Scott brought suit against Sanford in a federal court under the diverse-citizenship clause of the Constitution. The question of the constitutionality of the Missouri Compromise restriction had not been argued by counsel or examined by the judges in the state Court. It could not have been introduced into a decision by the federal Supreme Court without violating the Judiciary Act of 1789, which declared: "But no error shall be assigned or regarded as a ground of reversal . . . than such as appears on the face of the record."
6. Typescript copies of Missouri circuit court proceedings in Dred Scott Collection, MHS.
7. Roswell M. Field to Montgomery Blair, Dec. 24, 1854, copy in Dred Scott Collection, MHS. The copies of several letters from Field to Blair were presented to the Missouri Historical Society by Frederick Trevor Hill, who had the originals from a member of the Blair family. In another account offered many years later by a lawyer named Arba N. Crane (who had been associated with Field for a time) he, Crane, had first brought Dred Scott to Field's attention and had done most of the actual work on the case. See John W. Burgess, *The Middle Period, 1817–1858* (New York, 1897), 450–51; John F. Lee to Mary Louise Dalton, Feb. 15, 1907, Dred Scott Collection. But Crane, having been born in 1834, was only nineteen years old in 1853 and still a student in Vermont. He graduated from the Harvard Law School in 1856 and moved to St. Louis that same year (T. K. Skinker, "Memorial to Arba Nelson Crane," Dred Scott Collection). Crane's story has been accepted by a number of historians, including Vincent C. Hopkins, *Dred Scott's Case* (New York, 1951, 1967), 24–26, 30, n. 10. Hopkins even says that Crane "appeared for the Scotts" along with Field in the federal circuit court trial in 1854, then in a footnote he states correctly that Crane "did not arrive in St. Louis till 1856." It appears that Crane may have played some part in the proceedings by which the Scotts were manumitted in 1857. Otherwise, simple chronology explodes his claims, made, apparently, in bibulous old age.
8. Washington *Union*, Dec. 17, 1856; *National Intelligencer* (Washington), Dec. 24, 1856.
9. Charles Warren, *The Supreme Court in United States History*, rev. ed. (2 vols.; Boston, 1932), II, 281; Albert J. Beveridge, *Abraham Lincoln, 1809–1858* (2 vols.; Boston, 1928), II, 456; Avery O. Craven, *The Coming of the Civil War* (New York, 1942), 382; Elbert B. Smith, *The Death of Slavery* (Chicago, 1967), 145.

10. Hopkins, *Dred Scott's Case*, 23–24, 29–30, notes 7 and 8. Acceptance of the Hopkins explanation is perhaps best illustrated by its inclusion in J. G. Randall and David Donald, *The Civil War and Reconstruction*, 2nd ed. (Boston 1961), 109.

11. Stanley I. Kutler, ed., *The Dred Scott Decision, Law or Politics?* (Boston, 1967), xi.

12. Defendant's plea and Agreed Statement of Facts, both filed May 4, 1854, in the U.S. circuit court, St. Louis, photostatic copies in Dred Scott Collection, MHS. These and other principal documents are printed in Lawson, ed., *State Trials*, XIII, 246–51; also in *U.S. Supreme Court Reports*, 15 Lawyers Ed. 692–98. Sanford was also identified as Scott's owner in the preface to the July 4 pamphlet (see Lawson, 244), where Dred was made to say that about 18 months earlier, he had been "traded off to the defendant."

13. Walter Ehrlich, "Was the Dred Scott Case Valid?" *JAH*, LV (1968), 263, maintains that such a transfer "could not have happened" because Sanford was confined in an insane asylum during the entire period from March 6, 1857, until his death on May 5 that same year. This assumes that Sanford would have had to continue as owner until the Supreme Court delivered its decision. However, the suit was an action of trespass for offenses allegedly committed on January 1, 1853, and the grounds for the suit (and for appealing the adverse verdict) presumably would have continued to exist if Sanford had sold Scott sometime before March 6, 1857.

14. In "Was the Dred Scott Case Valid?" 262–63, Ehrlich points out that the Agreed Statement of Facts includes the egregious misstatement that it was John Emerson who sold Scott and his family to Sanford (Emerson, of course, had been dead since 1843). This may have been just a slip of the pen, or an effort to keep the facts simple, or a fiction employed to keep Mrs. Chaffee's name off the record. It adds to our doubt about Sanford's acknowledgment of ownership, but it proves nothing.

15. See note 10 above.

16. Hopkins's answer to this question is unsatisfactory. He says that after Sanford's death in 1857, Chaffee became his "logical successor" in administering the Emerson estate, but there is no explanation of how this was legally possible under those supposedly restrictive Missouri laws. It should be added, however, that when the Chaffees transferred ownership of Dred and his family to Taylor Blow in 1857 for purposes of manumission, they did so by quitclaim, thus leaving room for doubt about the true legal ownership of the Scotts even at that late date.

17. This is the explanation offered by Ehrlich, "Was the Dred Scott Case Valid?" 260–61.

18. In "Was the Dred Scott Case Valid?" 264, Ehrlich takes the contrary view that if Sanford's true relationship to the Scotts had been known, "perhaps history would never have heard of this case."

19. See above, 251, 254. The short-lived suits against Alexander Sanford, Samuel Russell, and Irene Emerson had been aimed at the three persons directly involved in holding the Scotts as slaves, although only one of them was the owner.

20. Historians who declare that Mrs. Chaffee transferred the Scotts to Sanford by a "fictitious sale" in order to set up a federal suit under the diverse-citizenship rule have apparently forgotten that she too was by 1853 a citizen of a state other than Missouri. However, a federal suit against her would have been virtually an attempt to carry an appeal from the highest court of a state to a lower federal court, and the latter might very well have decided that it was improper to accept jurisdiction. In addition, it was easier to construct the necessary charge of assault and false imprisonment against Sanford, since he frequently visited St. Louis. The old charge against Mrs. Chaffee could not be renewed because the statute of limitations for such actions was two years.

21. See above, 420–21. Chaffee, in a letter to the Springfield (Mass.) *Republican*, printed March 16, 1857, denied having any part in the suit or any knowledge of it until after it was "noticed for trial."

22. See, for example, *Morning Courier and New York Enquirer*, Dec. 18, 1856; *National Era* (Washington), March 19, 1857. The suspicion was not soon dispelled. In 1860, the Kentucky antislavery leader Cassius M. Clay declared that the Dred Scott decision was "gotten up entirely by the Democratic party." New York *Tribune*, Jan. 21, 1860.

23. Slason Thompson, *Eugene Field* (2 vols.; New York, 1901), I, 1–48, contains biographical information on Roswell M. Field, but his treatment of the Dred Scott case is confused. He credits Roswell Field with all the work done by Alexander P. Field.

24. *Morning Courier and New York Enquirer*, March 16, 1857; Walter Ehrlich, "History of the Dred Scott Case Through the Decision of 1857," Ph.D. dissertation, Washington University, 1950, p. 151.

25. The suit was brought under common rather than statute law, however; for Scott did not file the petition for leave to sue in accordance with the Missouri statute. Roswell M. Field to Montgomery Blair, March 12, 1856, typescript copy in Dred Scott Collection, MHS. This time, it should be noted, one suit was filed for Dred, Harriet, and the children, despite the possible technical barrier mentioned in note 2 of the preceding chapter. The point was apparently never raised in the trial.

26. Manuscript records and documents of the trial in the U.S. circuit court are in the office of the Clerk, United States District Court for Eastern Missouri, St. Louis. Suits under the diverse-citizenship clause at that time originated in the circuit court.

27. This was the complaint of a grand jury as quoted in the *Tri-Weekly Missouri Democrat*, April 21, 1854, clipping in Dred Scott Collection, MHS.

28. W. V. N. Bay, *Reminiscences of the Bench and Bar of Missouri* (St. Louis, 1878), 538–44; Roy T. King, "Robert William Wells, Jurist, Public Servant, and Designer of the Missouri State Seal," *Missouri Historical Review*, XXX (1936), 107–31. Wells was the federal district judge, sitting alone on the circuit court for this term because Justice James M. Wayne, with the Supreme Court holding an unusually long session, was unavailable for circuit duty.

29. Ms. U.S. circuit court records as cited in note 26 above.

30. By Article Three, Section Two, federal judicial power was also extended to con-

troversies "between a state, or the citizens thereof, and foreign states, citizens or subjects."

31. Wells to Montgomery Blair, Feb. 12, 1856, typescript copy, Dred Scott Collection, MHS. In a speech to a local Republican meeting in 1858, William H. Herndon pointed out that by virtue of the Dred Scott decision, a Negro in one state could not be sued in federal court by a citizen of another state for debt or breach of contract. This amounted to "a most glaring wrong and outrage upon the white man, by leaving him without remedy . . . in the United States Courts and by making the negro wholly irresponsible for his contracts." *Illinois State Journal* (Springfield), July 27, 1858.

32. *DSvS*, 453–54. Taney mistakenly asserted, however, that the action in the Missouri courts had been brought against the "same party"—that is, Sanford. The final paragraph of the Agreed Statement of Facts summarized *Scott v. Emerson* without mentioning Mrs. Emerson's name. Examination of the original manuscript in the Clerk's office (see note 26 above) reveals that whereas the main body of the statement was written by Field or his clerk (being in the same handwriting as Scott's replication), the addendum appears on an undated separate sheet in the handwriting of Sanford's attorney (or clerk), Hugh A. Garland. The Scott forces, of course, had no reason to want the *Emerson* case included in the record.

33. Field to Montgomery Blair, Jan. 7, 1855, typescript copy, Dred Scott Collection, MHS.

34. Ms. U.S. circuit court records as cited in note 26 above.

35. See note 32 above and Lawson, ed., *State Trials*, XIII, 250–51. The Agreed Statement, Sanford's pleas in bar, and Scott's replication were all filed on May 4, 1854.

36. Ms. U.S. circuit court records as cited in note 26 above; Lawson, ed., *State Trials*, XIII, 252.

37. Wells to Montgomery Blair, Feb. 12, 1856, typescript copy in Dred Scott Collection, MHS.

38. *DSvS*, 454. The Taney decision reversed the judgment for Sanford and ordered that the circuit court dismiss the suit for want of jurisdiction.

39. Ms. U.S. circuit court records as cited in note 26 above.

40. St. Louis *Morning Herald*, May 18, 1854, typescript copy of article headed, "Interesting Law Case—A Question of Slavery," in Dred Scott Collection, MHS.

41. Lawson, ed., *State Trials*, XIII, 243–45.

42. Field to Blair, Dec. 24, 1854; Jan. 7, 1855, typescript copies, Dred Scott Collection, MHS. According to William Ernest Smith, *The Francis Preston Blair Family in Politics* (2 vols.; New York, 1933), I, 385, Field had first written to Blair in May 1854, but the letter went unanswered because Blair was in California settling the estate of his brother James.

43. Bailey to Lyman Trumbull, May 12, 1857, Lyman Trumbull Papers, MDLC.

44. Smith, *Blair Family*, I, 96–97, 210–15, 380–82, 385–86; *National Intelligencer*, Dec. 24, 1856 (letter from Blair). According to the manuscript census returns for Missouri, Blair owned four slaves in 1840.

45. National *Intelligencer*, Dec. 24, 1856.

46. Case 3230, Docket G, p. 3388 (1854), ms. records, U.S. Supreme Court Library.

CHAPTER 12

1. David M. Potter, *The Impending Crisis, 1848–1861,* completed and edited by Don E. Fehrenbacher (New York, 1976), 199–208; Allan Nevins, *Ordeal of the Union* (2 vols.; New York, 1947), II, 416–19; Samuel A. Johnson, *The Battle Cry of Freedom: the New England Emigrant Aid Company in the Kansas Crusade* (Lawrence, Kans., 1954), 134–48; James D. Richardson, ed., *Messages and Papers of the Presidents* (11 vols.; Washington, D.C., 1913), IV, 2885–93; Richard H. Sewell, *Ballots for Freedom: Antislavery Politics in the United States, 1837–1860* (New York, 1976), 277–79; William Ernest Smith, *The Francis Preston Blair Family in Politics* (2 vols.; New York, 1933), I, 324–31.

2. Walter Ehrlich, "History of the Dred Scott Case Through the Decision of 1857," Ph.D. dissertation, Washington University, 1950, pp. 193–94. The antislavery *National Era* (Washington) called attention to the case in February 1856, but as late as December 25, 1856, it reported that Dred Scott claimed to have been born free while his mother was being held as a slave in federal territory north of 36° 30'.

3. A copy of the brief is in the Francis Preston Blair Family Papers, MDLC.

4. Field to Blair, Jan. 7, 1856, typescript copy in Dred Scott Collection, MHS.

5. Blair was no advocate of racial equality. He strongly favored colonization and as a member of Lincoln's cabinet developed negrophobic tendencies after the issuance of the Emancipation Proclamation. See especially the report of his racist speech at Rockville, Md., in the New York *Herald* and other major newspapers, Oct. 6, 1863.

6. This summary of the Blair brief differs sharply from the summary of Blair's February 1856 argument in Vincent C. Hopkins, *Dred Scott's Case* (New York, 1951), 33–39. The reason is that Hopkins somehow confused Blair's reargument in December 1856 with the brief of his first argument in February.

7. Hopkins, *Dred Scott's Case,* 46, note 24, says that Geyer appeared alone for Sanford at this hearing. He cites a statement to that effect in the Washington *Union,* March 19, 1857 (more than a year later). However, the Minutes of the Supreme Court, Vol. Q, p. 8271, in the Supreme Court Library, show plainly that Johnson participated in the argument.

8. Washington *Evening Star,* Feb. 12, 13, 14, 15, 1856; Washington *Union,* Feb. 14, 1856; New York *Tribune,* Feb. 20, 1856; Ehrlich, "Dred Scott Case," 197–200; Johnson to B. H. Richardson and others, March 6, 1858, published in Washington *Union,* March 18, 1858. Johnson declared that he and Geyer served without compensation.

9. New York *Tribune,* Feb. 26, 29; April 9, 11, 12, 1856. Official records of the Court do not indicate the times of the conferences, but the *Tribune* correspondent probably had accurate information on the subject from Justice McLean. See note 13 below.

10. *National Era*, Feb. 21, 1856; New York *Tribune* Feb., 15, 1856.

11. Jeter Allen Isely, *Horace Greeley and the Republican Party, 1853–1861* (Princeton, 1947), 226.

12. Francis P. Weisenburger, *The Life of John McLean* (Columbus, Ohio, 1937), 106–7. Isely, *Horace Greeley,* 226n, identified Harvey as "Index." Before he did so, historians generally attributed the correspondence to James S. Pike.

13. Justice Catron, writing to President-elect James Buchanan a year later, said of the Dred Scott case: "It was before the judges in conference on two several occasions about a year ago, when the judges expressed their views pretty much at large. All our opinions were published in the New York Tribune the next day after the opinions were expressed. This was of course a gross breach of confidence, as the information could only come from a judge who was present. This circumstance, I think, has made the Chief more wary than usual." The original of this letter, dated February 6, 1857, is in the James Buchanan Papers, Historical Society of Pennsylvania; it is published in Philip Auchampaugh, "James Buchanan, the Court and the Dred Scott Case," *Tennessee Historical Magazine,* IX (1926), 234.

14. New York *Tribune*, Feb. 18, 20, 29; April 9, 12, 1856.

15. Benjamin R. Curtis, ed., *A Memoir of Benjamin Robbins Curtis, LL.D.* (2 vols.; Boston, 1879), I, 180.

16. Samuel Tyler, *Memoir of Roger Brooke Taney, LL.D.*, 2nd ed. (Baltimore, 1876), 382–85, containing a letter to Tyler from Justice John A. Campbell, Nov. 24, 1870, with a confirmatory letter from Nelson, May 13, 1871. Campbell wrote two other accounts of *Dred Scott* decision-making, both more or less consistent with this one: in a eulogy of Benjamin R. Curtis delivered before the bar of the Supreme Court in 1874, 20 Wallace x–xi; and in a letter to George T. Curtis, Oct. 30, 1879, Campbell-Colton Papers, University of North Carolina.

17. Supreme Court Minutes, May 12, 1856, Vol. Q, pp. 8413–14, Supreme Court Library.

18. New York *Tribune*, May 13, 15, 1856.

19. Tyler, *Memoir of Taney,* 383, containing this sentence written by Campbell in 1870: "Justice Nelson hesitated, and proposed a re-argument of that and other questions to be had at the next term, and this was assented to, none objecting."

20. *CWAL*, II, 465.

21. Roy Franklin Nichols, *The Disruption of American Democracy* (New York, 1948), 44.

22. Richardson, *Messages and Papers,* IV, 2930–33.

23. *Ibid.,* 2934. Pierce's attorney general, Caleb Cushing had earlier stated in an official opinion that the Missouri Compromise restriction was unconstitutional, apparently because it forbade slavery "forever" in the region and thus invaded the equality of future states. See *Official Opinions of the Attorneys General of the United States,* VII, 574–76.

24. By using the phrase "future state" instead of "territory," Pierce stopped short of categorically denying the power of Congress to forbid slavery during the territo-

rial period, and to this extent he fell in with the strategy of evasion already adopted by Stephen A. Douglas. But his meaning was abundantly clear. The Kansas-Nebraska Act, after all, had been a measure for the organization of new territories, not for the admission of new states. Furthermore, in one paragraph of his message Pierce plainly suggested that the 36° 30' restriction, as applied to the territorial stage, had been a violation of the treaty with France for the purchase of Louisiana. "While it remains in a Territorial condition," he declared after quoting from the treaty, "its inhabitants are maintained and protected in the free enjoyment of their liberty and property." Thus he anticipated the principal theme of Justice Catron's concurring opinion in the Dred Scott case. See above, 402.

25. *CG*, 34–3, pp. 10–11, 15–16, 71–74, 85–87, and *passim;* New York *Tribune,* Dec. 16, 1856.

26. *Ibid.;* Baltimore *Sun,* Dec. 10, and New York *Journal of Commerce,* Dec. 18, 19, 1856, for reports of slave insurrections. A Washington correspondent of the New York *Courier and Enquirer* declared, Jan. 28, 1857: "The gay season is less brilliant than was expected. The prevailing characteristic of our society, as of our politics, appears to be a sullen reserve. Recent political events have left feelings of personal bitterness, wholly unprecedented, producing social isolation in place of the genial amenities of private life. The last levee of the President was almost unattended."

27. Curtis, *Memoir,* I, 240–41. There was some feeling that Blair waited too long before asking for help. According to James E. Harvey, New York *Tribune,* Dec. 17, 1856, Blair asked Senator William P. Fessenden of Maine, a moderate Republican, to join him as counsel and was told that it was too late. Blair himself said that he first tried to enlist the aid of a leading southern lawyer, then asked several northerners without success until Curtis joined him. *National Intelligencer* (Washington), Dec. 24, 1856.

28. New York *Tribune,* Dec. 15, 16, 17, 18, 19, 20, 22, 1856; New York *Journal of Commerce,* Dec. 17, 18, 19, 1856; Washington *Union,* Dec. 17, 1856.

29. *Argument of Montgomery Blair, Dred Scott vs. John F. A. Sanford, Supreme Court of the United States, December Term, 1856,* 4–5. A copy of this forty-page pamphlet is in the Blair Papers, MDLC. Blair also filed a supplementary brief dealing largely with congressional power over slavery in the territories.

30. From pages 4–5 of the brief submitted by Geyer for the reargument in the December term. A copy is in the Supreme Court Library.

31. *Blair Argument,* 5–16.

32. Geyer brief, 5–6.

33. *Ibid.,* 6–9.

34. *Blair Argument,* 17–18. "The court," said Blair, "did not mean that a decision of a State court was more conclusive as to the law on this than on any other subject, but merely that a writ of error to the judgment of the State court on this subject, as on every other which involved only State laws, could give no jurisdiction, and the judgment on this particular case was therefore conclusive."

35. *Ibid.,* 18–19. The case cited was *Ennis v. Smith,* 14 Howard 399, 423 (1852).

Blair, it appears, mistakenly believed that the military-sojourner argument had not been introduced in earlier *Dred Scott* litigation.

36. *Blair Argument*, 18.
37. *Ibid.* As one of his authorities, Blair cited *Swift v. Tyson*, 16 Peters 1 (1842), in which Justice Joseph Story, speaking for the Court, held that federal courts, in matters of general commercial law, need not follow state court decisions. For discussion of this subject, see Carl B. Swisher, *The Taney Period, 1836–1864*, Volume V of the Oliver Wendell Holmes Devise *History of the Supreme Court* (New York, 1974), 325–34.
38. *Blair Argument*, 19–21. Blair insisted, for example, that Lord Stowell's decision in *The Slave Grace*, 2 Haggard 94 (1827), was inapplicable because England had no express law against slavery that could work permanent emancipation. He added that two Maryland decisions rendered by the same court had recognized this distinction between the limited effect of English law and the permanent effect of Pennsylvania law, with its express constitutional and statutory prohibition of slavery.
39. *Blair Argument*, 21–26.
40. *Bank of Augusta v. Earle*, 13 Peters 519, 589 (1839).
41. *Scott v. Emerson*, 15 Missouri 577, 584.
42. Sources for this paragraph and those immediately following are: *Blair Argument*, 26–40; Geyer brief, 10–12; New York *Tribune*, Dec. 18, 1956 (summarizing Johnson's argument); George Ticknor Curtis, *Constitutional History of the United States* (2 vols.; New York, 1896), II, 499–517 (the text of his argument).

CHAPTER 13

1. Richard Malcolm Johnston and William Hand Browne, *Life of Alexander H. Stephens*, rev. ed. (Philadelphia, 1883), 318.
2. John P. Frank, *Justice Daniel Dissenting: A Biography of Peter V. Daniel, 1784–1860* (Cambridge, Mass., 1964), 257–58. Elizabeth Harris Daniel was the Justice's second wife and only half his age.
3. John A. Campbell to Samuel Tyler, Nov. 24, 1870, in Samuel Tyler, *Memoir of Roger Brooke Taney, LL.D.*, 2nd ed. (Baltimore, 1876), 383 (for other versions of the Campbell account, see note 16, Chapter XII, above); John Catron to James Buchanan, Feb. 19, 1857, Buchanan Papers, Historical Society of Pennsylvania, published in Philip Auchampaugh, "James Buchanan, the Court and the Dred Scott Case," *Tennessee Historical Magazine*, IX (1926), 236.
4. For Martin Van Buren's view that the Court majority was trying to preserve the "safety of the Union," see his *Inquiry into the Origin and Course of Political Parties in the United States* (New York, 1867), 362. For a sample of the intensity of southern feeling about the Missouri Compromise restriction, see Daniel's opinion in *DSvS*, 488–90.
5. Johnston and Browne, *Stephens*, 316. Blair informed Van Buren on February 5, 1857, that he thought outside pressure was being put on the court for a decision

against the Missouri Compromise restriction. Martin Van Buren Papers, MDLC.

6. Buchanan Papers, Historical Society of Pennsylvania; Auchampaugh, "Buchanan and the Dred Scott Case," 234–35.

7. Nelson's opinion is closer to 6000 words long if one counts his summary of the record. It was eventually published unchanged as a concurring opinion.

8. Buchanan Papers, Historical Society of Pennsylvania; Auchampaugh, "Buchanan and the Dred Scott Case," 236.

9. Tyler, *Memoir of Taney*, 384.

10. Buchanan Papers, Historical Society of Pennsylvania; Auchampaugh, "Buchanan and the Dred Scott Case," 236–37. This is in fact the standard interpretation. See, for example, Charles Warren, *The Supreme Court in United States History*, rev. ed. (2 vols.; Boston, 1932), II, 293; Alfred H. Kelly and Winfred A. Harbison, *The American Constitution, Its Origins and Development*, 4th ed. (New York, 1970), 385; G. Edward White, *The American Judicial Tradition* (New York, 1976), 78–79; Bernard Schwartz, *From Confederation to Nation: The American Constitution, 1835–1877* (Baltimore, 1973), 118–19.

11. Benjamin R. Curtis, ed., *A Memoir of Benjamin Robbins Curtis, LL.D.* (2 vols.; Boston, 1879), I, 234–35; Campbell letter in Tyler, *Memoir of Taney*, 384. (For two other Campbell versions, see note 16 in Chapter XII, above.) Reverdy Johnson, in a speech a year later, placed the blame on the two dissenters. See Tyler, *Memoir of Taney*, 385–91.

12. Allan Nevins, *The Emergence of Lincoln* (2 vols.; New York, 1950), II, 473–77.

13. Frank H. Hodder, "Some Phases of the Dred Scott Case," *MVHR*, XVI (1929), 3–22. Hodder thought that "Taney had a whole lot better anti-slavery record than Curtis," and that it was "time to take a little of that Curtis halo and give it to Taney." Hodder to Albert J. Beveridge, Feb. 9, 1927, Beveridge Papers, MDLC.

14. *DSvS*, 454, Wayne: "I shall neither read nor file an opinion of my own in this case, which I prepared when I supposed it might be necessary and proper for me to do so." Stephens, writing on January 1, 1857, declared: "The judges are all writing out their opinions, I believe, *seriatim*. The chief justice will give an elaborate one." Johnston and Browne, *Stephens*, 318. In his letter of February 6 to Buchanan, cited in note 6, above, Catron said that Daniel, in spite of his wife's death, would "surely deliver his own opinion in the case at length."

15. Campbell letter in Tyler, *Memoir of Taney*, 384; Curtis, *Memoir*, I, 206, 234–35; Alexander A. Lawrence, *James Moore Wayne, Southern Unionist* (Chapel Hill, N.C., 1943), 148–49, 154–55.

16. Buchanan Papers, Historical Society of Pennsylvania; Auchampaugh, "Buchanan and the Dred Scott Case," 236.

17. *Ibid.*, 237.

18. James D. Richardson, ed., *Messages and Papers of the Presidents* (11 vols.; Washington, D.C., 1913), IV, 2962. Buchanan went on to embrace the southern version of popular sovereignty: "It has ever been my individual opinion that under the Nebraska-Kansas act the appropriate period will be when the number

of actual residents in the Territory shall justify the formation of a constitution with a view to its admission as a State into the Union."

19. The story was retailed most dramatically by William H. Seward in a speech in the Senate, March 3, 1858. *CG*, 35–1, p. 941.

20. *DSvS*, 451, and see above, 379.

21. Curtis, *Memoir*, I, 193.

22. New York *Tribune*, March 7, 9, 1857; Washington *Evening Star*, March 7, 1857; New York *Journal of Commerce*, March 8, 9, 1857.

23. New York *Tribune*, March 9, 1857; Washington *Union*, March 11, 1857. This newspaper version was less than one-fourth the length of Taney's official opinion published in May.

24. McLean to Blair, March 30, 1857, Francis Preston Blair Papers, MDLC.

25. Harvey to McLean, April 3, 1857, John McLean Papers, MDLC.

26. Photocopies of the Curtis-Carroll correspondence, from originals in the National Archives, RG 267, are in the Carl B. Swisher Papers, MDLC. Most of the letters are published in Curtis *Memoir*, I, 212–13, 216.

27. The Curtis-Taney correspondence, with comment by Curtis, is in the Benjamin R. Curtis Papers, MDLC; it is printed in Curtis, *Memoir*, I, 213–15, 217–30. The dates were: Curtis to Taney, April 18, May 13, June 16; Taney to Curtis, April 28, June 11, June 20, 1857.

28. *Rules of the Supreme Court of the United States* (Washington, D.C., 1874), 398. Apparently the rule was not strictly enforced.

29. Taney to David M. Perine, June 16, 1857, Perine Papers, Maryland Historical Society.

30. Curtis resigned in a letter to the President dated September 1, 1857, but it is clear that he made up his mind to do so during the correspondence with Taney. To friends he explained his resignation on financial grounds, and his brother insisted that the quarrel with Taney "had no influence upon the determination to which he finally came," but this is difficult to believe. The letter of acknowledgment from Attorney General Jeremiah S. Black was coldly worded. Buchanan, in a show of meanness, had directed Black to eliminate the conventional words of praise that were included in the original draft. Curtis, *Memoir*, I, 243–50; Buchanan to Black, Sept. 15, 1857, transcript in Swisher Papers, MDLC; Richard H. Leach, "Justice Curtis and the Dred Scott Case," *Essex Institute Historical Collections*, XCIV (1958), 37–56.

31. Taney to Pierce, Aug. 29, 1857, Franklin Pierce Papers, MDLC.

32. Curtis *Memoir*, I, 229.

33. See note 23 above.

34. Supreme Court Records, RG 267, Opinions in Appellate Cases, Box no. 52, NA.

35. The rebuttal begins on page 427 as follows: "But, before we proceed to examine this part of the case, it may be proper to notice an objection taken to the judicial authority of this court to decide it. . . ."

36. The opening sentence of the passage is: "But the case of *The American and Ocean Insurance Companies vs. Canter*, 1 Pet., 511, has been quoted as establishing a different construction of this clause of the Constitution."

37.   Although there is no indication that this question was argued by counsel, it appears to have come up in conference; for Curtis in some degree anticipated Taney's argument. See above, 413–14.

CHAPTER 14

1.   Frederick S. Allis, Jr., "The Dred Scott Labyrinth," in H. Stuart Hughes et al., eds., *Teachers of History: Essays in Honor of Laurence Bradford Packard* (Ithaca, N.Y., 1954), 362.
2.   Some examples of the box-score analysis are: *The Case of Dred Scott* (New York: Tribune Association, 1860), 99–100; George Ticknor Curtis, *Constitutional History of the United States* (2 vols.; New York, 1896), II, 268–72.
3.   Three of the seven concluded that the case should be returned to the circuit court with the order to dismiss it for want of jurisdiction (Taney, Wayne, and Daniel); one justice concluded that the decision of the circuit court should be affirmed (Nelson); two justices indicated that either judgment would be satisfactory (Grier and Campbell); one justice said nothing about the form of the judgment (Catron).
4.   Allis, "Dred Scott Labyrinth," 362.
5.   See especially, Curtis, *Constitutional History*, II, 270–72.
6.   James Bradley Thayer, *Cases on Constitutional Law* (2 vols.; Cambridge, Mass., 1895), I, 480.
7.   Frank H. Hodder, in his influential article, "Some Phases of the Dred Scott Case," *MVHR*, XVI (1929), 12, asserted that Nelson's was "the only respectable opinion delivered by the Court."
8.   Curtis claimed the right to go to the merits while insisting that Taney had no such right after deciding that the circuit court had lacked jurisdiction. But he assumed that Taney was speaking officially for the Court majority, whereas he himself, as a dissenter, was contributing nothing to the authoritative decision. All dissenting opinion is on a level with dictum in the sense of being outside the *ratio decidendi*.
9.   Carl B. Swisher, *The Taney Period, 1836–1864*, Volume V of the Oliver Wendell Holmes Devise *History of the Supreme Court of the United States* (New York, 1974), 513–15.
10.   U.S. *v. Storer Broadcasting Co.*, 351 U.S. 192, 206, 213–14 (1956). See also the exchange between Harlan and Frankfurter in *Ferguson v. Moore-McCormack Lines*, 352 U.S. 521 (1957), reprinted in Glendon A. Schubert, *Constitutional Politics* (New York, 1960), 101–8, where the question was whether a justice who has voted against acceptance of jurisdiction by grant of certiorari is *required* to vote on the merits.
11.   "Opinions of the Justices of the Supreme Judicial Court on Questions Propounded by the Senate, March 26, 1857," 44 Maine Reports 505, 591 (1857). Parts of this interesting document are reprinted in Stanley I. Kutler, ed., *The Dred Scott Decision, Law or Politics?* (New York, 1967), 90–99. The Boston *Courier,* quoted in the Augusta (Ga.) *Constitutionalist,* May 31, 1857, took the

same view as Judge Davis, declaring: "When a judgment is given by a Court, this is taken as the opinion of all its members except so far as they expressly signify their dissent." This view is also argued at great length in Elbert William R. Ewing, *Legal and Historical Status of the Dred Scott Decision* (Washington, D.C., 1909), 34–49. But for a different view, see Thayer, *Cases*, I, 493–94.

12.   *DSvS*, 458. Said Nelson of the plea in abatement: "In the view we have taken of the case, it will not be necessary to pass upon this question, and we shall therefore proceed at once to an examination of the case upon its merits."

13.   It was Campbell who, in his later statements, gave the wrong impression that the conference decision remained final, and that it was a decision against the legality of taking up the plea in abatement, arrived at by a majority consisting of McLean, Catron, Grier, Campbell, and the latecomer, Nelson. "Each of these Judges," Campbell wrote in 1870, "has recorded in his opinion that there was nothing in the plea in abatement before the Court for review." But this is demonstrably untrue. Only two justices so stated in their opinions—McLean and Catron, and not even Campbell himself! Samuel Tyler, *Memoir of Roger Brooke Taney, LL.D.* (Baltimore, 1876), 383, and see the notes that follow.

14.   *Ibid.*, 384. Wayne's proposal, according to Campbell, "was assented to; some reserving to themselves to qualify their assent as the opinion might require." Writing in 1879 (see Chapter XII, note 16, above), Campbell said: "Justice Wayne . . . made the motion that the Chief Justice should prepare the opinion of the Court and discuss all of the questions in the cause. There was no debate about this. It seemed to be acquiesced in, though some did not approve it." Just how Taney, speaking for the Court, could have discussed all of the questions in the case, if the Court majority had ruled that the issue of Negro citizenship was not before the Court, Campbell never succeeded in explaining.

15.   *DSvS*, 458. Nelson stated the anti-Taney view first and then, as it were, gave rebuttal for the Taney side.

16.   *Ibid.*, 469.

17.   Tyler, *Memoir of Taney*, 383, and the other statements of Campbell cited in Chapter XII, note 16, above.

18.   Supreme Court Records, RG 267, Opinions in Appellate Cases, Box no. 52, NA; *DSvS*, 493.

19.   In a later passage, Campbell added to the confusion with this sentence: "And in so far as the argument of the Chief Justice upon the plea in abatement has a reference to the plaintiff or his family, in any of the conditions or circumstances of their lives as presented in the evidence, I concur in that portion of his opinion." However, Taney, in his discussion of the plea in abatement, said nothing at all about Dred Scott and his circumstances. Campbell was perhaps referring to another problem discussed by Taney in which he did speak of Scott's circumstances—namely, whether the merits of the case presented a jurisdictional question. So Campbell's use of the words "plea in abatement" in the sentence quoted above may have been a slip of the pen. *DSvS*, 518, and compare 400–404 with 427.

20.   Catron to Samuel Treat, May 31, 1857, Treat Papers, MHS. Concerning Taney's argument, which he labeled a "*dictum*," Catron declared, "It cannot

stand a moment in face of the dissenting opinions on this point." Catron insisted that five other justices agreed with him on the plea in abatement. However, he was counting not only Nelson, Grier, and Campbell, but also Curtis, which was certainly a mistake and shows how much confusion there was among the justices themselves. Catron, it should be noted, was alone in insisting that Taney's argument on Negro citizenship, rather than his argument on the Missouri Compromise, was *obiter dictum.*

21. Allis, "Dred Scott Labyrinth," 357. The three other justices who thought that the Court had decided against Negro citizenship were, of course, Taney, Wayne, and Daniel. For the statements of all five, see *DSvS*, 427, 455, 482, 549, 588–89. The Supreme Court itself later held that the Dred Scott decision had excluded Negroes from citizenship. Justice Samuel F. Miller, speaking for the Court in the *Slaughterhouse Cases*, 16 Wallace 36, 72–73 (1872), declared: "It had been held by this court, in the celebrated Dred Scott Case . . . that a man of African descent, whether a slave or not, was not and could not be a citizen of a State or of the United States."

22. *Buchner v. Chicago, Milwaukee & Northwestern Railroad Co.*, 60 Wisconsin 264 (1884).

23. *DSvS*, 549, 590.

24. Edward S. Corwin, "The Dred Scott Decision, in the Light of Contemporary Legal Doctrines," *AHR*, XVII (1911), 55–59. Corwin's article has been the most influential rebuttal to the charge of *obiter dictum*, but more than one historian has read it without grasping this particular point. See Allis, "Dred Scott Labyrinth," 355, 357, 358. Corwin, it must be added, never came to grips with the technical argument of Justice Curtis against jurisdiction. See above, 405.

25. *DSvS*, 426–27, 454, 456, 469, 492, 517–18, 529, 564, 633. Catron concluded by saying: "I concur with my brother judges that the plaintiff, Scott, is a slave, and was so when this suit was brought."

CHAPTER 15

1. David M. Potter, *The Impending Crisis, 1848–1861*, completed and edited by Don E. Fehrenbacher (New York, 1976), 283.

2. Frank H. Hodder, "Some Phases of the Dred Scott Case," *MVHR*, XVI (1929), 3–22; Bernard Schwartz, *From Confederation to Nation: The American Constitution, 1835–1877* (Baltimore, 1973), 117–18; Charles W. Smith, Jr., *Roger B. Taney: Jacksonian Jurist* (Chapel Hill, N.C., 1936), 155, 160–61. For a general comment on the motivation of the majority, see James A. Rawley, *Race and Politics: "Bleeding Kansas" and the Coming of the Civil War* (Philadelphia, 1969), 275–81.

3. *DSvS*, 399–400.

4. *Ibid.*, 530–32.

5. *Ibid.*, 400–403. See also Daniel's opinion on this issue, *ibid.*, 472–75, with a long quotation from the opinion of the Court in *Rhode Island v. Massachusetts*, in which Taney had opposed acceptance of jurisdiction.

6. *DSvS*, 565, 567; and see above, 405.
7. See, for example, the remarks of Justice John Marshall Harlan in *Giles v. Harris*, 189 U.S. 475, 498–501 (1903), and of his grandson, John Marshall Harlan, in *U.S. v. Storer Broadcasting Co.*, 351 U.S. 192, 206n (1956).
8. *DSvS*, 566. Precedent may have been stronger on Scott's side in the matter of waiver, however. See, for example, *Sheppard v. Graves*, 14 Howard 505, 510 (1852), one of the cases cited by Montgomery Blair.
9. *DSvS*, 403.
10. *Ibid*. Italics added. Duane D. Smith, "The Development of the Concept of Citizenship in American Constitutional Law," Ph.D. dissertation, Ohio State University, 1936, pp. 95–97.
11. *DSvS*, 403–4. Marvin Laurence Winitsky, "The Jurisprudence of Roger B. Taney," Ph.D. dissertation, UCLA, 1973, pp. 84–85, points out that Taney here contradicted his earlier opinion in *United States v. Rogers*, 4 Howard 567, 572 (1846), wherein he had described Indians as a subject people rather than as a group of foreign nations.
12. *DSvS*, 404. It should be added that since many states permitted aliens to vote, a considerable number of non-citizens were included in the "sovereign people," as Taney defined the phrase.
13. *Ibid.*, 404–5.
14. *Ibid.*, 405, and see above, 406–7.
15. Article Four, Section Two.
16. *DSvS*, 405–7.
17. *Ibid.*, 406.
18. *Ibid.*, 407. In passing, one may wonder what Taney meant by the "civilized portion" of the white race. Christendom, perhaps.
19. Charles Warren, *The Supreme Court in United States History*, rev. ed. (2 vols; Boston, 1932), II, 303.
20. *DSvS*, 408–9, 413–16. For a discussion of the Court's use of history, see Alfred H. Kelly, "Clio and the Court: An Illicit Love Affair," in Philip B. Kurland, ed., *1965 Supreme Court Review* (Chicago, 1965), 119–58.
21. This particular circularity in Taney's argument was pointed out in John Codman Hurd, *The Law of Freedom and Bondage in the United States* (2 vols.; Boston, 1858, 1862), II, 293n.
22. *DSvS*, 407, 409.
23. *Ibid.*, 409–10.
24. *Ibid.*, 410–12.
25. *Ibid.*, 412.
26. Winthrop D. Jordan, *White over Black: American Attitudes toward the Negro, 1550–1812* (Chapel Hill, N.C., 1968; Baltimore, 1969), 310–11, and see above, 16–18.
27. *DSvS*, 416.
28. *Ibid.*, 407 ("It is difficult at this day to realise . . ."), 410 ("The general words above quoted . . ."), 426 ("No one, we presume. . .").
29. *CWAL*, II, 403–4; Leon F. Litwack, *North of Slavery: The Negro in the Free States, 1790–1860* (Chicago, 1961); Ira Berlin, *Slaves Without Masters: The Free Negro in the Antebellum South* (New York, 1974).

30. *DSvS*, 416–17.
31. *Bank of Augusta v. Earle*, 13 Peters 519 (1839); *Louisville, Cincinnati and Charleston Railroad Company v. Letson*, 2 Howard 497, 558 (1844). The contradiction between the Court's ruling on corporate citizenship and Taney's rejection of Negro citizenship is noted briefly in R. Kent Newmyer, *The Supreme Court under Marshall and Taney* (New York, 1968), 133. Hurd, *Law of Freedom and Bondage*, 330 and note, after an elaborate analysis, concluded that Negroes were intended to be included as citizens under the diverse-citizenship clause but not under the privileges-and-immunities clause.
32. *Sturgis v. Crowninshield*, 4 Wheaton 122, 145–49 (1819); *Chirac v. Chirac*, 2 Wheaton 259, 269 (1817).
33. *DSvS*, 417–18, and compare with 405–6.
34. "These dicta," writes Edward S. Corwin, "are much too narrow to sustain the power which Congress has actually exercised on the subject." *The Constitution of the United States of America, Analysis and Interpretation* (Washington, D.C., 1953), 254.
35. *DSvS*, 418.
36. *Ibid.*, 418–19.
37. *Ibid.*, 419.
38. *Ibid.*, 415. The case was *Crandall v. the State*, 10 Connecticut 340 (1834).
39. *DSvS*, 419–20. In this passage, Taney again declared that Congress had no power under the Constitution to naturalize "the African race imported into or born in this country." This was dictum and purely arbitrary. The relevant clause says only that Congress shall have the power "to establish an uniform rule of naturalization." There is apparently no constitutional restriction on the power of Congress to make any non-citizen a citizen of the United States.
40. *Ibid.*, 420–21, 426.
41. *Ibid.*, 421.
42. *Ibid.*, 423–25. Curtis concurred with Taney on this point and used it to bolster his own argument, *ibid.*, 589. The fact remains that Taney, as an attorney, had participated in a case in which a Negro averred that he was a citizen under the diverse-citizenship clause, just like Dred Scott, but it was a friendly suit, and the Court's jurisdiction was not challenged. 2 Peters 664.
43. *DSvS*, 422–23, 425.
44. *Ibid.*, 425–26.
45. *Ibid.*, 426. Taney had used precisely the same phrase, "this unfortunate race," to designate Indians in *United States v. Rogers*. See note 11 above.
46. *DSvS*, 426–27.

CHAPTER 16

1. *DSvS*, 427–30; see above, 330–32.
2. It has been argued that Taney had to consider the constitutionality of the Missouri Compromise restriction because the rules of interstate comity and the precedent of *Strader v. Graham* did not apply to Scott's residence in Wisconsin Territory, where slavery was forbidden by *federal* law. Thus, Horace H. Hagan,

"The Dred Scott Decision," *Georgetown Law Journal*, XV (1926), 109–10: "The rule thus applied between equal sovereignties would not logically or necessarily apply where it was a question only of an apparent conflict between a law of the Federal Government and the laws of the State of Missouri. If the Federal law were constitutional, it was supreme and the laws of Missouri could not create a slave out of a man whom a valid enactment of a paramount power had declared to be free. Therefore, the vital question in the Dred Scott case, the question that could not be avoided, was the constitutionality of the Missouri Compromise." But Hagan was careless in his reading of *Strader* and of *Dred Scott* as well. In the former case, Taney had declared that a federal territorial law had no more extraterritorial force than a state law, and Nelson in *Dred Scott* said that this furnished a "conclusive answer to the distinction attempted to be set up between the extraterritorial effect of a state law and the Act of Congress in question." *DSvS*, 464. The distinction thus rejected by both Taney and Nelson is, of course, the very distinction drawn by Hagan. Which view is legally sounder does not matter. The point is that Taney could scarcely have used the Hagan argument to justify judicial review of the Missouri Compromise restriction. Another nominal reason for taking up the territorial question first was that it involved Scott's wife and children as well as himself, whereas he alone could claim freedom under the law of Illinois. But this would have made a difference only if Taney intended to *uphold* the Scotts' claim to freedom by virtue of their residence at Fort Snelling (in which case there would have been no need to examine the effect of Dred's residence in Illinois). As it was, however, Taney, after his ruling against the Missouri Compromise restriction, still had to consider whether Dred Scott had become a free man in Illinois.

3. *DSvS*, 432–42.
4. Francis S. Philbrick, ed., *The Laws of Illinois Territory, 1809–1818* (Springfield, Ill., 1950), cxxv–cxxvii. Gouverneur Morris wrote in 1803: "I knew as well then [in 1787] as I do now, that all North America must at length be annexed to us." It was Morris who drafted the territory clause in its final form. Max Farrand, ed., *The Records of the Federal Convention of 1787*, rev. ed. (4 vols.; New Haven, 1937), III, 401.
5. *DSvS*, 440.
6. "But it must be remembered," said Curtis in his dissent, "that this is a grant of power to the Congress—that it is therefore necessarily a grant of power to legislate—and, certainly, rules and regulations respecting a particular subject, made by the legislative power of a country, can be nothing but laws." *Ibid.*, 614.
7. Taney made much of the fact that the wording in the territory clause was strikingly different from the wording in Article One, Section Eight, empowering Congress "to exercise exclusive legislation in all cases whatsoever" over land ceded for the seat of the government (District of Columbia) and over places purchased by the federal government for forts, arsenals, dockyards, etc. But the reason for the stronger terminology here is obvious. Once a western territory was ceded by a state, there was no question as to jurisdiction, since the cession put the territory beyond the reach of state sovereignty. But in the case of forts,

dockyards, and the District of Columbia, the areas would be small enclaves of federal sovereignty within the boundaries of sovereign states, and so a more emphatic language seemed advisable. This explanation was presented in the argument of George Ticknor Curtis. See his *Constitutional History of the United States* (2 vols.; New York, 1896), II, 510.

8.   Farrand, *Records*, II, 324.
9.   *DSvS*, 434.
10. *Ibid.*, 434–35.
11. *Ibid.*, 438–39.
12. *American Insurance Co. v. Canter*, 1 Peters 511, 542–43, 546.
13. The specific issue in the case was whether Congress could delegate to territorial legislatures the power to establish courts with admiralty jurisdiction. Marshall held that Congress was not restricted by Article Three of the Constitution in legislating for the territories, giving as his reason the sentence quoted in the text. The reason was obviously broad enough to apply also to Article One—that is, Congress was not restricted to its delegated powers in legislating for the territories. But Taney insisted that the generalization referred only to Article Three, the judiciary article, and not to Article One, the legislative article. *DSvS*, 442–46. "And we are satisfied," Taney concluded, "that no one who reads attentively the page in Peters' Reports to which we have referred, can suppose that the attention of the court was drawn for a moment to the question now before this court, or that it meant in that case to say that Congress had a right to prohibit a citizen of the United States from taking any property which he lawfully held into a Territory of the United States." Instead, according to Taney, one must suppose that Marshall, speaking seven years after the settlement of the Missouri crisis, silently excepted slavery when he defined the territorial power of Congress in such emphatic and sweeping terms. In *Benner v. Porter*, 9 Howard 235, 242 (1850), Justice Nelson followed the Marshall line precisely when he declared: "They are legislative courts, Congress in the exercise of its powers in the organization and government of the Territories, combining the powers of both the Federal and State authorities." There was no dissent from Nelson's opinion.
14. *Ibid.*, 446–47. No doubt the most striking example is the contrast between the enormous reach of the due-process clause and the shrunken significance of the privileges-or-immunities clause of the Fourteenth Amendment, as a result of judicial interpretation.
15. *Ibid.*
16. *Ibid.*, 446–49. With his usual repetitiousness, Taney said all of this about four times. For the problem of colonies, see above, 585–87.
17. *Ibid.*, 450. Taney's argument at this point is similar to that of Thomas L. Clingman, congressman from North Carolina, in a letter published in the Washington *Globe*, Jan 13, 1857, at about the time when some of the justices were presumably working on their opinions.
18. *DSvS*, 450. For Stephen A. Douglas's curious misinterpretation of this passage, see above, 520–23.
19. *Ibid.*, 451.

20. Taney's word on this subject was by no means final, of course. See especially *Downes v. Bidwell*, 182 U.S. 244 (1901).
21. *DSvS*, 451–52.
22. Philbrick, *Laws of Illinois Territory*, cxxx–clvii, especially cxlviii, in a keen analysis of this part of Taney's opinion, says flatly that the latter "did not declare that the Missouri Compromise *violated* the Fifth Amendment." But few historians have read the opinion with as much care as Philbrick did. For the standard interpretation that Taney did in fact hold the 36° 30' restriction to be a violation of the due-process clause, see, for example, Allan Nevins, *The Emergence of Lincoln* (2 vols.; New York, 1950), I, 94; Alfred H. Kelly and Winfred A. Harbison, *The American Constitution, Its Origins and Development*, 4th ed. (New York, 1970), 388–89.
23. See, for example, the argument of Alvan Stewart, summarized in Jacobus tenBroek, *The Antislavery Origins of the Fourteenth Amendment* (Berkeley, 1951), 43–45; and the argument of Salmon P. Chase, summarized in Eric Foner, *Free Soil, Free Labor, Free Men: The Ideology of the Republican Party Before the Civil War (New York, 1970)*, 76–77.
24. The case was *Murray v. Hoboken Land & Improvement Co.*, 18 Howard 272 (1856), in which Justice Curtis declared (p. 276): "The article is a restraint on the legislative as well as on the executive and judicial powers of the government, and cannot be so construed as to leave congress free to make any process 'due process of law' by its mere will." Curtis was, in a sense, talking about congressional control of procedure, rather than substantive due process in its modern sense. But the fact that Taney did not cite this very recent case in his Dred Scott opinion lends support to the view that his use of the due-process clause was on the whole rather casual. See Howard Jay Graham, "Procedure to Substance: Extrajudicial Rise of Due Process, 1830–1860," in his *Everyman's Constitution: Historical Essays on the Fourteenth Amendment, the "Conspiracy Theory," and American Constitutionalism* (Madison, 1968), 242–65, and the authorities cited at 243n. For examples of southern nonjudicial invocation of the due-process clause, see the speech of Alexander Smyth of Virginia in the House of Representatives, January 28, 1820, *AC*, 16-1, col. 998; the speech of Francis W. Pickens of South Carolina in the House, January 21, 1836, *Register of Debates of Congress*, 24-1, cols. 2246–47; committee report of Henry L. Pinckney of South Carolina, May 18, 1836, on abolition in the District of Columbia, *House Reports*, 28-1, No. 691 (Serial 295), 14.
25. *DSvS*, 450: "and who had committed no offense against the law."
26. Philbrick *Laws of Illinois Territory*, 31.
27. *DSvS*, 626–27. In these instances, as well as in the case of the anti-gambling law, the forfeiture was not in the law but in the penalty for breaking it.
28. *Ibid.*, 448: "Whatever it acquires, it acquires for the benefit of the people of the several States who created it. It is their trustee acting for them." This is just ambiguous enough to avoid being unquestionably Calhounish. Taney did not return to this phraseology in his summary paragraph. See, however, Arthur Bestor, "State Sovereignty and Slavery: A Reinterpretation of Proslavery Constitutional Doctrine, 1846–1860," *Journal of the Illinois State Historical So-*

ciety, LIV (1961), 170, for the statement that the concept of trusteeship was "vital" to Taney's argument.

29. *DSvS*, 452.
30. *Ibid.*, 452–53.
31. *Ibid.*, 453–54.
32. *Ibid.*, 454.

CHAPTER 17

1. *DSvS*, 454–56. Wayne distinguished between writs of error to state courts and writs of error to lower federal courts. In the one instance, jurisdiction was limited; in the other it was not. In cases coming from state courts, the first question was whether the Supreme Court had jurisdiction. In cases coming from lower federal courts, the question was whether the lower court had had jurisdiction. And the Supreme Court had the right and duty to correct all errors made in the lower court—of merit as well as jurisdictional. Otherwise, Wayne said, the effect would be to enlarge the jurisdiction of lower federal courts by delimiting the Supreme Court's power of review. (Thus, in the Dred Scott case, the opposing argument would have limited the Supreme Court to correcting the error of accepting jurisdiction or the error of merit, but not both.)

2. Benjamin R. Curtis, ed., *A Memoir of Benjamin Robbins Curtis, LL.D.* (2 vols.; Boston, 1879), I, 193. Curtis made this remark in a letter to his uncle written February 27, 1857, just one week before the delivery of the Dred Scott decision. Curtis also said that Wayne had been "ill much of the winter," and that Daniel had been "prostrated for months" by the death of his wife.

3. John Charles Hogan, "The Role of Chief Justice Taney in the Decision of the Dred Scott Case," *Case and Comment*, LVIII (1953), 3–8. Hogan's conclusion was based in part on a quantified comparative study of the two justices' literary styles. See the comment of a doubter, Carl B. Swisher, *The Taney Period, 1836–1864*, Volume V of the Oliver Wendell Holmes Devise *History of the Supreme Court of the United States* (New York, 1974), 625n.

4. Memorandum, March 13, 1857, signed by William Thomas Carroll, Clerk of the Court, Supreme Court Records, RG 267, File 3230, Transcript of Record, NA.

5. After *Scott v. Emerson*, 15 Missouri 577 (1852), the most significant case was *Sylvia v. Kirby*, 17 Missouri 434 (1853).

6. *DSvS*, 464.

7. *Ibid.*, 464–65.

8. This in spite of the fact that the Court just nine months earlier, in *Pease v. Peck*, 18 Howard 595 (1856), held that when the decisions of a state supreme court on a given issue were not consistent, the U.S. Supreme Court did not feel bound to follow the last ones, but was instead free to follow its own convictions. For some hearsay evidence that the Court majority, with Justice Grier as its spokesman, took this step deliberately in order to free itself in the Dred Scott case from the obligation to follow *Scott v. Emerson*, see Curtis, *Memoir*, I, 210.

9. *DSvS*, 466–67.

10. *Ibid.*, 468. Nelson cited only one case, a British one. Obviously he could find no American precedent in rebuttal to *Rachel v. Walker*. During the reargument in December 1856, Catron directed a query on the subject to Jefferson Davis, then secretary of war. Davis replied that there was nothing in military regulations governing the use of servants in federal territory north of Missouri. "But, he added, "officers of the Army being, by law, allowed servants have always been in the habit of taking them to the Indian country, when their duties required their presence there, whether they are white men, free blacks or slaves, and the officer has been paid by the Government the amount allowed for their services in each case." Dunbar Rowland, ed., *Jefferson Davis, Constitutionalist: His Letters, Papers, and Speeches* (10 vols.; Jackson, Miss., 1923), III, 100.

11. *DSvS*, 460–61.

12. Although defense counsel had argued in *Scott v. Emerson* that Emerson's residence on free soil was temporary, this issue had not been decided in the Missouri supreme court. There, Judge Scott had overruled *Rachel* on other grounds and had, in effect, set aside the distinction between temporary and permanent residence. The headnote of *Scott v. Emerson* makes this clear: "The voluntary removal of a slave, by his master, to a State, Territory or Country in which slavery is prohibited, with a view to residence there, does not entitle the slave to sue for his freedom, in the courts of this State." In any case, Nelson did not cite *Scott v. Emerson* or any other authority but simply asserted that the question was "too plain to require argument."

13. 10 Howard 82, 93 (1851), and see William M. Wiecek, "*Somerset:* Lord Mansfield and the Legitimacy of Slavery in the Anglo-American World," *University of Chicago Law Review*, XLII (1974), 137–38.

14. In the House-Divided speech and in the debates with Douglas, *CWAL*, II, 465–67; III, 230–32, 251. Twice Lincoln mentioned the passage in Nelson's opinion, calling attention to its similarity to phrasing in the Kansas-Nebraska Act.

15. *DSvS*, 468.

16. *Ibid.*, 469.

17. *Ibid.*, 472–75, 493, 518–19; New York *Tribune*, March 7, 1857; Catron to Samuel Treat, May 31, 1857, Treat Papers, MHS; James Harvey to John McLean, April 3, 1857, McLean Papers, MDLC. One senses some feeling between Taney and Catron, whose opinion was placed last among the concurring justices. Catron told Treat that the Washington *Union* probably would not publish his opinion because of his disagreement with Taney. He wanted it published in a St. Louis newspaper and was willing to pay for it.

18. *DSvS*, 475–82.

19. *Ibid.*, 519.

20. *Ibid.*, 494–500; *Argument of Montgomery Blair, Dred Scott v. Sandford, Supreme Court of the United States, December Term 1855*, 18–19. The right of transit in Illinois was confirmed in *Willard v. the People*, 4 Scammon 461 (Ill., 1843). But attitudes were changing by the 1850s. See especially *Rodney v. Illi-*

nois Central Railroad, 19 Illinois 42 (1857), amounting to a refusal of comity rights to slavery.

21. *Argument of Blair*, 19–20. Lord Stowell had stressed the absence of positive law.

22. *DSvS*, 500.

23. *Ibid.*, 485–86. Prior to this discussion, however, Daniel had expatiated on the absolute sovereignty of nations to show that neither international law nor English law (including, presumably, law enunciated by Lord Stowell) had any binding force whatever within the United States (pp. 483–85).

24. *Ibid.*, 486–87. The case was *Lewis v. Fullerton*, 1 Randolph 15 (Va., 1821).

25. *DSvS*, 489–90.

26. *Ibid.*, 490–91. The pretension to such power, Daniel said, must be met with "antipathy and disgust at its sinister aspect" (p. 488).

27. *Ibid.*, 501, 509–10, 514. The public domain, Campbell said, lay within the jurisdiction of existing states as well as outside them. Thus, if the territory clause granted Congress plenary legislative power on domain outside state jurisdiction, why not also on public domain with the boundaries of a state?

28. *Ibid.*, 501–2.

29. *Ibid.*, 514–15.

30. *Ibid.*, 515. Edward S. Corwin, "The Dred Scott Decision in the Light of Contemporary Legal Doctrines," *AHR*, XVII (1911), 59, says that Campbell took the "extremest position" on the territorial question, and that his argument represented "the extremest Calhounism," but there appears to be little textual basis for this judgment.

31. *DSvS*, 500, 516. Twice, Campbell asserted that Congress could not regulate interstate trade in slaves and that this was settled doctrine of the Supreme Court. The basis for this dubious claim was apparently *Groves v. Slaughter*, 15 Peters 449 (1841), in which the subject was discussed only by concurring justices and not in the opinion of the Court. Henry Clay made a similar assertion during the debates on the Compromise of 1850. See *CG*, 31-1, p. 246, and also Arthur Bestor, "The American Civil War as a Constitutional Crisis," *AHR*, LXIX (1964), 341–43.

32. *DSvS*, 505, 516–17. Nine years earlier in a private letter and before his appointment to the Supreme Court, Campbell had insisted that Congress *did* have the power to prohibit slavery in the territories. Campbell to Calhoun, March 1, 1848, in Chauncey S. Boucher and Robert P. Brooks, eds., *Correspondence Addressed to John C. Calhoun, 1837–1849*, AHA *Annual Report*, 1929, pp. 430–34.

33. *DSvS*, 519–23. Wayne had delivered the opinion of the Court in *Cross v. Harrison*, 16 Howard 164 (1854), upholding the power of Congress to govern the territories under the territory clause, and he now seemed to be contradicting himself. Catron to Samuel Treat, May 31, 1857, Treat Papers, MHS.

34. *DSvS*, 523–24. There was manipulation here, of course. Virginia did not insist upon the prohibition of slavery in her deeds of cession. Catron was treating the Ordinance as a pact between Virginia and the other states.

35. *Ibid.*, 524–25. By stressing the word "liberty" instead of "property," antislavery spokesmen could argue that the treaty had the effect of freeing all slaves in Louisiana.

36. *Ibid.*, 528–29.

37. Glover Moore, *The Missouri Controversy, 1819–1821* (Lexington, Ky., 1953), 47–48; Andrew C. McLaughlin, *A Constitutional History of the United States* (New York, 1935), 377, with cases cited. Private contractual commitments in a treaty, such as confirmation of land titles, are a different matter, but they ordinarily must be fairly specific, in contrast with the vague statement about property rights in the Louisiana treaty, which did not even mention slavery.

38. *DSvS*, 526–28.

39. *Ibid.*, 527–29. Arthur Bestor, "State Sovereignty and Slavery: A Reinterpretation of Proslavery Constitutional Doctrine, 1846–1860," *Journal of the Illinois State Historical Society*, LIV (1961), 168n, is mistaken in saying that Catron found the 36° 30′ restriction, not unconstitutional, but merely "invalid."

40. For example, Swisher, *Taney Period*, 627–28; Charles W. Smith, Jr., *Roger B. Taney: Jacksonian Jurist* (Chapel Hill, N.C., 1936), 160–61.

41. *DSvS*, 531–33.

42. *Ibid.*, 564–67.

43. *Ibid.*, 567–71.

44. *Ibid.*, 571; *Gassies v. Ballon*, 6 Peters 761, 762 (1832). Whereas Taney and Curtis in *Dred Scott* were both seeking to convert a question of state citizenship into a question of national citizenship (with opposite results in mind), John Marshall in *Gassies* was simply providing a formula for determining state citizenship when national citizenship was not in doubt (because Gassies had been naturalized).

45. *DSvS*, 571–88.

46. *Ibid.*, 582–84.

47. *Ibid.* 549–50, 588–90.

48. *Ibid.*, 609–10; for McLean, 540.

49. *Ibid.*, 611–13.

50. *Ibid.*, 540, 614.

51. *Ibid.*, 623–24.

52. George T. Curtis, in his argument as counsel for Scott, emphasized that he would not talk about "general" principles. See his *Constitutional History of the United States* (2 vols.; New York, 1896), II, 501. Justice Curtis cited the example of *Loughborough v. Blake*, 5 Wheaton 317, 324 (1820), wherein John Marshall rejected a request that it apply the general principle of no taxation without representation.

53. *DSvS*, 624, 626–27; for McLean's brief statement, 547.

54. *Ibid.*, 557, 629–33; *New Orleans v. De Armas*, 9 Peters 224, 235 (1835).

55. *DSvS*, 557, 558, 561, 596–97.

56. *Ibid.*, 547–49, 624.

57. *Ibid.*, 548, 591, 593.

58. *Ibid.*, 598 601.

59. *Ibid.*, 557, 591–93.

60. *Ibid.*, 556–57, 563, 594–95, 604, and see note 8, above. Missouri had incorporated the common law by statute in 1816 when it was still a territory. Laws of a Public and General Nature of the District of Louisiana, of the Territory of Missouri, and of the State of Missouri up to the Year 1824 (2 vols.; Jefferson City, Mo., 1842), I, 436.

61. *DSvS*, 603. The cases were *Miller v. Austen,* 13 Howard 218 (1851); *Homer v. Brown,* 16 Howard 354 (1853).

CHAPTER 18

1. New York *Tribune,* March 7, 9–12, 16–17, 19–21, 25; April 11, 1857.

2. Chicago *Democratic-Press,* March 13, 1857; Chicago *Tribune,* March 12, 1857. For extensive quotations from press opinion, see Albert J. Beveridge, *Abraham Lincoln, 1809–1858* (2 vols.; Boston, 1928), II, 487–90; Charles Warren, *The Supreme Court in United States History,* rev. ed (2 vols; Boston, 1932), II, 304–9.

3. Louisville *Democrat,* March 8, 1857 (before even the newspaper summary had been published); New Orleans *Picayune,* March 20, 1857; Augusta *Constitutionalist,* March 15, 1857.

4. *New Hampshire Patriot* (Concord), March 18, 1857. Later, the state Democratic convention in Massachusetts resolved: "The duty of every good citizen to bow to the decision of the U.S. Supreme Court cannot be lost sight of; the purity and capacity of that august tribunal cannot be questioned." Boston *Advertiser,* Sept. 17, 1857.

5. Washington *Union,* March 6, 11, 12, 1857.

6. New York *Journal of Commerce,* March 11, 1857.

7. Philadelphia *Pennsylvanian,* March 10, 11, 1857, New York *Herald,* March 8, 1857; New Orleans *Picayune,* March 20, 1857; Augusta *Constitutionalist,* March 15, 1857; also the *New Hampshire Patriot,* March 18, 1857: "utterly demolishes the whole black republican platform."

8. Especially in Garrison's famous declaration that the Constitution was a "covenant with death" and an "agreement with hell," as he set fire to a copy of it. *The Liberator* (Boston), July 7, 1854.

9. Portland (Maine) *Eastern Argus,* March 13, 14, 1857; Philadelphia *Pennsylvanian,* March 11, 1857; New York *Journal of Commerce,* March 12, 1857; Richmond *Enquirer,* March 13, 1857; *Iowa State Democrat,* March 17, 1857. See also Albany *Argus,* quoted in Cleveland *Plain Dealer,* March 14, 1857; Washington *Union,* March 26, 1857. There were, it should be noted, some Republicans who saw the risks involved in unrestrained denunciation of the Court. They expressed their disapproval of the decision in less strident tones and repudiated any suggestion of offering resistance to it. See, for example, New York *Times,* March 7, 9, 1857.

10. Springfield *Argus,* quoted in Boston *Post,* June 1, 1857. Said the Cleveland *Plain Dealer,* March 16, 1857: "The decision confirms to this free soil hypocrite, by right of his wife, the body and blood of Dred Scott and his family."

11. Printed in New York *Tribune*, March 17, 1857. Chaffee also described himself
     as "possessed of no power to control—refused all right to influence the course of
     the defendant in the cause—and all the while feeling and openly expressing the
     fullest sympathy with Dred Scott and his family." What he seems to be saying is
     that, after learning about the case he tried to intervene and was rebuffed by
     Sanford.

12. Permanent Record Books, Missouri circuit court, St. Louis, Volume 26; Walter
     Ehrlich, History of the Dred Scott Case Through the Decision of 1857," Ph.D.
     dissertation, Washington University, 1950, pp. 381–82. In the Caleb Cushing
     Papers, MDLC, there is a letter from R. H. Gillet to Cushing dated November
     16, 1857, in which he says in part: "I saw Mr. [Montgomery] Blair this evening.
     He informed me that . . . before the suit was finally ended in the Supreme
     Court, Sanford had finally administered on the estate and the property was
     disposed of under Emerson's will and that Mrs. Emerson took him [Dred Scott]
     with other property as residuary legatee. That finding out the true state of the
     case, he Mr. B. wrote Chaffee on the subject and desired that Dred might be
     set free. That Chaffee conveyed him, or authorized B as his attorney to do so,
     for a nominal consideration to a person in St. Louis, who appeared in open
     court and the necessary proceedings were had to perfect his freedom. He thinks
     that Chaffee knew nothing of the early proceedings, if he did the later ones, and
     was not aware that Dred passed to his wife under the residuary clause in the
     will." This conflicts with other evidence that the Emerson estate had been long
     since settled (see above, pp. 249–50) and is the only contemporary indication
     that Blair had something to do with the manumission of Scott. Also in the
     Cushing Papers is a memorandum by Cushing of a conversation with R. G.
     Chapman at Salem on November 23. Chapman claimed that he "wrote the deed
     by which Dr. C[haffee] set Dred Scott free."

13. Sanford's probate records in St. Louis indicate that the inventory of his estate
     was not filed until December 3, 1858, by which time Dred Scott was dead.

14. In his letter to the Springfield *Republican* (note 11 above), Chaffee declared: "If
     in the distribution of the estate, of which this decision affirms these human
     beings to be part, it appears that I or mine consent to receive any part of the
     thirty pieces of silver, then, and not till then, let the popular judgment as well
     as the public press, fix on me the mark of a traitor to my conscience." Since his
     brother-in-law Sanford was still alive, Chaffee must have been referring to the
     Emerson estate. This suggests that he did not regard Sanford as the owner of
     Scott and that he thought the Emerson estate was *still* not settled. One suspects
     that either Chaffee was dissimulating or that he had been misled by his wife.
     See also above, 248, and note 41 below.

15. See, for example, Worcester *Bay State,* quoted in Boston *Post,* June 1, 1857. "It
     looks," said Caleb Cushing in a speech in October, 1857, "like a fancy case, got
     up and carried on for the public edification and amusement." See note 41
     below.

16. For example, Fred Rodell, "Dred Scott—A Century After," *Atlantic Monthly,*
     CC (Oct. 1957), 60–63; Elbert B. Smith, *The Death of Slavery: The United
     States, 1837–1865* (Chicago, 1967), 145. The historian Edward Channing

thought that William Lloyd Garrison or Benjamin F. Wade, or both, had something to do with arranging the Dred Scott case. Channing to Albert J. Beveridge, Jan. 27, 1927, Beveridge Papers, MDLC.

17. Carl B. Swisher, *The Taney Period, 1836–1864,* Volume V of the Oliver Wendell Holmes Devise *History of the Supreme Court* (New York, 1974), 640. Howard, a fellow Marylander and Democrat, had a family connection with Taney
through the Key family.

18. Taney to Benjamin R. Curtis, April 28, 1857, Curtis Papers, MDLC, printed in
Benjamin R. Curtis, ed., *A Memoir of Benjamin Robbins Curtis, LL.D.* (2 vols.;
Boston, 1879), I, 213–15.

19. Swisher, *Taney Period,* 641. The Senate in its special session of March 1857
failed to pass authorization of the printing. It was underwritten, however, by a
group of Democratic senators. The next session of the Senate agreed to pay the
bill. *CG,* 35-1, pp. 665–67.

20. John Appleton to Benjamin C. Howard, August 13, 1858 (responding to a query
of July 19), Howard Papers, Maryland Historical Society.

21. Swisher, *Taney Period,* 641.

22. Catron to Samuel Treat, May 31, 1857, Treat Papers, MHS. Catron wrote from
Nashville, where, perhaps at his urging, the *Union and American* published his
opinion on June 11–12. Contrary to his expectation, the Washington *Union* did
likewise on June 2. The *Union* published Taney's opinion beginning on May 26.
Acknowledgments in the John McLean Papers, MDLC, indicate that he mailed
out quite a few copies of a pamphlet edition of his opinion.

23. *DSvS,* 393–96; Swisher, *Taney Period,* 641–42. As Swisher points out, the
headnote in Taney's longhand is in the Howard Papers, Maryland Historical Society.

24. Blair to McLean, McLean Papers, MDLC.

25. New York *Express,* March 16, 23, 30, April 6, 1857; New York *Herald,* April 9,
1857. On Cheever, see the article by Frederick T. Persons in the *Dictionary of
American Biography,* IV, 48–49. Cheever was a sensationalist. As a pastor in
Salem during the 1830s, he published an anti-liquor article of such a highly per-
sonalized nature that the offending press was destroyed, and Cheever was assaulted on the street, convicted of libel, fined $1000, and sentenced to a month
in jail. In 1857, along with his anti-*Dred-Scott* sermons, he published *God
Against Slavery* (Cincinnati), a collection of more than twenty discourses, including a speech in which he compared Pierce's Kansas policy to "Nero's mad
malignity . . . in getting the neck of the people at one knot in the noose, and
under foot; a treason that cuts the jugular vein, and lets out the life blood, and,
if successful, would leave nothing but a trampled carcass, like the worn-out
corpses of European despotism." An effort to remove Cheever from his pas-
torate proved unsuccessful. Details are in New York *Tribune,* May 19, 1857,
and in the George Barrel Cheever Papers, American Antiquarian Society,
Worcester, Mass. Church politics of this kind could be as ruthless as public politics. On June 12, Cheever reported to his wife: "At our annual meeting we have
decapitated all the deacons. They demanded my resignation as pastor."

26. Quoted in Warren, *Supreme Court,* II, 306–7.

27. Providence *Post*, May 15, 1857; Charles Baumer Swaney, *Episcopal Methodism and Slavery* (Boston, 1926), 277. During the presidential campaign of the preceding year, the *Illinois State Register* (Springfield) had complained: "The pulpits of the country have been converted into stump rostrums, and the religious associations into Frémont clubs."

28. "A Legal Review of the Case of Dred Scott," published also as a pamphlet (Boston, 1857), in which the quotation is at page 9.

29. "The Decision of the Supreme Court in the Dred Scott Case," *Christian Examiner*, LXIII (July, 1857), 65–93, quotation at 88. The author was Nathan Hale, nephew of the famous spy and father of Edward Everett Hale. A journalist, he had published the *Boston Advertiser* for forty years.

30. Timothy Farrar, "The Dred Scott Case," *North American Review*, LXXXV (Oct. 1857), 392–415, quotations at 395, 415. This article and those discussed above were apparently reviews of Appleton's commercial edition of the decision.

31. *Ibid.*, 399, 414. Critics generally ignored Taney's claim to be canvassing the jurisdictional question throughout the whole of his opinion.

32. Theodore D. Woolsey, "Opinion of Judge Daniel in the Case of Dred Scott," and W. A. Learned, "Negro Citizenship," *New Englander*, XV (Aug. 1857), 345–65, 478–526.

33. *The Constitutional Power of Congress over the Territories* (Boston, 1857), revised as *The Just Supremacy of Congress over the Territories* (Boston, 1859); *A Review of the Decision of the Supreme Court of the United States in the Dred Scott Case* (Louisville, 1857).

34. Elbert B. Smith, *Magnificent Missourian: The Life of Thomas Hart Benton* (Philadelphia, 1958), 319. Other estimates are not that high. Swisher, *Taney Period*, 643n, pays the book little attention, saying that it was "longer but less precise" than the Farrar and Gray-Lowell pieces.

35. The full title is *Historical and Legal Examination of That Part of the Decision of the Supreme Court of the United States in the Dred Scott Case, Which Declares the Unconstitutionality of the Missouri Compromise Act, and the Self-Extension of the Constitution to Territories, Carrying Slavery Along with It* (New York, 1957). See especially pp. 11–16, 26–30, 35, 36–37, 61.

36. *The Law of Freedom and Bondage in the United States* (2 vols.; Boston, 1858, 1862). Robert M. Cover, *Justice Accused: Antislavery and the Judicial Process* (New Haven, 1975), 269n, says that Hurd relied more heavily on the legal philosophy of John Austin than any other antebellum American writer, but it is not quite accurate to accuse Hurd of "attacking natural law as a source of 'jurisprudence.'" Hurd in fact said that it *is* the source, but that the state determines in what respect. On Hurd, see the article by John E. Briggs in the *Dictionary of American Biography*, IX, 423.

37. *North American Review*, LXXIX (Jan. 1859), 279–80.

38. Hurd, *Law of Freedom and Bondage*, I, 560–70.

39. *Ibid.*, 589–92. Other relevant books soon published were Sidney George Fisher, *The Law of the Territories* (Philadelphia, 1859); Joel Parker, *Personal Liberty Laws (Statutes of Massachusetts) and Slavery in the Territories (Case of Dred Scott)* (Boston, 1861).

40. *De Bow's Review*, XXII (April 1857), 403. This premier southern magazine carried no significant analysis of the decision.

41. The speech was carried in a number of newspapers, such as the Providence *Post*, Nov. 5, 1857. A copy of the broadside edition is in the Cushing Papers, MDLC, accompanying a letter dated November 9 from Calvin C. Chaffee in which Chaffee challenged Cushing to produce his authority for the following sentence in the speech: "Meanwhile, by the death of Dr. Emerson and by marriage, Dred became the property of Dr. Chaffee, member of the last Congress from Massachusetts." Thus Chaffee was still prepared to dispute any statement that he had ever been the owner of Dred Scott. From a note of endorsement on the letter, it appears that Cushing, perhaps fearing a libel suit, met with Chaffee in the presence of Congressman Henry L. Dawes and agreed to modify the sentence in a revised edition of the speech. Cushing as attorney general had anticipated part of the Dred Scott decision by ruling that Negroes were not citizens and casting doubt on the constitutionality of the Missouri Compromise restriction. See *Official Opinions of the Attorneys General of the United States*, VII, 571, 576, VIII, 139, 142; and M. Michael Catherine Hodgson, *Caleb Cushing, Attorney General of the United States, 1853–1857* (Washington, D.C., 1955), 158–62.

42 Taney to Cushing, Nov. 9, 1857, Cushing Papers. MDLC. The Dred Scott decision also received high praise from Richard Rush, statesman and diplomat of the preceding generation, and son of the antislavery leader of Revolutionary times, Benjamin Rush. He said that Taney's opinion was a "masterpiece" and probably the most important decision ever rendered by the Court. Rush to Benjamin C. Howard, June 4, 1857, Howard Papers, Maryland Historical Society.

43. Samuel Tyler, *Memoir of Roger Brooke Taney, LL.D.*, 2nd ed. (Baltimore, 1876), 660–64.

44. J. H. Van Evrie, *The Dred Scott Decision* (New York, 1859), iii; George M. Fredrickson, *The Black Image in the White Mind: The Debate on Afro-American Character and Destiny, 1817–1914* (New York, 1971), 91–94. During the Civil War, Van Evrie became one of the leading propagandists against emancipation on racial grounds.

45. Benjamin Quarles, *Black Abolitionists* (New York, 1969), 230–34.

46. Bangor *Whig and Courier*, March 15, 1857.

47. Reprinted in *The Liberator*, April 3, 1857.

48. Louisville *Democrat*, April 8, 1857, "The late decision of the Supreme Court will have one happy effect," said the *Democrat*. "It will throw this whole negro controversy upon the real point at issue; and brush away the rubbish about free dirt [soil] and free labor. The real issue is the equality of the negro with the white man. On the Topeka constitution's racism, see also Portland *Eastern Argus*, April 2, 1857; Madison (Wis.) *Weekly Argus and Democrat*, June 23, 1857.

49. Draft of a speech, 1861, pp. 13, 16, Susan B. Anthony Papers, MDLC. At a meeting to protest the decision in Philadelphia on April 3, 1857, the black leader Robert Purvis declared that there was nothing new in the decision, that it was "in perfect keeping with the treatment of the colored people by the Ameri-

can Government from the beginning to this day." *The Liberator*, April 10, 1857.

50. An Ohio supreme court decision in 1831, *Gray v. Ohio*, 4 Ohio Reports 353, 354, had defined white as anything more than half white. All southern states that defined a Negro set the minimum at one-fourth Negro blood or less. See Ira Berlin, *Slaves Without Masters: The Free Negro in the Antebellum South* (New York, 1974), 161–62. The Tennessee provision is in Return J. Meigs and William F. Cooper, *The Code of Tennessee Enacted by the General Assembly of 1857–8* (Nashville, 1858), 687.

51. Leon F. Litwack, *North of Slavery: The Negro in the Free States, 1790–1860* (Chicago, 1961), 54–59; Henry Wilson, *History of the Rise and Fall of the Slave Power in America* (3 vols.; 1872–77), II, 638; Herbert Aptheker, *A Documentary History of the Negro People in the United States* (New York, 1951, 1969), 447–48, for example of a Negro whose pre-emption claim was canceled after he had invested much labor and money in it; Burlington (Vt.) *Free Press*, April 14, 1858, and New Orleans *Picayune*, April 22, 1858, on refusal of passports; Chicago *Tribune*, May 3, 1858, on pre-emption and command of vessels.

52. *Acts Passed at the Twelfth Session of the General Assembly of the State of Arkansas* (Little Rock, 1859), 175–78. The same session of the legislature forbade emancipation absolutely. *Ibid.*, 69. Florida and Missouri governors vetoed expulsion laws; Maryland voters rejected such a law by referendum. Mississippi and Tennessee legislatures turned against the idea. Conscience, economic considerations, and the secession crisis all worked against the movement. In addition, there was a somewhat delayed realization that re-enslaved blacks would make dangerous slaves. Berlin, *Slaves Without Masters*, 368–80.

53. "Opinions of the Justices of the Supreme Judicial Court on Questions Propounded by the Senate, March 26, 1857," 44 Maine Reports 505 (1857), excerpts in Stanley I. Kutler, ed., *The Dred Scott Decision, Law or Politics?* (New York, 1967), 90–99.

54. In 1854, Curtis had been influential in securing the indictment of Wendell Phillips, Theodore Parker, and several other persons in connection with the Anthony Burns rescue affair. For this he was denounced in the New York *Tribune* as "a slave-catching Judge, appointed to office as a reward for his professional support given to the Fugitive Slave bill." Said Curtis, "My duty is to administer the law. This will be done." A technical defect, pointed out by Curtis himself, resulted in an entry of *nolle prosequi*. Curtis, *Memoir*, I, 173–75, 177–78; Warren, *Supreme Court*, II, 272; *U.S. v. Stowell*, 27 Federal Cases 1350 (1854).

55. A senator under instruction from his legislature had three choices; he could obey, or disobey, or resign. During the great debates of 1850, for instance, Stephen A. Douglas said at one point: "If we are to take cognizance of the subject of slavery there [Utah and New Mexico], then I am compelled to vote according to my view of what is right under my instructions." *CG*, 31-1, p. 1143. On the other hand, George W. Jones of Iowa defied legislative instruction in 1858 to support administration policy in Kansas. *Iowa State Gazette* (Burlington), Feb. 18, 1858.

56. Norwich (Conn.) *Weekly Courier*, May 13, 1857; Providence *Post*, May 15, 1857; Portsmouth (N.H.) *Journal*, May 23, 1857.

57. Bangor *Whig and Courier*, May 2, 19, 1857.
58. Portsmouth *Journal*, June 20, 1857; Hurd, *Law of Freedom and Bondage*, II, 36, 40; *Acts and Resolves Passed by the General Court of Massachusetts in the Year 1857* (Boston, 1857), 635–36. On New York and Ohio, see notes 59–68 below. Pennsylvania passed no legislation on the subject, but for a time considerable excitement was caused by the joint resolution introduced by J. N. Harris, declaring that the Supreme Court "has become little else than the willing tool of pro-Slavery politicians, and has rendered a judgment in the Dred Scott case, which is a more monstrous prevarication of truth and right, than any to be found in the records of any nation calling itself free and enlightened." [Pennsylvania General Assembly], *Daily Legislative Record*, 1857 session, no. 53, pp. 1–3 (March 23, 1857); also no. 90, pp. 4–7, a committee report arguing that Negroes were citizens and denouncing the "startling and monstrous doctrine" that slavery was property under the Constitution.
59. *N.Y. Senate Journal*, 80 session, 1857, pp. 67, 354; *N.Y. Assembly Journal*, 80 session, 556, 861; New York *Tribune*, March 26, 1857, giving the Assembly vote as 75 to 27. The *Tribune* gave the measure no editorial support. See also Litwack, *North of Slavery*, 87–90. The property requirement for Negro suffrage, set in the state constitution of 1821 and reaffirmed in the constitution of 1846, was a $250 freehold. Various newspapers, getting their chronology confused, saw the proposal as a retaliation for *Dred Scott;* New Orleans *Picayune*, April 11, 18, 1857; New York *Journal of Commerce*, April 9, 1857; Washington *Union*, April 11, 1857.
60. *N.Y. Assembly Documents*, 80 session, 1857, no. 201, pp. 1–6 (also *Senate Document* no. 158). The quotation from Madison's Virginia Resolutions asserted the right of the state of "interpose" when the federal government exceeded its constitutional limits. The report was published in the New York *Herald*, April 12, 1857, with the extravagant comment: "Here are the elements of sedition, bad faith, discord, rebellion, and revolution."
61. Sickles was tried in 1859 for killing his wife's lover, Philip Barton Key, U.S. district attorney in Washington and son of Taney's brother-in-law, Francis Scott Key. Sickles pleaded temporary insanity, assertedly for the first time, in legal history, and was acquitted. W. A. Swanberg, *Sickles the Incredible* (New York, 1956), 37–67, 199–219.
62. *N.Y. Senate Journal*, 1857, pp. 1037–41; *N.Y. Assembly Journal*, 1857, pp. 1543–44; New York *Tribune*, April 18, 1857; New York *Herald*, April 18, 1857, said that the legislature had nullified the Dred Scott decision.
63. The census of 1860 showed about 49,000 Negroes in New York, many of them disfranchised by the property qualification. The five New England states with equal suffrage (all but Connecticut) had a total black population of approximately 16,000. It is difficult to accept the estimate of *Douglass' Monthly*, February, March 1859, pp. 21, 37, that of 13,675 black men over age twenty-one in the state, more than 10,000 voted in the gubernatorial election of 1858.
64. New Orleans *Picayune*, April 11, 18, 1857.
65. *The Tribune Almanac and Political Register for 1859*, 45. This was a lesser election for state offices below the office of governor.

66. Allan Nevins and Milton Halsey Thomas, eds., *The Diary of George Templeton Strong* (4 vols.; New York, 1952), II, 369.
67. *Douglass' Monthly*, Dec. 1860, p. 369, which added that many Republicans at the polls refused to touch a ticket in favor of the amendment.
68. *Acts . . . of Ohio*, 52nd assembly, 2nd session (1857), 170, 186; *ibid.*, 53rd assembly, 1st session (1858), 10, 19; Eugene H. Roseboom, *The Civil War Era, 1850–1873*, Volume IV of Carl Wittke, ed., *The History of the State of Ohio* (6 vols.; Columbus, 1944), pp. 326–29, 341–42. The visible admixture law, which meant that anyone of swarthy complexion (like Abraham Lincoln or his running-mate Hannibal Hamlin) could be challenged at the polls. It was declared unconstitutional by the state Supreme Court in *Anderson v. Millikin*, 9 Ohio State Reports 568, 579–80 (1859), and repealed by the next Republican legislature. The Ohio legislature in 1857 also passed a series of resolutions on the Dred Scott decision, including one declaring that it foreshadowed or included a guaranteed right of transit. *Ohio Senate Journal*, 52nd assembly, 2nd session, 425–26, 453–56; *Ohio House of Representatives Journal*, 52nd, 2nd, 565–66. A committee report in the Senate declared that the Dred Scott decision had "no parallel in wickedness in the history of the world," and that it would "take more than one decision fulminated by a jesuitical catholic judge to conquer a free protestant people." *Senate Journal*, 568–72 (Appendix).
69. Roseboom, *Civil War Era*, 325, 328. The panic began in Ohio with the failure of the Ohio Life Insurance Company of Cincinnati in August.
70. *CWAL*, II, 391.
71. *Ibid.*, 404. Speech of June 26, 1857 at Springfield in reply to one made two weeks earlier by Douglas.
72. *Ibid.*, 405.
73. *Ibid.*, 405, 408–9, 498; III, 80, 84, 146, 402, 504.
74. *Ibid.*, 177, 179. This was the debate at Charleston, September 18, 1858. *Douglas:* "He declared his utter opposition to the Dred Scott decision, and advanced as a reason that the court had decided that it was not possible for a negro to be a citizen. . . . If he is opposed to the Dred Scott decision for that reason he must be in favor of conferring . . . citizenship upon the negro!" *Lincoln:* "I mentioned in a certain speech of mine . . . that the Supreme Court had decided that a negro could not possibly be made a citizen, and without saying what was my ground of complaint in regard to that, or whether I had any ground of complaint, Judge Douglas has from that thing manufactured nearly every thing that he ever says about my disposition to produce an equality between the negroes and the white people. . . . Now my opinion is that the different States have the power to make a negro a citizen . . . if they choose. The Dred Scott decision decides that they have not that power. If the State of Illinois had that power I should be opposed to the exercise of it. . . . That is all I have to say about it."
75. Eric Foner, *Free Soil, Free Labor, Free Men: The Ideology of the Republican Party before the Civil War* (New York, 1970), 264–80; Eugene H. Berwanger, *The Frontier Against Slavery: Western Anti-Negro Prejudice and the Slavery Extension Controversy* (Urbana, Ill., 1967), 130–34. Leaders in the revival of the

colonization movement were the Blair family. Montgomery Blair, in recruiting Senator James R. Doolittle of Wisconsin, declared: "It would do more, too, than ten thousand speeches to define accurately our objects and disabuse the minds of the great body of the Southern people . . . that the Republicans wish to set negroes free among them to be their equals and consequently their rulers when they are numerous." William Ernest Smith, *The Francis Preston Blair Family in Politics* (2 vols.; New York, 1933), I, 443–50, especially p. 445. On Republican racial attitudes, see also John M. Rozett, "Racism and Republican Emergence in Illinois, 1848–1860: A Re-Evaluation of Republican Negrophobia," *CWH*, XXII (1976), 101–15.

76. Horace Greeley, *An Overland Journey from New York to San Francisco in the Summer of 1859* (New York, 1860), p. 37.

77. *N.Y. Assembly Documents*, 80th session, 1857, no. 201, p. 3; New York *Tribune*, March 11, 1857; Bangor *Whig and Courier*, March 15, 1857; *Ohio State Journal* (Columbus), March 11, 1857, declaring that the Dred Scott decision had transformed the territories into "one great slave pen," and that the federal government threatened to "cover our whole continent with slavery as the waters cover the sea."

78. On earlier nationalization of slavery, see above, 36–47, and for further discussion, see above, 487–88, 492–93.

79. For example, New York *Tribune*, March 12, 1857; Bangor *Whig and Courier*, March 15, 1857; *CWAL*, II, 401.

80. David M. Potter, *The Impending Crisis, 1848–1861*, completed and edited by Don E. Fehrenbacher (New York, 1976), 284.

81. *Ableman v. Booth*, 21 Howard 506, 520.

82. Charles Grove Haines, *The American Doctrine of Judicial Supremacy* (Los Angeles, 1932; New York, 1959), 27–28, 241–53, 332–34, and *passim*. Scholars favoring judicial activism object to the phrase "judicial supremacy," but it is scarcely more misleading than "judicial review" as a description of the power exercised by the Supreme Court in the twentieth century. The important point is the vast difference between the narrow and broad concepts of judicial review. For the complaints of the pro-activism writers, see F. D. G. Ribble, "Judicial Review and the Maintenance of the Federal System," in W. Melville Jones, ed., *Chief Justice John Marshall, A Reappraisal* (Ithaca, N.Y., 1956), 61–64; Charles L. Black, Jr., *The People and the Court: Judicial Review in a Democracy* (New York, 1960), 167–68; Eugene V. Rostow, *The Sovereign Prerogative: The Supreme Court and the Quest for Law* (New Haven, 1962), 89–90. Black, for example, says, "The very most the Court ever has is a veto." But this is surely a grossly understated description of the Court's modern policy-making role.

83. Unpublished opinion of Taney, May 28, 1832. See Chapter III, note 76 above. A transcript is in the Carl B. Swisher Papers, MDLC.

84. New York *Tribune*, Feb. 19, 1856.

85. *Ibid.*, March 12, 16, 1857.

86. *CWAL*, II, 401.

87. *Ibid.*, 400–403, 495; III, 255.

88. New York *Times*, June 23, 1857.
89. *Anderson v. Poindexter*, 6 Ohio State Reports 622. One of the concurring jus-
     tices, Jacob Brinkerhoff (chief rival claimant to authorship of the Wilmot Pro-
     viso), summed up in one sentence the new and radical northern attitude toward
     sojourn and transit: "Poindexter, having come into a free state otherwise than by
     escaping, was free; and having thus become free, could not again be reduced to
     slavery" (pp. 636–37).
90. *Lemmon v. the People*, 20 New York Reports 562. It was a 5-to-3 decision.
     Southern newspapers took much interest in the case. The *Charleston Courier* of
     April 14, 1857, for example, saw it as a test of sojourners' rights. See also Paul
     Finkelman, "A More Perfect Union? Slavery, Comity, and Federalism,
     1787–1861," Ph.D. dissertation, University of Chicago, 1976, pp. 312–32.
91. *Mitchell v. Lamar*, an unreported case, being a damage suit with a plea to the
     jurisdiction of the Court, just as in the case of *Dred Scott*. Chicago *Democratic
     Press*, May 15, quoted in New York *Evening Post*, May 20, 1857, and also in
     National Era (Washington), July 30, 1857.
92. The case was not reported. Taney's "supplement" is in Tyler, *Memoir of Taney*,
     578–608.
93. *Ibid.*, 578–79.
94. *Ibid.*, 583–89, 593.
95. George Ticknor Curtis, *Constitutional History of the United States* (2 vols.; New
     York, 1896), 276n.
96. Quoted from the New York *Independent*, April 3, 1886, in Warren, *Supreme
     Court*, II, 304.
97. Philadelphia *Pennsylvanian*, July 22, 1857.
98. Tyler, *Memoir of Taney*, 601.
99. *Ibid.*, 607–8.

CHAPTER 19

1. Augusta *Constitutionalist*, March 15, 1857.
2. Charleston *Mercury*, April 20, 21, 1857. The Richmond *South*, as quoted in the
    Madison (Wis.) *State Journal* of April 24, echoed the doubts of the *Mercury*:
    "Another such success as was achieved in the Kansas-Nebraska act, and the
    South would have been undone—so hardly was the victory won and so much of
    resentment and ferocious energy did it infuse in the ranks of the adversary. It
    seems as if the same consequence will follow from our recent triumphs in the
    Supreme Court." On the string of "empty" southern victories, see David M.
    Potter, *The Impending Crisis, 1848–1861*, completed and edited by Don E.
    Fehrenbacher (New York, 1976), 325–26.
3. Savannah (Ga.) *Republican*, March 12, 1857.
4. Albert J. Beveridge, at work upon his biography of Lincoln in the 1920s became
    convinced that the Dred Scott decision "literally saved the Republican Party
    from collapse." More than that, on the basis of finding less reference to *Dred
    Scott* in manuscript collections than he had expected, Beveridge became almost

obsessed with the idea that the public at large had no interest in the case until Republican leaders began to use it for propaganda purposes because they were "in a bad way for an issue" in early 1857. Beveridge to Frank L. Owsley, Nov. 24, 1926; to William E. Dodd, Dec. 13, 1926; to Justice Oliver Wendell Holmes, Jan. 27, 1927; to Frank H. Hodder, Feb. 3, 1927; to Nathaniel W. Stephenson, March 21, 1927; to Charles A. Beard, April 7, 1927, Beveridge Papers, MDLC; and see his *Abraham Lincoln, 1809–1858* (2 vols.; Boston, 1928), II, 497–99.

5. New York *Evening Post*, March 7, 1857; Chicago *Tribune*, March 12, 14, 16, 1857. See also Madison *State Journal*, March 17, 21, 1857; Bloomington (Ill.) *Pantagraph*, March 17, 1857, declaring: "One little step only remains: to decide all *State* prohibitions of Slavery to be void; and our enslavement is complete."

6. Allan Nevins, *The Emergence of Lincoln* (2 vols.; New York, 1950), I, 362; David Brion Davis, *The Slave Power Conspiracy and the Paranoid Style* (Baton Rouge, 1969), 5.

7. Quoted in Indianapolis *State Sentinel*, March 25, 1857.

8. *CG*, 35-1, pp. 385, 665. Harlan also argued that equal enjoyment of the public domain meant slaveholding rights on public lands within free states.

9. The quotation is from the House-Divided speech, June 16, 1858 *CWAL*, II, 467. See also *CWAL*, III, 27, 78, 250, 255.

10. Richard H. Sewell, *Ballots for Freedom: Antislavery Politics in the United States, 1837–1860* (New York, 1976), 301–2. See also Harry V. Jaffa, *Crisis of the House Divided: An Interpretation of the Issues in the Lincoln-Douglas Debates* (New York, 1959), 275–93.

11. The *Union* article was quoted in full and attacked by Douglas in the Senate on March 22, 1858, *CG*, 35-1, App., 199–200. The *Union* backed off a bit in some of its later editorials. There were scattered newspaper reports in 1857 of slaves being taken into free states and free territory, with the Dred Scott decision cited as justification. One southerner in Minnesota reportedly announced his intention of staying there permanently with his slaves. *Minnesota Republican* (St. Anthony), quoted in Baltimore *Sun*, June 11, 1857; Lafayette (Ind.) *Journal*, Nov. 17, 1857; Chicago *Tribune* Nov. 23, 1857. For further discussion, see above, 477–78.

12. *Ableman v. Booth*, 21 Howard 506; Carl B. Swisher, *The Taney Period, 1836–1864*, Volume V of the Oliver Wendell Holmes Devise *History of the Supreme Court of the United States* (New York, 1974), 653–75. There is a curious personal connection between the *Dred Scott* and *Booth* cases. Benammi S. Garland of St. Louis, who for some ten years acted as agent for John F. A. Sanford in respect to Dred Scott (employing counsel, collecting hire money, etc.), was the slaveholder whose forcible recapture of his escaped slave near Racine, Wisconsin, in 1854 set the stage for the Booth affair. *Ibid.*, 653–56; Vincent C. Hopkins, *Dred Scott's Case* (New York, 1951, 1967), 30.

13. Maurice S. Culp, "A Survey of the Proposals to Limit or Deny the Power of Judicial Review by the Supreme Court of the United States," *Indiana Law Journal*, IV (1928–29), 386–98, 474–90.

14. Especially by Charles Warren, who paid too much attention to the oratory of

John P. Hale and a few other radical Republicans. In his *The Supreme Court in United States History*, rev. ed. (2 vols.; Boston, 1932), II, 333, Warren writes, for example, of efforts in Congress "to weaken the authority of the Court, by a move to repeal the Twenty-Fifth Section of the Judiciary Act [of 1789] and to abolish the Court's jurisdiction on writs of error to State Courts; and bills for this purpose (originating in Ohio) were introduced in both the Senate and the House, in the spring of 1858." This sounds formidable, but it turns out that the bill in the Senate was introduced by George E. Pugh, a Democrat rather than a Republican; it was not reported favorably from committee and occasioned not a single vote or word of debate. *Senate Journal*, 35-1 (Serial 917), 365, 510, Warren says that Philemon Bliss, a Republican, introduced a similar bill in the House, but according to both the *CG*, 35-1, p. 1131, and the *House Journal*, 35-1 (Serial 940), 497, 708, the Bliss bill was for repeal of the *twenty-fourth* section of the Judiciary Act, a far less significant section. In any case, it was reported adversely and occasioned no debate.

15.   *CG*, 35-1, p. 943.

16.   *CWAL*, III, 232. William P. Fessenden of Maine had said about the same thing in the Senate on February 8, 1858. *CG*, 35-1, p. 617.

17.   Warren, *Supreme Court*, II, 357.

18.   See, for example, *Iowa State Democrat* (Davenport), March 17, April 3, Dec. 10, 1857; Portland (Me.) *Eastern Argus*, March 13, 16, 17, 24; May 20, 1857.

19.   James D. Richardson, ed., *Messages and Papers of the Presidents* (11 vols.; Washington, D.C., 1913), IV, 2962. Buchanan, in fact, had endorsed the southern position in his inaugural, before the decision was rendered. The Charleston *Courier*, March 9, 1857, said that Buchanan's statement, coupled with the Dred Scott decision, constituted a "repudiation of the wild doctrine of 'squatter sovereignty,' notwithstanding the induction of its patriotic, but mistaken, author and apostle [Lewis Cass] into the Cabinet."

20.   New York *Times*, June 23, 1857.

21.   Don E. Fehrenbacher, *Prelude to Greatness: Lincoln in the 1850's* (Stanford, 1962), 132, 134.

22.   *CG*, 34-3, pp. 67, 103–4; App., 104.

23.   Washington *Union*, June 23, 1857. The Memphis *Appeal*, June 24, 1857, published the entire speech, saying that the subjects in it were "ably handled." The Richmond *South* of June 20, quoted in the New York *Herald*, June 24, printed an extensive summary of the speech and said, "An unbiased judgment can no more resist his conclusions than a cultivated intelligence can refuse its homage to the ability of his performance." The *Herald* commented that this was Douglas's opening bid for the presidential nomination and foreshadowed his position as favorite of southern ultras against the Buchanan wing of the party.

24.   On Kansas in 1857–58, see Potter, *Impending Crisis*, 297–327; Nevins, *Emergence of Lincoln*, I, 133–75, 229–49; Roy Franklin Nichols, *The Disruption of American Democracy* (New York, 1948), 94–131; James A. Rawley, *Race and Politics: "Bleeding Kansas" and the Coming of the Civil War* (Philadelphia, 1969), 202–56. Documents are in *Transactions of the Kansas State Historical Society*, Volume V (1889–96), 264–561.

25. On Walker, see James P. Shenton, *Robert John Walker, a Politician from Jackson to Lincoln* (New York, 1961). On the Buchanan administration in general, see Nichols, *Disruption;* and Elbert B. Smith, *The Presidency of James Buchanan* (Lawrence, Kans., 1975).

26. See Walker's letter to Buchanan, June 28, 1857, *House Reports*, 36-1, no. 648 (Serial 1071), 115. This is the report of the Covode Committee investigating irregularities in the Buchanan administration (1860).

27. The Walker inaugural is in *KSHS Transactions*, V, 328–41.

28. Mobile *Advertiser*, July 26, 1857; also June 28, July 18, 21, 28, 31, 1857.

29. Charleston *Courier*, July 18, 22, Aug. 4, 1857.

30. Ulrich Bonnell Phillips, ed., *The Correspondence of Robert Toombs, Alexander H. Stephens, and Howell Cobb*, AHA *Annual Report*, 1911, II, 400–401. The theme of betrayal was common. For instance, the New Orleans *Crescent* of July 17, 1857, quoted in Avery O. Craven, *The Growth of Southern Nationalism, 1848–1861* (Baton Rouge, 1953), 284, said: "So far as Kansas is concerned, the South has been irredeemably sold by the administration—by an administration that went into power on her votes."

31. Columbus (Ga.) *Times and Sentinel*, quoted in Augusta *Constitutionalist*, July 16, 1857; Nevins, *Emergence of Lincoln*, I, 165–66.

32. Washington *Union*, July 7, 9, 14, 1857. *North Carolina Standard* (Raleigh), July 15, 1857; Wilmington (N.C.) *Journal*, July 10, 1857.

33. Buchanan to Walker, July 12, 1857, *House Reports*, 36-1, no. 648 (Serial 1071), 112–13.

34. Toombs to W. W. Burwell, July 11, 1857, *Correspondence of Toombs, Stephens, and Cobb*, 403.

35. Mobile *Advertiser*, Nov. 11, 1857; see also *Advertiser*, Nov. 28, 1857.

36. The New York *Herald*, June 24, 1857, said: "The plan of Mr. Douglas is to make Kansas a slave State, by . . . the process of adopting in Congress this forthcoming pro-slavery constitution, without referring it to a vote of the Kansas people." This was the *Herald's* reading of Douglas's Springfield speech.

37. *KSHS Transactions*, V, 403–8; Potter, *Impending Crisis*, 306.

38. Text of the constitution in *House Reports*, 35-1, No. 377 (Serial 966), 73–92. Article Seven, on slavery, at 81–82.

39. *Ibid.*, 89–90. Even after seven years, amendment could be achieved only with difficulty. A two-thirds vote of the legislature and a majority vote of registered voters were required just to call a convention.

40. Nevins, *Emergence of Lincoln*, I, 280–81.

41. Philip Shriver Klein, *President James Buchanan, a Biography* (University Park, Pa., 1962), 308; Potter, *Impending Crisis*, 313–14; Nevins, *Emergence*, I, 169–70.

42. Annual message, Dec. 8, 1857, Richardson, ed., *Messages and Papers*, IV, 2984.

43. New York *Times*, June 23, 1857. Douglas said twice in that speech that the free-staters and Republicans would be responsible, it being their policy "to produce strife, anarchy, and bloodshed in Kansas." For his denunciation of the Lecompton convention as illegitimate because Congress had not passed an enabling act,

see his Senate speech, Dec. 9, 1857, *CG*, 35-1, pp. 15–16. Douglas denied that a territorial legislature had the power on its own to call a constitutional convention. This was in sharp contrast with his argument in 1859 in his *Harper's* essay. See above, 519–20.

44. W. D. Porter to James H. Hammond, Dec. 28, 1857, Hammond Papers, MDLC; Charleston *Mercury*, Jan. 16, 1858; and see Harold S. Schultz, *Nationalism and Sectionalism in South Carolina, 1852–1860* (Durham, N.C., 1950), 168–69.

45. Douglas to Buchanan, Sept. 4, Oct. 8, 1857, in Robert W. Johannsen, ed., *The Letters of Stephen A. Douglas* (Urbana, Ill., 1961), 397–99, 401–2, in which Douglas speaks of Illinois as having been treated with "neglect and injustice." But see also David E. Meerse, "Origins of the Buchanan-Douglas Feud Reconsidered," *Journal of the Illinois State Historical Society*, LXVII (1974), 154–74, in which it is argued that Douglas really was not mistreated and that patronage problems had little to do with alienating him from Buchanan.

46. C. Goudy (Taylorville, Ill.) to Douglas, Dec. 20, 1857; James Williams (Belvidere, Ill.) to Douglas, Jan. 26, 1858; E. Currier (South Grove, Ill.) to Douglas, Jan. 29, 1858, Stephen A. Douglas Papers, University of Chicago. Also, Alvin Hovey (Mt. Vernon, Inc.) to Douglas, Dec. 21, 1857, *ibid.:* "You have occupied the only ground upon which the northern democracy can stand, and if you fail, our party in the free states is destroyed." Even the Charleston *Mercury*, Dec. 16, 1857, acknowledged that Douglas was acting out of necessity: "He had long acted fairly towards the South. We believe that he would still be disposed to continue this course; but in that course lies political ruin. Cast out of the Senate by the Legislature of Illinois, where would he be three years hence, in the great game of Presidential aspirations?" See also *Mercury*, Jan. 5, 1858.

47. Shenton, *Walker*, 173–74; Washington *Union*, Nov. 18, 1857.

48. Robert W. Johannsen, *Stephen A. Douglas* (New York, 1973), 586–92; Richardson, ed., *Messages and Papers*, IV, 2980–85.

49. *CG*, 35-1, pp. 14–19.

50. Jackson *Mississippian*, Dec. 7, 1858. On the Douglas-Buchanan quarrel in general, see Reinhard H. Luthin, "The Democratic Split During Buchanan's Administration," *Pennsylvania History*, II (1944), 13–35.

51. In the Senate, the debate was usually on the motion of Douglas to refer the Kansas portion of the annual message to his committee on territories. In the House, members often took advantage of gaining the floor to speak on Kansas, whatever the nominal subject under consideration. Thus, on January 29, when the committee of the whole was considering an invalids' pension bill, Thomas L. Anderson of Missouri delivered a long pro-Lecompton speech in which he asserted that slavery had been "established in the early ages of the world, under the express authority of Heaven." *CG*, 35-1, pp. 417–21.

52. *House Reports*, 35-1, No. 377 (Serial 966), 93–97. Stanton was a proslavery Tennessean who had served ten years in Congress. His letter defending himself is in *CG*, 35-1, pp. 596–97. Walker resigned in a long letter, Dec. 15, 1857, *KSHS Transactions*, V, 421–30.

53. Richardson, ed., *Messages and Papers*, IV, 3002–12. The historian George Ban-

croft, who had served with Buchanan in Polk's cabinet, tried in vain to dissuade the President, writing on December 5, 1857: "I entreat you, as one who most sincerely wishes honor and success to your administration, not to endorse the Lecompton Constitution." James Buchanan Papers, Historical Society of Pennsylvania.

54. W. D. Porter to James H. Hammond, Jan. 30, 1858, Hammond Papers, MDLC. Robert W. Barnwell stated the paradox when he wrote to Hammond January 18 that South Carolina would probably leave the Union over the issue, though it was "a feeble one." These and other letters to Hammond on the subject are quoted in Schultz, *Nationalism and Sectionalism*, 154n.

55. *CG*, 35-1, pp. 1–2, 38–41. These are the figures given in the *Congressional Globe* at the beginning of the session. In May 1858, two representatives from the newly admitted state of Minnesota took their seats. Both were Democrats. Also, in May, an Ohio Republican was unseated in an election contest and replaced by Democrat Clement L. Vallandigham. Early in the session, Nathaniel P. Banks resigned to accept election as governor of Massachusetts and his successor was promptly elected. These changes presumably account for the totals of 131 Democrats, 93 Republicans, and 14 Whig-Americans given in Thomas B. Alexander, *Sectional Stress and Party Strength: A Study of Roll-Call Voting Patterns in the United States House of Representatives, 1836–1860* (Nashville, 1967), 19. One newly elected Democrat in the Senate, Martin W. Bates of Delaware, never attended throughout the session, according to the record.

56. The vote was on the question of whether to refer the President's Kansas message to the committee on territories, controlled by administration supporters, or to a select committee with investigative authority. The question produced an all-night filibuster February 5–6 and a brawl on the floor of the House, begun by Lawrence M. Keitt, a South Carolina fire-eater, and Galusha A. Grow, radical Republican from Ohio. The anti-Lecompton victory was nullified when Speaker James L. Orr of South Carolina loaded the select committee with pro-Lecompton men. *CG*, 35-1, pp. 597–606, 621–23; Nichols, *Disruption*, 164–67.

57. Harris to John A. McClernand, Feb. 16, 1858, McClernand Papers, Illinois State Historical Library.

58. *CG*, 35-1, p. 140. "All other men are permitted to dissent but me," Douglas complained. "If I dissent, it disturbs the harmony of the Democratic party!"

59. *Ibid.*, 38, 209–12. Bliss's denunciation is especially interesting because he concentrated on Taney's ruling against Negro citizenship, calling it a "wicked edict" that had "hardly been surpassed in atrocity" since the revocation of the Edict of Nantes. Rivaling Bliss in denunciatory vehemence was E. P. Walton of Vermont. See *CG*, 35-1, App., 331–36.

60. *CG*, 35-1, pp. 315–21, 341–45.

61. *Ibid.*, 384–85, 402.

62. *Ibid.*, 852–55. Chaffee's speech was reprinted as an eight-page pamphlet with the title: *The Lecompton Constitution: A Measure to Africanize the Territories of the United States.* See also the remarks of Lyman Trumbull, p. 522; Benjamin F. Wade, p. 1114; and especially Jacob Collamer of Vermont, pp. 924–25.

63. *CG*, 35-1 , pp. 617, 1115.
64. The characterization is from Warren, *Supreme Court*, II, 326, who also called the speech "slanderous."
65. *CG*, 35-1, p. 941. See also, for a more ornate kind of invective, the speech of Owen Lovejoy, 752–754: "The demon of slavery has come forth from the tombs. It . . . dodges behind the national compact, and grins and chatters out its senile puerilities about constitutional sanction; and then, like a very fantastic ape, jumps upon the bench, puts on ermine and wig, and pronounces the dictum that a certain class of human beings have no rights which another certain class are bound to regard. . . . It claims the right to pollute the Territories with its slimy footsteps, and then makes its way to the very home of freedom in the free States, carried there on a constitutional palanquin, manufactured and borne aloft on the one side by a Democratic Executive, and on the other by a Democratic Jesuit judge!"
66. Samuel Tyler, *Memoir of Roger Brooke Taney, LL.D.*, 2nd ed. (Baltimore, 1876), 386, 391. Tyler devoted some eighteen pages to Seward's speech and rebuttal to it.
67. Senator Judah P. Benjamin, ten days later, *CG*, 35-1, p. 1071.
68. *Ibid.*, App., 403.
69. *CG*, 35-1, pp. 1065–72.
70. *Ibid.*, 524.
71. *Ibid.*, 615–16. Italics added to the Fessenden question.
72. *CG*, 35-1, App., 199–200.
73. See the exchange between Douglas and Lincoln on the subject in their debates at Ottawa and Freeport, August 21, 27, 1858, *CWAL*, III, 24–27, 69–70.
74. *CG*, 35-1, pp. 1261, 1264–65. On Crittenden, see Albert D. Kirwan, *John J. Crittenden: The Struggle for the Union* (Lexington, Ky., 1962), 321–29.
75. New York *Tribune*, March 29, 30, 31, 1858; Nevins, *Emergence of Lincoln*, I, 292–93; Potter, *Impending Crisis*, 322–23; Richardson, ed., *Messages and Papers*, IV, 3010.
76. *CG*, 35-1, pp. 1435–38. William Montgomery an anti-Lecompton Democrat from Pennsylvania, moved the Crittenden substitute in the House.
77. *U.S. Statutes at Large*, XI, 269–72.
78. *CG*, 35-1 pp. 1899, 1905–6. Thomas L. Harris, House leader of the anti-Lecompton Democrats, charged that the administration had "bought men like hogs in the market." Johannsen, *Douglas*, 613.
79. J. M. Davidson to Douglas, April 27, 1858, Douglas Papers, University of Chicago. "Any reconciliation between you and the Administration party soils you, yes, to be plain, degrades you and strikes you down from that high position where you have fearlessly and consistently battled." So wrote Usher F. Linder of Charleston, Ill., May 15, 1858. On Douglas's decision about the English bill, see especially Damon Wells, *Stephen Douglas, the Last Years, 1857–1861* (Austin, 1971), 46–51. I cannot agree, however, with Wells' judgment that "much southern anger with Douglas was short-lived." On the English bill generally, see Frank H. Hodder, "Some Aspects of the English Bill for the Admission of Kansas," AHA *Annual Report* 1906, I, 201–10.

80. James D. Tradewell to Hammond, Feb. 11, 1858, Hammond Papers, MDLC; also A. B. Crook to Hammond, Feb. 5, 1858; Hammond to William Gilmore Simms, Feb. 7, 1858, declaring: "I now say Lecompton or Separation."

81. Mobile *Register*, Jan. 8, 24, 1858; New York *Times*, Feb. 3, 1858; Jackson *Mississippian* (semi-weekly edition), Jan. 15, 1858, quoting Unionist papers favoring resistance or separation if Kansas should be rejected. *CG*, 35-1, p. 770, gives the heart of the Alabama resolutions preparing for a secession convention. See *ibid.*, 393, for the statement of Lucius J. Gartrell of Georgia: "Upon the action of this Congress, must depend the union or disunion of this great confederacy." Also p. 858, Reuben Davis of Mississippi: "Reject Kansas and the cordon is then completed, and the South forever degraded. . . . Against this final act of degradation I believe the South will resist—resist with arms." There is no general study of the secession movement of 1858.

82. Brown to Stephens, Feb. 9 and also March 26, 1858, *Correspondence of Toombs, Stephens, and Cobb*, 431–33.

83. Memphis *Appeal*, Feb. 6, 1858.

84. New Orleans *Picayune*, Feb. 4, 1858.

85. Brown to Stephens, May 7, 1858, *Correspondence of Toombs, Stephens, and Cobb*, 434.

86. Richmond *South*, quoted in Montgomery (Ala.) *Confederation*, May 4, 1858. The *Confederation* itself, May 17, said that ninety-nine out of a hundred Alabama Democrats would support the compromise. The Memphis *Appeal*, April 30, 1858, insisted that the difference between the English bill and the Crittenden-Montgomery amendment was as "between night and day." On the other hand, the Milledgeville (Ga.) *Southern Recorder*, May 11, 25, called the English bill a "complete surrender."

87. *KSHS Transactions*, V, 540.

88. *Ohio State Journal*, April 6, 1858; *Illinois State Journal*, Feb. 24, 1858.

89. *CG*, 35-1, pp. 3055–58; Johannsen, *Douglas*, 620–28; Nichols, *Disruption*, 211–13.

90. Quoted in Klein, *Buchanan*, 312.

91. The speech is in Paul M. Angle, ed., *Created Equal? The Complete Lincoln-Douglas Debates of 1858* (Chicago, 1958), 12–25.

92. Washington *Union*, July 13, 18, 20, 1858; Cobb to Alexander H. Stephens, Sept. 8, 1858, *Correspondence of Toombs, Stephens, and Cobb*, 442–44; Savannah *Morning News*, quoted in Savannah *Republican*, Aug. 13, 1858.

93. *Georgia Federal Union* (Milledgeville), Sept. 7, quoted in *North Carolina Standard* (Raleigh), Sept. 18, 1858; See also the quotations in Percy Lee Rainwater, *Mississippi, Storm Center of Secession, 1856–1861* (Baton Rouge, 1938), 65–66, including this from the *Southern Reveille* (Port Gibson), Sept. 17, 1858: "Let him go. He betrayed us at the moment, the only one, in which he could have eminently served us."

94. Charleston *Courier*, July 21, 1858; Jacksonian *Mississippian*, Dec. 7, 1858; Charleston *Mercury*, Aug. 10, 1858.

95. Charleston *Courier*, July 21, 1858; Columbus *Times and Sentinel*, quoted in Savannah *Republican*, Aug. 13, 1858; *Georgia Federal Union*, quoted in Savan-

nah *Republican*, Aug. 10, 1858; Savannah *Georgian*, quoted in Savannah *Republican*, Aug. 10, 1858; *South-Side Democrat*, quoted in *North Carolina Standard*, July 24, 1858.

CHAPTER 20

1. For differing views of whether a united Democratic party would have fared better in 1860, see Allan Nevins, *The Emergence of Lincoln* (2 vols.; New York, 1950), II, 312; and Don E. Fehrenbacher, *Prelude to Greatness: Lincoln in the 1850's* (Stanford, 1962), 159–60.
2. On the nomination, see Fehrenbacher, *Prelude to Greatness*, 48–69, but note the correction of Richard P. McCormick, *The Second American Party System: Party Formation in the Jacksonian Era* (Chapel Hill, N.C., 1966), 300n. During the debates, Douglas said of the nomination: "Probably this was the first time that such a thing was ever done." *CWAL*, III, 174. McCormick finds one earlier instance, however—that of Robert J. Walker by Mississippi Democrats in 1834.
3. Chicago *Tribune*, June 18, 1858. A secondary reason for the resolution was that Illinois Democrats were trying to make people believe that the real Republican choice for the Senate was the obnoxious editor of the Chicago *Democrat*, John Wentworth. See Don E. Fehrenbacher, *Chicago Giant: A Biography of "Long John" Wentworth* (Madison, Wis., 1957), 148–49, 157, 159; and Fehrenbacher, *Prelude to Greatness*, 65–68.
4. *CWAL*, II, 398–410, 461–69. The emphases are Lincoln's.
5. In his Senate speech of December 9, 1857, on the Lecompton constitution, Douglas said: "It is none of my business which way the slavery clause is decided. I care not whether it is voted down or voted up." The passage was frequently quoted by Lincoln and other Republicans as evidence of Douglas's moral neutralism on the issue of slavery. Lincoln, it should be noted, did not use the word "conspiracy" in the House-Divided address, but he did in later speeches.
6. Under the Dred Scott decision, Lincoln said, "squatter sovereignty" had been "squatted out of existence." *CWAL*, II, 464.
7. Paul M. Angle, ed., *Created Equal? The Complete Lincoln-Douglas Debates of 1858* (Chicago, 1958), 12–25.
8. The two men discussed the decision in other speeches during the 1858 campaign, but these are the ones most fully reported. See also summaries of Lincoln speeches at Carlinville, Bloomington, and Edwardsville, *CWAL*, III, 80–81, 89–90, 95–96.
9. Compare Lincoln's appeal to the Declaration of Independence in his Chicago speech with his remarks on race in the same speech and also with his repudiation of racial equality in the debates at Ottawa and Charleston, *CWAL*, II, 498–501; III, 16, 145–46.
10. Angle, ed., *Created Equal*, 14.
11. *CWAL*, III, 538.
12. *Ibid.*, II, 486–87.

13. Angle, ed., *Created Equal*, 58–59. These were his words at Springfield, but he said very much the same thing at Bloomington. See Robert W. Johannsen, *Stephen A. Douglas* (New York, 1973), 656.

14. *CWAL*, III, 1–37. All Democratic platforms since 1840 had ignored *McCulloch v. Maryland* (1819) by declaring: "Congress has no power to charter a national bank."

15. Charles H. Ray (an editor of the Chicago *Tribune*) to Elihu B. Washburne (member of Congress), probably Aug. 23, 1858, Washburne Papers, MDLC. On the debates generally, see Richard Allen Heckman, *Lincoln vs. Douglas: The Great Debates Campaign* (Washington, D.C., 1967).

16. Lincoln's restatement of and response to the seven Douglas questions may be found in *CWAL*, III, 40. He denied being pledged to repeal of the Fugitive Slave Act, pledged against admission of any more slave states, pledged to abolition of slavery in the District of Columbia, or pledged to the prohibition of interstate slave trade. He acknowledged only being pledged to the prohibition of slavery in the territories.

17. For example, in a letter apparently handed to Lincoln on the morning of the Freeport debate, Joseph Medill of the Chicago *Tribune* specifically recommended (in different phrasing) the first three of Lincoln's four questions. Medill to Lincoln, Aug. 27, 1858, Robert Todd Lincoln Collection, MDLC.

18. On the mythology of the second question, see Fehrenbacher, *Prelude to Greatness*, 122–28.

19. *CWAL*, III, 43, 53–54.

20. *Ibid.*, 230, 242, 250–51, 267–68, 277–78.

21. "The third question is the fundamental question put to Douglas at Freeport."— Harry V. Jaffa, *Crisis of the House Divided: An Interpretation of the Issues in the Lincoln-Douglas Debates* (New York, 1959), 352.

22. *Georgia Federal Union* (Milledgeville), Sept. 7, quoted in *North Carolina Standard* (Raleigh), Sept. 18, 1858. The Washington *Union*, Sept. 1, 1858, laid down as the condition of reconcilation that Douglas should "distinctly declare" that he would "acquiesce in and abide by the English bill."

23. *CWAL*, III, 43, 51–52.

24. *Ibid.*, 128–32, 316–18.

25. *Ibid.*, 132, 141–42, 269–70.

26. Richmond *Enquirer*, Sept. 10, 17, 30, 1858; Washington *Union*, Sept. 10, 14, 19, 1858; Fehrenbacher, *Prelude to Greatness*, 139, 191.

27. In the first category, for instance, the Mobile *Register*, Jackson *Mississippian*, and Charleston *Mercury*; in the second, the Richmond *Enquirer*, Augusta *Constitutionalist*, and Louisville *Democrat*; in the third, the Charleston *Courier*, Memphis *Appeal*, and Milledgeville *Southern Recorder*.

28. Mobile *Register*, Aug. 18, Sept. 26, 1858. See also Washington *Union*, Sept. 1, 1858; Jackson *Mississippian*, Sept. 24, 1858 (semi-weekly); Fehrenbacher, *Prelude to Greatness*, 135.

29. Caddo Gazette, quoted in *Illinois State Register* (Springfield), Oct. 11, 1858.

30. J. Henly Smith to Stephens from Washington, D.C., Aug. 3, 1858. Alexander H. Stephens Papers, MDLC.

31. Richmond *South*, quoted in Chicago *Times*, June 19, 1858. For other evidence of southern preference for Douglas over Lincoln, see Richmond *Enquirer*, June 15, 19, 22, 1858; New Orleans *Delta*, Aug. 14, quoted in Chicago *Press and Tribune*, Aug. 26, 1858; Montgomery *Confederation*, Aug. 30, 1858; Memphis *Appeal*, Sept. 9, 21, 25, 28, 1858; Louisville *Courier*, quoted in Memphis *Appeal*, Oct. 7, 1858; New York *Herald*, Oct. 4, 1858; Augusta *Constitutionalist*, Oct. 30, 1858.

32. Washington *Union*, Sept. 3, 1858; *North Carolina Standard*, Sept. 25, 1858 (see also July 24); Memphis *Avalanche*, quoted in Memphis *Appeal*, Sept. 7, 1858.

33. Columbia (S.C.) *Banner*, quoted in Jackson *Mississippian*, Sept. 24, 1858 (Semiweekly); *CWAL*, III, 550; Mobile *Register*, Aug. 4, Sept. 29, Oct. 22, 1858.

34. Nevins, *Emergence of Lincoln*, II, 41–42.

35. The Portland *Eastern Argus* printed the entire speech on September 13–14. It is reprinted, together with many of Davis's other New England speeches in Dunbar Rowland, ed., *Jefferson Davis, Constitutionalist: His Letters, Papers, and Speeches* (10 vols.; Jackson, Miss., 1923), III, 271–73, 274–81, 284–332.

36. *CWAL*, III, 295; Washington *States*, Oct. 22, 1858; Vicksburg *Whig*, quoted in Jackson *Mississippian*, Oct. 22, 1858; Mobile *Register*, Oct. 15, 1858; The *Mississippian* printed the Portland speech in full on Oct. 12. Douglas caused confusion by associating the speech with Bangor instead of Portland.

37. *National Intelligencer* (Washington), Nov. 27, 1858; Rowland, ed., *Davis Papers*, III, 344–45.

38. Jackson *Mississippian*, Oct. 29, 1858 (semi-weekly).

39. Quoted in *Illinois State Register*, Dec. 9, 1858.

40. In the statewide race for state treasurer, the Republicans won with a plurality of about four thousand votes. Thirteen of the twenty-five state senate seats were not at stake in 1858, and the Democrats held eight of them. Thus, in the election, the Democrats won forty-six legislative seats to forty-one for the Republicans. If the legislative vote had accurately reflected the popular vote, the Republicans would have won forty-four seats instead of forty-one, still two fewer than what they needed for a victory. See Fehrenbacher, *Prelude to Greatness*, 118–20, for discussion of the view that Lincoln lost because of an "antiquated" or "gerrymandered" legislative apportionment.

41. Douglas to Henry A. Wise, Nov. 7, 1858, in Robert W. Johannsen, ed., *The Letters of Stephen A. Douglas* (Urbana, Ill., 1961), 429.

42. *CG*, 35-1, pp. 1–2; 36-1, pp. 1–2; David M. Potter, *The Impending Crisis, 1848–1861*, completed and edited by Don E. Fehrenbacher (New York, 1976), 326.

43. Speaker elections, *CG*, 35-1, p. 2; 36-1, pp. 2, 52, 86–87, 158, 165, 170, 175, 188 . . . 650. Thomas S. Bocock of Virginia was the Democratic caucus nominee in 1859–60. The Republicans gained Senate seats in New Jersey, Rhode Island, Michigan, and Iowa. The Democrats made up their losses with four new members from the new states of Minnesota and Oregon.

44. David E. Meerse, "The Northern Democratic Party and the Congressional Elections of 1858," *CWH*, XIX (1973), 119–37, reprinted in Robert P. Swierenga, ed., *Beyond the Civil War Synthesis: Political Essays of the Civil War Era* (Westport, Conn., 1975), 79–97, attempts with only partial success to

minimize the influence of the Lecompton controversy on the elections of 1858 and to demonstrate that the election results were neither a serious setback for the Democratic party nor a reflection on Buchanan's presidential leadership. These conclusions are reached by some manipulative uses of the evidence, such as lumping pro-Lecompton and anti-Lecompton Democrats together in measuring party performance at the polls (thus discounting the split in the Democratic party, which was the most striking consequence of the Lecompton struggle), and such as stressing the fact that twenty-one out of twenty-six "consistent friends of the administration" won renomination while passing lightly over the fact that all but six of them were then beaten in the elections. What Meerse succeeds in demonstrating is that: (1) the Democrats improved their voting strength in a number of states that they had little or no hope of carrying in 1860 and at the same time lost ground badly in the states that they desperately needed to keep in the Democratic column; (2) Republican gains resulted more often from the recruitment of American voters than from cutting into Democratic strength; (3) other issues and influences besides Kansas affected the election results. One can scarcely quarrel with Meerse's conclusion that "Democratic congressional losses in 1858 were as much the result of power, prestige, and patronage as of unpopular Presidential policies about Kansas." But presumably the same statement with reverse emphasis would also be true. The "disaster" for Democrats in 1858 was concentrated in Pennsylvania, Indiana, and New Jersey, but Meerse treats those states as exceptions or as "atypical" (pp. 121, 135–36) and directs attention to statistical gains for the Democrats elsewhere. Those gains were in fact meaningless as far as the approaching presidential contest was concerned. The significant elections in 1858 were those in which the Republican party completed its rise to majoritarian status throughout the North. Meerse's study is nevertheless valuable for demonstrating that the Democratic party, with all its troubles, retained a remarkable vitality and was in no danger of going the way of the Federalists and Whigs. For further discussion, see above, 561–67.

45. Meerse, "Northern Democratic Party," 125–27, provides data for this summary, but his emphases are different from mine. Buchanan to his niece, Harriet Lane, Oct. 15, 1858, in John Bassett Moore, ed., *The Works of James Buchanan* (12 vols.; Philadelphia, 1908–11), X, 229. Buchanan was speaking of the election results in Pennsylvania.

46. Washington *Union*, Nov. 18, 1858.

47. Johannsen, *Douglas*, 682–83; George Fort Milton, *The Eve of Conflict: Stephen A. Douglas and the Needless War* (Boston, 1934), 358.

48. New York *Times*, Dec. 9, 10, 14, 1858; Johannsen, *Douglas*, 685–87.

49. In Memphis, for example, he was introduced by the former Whig senator, James C. Jones; in Mississippi by the former governor, Joseph Matthews; in Louisiana by Pierre Soulé, political opponent of John Slidell.

50. Jackson *Mississippian*, Dec. 7, 22, 1858; the latter quoted in Percy Lee Rainwater, *Mississippi, Storm Center of Secession, 1856–1861* (Baton Rouge, 1938), 66.

51. Speech at New Orleans, Dec. 6, shorthand transcription from New Orleans *Delta*, published in National *Intelligencer*, Dec. 29, 1858.

52. *Ibid.;* Johannsen, *Douglas*, 683–84; James D. Richardson, ed., *Messages and*

Papers of the Presidents (11 vols.; Washington, D.C., 1913), IV, 3040–42. In New Orleans, as if to emphasize the theme of expansion, Douglas's principal host was Pierre Soulé of Ostend Manifesto notoriety, and the coasting vessel he boarded there was the *Black Warrior*, whose seizure in 1854 had precipitated a crisis with Spain and led to the issuance of the "manifesto."

53. Washington *Union*, Dec. 19, 25, 1858; Jan. 13, 1859; New York *Times*, Jan. 11, 12, 13, 14, 24, 1859; Johannsen, *Douglas*, 688–90; Johannsen, ed., *Letters of Douglas*, 431–37.

54. *CG*, 35-2, pp. 1222–23. Hale's amendment was germane because the bill contained an appropriation for the taking of a census in Kansas. See *House Journal*, 35-2 (Serial 995), 382–99, for passage of the Oregon bill. The Democrats made extravagant claims for the population of Oregon. Joseph Lane, one of the senators-elect, said that estimates of only 40,000 were absurd and that the correct figure was about 90,000. Alexander H. Stephens suggested that it might be as much as 130,000 (*CG*, 35-2, pp. 943–45; *National Intelligencer*, Dec. 29, 1858). The census of 1860 showed 52,465 in Oregon and 106,390 in Kansas. The Oregon admission bill had been passed by the Senate in the preceding session. *Senate Journal*, 35-1 (Serial 917), 476–77. The Senate vote was 35 to 17 and mixed as to section and party. The Republicans were 11 to 6 in favor, whereas in the House nine months later, the Republicans voted 73 to 15 against admission. In between, Oregon's legislature elected two Democratic senators. See Henry H. Simms, "The Controversy over the Admission of the State of Oregon," *MVHR*, XXXII (1945), 355–74.

55. *CG*, 35-2, pp. 1222–25; Johannsen, *Douglas*, 694. Most historians other than Johannsen give the impression that the debate burst forth on February 23.

56. *CG*, 35-2, p. 1241.

57. Roy Franklin Nichols, *The Disruption of American Democracy* (New York, 1948), 230, 282. On Brown, see James Byrne Ranck, *Albert Gallatin Brown, Radical Southern Nationalist* (New York, 1937).

58. *CG*, 35-2, pp. 1241–43, for Brown's speech. The ensuing debate is at 1243–74.

59. *Ibid.*, 1264.

60. *Ibid.*, 1244–46, 1255, 1258–59.

61. *Ibid.*, 1243, 1247–48, 1256, 1259.

62. *Ibid.*, 1259.

63. *CG*, 35-1, pp. 1140–45, 1261, 1264; 35-2, pp. 1249–51.

64. James W. Singleton to Douglas, Feb. 20, 1859, Stephen A. Douglas Papers, University of Chicago.

65. Allan J. Green to James H. Hammond, March 7, 1858; William Porcher Miles to Hammond, Nov. 10, 1858, Hammond Papers, MDLC. For a number of such quotations from South Carolina on the emptiness of the Lecompton cause, see Harold S. Schultz, *Nationalism and Sectionalism in South Carolina, 1852–1860* (Durham, N.C., 1950), 154n.

66. Hammond to William Gilmore Simms, March 13, 1859; Orr to Hammond, Sept. 17, 1859, Hammond Papers, MDLC; Chesnut in speech on Sept. 28, 1859, quoted in Schultz, *Nationalism and Sectionalism*, 181; Toombs as reported in Augusta *Constitutionalist*, Sept. 14, 1859, and in his letter to Alex-

ander H. Stephens, Feb. 10, 1860, in Ulrich Bonnell Phillips, ed., *The Correspondence of Robert Toombs, Alexander H. Stephens, and Howell Cobb*, AHA *Annual Report*, 1911, II, 460–62.

67.   Memphis *Avalanche*, Sept. 8, 1859; also July 2, 1859, with the assertion that Douglas's doctrine was "more dangerous and fatal to the interests of the South than any ever advocated by the rankest abolitionist." This sort of statement was made more than once on the Senate floor; for instance, Alfred Iverson of Georgia, *CG*, 36-1, p. 382: "I consider his [Douglas's] doctrines . . . as unsound in theory and disastrous to us in practice as the Wilmot proviso."

68.   Zachariah Chandler of Michigan, Feb. 17, 1859, *CG*, 35-2, p. 1081.

CHAPTER 21

1.   Douglas to James W. Singleton, March 31; to J. B. Dorr, June 22; to John L. Peyton, Aug. 2, 1859, all in Robert W. Johannsen, ed., *The Letters of Stephen A. Douglas* (Urbana, Ill., 1961), 439, 446–47, 451–52. Administration leaders objected strongly to Douglas's introduction of the slave-trade issue. See Buchanan to Robert Tyler, June 27, 1859, in John Bassett Moore, ed., *The Works of James Buchanan* (12 vols.; Philadelphia, 1908–11), X, 325–26; Robert W. Johannsen, *Stephen A. Douglas* (New York, 1973), 705. On the move to revive the African slave trade there is a considerable literature. See David M. Potter, *The Impending Crisis, 1848–1861*, completed and edited by Don E. Fehrenbacher (New York, 1976), 395–401, with the citations there given; and Ronald T. Takaki, *A Pro-Slavery Crusade: The Agitation to Reopen the African Slave Trade* (New York, 1971).

2.   Douglas to the San Francisco *National*, Aug. 16, 1859 (published Sept. 16, 1859, and also published as a pamphlet), in Johannsen, ed., *Letters of Douglas*, 453–66.

3.   Robert W. Johannsen, "Stephen A. Douglas, 'Harper's Magazine,' and Popular Sovereignty," *MVHR*, XLV (1959), 606–31. The text of the essay is reprinted and hereafter cited in Harry V. Jaffa and Robert W. Johannsen, eds., *In the Name of the People: Speeches and Writings of Lincoln and Douglas in the Ohio Campaign of 1859* (Columbus, 1959), 58–125.

4.   Johannsen, "Harper's Magazine," 622.

5.   *Ibid.*, 623–26; Curtis, *The Just Supremacy of Congress over the Territories* (Boston, 1859); Johnson, *Remarks on Popular Sovereignty, As Maintained and Denied Respectively by Judge Douglas and Attorney-General Black* (Baltimore, 1859); Greeley, "History Vindicated: A Letter to the Hon. Stephen A. Douglas on His 'Harper' Essay," New York *Tribune*, Oct. 15, 1859; Black, *Observations on Senator Douglas's Views of Popular Sovereignty, as Expressed in Harper's Magazine for Sept., 1859* (Washington, D.C., 1859), also published in the Washington *Constitution* (new name of the Washington *Union*, organ of the administration), Sept. 10, 1859; reprinted in Jaffa and Johannsen, eds., *In the Name of the People*, 173–99.

6.   *Ibid.*, 219.

7. *CWAL*, III, 405.
8. Johannsen, "Harper's Magazine," 626–27.
9. See, for example, the *National Era* (Washington), Aug. 25, 1859, maintaining that judicial supremacy was "Federalist doctrine"; also the speech of Jacob Collamer of Vermont in the Senate, March 8, 1860, *CG*, 36–1, p. 1055, maintaining that the United States, since it was not a party to the suit, was not bound by the Dred Scott decision.
10. *DSvS*, 452.
11. Memphis *Avalanche*, Aug. 31, 1859. "This whole question," complained the New York *Times* on October 4, 1859, "is rapidly passing out of the field of practical politics. The distinctions made upon the point are becoming too narrow and refined for popular interest, especially as no occasion is likely to arise speedily for the application of any of these diverse theories.
12. The phrase is that of George E. Pugh, Jan. 12, 1860, *CG*, 36–1, p. 423.
13. Jackson *Mississippian*, Aug. 23, 1859; Memphis *Avalanche*, July 2, 1859.
14. Jaffa and Johannsen, eds., *In the Name of the People*, 65.
15. *Ibid.*, 89–92; *Senate Reports*, 35–1, No. 82 (Serial 938), 62–64. These views also seemed to conflict with Douglas's attitude toward the Mormons in Utah. In his Springfield speech of June 12, 1857, Douglas had proposed repeal of the Utah organic act, thereby "blotting the territorial government out of existence." New York *Times*, June 23, 1857. See the comment of Senator James S. Green of Missouri, *CG*, 35–2, p. 1253.
16. *Barron v. Baltimore*, 7 Peters 243.
17. Jaffa and Johannsen, eds., *In the Name of the People*, 103.
18. In state courts *Barron v. Baltimore* had sometimes been ignored. William Winslow Crosskey, "Charles Fairman, 'Legislative History,' and the Constitutional Limitations on State Authority," *University of Chicago Law Review*, XXII (1954), 141–42.
19. Johannsen, "Harper's Magazine," 620, and *Douglas*, 709, summarizes the passage but does not analyze it.
20. *DSvS*, 450; Jaffa and Johannsen, eds., *In the Name of the People*, 99–100. ·
21. Beginning with *Gitlow v. New York*, 263 U.S. 652 (1925).
22. Jaffa and Johannsen, eds., *In the Name of the People*, 100–103.
23. *Ibid.*, 103–7.
24. The Richmond *Enquirer* is quoted with other similar comments in Johannsen, *Douglas*, 710. Brown, with a party of twenty-two men, captured the federal arsenal at Harpers Ferry on October 16, 1859, and held it for two days before being taken prisoner. See Potter, *Impending Crisis*, 356–84.
25. Mobile *Register*, Sept. 10, 1859; New Orleans *True Delta* (weekly), March 10, 1860; Louisville *Democrat*, quoted in Memphis *Appeal*, Sept. 9, 1859.
26. James D. Richardson, ed., *Messages and Papers of the Presidents* (11 vols.; Washington, D.C., 1913), IV, 3085–86. Toombs pronounced the message "satisfactory to the South on the slavery question." Ulrich Bonnell Phillips, ed., *The Correspondence of Robert Toombs, Alexander H. Stephens, and Howell Cobb*, AHA *Annual Report*, 1911, II, 452.
27. Horace White published an editorial in the Chicago *Press and Tribune*, Dec. 24,

1858, calling upon the legislatures of Kansas and Nebraska territories to put the principle of "unfriendly legislation" into effect by abolishing slavery. He sent copies to members of the legislatures. White to Lyman Trumbull, Dec. 28, 1858; Jan. 10, 1859, Trumbull Papers, MDLC. See also Joseph Logsdon, *Horace White, Nineteenth Century Liberal* (Westport, Conn., 1971), 57–58.

28. *CG*, 35-2, p. 1247.
29. Daniel W. Wilder, *Annals of Kansas* (Topeka, 1886), 252; J. Sterling Morton et al., *Illustrated History of Nebraska* (3 vols.; Lincoln, 1905), I, 368–69. Kansas abolished slavery in 1860; Nebraska, in 1861. Wilder, 295; Morton, I, 443.
30. Avery O. Craven, *The Growth of Southern Nationalism, 1848–1861* (Baton Rouge, 1953), 307.
31. Jeremiah Lynch, *The Life of David C. Broderick, a Senator of the Fifties* (New York, 1911), 229; David A. Williams, *David C. Broderick, a Political Portrait* (San Marino, Calif., 1969), 230–44.
32. Potter, *Impending Crisis*, 387.
33. Craven, *Southern Nationalism*, 251. The abridgment was published as *Compendium of the Impending Crisis of the South* (New York, 1860). On Helper, see Hugh C. Bailey, *Hinton Rowan Helper, Abolitionist-Racist* (University, Ala., 1965).
34. *CG*, 36-1, pp. 2–650 *passim;* Ollinger Crenshaw, "The Speakership Contest of 1859–1860; John Sherman's Election a Cause of Disruption?" *MVHR*, XXIX (1942), 323–38. To southerners, says Crenshaw, the election of Sherman would have been "tantamount to incitement of servile rebellion." See also Johannsen, *Douglas*, 717–21; Potter, *Impending Crisis*, 387–90; Allan Nevins, *The Emergence of Lincoln* (2 vols.; New York, 1950), II, 116–22.
35. Toombs to Alexander H. Stephens, Jan. 31, 1860, in *Correspondence of Toombs, Stephens, and Cobb*, 458–59.
36. *CG*, 36-1, pp. 641, 650. McClernand on one ballot received ninety-one votes; Thomas S. Bocock, nominee of the Democratic caucus, had never gotten more than eighty-eight. Numerous southerners made short speeches as they voted for McClernand, stating that they did not agree with him on the territorial issue. *Ibid.*, 642–45. The final vote was Pennington, 117; McClernand, 85; scattered, 15.
37. *Ibid.*, 29, 98.
38. *Ibid.*, 162, 176–80.
39. *Ibid.*, 176–86, 415–17. For the Campbell passage, see *DSvS*, 514, and above, 400. For an interesting exchange between Pugh and Jefferson Davis on the latter's Portland speech, see *CG*, 36-1, p. 419.
40. *Ibid.*, 379–85, 415–27, 494, 658; James Byrne Ranck, *Albert Gallatin Brown, Radical Southern Nationalist* (New York, 1937), 183.
41. Roy Franklin Nichols, *The Disruption of American Democracy* (New York, 1948), 283.
42. *CG*, 36-1, pp. 658, 935.
43. *Senate Journal*, 36-1 (Serial 1022), 507–10, 515–17.
44. *CG*, 36-1, p. 2344. The Memphis *Avalanche*, Feb. 22, 1860, explained matters in the same terms. The South, it said, did not want a territorial slave code but

only "recognition of the power and duty of the Federal government" to give protection to slavery in the territories if it should "at any time become necessary."

45. Jackson *Mississippian*, Feb. 7, 28, March 6, 1860. See note 29 above.

46. *Senate Journal*, 36-1 (Serial 1022), 182 (Feb. 23, 1860), 587–88 (June 8, committee discharged from further consideration).

47. *CG*, 36-1, p. 1970. The House of Representatives, it should be noted, passed a bill admitting Kansas to statehood (April 12), 134 to 73, but it was postponed in the Senate, 32 to 27, Pugh voting with the Republican minority. The House also passed legislation disallowing all proslavery legislation in New Mexico (May 10), 97 to 90, but the measure was reported unfavorably by the Senate committee on territories. *Ibid.*, 1672, 2625; *House Journal*, 36-1 (Serials 1041–42), 303, 815–16; *Senate Journal*, 36-1 (Serial 1022), 587.

48. Johannsen, *Douglas*, 734–39; Nichols, *Disruption*, 276–82; George Fort Milton, *The Eve of Conflict: Stephen A. Douglas and the Needless War* (Boston, 1934), 403–8; Damon Wells, *Stephen Douglas, the Last Years, 1857–1861* (Austin, 1971), 212–15.

49. Memphis *Avalanche*, Feb. 6, March 17, 1860; Craven, *Southern Nationalism*, 320–22; Dwight Lowell Dumond, *The Secession Movement, 1860–1861* (New York, 1931), 33–35; Austin L. Venable, "The Conflict Between the Douglas and Yancey Forces in the Charleston Convention," *JSH*, VIII (1942), 226–41. The Alabama resolutions are in *Official Proceedings of the Democratic National Convention Held in 1860* (Cleveland, 1860), 56–57. The Arkansas delegates had likewise been instructed to retire if slave-code demands were not met. *Ibid.*, 63.

50. M[urat] Halstead, *Caucuses of 1860: A History of the National Political Conventions of the Current Presidential Campaign* (Columbus, 1860), 36. Douglas eventually found it necessary to make a public denial of having authorized withdrawal of his name. Johannsen, *Douglas*, 758.

51. *Official Proceedings*, 20.

52. *Ibid.*, 36–65. One Arkansas delegate remained; one Delaware delegate left.

53. *Ibid.*, 71–97; Johannsen, *Douglas*, 757. The decision seemed to be a change of convention rules, which specified two-thirds of the "votes given." But Caleb Cushing, the doughface chairman of the convention, ruled otherwise and was sustained by a convention vote.

54. Halstead, *Caucuses of 1860*, p. 109.

55. *Ibid.*, 103; Johannsen, *Douglas*, 765–66.

56. *CG*, 36-1, pp. 2100, 2120–22, 2143–56, 2211–14; App., 301–16, 338–45.

57. *CG*, 36-1, p. 2230.

58. *Ibid.*, 2234, 2241; App., 344.

59. *Official Proceedings*, 95–156; Johannsen, *Douglas*, 767–72.

60. Halstead, *Caucuses of 1860*, 217–27; William C. Davis, *Breckinridge: Statesman, Soldier, Symbol* (Baton Rouge, 1974), 222–26. According to Davis, Breckinridge accepted the nomination "as a stratagem to bring about Douglas' withdrawal."

61. *Official Proceedings*, 176–77.

62. Arthur M. Schlesinger, et al., eds., *History of American Presidential Elections, 1789–1968* (4 vols.; New York, 1971), II, 1040, 1126.

63. For differing views on whether the Republican platform of 1860 amounted to a conservative retreat from party principles of 1850, see: Reinhard H. Luthin, *The First Lincoln Campaign* (Cambridge, Mass., 1944), 148–49; Jeter Allen Isely, *Horace Greeley and the Republican Party, 1853–1861, a Study of the New York Tribune* (Princeton, 1947), 288–89; Don E. Fehrenbacher, *Prelude to Greatness: Lincoln in the 1850's* (Stanford, 1962), 156–57n; Eric Foner, *Free Soil, Free Labor, Free Men: The Ideology of the Republican Party Before the Civil War* (New York, 1970), 132–33; Potter, *Impending Crisis*, 422n.

64. See, for example, the New Orleans *Bee*, May 21, June 25, in Dwight Lowell Dumond, ed., *Southern Editorials on Secession* (New York, 1931), 103–5, 131–33.

65. Schlesinger, ed., *Presidential Elections*, II, 1125.

66. Fusion tickets were arranged in Pennsylvania, New Jersey, New York, and Rhode Island. See Potter, *Impending Crisis*, 437–38.

67. Dumond, ed., *Southern Editorials*, 153.

68. Frank Moore, ed., *The Rebellion Record: A Diary of American Events, with Documents, Narratives, Illustrative Incidents, Poetry, etc.* (12 vols.; New York, 1861–68), I, 3–4 (documents).

69. *CG*, 36-2, p. 3 (Dec. 4, 1860).

70. Dumond, ed., *Southern Editorials*, 178–81, 201–3.

71. R. S. Holt to Joseph Holt, Nov. 9, 1860, Holt Papers, MDLC; Ollinger Crenshaw, *The Slave States in the Presidential Election of 1860* (Baltimore, 1945), 89–107; Wendell G. Addington, "Slave Insurrections in Texas," *JNH*, XXXV (1950), 408–34; William L. Barney, *The Secessionist Impulse: Alabama and Mississippi in 1860* (Princeton, 1974), 163–80; Steven A. Channing, *Crisis of Fear: Secession in South Carolina* (New York, 1970), 264–73. On similar fear during the 1856 campaign, see Harvey Wish, "The Slave Insurrection Panic of 1856," *JSH*, V (1939), 206–22.

72. *CG*, 36-2, pp. 24, 114, 158. The chairman of the committee was Crittenden's colleague, Lazarus W. Powell of Kentucky, who introduced the resolution creating it. The members included Douglas, Davis, Seward, Toombs, and Hunter. See Albert D. Kirwan, *John J. Crittenden: The Struggle for the Union* (Lexington, Ky., 1962), 374–404; Potter, *Impending Crisis*, 530–33; Dumond, *Secession Movement*, 158–61.

73. For example, Albert Gallatin Brown in 1848 had called the Missouri Compromise "a fungus, an excrescence, a political monstrosity" and the "most fatal error" in the whole history of slavery legislation. *CG*, 30-1, App., 647.

74. *CG*, 36-2, p. 114. The four accompanying resolutions proposed changes in the Fugitive Slave Law, urged repeal of personal liberty laws, and called for stringent enforcement of the laws against the African slave trade.

75. *Senate Reports*, 36–2, No. 288 (Serial 1090), 4–8; *CG*, 36-2, p. 1405; L. E. Chittenden, *A Report of the Debates and Proceedings in the Secret Sessions of the Conference Convention, for Proposing Amendments to the Constitution of the United States, Held at Washington, D.C. in February, A.D. 1861* (New

York, 1864); Robert Gray Gunderson, *Old Gentlemen's Convention: The Washington Peace Conference of 1861* (Madison, Wis., 1961), with the text of the proposed seven-section amendment to the Constitution on pp. 107–9. One major change was that the 36° 30′ provision would apply only to "present territory"—a concession to the Republicans.

76. Evansville *Journal*, Feb. 12, 1861, in Howard Cecil Perkins, ed., *Northern Editorials on Secession* (2 vols.; New York, 1942), I, 316–17.

77. *CWAL*, IV, 440. See Potter, *Impending Crisis*, 550–53, 558–59. Some historians have maintained that Lincoln opposed compromise for fear of disrupting the Republican party. See, for example, Philip Shriver Klein, *President James Buchanan, a Biography* (University Park, Pa., 1962), 386; and see the comment of Elbert B. Smith in his *The Presidency of James Buchanan* (Lawrence, Kan., 1975), 157–58.

78. See the Richmond *Enquirer* editorial, Jan. 29, 1861, in Dumond, ed., *Southern Editorials*, 426–28.

79. David M. Potter, *Lincoln and His Party in the Secession Crisis* (New Haven, 1942, 1962), xviii–xxiii; Potter, *Impending Crisis*, 553–54.

80. Notably Charles Francis Adams on the House "Committee of 33." Even Lincoln said that he did not care much about New Mexico. But admission was defeated with little support from Republicans. *CG*, 36-2, pp. 1326–27; *CWAL*, IV, 183; Potter, *Impending Crisis*, 530, 533–34; Martin Duberman, *Charles Francis Adams, 1807–1886* (Boston, 1961), 227–48.

81. *CG*, 36-2, pp. 1285, 1403. The House passed the amendment 133 to 65, with about 40 per cent of Republicans voting in favor. The Senate passed it by a bare two-thirds majority, 24 to 12, with Republicans supplying 8 of the affirmative votes and all of the negative ones. This "13th Amendment" was endorsed by Lincoln in his inaugural and ratified by two states.

82. *Ibid.*, 1391.

83. *CWAL*, IV, 150, 152, 153, 183.

84. Utica *Observer*, Jan. 7, 1861, in Perkins, ed., *Northern Editorials*, I, 296–98.

85. The Crittenden plan was endorsed by the legislatures of Tennessee, Delaware, and Kentucky. *House Miscellaneous Documents*, 36-2, Nos. 21, 27 (Serial 1103); *House Executive Documents*, 36-2, No. 55 (Serial 1100). Reverdy Johnson, at the Washington Peace Conference, argued that the South would be giving up a major part of what it had gained in the Dred Scott decision. Chittenden, *Debates and Proceedings*, 90.

86. James Ford Rhodes, *History of the United States from the Compromise of 1850 to the Final Restoration of Home Rule at the South in 1877* (7 vols.; New York, 1893–1906), III, 261. As authority, Rhodes cited *Appleton's Annual Cyclopædia* for 1861. But he might also have drawn upon newspaper editorials, such as that of the New Orleans *Bee*, Jan. 16, 1861, quoted in Dumond, *Secession Movement*, 168n. The *Bee* declared: "We believe that with the possible exception of a few New England States, there is not a non-slaveholding Commonwealth of which the people would not accept the Crittenden amendments by an overwhelming majority." Rhodes in turn was often cited by later historians, who also relied heavily on the assertion of Horace Greeley that in a popular referendum

the Crittenden Compromise would have prevailed by an "overwhelming majority." Greeley, *Recollections of a Busy Life* (New York, 1868), 397; Potter, *Lincoln and His Party*, 195–200; Kirwan, *Crittenden*, 404. That the Crittenden plan had strong support in the North is undeniable; that it had majority support can neither be proved nor disproved.

87. *CG*, 36-2, p. 33 (Dec. 10, 1860).
88. *CWAL*, III, 547–48.

CHAPTER 22

1. Taney to George W. Hughes, Aug. 22, 1860, in Samuel Tyler, *Memoir of Roger Brooke Taney, LL.D.*, 2nd ed. (Baltimore, 1876), 405–8.
2. *Ibid.*
3. Taney to J. Mason Campbell, Oct. 19, 1860, Benjamin C. Howard Papers, Maryland Historical Society.
4. James D. Richardson, ed., *Messages and Papers of the Presidents* (11 vols.; Washington, D.C., 1913), V, 3157–70.
5. Roger B. Taney Papers, MDLC. Six states, said Taney, had left the Union. This would date the writing of the document soon after the secession of Louisiana on January 26, 1861, since Texas on February 1 became the seventh state to secede. Taney also declared that Congress had been "in session for two thirds of the time allotted by the Constitution," which suggests the first two or three days in February. Both of these statements were made in the second half of the fragment, however. The earlier pages could have been written at an earlier date.
6. The advertisement actually appeared in the Boston *Gazette and Country Journal*, July 22, 1776, simultaneously with publication of the Declaration of Independence—not the Constitution as Taney stated—an important difference of eleven years.
7. *CWAL*, IV, 262–271.
8. New York *Tribune*, March 6, 1861.
9. Carl B. Swisher, *Roger B. Taney* (New York, 1935), 155–57, 196–97; and see above, 441.
10. Notably, the mayor of Baltimore, George W. Brown; and Charles and Frank Key Howard, son-in-law and grandson, respectively, of Taney's brother-in-law, Francis Scott Key. See Dean Sprague, *Freedom Under Lincoln* (Boston, 1965), 1–56, 190–91, 209–11, 284.
11. Taney to Pierce, June 12, 1861, Franklin Pierce Papers, MCLC.
12. Ex parte Merryman, 17 Federal Cases 144 (No. 9487); Carl B. Swisher, *The Taney Period, 1836–1864*, Volume V of the Oliver Wendell Holmes Devise *History of the Supreme Court of the United States* (New York, 1974), 844–54; Marvin R. Cain, *Lincoln's Attorney General: Edward Bates of Missouri* (Columbia, Mo., 1965), 144–51; David M. Silver, *Lincoln's Supreme Court* (Urbana, Ill., 1956), 27–36.
13. Taney to Conway Robinson, April 10, 1863, in Tyler, *Memoir of Taney*. 461.
14. Taney to David M. Perine, Aug. 6, 1863, in Tyler, *Memoir of Taney*, 454.

15. Swisher, *Taney,* 570–71.
16. McHenry Howard to Bernard C. Steiner, May 1, 1919, Howard Papers, Maryland Historical Society. See Walker Lewis, *Without Fear or Favor: A Biography of Chief Justice Roger Brooke Taney* (Boston, 1965), 465; Bernard C. Steiner, *Life of Roger Brooke Taney* (Baltimore, 1922), 503.
17. Taney to J. Mason Campbell, October 2, 1856, in the possession of Mrs. Carl B. Swisher of Baltimore, who kindly provided me with a copy. Part of the letter is quoted in Swisher, *Taney,* 492–93.
18. Swisher, *Taney Period,* 722. The story of the tragic summer at Old Point is also told in Swisher, *Taney,* 465–71; Lewis, *Without Fear or Favor,* 377–81. Taney's lingering heartsickness is revealed in letters to David M. Perine, April 14, June 6, Aug. 12, 1856, Perine Papers, Maryland Historical Society.
19. Cincinnati *Enquirer,* quoted in Charleston *Courier,* April 1, 1857; Frank H. Hodder, "Some Phases of the Dred Scott Case," *MVHR,* XVI (1929), 17; Charles W. Smith, Jr. *Roger B. Taney, Jacksonian Jurist* (Chapel Hill, N.C., 1936), 147; Lewis, *Without Fear or Favor,* 360; Robert M. Spector, "Lincoln and Taney: A Study in Constitutional Polarization," *American Journal of Legal History,* XV (1971), 212. On Taney's manumissions and defense of the abolitionist minister, see Swisher, *Taney,* 94–98; Lewis, *Without Fear or Favor,* 44, 76–79.
20. See especially Charles Sellers, "The Travail of Slavery," in Sellers, ed., *The Southerner as American* (Chapel Hill, N.C., 1960), 40–71.
21. C. Vann Woodward, *The Burden of Southern History,* rev. ed. (Baton Rouge, 1968), 57. See Steven A. Channing, *Crisis of Fear: Secession in South Carolina* (New York, 1970); Clement Eaton, *The Freedom-of-Thought Struggle in the Old South* (New York, 1964), 89–117. Taney revealed his deep gloom about the nation's future in conversations with the British consul at Richmond during May, 1857. G. P. R. James to Lord Clarendon, May 30, 1857, quoted in Allan Nevins, *The Emergence of Lincoln* (2 vols.; New York, 1950), I, 117.
22. Daniel to Van Buren, Nov. 1, 1847, Martin Van Buren Papers, MDLC.
23. Bernard Schwartz, *The Reins of Power: A Constitutional History of the United States* (New York, 1963), 86; Carl B. Swisher, "Dred Scott Case," in James Truslow Adams and R. V. Coleman, eds., *Dictionary of American History,* 2nd ed. (5 vols.; New York, 1946), II, 168; Robert K. Carr, *The Supreme Court and Judicial Review* (New York, 1942), 208. Robert H. Jackson, in *The Struggle for Judicial Supremacy* (New York, 1941), 327, wrote that hope for a peaceful settlement "vanished when the Supreme Court held that the Constitution would allow no compromise about the existence of slavery in the territories." Leo Pfeffer, in *This Honorable Court* (Boston, 1965), 158, declared: "If war was not inevitable, the decision made it so." See also Bruce Catton, *The American Heritage Picture History of the Civil War* (2 vols.; New York, 1960), I, 40; R. Kent Newmyer, *The Supreme Court under Marshall and Taney* (New York, 1968), 139.
24. Charles Warren, *The Supreme Court in United States History,* rev. ed. (2 vols.; Boston, 1932), II, 357. The New York *Times,* Oct. 14, 1864, said that the Dred Scott decision "contributed more than all other things combined to the election of President Lincoln."

25. *Ibid.*, June 23, 1857. See above, 455–57.
26. Lincoln also carried California and Oregon with pluralities and won 4 of 7 New Jersey electoral votes even though he was outvoted there. In the nation as a whole, he won approximately 1.9 million votes out of a total of 4.7 million. In the free states, however, he won approximately 54 per cent of the popular vote. In the electoral college, he won 180 votes out of 303. Combining the popular votes of his three opponents would have deprived him only of 11 electoral votes in New Jersey, Oregon, and California, leaving him still with a clear majority of 169.
27. Nevins, *Emergence of Lincoln*, II, 312; Warren, *Supreme Court*, II, 356–57.
28. Statistics of the presidential elections of 1856 and 1860 are taken from W. Dean Burnham, *Presidential Ballots, 1836–1892* (Baltimore, 1955).
29. Statistics of the state elections of 1857 and 1858 are taken from *The Tribune Almanac* (New York) for 1858 and 1859.
30. See, for example, Ronald P. Formisano, *The Birth of Mass Political Parties: Michigan, 1827–1861* (Princeton, 1971); Michael Fitzgibbon Holt, *Forging a Majority: The Formation of the Republican Party in Pittsburgh, 1848–1860* (New Haven, 1969).
31. Cain, *Lincoln's Attorney General*, 98–99.
32. Lawrence Bruser, "Political Antislavery in Connecticut, 1844–1858," Ph.D. dissertation, Columbia University, 1974, p. 396, finds that the Dred Scott decision was "a boon" to the "political fortunes" of the Connecticut opposition coalition that was still in the process of becoming the Republican party. Yet, as the charts indicate, it was the Connecticut Democrats who made gains in 1857. And Bruser himself says (p. 410): "The huge Fremont majority of [the previous] November had disappeared." The Democrats profited from intense factionalism among their opponents in 1857, but it appears that they were unhurt by *Dred Scott*. It should be noted that Democratic divisions in 1858 and 1860 could not be incorporated into the chart which thus in a sense understates the party's decline in those years.

CHAPTER 23

1. St. Louis *Evening News*, April 3, 1857; St. Louis *Ledger*, quoted in Worcester (Mass.) *Sun*, May 29, 1857; New York *Herald*, Sept. 22, 1858; *Revised Statutes of the State of Missouri, 1854–55* (2 vols.; Jefferson City, 1856), II, 1094–95. The bonds for good behavior are in the Dexter P. Tiffany Collection, MHS. They give Dred's occupation as porter and Harriet's as "washer." See also Donnie D. Bellamy, "Free Blacks in Antebellum Missouri, 1820–1860," *Missouri Historical Review*, LXVII (1973), 198–226, especially 204–5.
2. New York *Herald*, Sept. 22, 1858; J. Hugo Grimm to Charles Van Ravenswaay, Oct. 29, 1946, citing 1867 records of Calvary Cemetery, Dred Scott Collection, MHS; John A. Bryan, "The Blow Family and Their Slave Dred Scott," *Missouri Historical Society Bulletin*, V (1948), 25; New York *Times*, July 26, 1957, p. 37; St. Louis *Post-Dispatch*, Sept. 17, 1957, p. 3B.

3. St. Louis *Globe-Democrat*, Jan. 10, 1886; Vincent C. Hopkins, *Dred Scott's Case* (New York, 1951, 1967), 177.

4. Springfield (Mass.) *Republican*, Aug. 9, 1896; Feb. 12, 1903; *Biographical Directory of the American Congress, 1774–1961* (Washington, D.C., 1961), 676.

5. Essays on Blow, Drake, and Gamble in the *Dictionary of American Biography*, II, 391–92; V, 425–26; VII, 120–21, all by Thomas S. Barclay; Barclay, *The Liberal Republican Movement in Missouri, 1865–1871* (Columbia, Mo., 1926); William E. Parrish, *Missouri Under Radical Rule* (Columbia, Mo., 1965); Wilbert Henry Rosin, "Hamilton Rowan Gamble, Missouri's Civil War Governor," Ph.D. dissertation, University of Missouri, 1960; William Ernest Smith, *The Francis Preston Blair Family in Politics* (2 vols.; New York, 1933), II, 19–89, and *passim*.

6. St. Louis *Globe-Democrat*, Oct. 9, 1904; Irving Dilliard, "Dred Scott Eulogized by James Milton Turner," *JNH* (1941), 1–11. On Turner generally, see Dilliard, "James Milton Turner: A Little Known Benefactor of His People," *JNH*, XIX (1934), 372–411; Lawrence O. Christensen, "J. Milton Turner: An Appraisal," *Missouri Historical Review*, LXX (1975), 1–19; and Dilliard's article on Turner in the *Dictionary of American Biography*, XIX, 66–67.

7. Dalton to Hill, Feb. 11, March 13, 1907; notes taken by Dalton in conversation with Mrs. Blow, Feb. 18, 1907, Dred Scott Collection, MHS; Frederick Trevor Hill, *Decisive Battles of the Law* (New York, 1907), 116; Frank H. Hodder, "Some Phases of the Dred Scott Case," *MVHR*, XVI (1929), 4; Avery O. Craven, *The Coming of the Civil War* (New York, 1942), 381; Thomas S. Barclay, "Dred Scott," *Dictionary of American Biography*, XVI, 488–89. None of the historians cited authority *specifically* for the attribution of shiftlessness. But Hodder did cite Hill otherwise; Craven acknowledged that he had followed Hodder's article "rather closely" in his treatment of the Dred Scott case; Barclay cited the Hodder article. Edward Channing, citing Hill as one of his authorities, declared: "Dred seems to have been a rather inefficient negro, who may have made a good household servant, but was hardly capable of looking out for himself and his family." *A History of the United States* (6 vols.; New York, 1905–25), VI, 187. Albert J. Beveridge in correspondence agreed with Hodder that Scott was a "worthless nigger," but he did not say so in his biography of Lincoln. Beveridge to Hodder, Feb. 22, 1927, Beveridge Papers, MDLC.

8. John A. Bryan, "The Blow Family and Their Slave Dred Scott," *Missouri Historical Society Bulletin*, IV (1948), 228; Duane Meyer, *The Heritage of Missouri*, rev. ed. (Hazelwood, Mo., 1970), 332. For the view that historians have done Scott a "serious injustice," see the essay by Louis Ruchames in John A. Garraty, ed., *Encyclopedia of American Biography* (New York, 1974), 974.

9. Mary Louise Dalton admitted that she herself probably influenced Mrs. Blow to believe that Scott lived twenty years after his manumission. One must consider the possibility that Dred's shiftlessness was as much her idea as Mrs. Blow's recollection. See her letter to Hill, March 13, 1907, cited in note 7 above.

10. Fred Rodell, "Dred Scott, a Century After," *Atlantic Monthly*, CC (Oct. 1957), 61–62; *Reader's Digest Family Encyclopedia of American History* (Pleasantville, N.Y., 1975), 358. See above, 271–76.

11. For Buchanan's citation of the Dred Scott decision in his vetoes of the home-stead and college land-grant bills, see John Bassett Moore, ed., *The Works of James Buchanan* (12 vols.; Philadelphia, 1908–11), X, 307–8, 446. Justice Felix Frankfurter is said to have remarked that after the Civil War, the Dred Scott decision was never mentioned by members of the Supreme Court any more than ropes and scaffolds were ever mentioned in a family that had lost one of its number to the hangman. Bruce Catton, "The Dred Scott Case," in John A. Garraty, ed., *Quarrels That Have Shaped the Constitution* (New York, 1964), 89. Philip B. Kurland, in *Politics, the Constitution, and the Warren Court* (Chicago, 1970), 200, says: "The tragedy of Dred Scott remains a ghost of terrifying proportions."

12. Patricia C. Acheson, *The Supreme Court: America's Judicial Heritage* (New York, 1961), 120.

13. Edward S. Corwin, "The Dred Scott Decision in the Light of Contemporary Legal Doctrines," *AHR*, XVII (1911), 52–69, especially 68–69, originally a paper read at the 1910 meeting of the AHA; Charles Warren, *The Supreme Court in United States History*, rev. ed. (2 vols.; Boston, 1932), II, 316–17.

14. Charles Evans Hughes, *The Supreme Court of the United States* (New York, 1928), 50–51. The book consists of six lectures delivered by Hughes at Columbia University in 1927. Numerous writers express the same opinion. For instance, Walter F. Murphy, *Congress and the Court* (Chicago, 1962), 31, speaks of the "disastrous effect of *Dred Scott* on the Court's prestige," and Robert H. Jackson, *The Struggle for Judicial Supremacy* (New York, 1941), 326, says that in 1861, "judicial power was all but extinct."

15. Stanley I. Kutler, *Judicial Power and Reconstruction Politics* (Chicago, 1968), 1–29; Bernard Schwartz, *From Confederation to Nation: The American Constitution, 1835–1877* (Baltimore, 1973), 183–87.

16. Carl B. Swisher, *The Taney Period, 1836–1864*, Volume V of the Oliver Wendell Holmes Devise *History of the Supreme Court of the United States* (New York, 1974), 858–64, 872–75, 889–92, 929; Alexander A. Lawrence, *James Moore Wayne, Southern Unionist* (Chapel Hill, N.C., 1943), 180–85; David M. Silver, *Lincoln's Supreme Court* (Urbana, 1956), 14–24. See the New York *Tribune,* July 14, 1861, for Catron's charge to a St. Louis grand jury in which he declared that armed resistance to federal authority was treason. Samuel Nelson also continued on the Court but was generally opposed to the war. He and Nathan Clifford (appointed by Buchanan to replace Curtis), together with Taney, formed a threesome hostile to the Lincoln administration. Curtis, who spent considerable time in wartime Washington arguing cases before the Supreme Court, was also an opponent of the Lincoln government. He denounced the Emancipation Proclamation and published a pamphlet accusing Lincoln of assuming dictatorial power. Benjamin R. Curtis, *Executive Power* (Boston, 1862), reprinted in Benjamin R. Curtis, ed., *A Memoir of Benjamin Robbins Curtis, LL.D.* (2 vols.; Boston, 1879), II, 306–35. On *Ex parte Merryman*, see above, 556.

17. George W. Woodward to Jeremiah S. Black, Nov. 28, 1860, Black Papers, MDLC; New York Daily News, Nov. 28, 1860; Sidney Webster to Caleb Cush-

ing, Nov. 27, 1860; Cushing to George M. Browne, Jan. 26, 1861, Cushing
Papers, MDLC; Taney to Ellis Lewis, Dec. 24, 1860, Lewis Papers, Historical
Society of Pennsylvania (photocopy in Carl B. Swisher Papers, MDLC). On
Taney's financial troubles, see Carl B. Swisher, *Roger B. Taney* (New York,
1935), 575–76. On May 25, 1864, just a few months before his death, Taney
wrote to an old friend, David M. Perine: "Can you lend me three hundred
dollars? I must tell you honestly, I do not know when I can repay you. But I
must first begin a rigid economy, and change the habits of my life in that respect, or my family will be literally destitute when I die." Perine Papers, Maryland Historical Society (transcript in Swisher Papers, MDLC).

18. *CG*, 38-2, p. 1014.

19. Swisher, *Taney*, 566–72.

20. Taney, at the time of the Merryman affair, thought that he would be arrested.
     Ibid., 553; Samuel Tayler, ed., *Memoir of Roger Brooke Taney, LL.D.*, 2nd ed.
     (Baltimore, 1876), 427. According to a memorandum by Ward Hill Lamon in
     the Lamon Papers, Huntington Library, the Lincoln administration determined
     to arrest Taney and a warrant was issued. Lincoln left it to the discretion of
     Lamon as U.S. Marshal for the District of Columbia as to whether to make the
     arrest or not. Lamon decided against it. The story is difficult to believe, for it
     seems unlikely that Lincoln would have left such a critical decision to a minor
     official.

21. Silver, *Lincoln's Supreme Court*, 31, 34–36; Swisher, *Taney*, 568–69; Tyler,
     ed., *Memoir of Taney*, 432–35; *CWAL*, IV, 429–31; *Official Opinions of the At-
     torneys General of the United States*, X, 74–92. The New York *Herald* of June
     2, 1861, printed a report from its Baltimore correspondent, dated May 31 and
     declaring: "Judge Taney received a letter from the President yesterday, in
     regard to this [Merryman] case." No copy of the letter has ever been found,
     however.

22. *CG*, 37-2, pp. 2041–54, 2066–68, 2618, 2769; New York *Tribune*, June 18,
     1862; Kutler, *Judicial Power*, 27. At one point, William P. Fessenden did assert
     that his vote on the bill would not be controlled by "the opinion of this chief jus-
     tice or that," but he was commenting on Joseph Story's opinion in *Prigg v.
     Pennsylvania*. *CG*, 37-2, pp. 2050–51.

23. *Official Opinions of Attorneys General*, X, 382–413, especially 409–13; Marvin
     R. Cain, *Lincoln's Attorney General: Edward Bates of Missouri* (Columbia, Mo.,
     1965), 222–25. The New York *Times* of December 27, 1862, hailed the Bates
     opinion as a "blow dealt at that worst of judicial enormities—the Dred Scott
     decision."

24. *CG*, 38-1, pp. 136–64.

25. Most notably by Silver, *Lincoln's Supreme Court*, with chapter titles and sub-
     heads such as these: "Disaster Stalks," "Shatter the Court," "Threats and
     Threats Again," and "The Court Again in Peril." See also James G. Randall,
     Constitutional Problems Under Lincoln, rev. ed. (Urbana, Ill., 1951), 9n; Robert
     G. McCloskey, *The American Supreme Court* (Chicago, 1960), 99–100; and the
     quotation from Edward S. Corwin on p. 573 above.

26. Chicago *Tribune*, March 4, 1861; New York *Tribune*, Dec. 12, 1861. See also

the Cincinnati *Commercial*, Nov. 3, 1860, in Howard Cecil Perkins, ed., *Northern Editorials on Secession* (2 vols.; New York, 1942), I, 74–76.

27. *CG*, 37-2, pp. 8, 26–28. Silver, *Lincoln's Supreme Court*, 43, after quoting from the Hale resolution, comments: "The Radicals had unveiled their plan to scuttle the Taney Supreme Court." Yet he names no other "Radicals" involved.

28. *U.S. Statutes at Large*, XII, 576–77; Kutler, *Judicial Power*, 16–18. In 1863, Congress increased the number of justices to ten, thus indulging in a minimal "packing" of the Court. *U.S. Statutes at Large*, XII, 794–95.

29. *Ex parte Vallandigham*, 1 Wallace 243; Swisher, *Taney Period*, 925–27; Randall, *Constitutional Problems*, 176–79. The most important war-related decision of the wartime Court was in the *Prize Cases*, 2 Black 635 (1863). The Court by a 5 to 4 vote, upheld the legality of the blockade proclaimed by Lincoln in April 1861, even though Congress did not recognize a state of war until July.

30. Lincoln's five appointments were Noah H. Swayne of Ohio, Samuel F. Miller of Iowa, David Davis of Illinois, Stephen J. Field of California, and Salmon P. Chase of Ohio. See Silver, *Lincoln's Supreme Court*, 57–93, 185–209.

31. Chicago *Tribune*, Oct. 14, 1864; Allan Nevins and Milton Halsey Thomas, eds., *The Diary of George Templeton Strong* (4 vols.; New York, 1952), III, 500–501.

32. New York *Times*, Oct. 14, 1864. The Chicago *Tribune* said that Taney's "other relations to public and private life have been eminently useful and honorable." The New York *Tribune* of the same date declared: "He was the product of circumstances which (we trust) will mold the character of no future Chief Justice of the United States; but it were unjust to presume that he did not truly and earnestly seek the good of his country." Taney himself was never as generous in his judgment of Republican motives. In his private relations, however, the Chief Justice seldom allowed political feeling to affect his sense of propriety. The member of the Lincoln administration with the highest opinion of Taney was the only one in frequent contact with him, Attorney General Edward Bates, who called him "a model of a presiding officer; and the last specimen within my knowledge, of a graceful and polished old fashioned gentleman." Howard K. Beale, ed., *The Diary of Edward Bates, 1859–1866*, AHA *Annual Report*, 1930, IV, 418. Bates was the only member of the cabinet who went to Frederick, Md., for the funeral. Lincoln and three cabinet members attended the brief ceremony held in Washington. Taney's graciousness also won the friendship of the new Republican justices, particularly Samuel F. Miller, who reportedly declared: "Before the first term of my service in the Court had passed, I more than liked him; I loved him." Charles Fairman, *Mr. Justice Miller and the Supreme Court, 1862–1890* (Cambridge, Mass., 1939), 52–53. In bar proceedings taking note of Taney's death, perhaps the most eloquent eulogy was delivered by Benjamin R. Curtis, with whom he had quarreled so bitterly in the aftermath of the Dred Scott decision. See Tyler, ed., *Memoir of Taney*, 509–16.

33. "Roger Brooke Taney," *Atlantic Monthly*, XV (Feb. 1865), 151–61, especially 159, 160. Although the essay was unsigned, it has been attributed to Charles M. Ellis, a Boston lawyer. Walker Lewis, *Without Fear of Favor: A Biography of Chief Justice Roger Brooke Taney* (Boston, 1965), 481.

34. *CG*, 38-2, pp. 1012–17; Kutler, *Judicial Power*, 24–25. Trumbull, in no sense a

conservative at this time, called Taney "a great and learned and an able man." Sumner was cut off without being able to finish his remarks, the remainder of which are published in *The Works of Charles Sumner* (15 vols.; Boston, 1870–83), IX, 270–310. The most vicious denunciation of Taney appeared in the summer of 1865 in the form of a pamphlet entitled *The Unjust Judge–A Memorial of Roger Brooke Taney, Late Chief Justice of the United States*, which declared that as a judge, Taney was, "next to Pontius Pilate, perhaps the worst that ever occupied the seat of judgment among men." Lewis, *Without Fear or Favor*, 477–92, offers evidence that the anonymous author was Charles Sumner, but Sumner's biographer finds the argument unconvincing. See David Donald, *Charles Sumner and the Rights of Man* (New York, 1970), 193n.

35.   The most notable instances of congressional intervention were the withdrawal of the Court's appellate jurisdiction under the Habeas Corpus Act of 1867 (in order to prevent a decision detrimental to military Reconstruction in the pending case *Ex parte McCardle*), and the reduction of Court membership from ten to seven in 1866 in order to prevent Andrew Johnson from making appointments. Other measures curbing the Court were proposed and rejected. For example, in 1868, the House of Representatives passed a bill requiring a two-thirds vote in decisions invalidating congressional legislation, but the Senate withheld its approval. Kutler, *Judicial Power*, 35, 48–113; Charles Fairman, *Reconstruction and Reunion, 1864–88, Part One*, Volume VI of the Oliver Wendell Holmes Devise *History of the Supreme Court of the United States* (New York, 1971), 459–78; Maurice S. Culp, "A Survey of the Proposals to Limit or Deny the Power of Judicial Review by the Supreme Court of the United States," *Indiana Law Journal*, IV (1929), 386–98, 474–90; Stuart S. Nagel, "Court-Curbing Periods in American History," *Vanderbilt Law Review*, XVIII (1965), 925–44. Nagel classifies the years 1858 to 1869 as a "high frequency" period in "court-curbing" because twenty-two bills were *introduced* in Congress during that time, but only during Reconstruction were any significant measures passed.

36.   Theodore Calvin Pease and James G. Randall, eds., *The Diary of Orville Hickman Browning* (2 vols.; Springfield, Ill., 1925, 1933), II, 54. According to Browning, Chase said that Taney had been "cruelly misrepresented in regard to his opinion in the Dred Scott case." Stevens's speech is in *CG*, 39-1, pp. 72–75. For an example of the Democratic argument that he was denouncing, see the remarks of Andrew J. Rogers of New Jersey on a bill for Negro suffrage in the District of Columbia, *ibid.*, 196–97. Said Rogers, "The wisdom of ages, for more than five thousand years, and the most enlightened Governments that ever existed upon the face of the earth have handed down to us that grand principle that all Governments of a civilizing character have been and were intended especially for the benefit of white men and white women, and not for those who belong to the negro, Indian, or mulatto race."

37.   *Ex parte Milligan*, 4 Wallace 2 (1866), holding that military trial of civilians was illegal except in a theater of war; *CG*, 39-2, p. 251; Chicago *Tribune*, Jan. 5, 1867; Cleveland *Herald*, quoted along with many other editorial comments in Warren, *Supreme Court*, II, 428–42, especially 432; *Plessy v. Ferguson*, 163 U.S. 537, 559 (1896); Fairman, *Reconstruction and Reunion*, 200–222; *Com-*

plete Presidential Press Conferences of Franklin D. Roosevelt (25 vols.; New York, 1972), V, no. 209, p. 315 (May 31, 1935). Justice Wiley Rutledge, after dissenting in *In re Yamashita*, 327 U.S. 1 (1946), concerning the summary conviction of a Japanese general, wrote that the case would "outrank Dred Scott in the annals of the Court." Rutledge to John P. Frank, quoted in Frank's *Marble Palace: The Supreme Court in American Life* (New York, 1961), 137.

38. Derrick A. Bell, Jr., ed., *Race, Racism, and American Law* (Boston, 1973), 21.

39. *CG*, 39-1, pp. 504, 1776. In general, see Fairman, *Reconstruction and Reunion*, 1169–1204, 1260–1300; Herman Belz, *A New Birth of Freedom: The Republican Party and Freedmen's Rights, 1861–1866* (Westport, Conn., 1976), 113–37; Joseph B. James, *The Framing of the Fourteenth Amendment* (Urbana, Ill., 1956, 1965).

40. *Slaughterhouse Cases*, 16 Wallace 36 (1873); *U.S. v. Cruikshank*, 92 U.S. 542 (1876); *U.S. v. Harris*, 106 U.S. 629 (1883); *Civil Rights Cases*, 109 U.S. 3 (1883); *Plessy v. Ferguson*, 163 U.S. 537 (1896); *Cummings v. County Board of Education*, 175 U.S. 528 (1899); *Ex parte Virginia*, 100 U.S. 339 (1880); *U.S. v. Reese*, 92 U.S. 214 (1876); *Williams v. Mississippi*, 170 U.S. 213 (1898); Loren P. Beth, *The Development of the American Constitution, 1877–1917* (New York, 1971), 191–203; Loren Miller, *The Petitioners: The Story of the Supreme Court of the United States and the Negro* (New York, 1966), 102–82; Alfred H. Kelly and Winfred A. Harbison, *The American Constitution, Its Origin and Development*, 4th ed. (New York, 1970), 490–94. There were exceptions to the general trend. For instance, in *Guinn v. United States*, 238 U.S. 347 (1915), the Court belatedly outlawed the notorious grandfather clause. See also Charles A. Miller, "Constitutional Law and the Rhetoric of Race," in Donald Fleming and Bernard Bailyn, eds., *Perspectives in American History*, Volume V: *Law in American History* (Cambridge, Mass., 1971), 166–71, for discussion of the three-step process in the judicial arguments "used to invalidate federal legislation forbidding racial discrimination and, at the same time, to uphold state legislation requiring it." First there was a state-centered definition of power, then assertion of the wrongheadedness of Negroes for believing they were being treated as inferiors, and finally intimation that racial inferiority might be objectively true.

41. *United States v. County Board of Education*, 372 Federal Reporter, 2nd Series, 836, 873 (1966).

42. Miller, *Petitioners*, 116.

43. For instance, *M.C. & L.M. Railway v. Swan*, 111 U.S. 379, 383 (1884); *Kelly v. Strouse*, 116 Georgia 872, 886 (1903); *Birmingham Post Company v. Brown*, 217 Federal Reporter, 2nd Series 127, 130, 131 (1954).

44. *Jackson v. Steamboat Magnolia*, 20 Howard 296, 334 (1858); *South Carolina v. United States*, 199 U.S. 437, 448–49 (1905); *Home Building & Loan Association v. Blaisdell*, 290 U.S. 398, 450 (1934); *Des Moines Joint Land Bank v. Nordholm*, 217 Iowa 1319, 1386 (1934); *State ex rel. Diederichs v. State Highway Commission*, 89 Montana 205, 210 (1931); *Graham v. Board of Examiners*, 116 Montana 584, 598–99 (1945); *State ex rel. State Aeronautics Commission v. Board of Examiners*, 121 Montana 402, 429–30 (1948); *Cottingham v. Board of Examiners*, 134 Montana 1, 38 (1958); *Borino v. Lounsbury*, 86 Connecticut

622, 627–28 (1913); *Pennsylvania Co., etc. v. Scott*, 346 Pennsylvania 13, 26n (1942).

45. Miller then proceeded to insist that most civil rights were associated with state citizenship, rather than federal citizenship, thus rendering the privileges-and-immunities clause of the Fourteenth Amendment virtually useless. 16 Wallace 36, 72–80 (1873).

46. *State ex rel. Wettengel v. Zimmerman*, 249 Wisconsin 237, 241–42 (1946). In *Steuart v. State ex. rel. Dolcimascolo*, 119 Florida 117, 121, a dissenting judge quoted Taney and revived his idea that a state, being sovereign, could confer citizenship within its own boundaries upon a person not a United States citizen.

47. *United States v. Kagama*, 118 U.S. 375, 380 (1886). See also *Murphy v. Ramsey*, 114 U.S. 15, 44 (1885).

48. *Mormon Church v. United States*, 136 U.S. 1, 42. Chief Justice Melville W. Fuller, dissenting, insisted that the power to govern was granted in the territory clause. *Ibid.*, 67.

49. *De Lima v. Bidwell*, 182 U.S. 1, 196 (1901). In another rather fuzzy sentence, Brown declared: "It is an authority which arises, not necessarily from the territorial clause of the Constitution, but from the necessities of the case." See also *Downes v. Bidwell*, 182 U.S. 244, 250 (1901); *Shively v. Bowlby*, 152 U.S. 1, 48 (1894).

50. *Hooven and Allison v. Evatt*, 324 U.S. 652, 673. See also *Putty v. United States*, 220 Federal Reports, 2nd Series 473, 475 (1955).

51. *Hornbuckle v. Toombs*, 85 U.S. 648, 655 (1874); *Civil Rights Cases*, 109 U.S. 3, and especially 19 (1883). See also *National Bank v. County of Yankton*, 101 U.S. 129, 133 (1879), in which Chief Justice Morrison R. Waite declared of the territories: "Their relation to the general government is much the same as that which counties bear to the respective States." Also *Simms v. Simms*, 175 U.S. 162, 168 (1899); *Utter v. Franklin*, 172 U.S. 416, 423 (1899); *Binns v. United States*, 194 U.S. 486, 491 (1904). The most thorough legal study of territorial government is J. W. Smurr, *Territorial Jurisprudence: What the Judges Said About Frontier Government in the United States of America During the Years 1787–1900* (Ann Arbor, Mich., 1970).

52. *National Bank v. County of Yankton*, 101 U.S. 129, 133; *Murphy v. Ramsey*, 114 U.S. 15, 45. See also *Territory v. Blomberg*, 2 Arizona 204, 207 (1886); *Cases v. United States*, 131 Federal Reporter, 2nd Series 916, 920.

53. *Congressional Record*, 47-1, p. 1158. See *DSvS*, 449.

54. *Murphy v. Ramsey*, 114 U.S. 15 (1885); *Davis v. Beason*, 133 U.S. 333 (1890); *Mormon Church v U.S.*, 136 U.S. 1 (1890); Smurr, *Territorial Jurisprudence*, 84–91.

55. *Congressional Record*, 55-3, pp. 20, 93–96; Carl B. Swisher, *American Constitutional Development* (Boston, 1943), 459–72. The Vest resolution was debated extensively but never acted upon. *Senate Journal*, 55-3 (Serial 3724), 75, 80, 83, 91, 93, 96, 98, 99, 101–2.

56. *Congressional Record*, 55-3, pp. 290–92.

57. *Downes v. Bidwell*, 182 U.S. 244, 273–74 (1901). See *House Documents*, 56-2, No. 509 (Serial 4171), containing the records, briefs, and arguments of counsel in the *Insular Cases*, especially pp. 58–59, 166, 212, 244, 308, 392–93, 421.

58. [Finley Peter Dunne], "The Supreme Court's Decisions," in his *Mr. Dooley's Opinions* (New York, 1901), 24–25.

59. *Downes v. Bidwell*, 182 U.S. 244, 291, 360–61; Smurr, *Territorial Jurisprudence*, 354–81. The specific issue in the *Insular Cases* was whether Congress could impose import duties on goods coming from Puerto Rico and the other new island possessions.

60. *Congressional Record*, 55-3, p. 639.

61. C. Vann Woodward, *The Strange Career of Jim Crow*, 2nd ed. (New York, 1966), 74.

62. Elbert William R. Ewing, *Legal and Historical Status of the Dred Scott Decision* (Washington, D.C., 1909).

63. William E. Mikell, "Roger Brooke Taney," in William Draper Lewis, ed., *Great American Lawyers* (12 vols.; Philadelphia, 1908), IV, 75–194, especially 128, 162, 167–77.

64. *Ibid.*, 150, 154n, 165, 183; Ewing, *Dred Scott Decision*, 7–8, 187, 196, 203, 223. Mikell resumed his defense of Taney 16 years later (by which time he had become dean of the University of Pennsylvania Law School), declaring that Taney's Dred Scott opinion was "a masterpiece of judicial reasoning," which provoked a "tornado of abuse and hate." "Chief Justice Roger Brooke Taney," *University of West Virginia Law Quarterly*, XXX (1924), 87–103, especially 102.

65. Edward S. Corwin, "The Dred Scott Decision, in the Light of Contemporary Legal Doctrines," *AHR*, XVII (1911), 52–69.

66. Horace H. Hagan, "The Dred Scott Decision," *Georgetown Law Journal*, XV (1927), 95–114, especially 95, 112n, 113. For discussion of another point made by Hagan, see above, 675–76.

67. Wallace Mendelson, "The Dred Scott Case Revisited," *Louisiana Law Review*, VII (1947), 398–405; "Chief Justice Taney—Jacksonian Judge," *University of Pittsburgh Law Review*, XII (1951), 381–93; "Dred Scott's Case Reconsidered," *Minnesota Law Review*, XXXVIII (1953), 16–28, especially 16. See also F. Dumont Smith, "Roger Brooke Taney," *Texas Law Review*, I (1923), 261–80; Walter P. Armstrong, "The Rehabilitation of Roger B. Taney," *Tennessee Law Review*, XIV (1936), 205–18.

68. Alexander M. Bickel, *The Supreme Court and the Idea of Progress* (New York, 1970), 41; David M. Potter, *The Impending Crisis, 1848–1861*, completed and edited by Don E. Fehrenbacher (New York, 1976), 293.

69. Ray Allen Billington, ed., *Frontier and Section: Selected Essays of Frederick Jackson Turner* (Englewood Cliffs, N.J., 1961), 52, 72, 86–87; Charles A. Beard and Mary R. Beard, *The Rise of American Civilization* (2 vols.; New York, 1927), I, 557; Richard Hofstadter, *The Progressive Historians: Turner, Beard, Parrington* (New York, 1968), 52, 85, 95, 128, 302, 326–27; Staughton Lynd, "On Turner, Beard and Slavery," *JNH*, XLVIII (1963), 235–50, reprinted in Lynd, *Class Conflict, Slavery, and the United States Constitution* (Indianapolis, 1967), 135–52; Arthur M. Schlesinger, Jr., *The Age of Jackson* (Boston, 1946), 325, 486–87, 516–17.

70. On the work and influence of William A. Dunning, Ulrich B. Phillips, Frank L. Owsley, Charles W. Ramsdell, E. Merton Coulter, Avery O. Craven, James G. Randall, and others, see Thomas J. Pressly, *Americans Interpret Their Civil War*

(Princeton, 1954; New York, 1966), 265–328. See also Don E. Fehrenbacher, "Disunion and Reunion," in John Higham, eds., *The Reconstruction of American History* (New York, 1962), 108–14.

71. Warren, *Supreme Court*, II, 300–19; Albert J. Beveridge, *Abraham Lincoln, 1809–1858* (2 vols.; Boston, 1928), II, 486–99; Beveridge to William E. Dodd, Dec. 13, 1926; to Oliver Wendell Holmes, Jan 27, 1927; to Charles A. Beard, April 7, 1927, Beveridge Papers, MDLC.

72. Moore, ed., *Works of Buchanan*, X, 106–7; Frank H. Hodder, "Some Phases of the Dred Scott Case," *MVHR*, XVI (1929), 22; Beveridge to Hodder, Feb. 22, 1927, Beveridge Papers, MDLC.

73. Charles Evans Hughes, "Roger Brooke Taney," *American Bar Association Journal*, XVII (1931), 785–90. Hughes also spoke of the "violent and malignant attack upon the decision."

74. Swisher, *Taney*, 495–523, especially 503–5.

75. Charles W. Smith, Jr., *Roger B. Taney: Jacksonian Jurist* (Chapel Hill, N.C., 1936), 147, 154, 155–76, 210.

76. Felix Frankfurter, *The Commerce Clause Under Marshall, Taney and Waite* (Chapel Hill, N.C., 1937; Chicago, 1964), 49, 66–68, 73. Frankfurter first published his lecture on Taney in the *Harvard Law Review*, XLIX (1936), 1286–1302. As authority for his statements about Taney's attitude toward slavery, he cited the Swisher biography, but he appears not to have read it very carefully. In 1953, he named Marshall, Taney, and Hughes as the three greatest chief justices. Philip Elman, ed., *Of Law and Men: Papers and Addresses of Felix Frankfurter, 1939–56* (New York, 1956), 113.

77. For example, Benjamin Fletcher Wright, Jr., *The Contract Clause of the Constitution* (Cambridge, Mass., 1938), 62–88, 245–46; Ben W. Palmer, *Marshall and Taney, Statesmen of the Law* (Minneapolis, 1939), 145–275. Wright argued that there was continuity between Marshall and Taney in interpretation of the contract clause. Palmer asked "Which was the greater judge, John Marshall or Roger Brooke Taney?" and returned an equivocal answer (256, 271).

78. Marvin Laurence Winitsky, "The Jurisprudence of Roger B. Taney," Ph.D. dissertation, UCLA, 1973, is generally an evenhanded study but more critical of Taney's slavery decisions. See also Arthur Bestor, "State Sovereignty and Slavery: A Reinterpretation of Proslavery Constitutional Doctrine, 1846–1860," *Journal of the Illinois State Historical Society*, LIV (1961), 117–80; William M. Wiecek, "Slavery and Abolition Before the United States Supreme Court, 1820–1860," *JAH*, LXV (1978), 34–59.

79. Albert P. Blaustein and Roy M. Mersky, "Rating Supreme Court Justices," *American Bar Association Journal*, LVIII (1972), 1183–89. The other three nineteenth-century justices rated "great" were John Marshall, Joseph Story, and John Marshall Harlan.

80. New York *Times*, March 3, 1957, p. 67.

81. Rodell, "Dred Scott," 63. See also Potter, *Impending Crisis*, 286.

82. Rodell, "Dred Scott," 60. The Warren Court has been the subject of much scholarly interpretation and argument. See, for example, Archibald Cox, *The Warren Court: Constitutional Decision as an Instrument of Reform* (Cambridge,

Mass., 1968); Clifford M. Lytle, *The Warren Court and Its Critics* (Tucson, Ariz., 1968); Philip B. Kurland, *Politics, the Constitution, and the Warren Court* (Chicago, 1970); Robert G. McCloskey, *The Modern Supreme Court* (Cambridge, Mass., 1972), 129–366.

83. Jethro K. Lieberman, *Milestones: 200 Years of American Law, Milestones in Our Legal History* (New York, 1976), vi–vii. The Declaration of Independence and the Constitution were recognized as pre-eminent and included without balloting. The eighteen milestones chosen by ballot were: (1) *Marbury v. Madison* (1803); (2) Warren Court (1953–69); (3) *United States v. Nixon* (1974); (4) *Miranda v. Arizona* (1966); (5) *Brown v. Board of Education* (1954); (6) *Dred Scott v. Sandford* (1857); (7) Social Security Act (1935); (8) *Dartmouth College v. Woodward* (1819); (9) *In re Gault* (1967); (10) *Schechter v. United States* (1935); (11) *Baker v. Carr* (1962); (12) Marshall Court (1801–35); (13) *Gideon v. Wainwright* (1963); (14) Fourteenth Amendment (1868); (15) *Erie v. Tompkins* (1938); (16) *Mapp v. Ohio* (1961); (17) *McCulloch v. Maryland* (1819); (18) *Roe v. Wade* (1973).

84. *Ibid.;* Hughes, "Taney," 787.

85. Alexis de Tocqueville, *Democracy in America*, edited by Phillips Bradley (2 vols., Vintage: New York, 1945), I, 290.

86. Adolf A. Berle, *The Three Faces of Power* (New York, 1967), 3. See also Philip B. Kurland, "Government by Judiciary," *Modern Age*, XX (1976), 358–71; Raoul Berger, *Government by Judiciary: The Transformation of the Fourteenth Amendment* (Cambridge, Mass., 1977).

87. See Ward E. Y. Elliott, *The Rise of Guardian Democracy: The Supreme Court's Role in Voting Rights Disputes, 1845–1969* (Cambridge, Mass., 1974), 1–33.

88. For example, *Powell v. McCormack*, 395 U.S. 486 (1969), and *United States v. Nixon*, 418 U.S. 683 (1974), present significant questions about the capacity of the Supreme Court to limit the powers of Congress and the president. The range of possibilities for judicial intervention is suggested in *Mora v. McNamara*, 389 U.S. 934 (1967), in which the Court was asked to issue a judgment declaring that military operations in Vietnam were illegal. Certiorari was denied, with two justices dissenting.

Index